Lawrence A. Canton
February 15, 1940
D0369222

American Historical Series

GENERAL EDITOR

CHARLES H. HASKINS

Professor of History in Harvard University

THE AGE OF THE REFORMATION

BY

PRESERVED SMITH, Ph.D.

NEW YORK

HENRY HOLT AND COMPANY

November, 1938

PRINTED IN U.S.A.

VITÂ
CARIORI
FILIOLAE
PRISCILLAE
SACRUM

PREFACE

The excuse for writing another history of the Reformation is the need for putting that movement in its proper relations to the economic and intellectual revolutions of the sixteenth century. The labor of love necessary for the accomplishment of this task has employed most of my leisure for the last six years and has been my companion through vicissitudes of sorrow and of joy. A large part of the pleasure derived from the task has come from association with friends who have generously put their time and thought at my disposal. First of all, Professor Charles H. Haskins, of Harvard, having read the whole in manuscript and in proof with care, has thus given me the unstinted benefit of his deep learning, and of his ripe and sane judgment. Next to him the book owes most to my kind friend, the Rev. Professor William Walker Rockwell, of Union Seminary, who has added to the many other favors he has done me a careful revision of Chapters I to VIII, Chapter XIV, and a part of Chapter IX. Though unknown to me personally, the Rev. Dr. Peter Guilday, of the Catholic University of Washington, consented, with gracious, characteristic urbanity, to read Chapters VI and VIII and a part of Chapter I. I am grateful to Professor N. S. B. Gras, of the University of Minnesota, for reading that part of the book directly concerned with economics (Chapter XI and a part of Chapter X); and to Professor Frederick A. Saunders, of Harvard, for a like service in technical revision of the section on science in Chapter XII. While acknowledging with hearty thanks the priceless services of these eminent scholars, it is only fair to relieve them of all responsibility for any rash statements that may have escaped their scrutiny, as well as for any conclusions from which they might dissent.

For information about manuscripts and rare books in Europe my thanks are due to my kind friends: Mr. P. S. Allen, Librarian of Merton College, Oxford, the so successful editor of Erasmus's Epistles; and Professor Carrington Lancaster, of Johns Hopkins University. To several libraries I owe much for the use of books. My friend, Professor Robert S. Fletcher, Librarian of Amherst College, has often sent me volumes from that excellent store of books. My sister, Professor Winifred Smith, of Vassar College, has added to many loving services, this: that during my four years at Poughkeepsie, I was enabled to use the Vassar library. For her good offices, as well as for the kindness of the librarian, Miss Amy Reed, my thanks. My father, the Rev. Dr. Henry Preserved Smith, professor and librarian at Union Theological Seminary, has often sent me rare books from that library; nor can I mention this, the least of his favors, without adding that I owe to him much both of the inspiration to follow and of the means to pursue a scholar's career. My thanks are also due to the libraries of Columbia and Cornell for the use of books. But the work could not easily have been done at all without the facilities offered by the Harvard Library. When I came to Cambridge to enjoy the riches of this storehouse, I found the great university not less hospitable to the stranger within her gates than she is prolific in great sons. After I was already deep in debt to the librarian, Mr. W. C. Lane, and to many of the professors, a short period in the service of Harvard, as lecturer in history, has made me feel that I am no longer a stranger, but that I can count myself, in some sort, one of her citizens and foster sons, at least a *dimidiatus alumnus*.

This book owes more to my wife than even she perhaps quite realizes. Not only has it been her study, since our marriage, to give me freedom for my work, but her literary advice, founded on her own experience as writer and critic, has been of the highest value, and she has carefully read the proofs.

PRESERVED SMITH.

Cambridge,
Massachusetts,
May 16, 1920.

CONTENTS

THE AGE OF THE REFORMATION

CHAPTER I

THE OLD AND THE NEW

§ 1. The World

Though in some sense every age is one of transition and every generation sees the world remodelled, there sometimes comes a change so startling and profound that it seems like the beginning of a new season in the world's great year. The snows of winter melt for weeks, the cold winds blow and the cool rains fall, and we see no change until, almost within a few days, the leaves and blossoms put forth their verdure, and the spring has come.

1483–1546

Such a change in man's environment and habits as the world has rarely seen, took place in the generation that reached early manhood in the year 1500. In the span of a single life—for convenience let us take that of Luther for our measure—men discovered, not in metaphor but in sober fact, a new heaven and a new earth. In those days masses of men began to read many books, multiplied by the new art of printing. In those days immortal artists shot the world through with a matchless radiance of color and of meaning. In those days Vasco da Gama and Columbus and Magellan opened the watery ways to new lands beyond the seven seas. In those days Copernicus established the momentous truth that the earth was but a tiny planet spinning around a vastly greater sun. In those days was in large part accomplished the economic shift from medieval gild to modern production by capital and wages. In those days wealth was piled up in the coffers of the merchants, and a new power was given to the life of the individual, of the nation, and of the third estate. In those days the monarchy of the Roman church was broken, and large portions of her dominions seceded to form new organizations, governed by other powers and animated by a different spirit.

Antecedents of the Reformation

Other generations have seen one revolution take place at a time, the sixteenth century saw three, the Rise of Capitalism, the end of the Renaissance, and the beginning of the Reformation. All three, interacting, modifying each other, conflicting as they sometimes did, were equally the consequences, in different fields, of antecedent changes in man's circumstances. All life is an adaptation to environment; and thus from every alteration in the conditions in which man lives, usually made by his discovery of new resources or of hitherto unknown natural laws, a change in his habits of life must flow. Every revolution is but an adjustment to a fresh situation, intellectual or material, or both.

Economic

Certainly, economic and psychological factors were alike operative in producing the three revolutions. The most general economic force was the change from "natural economy" to "money economy," *i. e.* from a society in which payments were made chiefly by exchange of goods, and by services, to one in which money was both the agent of exchange and standard of value. In the Middle Ages production had been largely cooperative; the land belonged to the village and was apportioned out to each husbandman to till, or to all in common for pasture. Manufacture and commerce were organized by the gild—a society of equals, with the same course of labor and the same reward for each, and with no distinction save that founded on seniority—apprentice, workman, master-workman. But in the later Middle Ages, and more rapidly at their close, this system broke down under the necessity for larger capital in production and the possibility of supplying it by the increase of wealth and of banking technique that made possible investment, rapid turn-over of capital, and corporate partnership. The increase of wealth and the changed mode of its production has been in large part the cause of three developments which in their turn became causes of revolution: the rise of the bourgeoisie, of nationalism, and of individualism.

The bourgeoisie

Just as the nobles were wearing away in civil strife and were seeing their castles shot to pieces by cannon, just as the clergy were wasting in supine indolence and were riddled by the mockery of humanists, there arose a new class, eager and able to take the helm of civilization, the moneyed men of city and of trade. *Nouveaux riches* as they were, they had an appetite for pleasure and for ostentation unsurpassed by any, a love for the world and an impatience of the meek and lowly church, with her ideal of poverty and of chastity. In their luxurious and leisured homes they sheltered the arts that made life richer and the philosophy, or religion, that gave them a good conscience in the work they loved. Both Renaissance and Reformation were dwellers in the cities and in the marts of commerce.

National states

It was partly the rise of the third estate, but partly also cultural factors, such as the perfecting of the modern tongues, that made the national state one of the characteristic products of modern times. Commerce needs order and strong government; the men who paid the piper called the tune; police and professional soldiery made the state, once so racked by feudal wars, peaceful at home and dreaded abroad. If the consequence of this was an increase in royal power, the kings were among those who had greatness thrust upon them, rather than achieving it for themselves.

They were but the symbols of the new, proudly conscious nation, and the police commissioners of the large bankers and traders.

Individualism

The reaction of nascent capitalism on the individual was no less marked than on state and society, though it was not the only cause of the new sense of personal worth. Just as the problems of science and of art became most alluring, the man with sufficient leisure and resource to solve them was developed by economic forces. In the Middle Ages men had been less enterprising and less self-conscious. Their thought was not of themselves as individuals so much as of their membership in groups. The peoples were divided into well-marked estates, or classes; industry was co-operative; even the great art of the cathedrals was rather gild-craft than the expression of a single genius; even learning was the joint property of universities, not the private accumulation of the lone scholar. But with every expansion of the ego either through the acquisition of wealth or of learning or of pride in great exploits, came a rising self-consciousness and self-confidence, and this was the essence of the individualism so often noted as one of the contrasts between modern and medieval times. The child, the savage, and to a large extent the undisciplined mind in all periods of life and of history, is conscious only of object; the trained and leisured intellect discovers, literally by "reflection," the subjective. He is then no longer content to be anything less than himself, or to be lost in anything greater.

Just as men were beginning again to glory in their own powers came a series of discoveries that totally transformed the world they lived in. So vast a change is made in human thought and habit by some apparently trivial technical inventions that it sometimes seems as if the race were like a child that had boarded a locomotive and half accidentally started it, but could neither guide nor stop it. Civilization was born with the great inventions of fire, tools, the domestication of animals, writing, and navigation, all of them, together with important astronomical discoveries, made prior to the beginnings of recorded history. On this capital mankind traded for some millenniums, for neither classic times nor the Dark Ages added much to the practical sciences. But, beginning with the thirteenth century, discovery followed discovery, each more important in its consequences than its last. One of the first steps was perhaps the recovery of lost ground by the restoration of the classics. Gothic art and the vernacular literatures testify to the intellectual activity of the time, but they did not create the new elements of life that were brought into being by the inventors.

Inventions

What a difference in private life was made by the introduction of chimneys and glass windows, for glass, though known to antiquity, was not commonly applied to the openings that, as the etymology of the English word implies, let in the wind! By the fifteenth century the power of lenses to magnify and refract had been utilized, as mirrors, then as spectacles, to be followed two centuries later by telescopes and microscopes. Useful chemicals were now first applied to various manufacturing processes, such as the tinning of iron. The compass, with its weird power of pointing north, guided the mariner on uncharted seas. The obscure inventor of gunpowder revolutionized the art of war more than all the famous conquerors had done, and the polity of states more than any of the renowned legislators of antiquity. The equally obscure inventor of mechanical clocks—a great improvement on the older sand-glasses, water-glasses, and candles—made possible a new precision and regularity of daily life, an untold economy of time and effort.

Printing

But all other inventions yield to that of printing, the glory of John Gutenberg of Mayence, one of those poor and in their own times obscure geniuses who carry out to fulfilment a great idea at much sacrifice to themselves. The demand for books had been on the increase for a long time, and every effort was made to reproduce them as rapidly and cheaply as possible by the hand of expert copyists, but the applications of this method produced slight result. The introduction of paper, in place of the older vellum or parchment, furnished one of the indispensable pre-requisites to the multiplication of cheap volumes. In the early fifteenth century, the art of the wood-cutter and engraver had advanced sufficiently to allow some books to be printed in this manner, *i. e.* from carved blocks. This was usually, or at first, done only with books in which a small amount of text went with a large amount of illustration. There are extant, for example, six editions of the *Biblia Pauperum,* stamped by this method. It was afterwards applied, chiefly in Holland, to a few other books for which there was a large demand, the Latin grammar of Donatus, for example, and a guide-book to Rome known as the *Mirabilia Urbis Romae.* But at best this method was extremely unsatisfactory; the blocks soon wore out, the text was blurred and difficult to read, the initial expense was large.

The essential feature of Gutenberg's invention was therefore not, as the name implies, printing, or impression, but typography, or the use of type. The printer first had a letter cut in hard metal, this was called the punch; with it he stamped a mould known as the matrix in which he was able to found a large number of exactly identical types of metal, usually of lead. These, set side by side in a case, for the first time made it possible satisfactorily to print at reasonable cost a large number of copies of the same text, and, when that was done, the types could be taken apart and used for another work.

The earliest surviving specimen of printing—not counting a few undated letters of indulgence—is a fragment on the last judgment completed at Mayence before 1447. In 1450 Gutenberg made a partnership with the rich goldsmith John Fust, and from their press issued, within the next five years, the famous Bible with 42 lines to a page, and a Donatus (Latin grammar) of 32 lines. The printer of the Bible with 36 lines to a page, that is the next oldest surviving monument, was apparently a helper of Gutenberg, who set up an independent press in 1454. Legible, clean-cut, comparatively cheap, these books demonstrated once for all the success of the new art, even though, for illuminated initials, they were still dependent on the hand of the scribe.

Books and Reading

In those days before patents the new invention spread with wonderful rapidity, reaching Italy in 1465, Paris in 1470, London in 1480, Stockholm in 1482, Constantinople in 1487, Lisbon in 1490, and Madrid in 1499. Only a few backward countries of Europe remained without a press. By the year 1500 the names of more than one thousand printers are known, and the titles of about 30,000 printed works. Assuming that the editions were small, averaging 300 copies, there would have been in Europe by 1500 about 9,000,000 books, as against the few score thousand manuscripts that lately had held all the precious lore of time. In a few years the price of books sank to one-eighth of what it had been before. "The gentle reader" had started on his career.

The importance of printing cannot be over-estimated. There are few events like it in the history of the world. The whole gigantic swing of modern democracy and of the scientific spirit was released by it. The veil of the temple of religion and of knowledge was rent in twain, and the arcana of the priest and clerk exposed to the gaze of the people. The reading public became the supreme court before whom, from this time, all cases must be argued. The conflict of opinions and parties, of privilege and freedom, of science and obscurantism, was transferred from the secret chamber of a small, privileged, professional, and sacerdotal coterie to the arena of the reading public.

Exploration

It is amazing, but true, that within fifty years after this exploit, mankind should have achieved another like unto it in a widely different sphere. The horror of the sea was on the ancient world; a heart of oak and triple bronze was needed to venture on the ocean, and its annihilation was one of the blessings of the new earth promised by the Apocalypse. All through the centuries Europe remained sea-locked, until the bold Portuguese mariners venturing ever further and further south along the coast of Africa, finally doubled the Cape of Good Hope—a feat first performed by Bartholomew Diaz in 1486, though it was not until 1498 that Vasco da Gama reached India by this method.

Still unconquered lay the stormy and terrible Atlantic,

> Where, beyond the extreme sea-wall, and between the remote
> sea-gates,
> Waste water washes, and tall ships founder, and deep death
> waits.

But the ark of Europe found her dove—as the name Columbus signifies—to fly over the wild, western waves, and bring her news of strange countries. The effect of these discoveries, enormously and increasingly important from the material standpoint, was first felt in the widening of the imagination. Camoens wrote the epic of Da Gama, More placed his Utopia in America, and Montaigne speculated on the curious customs of the redskins. Ariosto wrote of the wonders of the new world in his poem, and Luther occasionally alluded to them in his sermons.

Universities

If printing opened the broad road to popular education, other and more formal means to the same end were not neglected. One of the great innovations of the Middle Ages was the university. These permanent corporations, dedicated to the advancement of learning and the instruction of youth, first arose, early in the twelfth century, at Salerno, at Bologna and at Paris. As off-shoots of these, or in imitation of them, many similar institutions sprang up in every land of western Europe. The last half of the fifteenth century was especially rich in such foundations. In Germany, from 1450 to 1517, no less than nine new academies were started: Greifswald 1456, Freiburg in the Breisgau 1460, Basle 1460, Ingolstadt 1472, Trèves 1473, Mayence 1477, Tübingen 1477, Wittenberg 1502, and Frankfort on the Oder 1506. Though generally founded by papal charter, and maintaining a strong ecclesiastical flavor, these institutions were under the direction of the civil government.

In France three new universities opened their doors during the same period: Valence 1459, Nantes 1460, Bourges 1464. These were all placed under the general supervision of the local bishops. The great university of Paris was gradually changing its character. From the most cosmopolitan and international of bodies it was fast becoming strongly nationalist, and was the chief center of an Erastian Gallicanism. Its tremendous weight cast against the Reformation was doubtless a chief reason for the failure of that movement in France.

Spain instituted seven new universities at this time: Barcelona 1450, Saragossa 1474, Palma 1483, Sigüenza 1489, Alcalá 1499, Valencia 1500, and Seville 1504. Italy and England remained content with the academies they already had, but many of the smaller countries now started native universities. Thus Pressburg was founded in Hungary in 1465, Upsala in Sweden in 1477, Copenhagen in 1478, Glasgow in 1450, and Aberdeen in 1494. The number of students in each foundation fluctuated, but the total was steadily on the increase.

Naturally, the expansion of the higher education brought with it an increase in the number and excellence of the schools. Particularly notable is the work of the Brethren of the Common Life, who devoted themselves almost exclusively to teaching boys. Some of their schools, as Deventer, attained a reputation like that of Eton or Rugby today.

The spread of education was not only notable in itself, but had a more direct result in furnishing a shelter to new movements until they were strong enough to do without such support. It is significant that the Reformations of Wyclif, Huss, and Luther, all started in universities.

Growth of intelligence

As the tide rolls in, the waves impress one more than the flood beneath them. Behind, and far transcending, the particular causes of this and that development lies the operation of great biological laws, selecting a type for survival, transforming the mind and body of men slowly but surely. Whether due to the natural selection of circumstance, or to the inward urge of vital force, there seems to be no doubt that the average intellect, not of leading thinkers or of select groups, but of the European races as a whole, has been steadily growing greater at every period during which it can be measured. Moreover, the monastic vow of chastity tended to sterilize and thus to eliminate the religiously-minded sort. Operating over a long period, and on both sexes, this cause of the growing secularization of the world, though it must not be exaggerated, cannot be overlooked.

§ 2. The Church

Over against "the world," "the church." . . . As the Reformation was primarily a religious movement, some account of the church in the later Middle Ages must be given. How Christianity was immaculately conceived in the heart of the Galilean carpenter and born with words of beauty and power such as no other man ever spoke; how it inherited from him its background of Jewish monotheism and Hebrew Scripture; how it was enriched, or sophisticated, by Paul, who assimilated it to the current mysteries with their myth of a dying and rising god and of salvation by sacramental rite; how it decked itself in the white robes of Greek philosophy and with many a gewgaw of ceremony and custom snatched from the flamen's vestry; how it created a pantheon of saints to take the place of the old polytheism; how it became first the chaplain and then the heir of the Roman Empire, building its church on the immovable rock of the Eternal City, asserting like her a dominion without bounds of space or time; how it conquered and tamed the barbarians;—all this lies outside the scope of the present work to describe. But of its later fortunes some brief account must be given.

Innocent III 1198–1216

By the year 1200 the popes, having emerged triumphant from their long strife with the German emperors, successfully asserted their claim to the suzerainty of all Western Europe. Innocent III took realms in fief and dictated to kings. The pope, asserting that the spiritual power was as much superior to the civil as the sun was brighter than the moon, acted as the vicegerent of God on earth. But this supremacy did not last long unquestioned. Just a century after Innocent III, Boniface VIII was worsted in a quarrel with Philip IV of France, and his successor, Clement V, a Frenchman, by transferring the papal capital to Avignon, virtually made the supreme pontiffs subordinate to the French government and thus weakened their influence in the rest of Europe. This "Babylonian Captivity" was followed by a greater misfortune to the pontificate, the Great Schism, for the effort to transfer the papacy back to Rome led to the election of two popes, who, with their successors, respectively ruled and mutually anathematized each other from the two rival cities. The difficulty of deciding which was the true successor of Peter was so great that not only were the kingdoms of Europe divided in their allegiance, but doctors of the church and canonized saints could be found among the supporters of either line. There can be no doubt that respect for the pontificate greatly suffered by the schism, which was in some respects a direct preparation for the greater division brought about by the Protestant secession.

Boniface VIII 1294–1303

The Babylonian Captivity 1309–76

The Great Schism 1378–1417

The attempt to end the schism at the Council of Pisa resulted only in the election of a third pope. The situation was finally dealt with by the Council of Constance which deposed two of the popes and secured the voluntary abdication of the third. The synod further strengthened the church by executing the heretics Huss and Jerome of Prague, and by passing decrees intended to put the government of the church in the hands of representative assemblies. It asserted that it

Councils Pisa, 1409

Constance 1414–18

had power directly from Christ, that it was supreme in matters of faith, and in matters of discipline so far as they affected the schism, and that the pope could not dissolve it without its own consent. By the decree *Frequens* it provided for the regular summoning of councils at short intervals. Beyond this, other efforts to reform the morals of the clergy proved abortive, for after long discussion nothing of importance was done.

Basle 1431–43

For the next century the policy of the popes was determined by the wish to assert their superiority over the councils. The Synod of Basle reiterated all the claims of Constance, and passed a number of laws intended to diminish the papal authority and to deprive the pontiff of much of his ill-gotten revenues—annates, fees for investiture, and some other taxes. It was successful for a time because protected by the governments of France and Germany, for, though dissolved by Pope Eugene IV in 1433, it refused to listen to his command and finally extorted from him a bull ratifying the conciliar claims to supremacy.

In the end, however, the popes triumphed. The bull *Execrabilis* denounced as a damnable abuse the appeal to a future council, and the *Pastor Aeternus* reasserted in sweeping terms the supremacy of the pope, repealing all decrees of Constance and Basle to the contrary, as well as other papal bulls.

1458

1516

The secularization of the papacy

At Rome the popes came to occupy the position of princes of one of the Italian states, and were elected, like the doges of Venice, by a small oligarchy. Within seventy years the families of Borgia, Piccolomini, Rovere, and Medici were each represented by more than one pontiff, and a majority of the others were nearly related by blood or marriage to one of these great stocks. The cardinals were appointed from the pontiff's sons or nephews, and the numerous other offices in their patronage, save as they were sold, were distributed to personal or political friends.

Nicholas V 1447–55

Like other Italian princes the popes became, in the fifteenth century, distinguished patrons of arts and letters. The golden age of the humanists at Rome began under Nicholas V who employed a number of them to make translations from Greek. It is characteristic of the complete secularization of the States of the Church that a number of the literati pensioned by him were skeptics and scoffers. Valla, who mocked the papacy, ridiculed the monastic orders, and attacked the Bible and Christian ethics, was given a prebend; Savonarola, the most earnest Christian of his age, was put to death.

1453

The fall of Constantinople gave a certain European character to the policy of the pontiffs after that date, for the menace of the Turk seemed so imminent that the heads of Christendom did all that was possible to unite the nations in a crusade. This was the keynote of the statesmanship of Calixtus III and of his successor, Pius II. Before his elevation to the see of Peter this talented writer, known to literature as Aeneas Sylvius, had, at the Council of Basle, published a strong argument against the extreme papal claims, which he afterwards, as pope, retracted. His zeal against the Turk and against his old friends the humanists lent a moral tone to his pontificate, but his feeble attempts to reform abuses were futile.

Calixtus III 1455–8

Pius II 1458–64

Paul II 1464–71

Sixtus IV 1471–84

The colorless reign of Paul II was followed by that of Sixtus IV, a man whose chief passion was the aggrandizement of his family. He carried nepotism to an extreme and by a policy of judicial murder very nearly exterminated his rivals, the Colonnas.

Innocent VIII 1484–92

The enormous bribes paid by Innocent VIII for his election were recouped by his sale of offices and spiritual graces, and by taking a tribute from the Sultan, in return for which he refused to proclaim a crusade. The most important act of his pontificate was the publication of the bull against witchcraft.

Alexander VI 1492–1503

The name of Alexander VI has attained an evil eminence of infamy on account of his own crimes and vices and those of his children, Caesar Borgia and Lucretia. One proof that the public conscience of Italy, instead of being stupified by the orgy of wickedness at Rome was rather becoming aroused by it, is found in the appearance, just at this time, of a number of preachers of repentance. These men, usually friars, started "revivals" marked by the customary phenomena of sudden conversion, hysteria, and extreme austerity. The greatest of them all was the Dominican Jerome Savonarola who, though of mediocre intellectual gifts, by the passionate fervor of his convictions, attained the position of a prophet at Florence. He began preaching here in 1482, and so stirred his audiences that many wept and some were petrified with horror. His credit was greatly raised by his prediction of the invasion of Charles VIII of France in 1494. He succeeded in driving out the Medici and in introducing a new constitution of a democratic nature, which he believed was directly sanctioned by God. He attacked the morals of the clergy and of the people and, besides renovating his own order, suppressed not only public immorality but all forms of frivolity. The people burned their cards, false hair, indecent pictures, and the like; many women left their husbands and entered the cloister; gamblers were tortured and blasphemers had their tongues pierced. A police was instituted with power of searching houses.

Savonarola 1452–98

It was only the pope's fear of Charles VIII that prevented his dealing with this dangerous reformer, who now began to attack the vices of the curia. In 1495, however, the friar was summoned to Rome, and refused to go; he was then forbidden to preach, and disobeyed. In Lent 1496 he proclaimed the duty of resisting the pope when in error. In November a new brief proposed changes in the constitution of his order which would bring him more directly under the power of Rome. Savonarola replied that he did not fear the excommunication of the sinful church, which, when launched against him May 12, 1497, only made him more defiant. Claiming to be commissioned directly from God, he appealed to the powers to summon a general council against the pope.

At this juncture one of his opponents, a Franciscan, Francis da Puglia, proposed to him the ordeal by fire, stating that though he expected to be burnt he was willing to take the risk for the sake of the faith. The challenge refused by Savonarola was taken up by his friend Fra Domenico da Pescia, and although forbidden by Alexander, the ordeal was sanctioned by the Signory and a day set. A dispute as to whether Domenico should be allowed to take the host or the crucifix into the flames prevented the experiment from taking place, and the mob, furious at the loss of its promised spectacle, refused further support to the discredited leader. For some years, members of his own order, who resented the severity of his reform, had cherished a grievance against him, and now they had their chance. Seized by the Signory, he was tortured and forced to confess that he was not a prophet, and on May 22, 1498, was condemned, with two companions, to be hung. After the speedy execution of the sentence, which the sufferers met calmly, their bodies were burnt. All effects of Savonarola's career, political, moral, and religious, shortly disappeared.

Alexander was followed by a Rovere who took the name of Julius II. Notwithstanding his advanced age this pontiff proved one of the most vigorous and able

Julius II
1503–13

statesman of the time and devoted himself to the aggrandizement, by war and diplomacy, of the Papal States. He did not scruple to use his spiritual thunders against his political enemies, as when he excommunicated the Venetians. He found himself at odds with both the Emperor Maximilian and Louis XII of France, who summoned a schismatic council at Pisa. Supported by some of the cardinals this body revived the legislation of Constance and Basle, but fell into disrepute when, by a master stroke of policy, Julius convoked a council at Rome. This synod, the Fifth Lateran, lasted for four years, and endeavored to deal with a crusade and with reform. All its efforts at reform proved abortive because they were either choked, while in course of discussion, by the Curia, or, when passed, were rendered ineffective by the dispensing power.

1509

1511

1512–16

Leo X 1513–21

While the synod was still sitting Julius died and a new pope was chosen. This was the son of Lorenzo the Magnificent, the Medici Leo X. Having taken the tonsure at the age of seven, and received the red hat six years later, he donned the tiara at the early age of thirty-eight. His words, as reported by the Venetian ambassador at Rome, "Let us enjoy the papacy, since God has given it to us," exactly express his program. To make life one long carnival, to hunt game and to witness comedies and the antics of buffoons, to hear marvellous tales of the new world and voluptuous verses of the humanists and of the great Ariosto, to enjoy music and to consume the most delicate viands and the most delicious wines—this was what he lived for. Free and generous with money, he prodigally wasted the revenues of three pontificates. Spending no less than 6000 ducats a month on cards and gratuities, he was soon forced to borrow to the limit of his credit. Little recked he that Germany was being reft from the church by a poor friar. His irresolute policy was incapable of pursuing any public end consistently, save that he employed the best Latinists of the time to give elegance to his state papers. His method of governing was the purely personal one, to pay his friends and flatterers at the expense of the common good. One of his most characteristic letters expresses his intention of rewarding with high office a certain gentleman who had given him a dinner of lampreys.

§ 3. Causes of the Reformation

Corruption of the church not a main cause of the Reformation

In the eyes of the early Protestants the Reformation was a return to primitive Christianity and its principal cause was the corruption of the church. That there was great depravity in the church as elsewhere cannot be doubted, but there are several reasons for thinking that it could not have been an important cause for the loss of so many of her sons. In the first place there is no good ground for believing that the moral condition of the priesthood was worse in 1500 than it had been for a long time; indeed, there is good evidence to the contrary, that things were tending to improve, if not at Rome yet in many parts of Christendom. If objectionable practices of the priests had been a sufficient cause for the secession of whole nations, the Reformation would have come long before it actually did. Again, there is good reason to doubt that the mere abuse of an institution has ever led to its complete overthrow; as long as the institution is regarded as necessary, it is rather mended than ended. Thirdly, many of the acts that seem corrupt to us, gave little offence to contemporaries, for they were universal. If the church sold offices and justice, so did the civil governments. If the clergy lived impure lives, so did the laity. Probably the standard of the church (save in special circumstances) was no worse than that of civil life, and in some respects it was rather more decent. Finally, there is some reason to suspect of exaggeration the charges preferred by the innovators. Like all reformers they made the most of their enemy's faults. Invective like theirs is common to every generation and to all spheres of life. It is true that the denunciation of the priesthood comes not only from Protestants and satirists, but from popes and councils and canonized saints, and that it bulks large in medieval literature. Nevertheless, it is both *a priori* probable and to some extent historically verifiable that the evil was more noisy, not more potent, than the good. But though the corruptions of the church were not a main cause of the Protestant secession, they furnished good excuses for attack; the Reformers were scandalized by the divergence of the practice and the pretensions of the official representatives of Christianity, and their attack was envenomed and the break made easier thereby. It is therefore necessary to say a few words about those abuses at which public opinion then took most offence.

Abuses: Financial

Many of these were connected with money. The common man's conscience was wounded by the smart in his purse. The wealth of the church was enormous, though exaggerated by those contemporaries who estimated it at one-third of the total real estate of Western Europe. In addition to revenues from her own land the church collected tithes and taxes, including "Peter's pence" in England, Scandinavia and Poland. The clergy paid dues to the curia, among them the *servitia* charged on the bishops and the annates levied on the income of the first year for each appointee to high ecclesiastical office, and the price for the archbishop's pall. The priests recouped themselves by charging high fees for their ministrations. At a time when the Christian ideal was one of "apostolic poverty" the riches of the clergy were often felt as a scandal to the pious.

Simony

Though the normal method of appointment to civil office was sale, it was felt as a special abuse in the church and was branded by the name of simony. Leo X made no less than 500,000 ducats [1] annually from the sale of more than 2000 offices, most of which, being sinecures, eventually came to be regarded as annuities, with a salary amounting to about 10 per cent. of the purchase price.

Justice was also venal, in the church no less than in the state. Pardon was obtainable for all crimes for, as a papal vice-chamberlain phrased it, "The Lord wishes not the death of a sinner but that he should pay and live." Dispensations from the laws against marriage within the prohibited degrees were sold. Thus an ordinary man had to pay 16 grossi [2] for dispensation to marry a woman who stood in "spiritual relationship" [3] to him; a noble had to pay 20 grossi for the same privilege, and a prince or duke 30 grossi. First cousins might marry for the payment of 27 grossi; an uncle and niece for from three to four ducats, though this was later raised to as much as sixty ducats, at least for nobles. Marriage within the first degree of affinity (a deceased wife's mother or daughter by another husband) was at one time sold for about ten ducats; marriage within the second degree [4] was per-

[1] A ducat was worth intrinsically $2.25, or nine shillings, at a time when money had a much greater purchasing power than it now has.

[2] The grossus, English groat, German Groschen, was a coin which varied considerably in value. It may here be taken as intrinsically worth about 8 cents or four pence, at a time when money had many times the purchasing power that it now has.

[3] A spiritual relationship was established if a man and woman were sponsors to the same child at baptism.

[4] Presumably of affinity, *i.e.*, a wife's sister, but there is nothing to

mitted for from 300 to 600 grossi. Hardly necessary to add, as was done: "Note well, that dispensations or graces of this sort are not given to poor people."[1] Dispensations from vows and from the requirements of ecclesiastical law, as for example those relating to fasting, were also to be obtained at a price.

Indulgences

One of the richest sources of ecclesiastical revenue was the sale of indulgences, or the remission by the pope of the temporal penalties of sin, both penance in this life and the pains of purgatory. The practice of giving these pardons first arose as a means of assuring heaven to those warriors who fell fighting the infidel. In 1300 Boniface VIII granted a plenary indulgence to all who made the pilgrimage to the jubilee at Rome, and the golden harvest reaped on this occasion induced his successors to take the same means of imparting spiritual graces to the faithful at frequent intervals. In the fourteenth century the pardons were extended to all who contributed a sum of money to a pious purpose, whether they came to Rome or not, and, as the agents who were sent out to distribute these pardons were also given power to confess and absolve, the papal letters were naturally regarded as no less than tickets of admission to heaven. In the thirteenth century the theologians had discovered that there was at the disposal of the church and her head an abundant "treasury of the merits of Christ and the saints," which might be applied vicariously to anyone by the pope. In the fifteenth century the claimed power to free living men from purgatory was extended to the

show that this law did not also apply to consanguinity, and at one time the pope proposed that the natural son of Herry VIII, the Duke of Richmond, should marry his half sister, Mary.

[1] "Nota diligenter, quod huiusmodi gratiae et dispensationes non conceduntur pauperibus." *Taxa cancellariae apostolicae,* in E. Friedberg: *Lehrbuch des katholischen und evangelischen Kirchenrechts,* 1903, pp. 389ff.

dead, and this soon became one of the most profitable branches of the "holy trade."

The means of obtaining indulgences varied. Sometimes they were granted to those who made a pilgrimage or who would read a pious book. Sometimes they were used to raise money for some public work, a hospital or a bridge. But more and more they became an ordinary means for raising revenue for the curia. How thoroughly commercialized the business of selling grace and remission of the penalties of sin had become is shown by the fact that the agents of the pope were often bankers who organized the sales on purely business lines in return for a percentage of the net receipts plus the indirect profits accruing to those who handle large sums. Of the net receipts the financiers usually got about ten per cent.; an equal amount was given to the emperor or other civil ruler for permitting the pardoners to enter his territory, commissions were also paid to the local bishop and clergy, and of course the pedlars of the pardons received a proportion of the profits in order to stimulate their zeal. On the average from thirty to forty-five per cent. of the gross receipts were turned into the Roman treasury.

It is natural that public opinion should have come to regard indulgences with aversion. Their bad moral effect was too obvious to be disregarded, the compounding with sin for a payment destined to satisfy the greed of unscrupulous prelates. Their economic effects were also noticed, the draining of the country of money with which further to enrich a corrupt Italian city. Many rulers forbade their sale in their territories, because, as Duke George of Saxony, a good Catholic, expressed it, before Luther was heard of, "they cheated the simple layman of his soul." Hutten mocked at Pope Julius II for selling to others the heaven he could not win himself. Pius II was obliged

Pius II 1458–64

to confess: "If we send ambassadors to ask aid of the princes, they are mocked; if we impose a tithe on the clergy, appeal is made to a future council; if we publish an indulgence and invite contributions in return for spiritual favors, we are charged with greed. People think all is done merely for the sake of extorting money. No one trusts us. We have no more credit than a bankrupt merchant."

Immorality of clergy

Much is said in the literature of the latter Middle Ages about the immorality of the clergy. This class has always been severely judged because of its high pretensions. Moreover the vow of celibacy was too hard to keep for most men and for some women; that many priests, monks and nuns broke it cannot be doubted. And yet there was a sprinkling of saintly parsons like him of whom Chancer said

> Who Christes lore and his apostles twelve
> He taught, but first he folwed it himselve,

and there were many others who kept up at least the appearance of decency. But here, as always, the bad attracted more attention than the good.

The most reliable data on the subject are found in the records of church visitations, both those undertaken by the Reformers and those occasionally attempted by the Catholic prelates of the earlier period. Everywhere it was proved that a large proportion of the clergy were both wofully ignorant and morally unworthy. Besides the priests who had concubines, there were many given to drink and some who kept taverns, gaming rooms and worse places. Plunged in gross ignorance and superstition, those blind leaders of the blind, who won great reputations as exorcists or as wizards, were unable to understand the Latin service, and sometimes to repeat even the Lord's prayer or creed in any language.

Piety

The Reformation, like most other revolutions, came not at the lowest ebb of abuse, but at a time when the tide had already begun to run, and to run strongly, in the direction of improvement. One can hardly find a sweeter, more spiritual religion anywhere than that set forth in Erasmus's *Enchiridion,* or in More's *Utopia,* or than that lived by Vitrier and Colet. Many men, who had not attained to this conception of the true beauty of the gospel, were yet thoroughly disgusted with things as they were and quite ready to substitute a new and purer conception and practice for the old, mechanical one.

Evidence for this is the popularity of the Bible and other devotional books. Before 1500 there were nearly a hundred editions of the Latin Vulgate, and a number of translations into German and French. There were also nearly a hundred editions, in Latin and various vernaculars, of *The Imitation of Christ.* There was so flourishing a crop of devotional handbooks that no others could compete with them in popularity. For those who could not read there were the *Biblia Pauperum,* picture-books with a minimum of text, and there were sermons by popular preachers. If some of these tracts and homilies were crude and superstitious, others were filled with a spirit of love and honesty. Whereas the passion for pilgrimages and relics seemed to increase, there were men of clear vision to denounce the attendant evils. A new feature was the foundation of lay brotherhoods, like that of the Common Life, with the purpose of cultivating a good character in the world, and of rendering social service. The number of these brotherhoods was great and their popularity general.

Clash of new spirit with old institutions

Had the forces already at work within the church been allowed to operate, probably much of the moral reform desired by the best Catholics would have been accomplished quietly without the violent rending of Christian unity that actually took place. But the fact is, that such reforms never would or could have satisfied the spirit of the age. Men were not only shocked by the abuses in the church, but they had outgrown some of her ideals. Not all of her teaching, nor most of it, had become repugnant to them, for it has often been pointed out that the Reformers kept more of the doctrines of Catholicism than they threw away, but in certain respects they repudiated, not the abuse but the very principle on which the church acted. In four respects, particularly, the ideals of the new age were incompatible with those of the Roman communion.

Sacramental theory of the church

The first of these was the sacramental theory of salvation and its corollary, the sacerdotal power. According to Catholic doctrine grace is imparted to the believer by means of certain rites: baptism, confirmation, the eucharist, penance, extreme unction, holy orders, and matrimony. Baptism is the necessary prerequisite to the enjoyment of the others, for without it the unwashed soul, whether heathen or child of Christian parents, would go to eternal fire; but the "most excellent of the sacraments" is the eucharist, in which Christ is mysteriously sacrificed by the priest to the Father and his body and blood eaten and drunk by the worshippers. Without these rites there was no salvation, and they acted automatically (*ex opere operato*) on the soul of the faithful who put no active hindrance in their way. Save baptism, they could be administered only by priests, a special caste with "an indelible character" marking them off from the laity. Needless to remark the immense power that this doctrine gave the clergy in a believing age. They were made the arbiters of each man's eternal destiny, and their moral character had no more to do with their binding and loosing sentence than does the moral character of a secular officer affect his official acts. Add to this that the priests were unbound by ties of family, that by confession they entered into everyone's private life, that they were not amenable to civil justice —and their position as a privileged order was secure. The growing self-assurance and enlightenment of a nascent individualism found this distinction intolerable.

Other-worldliness

Another element of medieval Catholicism to clash with the developing powers of the new age was its pessimistic and ascetic other-worldliness. The ideal of the church was monastic; all the pleasures of this world, all its pomps and learning and art were but snares to seduce men from salvation. Reason was called a barren tree but faith was held to blossom like the rose. Wealth was shunned as dangerous, marriage deprecated as a necessary evil. Fasting, scourging, celibacy, solitude, were cultivated as the surest roads to heaven. If a good layman might barely shoulder his way through the strait and narrow gate, the highest graces and heavenly rewards were vouchsafed to the faithful monk. All this grated harshly on the minds of the generations that began to find life glorious and happy, not evil but good.

Worship of saints

Third, the worship of the saints, which had once been a stepping-stone to higher things, was now widely regarded as a stumbling-block. Though far from a scientific conception of natural law, many men had become sufficiently monistic in their philosophy to see in the current hagiolatry a sort of polytheism. Erasmus freely drew the parallel between the saints and the heathen deities, and he and others scourged the grossly materialistic form which this worship often took. If we may believe him, fugitive nuns prayed for help in hiding their sin; merchants for a rich haul; gamblers for luck; and prostitutes for generous patrons. Margaret of Navarre tells as an actual fact of a man who prayed for help in seducing his neighbor's wife, and similar instances of perverted piety are not wanting. The passion for the relics of the saints led to an enormous traffic in spurious articles. There appeared to be enough of the wood of the true cross, said Erasmus, to make a ship; there were exhibited five shin-bones of the ass on which Christ rode, whole bottles of the Virgin's milk, and several complete bits of skin saved from the circumcision of Jesus.

Temporal power of the church

Finally, patriots were no longer inclined to tolerate the claims of the popes to temporal power. The church had become, in fact, an international state, with its monarch, its representative legislative assemblies, its laws and its code. It was not a voluntary society, for if citizens were not born into it they were baptized into it before they could exercise any choice. It kept prisons and passed sentence (virtually if not nominally) of death; it treated with other governments as one power with another; it took principalities and kingdoms in fief. It was supported by involuntary contributions.[1]

The expanding world had burst the bands of the old church. It needed a new spiritual frame, and this frame was largely supplied by the Reformation. Prior to that revolution there had been several distinct efforts to transcend or to revolt from the limitations imposed by the Catholic faith; this was done by the mystics, by the pre-reformers, by the patriots and by the humanists.

§ 4. The Mystics

One of the earliest efforts to transcend the economy of salvation offered by the church was made by a school of mystics in the fourteenth and fifteenth cen-

[1] Maitland: *Canon Law in the Church of England,* p. 100.

tury. In this, however, there was protest neither against dogma nor against the ideal of other-worldliness, for in these respects the mystics were extreme conservatives, more religious than the church herself. They were like soldiers who disregarded the orders of their superiors because they thought these orders interfered with their supreme duty of harassing the enemy. With the humanists and other deserters they had no part nor lot; they sought to make the church more spiritual, not more reasonable. They bowed to her plan for winning heaven at the expense of earthly joy and glory; they accepted her guidance without question; they rejoiced in her sacraments as aids to the life of holiness. But they sorrowed to see what they considered merely the means of grace substituted for the end sought; they were insensibly repelled by finding a mechanical instead of a personal scheme of salvation, an almost commercial debit and credit of good works instead of a life of spontaneous and devoted service. Feeling as few men have ever felt that the purpose and heart of religion is a union of the soul with God, they were shocked to see the interposition of mediators between him and his creature, to find that instead of hungering for him men were trying to make the best bargain they could for their own eternal happiness. While rejecting nothing in the church they tried to transfigure everything. Accepting priest and sacrament as aids to the divine life they declined to regard them as necessary intermediaries.

Eckhart, 1260–1327

The first of the great German mystics was Master Eckhart, a Dominican who lived at Erfurt, in Bohemia, at Paris, and at Cologne. The inquisitors of this last place summoned him before their court on the charge of heresy, but while his trial was pending he died. He was a Christian pantheist, teaching that God was the only true being, and that man was capable of reaching the absolute. Of all the mystics he was the most speculative and philosophical. Both Henry Suso and John Tauler were his disciples. Suso's ecstatic piety was of the ultra-medieval type, romantic, poetic, and bent on winning personal salvation by the old means of severe self-torture and the constant practice of good works. Tauler, a Dominican of Strassburg, belonged to a society known as The Friends of God. Of all his contemporaries he in religion was the most social and practical. His life was that of an evangelist, preaching to laymen in their own vernacular the gospel of a pure life and direct communion with God through the Bible and prayer. Like many other popular preachers he placed great emphasis on conversion, the turning (*Kehr*) from a bad to a good life. Simple faith is held to be better than knowledge or than the usual works of ecclesiastical piety. Tauler esteemed the holiest man he had ever seen one who had never heard five sermons in his life. All honest labor is called God's service, spinning and shoe-making the gifts of the Holy Spirit. Pure religion is to be "drowned in God," "intoxicated with God," "melted in the fire of his love." Transcending the common view of the average Christian that religion's one end was his own salvation, Tauler taught him that the love of God was greater than this. He tells of a woman ready to be damned for the glory of God—"and if such a person were dragged into the bottom of hell, there would be the kingdom of God and eternal bliss in hell."

Suso, 1300–66

Tauler c. 1300–61

One of the fine flowers of German mysticism is a book written anonymously—"spoken by the Almighty, Eternal God, through a wise, understanding, truly just man, his Friend, a priest of the Teutonic Order at Frankfort." *The German Theology*, as it was named by Luther, teaches in its purest form entire abandonment to God, simple passivity in his hands, utter self-

The German Theology

denial and self-surrender, until, without the interposition of any external power, and equally without effort of her own, the soul shall find herself at one with the bridegroom. The immanence of God is taught; man's helpless and sinful condition is emphasized; and the reconciliation of the two is found only in the unconditional surrender of man's will to God. "Put off thine own will and there will be no hell."

Tauler's sermons, first published 1498, had an immense influence on Luther. They were later taken up by the Jesuit Canisius who sought by them to purify his church. *The German Theology* was first published by Luther in 1516, with the statement that save the Bible and St. Augustine's works, he had never met with a book from which he had learned so much of the nature of "God, Christ, man, and all things." But other theologians, both Protestant and Catholic, did not agree with him. Calvin detected secret and deadly poison in the author's pantheism, and in 1621 the Catholic Church placed his work on the Index.

1543

The Netherlands also produced a school of mystics, later in blooming than that of the Germans and greater in its direct influence. The earliest of them was John of Ruysbroeck, a man of visions and ecstasies. He strove to make his life one long contemplation of the light and love of God. Two younger men, Gerard Groote and Florence Radewyn, socialized his gospel by founding the fellowship of the Brethren of the Common Life. Though never an order sanctioned by the church, they taught celibacy and poverty, and devoted themselves to service of their fellows, chiefly in the capacity of teachers of boys.

Ruysbroeck, 1293–1381

Groote, 1340–84 Radewyn, 1350–1400

The fifteenth century's rising tide of devotion brought forth the most influential of the products of all the mystics, the *Imitation of Christ* by Thomas à Kempis. Written in a plaintive minor key of resig-

Thomas à Kempis, c. 1380–1471

nation and pessimism, it sets forth with much artless eloquence the ideal of making one's personal life approach that of Christ. Humility, self-restraint, asceticism, patience, solitude, love of Jesus, prayer, and a diligent use of the sacramental grace of the eucharist are the means recommended to form the character of the perfect Christian. It was doubtless because all this was so perfect an expression of the medieval ideal that it found such wide and instant favor. There is no questioning of dogma, nor any speculation on the positions of the church; all this is postulated with childlike simplicity. Moreover, the ideal of the church for the salvation of the individual, and the means supposed to secure that end, are adopted by à Kempis. He tacitly assumes that the imitator of Christ will be a monk, poor and celibate. His whole endeavor was to stimulate an enthusiasm for privation and a taste for things spiritual, and it was because in his earnestness and single-mindedness he so largely succeeded that his book was eagerly seized by the hands of thousands who desired and needed such stimulation and help. The Dutch canon was not capable of rising to the heights of Tauler and the Frankfort priest, who saw in the love of God a good in itself transcending the happiness of one's own soul. He just wanted to be saved and tried to love God for that purpose with all his might. But this careful self-cultivation made his religion self-centered; it was, compared even with the professions of the Protestants and of the Jesuits, personal and unsocial.

Notwithstanding the profound differences between the Mystics and the Reformers, it is possible to see that at least in one respect the two movements were similar. It was exactly the same desire to get away from the mechanical and formal in the church's scheme of salvation, that animated both. Tauler and Luther both deprecated good works and sought justification in faith only. Important as this is, it is possible to see why the mystics failed to produce a real revolt from the church, and it is certain that they were far more than the Reformers fundamentally, even typically Catholic. It is true that mysticism is at heart always one, neither national nor confessional. But Catholicism offered so favorable a field for this development that mysticism may be considered as the efflorescence of Catholic piety *par excellence*. Hardly any other expression of godliness as an individual, vital thing, was possible in medieval Christendom. There is not a single idea in the fourteenth and fifteenth century mysticism which cannot be read far earlier in Augustine and Bernard, even in Aquinas and Scotus. It could never be anything but a sporadic phenomenon because it was so intensely individual. While it satisfied the spiritual needs of many, it could never amalgamate with other forces of the time, either social or intellectual. As a philosophy or a creed it led not so much to solipsism as to a complete abnegation of the reason. Moreover it was slightly morbid, liable to mistake giddiness of starved nerve and emotion for a moment of vision and of union with God. How much more truly than he knew did Ruysbroeck speak when he said that the soul, turned inward, could see the divine light, just as the eyeball, sufficiently pressed, could see the flashes of fire in the mind!

Mysticism

§ 5. Pre-reformers

The men who, in later ages, claimed for their ancestors a Protestantism older than the Augsburg Confession, referred its origins not to the mystics nor to the humanists, but to bold leaders branded by the church as heretics. Though from the earliest age Christendom never lacked minds independent enough to differ from authority and characters strong enough to attempt to cut away what they considered rotten in ecclesiastical doctrine and practice, the first heretics that can really be considered as harbingers of the Reformation were two sects dwelling in Southern France, the Albigenses and the Waldenses. The former, first met with in the eleventh century, derived part of their doctrines from oriental Manichaeism, part from primitive gnosticism. The latter were the followers of Peter Waldo, a rich merchant of Lyons who, about 1170, sold his goods and went among the poor preaching the gospel. Though quite distinct in origin both sects owed their success with the people to their attacks on the corrupt lives of the clergy, to their use of the vernacular New Testament, to their repudiation of part of the sacramental system, and to their own earnest and ascetic morality. The story of their savage suppression, at the instigation of Pope Innocent III, in the Albigensian crusade, is one of the darkest blots on the pages of history. A few remnants of them survived in the mountains of Savoy and Piedmont, harried from time to time by blood-thirsty pontiffs. In obedience to a summons of Innocent VIII King Charles VIII of France massacred many of them.

Albigenses

Waldenses

1209–29

1487

The spiritual ancestors of Luther, however, were not so much the French heretics as two Englishmen, Occam and Wyclif. William of Occam, a Franciscan who taught at Oxford, was the most powerful scholastic critic of the existing church. Untouched by the classic air breathed by the humanists, he said all that could be said against the church from her own medieval standpoint. He taught determinism; he maintained that the final seat of authority was the Scripture; he showed that such fundamental dogmas as the existence of God, the Trinity, and the Incarnation, cannot be deduced by logic from the given premises; he pro-

Occam, † c. 1349

posed a modification of the doctrine of transubstantiation in the interests of reason, approaching closely in his ideas to the "consubstantiation" of Luther. Defining the church as the congregation of the faithful, he undermined her governmental powers. This, in fact, is just what he wished to do, for he went ahead of almost all his contemporaries in proposing that the judicial powers of the clergy be transferred to the civil government. Not only, in his opinion, should the civil ruler be totally independent of the pope, but even such matters as the regulation of marriage should be left to the common law.

Wyclif, 1324–84

A far stronger impression on his age was made by John Wyclif, the most significant of the Reformers before Luther. He, too, was an Oxford professor, a schoolman, and a patriot, but he was animated by a deeper religious feeling than was Occam. In 1361 he was master of Balliol College, where he lectured for many years on divinity. At the same time he held various benefices in turn, the last, the pastorate of Lutterworth in Leicestershire, from 1374 till his death. He became a reformer somewhat late in life owing to study of the Bible and of the bad condition of the English church. At the peace congress at Bruges as a commissioner to negotiate with papal ambassadors for the relief of crying abuses, he became disillusioned in his hope for help from that quarter. He then turned to the civil government, urging it to regain the usurped authority of the church. This plan, set forth in voluminous writings, in lectures at Oxford and in popular sermons in London, soon brought him before the tribunal of William Courtenay, Bishop of London, and, had he not been protected by the powerful prince, John of Lancaster, it might have gone hard with him. Five bulls launched against him by Gregory XI from Rome only confirmed him in his course, for he ap-

1374

1377

pealed from them to Parliament. Tried at Lambeth he was forbidden to preach or teach, and he therefore retired for the rest of his life to Lutterworth. He continued his literary labors, resulting in a vast host of pamphlets. 1378

Examining his writings we are struck by the fact that his program was far more religious and practical than rational and speculative. Save transubstantiation, he scrupled at none of the mysteries of Catholicism. It is also noticeable that social reform left him cold. When the laborers rose under Wat Tyler, Wyclif sided against them, as he also proposed that confiscated church property be given rather to the upper classes than to the poor. The real principles of Wyclif's reforms were but two: to abolish the temporal power of the church, and to purge her of immoral ministers. It was for this reason that he set up the authority of Scripture against that of tradition; it was for this that he doubted the efficacy of sacraments administered by priests living in mortal sin; it was for this that he denied the necessity of auricular confession; it was for this that he would have placed the temporal power over the spiritual. The bulk of his writings, in both Latin and English, is fierce, measureless abuse of the clergy, particularly of prelates and of the pope. The head of Christendom is called Antichrist over and over again; the bishops, priests and friars are said to have their lips full of lies and their hands of blood; to lead women astray; to live in idleness, luxury, simony and deceit; and to devour the English church. Marriage of the clergy is recommended. Indulgences are called a cursed robbery. 1381

To combat the enemies of true piety Wyclif relied on two agencies. The first was the Bible, which, with the assistance of friends, he Englished from the Vulgate. None of the later Reformers was more bent upon giving the Scriptures to the laity, and none attributed to it a higher degree of inspiration. As a second measure Wyclif trained "poor priests" to be wandering evangelists spreading abroad the message of salvation among the populace. For a time they attained considerable success, notwithstanding the fact that the severe persecution to which they were subjected caused all of Wyclif's personal followers to recant. The passage of the act *De Haeretico Comburendo* was not, however, in vain, for in the fifteenth century a number of common men were found with sufficient resolution to die for their faith. It is probable that, as Cuthbert Tunstall, Bishop of London wrote in 1523, the Lollards, as they were called, were the first to welcome Lutheranism into Britain.

1401

But if the seed produced but a moderate harvest in England it brought forth a hundred-fold in Bohemia. Wyclif's writings, carried by Czech students from Oxford to Prague, were eagerly studied by some of the attendants at that university, the greatest of whom was John Huss. Having taken his bachelor's degree there in 1393, he had given instruction since 1398 and became the head of the university (Rector) for the year 1402. Almost the whole content of his lectures, as of his writings, was borrowed from Wyclif, from whom he copied not only his main ideas but long passages verbatim and without specific acknowledgment. Professors and students of his own race supported him, but the Germans at the university took offence and a long struggle ensued, culminating in the secession of the Germans in a body in 1409 to found a new university at Leipsic. The quarrel, having started over a philosophic question,—Wyclif and Huss being realists and the Germans nominalists,—took a more serious turn when it came to a definition of the church

Huss, 1369–1415

and of the respective spheres of the civil and ecclesiastical authorities. Defining the church as the body of the predestinate, and starting a campaign against indulgences, Huss soon fell under the ban of his superiors. After burning the bulls of John XXIII Huss withdrew from Prague. Summoned to the Council of Constance, he went thither, under safe-conduct from the Emperor Sigismund, and was immediately cast into a noisome dungeon. 1411 1412

The council proceeded to consider the opinions of Wyclif, condemning 260 of his errors and ordering his bones to be dug up and burnt, as was done twelve years later. Every effort was then made to get Huss to recant a list of propositions drawn up by the council and attributed to him. Some of these charges were absurd, as that he was accused of calling himself the fourth person of the Trinity. Other opinions, like the denial of transubstantiation, he declared, and doubtless with truth, that he had never held. Much was made of his saying that he hoped his soul would be with the soul of Wyclif after death, and the emperor was alarmed by his argument that neither priest nor king living in mortal sin had a right to exercise his office. He was therefore condemned to the stake. 1414

His death was perfect. His last letters are full of calm resolution, love to his friends, and forgiveness to his enemies. Haled to the cathedral where the council sat on July 6, 1415, he was given one last chance to recant and save his life. Refusing, he was stripped of his vestments, and a paper crown with three demons painted on it put on his head with the words, "We commit thy soul to the devil"; he was then led to the public square and burnt alive. Sigismund, threatened by the council, made no effort to redeem his safe-conduct, and in September the reverend fathers passed a decree that no safe-conduct to a heretic, and no pledge prejudicial to the Catholic faith, could be considered binding. Among the large concourse of divines not one voice was raised against this treacherous murder.

Huss's most prominent follower, Jerome of Prague, after recantation, returned to his former position and was burnt at Constance on May 30, 1416. A bull of 1418 ordered the similar punishment of all heretics who maintained the positions of Wyclif, Huss, or Jerome of Prague.

As early as September a loud remonstrance against the treatment of their master was voiced by the Bohemian Diet. The more radical party, known as Taborites, rejected transubstantiation, worship of the saints, prayers for the dead, indulgences, auricular confession, and oaths. They allowed women to preach, demanded the use of the vernacular in divine service and the giving of the cup to the laity. A crusade was started against them, but they knew how to defend themselves. The Council of Basle was driven to negotiate with them and ended by a compromise allowing the cup to the laity and some other reforms. Subsequent efforts to reduce them proved futile. Under King Podiebrad the Utraquists maintained their rights.

1431–6

Some Hussites, however, continued as a separate body, calling themselves Bohemian Brethren. First met with in 1457 they continue to the present day as Moravians. They were subject to constant persecution. In 1505 the Catholic official James Lilienstayn drew up an interesting list of their errors. It seems that their cardinal tenet was the supremacy of Scripture, without gloss, tradition, or interpretation by the Fathers of the church. They rejected the primacy of the pope, and all ceremonies for which authority could not be found in the Bible, and they denied the efficacy of masses for the dead and the validity of indulgences.

With much reason Wyclif and Huss have been called "Reformers before the Reformation." Luther himself, not knowing the Englishman, recognized his deep indebtedness to the Bohemian. All of their program, and more, he carried through. His doctrine of justification by faith only, with its radical transformation of the sacramental system, cannot be found in these his predecessors, and this was a difference of vast importance.

§ 6. Nationalizing the Churches

Inevitably, the growth of national sentiment spoken of above reacted on the religious institutions of Europe. Indeed, it was here that the conflict of the international, ecclesiastical state, and of the secular governments became keenest. Both kings and people wished to control their own spiritual affairs as well as their temporalities.

The ecclesia Anglicana

England traveled farthest on the road towards a national church. For three centuries she had been asserting the rights of her government to direct spiritual as well as temporal matters. The Statute of Mortmain forbade the alienation of land from the jurisdiction of the civil power by appropriating it to religious persons. The withdrawing of land from the obligation to pay taxes and feudal dues was thus checked. The encroachment of the civil power, both in England and France, was bitterly felt by the popes. Boniface VIII endeavored to stem the flood by the bull *Clericis laicos* forbidding the taxation of clergy by any secular government, and the bull *Unam Sanctam* asserting the universal monarchy of the Roman pontiff in the strongest possible terms. But these exorbitant claims were without effect. The Statute of Provisors forbade the appointment to English benefices by the pope, and the Statute of Praemunire took away the right of Eng-

1279

1296

1302

1351 and 1390

1353 and 1393

lish subjects to appeal from the courts of their own country to Rome. The success of Wyclif's movement was largely due to his patriotism. Though the signs of strife with the pope were fewer in the fifteenth century, there is no doubt that the national feeling persisted.

The Gallican Church

France manifested a spirit of liberty hardly less fierce than that of England. It was the French King Philip the Fair who humiliated Boniface VIII so severely that he died of chagrin. During almost the whole of the fourteenth century the residence of a pope subservient to France at Avignon prevented any difficulties, but no sooner had the Council of Constance restored the head of the unified church to Rome than the old conflict again burst forth. The extreme claims of the Gallican church were asserted in the law known as the Pragmatic Sanction of Bourges, by which the pope was left hardly any right of appointment, of jurisdiction, or of raising revenue in France. The supremacy of a council over the pope was explicitly asserted, as was the right of the civil magistrate to order ecclesiastical affairs in his dominions. When the pontiffs refused to recognize this almost schismatical position taken by France, the Pragmatic Sanction was further fortified by a law sentencing to death any person who should bring into the country a bull repugnant to it. Strenuous efforts of the papacy were directed to secure the repeal of this document, and in 1461 Pius II induced Louis XI to revoke it in return for political concessions in Naples. This action, opposed by the University and Parlement of Paris, proved so unpopular that two years later the Gallican liberties were reasserted in their full extent.

1438

Harmony was established between the interests of the curia and of the French government by the compromise known as the Concordat of Bologna. The

1516

concessions to the king were so heavy that it was difficult for Leo X to get his cardinals to consent to them. Almost the whole power of appointment, of jurisdiction, and of taxation was put into the royal hands, some stipulations being made against the conferring of benefices on immoral priests and against the frivolous imposition of ecclesiastical punishments. What the pope gained was the abandonment of the assertion made at Bourges of the supremacy of a general council. The Concordat was greeted by a storm of protest in France. The Sorbonne refused to recognize it and appealed at once to a general council. The king, however, had the refractory members arrested and decreed the repeal of the Pragmatic Sanction in 1518.

In Italy and Germany the growth of a national state was retarded by the fact that one was the seat of the pope, the other of the emperor, each of them claiming a universal authority. Moreover, these two powers were continually at odds. The long investiture strife, culminating in the triumph of Gregory VII at Canossa and ending in the Concordat of Worms, could not permanently settle the relations of the two. Whereas Aquinas and the Canon Law maintained the superiority of the pope, there were not lacking asserters of the imperial preëminence. William of Occam's argument to prove that the emperor might depose an heretical pope was taken up by Marsiglio of Padua, whose *Defender of the Peace* ranks among the ablest of political pamphlets. In order to reduce the power of the pope, whom he called "the great dragon and old serpent," he advanced the civil government to a complete supremacy in ecclesiastical affairs. He stated that the only authority in matters of faith was the Bible, with the necessary interpretation given it by a general council composed of both clergy and laymen; that the emperor had the right to convoke and

Italy

1077

1122

c. 1324

direct this council and to punish all priests, prelates and the supreme pontiff; that the Canon Law had no validity; that no temporal punishment should be visited on heresy save by the state, and no spiritual punishment be valid without the consent of the state.

Germany

With such a weapon in their hands the emperors might have taken an even stronger stand than did the kings of England and France but for the lack of unity in their dominions. Germany was divided into a large number of practically independent states. It was in these and not in the empire as a whole that an approach was made to a form of national church, such as was realized after Luther had broken the bondage of Rome. When Duke Rudolph IV of Austria in the fourteenth century stated that he intended to be pope, archbishop, archdeacon and dean in his own land, when the dukes of Bavaria, Saxony and Cleves made similar boasts, they but put in a strong form the program that they in part realized. The princes gradually acquired the right of patronage to church benefices, and they permitted no bulls to be published, no indulgences sold, without their permission. The Free Cities acted in much the same way. The authority of the German states over their own spiritualities was no innovation of the heresy of Wittenberg.

For all Germany's internal division there was a certain national consciousness, due to the common language. In no point were the people more agreed than in their opposition to the rule of the Italian Curia.

1382

At one time the monasteries of Cologne signed a compact to resist Gregory XI in a proposed levy of tithes, stating that, "in consequence of the exactions by which the Papal Court burdens the clergy the Apostolic See has fallen into contempt and the Catholic faith in these parts seems to be seriously imperiled."

Again, a Knight of the Teutonic Order in Prussia 1430 wrote: "Greed reigns supreme in the Roman Court, and day by day finds new devices and artifices for extorting money from Germany under pretext of ecclesiastical fees. Hence arise much outcry, complaint and heart-burning. . . . Many questions about the papacy will be answered, or else obedience will ultimately be entirely renounced to escape from these outrageous exactions of the Italians."

The relief expected from the Council of Basle failed, and abuses were only made worse by a compact between Frederick III and Nicholas V, known as the Concordat of Vienna. This treaty was by no means 1448 comparable with the English and French legislation, but was merely a division of the spoils between the two supreme rulers at the expense of the people. The power of appointment to high ecclesiastical positions was divided, annates were confirmed, and in general a considerable increase of the authority of the Curia was established.

Protests began at once in the form of "Gravamina," or lists of grievances drawn up at each Diet as a petition, and in part enacted into laws. In 1452 the Spiritual Electors demanded that the emperor proceed with reform on the basis of the decrees of Constance. In 1457 the clergy refused to be taxed for a crusade. In 1461 the princes appealed against the sale of indulgences. The Gravamina of this year were very bitter, complaining of the practice of usury by priests, of the pomp of the cardinals and of the pope's habit of giving promises of preferment to certain sees and then declaring the places vacant on the plea of having made a "mental reservation" in favor of some one else. The Roman clergy were called in this bill of grievances "public fornicators, keepers of concubines, ruffians, pimps and sinners in various other respects." Drastic proposals of reform were defeated by the pope.

Gravamina

The Gravamina continued. Those of 1479 appealed against the Mendicant Orders and against the appointment of foreigners. They clamored for a new council and for reform on the basis of the decrees of Basle; they protested against judicial appeals to Rome, against the annates and against the crusade tax. It was stated that the papal appointees were rather fitted to be drivers of mules than pastors of souls. Such words found a reverberating echo among the people. The powerful pen of Gregory of Heimburg, sometimes called "the lay Luther," roused his countrymen to a patriotic stand against the Italian usurpation.

The Diet of 1502 resolved not to let money raised by indulgences leave Germany, but to use it against the Turks. Another long list of grievances relating to the tyranny and extortion of Rome was presented in 1510. The acts of the Diet of Augsburg in the summer of 1518 are eloquent testimony to the state of popular feeling when Luther had just begun his career. To this Diet Leo X sent as special legate Cardinal Cajetan, requesting a subsidy for a crusade against the Turk. It was proposed that an impost of ten per cent. be laid on the incomes of the clergy and one of five per cent. on the rich laity. This was refused on account of the grievances of the nation against the Curia, and refused in language of the utmost violence. It was stated that the real enemy of Christianity was not the Turk but "the hound of hell" in Rome. Indulgences were branded as blood-letting.

When such was the public opinion it is clear that Luther only touched a match to a heap of inflammable material. The whole nationalist movement redounded to the benefit of Protestantism. The state-churches of northern Europe are but the logical development of previous separatist tendencies.

§ 7. The Humanists

But the preparation for the great revolt was no less thorough on the intellectual than it was on the religious and political sides. The revival of interest in classical antiquity, aptly known as the Renaissance, brought with it a searching criticism of all medieval standards and, most of all, of medieval religion. The Renaissance stands in the same relationship to the Reformation that the so-called "Enlightenment" stands to the French Revolution. The humanists of the fifteenth century were the "philosophers" of the eighteenth.

The new spirit was born in Italy. If we go back as far as Dante we find, along with many modern elements, such as the use of the vernacular, a completely medieval conception of the universe. His immortal poem is in one respect but a commentary on the *Summa theologiae* of Aquinas; it is all about the other world. The younger contemporaries of the great Florentine began to be restless as the implications of the new spirit dawned on them. Petrarch lamented that literary culture was deemed incompatible with faith. Boccaccio was as much a child of this world as Dante was a prophet of the next. Too simple-minded deliberately to criticize doctrine, he was instinctively opposed to ecclesiastical professions. Devoting himself to celebrating the pleasures and the pomp of life, he took especial delight in heaping ridicule on ecclesiastics, representing them as the quintessence of all impurity and hypocrisy. The first story in his famous Decameron is of a scoundrel who comes to be reputed as a saint, invoked as such and performing miracles

Dante, 1265–1321

Petrarch, 1304–74

Boccaccio, 1313–75

after death. The second story is of a Jew who was converted to Christianity by the wickedness of Rome, for he reasoned that no cult, not divinely supported, could survive such desperate depravity as he saw there. The third tale, of the three rings, points the moral that no one can be certain what religion is the true one. The fourth narrative, like many others, turns upon the sensuality of the monks. Elsewhere the author describes the most absurd relics, and tells how a priest deceived a woman by pretending that he was the angel Gabriel. The trend of such a work was naturally the reverse of edifying. The irreligion is too spontaneous to be called philosophic doubt; it is merely impiety.

Valla, 1406–56

But such a sentiment could not long remain content with scoffing. The banner of pure rationalism, or rather of conscious classical skepticism, was raised by a circle of enthusiasts. The most brilliant of them, and one of the keenest critics that Europe has ever produced, was Lorenzo Valla, a native of Naples, and for some years holder of a benefice at Rome. Such was the trenchancy and temper of his weapons that much of what he advanced has stood the test of time.

The Donation of Constantine

The papal claim to temporal supremacy in the Western world rested largely on a spurious document known as the Donation of Constantine. In this the emperor is represented as withdrawing from Rome in order to leave it to the pope, to whom, in return for being cured of leprosy, he gives the whole Occident. An uncritical age had received this forgery for five or six centuries without question. Doubt had been cast on it by Nicholas of Cusa and Reginald Peacock, but Valla demolished it. He showed that no historian had spoken of it; that there was no time at which it could have occurred; that it is contradicted by other contemporary acts; that the barbarous style contains expressions of Greek, Hebrew, and German origin; that the testimony of numismatics is against it; and that the author knew nothing of the antiquities of Rome, into whose council he introduced satraps. Valla's work was so thoroughly done that the document, embodied as were its conclusions in the Canon Law, has never found a reputable defender since. In time the critique had an immense effect. Ulrich von Hutten published it in 1517, and in the same year an English translation was made. In 1537 Luther turned it into German.

Valla attacks the Pope

And if the legality of the pope's rule was so slight, what was its practical effect? According to Valla, it was a "barbarous, overbearing, tyrannical, priestly domination." "What is it to you," he apostrophizes the pontiff, "if our republic is crushed? You have crushed it. If our temples have been pillaged? You have pillaged them. If our virgins and matrons have been violated? You have done it. If the city is innundated with the blood of citizens? You are guilty of it all."

Annotations on the New Testament

Valla's critical genius next attacked the schoolman's idol Aristotle and the humanist's demigod Cicero. More important were his *Annotations on the New Testament,* first published by Erasmus in 1505. The Vulgate was at that time regarded, as it was at Trent defined to be, the authentic or official form of the Scriptures. Taking in hand three Latin and three Greek manuscripts, Valla had no difficulty in showing that they differed from one another and that in some cases the Latin had no authority whatever in the Greek. He pointed out a number of mistranslations, some of them in passages vitally affecting the faith. In short he left no support standing for any theory of verbal inspiration. He further questioned, and successfully, the authorship of the Creed attributed to the Apostles, the authenticity of the writings of Dionysius the Areopagite and of the letter of Christ to King Abgarus, preserved and credited by Eusebius.

Attack on Christian ethics

His attack on Christian ethics was still more fundamental. In his *Dialogue on Free Will* he tried with ingenuity to reconcile the freedom of the will, denied by Augustine, with the foreknowledge of God, which he did not feel strong enough to dispute. In his work on *The Monastic Life* he denied all value to asceticism. Others had mocked the monks for not living up to their professions; he asserted that the ideal itself was mistaken. But it is the treatise *On Pleasure* that goes the farthest. In form it is a dialogue on ethics; one interlocutor maintaining the Epicurean, the second the Stoical, and the third the Christian standard. The sympathies of the author are plainly with the champion of hedonism, who maintains that pleasure is the supreme good in life, or rather the only good, that the prostitute is better than the nun, for the one makes men happy, the other is dedicated to a painful and shameful celibacy; that the law against adultery is a sort of sacrilege; that women should be common and should go naked; and that it is irrational to die for one's country or for any other ideal. . . . It is noteworthy that the representative of the Christian standpoint accepts tacitly the assumption that happiness is the supreme good, only he places that happiness in the next life.

Valla's ideas obtained throughout a large circle in the half-century following his death. Masuccio indulged in the most obscene mockery of Catholic rites. Poggio wrote a book against hypocrites, attacking the monks, and a joke-book largely at the expense of the faithful. Machiavelli assailed the papacy with great ferocity, attributing to it the corruption of Italian morals and the political disunion and weakness of

Machiavelli, 1469–1530

Italy, and advocating its annihilation. In place of Christianity, habitually spoken of as an exploded superstition, dangerous to the state, he would put the patriotic cults of antiquity.

It is not strange, knowing the character of the popes, that pagan expressions should color the writings of their courtiers. Poggio was a papal secretary, and so was Bembo, a cardinal who refused to read Paul's epistles for fear of corrupting his Latinity. In his exquisite search for classical equivalents for the rude phrases of the gospel, he referred, in a papal breve, to Christ as "Minerva sprung from the head of Jove," and to the Holy Ghost as "the breath of the celestial Zephyr." Conceived in the same spirit was a sermon of Inghirami heard by Erasmus at Rome on Good Friday 1509. Couched in the purest Ciceronian terms, while comparing the Saviour to Curtius, Cecrops, Aristides, Epaminondas and Iphigenia, it was mainly devoted to an extravagant eulogy of the reigning pontiff, Julius II.

But all the Italian humanists were not pagans. There arose at Florence, partly under the influence of the revival of Greek, partly under that of Savonarola, a group of earnest young men who sought to invigorate Christianity by infusing into it the doctrines of Plato. The leaders of this Neo-Platonic Academy, Pico della Mirandola and Marsiglio Ficino, sought to show that the teachings of the Athenian and of the Galilean were the same. Approaching the Bible in the simple literary way indicated by classical study, Pico really rediscovered some of the teachings of the New Testament, while in dealing with the Old he was forced to adopt an ingenious but unsound allegorical interpretation. "Philosophy seeks the truth," he wrote, "theology finds it, religion possesses it." His extraordinary personal influence extended through

Pico della Mirandola, 1462–94

lands beyond the Alps, even though it failed in accomplishing the rehabilitation of Italian faith.

Faber Stapulensis, c. 1455–1536

The leader of the French Christian Renaissance, James Lefèvre d'Étaples, was one of his disciples. Traveling in Italy in 1492, after visiting Padua, Venice and Rome, he came to Florence, learned to know Pico, and received from him a translation of Aristotle's Metaphysics made by Cardinal Bessarion. Returning to Paris he taught, at the College of Cardinal Lemoine, mathematics, music and philosophy. He did not share the dislike of Aristotle manifested by most of the humanists, for he shrewdly suspected that what was offensive in the Stagyrite was due more to his scholastic translators and commentators than to himself. He therefore labored to restore the true text, on which he wrote a number of treatises. It was with the same purpose that he turned next to the early Fathers and to the writer called Dionysius the Areopagite. But he did not find himself until he found the Bible. In 1509 he published the *Quintuplex Psalterium,* the first treatise on the Psalms in which the philological and personal interest was uppermost. Hitherto it had not been the Bible that had been studied so much as the commentaries on it, a dry wilderness of arid and futile subtlety. Lefèvre tried to see simply what the text said, and as it became more human it became, for him, more divine. His preface is a real cry of joy at his great discovery. He did, indeed, interpret everything in a double sense, literal and spiritual, and placed the emphasis rather on the latter, but this did not prevent a genuine effort to read the words as they were written. Three years later he published in like manner the Epistles of St. Paul, with commentary. Though he spoke of the apostle as a simple instrument of God, he yet did more to uncover his personality than any of the previous commentators. Half mystic as he was, Lefèvre discovered in Paul the doctrine of justification by faith only. To I Corinthians viii, he wrote: "It is almost profane to speak of the merit of works, especially towards God. . . . The opinion that we can be justified by works is an error for which the Jews are especially condemned. . . . Our only hope is in God's grace." Lefèvre's works opened up a new world to the theologians of the time. Erasmus's friend Beatus Rhenanus wrote that the richness of the *Quintuplex Psalter* made him poor. Thomas More said that English students owed him much. Luther used the two works of the Frenchman as the texts for his early lectures. From them he drew very heavily; indeed it was doubtless Lefèvre who first suggested to him the formula of his famous "sola fide."

Colet, † 1519

The religious renaissance in England was led by a disciple of Pico della Mirandola, John Colet, a man of remarkably pure life, and Dean of St. Paul's. He wrote, though he did not publish, some commentaries on the Pauline epistles and on the Mosaic account of creation. Though he knew no Greek, and was not an easy or elegant writer of Latin, he was allied to the humanists by his desire to return to the real sources of Christianity, and by his search for the historical sense of his texts. Though in some respects he was under the fantastic notions of the Areopagite, in others his interpretation was rational, free and undogmatic. He exercised a considerable influence on Erasmus and on a few choice spirits of the time.

The humanism of Germany centered in the universities. At the close of the fifteenth century new courses in the Latin classics, in Greek and in Hebrew, began to supplement the medieval curriculum of logic and philosophy. At every academy there sprang up a circle of "poets," as they called themselves, often of lax morals and indifferent to religion, but earnest in their championship of culture. Nor were these circles confined entirely to the seats of learning. Many a city had its own literary society, one of the most famous being that of Nuremberg. Conrad Mutianus Rufus drew to Gotha, where he held a canonry, a group of disciples, to whom he imparted the Neo-Platonism he had imbibed in Italy. Disregarding revelation, he taught that all religions were essentially the same. "I esteem the decrees of philosophers more than those of priests," he wrote.

Mutian, 1471–1526

What Lefèvre and Colet had done for the New Testament, John Reuchlin did for the Old. After studying in France and Italy, where he learned to know Pico della Mirandola, he settled at Stuttgart and devoted his life to the study of Hebrew. His *De Rudimentis Hebraicis,* a grammar and dictionary of this language, performed a great service for scholarship. In the late Jewish work, the *Cabbala,* he believed he had discovered a source of mystic wisdom. The extravagance of his interpretations of Scriptual passages, based on this, not only rendered much of his work nugatory, but got him into a great deal of trouble. The converted Jew, John Pfefferkorn, proposed, in a series of pamphlets, that Jews should be forbidden to practise usury, should be compelled to hear sermons and to deliver up all their Hebrew books to be burnt, except the Old Testament. When Reuchlin's aid in this pious project was requested it was refused in a memorial dated October 6, 1510, pointing out the great value of much Hebrew literature. The Dominicans of Cologne, headed by their inquisitor, James Hochstraten, made this the ground for a charge of heresy. The case was appealed to Rome, and the trial, lasting six years, excited the interest of all Europe. In Germany it was argued with much heat in a host of pam-

Reuchlin, 1455–1522

1506

phlets, all the monks and obscurantists taking the side of the inquisitors and all the humanists, save one, Ortuin Gratius of Cologne, taking the part of the scholar. The latter received many warm expressions of admiration and support from the leading writers of the time, and published them in two volumes, the first in 1514, under the title *Letters of Eminent Men.* It was this that suggested to the humanist, Crotus Rubeanus, the title of his satire published anonymously, *The Letters of Obscure Men.* In form it is a series of epistles from monks and hedge-priests to Ortuin Gratius. Writing in the most barbarous Latin, they express their admiration for his attack on Reuchlin and the cause of learning, gossip about their drinking-bouts and pot-house amours, expose their ignorance and gullibility, and ask absurd questions, as, whether it is a mortal sin to salute a Jew, and whether the worms eaten with beans and cheese should be considered meat or fish, lawful or not in Lent, and at what stage of development a chick in the egg becomes meat and therefore prohibited on Fridays. The satire, coarse as it was biting, failed to win the applause of the finer spirits, but raised a shout of laughter from the students, and was no insignificant factor in adding to contempt for the church. The first book of these *Letters,* published in 1515, was followed two years later by a second, even more caustic than the first. This supplement, also published without the writer's name, was from the pen of Ulrich von Hutten.

Epistolae Obscurorum Virorum

This brilliant and passionate writer devoted the greater part of his life to war with Rome. His motive was not religious, but patriotic. He longed to see his country strong and united, and free from the galling oppression of the ultramontane yoke. He published Valla's *Donation of Constantine,* and wrote epigrams on the popes. His dialogue *Fever the First* is a vitri-

Hutten, 1488–1523

olic attack on the priests. His *Vadiscus or the Roman Trinity* scourges the vices of the curia where three things are sold: Christ, places and women. When he first heard of Luther's cause he called it a quarrel of monks, and only hoped they would all destroy one another. But by 1519 he saw in the Reformer the most powerful of allies against the common foe, and he accordingly embraced his cause with habitual zeal. His letters at this time breathe out fire and slaughter against the Romanists if anything should happen to Luther. In 1523, he supported his friend Francis von Sickingen, in the attempt to assert by force of arms the rights of the patriotic and evangelic order of knights. When this was defeated, Hutten, suffering from a terrible disease, wandered to Switzerland, where he died, a lonely and broken exile. His epitaph shall be his own lofty poem:

1520

> I have fought my fight with courage,
> Nor have I aught to rue,
> For, though I lost the battle,
> The world knows, I was true!

Erasmus, 1466–1536

The most cosmopolitan, as well as the greatest, of all the Christian humanists, was Desiderius Erasmus of Rotterdam. Though an illegitimate child, he was well educated and thoroughly grounded in the classics at the famous school of Deventer. At the age of twenty he was persuaded, somewhat against his will, to enter the order of Augustinian Canons at Steyn. Under the patronage of the Bishop of Cambrai he was enabled to continue his studies at Paris. For the next ten years he wandered to England, to various places in Northern France and Flanders, and Italy, learning to know many of the intellectual leaders of the time. From 1509–14 he was in England, part of the time lecturing at Cambridge. He then spent some

1499–1509

years at Louvain, seven years at Basle and six years at Freiburg in the Breisgau, returning to Basle for the last year of his life.

Until he was over thirty Erasmus's dominant interest was classical literature. Under the influence of Colet and of a French Franciscan, John Vitrier, he turned his attention to liberalizing religion. His first devotional work, *The Handbook of the Christian Knight,* perfectly sets forth his program of spiritual, as opposed to formal, Christianity. It all turns upon the distinction between the inner and the outer man, the moral and the sensual. True service of Christ is purity of heart and love, not the invocation of saints, fasting and indulgences.

Enchiridion Militis Christiani, 1503

In *The Praise of Folly* Erasmus mildly rebukes the foibles of men. There never was kindlier satire, free from the savage scorn of Crotus and Hutten, and from the didactic scolding of Sebastian Brant, whose *Ship of Fools* was one of the author's models. Folly is made quite amiable, the source not only of some things that are amiss but also of much harmless enjoyment. The besetting silliness of every class is exposed: of the man of pleasure, of the man of business, of women and of husbands, of the writer and of the pedant. Though not unduly emphasized, the folly of current superstitions is held up to ridicule. Some there are who have turned the saints into pagan gods; some who have measured purgatory into years and days and cheat themselves with indulgences against it; some theologians who spend all their time discussing such absurdities as whether God could have redeemed men in the form of a woman, a devil, an ass, a squash or a stone, others who explain the mystery of the Trinity.

1511

1494

In following up his plan for the restoration of a simpler Christianity, Erasmus rightly thought that a return from the barren subtleties of the schoolmen to the primitive sources was essential. He wished to reduce Christianity to a moral, humanitarian, undogmatic philosophy of life. His attitude towards dogma was to admit it and to ignore it. Scientific enlightenment he welcomed more than did either the Catholics or the Reformers, sure that if the Sermon on the Mount survived, Christianity had nothing to fear. In like manner, while he did not attack the cult and ritual of the church, he never laid any stress on it. "If some dogmas are incomprehensible and some rites superstitious," he seemed to say, "what does it matter? Let us emphasize the ethical and spiritual content of Christ's message, for if we seek his kingdom, all else needful shall be added unto us." His favorite name for his religion was the "philosophy of Christ," and it is thus that he persuasively expounds it in a note, in his Greek Testament, to Matthew xi, 30:

Philosophy of Christ

> Truly the yoke of Christ would be sweet and his burden light, if petty human institutions added nothing to what he himself imposed. He commanded us nothing save love one for another, and there is nothing so bitter that charity does not soften and sweeten it. Everything according to nature is easily borne, and nothing accords better with the nature of man than the philosophy of Christ, of which almost the sole end is to give back to fallen nature its innocence and integrity. . . . How pure, how simple is the faith that Christ delivered to us! How close to it is the creed transmitted to us by the apostles, or apostolic men. The church, divided and tormented by discussions and by heresy, added to it many things, of which some can be omitted without prejudice to the faith. . . . There are many opinions from which impiety may be begotten, as for example, all those philosophic doctrines on the reason of the nature and the distinction of the persons of the Godhead. . . . The sacraments themselves were instituted for the salvation of men, but we abuse them for lucre, for vain glory or for the oppression of the humble. . . . What rules, what superstitions we have about vestments! How many are judged as to

their Christianity by such trifles, which are indifferent in themselves, which change with the fashion and of which Christ never spoke! . . . How many fasts are instituted! And we are not merely invited to fast, but obliged to, on pain of damnation. . . . What shall we say about vows . . . about the authority of the pope, the abuse of absolutions, dispensations, remissions of penalty, law-suits, in which there is much that a truly good man cannot see without a groan? The priests themselves prefer to study Aristotle than to ply their ministry. The gospel is hardly mentioned from the pulpit. Sermons are monopolized by the commissioners of indulgences; often the doctrine of Christ is put aside and suppressed for their profit. . . . Would that men were content to let Christ rule by the laws of the gospel and that they would no longer seek to strengthen their obscurant tyranny by human decrees!

Colloquies

In the *Familiar Colloquies,* first published in 1518 and often enlarged in subsequent editions, Erasmus brought out his religious ideas most sharply. Enormous as were the sales and influence of his other chief writings, they were probably less than those of this work, intended primarily as a text-book of Latin style. The first conversations are, indeed, nothing more than school-boy exercises, but the later ones are short stories penned with consummate art. Erasmus is almost the only man who, since the fall of Rome, has succeeded in writing a really exquisite Latin. But his supreme gift was his dry wit, the subtle faculty of exposing an object, apparently by a simple matter-of-fact narrative, to the keenest ridicule. Thus, in the *Colloquies,* he describes his pilgrimage to St. Thomas's shrine at Canterbury, the bloody bones and the handkerchief covered with the saint's rheum offered to be kissed—all without a disapproving word and yet in such a way that when the reader has finished it he wonders how anything so silly could ever have existed. Thus again he strips the worship of Mary, and all the stupid and wrong projects she is asked to abet. In the conversation called *The Shipwreck,* the people pray to the Star of the Sea exactly as they did in pagan times, only it is Mary, not Venus that is meant. They offer mountains of wax candles to the saints to preserve them, although one man confides to his neighbor in a whisper that if he ever gets to land he will not pay one penny taper on his vow. Again, in the *Colloquy on the New Testament,* a young man is asked what he has done for Christ. He replies:

> A certain Franciscan keeps reviling the New Testament of Erasmus in his sermons. Well, one day I called on him in private, seized him by the hair with my left hand and punished him with my right. I gave him so sound a drubbing that I reduced his whole face to a mere jelly. What do you say to that? Isn't that maintaining the gospel? And then, by way of absolution for his sins I took this book [Erasmus's New Testament, a folio bound with brass] and gave him three resounding whacks on the head in the name of the Father and of the Son and of the Holy Ghost.

"That," replies his friend, "was truly evangelic; defending the gospel by the gospel. But really it is time you were turning from a brute beast into a man."

Methods of argument

So it was that the man who was at once the gentlest Christian, the leading scholar, and the keenest wit of his age insinuated his opinions without seeming to attack anything. Where Luther battered down, he undermined. Even when he argued against an opinion he called his polemic a "Conversation"—for that is the true meaning of the word Diatribe. With choice of soft vocabulary, of attenuated forms, of double negatives, he tempered exquisitely his Latin. Did he doubt anything? Hardly, "he had a shade of doubt" (*subdubito*). Did he think he wrote well? Not at all, but he confessed that he produced "something more like Latin than the average" (*paulo latinius*). Did he like anything? If so, he only admitted—except when he was addressing his patrons—"that he was not altogether averse to it." But all at once from these feather-light touches, like those of a Henry James, comes the sudden thrust that made his stylus a dagger. Some of his epigrams on the Reformation have been quoted in practically every history of the subject since, and will be quoted as often again.

His wit

But it was not a few perfect phrases that made him the power that he was, but an habitual wit that never failed to strip any situation of its vulgar pretense. When a canon of Strassburg Cathedral was showing him over the chapter house and was boasting of the rule that no one should be admitted to a prebend who had not sixteen quarterings on his coat of arms, the humanist dropped his eyes and remarked demurely, with but the flicker of a smile, that he was indeed honored to be in a religious company so noble that even Jesus could not have come up to its requirements. The man was dumfounded, he almost suspected something personal; but he never forgot the salutary lesson so delicately conveyed.

Erasmus was a man of peace; he feared "the tumult" which, if we trust a letter dated September 9, 1517—though he sometimes retouched his letters on publishing them—he foresaw. "In this part of the world," he wrote, "I am afraid that a great revolution is impending." It was already knocking at the door!

CHAPTER II

GERMANY

§ 1. The Leader

It is superfluous in these days to point out that no great historical movement is caused by the personality, however potent, of a single individual. The men who take the helm at crises are those who but express in themselves what the masses of their followers feel. The need of leadership is so urgent that if there is no really great man at hand, the people will invent one, endowing the best of the small men with the prestige of power, and embodying in his person the cause for which they strive. But a really strong personality to some extent guides the course of events by which he is carried along. Such a man was Luther. Few have ever alike represented and dominated an age as did he. His heart was the most passionately earnest, his will the strongest, his brain one of the most capacious of his time; above all he had the gift of popular speech to stamp his ideas into the fibre of his countrymen. If we may borrow a figure from chemistry, he found public opinion a solution supersaturated with revolt; all that was needed to precipitate it was a pebble thrown in, but instead of a pebble he added the most powerful reägent possible.

Luther, 1483–1546

On that October day when Columbus discovered the new world, Martin, a boy of very nearly nine, was sitting at his desk in the school at Mansfeld. Though both diligent and quick, he found the crabbed Latin primer, itself written in abstract Latin, very difficult, and was flogged fourteen times in one morning by brutal masters for faltering in a declension. When he returned home he found his mother bending under a load of wood she had gathered in the forest. Both she and his father were severe with the children, whipping them for slight faults until the blood came. Nevertheless, as the son himself recognized, they meant heartily well by it. But for the self-sacrifice and determination shown by the father, a worker in the newly opened mines, who by his own industry rose to modest comfort, the career of the son would have been impossible.

Fully as much as by bodily hardship the boy's life was rendered unhappy by spiritual terrors. Demons lurked in the storms, and witches plagued his good mother and threatened to make her children cry themselves to death. God and Christ were conceived as stern and angry judges ready to thrust sinners into hell. "They painted Christ," says Luther—and such pictures can still be seen in old churches—"sitting on a rainbow with his Mother and John the Baptist on either side as intercessors against his frightful wrath."

At thirteen he was sent away to Magdeburg to a charitable school, and the next year to Eisenach, where he spent three years in study. He contributed to his support by the then recognized means of begging, and was sheltered by the pious matron Ursula Cotta. In 1501 he matriculated at the old and famous university of Erfurt. The curriculum here consisted of logic, dialectic, grammar, and rhetoric, followed by arithmetic, ethics, and metaphysics. There was some natural science, studied not by the experimental method, but wholly from the books of Aristotle and his medieval commentators, and there were also a few courses in literature, both in the Latin classics and in their later imitators. Ranking among the better

Erfurt

scholars Luther took the degrees of bachelor in 1502 and of master of arts in 1505, and immediately began the study of jurisprudence. While his diligence and good conduct won golden words from his preceptors he mingled with his comrades as a man with men. He was generous, even prodigal, a musician and a "philosopher"; in disputations he was made "an honorary umpire" by his fellows and teachers. "Fair fortune and good health are mine," he wrote a friend on September 5, 1501, "I am settled at college as pleasantly as possible."

For the sudden change that came over his life at the age of twenty-one no adequate explanation has been offered. Pious and serious as he was, his thoughts do not seem to have turned towards the monastic life as a boy, nor are the old legends of the sudden death of a friend well substantiated. As he was returning to Erfurt from a visit home, he was overtaken by a terrific thunderstorm, in which his excited imagination saw a divine warning to forsake the "world." In a fright he vowed to St. Ann to become a monk and, though he at once regretted the rash promise, on July 17, 1505, he discharged it by entering the Augustinian friary at Erfurt. After a year's novitiate he took the irrevocable vows of poverty, chastity, and obedience. In 1507 he was ordained priest. In the winter of 1510–1 he was sent to Rome on business of the order, and there saw much of the splendour and also of the corruption of the capital of Christendom. Having started, in 1508, to teach Aristotle at the recently founded University of Wittenberg, a year later he returned to Erfurt, but was again called to Wittenberg to lecture on the Bible, a position he held all his life.

1511

During his first ten years in the cloister he underwent a profound experience. He started with the horrible and torturing idea that he was doomed to hell.

"What can I do," he kept asking, "to win a gracious God?" The answer given him by his teachers was that a man must work out his own salvation, not entirely, but largely, by his own efforts. The sacraments of the church dispensed grace and life to the recipient, and beyond this he could merit forgiveness by the asceticism and privation of the monastic life. Luther took this all in and strove frantically by fasting, prayer, and scourging to fit himself for redemption. But though he won the reputation of a saint, he could not free himself from the desires of the flesh. He was helpless; he could do nothing. Then he read in Augustine that virtue without grace is but a specious vice; that God damns and saves utterly without regard to man's work. He read in Tauler and the other mystics that the only true salvation is union with God, and that if a man were willing to be damned for God's glory he would find heaven even in hell. He read in Lefèvre d'Étaples that a man is not saved by doing good, but by faith, like the thief on the cross.

Justification by faith only

In May, 1515, he began to lecture on Paul's Epistles to the Romans, and pondered the verse (i, 17) "The just shall live by his faith." All at once, so forcibly that he believed it a revelation of the Holy Ghost, the thought dawned upon him that whereas man was impotent to do or be good, God was able freely to make him so. Pure passivity in God's hands, simple abandonment to his will was the only way of salvation; not by works but by faith in the Redeemer was man sanctified. The thought, though by no means new in Christianity, was, in the application he gave it, the germ of the religious revolution. In it was contained the total repudiation of the medieval ecclesiastical system of salvation by sacrament and by the good works of the cloister. To us nowadays the thought seems remote; the question which called it forth outworn. But to the sixteenth century it was as intensely practical as social reform is now; the church was everywhere with her claim to rule over men's daily lives and over their souls. All progress was conditioned on breaking her claims, and probably nothing could have done it so thoroughly as this idea of justification by faith only.

The thought made Luther a reformer at once. He started to purge his order of Pharisaism, and the university of the dross of Aristotle. Soon he was called upon to protest against one of the most obtrusive of the "good works" recommended by the church, the purchase of indulgences. Albert of Hohenzollern was elected, through political influence and at an early age, to the archiepiscopal sees of Magdeburg and Mayence, this last carrying with it an electorate and the primacy of Germany. For confirmation from the pope in the uncanonical occupation of these offices, Albert paid a huge sum, the equivalent of several hundred thousand dollars today. Mayence was already in debt and the young archbishop knew not where to turn for money. To help him, and to raise money for Rome, Leo X declared an indulgence. In order to get as large a profit as possible Albert employed as his chief agent an unscrupulous Dominican named John Tetzel. This man went around the country proclaiming that as soon as the money clinked in the chest the soul of some dead relative flew from purgatory, and that by buying a papal pardon the purchaser secured plenary remission of sins and the grace of God.

Tetzel

The indulgence-sellers were forbidden to enter Saxony, but they came very near it, and many of the people of Wittenberg went out to buy heaven at a bargain. Luther was sickened by seeing what he believed to be the deception of the poor people in being taught to rely on these wretched papers instead of on real, lively faith. He accordingly called their value in question in Ninety-five Theses, or heads for a scholastic debate, which he nailed to the door of the Castle Church on October 31, 1517. He pointed out that the doctrine of the church was very uncertain, especially in regard to the freeing of souls from purgatory; that contrition was the only gate to God's pardon; that works of charity were better than buying of indulgences, and that the practices of the indulgence-sellers were extremely scandalous and likely to foment heresy among the simple. In all this he did not directly deny the whole value of indulgences, but he pared it down to a minimum.

The Ninety-five Theses, 1517

The Theses were printed by Luther and sent around to friends in other cities. They were at once put into German, and applauded to the echo by the whole nation. Everybody had been resentful of the extortion of greedy ecclesiastics and disgusted with their hypocrisy. All welcomed the attack on the "holy trade," as its supporters called it. Tetzel was mobbed and had to withdraw in haste. The pardons no longer had any sale. The authorities took alarm at once. Leo X directed the general of the Augustinians to make his presumptuous brother recant. The matter was accordingly brought up at the general chapter of the Order held at Heidelberg in May. Luther was present, was asked to retract, and refused. On the contrary he published a Sermon on Indulgence and Grace and a defence of the Theses stating his points more strongly than before.

February 3, 1518

The whole of Germany was now in commotion. The Diet which met at Augsburg in the summer of 1518 was extremely hostile to the pope and to his legate, Cardinal Cajetan. At the instance of this theologian, who had written a reply to the Theses, and of the Dominicans, wounded in the person of Tetzel, Luther was summoned to Rome to be tried. On August 5 the

Emperor Maximilian promised his aid to the pope, and, in order to expedite matters, the latter changed the summons to Rome to a citation before Cajetan at Augsburg, at the same time instructing the legate to seize the heretic if he did not recant. At this juncture Luther was not left in the lurch by his own sovereign, Frederic the Wise, Elector of Saxony, through whom an imperial safe-conduct was procured. Armed with this, the Wittenberg professor appeared before Cajetan at Augsburg, was asked to recant two of his statements on indulgences, and refused. A few days later Luther drew up an appeal "from the pope badly informed to the pope to be better informed," and in the following month appealed again from the pope to a future oecumenical council. In the meantime Leo X, in the bull *Cum postquam*, authoritatively defined the doctrine of indulgences in a sense contrary to the position of Luther.

October 12–14, 1518

The next move of the Vicar of Christ was to send to Germany a special agent, the Saxon Charles von Miltitz, with instructions either to cajole the heretic into retraction or the Elector into surrendering him. In neither of these attempts was he successful. At an interview with Luther the utmost he could do was to secure a general statement that the accused man would abide by the decision of the Holy See, and a promise to keep quiet as long as his opponents did the same.

January, 1519

Such a compromise was sure to be fruitless, for the champions of the church could not let the heretic rest for a moment. The whole affair was given a wider publicity than it had hitherto attained, and at the same time Luther was pushed to a more advanced position than he had yet reached, by the attack of a theologian of Ingolstadt, John Eck. When he assailed the Theses on the ground that they seriously impaired the authority of the Roman see, Luther retorted:

> The assertion that the Roman Church is superior to all other churches is proved only by weak and vain papal decrees of the last four hundred years, and is repugnant to the accredited history of the previous eleven hundred years, to the Bible, and to the decree of the holiest of all councils, the Nicene.

The Leipzig Debate, 1519

A debate on this and other propositions between Eck on the one side and Luther and his colleague Carlstadt on the other took place at Leipzig in the days from June 27 to July 16, 1519. The climax of the argument on the power of popes and councils came when Eck, skilfully manoeuvring to show that Luther's opinions were identical with those of Huss, forced from his opponent the bold declaration that "among the opinions of John Huss and the Bohemians many are certainly most Christian and evangelic, and cannot be condemned by the universal church." The words sent a thrill through the audience and throughout Christendom. Eck could only reply: "If you believe that a general council, legitimately convoked, can err, you are to me a heathen and a publican." Reconciliation was indeed no longer possible. When Luther had protested against the abuse of indulgences he did so as a loyal son of the church. Now at last he was forced to raise the standard of revolt, at least against Rome, the recognized head of the church. He had begun by appealing from indulgence-seller to pope, then from the pope to a universal council; now he declared that a great council had erred, and that he would not abide by its decision. The issue was a clear one, though hardly recognized as such by himself, between the religion of authority and the right of private judgment.

His opposition to the papacy developed with extraordinary rapidity. His study of the Canon Law made him, as early as March, 1519, brand the pope as either Antichrist or Antichrist's apostle. He applauded Melanchthon, a brilliant young man called to teach at Wittenberg in 1518, for denying transubstantiation. He declared that the cup should never have been withheld from the laity, and that the mass considered as a good work and a sacrifice was an abomination. His eyes were opened to the iniquities of Rome by Valla's exposure of the Donation of Constantine, published by Ulrich von Hutten in 1519. After reading it he wrote:

> Good heavens! what darkness and wickedness is at Rome! You wonder at the judgment of God that such unauthentic, crass, impudent lies not only lived but prevailed for many centuries, that they were incorporated into the Canon Law, and (that no degree of horror might be wanting) that they became as articles of faith.

Like German troops Luther was best in taking the offensive. These early years when he was standing almost alone and attacking one abuse after another, were the finest of his whole career. Later, when he came to reconstruct a church, he modified or withdrew much of what he had at first put forward, and reintroduced a large portion of the medieval religiosity which he had once so successfully and fiercely attacked. The year 1520 saw him at the most advanced point he ever attained. It was then that he produced, with marvellous fecundity, a series of pamphlets unequalled by him and unexcelled anywhere, both in the incisive power of their attack on existing institutions and in the popular force of their language.

To the Christian Nobility, 1520

His greatest appeal to his countrymen was made in his *Address to the Christian Nobility of the German Nation on the Improvement of the Christian Estate.* In this he asserts the right of the civil power to reform the spiritual, and urges the government to exercise this right. The priests, says he, defend themselves against all outside interference by three "walls," of which the first is the claim that the church is superior to the state, in case the civil authority presses them; the second, the assertion, if one would correct them by the Bible, that no one can interpret it but the pope; the third, if they are threatened with a general council, the contention that no one can convoke such a council save the pope. Luther demolishes these walls with words of vast import. First, he denies any distinction between the spiritual and temporal estates. Every baptized Christian, he asserts, is a priest, and in this saying he struck a mortal blow at the great hierarchy of privilege and theocratic tyranny built up by the Middle Ages. The second wall is still frailer than the first, says the writer, for anyone can see that in spite of the priests' claims to be masters of the Bible they never learn one word of it their whole life long. The third wall falls of itself, for the Bible plainly commands everyone to punish and correct any wrong-doer, no matter what his station.

Reform measures

After this introduction Luther proposes measures of reform equally drastic and comprehensive. The first twelve articles are devoted to the pope, the annates, the appointment of foreigners to German benefices, the appeal of cases to Rome, the asserted authority of the papacy over bishops, the emperor, and other rulers. All these abuses, as well as jubilees and pilgrimages to Rome should be simply forbidden by the civil government. The next three articles deal with sacerdotal celibacy, recommending that priests be allowed to marry, and calling for the suppression of many of the cloisters. It is further urged that foundations for masses and for the support of idle priests be abolished, that various vexatious provisions of the Canon Law be repealed, and that begging on any pretext be prohibited. The twenty-fourth article deals with the Bohemian schism, saying that Huss was wrongly burned, and calling for union with the Hussites who deny transubstantiation and demand the cup for the laity. Next, the writer takes up the reform of education in the interests of a more biblical religion. Finally, he urges that sumptuary laws be passed, that a bridle be put in the mouth of the great monopolists and usurers, and that brothels be no longer tolerated.

Of all the writer's works this probably had the greatest and most immediate influence. Some, indeed, were offended by the violence of the language, defended by Luther from the example of the Bible and by the necessity of rousing people to the enormities he attacked. But most hailed it as a "trumpet-blast" calling the nation to arms. Four thousand copies were sold in a few days, and a second edition was called for within a month. Voicing ideas that had been long, though vaguely, current, it convinced almost all of the need of a reformation. According to their sympathies men declared that the devil or the Holy Ghost spoke through Luther.

The Babylonian Captivity, 1520

Though less popular both in form and subject, *The Babylonian Captivity of the Church* was not less important than the *Address to the German Nobility*. It was a mortal blow at the sacramental system of the church. In judging it we must again summon the aid of our historical imagination. In the sixteenth century dogmas not only seemed but were matters of supreme importance. It was just by her sacramental system, by her claim to give the believer eternal life and salvation through her rites, that the church had imposed her yoke on men. As long as that belief remained intact progress in thought, in freedom of conscience, in reform, remained difficult. And here, as is frequently the case, the most effective arguments were not those which seem to us logically the strongest. Luther made no appeal to reason as such. He appealed to the Bible, recognized by all Christians as an authority, and showed how far the practice of the church had degenerated from her standard. In the first place he reduced the number of sacraments, denying that name to matrimony, orders, extreme unction and confirmation. In attacking orders he demolished the priestly ideal and authority. In reducing marriage to a civil contract he took a long step towards the secularization of life. Penance he considered a sacrament in a certain sense, though not in the strict one, and he showed that it had been turned by the church from its original significance of "repentance" [1] to that of sacramental penance, in which no faith was required but merely an automatic act. Baptism and the eucharist he considered the only true sacraments, and he seriously criticized the prevalent doctrine of the latter. He denied that the mass is a sacrifice or a "good work" pleasing to God and therefore beneficial to the soul either of living or of dead. He denied that the bread and wine are transubstantiated into the body and blood of Jesus, though he held that the body and blood are really present with the elements. He demanded that the cup be given to the laity.

Sacraments

The whole trend of Luther's thought at this time was to oppose the Catholic theory of a mechanical distribution of grace and salvation (the so-called *opus operatum*) by means of the sacraments, and to substitute for it an individual conception of religion in which faith only should be necessary. How far he carried this idea may be seen in his *Sermon on the New Testament, that is on the Holy Mass*,[2] published in the same year as the pamphlets just analysed. In it he makes the essence of the sacrament forgiveness, and the vehicle of this forgiveness the word of God apprehended by

1 In Latin *penitentia* means both penance and repentance.

2 *Cf.* Matthew, xxvi, 28.

faith, *not* the actual participation in the sacred bread and wine. Had he always been true to this conception he would have left no place for sacrament or priest at all. But in later years he grew more conservative, until, under slightly different names, almost the old medieval ideas of church and religion were again established, and, as Milton later expressed it, "New presbyter was but old priest writ large."

§ 2. The Revolution

Germany

Although the Germans had arrived, by the end of the fifteenth century, at a high degree of national self-consciousness, they had not, like the French and English, succeeded in forming a corresponding political unity. The Holy Roman Empire of the German Nation, though continuing to assert the vast claims of the Roman world-state, was in fact but a loose confederacy of many and very diverse territories. On a map drawn to the scale 1: 6,000,000 nearly a hundred separate political entities can be counted within the limits of the Empire and there were many others too small to appear. The rulers of seven of these territories elected the emperor; they were the three spiritual princes, the Archbishops of Mayence, Trèves and Cologne, the three German temporal princes, the Electors of the Rhenish Palatinate, Saxony, and Brandenburg, and in addition the King of Bohemia, who, save for purposes of the imperial choice, did not count as a member of the Germanic body. Besides these there were some powerful dukedoms, like Austria and Bavaria, and numerous smaller bishoprics and counties. There were also many free cities, like Augsburg and Nuremberg, small aristocratic republics. Finally there was a large body of "free knights" or barons, whose tiny fiefs amounted often to no more than a castle and a few acres, but who owned no feudal superior save the emperor. The unity of the Empire was expressed not only in the person of the emperor, but in the Diet which met at different places at frequent intervals. Its authority, though on the whole increasing, was small.

With no imperial system of taxation, no professional army and no centralized administration, the real power of the emperor dwindled. Such as it was he derived it from the fact that he was always elected from one of the great houses. Since 1438 the Hapsburgs, Archdukes of Austria, had held the imperial office. Since 1495 there was also an imperial supreme court of arbitration. The first imperial tax was levied in 1422 to equip a force against the Hussites. In the fifteenth century also the rudiments of a central administration were laid in the division of the realm into ten "circles," and the levy of a small number of soldiers. And yet, at the time of the Reformation, the Empire was little better than a state in dissolution through the centrifugal forces of feudalism.

1495

So little was the Empire an individual unit that the policy of her rulers themselves was not imperial. The statesmanship of Maximilian was something smaller than national; it was that of his Archduchy of Austria. The policy of his successor, on the other hand, was determined by something larger than Germany, the consideration of the Spanish and Burgundian states that he also ruled. Maximilian tried in every way to aggrandize his personal power, not that of the German nation. The Diet of Worms of 1495 tried to remodel the constitution. It proclaimed a perpetual public peace, provided that those who broke it should be outlawed, and placed the duty of executing the ban upon all territories within ninety miles of the offender. It also passed a bill for taxation, called the "common penny," which combined features of a poll tax, an in-

Maximilian I, 1493–1519

come tax and a property tax. The difficulty of collecting it was great; Maximilian himself as a territorial prince tried to evade it instead of setting his subjects the good example of paying it. He probably derived no more than the trifling sum of 50,000–100,000 gulden from it annually. The Diet also revived the Supreme Court and gave it a permanent home at Frankfort-on-the-Main. Feeble efforts to follow up this beginning of reform were made in subsequent Diets, but they failed owing to the insuperable jealousies of the princes and because the party of national unity lost the sympathy of the common people, to whom alone they could look for support.

Maximilian's external policy, though adventurous and unstable, was somewhat more successful. His only principle was to grasp whatever opportunity seemed to offer. Thus at one time he seriously proposed to have himself elected pope. His marriage with Mary, the daughter of Charles the Bold, added to the estates of his house Burgundy—the land comprising what is now Belgium, Luxemburg, most of Holland and large portions of north-eastern France. On the death of Mary, in 1482, Maximilian had much trouble in getting himself acknowledged as regent of her lands for their son Philip the Handsome. A part of the domain he also lost in a war with France. This was more than made up, however, by the brilliant match he made for Philip in securing for him the hand of Mad Joanna, the daughter and heiress of Ferdinand and Isabella of Spain. This marriage produced two sons, Charles and Ferdinand. The deaths of Isabella (1504), of Philip (1506) and of Ferdinand of Aragon (1516) left Charles at the age of sixteen the ruler of Burgundy and of Spain with its immense dependencies in Italy and in America. From this time forth the policy of Maximilian concentrated in the effort to

Charles V, 1500–58

secure the succession of his eldest grandson to the imperial throne.

When Maximilian died on January 12, 1519, there were several candidates for election. So little was the office considered national that the kings of France and England entered the lists, and the former, Francis I, actually at one time secured the promise of votes from the majority of electors. Pope Leo made explicit engagements to both Charles and Francis to support their claims, and at the same time instructed his legate to labor for the choice of a German prince, either Frederic of Saxony, if he would in return give up Luther, or else Joachim of Brandenburg. But at no time was the election seriously in doubt. The electors followed the only possible course in choosing Charles on June 28. They profited, however, by the rivalry of the rich king of France to extort enormous bribes and concessions from Charles. The banking house of Fugger supplied the necessary funds, and in addition the agents of the emperor-elect were obliged to sign a "capitulation" making all sorts of concessions to the princes. One of these, exacted by Frederic of Saxony in the interest of Luther, was that no subject should be outlawed without being heard.

The settlement of the imperial election enabled the pope once more to turn his attention to the suppression of the rapidly growing heresy. After the Leipzig debate the universities of Cologne and Louvain had condemned Luther's positions. Eck went to Rome in March, 1520, and impressed the curia, which was already planning a bull condemning the heretic, with the danger of delay. After long discussions the bull *Exsurge Domine* was ratified by the College of Cardinals and promulgated by Leo on June 15. In this, forty-one of Luther's sayings, relating to the sacraments of penance and the eucharist, to indulgences and

Bull against Luther, 1520

the power of the pope, to free will and purgatory, and to a few other matters, were anathematized as heretical or scandalous or false or offensive to pious ears. His books were condemned and ordered to be burnt, and unless he should recant within sixty days of the posting of the bull in Germany he was to be considered a heretic and dealt with accordingly. Eck was entrusted with the duty of publishing this fulmination in Germany, and performed the task in the last days of September.

The time given Luther in which to recant therefore expired two months later. Instead of doing so he published several answers to "the execrable bull of Antichrist," and on December 10 publicly and solemnly burnt it, together with the whole Canon Law. This he had come to detest, partly as containing the "forged decretals," partly as the sanction for a vast mechanism of ecclesiastical use and abuse, repugnant to his more personal theology. The dramatic act, which sent a thrill throughout Europe, symbolized the passing of some medieval accretions on primitive Christianity. There was nothing left for the pope but to excommunicate the heretic, as was done in the bull *Decet Pontificem Romanum* drawn up at Rome in January, and published at Worms on May 6.

1521

In the meantime Charles had come to Germany. For more than a year after his election he remained in Spain, where his position was very insecure on account of the revolt against his Burgundian officers. Arriving in the Netherlands in the summer of 1520 Charles was met by the special nuncios of the pope, Caracciolo and Aleander. After he was crowned emperor at Aix-la-Chapelle, he opened his first Diet, at Worms.

October 23, 1520

January 27, 1521

The Diet of Worms

Before this august assembly came three questions of highest import. The first related to the dynastic policy of the Hapsburgs. For the chronic war with France an army of 24,000 men and a tax of 128,000 gulden was voted. The disposition of Württemberg caused some trouble. Duke Ulrich had been deposed for rebellion in 1518, and his land taken from him by the Swabian League and sold to the emperor in 1520. Together with the Austrian lands, which Charles secretly handed over to his young brother Ferdinand, this territory made the nucleus of Hapsburg power in Germany.

Council of Regency

The Diet then took up the question of constitutional reform. In order to have a permanent administrative body, necessary during the long absences of the emperor, an Imperial Council of Regency was established and given a seat at Nuremberg. The emperor nominated the president and four of the twenty-two other members; each of the six German electors nominated one member; six were chosen by the circles into which the Empire was divided and six were elected by the other estates. The powers of the council were limited to the times when the emperor was away.

The third question treated by the Diet was the religious one. As usual, they drew up a long list of grievances against the pope, to which many good Catholics in the assembly subscribed. Next they considered what to do with Luther. Charles himself, who could speak no language but French, and had no sympathy whatever with a rebel from any authority spiritual or temporal, would much have preferred to outlaw the Wittenberg professor at once, but he was bound by his promise to Frederic of Saxony. Of the six electors, who sat apart from the other estates, Frederic was strongly for Luther, the Elector Palatine was favorably inclined towards him, and the Archbishop of Mayence represented a mediating policy. The other three electors were opposed. Among the lesser princes a considerable minority was for Luther, whereas among the representatives of the free cities and of the knights, probably a majority were his followers. The common people, though unrepresented, applauded Luther, and their clamors could not pass unheeded even by the aristocratic members of the Diet. The debate was opened by Aleander in a speech dwelling on the sacramental errors of the heretic and the similarity of his movement to that of the detested Bohemians. After a stormy session the estates decided to summon the bold Saxon before them and accordingly a citation, together with a safe-conduct, was sent him.

February 13

Though there was some danger in obeying the summons, Luther's journey to Worms was a triumphal progress. Brought before the Diet in the late afternoon of April 17, he was asked if a certain number of books, the titles of which were read, were his and if he would recant the heresy contained in them. The form of the questions took him by surprise, for he had expected to be confronted with definite charges and to be allowed to defend his positions. He accordingly asked for time, and was granted one more day. On his second appearance he made a great oration admitting that the books were his and closing with the words:

April 18, 1521

> Unless I am convicted by Scripture or by right reason (for I trust neither popes nor councils since they have often erred and contradicted themselves) . . . I neither can nor will recant anything since it is neither safe nor right to act against conscience. God help me. Amen.

There he stood, braving the world, for he could do no other. . . . He left the hall the hero of his nation.

Hoping still to convince him of error, Catholic theologians held protracted but fruitless conferences with him before his departure from Worms on the 26th of

April. The sympathy of the people with him was shown by the posting at Worms of placards threatening his enemies. Charles was sincerely shocked and immediately drew up a statement that he would hazard life and lands on the maintenance of the Catholic faith of his fathers. An edict was drafted by Aleander on the model of one promulgated in September in the Netherlands. The Edict of Worms put Luther under the ban of the Empire, commanded his surrender to the government at the expiration of his safe-conduct, and forbade all to shelter him or to read his writings. Though dated on May 8, to make it synchronize with a treaty between Charles and Leo, the Edict was not passed by the Diet until May 26. At this time many of the members had gone home, and the law was forced on the remaining ones, contrary to the wishes of the majority, by intrigue and imperial pressure.

Luther banned

After leaving Worms Luther was taken by his prince, Frederic the Wise, and placed for safe keeping in the Wartburg, a fine old castle near Eisenach. Here he remained in hiding for nearly a year, while doing some of his most important work. Here he wrote his treatise *On Monastic Vows,* declaring that they are wrong and invalid and urging all priests, nuns and monks to leave the cloister and to marry. In thus freeing thousands of men and women from a life often unproductive and sterile Luther achieved one of the greatest of his practical reforms. At the Wartburg also Luther began his translation of the Bible. The New Testament appeared in September 1522, and the Old Testament followed in four parts, the last published in 1532.

The Wartburg

While Luther was in retirement at the Wartburg, his colleagues Carlstadt and Melanchthon, and the Augustinian friar Gabriel Zwilling, took up the movement at Wittenberg and carried out reforms more radical

The radicals

than those of their leader. The endowments of masses were confiscated and applied to the relief of the poor on new and better principles. Prostitution was suppressed. A new order of divine service was introduced, in which the words purporting that the mass was a sacrifice were omitted, and communion was given to the laity in both kinds. Priests were urged to marry, and monks were almost forced to leave the cloister. An element of mob violence early manifested itself both at Wittenberg and elsewhere. An outbreak at Erfurt against the clergy occurred in June, 1521, and by the end of the year riots took place at Wittenberg.

Even now, at the dawn of the revolution, appeared the beginnings of those sects, more radical than the Lutheran, commonly known as Anabaptist. The small industrial town of Zwickau had long been a hotbed of Waldensian heresy. Under the guidance of Thomas Münzer the clothweavers of this place formed a religious society animated by the desire to renovate both church and state by the readiest and roughest means. Suppression of the movement at Zwickau by the government resulted only in the banishment, or escape, of some of the leaders. Three of them found their way to Wittenberg, where they proclaimed themselves prophets divinely inspired, and conducted a revival marked with considerable, though harmless, extravagance.

December 27, 1521

As the radicals at Wittenberg made the whole of Northern Germany uneasy, the Imperial Council of Regency issued a mandate forbidding all the innovations and commanding the Elector of Saxony to stop them. It is remarkable that Luther in this felt exactly as did the Catholics. Early in March he returned to Wittenberg with the express purpose of checking the reforms which had already gone too far

January 20, 1522

for him. His personal ascendency was so great that he found no trouble in doing so. Not only the Zwickau prophets, but Carlstadt and Zwilling were discredited. Almost all their measures were repealed, including those on divine service which was again restored almost to the Catholic form. Not until 1525 were a simple communion service and the use of German again introduced.

Rebellion of the knights, 1522–3

It soon became apparent that all orders and all parts of Germany were in a state of ferment. The next manifestation of the revolutionary spirit was the rebellion of the knights. This class, now in a state of moral and economic decay, had long survived any usefulness it had ever had. The rise of the cities, the aggrandizement of the princes, and the change to a commercial from a feudal society all worked to the disadvantage of the smaller nobility and gentry. About the only means of livelihood left them was freebooting, and that was adopted without scruple and without shame. Envious of the wealthy cities, jealous of the greater princes and proud of their tenure immediately from the emperor, the knights longed for a new Germany, more centralized, more national, and, of course, under their special direction. In the Lutheran movement they thought they saw their opportunity; in Ulrich von Hutten they found their trumpet, in Francis von Sickingen their sword. A knight himself, but with possessions equal to those of many princes, a born warrior, but one who knew how to use the new weapons, gold and cannon, Sickingen had for years before he heard of Luther kept aggrandizing his power by predatory feuds. So little honor had he, that, though appointed to high military command in the campaign against France, he tried to win personal advantage by treason, playing off the emperor against King Francis, with whom, for a long time, he almost openly sided. In 1520 he fell under the influence of Hutten, who urged him to espouse the cause of the "gospel" as that of German liberty. By August 1522 he became convinced that the time was ripe for action, and issued a manifesto proclaiming that the feudal dues had become unbearable, and giving the impression that he was acting as an ally of Luther, although the latter knew nothing of his intentions and would have heartily disapproved of his methods.

Sickingen's first march was against Trèves. The archbishop's "unchristian cannon" forced him to retire from this city. On October 10 the Council of Regency declared him an outlaw. A league formed by Trèves, the Palatinate and Hesse, defeated him and captured his castle at Landstuhl in May, 1523. Mortally wounded he died on May 7.

Alike unhurt and unhelped by such incidents as the revolt of the knights, the main current of religious revolution swept onwards. Leo X died on December 1, 1521, and in his place was elected Adrian of Utrecht, a man of very different character. Though he had already taken a strong stand against Luther, he was deeply resolved to reform the corruption of the church. To the Diet called at Nuremberg in the latter part of 1522 he sent as legate Chieregato with a brief demanding the suppression of the schism. It was monstrous, said he, that one little brother should seduce a whole nation from the path trodden by so many martyrs and learned doctors. Do you suppose, he asked, that the people will longer respect civil government if they are taught to despise the canons and decrees of the spiritual power? At the same time Adrian wrote to Chieregato:

Adrian VI, 1522–3

Diet of Nuremberg, 1522

> Say that we frankly confess that God permits this persecution of his church on account of the sins of men, especially those of the priests and prelates. . . . We

> know that in this Holy See now for some years there have been many abominations, abuses in spiritual things, excesses in things commanded, in short, that all has become perverted. . . . We have all turned aside in our ways, nor was there, for a long time, any who did right,—no, not one.

This confession rather strengthened the reform party, than otherwise, making its demands seem justified; and all that the Diet did towards the settlement of the religious question was to demand that a council, with representation of the laity, should be called in a German city. A long list of grievances against the church was again drawn up and laid before the emperor.

The same Diet took up other matters. The need for reform and the impotence of the Council of Regency had both been demonstrated by the Sickingen affair. A law against monopolies was passed, limiting the capital of any single company to fifty thousand gulden. In order to provide money for the central government a customs duty of 4 per cent. ad valorem was ordered. Both these measures weighed on the cities, which accordingly sent an embassy to Charles. They succeeded in inducing him to disallow both laws.

Diet of Nuremberg 1524

The next Diet, which assembled at Nuremberg early in 1524, naturally refrained from passing more futile laws for the emperor to veto, but on the other hand it took a stronger stand than ever on the religious question. The Edict of Worms was still nominally in force and was still to all intents and purposes flouted. Luther was at large and his followers were gaining. In reply to a demand from the government that the Edict should be strictly carried out, the Diet passed a resolution that it should be observed by each state as far as its prince deemed it possible. Despairing of an oecumenical council the estates demanded that a

German national synod be called at Spires before the close of the year with power to decide on what was to be done for the time being.

There is no doubt that by this time the public opinion of North Germany, at least, was thoroughly Lutheran. Ferdinand hardly exaggerated when he wrote his brother that throughout the Empire there was scarce one person in a thousand not infected with the new doctrines. The place now occupied by newspapers and weekly reviews was taken by a vast swarm of pamphlets, most of which have survived. Those of the years immediately following the Diet of Worms reveal the first enthusiasm of the people for the "gospel." The greater part of the broadsides produced are concerned with the leader and his doctrines. The comparison of him to Huss was a favorite one. One pamphleteer, at least, drew the parallel between his trial at Worms and that of Christ before Pilate. The whole bent of men's minds was theological. Doctrines which now seem a little quaint and trite were argued with new fervor by each writer. The destruction of images, the question of the real presence in the sacrament, justification by faith, and free will were disputed. Above all the Bible was lauded in the new translation, and the priests continued, as before, to be the favorite butt of sarcasm.

1523

Popular pamphlets

Among the very many writers of these tracts the playwright of Nuremberg, Hans Sachs, took a prominent place. In 1523 he published his poem on "the Nightingale of Wittenberg, whose voice sounds in the glorious dawn over hill and dale." This bird is, of course, Luther, and the fierce lion who has sought his life is Leo. The next year Hans Sachs published no less than three pamphlets favoring the reform. They were: 1. A Disputation between a Canon and a Shoemaker, defending the Word of God and the Christian

Hans Sachs

Estate. 2. Conversation on the Hypocritical Works of the Clergy and their Vows, by which they hope to be saved to the disparagement of Christ's Blood. 3. A Dialogue against the Roman Avarice. Multiply these pamphlets, the contents of which is indicated by their titles, by one hundred, and we arrive at some conception of the pabulum on which the people grew to Protestantism. Of course there were many pamphlets on the other side, but here, as in a thousand other cases, the important thing proved to be to have the cause ventilated. So long as discussion was forced in the channels selected by the reformers, even the interest excited by their adversaries redounded ultimately to their advantage.

The Peasants' War, 1524–5

The denunciation of authority, together with the message of the excellence of the humblest Christian and the brotherhood of man, powerfully contributed to the great rising of the lower classes, known as the Peasants' War, in 1524–5. It was not, as the name implied, confined to the rustics, for probably as large a proportion of the populace of cities as of the tillers of the soil joined it. Nor was there in it anything entirely new. The cry for justice was of long standing, and every single element of the revolt, including the hatred of the clergy and demand for ecclesiastical reform, is to be found also in previous risings. Thus, the rebellion of peasants under Hans Böhm, commonly called the Piper of Niklashausen, in 1476, was brought about by a religious appeal. The leader asserted that he had special revelations from the Virgin Mary that serfdom was to be abolished, and the kingdom of God to be introduced by the levelling of all social ranks; and he produced miracles to certify his divine calling. There had also been two risings, closely connected, the first, in 1513, deriving its name of "Bundschuh" from the peasant's tied shoe, a class emblem, and the second, in 1514, called "Poor Conrad" after the peasant's nickname. If the memory of the suppression of all these revolts might dampen the hopes of the poor, on the other hand the successful rise of the Swiss democracy was a perpetual example and encouragement to them.

Causes

The most fundamental cause of all these risings alike was, of course, the cry of the oppressed for justice. This is eternal, as is also one of the main alignments into which society usually divides itself, the opposition of the poor and the rich. It is therefore not very important to inquire whether the lot of the third estate was getting better or worse during the first quarter of the sixteenth century. In either case there was a great load of wrong and tyranny to be thrown off. But the question is not uninteresting in itself. As there are diametrically opposite answers to it, both in the testimony of contemporaries and in the opinion of modern scholars, it is perhaps incapable of being answered. In some districts, and in some respects, the lot of the poor was becoming a little easier; in other lands and in different ways it was becoming harder. The time was one of general prosperity, in which the peasant often shared. The newer methods of agriculture, manufacture and commerce benefited him who knew how to take advantage of them. That some did so may be inferred from the statement of Sebastian Brant that the rustics dress like nobles, in satin and gold chains. On the other hand the rising prices would bear hard on those laborers dependent on fixed wages, though relieving the burden of fixed rents. The whole people, except the merchants, disliked the increasing cost of living and legislated against it to the best of their ability. Complaints against monopoly were common, and the Diets sometimes enacted laws against them. Foreign trade was looked on with suspicion as draining the country of silver and gold. Again, although the peasants benefited by the growing stability of government, they felt as a grievance the introduction of the new Roman law with its emphasis upon the rights of property and of the state. Burdens directly imposed by the territorial governments were probably increasing. If the exactions from the landlords were not becoming greater, it was simply because they were always at a maximum. At no time was the rich gentleman at a loss to find law and precedent for wringing from his serfs and tenants all that they could possibly pay. The peasants were of three classes: the serfs, the tenants who paid a quit-rent, and hired laborers. The former, more than the others, perhaps, had now arrived at the determination to assert their rights. For them the Peasants' War was the inevitable break with a long economic past, now intolerable and hopeless. There is some evidence to show that the number of serfs was increasing. This process, by menacing the freedom of the others, united all in the resolve to stop the gradual enslavement of their class, and to reckon with those who benefited by it.

Peasant classes

How little new there was in the ideals of the last and most terrible of the peasant risings may be seen by a study of the programs of reform put forward from time to time during the preceding century. There is nothing in the manifestos of 1525 that may not be found in the pamphlets of the fifteenth century. The grievances are the same, and the hope of a completely renovated and communized society is the same. One of the most influential of these socialistic pamphlets was the so-called *Reformation of the Emperor Sigismund*, written by an Augsburg clergyman about 1438, first printed in 1476, and reprinted a number of times before the end of the century. Its title bears witness to the Messianic belief of the people that one of their great, old emperors should sometime return and restore the world to a condition of justice and happiness. The present tract preached that "obedience was dead and justice sick"; it attacked serfdom as wicked, denounced the ecclesiastical law and demanded the freedom given by Christ.

The same doctrine, adapted to the needs of the time, is preached in the *Reformation of the Emperor Frederic III,* published anonymously in 1523. Though more radical than Luther it reflects some of his ideas. Still more, however, does it embody the reforms proposed at Nuremberg in 1523. It may probably have been written by George Rüxner, called Jerusalem, an Imperial Herald prominent in these circles. It advocated the abolition of all taxes and tithes, the repeal of all imperial civil laws, the reform of the clergy, the confiscation of ecclesiastical property, and the limitation of the amount of capital allowed any one merchant to 10,000 gulden.

Though there was nothing new in either the manner of oppression or in the demands of the third estate during the last decade preceding the great rebellion, there does seem to be a new atmosphere, or tone, in the literature addressed to the lower classes. While on the one hand the poor were still mocked and insulted as they always had been by foolish and heartless possessors of inherited wealth and position, from other quarters they now began to be also flattered and courted. The peasant became in the large pamphlet literature of the time an ideal figure, the type of the plain, honest, God-fearing man. Nobles like Duke Ulrich of Württemberg affected to be called by popular nicknames. Carlstadt and other learned men proclaimed that the peasant knew better the Word of God and the way of salvation than did the learned. Many radical preachers, especially the Anabaptist

The peasant idealized

Münzer, carried the message of human brotherhood to the point of communism. There were a number of lay preachers, the most celebrated being the physician Hans Maurer, who took the sobriquet "Karsthans." This name, "the man with the hoe," soon became one of the catch-words of the time, and made its way into popular speech as a synonym for the simple and pious laborer. Hutten took it up and urged the people to seize flails and pitchforks and smite the clergy and the pope as they would the devil. Others preached hatred of the Jews, of the rich, of lawyers. Above all they appealed to the Bible as the divine law, and demanded a religious reform as a condition and preliminary to a thorough renovation of society. Although Luther himself from the first opposed all forms of violence, his clarion voice rang out in protest against the injustice of the nobles. "The people neither can nor will endure your tyranny any longer," he said to them in 1523, "God will not endure it; the world is not what it once was when you drove and hunted men like wild beasts."

1521

The rising began at Stühlingen, not far from the Swiss frontier, in June 1524, and spread with considerable rapidity northward, until the greater part of Germany was in the throes of revolution. The rebels were able to make headway because most of the regular troops had been withdrawn to the Turkish front or to Italy to fight the emperor's battle against France. In South Germany, during the first six months, the gatherings of peasants and townsmen were eminently peaceable. They wished only to negotiate with their masters and to secure some practical reforms. But when the revolt spread to Franconia and Saxony, a much more radically socialistic program was developed and the rebels showed themselves readier to enforce their demands by arms. For the year 1524 there was no general manifesto put forward, but there were negotiations between the insurgents and their quondam masters. In this district or in that, lists of very specific grievances were presented and redress demanded. In some cases merely to gain time, in others sincerely, the lords consented to reply to these petitions. They denied this or that charge, and they promised to end this or that form of oppression. Neither side was prepared for civil war. In all it was more like a modern strike than anything else.

The Twelve Articles

In the early months of 1525 several programs were drawn up of a more general nature than those previously composed, and yet by no means radical. The most famous of these was called *The Twelve Articles,* printed and widely circulated in February. The exact place at which they originated is unknown. The authorship has been much disputed, and necessarily so, for they were the work of no one brain, but were as composite a production as is the Constitution of the United States. The material in them is drawn from the mouths of a whole people. Far more than in other popular writings one feels that they are the genuine expression of the public opinion of a great class. Probably their draftsman was Sebastian Lotzer, the tanner who for years past had preached apostolic communism. It is not impossible that the Anabaptist Balthasar Hübmaier had a hand in them. Their demands are moderate and would be considered matters of self-evident justice to-day. The first article is for the right of each community to choose its own pastor; the second protests against the minor tithes on vegetables paid to the clergy, though expressly admitting the legality of the tithes on grain. The third article demands freedom for the serfs, the fourth and fifth ask for the right to hunt and to cut wood in the forests. The sixth, seventh and eighth articles protest against excessive forced labor, illegal payments and exorbitant rents. The ninth article denounces the new (Roman) law, and requests the reëstablishment of the old (German) law. The tenth article voices the indignation of the poor at the enclosure by the rich of commons and other free land. The eleventh demands the abolition of the heriot, or inheritance tax, by which the widow of a rustic was obliged to yield to her lord the best head of cattle or other valuable possession. The final article expresses the willingness of the insurgents to have all their demands submitted to the Word of God. Both here and in the preamble the entire assimilation of divine and human law is postulated, and the charge that the Lutheran Gospel caused sedition, is met.

Other manifestos

Though the *Twelve Articles* were adopted by more of the bands of peasants than was any other program, yet there were several other manifestos drawn up about the same time. Thus, in the *Fifty-nine Articles* of the Stühlingen peasants the same demands are put forth with much more detail. The legal right to trial by due process of law is asserted, and vexatious payments due to a lord when his peasant marries a woman from another estate, are denounced. But here, too, and elsewhere, the fundamental demands were the same: freedom from serfdom, from oppressive taxation and forced labor, and for unrestricted rights of hunting and woodcutting in the forests. Everywhere there is the same claim that the rights of the people are sanctioned by the law of God, and generally the peasants assume that they are acting in accordance with the new "gospel" of Luther. The Swabians expressly submitted their demands to the arbitration of a commission of four to consist of a representative of the emperor, Frederic of Saxony, Luther and either Melanchthon or Bugenhagen.

Münzer

When the revolt reached the central part of Germany it became at once more socialistic and more bloody. The baleful eloquence of Thomas Münzer was exerted at Mühlhausen to nerve the people to strike down the godless with pitiless sword. Already in September 1524 he preached: "On! on! on! This is the time when the wicked are as fearful as hounds. . . . Regard not the cries of the godless. . . . On, while the fire is hot. Let not your swords be cold from blood. Smite bang, bang on the anvil of Nimrod; cast his tower to the ground!" Other leaders took up the message and called for the extirpation of the tyrants, including both the clergy and the lords. Communism was demanded as in the apostolic age; property was denounced as wrong. Regulation of prices was one measure put forward, and the committing of the government of the country to a university another.

The propaganda of deeds followed close upon the propaganda of words. During the spring of 1525 in central Germany forty-six cloisters and castles were burned to the ground, while violence and rapine reigned supreme with all the ferocity characteristic of class warfare. On Easter Sunday, April 16, one of the best-armed bands of peasants, under one of the most brutal leaders, Jäcklein Rohrbach, attacked Weinsberg. The count and his small garrison of eighteen knights surrendered and were massacred by the insurgents, who visited mockery and insult upon the countess and her daughters. Many of the cities joined the peasants, and for a short time it seemed as if the rebellion might be successful.

Suppression of the rising

But in fact the insurgents were poorly equipped, untrained, without coöperation or leadership. As soon as the troops which won the battle of Pavia in Italy were sent back to Germany the whole movement collapsed. The Swabian League inflicted decisive de-

February 24, 1525

feats upon the rebels at Leipheim on April 4, and at Wurzach ten days later. Other blows followed in May. In the center of Germany the Saxon Electorate lay supine. Frederic the Wise died in the midst of the tumult after expressing his opinion that it was God's will that the common man should rule, and that it would be wrong to resist the divine decree. His young neighbor, Philip, Landgrave of Hesse, acted vigorously. After coming to terms with his own subjects by negotiations, he raised troops and met a band of insurgents at Frankenhausen. He wished to treat with them also, but Münzer's fanaticism, promising the deluded men supernatural aid, nerved them to reject all terms. In the very ancient German style they built a barricade of wagons, and calmly awaited the attack of the soldiers. Undisciplined and poorly armed, almost at the first shot they broke and fled in panic, more than half of them perishing on the field. Münzer was captured, and, after having been forced by torture to sign a confession of his misdeeds, was executed. After this there was no strength left in the peasant cause. The lords, having gained the upper hand, put down the rising with great cruelty. The estimates of the numbers of peasants slain vary so widely as to make certainty impossible. Perhaps a hundred thousand in all perished. The soldiers far outdid the rebels in savage reprisals. The laborers sank back into a more wretched state than before; oppression stalked with less rebuke than ever through the land.

May 5, 1525

May 15

§ 3. The Formation of the Protestant Party

Defections from Luther

In the sixteenth century politics were theological. The groups into which men divided had religious slogans and were called churches, but they were also political parties. The years following the Diet of

Worms saw the crystallization of a new group, which was at first liberal and reforming and later, as it grew in stability, conservative. At Worms almost all the liberal forces in Germany had been behind Luther, the intellectuals, the common people with their wish for social amelioration, and those to whom the religious issue primarily appealed. But this support offered by public opinion was vague; in the next years it became both more definite and more limited. At the same time that city after city and state after state was openly revolting from the pope, until the Reformers had won a large constituency in the Imperial Diets and a place of constitutional recognition, there was going on another process by which one after another certain elements at first inclined to support Luther fell away from him. During these years he violently dissociated himself from the extreme radicals and thus lost the support of the proletariat. In the second place the growing definiteness and narrowness of his dogmatism, and his failure to show hospitality to science and philosophy alienated a number of intellectuals. Third, a great schism weakened the Protestant church. But these losses were counterbalanced by two gains. The first was the increasing discipline and coherence of the new churches; the second was their gradual but rapid attainment of the support of the middle and governing classes in many German states.

The Radicals

Luther's struggle with radicalism had begun within a year after his stand at Worms. He had always been consistently opposed to mob violence, even when he might have profited by it. At Worms he disapproved Hutten's plans for drawing the sword against the Romanists. When, from his "watchtower," he first spied the disorders at Wittenberg, he wrote that notwithstanding the great provocation given to the common man by the clergy, yet tumult was the work of the devil. When he returned home he preached that the only weapon the Christian ought to use was the Word. "Had I wished it," said he then, "I might have brought Germany to civil war. Yes, at Worms I might have started a game that would not have been safe for the emperor, but it would have been a fool's game. So I did nothing, but only let the Word act." Driven from Wittenberg, the Zwickau prophets, assisted by Thomas Münzer, continued their agitation elsewhere. As long as their propaganda was peaceful Luther was inclined to tolerate it. "Let them teach what they like," said he, "be it gospel or lies." But when they began to preach a campaign of fire and sword, Luther wrote, in July 1524, to his elector begging him "to act vigorously against their storming and ranting, in order that God's kingdom may be advanced by word only, as becomes Christians, and that all cause of sedition may be taken from the multitude [Herr Omnes, literally Mr. Everybody], more than enough inclined to it already."

Exhortation to Peace

When the revolt at last broke out Luther was looked up to and appealed to by the people as their champion. In April 1525 he composed an *Exhortation to Peace on the Twelve Articles of the Swabian Peasants,* in which he distributed the blame for the present conditions liberally, but impartially, on both sides, aristocrats and peasants. To the former he said that their tyranny, together with that of the clergy, had brought this punishment on themselves, and that God intended to smite them. To the peasants he said that no tyranny was excuse for rebellion. Of their articles he approved of two only, that demanding the right to choose their pastors and that denouncing the heriot or death-duty. Their second demand, for repeal of some of the tithes, he characterized as robbery, and the third, for freedom of the serf, as unjustified because it made Christian liberty a merely external thing, and because Paul had said that the bondman should not seek to be free (I Cor. vii, 20 f). The other articles were referred to legal experts.

The peasants denounced

Hardly had this pamphlet come from the press before Luther heard of the deeds of violence of Rohrbach and his fellows. Fearing that complete anarchy would result from the triumph of the insurgents, against whom no effective blow had yet been struck, he wrote a tract *Against the Thievish, Murderous Hordes of Peasants.* In this he denounced them with the utmost violence of language, and urged the government to smite them without pity. Everyone should avoid a peasant as he would the devil, and should join the forces to slay them like mad dogs. "If you die in battle against them," said he to the soldiers, "you could never have a more blessed end, for you die obedient to God's Word in Romans 13, and in the service of love to free your neighbor from the bands of hell and the devil." A little later he wrote: "It is better that all the peasants be killed than that the princes and magistrates perish, because the rustics took the sword without divine authority. The only possible consequence of their Satanic wickedness would be the diabolic devastation of the kingdom of God." And again: "One cannot argue reasonably with a rebel, but one must answer him with the fist so that blood flows from his nose." Melanchthon entirely agreed with his friend. "It is fairly written in Ecclesiasticus xxxiii," said he, "that as the ass must have fodder, load, and whip, so must the servant have bread, work, and punishment. These outward, bodily servitudes are needful, but this institution [serfdom] is certainly pleasing to God."

Inevitably such an attitude alienated the lower classes. From this time, many of them looked not to the Lutheran but to the more radical sects, called Anabaptists, for help. The condition of the Empire at this time was very similar to that of many countries today, where we find two large upper and middle-class parties, the conservative (Catholic) and liberal (Protestant) over against the radical or socialistic (Anabaptist).

The Anabaptists

The most important thing about the extremists was not their habit of denying the validity of infant baptism and of rebaptizing their converts, from which they derived their name. What really determined their view-point and program was that they represented the poor, uneducated, disinherited classes. The party of extreme measures is always chiefly constituted from the proletariat because it is the very poor who most pressingly feel the need for change and because they have not usually the education to judge the feasibility of the plans, many of them quack nostrums, presented as panaceas for all their woes. A complete break with the past and with the existing order has no terrors for them, but only promise.

A radical party almost always includes men of a wide variety of opinions. So the sixteenth century classed together as Anabaptists men with not only divergent but with diametrically opposite views on the most vital questions. Their only common bond was that they all alike rejected the authoritative, traditional, and aristocratic organization of both of the larger churches and the pretensions of civil society. It is easy to see that they had no historical perspective, and that they tried to realize the ideals of primitive Christianity, as they understood it, without reckoning the vast changes in culture and other conditions, and yet it is impossible not to have a deep sympathy with the men most of whose demands were just and who sealed their faith with perpetual martyrdom. Not-

Spread of radicalism

withstanding the heavy blow to reform given in the crushing of the peasants' rising, radical doctrines continued to spread among the people. As the poor found their spiritual needs best supplied in the conventicle of dissent, official Lutheranism became an established church, predominantly an aristocratic and middle-class party of vested interest and privilege.

It is sometimes said that the origin and growth of the Anabaptists was due to the German translation of the Bible. This is not true and yet there is little doubt that the publication of the German version in 1522 and the years immediately following, stimulated the growth of many sects. The Bible is such a big book, and capable of so many different interpretations, that it is not strange that a hundred different schemes of salvation should have been deduced from it by those who came to it with different prepossessions. While many of the Anabaptists were perfect quietists, preaching the duty of non-resistance and the wickedness of bearing arms, even in self-defence, others found sanction for quite opposite views in the Scripture, and proclaimed that the godless should be exterminated as the Canaanites had been. In ethical matters some sects practised the severest code of morals, while others were distinguished by laxity. By some marriage was forbidden; others wanted all the marriage they could get and advocated polygamy. The religious meetings were similar to "revivals," frequently of the most hysterical sort. Claiming that they were mystically united to God, or had direct revelations from him, they rejected the ceremonies and sacraments of historic Christianity, and sometimes substituted for them practices of the most absurd, or most doubtful, character. When Melchior Rink preached, his followers howled like dogs, bellowed like cattle, neighed like horses, and brayed like asses—some of them very naturally, no doubt. In certain extreme cases the meetings ended in debauchery, while we know of men who committed murder in the belief that they were directed so to do by special revelation of God. Thus at St. Gall one brother cut another's throat, while one of the saints trampled his wife to death under the influence of the spirit. But it is unfair to judge the whole movement by these excesses.

The new sectaries, of course, ran the gauntlet of persecution. In 1529 the emperor and Diet at Spires passed a mandate against them to this effect: "By the plenitude of our imperial power and wisdom we ordain, decree, oblige, declare, and will that all Anabaptists, men and women who have come to the age of understanding, shall be executed and deprived of their natural life by fire, sword, and the like, according to opportunity and without previous inquisition of the spiritual judges." Lutherans united with Catholics in passing this edict, and showed no less alacrity in executing it. As early as 1525 the Anabaptists were persecuted at Zurich, where one of their earliest communities sprouted. Some of the leaders were drowned, others were banished and so spread their tenets elsewhere. Catholic princes exterminated them by fire and sword. In Lutheran Saxony no less than thirteen of the poor non-conformists were executed, and many more imprisoned for long terms, or banished.

And yet the radical sects continued to grow. The dauntless zeal of Melchior Hofmann braved all for the propagation of their ideas. For a while he found a refuge at Strassburg, but this city soon became too orthodox to hold him. He then turned to Holland, where the seed sowed fell into fertile ground. Two Dutchmen, the baker John Matthys of Haarlem and the tailor John Beuckelssen of Leyden went to the episcopal city of Münster in Westphalia near the Dutch

Münster

border, and rapidly converted the mass of the people to their own belief in the advent of the kingdom of God on earth. An insurrection expelled the bishop's government and installed a democracy in February, 1534. After the death of Matthys on April 5, a rising of the people against the dictatorial power of Beucklessen was suppressed by this fanatic who thereupon crowned himself king under the title of John of Leyden. Communism of goods was introduced and also polygamy. The city was now besieged by its suzerain, the Bishop of Münster, and after horrible sufferings had been inflicted on the population, taken by storm on June 25, 1535. The surviving leaders were put to death by torture.

The defeat itself was not so disastrous to the Anabaptist cause as were the acts of the leaders when in power. As the Reformer Bullinger put it: "God opened the eyes of the governments by the revolt at Münster, and thereafter no one would trust even those Anabaptists who claimed to be innocent." Their lack of unity and organization told against them. Nevertheless the sect smouldered on in the lower classes, constantly subject to the fires of martyrdom, until, toward the close of the century, it attained some cohesion and respectability. The later Baptists, Independents, and Quakers all inherited some portion of its spiritual legacies. To the secular historian its chief interest is in the social teachings, which consistently advocated tolerance, and frequently various forms of anarchy and socialism.

Defection of the humanists

Next to the defection of the laboring masses, the severest loss to the Evangelical party in these years was that of a large number of intellectuals, who, having hailed Luther as a deliverer from ecclesiastical bondage, came to see in him another pope, not less tyrannous than he of Rome. Reuchlin the Hebrew scholar and Mutian the philosopher had little sympathy with any dogmatic subtlety. Zasius the jurist was repelled by the haste and rashness of Luther. The so-called "godless painters" of Nuremberg, George Penz and the brothers Hans and Bartholomew Beham, having rejected in large part Christian doctrine, were naturally not inclined to join a new church, even when they deserted the old.

But a considerable number of humanists, and those the greatest, after having welcomed the Reformation in its first, most liberal and hopeful youth, deliberately turned their backs on it and cast in their lot with the Roman communion. The reason was that, whereas the old faith mothered many of the abuses, superstitions, and dogmatisms abominated by the humanists, it had also, at this early stage in the schism, within its close a large body of ripe, cultivated, fairly tolerant opinion. The struggling innovators, on the other hand, though they purged away much obsolete and offensive matter, were forced, partly by their position, partly by the temper of their leaders, to a raw self-assertiveness, a bald concentration on the points at issue, incompatible with winsome wisdom, or with judicial fairness. How the humanists would have chosen had they seen the Index and Loyola, is problematical; but while there was still hope of reshaping Rome to their liking they had little use for Wittenberg.

Rubeanus

> I admit that for some years I was very favorably inclined to Luther's enterprise [wrote Crotus Rubeanus in 1531], but when I saw that nothing was left untorn and undefiled . . . I thought the devil might bring in great evil in the guise of something good, using Scripture as his shield. So I decided to remain in the church in which I was baptized, reared and taught. Even if some fault might be found in it, yet in time it might have been im-

proved, sooner, at any rate, than in the new church which in a few years has been torn by so many sects.

Wilibald Pirckheimer, the Greek scholar and historian of Nuremberg, hailed Luther so warmly at first that he was put under the ban of the bull *Exsurge Domine.* By 1529, however, he had come to believe him insolent, impudent, either insane or possessed by a devil.

> I do not deny [he wrote] that at the beginning all Luther's acts did not seem to be vain, since no good man could be pleased with all those errors and impostures that had accumulated gradually in Christianity. So, with others, I hoped that some remedy might be applied to such great evils, but I was cruelly deceived. For, before the former errors had been extirpated, far more intolerable ones crept in, compared to which the others seemed child's play.

Appeal to Erasmus

To Erasmus, the wise, the just, all men turned as to an arbiter of opinion. From the first, Luther counted on his support, and not without reason, for the humanist spoke well of the Theses and commentaries of the Wittenberger. On March 28, 1519, Luther addressed a letter to him, as "our glory and hope," acknowledging his indebtedness and begging for support. Erasmus answered in a friendly way, at the same time sending a message encouraging the Elector Frederic to defend his innocent subject.

Dreading nothing so much as a violent catastrophe, the humanist labored for the next two years to find a peaceful solution for the threatening problem. Seeing that Luther's two chief errors were that he "had attacked the crown of the pope and the bellies of the monks," Erasmus pressed upon men in power the plan of allowing the points in dispute to be settled by an impartial tribunal, and of imposing silence on both parties. At the same time he begged Luther to do nothing violent and urged that his enemies be not allowed to take extreme measures against him. But after the publication of the pamphlets of 1520 and of the bull condemning the heretic, this position became untenable. Erasmus had so far compromised himself in the eyes of the inquisitors that he fled from Louvain in the autumn of 1521, and settled in Basle. He was strongly urged by both parties to come out on one side or the other, and he was openly taunted by Ulrich von Hutten, a hot Lutheran, for cowardice in not doing so. Alienated by this and by the dogmatism and intolerance of Luther's writings, Erasmus finally defined his position in a *Diatribe on Free Will.* As Luther's theory of the bondage of the will was but the other side of his doctrine of justification by faith only—for where God's grace does all there is nothing left for human effort—Erasmus attacked the very center of the Evangelical dogmatic system. The question, a deep psychological and metaphysical one, was much in the air, Valla having written on it a work published in 1518, and Pomponazzi having also composed a work on it in 1520, which was, however, not published until much later. It is noticeable that Erasmus selected this point rather than one of the practical reforms advocated at Wittenberg, with which he was much in sympathy. Luther replied in a volume on *The Bondage of the Will* reasserting his position more strongly than ever. How theological, rather than philosophical, his opinion was may be seen from the fact that while he admitted that a man was free to choose which of two indifferent alternatives he should take, he denied that any of these choices could work salvation or real righteousness in God's eyes. He did not hesitate to say that God saved and damned souls irrespective of merit. Erasmus answered again in a large work, the *Hyperaspistes* (*Heavy-Armed Soldier*), which came

1524

1525

1526–7 out in two parts. In this he offers a general critique of the Lutheran movement. Its leader, he says, is a dogmatist, who never recoils from extremes logically demanded by his premises, no matter how repugnant they may be to the heart of man. But for himself he is a humanist, finding truth in the reason as well as in the Bible, and abhorring paradoxes.

The controversy was not allowed to drop at this point. Many a barbed shaft of wit-winged sarcasm was shot by the light-armed scholar against the ranks of the Reformers. "Where Lutheranism reigns," he wrote Pirckheimer, "sound learning perishes." "With disgust," he confessed to Ber, "I see the cause of Christianity approaching a condition that I should be very unwilling to have it reach . . . While we are quarreling over the booty the victory will slip through our fingers. It is the old story of private interests destroying the commonwealth." Erasmus first expressed the opinion, often maintained since, that Europe was experiencing a gradual revival both of Christian piety and of sound learning, when Luther's boisterous attack plunged the world into a tumult in which both were lost sight of. On March 30, 1527, he wrote to Maldonato:

> I brought it about that sound learning, which among the Italians and especially among the Romans savored of nothing but pure paganism, began nobly to celebrate Christ, in whom we ought to boast as the sole author of both wisdom and happiness if we are true Christians. . . . I always avoided the character of a dogmatist, except in certain *obiter dicta* which seemed to me conducive to correct studies and against the preposterous judgments of men.

In the same letter he tells how hard he had fought the obscurantists, and adds: "While we were waging a fairly equal battle against these monsters, behold

Luther suddenly arose and threw the apple of Discord into the world."

In short, Erasmus left the Reformers not because they were too liberal, but because they were too conservative, and because he disapproved of violent methods. His gentle temperament, not without a touch of timidity, made him abhor the tumult and trust to the voice of persuasion. In failing to secure the support of the humanists Protestantism lost heavily, and especially abandoned its chance to become the party of progress. Luther himself was not only disappointed in the disaffection of Erasmus, but was sincerely repelled by his rationalism. A man who could have the least doubt about a doctrine was to him "an Arian, an atheist, and a skeptic." He went so far as to say that the great Dutch scholar's primary object in publishing the Greek New Testament was to make readers doubtful about the text, and that the chief end of his *Colloquies* was to mock all piety. Erasmus, whose services to letters were the most distinguished and whose ideal of Christianity was the loveliest, has suffered far too much in being judged by his relation to the Reformation. By a great Catholic [1] he has been called "the glory of the priesthood and the shame," by an eminent Protestant scholar [2] "a John the Baptist and Judas in one."

Sacramentarian schism

The battle with the humanists was synchronous with the beginnings of a fierce internecine strife that tore the young evangelical church into two parts. Though the controversy between Luther and his principal rival, Ulrich Zwingli, was really caused by a wide difference of thought on many subjects, it focused its rays, like a burning-glass, upon one point, the doctrine of the real presence of the body and blood of Christ in the

[1] Alexander Pope.

[2] Walther Köhler.

eucharist. The explanation of this mystery evolved in the Middle Ages and adopted by the Lateran Council of 1215, was the theory, called "transubstantiation," that the substance of the bread turned into the substance of the body, and the substance of the wine into the substance of the blood, without the "accidents" of appearance and taste being altered. Some of the later doctors of the church, Durand and Occam, opposed this theory, though they proposed a nearly allied one, called "consubstantiation," that the body and blood are present with the bread and wine. Wyclif and others, among whom was the Italian philosopher Pico della Mirandola, proposed the theory now held in most Protestant churches that the bread and wine are mere symbols of the body and blood.

Symbolism

At the dawn of the Reformation the matter was brought into prominence by the Dutch theologian Hoen, from whom the symbolic interpretation was adopted first by Carlstadt and then by the Swiss Reformers Zwingli and Oecolampadius. Luther himself wavered. He attacked the sacrifice of the mass, in which he saw a "good work" repugnant to faith, and a great practical abuse, as in the endowed masses for souls, but he finally decided on the question of the real presence that the words "this is my body" were "too strong for him" and meant just what they said.

After a preliminary skirmish with Carlstadt, resulting in the latter's banishment from Saxony, there was a long and bitter war of pens between Wittenberg and the Swiss Reformers. Once the battle was joined it was sure to be acrimonious because of the self-consciousness of each side. Luther always assumed that he had a monopoly of truth, and that those who proposed different views were infringing his copyright, so to speak. "Zwingli, Carlstadt and Oecolampadius would never have known Christ's gospel rightly," he opined, "had not Luther written of it first." He soon compared them to Absalom rebelling against his father David, and to Judas betraying his Master. Zwingli on his side was almost equally sure that he had discovered the truth independently of Luther, and, while expressing approbation of his work, refused to be called by his name. His invective was only a shade less virulent than was that of his opponent.

The substance of the controversy was far from being the straight alignment between reason and tradition that it has sometimes been represented as. Both sides assumed the inerrancy of Scripture and appealed primarily to the same biblical arguments. Luther had no difficulty in proving that the words "hoc est corpus meum" meant that the bread was the body, and he stated that this must be so even if contrary to our senses. Zwingli had no difficulty in proving that the thing itself was impossible, and therefore inferred that the biblical words must be explained away as a figure of speech. In a long and learned controversy neither side convinced the other, but each became so exasperated as to believe the other possessed of the devil. In the spring of 1529 Lutherans joined Catholics at the Diet of Spires in refusing toleration to the Zwinglians.

The division of Protestants of course weakened them. Their leading statesman, Philip, Landgrave of Hesse, seeing this, did his best to reconcile the leaders. For several years he tried to get them to hold a conference, but in vain. Finally, he succeeded in bringing together at his castle at Marburg on the Lahn, Luther, Melanchthon, Zwingli, Oecolampadius, and a large number of other divines. The discussion here only served to bring out more strongly the irreconcilability of the two "spirits." Shortly afterwards, when the question of a political alliance came up, the Saxon theologians drafted a memorial stating that

Marburg colloquy October 1–3, 1529

they would rather make an agreement with the heathen than with the "sacramentarians." The same attitude was preserved at the Diet of Augsburg, where the Lutherans were careful to avoid all appearance of friendship with the Zwinglians lest they should compromise their standing with the Catholics. Zwingli and his friends were hardly less intransigeant.

1530

October 11, 1531

When Zwingli died in battle with the Catholic cantons and when Oecolampadius succumbed to a fever a few weeks later, Luther loudly proclaimed that this was a judgment of God and a triumph for his own party. Though there was no hope of reconciling the Swiss, the South German Zwinglians, headed by the Strassburg Reformers Bucer and Capito, hastened to come to an understanding with Wittenberg, without which their position would have been extremely perilous. Bucer claimed to represent a middle doctrine, such as was later asserted by Calvin. As no middle ground is possible, the doctrine is unintelligible, being, in fact, nothing but the statement, in strong terms, of two mutually exclusive propositions. After much humiliation the divines succeeded, however, in satisfying Luther, with whom they signed the Wittenberg Concord on May 29, 1536. The Swiss still remained without the pale, and Luther's hatred of them grew with the years. Shortly before his death he wrote that he would testify before the judgment-seat of God his loathing for the sacramentarians. He became more and more conservative, bringing back to the sacrament some of the medieval superstitions he had once expelled. He began again to call it an offering and a sacrifice and again had it elevated in church for the adoration of the faithful. He wavered on this point, because, as he said, he doubted whether it were more his duty to "spite" the papists or the sacramentarians. He finally decided on the latter, "and if necessary," continued he, "I will have the host elevated three, seven, or ten times, for I will not let the devil teach me anything in my church."

Growth of Lutheranism in middle and upper classes

Notwithstanding the bitter controversies just related Lutheranism flourished mightily in the body of the people who were neither peasants nor intellectuals nor Swiss. The appeal was to the upper and middle classes, sufficiently educated to discard some of the medievalism of the Roman Church and impelled also by nationalism and economic self-interest to turn from the tyranny of the pope. City after city and state after state enlisted under the banner of Luther. He continued to appeal to them through the press. As a popular pamphleteer he must be reckoned among the very ablest. His faults, coarseness and unbridled violence of language, did not alienate most of his contemporaries. Even his Latin works, too harshly described by Hallam as "bellowing in bad Latin," were well adapted to the spirit of the age. But nothing like his German writings had ever been seen before. In lucidity and copiousness of language, in directness and vigor, in satire and argument and invective, in humor and aptness of illustration and allusion, the numerous tracts, political and theological, which poured from his pen, surpassed all that had hitherto been written and went straight to the hearts of his countrymen. And he won his battle almost alone, for Melanchthon, though learned and elegant, had no popular gifts, and none of his other lieutenants could boast even second-rate ability.

German Bible, 1522–32

Among his many publications a few only can be singled out for special mention. The continuation of the German Bible undoubtedly helped his cause greatly. In many things he could appeal to it against the Roman tradition, and the very fact that he claimed to do so while his opponents by their attitude seemed to shrink from this test, established the Protestant claim to be evangelical, in the eyes of the people. Next came his hymns, many popular, some good and one really great. *Ein' feste Burg* has been well called by Heine the Marseillaise of the Reformation. The Longer and Shorter Catechisms educated the common people in the evangelical doctrine so well that the Catholics were forced to imitate their enemy, though tardily, by composing, for the first time, catechisms of their own.

Hymns, 1528

Catechisms, 1529

Having overthrown much of the doctrine and discipline of the old church Luther addressed himself with admirable vigor and great success to the task of building up a substitute for it. In this the combination of the conservative and at the same time thoroughly popular spirit of the movement manifested itself. In divine service the vernacular was substituted for Latin. New emphasis was placed upon preaching, Bible-reading and hymn-singing. Mass was no longer incomprehensible, but was an act of worship in which all could intelligently participate; bread and wine were both given to the laity, and those words of the canon implying transubstantiation and sacrifice were omitted. Marriage was relegated from the rank of a sacrament to that of a civil contract. Baptism was kept in the old form, even to the detail of exorcizing the evil spirit. Auricular confession was permitted but not insisted upon.

Church government

The problems of church government and organization were pressing. Two alternatives were theoretically possible, congregationalism or state churches. After some hesitation, Luther was convinced by the extravagances of Münzer and his ilk that the latter was the only practicable course. The governments of the various German states and cities were now given supreme power in ecclesiastical matters. They took over the property belonging to the old church and administered it generally for religious or educational or charitable purposes. A system of church-visitation was started, by which the central authority passed upon the competence of each minister. Powers of appointment and removal were vested in the government. The title and office of bishop were changed in most cases to that of "superintendent," though in some German sees and generally in Sweden the name bishop was retained.

Lutheran accessions

How genuinely popular was the Lutheran movement may be seen in the fact that the free cities, Nuremberg, Augsburg, Strassburg, Ulm, Lübeck, Hamburg, and many others, were the first to revolt from Rome. In other states the government led the way. Electoral Saxony evolved slowly into complete Protestantism. Though the Elector Frederic sympathized with almost everything advanced by his great subject, he was too cautious to interfere with vested interests of ecclesiastical property and endowments. On his death his brother John succeeded to the title, and came out openly for all the reforms advocated at Wittenberg. The neighboring state of Hesse was won about 1524, though the official ordinance promulgating the evangelical doctrine was not issued until 1526. A very important acquisition was Prussia. Hitherto it had been governed by the Teutonic Order, a military society like the Knights Templars. Albert of Brandenburg became Grand Master in 1511, and fourteen years later saw the opportunity of aggrandizing his personal power by renouncing his spiritual ties. He accordingly declared the Teutonic Order abolished and himself temporal Duke of Prussia, shortly afterwards marrying a daughter of the king of Denmark. He swore allegiance to the king of Poland.

May, 5, 1525

1524–5

1525

Albert of Brandenburg, 1490–1568

The growth of Lutheranism unmolested by the imperial government was made possible by the absorption of the emperor's energies in his rivalry with France and Turkey and by the decentralization of the Empire. Leagues between groups of German states had been quite common in the past, and a new stimulus to their formation was given by the common religious interest. The first league of this sort was that of Ratisbon, between Bavaria and other South German principalities; its purpose was to carry out the Edict of Worms. This was followed by a similar league in North Germany between Catholic states, known as the League of Dessau, and a Protestant confederation known as the League of Torgau.

Leagues

1524

1525

Diet of Spires, 1526

The Diet held at Spires in the summer of 1526 witnessed the strength of the new party, for in it the two sides treated on equal terms. Many reforms were proposed, and some carried through against the obstruction by Ferdinand, the emperor's brother and lieutenant. The great question was the enforcement of the Edict of Worms, and on this the Diet passed an act, known as a Recess, providing that each state should act in matters of faith as it could answer to God and the emperor. In effect this allowed the government of every German state to choose between the two confessions, thus anticipating the principle of the Religious Peace of Augsburg of 1555.

The relations of the two parties were so delicate that it seemed as if a general religious war were imminent. In 1528 this was almost precipitated by a certain Otto von Pack, who assured the Landgrave of Hesse that he had found a treaty between the Catholic princes for the extirpation of the Lutherans and for the expropriation of their champions, the Elector of Saxony and Philip of Hesse himself. This was false, but the landgrave armed and attacked the Bishops of Würzburg and Bamberg, named by Pack as parties to the treaty, and he forced them to pay an indemnity.

Recess of Spires, 1529

The Diet which met at Spires early in 1529 endeavored to deal as drastically as possible with the schism. The Recess passed by the Catholic majority on April 7 was most unfavorable to the Reformers, repealing the Recess of the last Diet in their favor. Catholic states were commanded to execute the persecuting Edict of Worms, although Lutheran states were forbidden to abolish the office of the (Catholic) mass, and also to allow any further innovations in their own doctrines or practices until the calling of a general council. The princes were forbidden to harbor the subjects of another state. The Evangelical members of the Diet, much aggrieved at this blow to their faith, published a Protest taking the ground that the Recess of 1526 had been in the nature of a treaty and could not be abrogated without the consent of both parties to it. As the government of Germany was a federal one, this was a question of "states' rights," such as came up in our own Civil War, but in the German case it was even harder to decide because there was no written Constitution defining the powers of the national government and the states. It might naturally be assumed that the Diet had the power to repeal its own acts, but the Evangelical estates made a further point in their appeal to the emperor, by alleging that the Recess of 1526 had been passed unanimously and could only be repealed by a unanimous vote. The Protest and the appeal were signed by the Elector of Saxony, the Landgrave of Hesse, a few smaller states, and fourteen free cities. From the Protest they became immediately known as "the Protesting Estates," and subsequently the name Protestant was given to all those who left the Roman communion.

Protest, April 19

April 25

§ 4. The Growth of Protestantism until the Death of Luther

Certain states having announced that they would not be bound by the will of the majority, the question naturally came up as to how far they would defend this position by arms. Luther's advice was asked and given to the effect that all rebellion or forcible resistance to the constituted authorities was wrong. Passive resistance, the mere refusal to obey the command to persecute or to act otherwise contrary to God's law, he thought was right, but he discountenanced any other measures, even those taken in self-defence. All Germans, said he, were the emperor's subjects, and the princes should not shield Luther from him, but leave their lands open to his officers to do what they pleased. This position Luther abandoned a year later, when the jurists pointed out to him that the authority of the emperor was not despotic but was limited by law.

March 6, 1530

The Protest and Appeal of 1529 at last aroused Charles, slow as he was, to the great dangers to himself that lurked in the Protestant schism. Having repulsed the Turk and having made peace with France and the pope he was at last in a position to address himself seriously to the religious problem. Fully intending to settle the trouble once for all, he came to Germany and opened a Diet at Augsburg to which were invited not only the representatives of the various states but a number of leading theologians, both Catholic and Lutheran, all except Luther himself, an outlaw by the Edict of Worms.

June 20, 1530

The first action taken was to ask the Lutherans to state their position and this was done in the famous Augsburg Confession, read before the Diet by the Saxon Chancellor Brück. It had been drawn up by

June 25

Melanchthon in language as near as possible to that of the old church. Indeed it undertook to prove that there was in the Lutheran doctrine "nothing repugnant to Scripture or to the Catholic church or to the Roman church." Even in the form of the Confession published 1531 this Catholicizing tendency is marked, but in the original, now lost, it was probably stronger. The reason of this was not, as generally stated, Melanchthon's "gentleness" and desire to conciliate all parties, for he showed himself more truculent to the Zwinglians and Anabaptists than did Luther. It was due to the fact that Melanchthon was at heart half a Catholic, so much so, indeed, that Contarini and others thought it quite possible that he might come over to them. In the present instance he made his doctrine conform to the Roman tenets to such an extent that (in the lost original, as we may judge by the Confutation) even transubstantiation was in a manner accepted. The first part of the Confession is a creed; the second part takes up certain abuses, or reforms, namely: the demand of the cup for the laity, the marriage of priests, the mass, as an *opus operatum* or as celebrated privately, fasting and traditions, monastic vows and the power of the pope.

Melanchthon

But the concessions did not satisfy the Catholics. A Refutation was prepared by Eck and others and read before the Diet on August 3. Negotiations continued and still further concessions were wrung from Melanchthon, concessions of so dangerous a nature that his fellow-Protestants denounced him as an enemy of the faith and appealed to Luther against him. Melanchthon had agreed to call the mass a sacrifice, if the word were qualified by the term "commemorative," and also promised that the bishops should be restored to their ancient jurisdictions, a measure justified by him as a blow at turbulent sectaries but one also most perilous to Lutherans. On the other hand, Eck made some concessions, mostly verbal, about the doctrine of justification and other points.

That with this mutually conciliatory spirit an agreement failed to materialize only proved how irreconcilable were the aims of the two parties. The Diet voted that the Confession had been refuted and that the Protestants were bound to recant. The emperor promised to use his influence with the pope to call a general council to decide doubtful points, but if the Lutherans did not return to the papal church by April 15, 1531, they were threatened with coercion.

September 22

League of Schmalkalden

To meet this perilous situation a closer alliance was formed by the Protestant states at Schmalkalden in February 1531. This league constantly grew by the admission of new members, but some attempts to unite with the Swiss proved abortive.

On January 5, 1531, Ferdinand was elected King of the Romans—the title taken by the heir to the Empire—by six of the electors against the vote of Saxony. Three months later when the time granted the Lutherans expired, the Catholics were unable to do anything, and negotiations continued. These resulted in the Peace of Nuremberg, a truce until a general council should be called. It was an important victory for the Lutherans, who were thus given time in which to grow.

July 23, 1532

The seething unrest which found expression in the rebellion of the knights, of the peasants and of the Anabaptists at Münster, has been described. One more liberal movement, which also failed, must be mentioned at this time. It was as little connected with religion as anything in that theological age could be. The city of Lübeck, under its burgomaster George Wullenwever, tried to free itself from the influence of Denmark and at the same time to get a more popular

Lübeck, 1533–1535

government. In 1536 it was conquered by Christian III of Denmark, and the old aristocratic constitution restored. The time was not ripe for the people to assert its rights in North Germany.

May, 1534

The growth of Protestantism was at times assisted by force of arms. Thus, Philip of Hesse restored the now Protestant Duke Ulrich of Württemberg, who had been expelled for his tyranny by the Swabian League fifteen years before. This triumph was the more marked because the expropriated ruler was Ferdinand, King of the Romans. If in such cases it was the government which took the lead, in others the government undoubtedly compelled the people to continue Catholic even when there was a strongly Protestant public opinion. Such was the case in Albertine Saxony,[1] whose ruler, Duke George, though an estimable man in many ways, was regarded by Luther as the instrument of Satan because he persecuted his Protestant subjects. When he died, his brother, the Protestant Henry the Pious, succeeded and introduced the Reform amid general acclamation. Two years later this duke was followed by his son, the versatile but treacherous Maurice. In the year 1539 a still greater acquisition came to the Schmalkaldic League in the conversion of Brandenburg and its Elector Joachim II.

April, 1539

Philip of Hesse, 1504–67

Shortly afterwards the world was scandalized by the bigamy of Philip of Hesse. This prince was utterly spoiled by his accession to the governing power at the age of fifteen. Though he lived in flagrant immorality, his religion, which, soon after he met Luther at Worms, became the Evangelical, was real enough to make his sins a burden to conscience. Much attracted

[1] Saxony had been divided in 1485 into two parts, the Electorate, including Wittenberg, Weimar and Eisenach, and the Duchy, including Leipzig and Dresden. The former was called after its first ruler Ernestine, the latter Albertine.

by the teachings of some of the Anabaptists and Carlstadt that polygamy was lawful, and by Luther's assertion in the *Babylonian Captivity* that it was preferable to divorce, he begged to be allowed to take more wives, but was at first refused. His conscience was quickened by an attack of the syphilis in 1539, and at that time he asked permission to take a second wife and received it, on December 10, from Luther, Melanchthon, and Bucer. His secret marriage to Margaret von der Saal took place in the presence of Melanchthon, Bucer, and other divines. Luther advised him to keep the matter secret and if necessary even to "tell a good strong lie for the sake and good of the Christian church." Of course he was unable to conceal his act, and his conduct, and that of his spiritual advisers, became a just reproach to the cause. As no material advantages were lost by it, Philip might have reversed the epigram of Francis I and have said that "nothing was lost but honor." Neither Germany nor Hesse nor the Protestant church suffered directly by his act. Indeed it lead indirectly to another territorial gain. Philip's enemy Duke Henry of Brunswick, though equally immoral, attacked him in a pamphlet. Luther answered this in a tract of the utmost violence, called *Jack Sausage*. Henry's rejoinder was followed by war between him and the Schmalkaldic princes, in which he was expelled from his dominions and the Reformation introduced.

1526

March 4, 1540

1541

Further gains followed rapidly. The Catholic Bishop of Naumburg was expelled by John Frederic of Saxony, and a Lutheran bishop instituted instead. About the same time the great spiritual prince, Hermann von Wied, Archbishop Elector of Cologne, became a Protestant, and invited Melanchthon and Bucer to reform his territories. One of the last gains, before the Schmalkaldic war, was the Rhenish Palatinate, under

1541

its Elector Frederic III. His troops fought then on the Protestant side, though later he turned against that church. 1545

The opportunity of the Lutherans was due to the engagements of the emperor with other enemies. In 1535 Charles undertook a successful expedition against Tunis. The war with France simmered on until the Truce of Nice, intended to be for ten years, signed between the two powers in 1538. In 1544 war broke out again, and fortune again favored Charles. He invaded France almost to the gates of Paris, but did not press his advantage and on September 18 signed the Peace of Crépy giving up all his conquests.

Unable to turn his arms against the heretics, Charles continued to negotiate with them. The pressure he brought to bear upon the pope finally resulted in the summoning by Paul III of a council to meet at Mantua the following year. The Protestants were invited to send delegates to this council, and the princes of that faith held a congress at Schmalkalden to decide on their course. Hitherto the Lutherans had called themselves a part of the Roman Catholic church and had always appealed to a future oecumenical or national synod. They now found this position untenable, and returned the papal citation unopened. Instead, demands for reform, known as the Schmalkaldic Articles, were drawn up by Luther. The four principal demands were (1) recognition of the doctrine of justification by faith only, (2) abolition of the mass as a good work or *opus operatum,* (3) alienation of the foundations for private masses, (4) removal of the pretentions of the pope to headship of the universal church. As a matter of fact the council was postponed.

June 2, 1536

February, 1537

Failing to reach a permanent solution by this method, Charles was again forced to negotiate. The

April 19, 1539

Treaty of Frankfort agreed to a truce varying in length from six to fifteen months according to circumstances. This was followed by a series of religious conferences with the purpose of finding some means of reconciling the two confessions. Among the first of these were the meetings at Worms and Hagenau. Campeggio and Eck were the Catholic leaders, Melanchthon the spokesman for the Lutherans. Each side had eleven members on the commission, but their joint efforts were wrecked on the plan for limiting the papal power and on the doctrine of original sin. When the Diet of Ratisbon was opened in the spring of 1541 a further conference was held at which the two parties came closer to each other than they had done since Augsburg. The Book of Ratisbon was drawn up, emphasizing the points of agreement and slurring over the differences. Contarini made wide concessions, later condemned by the Catholics, on the doctrine of justification. Discussion of the nature of the church, the power of the pope, the invocation of saints, the mass, and sacerdotal celibacy seemed likely to result in some *modus vivendi.* What finally shattered the hopes of union was the discussion of transubstantiation and the adoration of the host. As Contarini had found in the statements of the Augsburg Confession no insuperable obstacle to an understanding he was astonished at the stress laid on them by the Protestants now.

Religious Colloquies

1540–1

1542

It is not remarkable that with such results the Diet of Spires should have avoided the religious question and have devoted itself to more secular matters, among them the grant to the emperor of soldiers to fight the Turk. Of this Diet Bucer wrote "The Estates act under the wrath of God. Religion is relegated to an agreement between cities. . . . The cause of our evils is that few seek the Lord earnestly, but most fight against him, both among those who have rejected, and of those who still bear, the papal yoke." At the Diet of Spires two years later the emperor promised the Protestants, in return for help against France, recognition until a German National Council should be called. For this concession he was sharply rebuked by the pope. The Diet of Worms contented itself with expressing its general hope for a "Christian reformation."

1545

During his later years Luther's polemic never flagged. His last book, *Against the Papacy of Rome, founded by the Devil,* surpassed Cicero and the humanists and all that had ever been known in the virulence of its invective against "the most hellish father, St. Paul, or Paula III" and his "hellish Roman church." "One would like to curse them," he wrote, "so that thunder and lightning would strike them, hell fire burn them, the plague, syphilis, epilepsy, scurvy, leprosy, carbuncles, and all diseases attack them"—and so on for page after page. Of course such lack of restraint largely defeated its own ends. The Swiss Reformer Bullinger called it "amazingly violent," and a book than which he "had never read anything more savage or imprudent." Our judgment of it must be tempered by the consideration that Luther suffered in his last years from a nervous malady and from other painful diseases, due partly to overwork and lack of exercise, partly to the quantities of alcohol he imbibed, though he never became intoxicated.

1545

Nevertheless, the last twenty years of his life were his happiest ones. His wife, Catherine von Bora, an ex-nun, and his children, brought him much happiness. Though the wedding gave his enemies plenty of openings for reviling him as an apostate, and though it drew from Erasmus the scoffing jest that what had begun as a tragedy ended as a comedy, it

June 13, 1525

crowned his career, symbolizing the return from medieval asceticism to modern joy in living. Dwelling in the fine old friary, entertaining with lavish prodigality many poor relatives, famous strangers, and students, notwithstanding unremitting toil and not a little bodily suffering, he expanded in his whole nature, mellowing in the warmth of a happy fireside climate. His daily routine is known to us intimately through the adoring assiduity of his disciples, who noted down whole volumes of his *Table Talk*.

Death and character of Luther

On Febrary 18, 1546, he died. Measured by the work that he accomplished and by the impression that his personality made both on contemporaries and on posterity, there are few men like him in history. Dogmatic, superstitious, intolerant, overbearing, and violent as he was, he yet had that inscrutable prerogative of genius of transforming what he touched into new values. His contemporaries bore his invective because of his earnestness; they bowed to "the almost disgraceful servitude" which, says Melanchthon, he imposed upon his followers, because they knew that he was leading them to victory in a great and worthy cause. Even so, now, many men overlook his narrowness and bigotry because of his genius and bravery.

His grandest quality was sincerity. Priest and public man as he was, there was not a line of hypocrisy or cant in his whole being. A sham was to him intolerable, the abomination of desolation standing where it ought not. Reckless of consequences, of danger, of his popularity, and of his life, he blurted out the whole truth, as he saw it, "despite all cardinals, popes, kings and emperors, together with all devils and hell." Whether his ideal is ours or not, his courage in daring and his strength to labor for it must command our respect.

Next to his earnestness he owed his success to a

His eloquence

wonderful gift of language that made him the tongue, as well as the spear-point, of his people. In love of nature, in wonder, in the power to voice some secret truth in a phrase or a metaphor, he was a poet. He looked out on the stars and considered the "good master-workman" that made them, on the violets "for which neither the Grand Turk nor the emperor could pay," on the yearly growth of corn and wine, "as great a miracle as the manna in the wilderness," on the "pious, honorable birds" alert to escape the fowler's net, or holding a Diet "in a hall roofed with the vault of heaven, carpeted with the grass, and with walls as far as the ends of the earth." Or he wrote to his son a charming fairy-tale of a pleasant garden where good children eat apples and pears and cherries and plums, and where they ride on pretty ponies with golden reins and silver saddles and dance all day and play with whistles and fifes and little cross-bows.

Luther's character combined traits not usually found in the same nature. He was both a dreamy mystic and a practical man of affairs; he saw visions and he knew how to make them realities; he was a God-intoxicated prophet and a cool calculator and hard worker for results. His faith was as simple and passionate as his dogmatic distinctions were often sophistical and arid. He could attack his foes with berserker fury, and he could be as gentle with a child as only a woman can. His hymns soar to heaven and his coarse jests trail in the mire. He was touched with profound melancholy and yet he had a wholesome, ready laugh. His words are now brutal invectives and again blossom with the most exquisite flowers of the soul—poetry, music, idyllic humor, tenderness. He was subtle and simple; superstitious and wise; limited in his cultural sympathies, but very great in what he achieved.

§ 5. The Religious War and the Religious Peace

The Schmalkaldic War, 1546–7

Hardly had Luther been laid to rest when the first general religious war broke out in Germany. There had been a few small wars of this character before, such as those of Hesse against Bamberg and Würzburg, and against Württemberg, and against Brunswick. But the conflicts had been successfully "localized." Now at last was to come a general battle, as a foretaste of the Thirty Years War of the next century.

It has sometimes been doubted whether the Schmalkaldic War was a religious conflict at all. The emperor asserted that his sole object was to reduce rebellious subjects to obedience. Several Protestant princes were his allies, and the territories he conquered were not, for the most part, forced to give up their faith. Nevertheless, it is certain that the fundamental cause of the strain was the difference of creed. A parallel may be found in our own Civil War, in which Lincoln truly claimed that he was fighting only to maintain the union, and yet it is certain that slavery furnished the underlying cause of the appeal to arms.

It has recently been shown that the emperor planned the attack on his Protestant subjects as far back, at least, as 1541. All the negotiations subsequent to that time were a mere blind to disguise his preparations. For he labored indefatigably to bring about a condition in which it would be safe for him to embark on the perilous enterprise. Though he was a dull man he had the two qualities of caution and persistence that stood him in better stead than the more showy talents of other statesmen. If, with his huge resources, he never did anything brilliant, still less did he ever take a gambler's chance of failing.

The opportune moment came at last in the spring of 1546. Two years before, he had beaten France with the help of the Protestants, and had imposed upon her as one condition of peace that she should make no allies within the Empire. In November of the same year he made an alliance with Paul III, receiving 200,000 ducats in support of his effort to extirpate the heresy.

Other considerations impelled him to attack at once. The secession of Cologne and the Palatinate from the Catholic communion gave the Protestants a majority in the Electoral College. Still more decisive was it that Charles was able at this time by playing upon the jealousies and ambitions of the states, to secure important allies within the Empire, including some of the Protestant faith. First, Catholic Bavaria forgot her hatred of Austria far enough to make common cause against the heretics. Then, two great Protestant princes, Maurice of Albertine Saxony and John von Küstrin—a brother of Joachim II, Elector of Brandenburg—abandoned their coreligionists and bartered support to the emperor in return for promises of aggrandizement.

January 1546

A final religious conference held at Ratisbon demonstrated more clearly than ever the hopelessness of conciliation. Whereas a semi-Lutheran doctrine of justification was adopted, the Protestants prepared two long memoirs rejecting the authority of the council recently convened at Trent. And then, in the summer, war broke out. At this moment the forces of the Schmalkaldic League were superior to those of its enemies. But for poor leadership and lack of unity in command they would probably have won.

Towards the last of August and early in September the Protestant troops bombarded the imperial army at Ingolstadt, but failed to follow this up by a decisive attack, as was urged by General Schärtlin of Augsburg. Lack of equipment was partly responsible for this failure. When the emperor advanced, the Elector of Saxony and the Landgrave of Hesse retired each to his own land. Another futile attempt of the League was a raid on the Tyrol, possibly influenced by the desire to strike at the Council of Trent, certainly by no sound military policy. The effect of these indecisive counsels was that Charles had little trouble in reducing the South German rebels, Augsburg, Ulm, Nuremberg, and Württemberg. The Elector Palatine hastened to come to terms by temporarily abandoning his religion. A counter-reformation was also effected in Cologne. Augsburg bought the emperor's pardon by material concessions.

February, 1547

October, 1546

In the meantime Duke Maurice of Albertine Saxony, having made a bargain with the emperor, attacked his second cousin the Elector. Though Maurice was not obliged to abjure his faith, his act was naturally regarded as one of signal treachery and he was henceforth known by the nickname "Judas." Maurice conquered most of his cousin's lands, except the forts of Wittenberg and Gotha. Charles's Spanish army under Alva now turned northward, forced a passage of the Elbe and routed the troops of John Frederic at the battle of Mühlberg, near Torgau, on April 24, 1547. John Frederic was captured wounded, and kept in durance several years. Wittenberg capitulated on May 19, and just a month later Philip of Hesse surrendered at Halle. He also was kept a prisoner for some years. Peace was made by the mediation of Brandenburg. The electoral vote of Saxony was given to Maurice, and with it the best part of John Frederic's lands, including Wittenberg. No change of religion was required. The net result of the war was to increase the imperial power, but to put a very slight check upon the expansion of Protestantism.

And yet it was for precisely this end that Charles chiefly valued his authority. Immediately, acting independently of the pope, he made another effort to restore the confessional unity of Germany. The Diet of Augsburg accepted under pressure from him a decree called the Interim because it was to be valid only until the final decisions of a general council. Though intended to apply only to Protestant states—the Catholics had, instead, a *formula reformationis*—the Interim, drawn up by Romanist divines, was naturally Catholic in tenor. The episcopal constitution was restored, along with the canon of the mass, the doctrine of the seven sacraments, and the worship of saints. On some doctrinal points vagueness was studied. The only concessions made to the Reformation were the *pro tempore* recognition of the marriage of the clergy and the giving of the cup to the laity. Various other details of practical reform were demanded. The Interim was intensely unpopular with both parties. The pope objected to it and German Catholics, especially in Bavaria, strongly opposed it. The South German Protestant states accepted it only under pressure. Maurice of Saxony adopted it in a modified form, known as the Leipzig Interim, in December 1548. The assistance rendered him by Melanchthon caused a fierce attack on the theologian by his fellow-Lutherans. In enforcing the Interim Maurice found his own profit, for when Magdeburg won the nickname of "our Lord God's pulpit" by refusing to accept it, Maurice was entrusted with the execution of the imperial ban, and captured the city on November 9, 1551.

1547–8

The Interim, June 30, 1548

Germany now fell into a confused condition, every state for itself. The emperor found his own difficulties in trying to make his son Philip successor to his brother Ferdinand. His two former Protestant allies, Maurice and John von Küstrin, made an alliance with France and with other North German princes and forced the emperor to conclude the Convention of Passau. This guaranteed afresh the religious freedom of the Lutherans until the next Diet, and forced the liberation of John Frederic and Philip of Hesse. Charles did not loyally accept the conditions of this agreement, but induced Albert, Margrave of Brandenburg-Culmbach, to attack the confederate princes in the rear. After Albert had laid waste a portion of North Germany he was defeated by Maurice at the battle of Sievershausen. Mortally wounded, the brilliant but utterly unscrupulous victor died, at the age of thirty-two, soon after the battle. As the conflict had by this time resolved itself into a duel between him and Charles, the emperor was now at last able to put through, at the Diet of Augsburg, a settlement of the religious question.

1552

July 9, 1553

Religious Peace of Augsburg, September 25, 1555

The principles of the Religious Peace were as follows:

(1) A truce between states recognizing the Augsburg Confession and Catholic states until union was possible. All other confessions were to be barred—a provision aimed chiefly at Calvinists.

(2) The princes and governments of the Free Cities were to be allowed to choose between the Roman and the Lutheran faith, but their subjects must either conform to this faith—on the maxim famous as *cujus regio ejus religio*—or emigrate. In Imperial Free Cities, however, it was specially provided that Catholic minorities be tolerated.

(3) The "ecclesiastical reservation," or principle that when a Catholic spiritual prince became Protestant he should be deposed and a successor appointed

so that his territory might remain under the church. In respect to this Ferdinand privately promised to secure toleration for Protestant subjects in the land of such a prince. All claims of spiritual jurisdiction by Catholic prelates in Lutheran lands were to cease. All estates of the church confiscated prior to 1552 were to remain in the hands of the spoliators, all seized since that date to be restored.

The Peace of Augsburg, like the Missouri Compromise, only postponed civil war and the radical solution of a pressing problem. But as we cannot rightly censure the statesmen of 1820 for not insisting on emancipation, for which public opinion was not yet prepared, so it would be unhistorical and unreasonable to blame the Diet of Augsburg for not granting the complete toleration which we now see was bound to come and was ideally the right thing. Mankind is educated slowly and by many hard experiences. Europe had lain so long under the domination of an authoritative ecclesiastical civilization that the possibility of complete toleration hardly occurred to any but a few eccentrics. And we must not minimize what the Peace of Augsburg actually accomplished. It is true that choice of religion was legally limited to two alternatives, but this was more than had been allowed before. It is true that freedom of even this choice was complete only for the rulers of the territories or Free Cities; private citizens might exercise the same choice only on leaving their homes. The hardship of this was somewhat lessened by the consideration that in any case the nonconformist would not have to go far before finding a German community holding the Catholic or Lutheran opinions he preferred. Finally, it must be remembered that, if the Peace of Augsburg aligned the whole nation into two mutually hostile camps, it at least kept them from war for more than

Actual results

half a century. Nor was this a mere accident, for the strain was at times severe. When the imperial knight, Grumbach, broke the peace by sacking the city of Würzburg, he was put under the ban, captured and executed. His protector, Duke John Frederic of Saxony, was also captured and kept in confinement in Austria until his death.

1563–7

Notwithstanding such an exhibition of centralized power, it is probable that the Peace of Augsburg increased rather than diminished the authority of the territorial states at the expense of the imperial government. Charles V, worn out by his long and unsuccessful struggle with heresy, after giving the Netherlands to his son Philip in 1555, abdicated the crown of the Empire to his brother Ferdinand in 1556. He died two years later in a monastery, a disappointed man, having expressed the wish that he had burned Luther at Worms. The energies of Ferdinand were largely taken up with the Turkish war. His son, Maximilian II, was favorably inclined to Protestantism.

Ferdinand, 1556–64

Maximilian II, 1564–76

Catholic reaction

Before Maximilian's death, however, a reaction in favor of Catholicism had already set in. The last important gains to the Lutheran cause in Germany came in the years immediately following the Peace of Augsburg. Nothing is more remarkable than the fact that practically all the conquests of Protestantism in Europe were made within the first half century of its existence. After that for a few years it lost, and since then has remained, geographically speaking, stationary in Europe. It is impossible to get accurate statistics of the gains and losses of either confession. The estimate of the Venetian ambassador that only one-tenth of the German empire was Catholic in 1558 is certainly wrong. In 1570, at the height of the Protestant tide, probably 70 per cent. of Germans—including Austrians—were Protestant. In 1910 the Germans of the

German Empire and of Austria were divided thus: Protestants 37,675,000; Catholics 29,700,000. The Protestants were about 56 per cent., and this proportion was probably about that of the year 1600.

Lutheran schisms

Historically, the final stemming of the Protestant flood was due to the revival of energy in the Catholic Church and to the internal weakness and schism of the Protestants. Even within the Lutheran communion fierce conflicts broke out. Luther's lieutenants fought for his spiritual heritage as the generals of Alexander fought for his empire. The center of these storms was Melanchthon until death freed him from "the rage of the theologians." Always half Catholic, half Erasmian at heart, by his endorsement of the Interim, and by his severe criticisms of his former friends Luther and John Frederic, he brought on himself the bitter enmity of those calling themselves "Gnesio-Lutherans," or "Genuine Lutherans." Melanchthon abolished congregational hymn-singing, and published his true views, hitherto dissembled, on predestination and the sacrament. He was attacked by Flacius the historian, and by many others. The dispute was taken up by still others and went to such lengths that for a minor heresy a pastor, Funck, was executed by his fellow-Lutherans in Prussia, in 1566. "Philippism" as it was called, at first grew, but finally collapsed when the Formula of Concord was drawn up in 1580 and signed by over 8000 clergy. This document is to the Lutheran Church what the decrees of Trent were to the Catholics. The "high" doctrine of the real presence was strongly stated, and all the sophistries advanced to support it canonized. The sacramental bread and wine were treated with such superstitious reverence that a Lutheran priest who accidentally spilled the latter was punished by having his fingers cut off. Melanchthon was against such "remnants of

April 19, 1560

papistry" which he rightly named "artolatry" or "bread-worship."

But the civil wars within the Lutheran communion were less bitter than the hatred for the Calvinists. By 1550 their mutual detestation had reached such a point that Calvin called the Lutherans "ministers of Satan" and "professed enemies of God" trying to bring in "adulterine rites" and vitiate the pure worship. The quarrel broke out again at the Colloquy of Worms. Melanchthon and others condemned Zwingli, thus, in Calvin's opinion, "wiping off all their glory." Nevertheless Calvin himself had said, in 1539, that Zwingli's opinion was false and pernicious. So difficult is the path of orthodoxy to find! In 1557 the Zwinglian leader M. Schenck wrote to Thomas Blaurer that the error of the papists was rather to be borne than that of the Saxons. Nevertheless Calvinism continued to grow in Germany at the expense of Lutheranism. Especially after the Formula of Concord the "Philippists" went over in large numbers to the Calvinists.

Effect on the nation

The worst thing about these distressing controversies was that they seemed to absorb the whole energies of the nation. No period is less productive in modern German history than the age immediately following the triumph of the Reformation. The movement, which had begun so liberally and hopefully, became, temporarily at least, narrower and more bigoted than Catholicism. It seemed as if Erasmus had been quite right when he said that where Lutheranism reigned culture perished. Of these men it has been said—and the epigram is not a bad one—that they made an intellectual desert and called it religious peace.

And yet we should be cautious in history of assuming *post hoc propter hoc*. That there was nothing necessarily blighting in Protestantism is shown by the examples of England and Poland, where the Reform was followed by the most brilliant literary age in the annals of these peoples. The latter part of the sixteenth century was also the great period of the literature of Spain and Portugal, which remained Catholic, whereas Italy, equally Catholic, notably declined in artistic production and somewhat also in letters. The causes of the alterations, in various peoples, of periods of productivity and of comparative sterility, are in part inscrutable. In the present case, it seems that when a relaxation of intellectual activity is visible, it was not due to any special quality in Protestantism, but was rather caused by the heat of controversy.

16th century literature

§ 7. Note on Scandinavia, Poland, and Hungary

A few small countries bordering on the Empire, neither fully in the central stream of European culture, nor wholly outside of it, may be treated briefly. All of them were affected by the Protestant revolution, the Teutonic peoples permanently, the others transiently.

Scandinavia looms large in the Middle Ages as the home of the teeming multitudes of emigrants, Goths and Vandals, who swarmed over the Roman Empire. Later waves from Denmark and the contiguous portion of Germany flooded England first in the Anglo-Saxon conquest and then in the Danish. The Normans, too, originally hailed from Scandinavia. But though the sons of the North conquered and colonized so much of the South, Scandinavia herself remained a small people, neither politically nor intellectually of the first importance. The three kingdoms of Denmark, Norway, and Sweden became one in 1397; and, after Sweden's temporary separation from the other two, were again united. The fifteenth century saw the great aggrandizement of the power of the prelates and of the larger nobles at the expense of the *bönder,* who, from a class of free and noble small proprietors degenerated not only into peasants but often into serfs.

1513

When Christian II succeeded to the throne, it was as the papal champion. His attempt to consolidate his power in Sweden by massacring the magnates under

November 8–11, 1520

the pretext that they were hostile to the pope, an act called the "Stockholm bath of blood," aroused the people against him in a war of independence.

Denmark

Christian found Denmark also insubordinate. It is true that he made some just laws, protecting the people and building up their prosperity, but their support was insufficient to counterbalance the hatred of the great lords spiritual and temporal. He was quick to see in the Reformation a weapon against the prelates, and appealed for help to Wittenberg as early as 1519. His endeavors throughout 1520 to get Luther himself to visit Denmark failed, but early in 1521 he succeeded in attracting Carlstadt for a short visit. This effort, however, cost him his throne, for he was expelled on April 13, 1523, and wandered over Europe

1559

in exile until his death.

The Duke of Schleswig-Holstein, to whom the crown was offered, reigned for ten years as Frederic I. Though his coronation oath bound him to do nothing against the church, he had only been king for three years before he came out openly for the Reformation. In this again we must see primarily a policy, rather than a conviction. He was supported, however, by the common people, who had been disgusted by the indul-

1516–19

gences sold by Arcimboldi and by the constant corruption of the higher clergy. The cities, as in Germany, were the strongest centers of the movement. The Diet of 1527 decreed that Lutherans should be recognized on equal terms with Catholics, that marriage of priests and the regular clergy be allowed. In 1530 a Lutheran confession was adopted.

Christian III, who reigned until 1559, took the final step, though at the price of a civil war. His victory enabled him to arrest all the bishops, August 20, 1536, and to force them to renounce their rights and properties in favor of the crown. Only one, Bishop Rönnow of Roskilde, refused, and was consequently held prisoner until his death. The Diet of 1536 abolished Catholicism, confiscated all church property and distributed it between the king and the temporal nobles. Bugenhagen was called from Wittenberg to organize the church on Lutheran lines. In the immediately following years the Catholics were deprived of their civil rights. The political benefits of the Reformation inured primarily to the king and secondarily to the third estate.

1537–9

Norway

Norway was a vassal of Denmark from 1380 till 1814. At no time was its dependence more complete than in the sixteenth century. Frederic I introduced the Reformation by royal decree as early as 1528, and Christian III put the northern kingdom completely under the tutelage of Denmark, in spiritual as well as in temporal matters. The adoption of the Reformation here as in Iceland seemed to be a matter of popular indifference.

1536

Sweden

Gustavus Vasa, 1523–60

After Sweden had asserted her independence by the expulsion of Christian II, Gustavus Vasa, an able ruler, ascended the throne. He, too, saw in the Reformation chiefly an opportunity for confiscating the goods of the church. The way had, indeed, been prepared by a popular reformer, Olaus Petri, but the king made the movement an excuse to concentrate in his own hands the spiritual power. The Diet of Westeras passed the necessary laws, at the same time expelling the chief leader of the Romanist party, John Brask,

1527

Bishop of Linköping. The Reformation was entirely Lutheran and extremely conservative. Not only the Anabaptists, but even the Calvinists, failed to get any hold upon the Scandinavian peoples. In many ways the Reformation in Sweden was parallel to that in England. Both countries retained the episcopal organization founded upon the "apostolical succession." Olaus Magni, Bishop of Westeras, had been ordained at Rome in 1524, and in turn consecrated the first Evangelical Archbishop, Lawrence Petri, who had studied at Wittenberg, and who later translated the Bible into Swedish and protected his people from the inroads of Calvinism. The king, more and more absolutely the head of the church, as in England, did not hesitate to punish even prominent reformers when they opposed him. The reign of Gustavus's successor, Eric XIV, was characterless, save for the influx of Huguenots strengthening the Protestants. King John III made a final, though futile, attempt to reunite with the Roman Church. As Finland was at this time a dependency of Sweden, the Reformation took practically the same course as in Sweden itself.

Petri 1499–1573

1541

Eric XIV, 1560–8

John III, 1569–92

A complete contrast to Sweden is furnished by Poland. If in the former the government counted for almost everything, in the latter it counted for next to nothing. The theater of Polish history is the vast plain extending from the Carpathians to the Düna, and from the Baltic almost to the Black Sea and the Sea of Azov. This region, lacking natural frontiers on several sides, was inhabited by a variety of races: Poles in the west, Lithuanians in the east, Ruthenians in the south and many Germans in the cities. The union of the Polish and Lithuanian states was as yet a merely personal one in the monarch. Since the fourteenth century the crown of Poland had been elective, but the grand-ducal crown of Lithuania was he-

Poland

reditary in the famous house of Jagiello, and the advantages of union induced the Polish nobility regularly to elect the heir to the eastern domain their king. Though theoretically absolute, in practice the king had been limited by the power of the nobles and gentry, and this limitation was given a constitutional sanction in the law *Nihil novi,* forbidding the monarch to pass laws without the consent of the deputies of the magnates and lesser nobles.

1505

Sigismund I, 1506–48

The foreign policy of Sigismund I was determined by the proximity of powerful and generally hostile neighbors. It would not be profitable in this place to follow at length the story of his frequent wars with Muscovy and with the Tartar hordes of the Crimea, and of his diplomatic struggles with the Turks, the Empire, Hungary, and Sweden. On the whole he succeeded not only in holding his own, but in augmenting his power. He it was who finally settled the vexatious question of the relationship of his crown to the Teutonic Order, which, since 1466, had held Prussia as a fief, though a constantly rebellious and troublesome one. The election of Albert of Brandenburg as Grand Master of the Order threatened more serious trouble, but a satisfactory solution of the problem was found when Albert embraced the Lutheran faith and secularized Prussia as an hereditary duchy, at the same time swearing allegiance to Sigismund as his suzerain. Many years later Sigismund's son conquered and annexed another domain of the Teutonic order further north, namely Livonia. War with Sweden resulted from this but was settled by the cession of Esthonia to the Scandinavian power.

1511

1525

1561

Internally, the vigorous Jagiello strengthened both the military and financial resources of his people. To meet the constant inroads of the Tartars he established the Cossacks, a rough cavalry formed of the hunters, fishers, and graziers of the Ukraine, quite analogous to the cowboys of the American Wild West. From being a military body they developed into a state and nation that occupied a special position in Poland and then in Russia. Sigismund's fiscal policy, by recovering control of the mint and putting the treasury into the hands of capable bankers, effectively provided for the economic life of the government.

Reformation

Poland has generally been as open to the inroads of foreign ideas as to the attacks of enemies; a peculiar susceptibility to alien culture, due partly to the linguistic attainments of many educated Poles and partly to an independent, almost anarchical disposition, has made this nation receive from other lands more freely than it gives. Every wave of new ideas innundates the low-lying plain of the Vistula. So the Reformation spread with amazing rapidity, first among the cities and then among the peasants of that land. In the fifteenth century the influence of Huss and the humanists had in different ways formed channels facilitating the inrush of Lutheranism. The unpopularity of a wealthy and indolent church predisposed the body politic to the new infection. Danzig, that "Venice of the North," had a Lutheran preacher in 1518; while the Edict of Thorn, intended to suppress the heretics, indicates that as early as 1520 they had attracted the attention of the central government. But this persecuting measure, followed thick and fast by others, only proved how little the tide could be stemmed by paper barriers. The cities of Cracow, Posen, and Lublin, especially susceptible on account of their German population, were thoroughly infected before 1522. Next, the contagion attacked the country districts and towns of Prussia, which had been pretty thoroughly converted prior to its secularization.

The first political effect of the Reformation was to

stimulate the unrest of the lower classes. Riots and rebellions, analogous to those of the Peasants' War in Germany, followed hard upon the preaching of the "gospel." Sigismund could restore order here and there, as he did at Danzig in 1526 by a military occupation, by fining the town and beheading her six leading innovators, but he could not suppress the growing movement. For after the accession of the lower classes came that of the nobles and gentry who bore the real sovereignty in the state. Seeing in the Reformation a weapon for humiliating and plundering the church, as well as a key to a higher spiritual life, from one motive or the other, they flocked to its standard, and, under leadership of their greatest reformer, John Laski, organized a powerful church.

Sigismund II 1548–72

The reign of Sigismund II saw the social upheaval by which the nobility finally placed the power firmly in their own hands, and also the height of the Reformation. By a law known as the "Execution" the assembly of nobles finally got control of the executive as well as of the legislative branch of the government. At the same time they, with the cordial assistance of the king, bound the country together in a closer bond known as the Union of Lublin. Though Lithuania and Prussia struggled against incorporation with Poland, both were forced to submit to a measure that added power to the state and opened to the Polish nobility great opportunity for political and economic exploitation of these lands. Not only the king, but the magnates and the cities were put under the heel of the ruling caste. This was an evolution opposite to that of most European states, in which crown and bourgeoisie subdued the once proud position of the baronage. But even here in Poland one sees the rising influence of commerce and the money-power, in that the Polish nobility was largely composed of small

1569

gentry eager and able to exploit the new opportunities offered by capitalism. In other countries the old privilege of the sword gave way to the new privilege of gold; in Poland the sword itself turned golden, at least in part; the blade kept its keen, steel edge, but the hilt by which it was wielded glittered yellow.

Protestantism

Unchecked though they were by laws, the Protestants soon developed a weakness that finally proved fatal to their cause, lack of organization and division into many mutually hostile sects. The Anabaptists of course arrived, preached, gained adherents, and were suppressed. Next came a large influx of Bohemian Brethren, expelled from their own country and migrating to a land of freedom, where they soon made common cause with the Lutherans. Calvinists propagated the seeds of their faith with much success. Finally the Unitarians, led by Lelio Sozini, found a home in Poland and made many proselytes, at last becoming so powerful that they founded the new city of Racau, whence issued the famous Racovian Catechism. At one time they seemed about to obtain the mastery of the state, but the firm union of the Trinitarian Protestants at Sandomir checked them until all of them were swept away together by the resurging tide of Catholicism. Several versions of the Bible, Lutheran, Socinian, and Catholic, were issued.

1537

1548

1558

1570

So powerful were the Evangelicals that at the Diet of 1555 they held services in the face of the Catholic king, and passed a law abolishing the jurisdiction of the ecclesiastical courts. This measure, of course, allowed freedom of all new sects, both those then in control of the Diet and the as yet unfledged Antitrinitarians. Nevertheless a strong wish was expressed for a national, Protestant church, and had Sigismund had the advantages, as he had the matrimonial difficulties, of Henry VIII, he might have established such a body. But he never quite dared to take the step, dreading the hostility of Catholic neighbors. Singularly enough the championship of the Catholic cause was undertaken by Greek-Catholic Muscovy, whose Czar, Ivan, represented his war against Poland as a crusade against the new iconoclasts. Unable to act with power, Sigismund cultivated such means of combating Protestantism as were ready to his hand. His most trenchant weapon was the Order of Jesuits, who were invited to come in and establish schools. Moreover, the excellence of their colleges in foreign lands induced many of the nobility to send their sons to be educated under them, and thus were prepared the seeds of the Counter-Reformation.

1562

The death of Sigismund without an heir left Poland for a time masterless. During the interregnum the Diet passed the Compact of Warsaw by which absolute religious liberty was granted to all sects—"Dissidentes de Religione"—without exception. But, liberal though the law was, it was vitiated in practice by the right retained by every master of punishing his serfs for religious as well as for secular causes. Thus it was that the lower classes were marched from Protestant pillar to Catholic post and back without again daring to rebel or to express any choice in the matter.

January 28, 1573

The election of Henry of Valois, a younger son of Catharine de' Medici, was made conditional on the acceptance of a number of articles, including the maintenance of religious liberty. The prince acceded, with some reservations, and was crowned on February 21, 1574. Four months later he heard of the death of his brother, Charles IX, making him king of France. Without daring to ask leave of absence, he absconded from Poland on June 18, thereby abandoning a throne which was promptly declared vacant.

Henry May 11, 1573

The new election presented great difficulties, and

almost led to civil war. While the Senate declared for the Hapsburg Maximilian II, the Diet chose Stephen Báthory, prince of Transylvania. Only the unexpected death of Maximilian prevented an armed collision between the two. Báthory, now in possession, forced his recognition by all parties and led the land of his adoption into a period of highly successful diplomacy and of victorious war against Muscovy. His religious policy was one of pacification, conciliation, and of supporting inconspicuously the Jesuit foundations at Wilna, Posen, Cracow, and Riga. But the full fruits of their propaganda, resulting in the complete reconversion of Poland to Catholicism were not reaped until the reign of his successor, Sigismund III, a Vasa, of Sweden.

Stephen Báthory, 1576–86

Sigismund III, 1586–1632

Bohemia

Bohemia, a Slav kingdom long united historically and dynastically with the Empire, as the home of Huss, welcomed the Reformation warmly, the Brethren turning first to Luther and then to Calvin. After various efforts to suppress and banish them had failed of large success, the Compact of 1567 granted toleration to the three principal churches. As in Poland, the Jesuits won back the whole land in the next generation, so that in 1910 there were in Bohemia 6,500,000 Catholics and only 175,000 Protestants.

Hungary, 1526

Hungary was so badly broken by the Turks at the battle of Mohács that she was able to play but little part in the development of Western civilization. Like her more powerful rival, she was also distracted by internal dissention. After the death of her King Lewis at Mohács there were two candidates for the throne, Ferdinand the Emperor's brother and John Zapolya, "woiwod" or prince of Transylvania. Protestantism had a considerable hold on the nobles, who, after the shattering of the national power, divided a portion of the goods of the church between them.

Zapolya, 1526–40

The Unitarian movement was also strong for a time, and the division this caused proved almost fatal to the Reformation, for the greater part of the kingdom was won back to Catholicism under the Jesuits' leadership. In 1910 there were about 8,600,000 Catholics in Hungary and about 3,200,000 Protestants.

1576–1612

Transylvania

Transylvania, though a dependency of the Turks, was allowed to keep the Christian religion. The Saxon colonists in this state welcomed the Reformation, formally recognizing the Augsburg Confession in a synod of 1572. Here also the Unitarians attained their greatest strength, being recruited partly from those expelled from Poland. They drew their inspiration not merely from Sozini, but from a variety of sources, for the doctrine appeared simultaneously among certain Anabaptist and Spiritualist sects. Toleration was granted them on the same terms as other Christians. The name "Unitarian" first appears in a decree of the Transylvania Diet of the year 1600. An appreciable body of this persuasion still remains in the country, together with a number of Lutherans, Calvinists, and Romanists, but the large majority of the people belong to two Greek Catholic churches.

CHAPTER III

SWITZERLAND

§ 1. Zwingli

The Swiss Confederation

Amid the snow-clad Alps and azure lakes of Switzerland there grew up a race of Germans which, though still nominally a part of the Empire, had, at the period now considered, long gone on its own distinct path of development. Politically, the Confederacy arose in a popular revolt against the House of Austria. The federal union of the three forest cantons of Uri, Schwyz, and Unterwalden, first entered into in 1291 and made permanent in 1315, was strengthened by the admission of Lucerne (1332), Zug (1352), Glarus (1351) and of the Imperial Cities of Zurich (1351) and Berne (1353). By the admission of Freiburg and Solothurn (1481), Basle (1501), Schaffhausen (1501) and Appenzell (1513) the Confederacy reached the number of thirteen cantons at which it remained for many years. By this time it was recognized as a practically independent state, courted by the great powers of Europe. Allied to this German Confederacy were two Romance-speaking states of a similar nature, the Confederacies of the Valais and of the Grisons.

The Swiss were then the one free people of Europe. Republican government by popular magistrates prevailed in all the cantons. Liberty was not quite democratic, for the cantons ruled several subject provinces, and in the cities a somewhat aristocratic electorate held power; nevertheless there was no state in Europe approaching the Swiss in self-government. Though they were generally accounted the best soldiers of the day, their military valor did not redound to their own advantage, for the hardy peasantry yielded to the solicitations of the great powers around them to enter into foreign, mercenary service. The influential men, especially the priests, took pensions from the pope or from France or from other princes, in return for their labors in recruiting. The system was a bad one for both sides. Swiss politics were corrupted and the land drained of its strongest men; whereas the princes who hired the mercenaries often found to their cost that such soldiers were not only the most formidable to their enemies but also the most troublesome to themselves, always on the point of mutiny for more pay and plunder. The Swiss were beginning to see the evils of the system, and prohibited the taking of pensions in 1503, though this law remained largely a dead letter. The reputation of the mountaineers suffered a blow in their defeat by the French at Marignano, followed by a treaty with France, intended by that power to make Switzerland a permanent dependency in return for a large annual subsidy payable to each of the thirteen cantons and to the Grisons and Valais as well. The country suffered from faction. The rural or "Forest" cantons were jealous of the cities, and the latter, especially Berne, the strongest, pursued selfish policies of individual aggrandizement at the expense of their confederates.

September 13–14, 1515

As everywhere else, the cities were the centers of culture and of social movements. Basle was famous for its university and for the great printing house of Froben. Here Albert Dürer had stayed for a while during his wandering years. Here Sebastian Brant had studied and had written his famous satire. Here the great Erasmus had come to publish his New Testament.

But the Reformation in Switzerland was only in

1521–9

part a child of humanism. Nationalism played its rôle in the revolt from Rome, memories of councils lingered at Constance and Basle, and the desire for a purer religion made itself felt among the more earnest. Switzerland had at least one great shrine, that of Einsiedeln; to her Virgin many pilgrims came yearly in hopes of the plenary indulgence, expressly promising forgiveness of both guilt and penalty of sin. Berne was the theater of one of the most reverberating scandals enacted by the contemporary church. A passionately contested theological issue of the day was whether the Virgin had been immaculately conceived. This was denied by the Dominicans and asserted by the Franciscans. Some of the Dominicans of the friary at Berne thought that the best way to settle the affair was to have a direct revelation. For their fraudulent purposes they conspired with John Jetzer, a lay brother admitted in 1506, who died after 1520. Whether as a tool in the hands of others, or as an imposter, Jetzer produced a series of bogus apparitions, bringing the Virgin on the stage and making her give details of her conception sufficiently gross to show that it took place in the ordinary, and not in the immaculate, manner. When the fraud was at last discovered by the authorities, four of the Dominicans involved were burnt at the stake.

The Jetzer scandal

1509

But the vague forces of discontent might never have crystallized into a definite movement save for the leadership of Ulrich Zwingli. He was born, January 1, 1484, on the Toggenburg, amidst the lofty mountains, breathing the atmosphere of freedom and beauty from the first. As he wandered in the wild passes he noticed how the marmots set a sentry to warn them of danger, and how the squirrel crossed the stream on a chip. When he returned to the home of his father, a local magistrate in easy circumstances, he heard

Zwingli

stirring tales of Swiss freedom and Swiss valor that planted in his soul a deep love of his native land. The religion he learned was good Catholic; and the element of popular superstition in it was far less weird and terrible than in Northern Germany. He remembered one little tale told him by his grandmother, how the Lord God and Peter slept together in the same bed, and were wakened each morning by the housekeeper coming in and pulling the hair of the outside man.

Education began early under the tuition of an uncle, the parish priest. At ten Ulrich was sent to Basle to study. Here he progressed well, becoming the head scholar, and here he developed a love of music and considerable skill in it. Later he went to school at Berne, where he attracted the attention of some friars who tried to guide him into their cloister, an effort apparently frustrated by his father. In the autumn of 1498 he matriculated at Vienna. For some unknown cause he was suspended soon afterwards, but was readmitted in the spring of 1500. Two years later he went to Basle, where he completed his studies by taking the master's degree. While here he taught school for a while. Theology apparently interested him little; his passion was for the humanities, and his idol was Erasmus. Only in 1513 did he begin to learn Greek.

1506

If, at twenty-two, before he had reached the canonical age, Zwingli took orders, and became parish priest at Glarus, it was less because of any deep religious interest than because he found in the clerical calling the best opportunity to cultivate his taste for letters. He was helped financially by a papal pension of fifty gulden per annum. His first published work was a fable. The lion, the leopard, and the fox (the Emperor, France, and Venice) try to drive the ox (Swit-

1510

zerland) out of his pasture, but are frustrated by the herdsman (the pope). The same tendencies—papal, patriotic, and political—are shown in his second book, an account of the relations between the Swiss and French, and in *The Labyrinth,* an allegorical poem. The various nations appear again as animals, but the hero, Theseus, is a patriot guided by the Ariadne thread of reason, while he is vanquishing the monsters of sin, shame, and vice. Zwingli's natural interest in politics was nourished by his experiences as field chaplain of the Swiss forces at the battles of Novara and Marignano.

1512
1516
1513
1515

Was he already a Reformer? Not in the later sense of the word, but he was a disciple of Erasmus. Capito wrote to Bullinger in 1536: "While Luther was in the hermitage and had not yet emerged into the light, Zwingli and I took counsel how to cast down the pope. For then our judgment was maturing under the influence of Erasmus's society and by reading good authors." Though Capito over-estimated the opposition of the young Swiss to the papacy, he was right in other respects. Zwingli's enthusiasm for the prince of humanists, perfectly evident in his notes on St. Paul, stimulated him to visit the older scholar at Basle in the spring of 1516. Their correspondence began at the same time. Is it not notable that in *The Labyrinth* the thread of Ariadne is not religion, but reason? His religious ideal, as shown by his notes on St. Paul, was at this time the Erasmian one of an ethical, undogmatic faith. He interpreted the Apostle by the Sermon on the Mount and by Plato. He was still a good Catholic, without a thought of breaking away from the church.

October, 1516–December, 1518

From Glarus Zwingli was called to Einsiedeln, where he remained for two years. Here he saw the superstitious absurdities mocked by Erasmus. Here, too, he first came into contact with indulgences, sold throughout Switzerland by Bernard Samson, a Milanese Franciscan. Zwingli did not attack them with the impassioned zeal of Luther, but ridiculed them as "a comedy." His position did not alienate him from the papal authorities, for he applied for, and received, the appointment of papal acolyte. How little serious was his life at this time may be seen from the fact that he openly confessed that he was living in unchastity and even joked about it.

September 1, 1518

Notwithstanding his peccadillos, as he evidently regarded them, high hopes were conceived of his abilities and independence of character. When a priest was wanted at Zurich, Zwingli applied for the position and, after strenuous canvassing, succeeded in getting it.

January 1, 1519

Soon after this came the turning-point in Zwingli's life, making of the rather worldly young man an earnest apostle. Two causes contributed to this. The first was the plague. Zwingli was taken sick in September and remained in a critical condition for many months. As is so often the case, suffering and the fear of death made the claims of the other world so terribly real to him that, for the first time, he cried unto God from the depths, and consecrated his life to service of his Saviour.

1519

The second influence that decided and deepened Zwingli's life was that of Luther. He first mentions him in 1519, and from that time forth, often. All his works and all his acts thereafter show the impress of the Wittenberg professor. Though Zwingli himself sturdily asserted that he preached the gospel before he heard of Luther, and that he learned his whole doctrine direct from the Bible, he deceived himself, as many men do, in over-estimating his own originality. He was truly able to say that he had formulated some of his ideas, in dependence on Erasmus, before he heard of the Saxon; and he still retained his capacity for private judgment afterwards. He never followed any man slavishly, and in some respects he was more radical than Luther; nevertheless it is true that he was deeply indebted to the great German.

Significantly enough, the first real conflict broke out at Zurich early in 1520. Zwingli preached against fasting and monasticism, and put forward the thesis that the gospel alone should be the rule of faith and practice. He succeeded in carrying through a practical reform of the cathedral chapter, but was obliged to compromise on fasting. Soon afterwards Zurich renounced obedience to the bishop. The Forest Cantons, already jealous of the prosperity of the cities, endeavored to intervene, but were warned by Zwingli not to appeal to war, as it was an unchristian thing. Opposition only drove his reforming zeal to further efforts.

In the spring of 1522 Zwingli formed with Anna Reinhard Meyer a union which he kept secret for two years, when he married her in church. In the marriage itself, though it was by no means unhappy, there was something lacking of fine feeling and of perfect love.

Reformation in Zurich

As the reform progressed, the need of clarification was felt. This was brought about by the favorite method of that day, a disputation. The Catholics tried in vain to prevent it, and it was actually held in January, 1523, on 67 theses drawn up by Zwingli. Here, as so often, it was found that the battle was half won when the innovators were heard. They themselves attributed this to the excellence of their cause; but, without disparaging that, it must be said that, as the psychology of advertising has shown, any thesis presented with sufficient force to catch the public ear, is

October 27, 1523

sure to win a certain number of adherents. The Town Council of Zurich ordered the abolition of images and of the mass. The opposition of the cathedral chapter considerably delayed the realization of this program. In December the Council was obliged to concede further discussion. It was not until Wednesday, April 12, 1525, that mass was said for the last time in Zurich. Its place was immediately taken, the next day, Maundy Thursday, by a simple communion service. At the same time the last of the convents were suppressed, or put in a condition assuring their eventual extinction. Other reforms included the abolition of processions, of confirmation and of extreme unction. With homely caution, a large number of simple souls had this administered to them just before the time allotted for its last celebration. Organs were taken out of the churches, and regular lectures on the Bible given.

Alarmed by these innovations the five original cantons,—Unterwalden, Uri, Schwyz, Lucerne and Zug,—formed a league in 1524 to suppress the "Hussite, Lutheran, and Zwinglian heresies." For a time it looked like war. Zwingli and his advisers drew up a remarkably thorough plan of campaign, including a method of securing allies, many military details, and an ample provision for prayer for victory. War, however, was averted by the mediation of Berne as a friend of Zurich, and the complete religious autonomy of each canton was guaranteed.

The Swiss Reformation had to run the same course of separation from the humanists and radicals, and of schism, as did the German movement. Though Erasmus was a little closer to the Swiss than he had been to the Saxon Reformers, he was alienated by the outrageous taunts of some of them and by the equally unwarranted attempts of others to show that he agreed with them. "They falsely call themselves evangelical," he opined, "for they seek only two things: a salary and a wife."

Then came the break with Luther, of which the story has already been told. The division was caused neither by jealousy, nor by the one doctrine—that of the real presence—on which it was nominally fought. There was in reality a wide difference between the two types of thought. The Saxon was both a mystic and a schoolman; to him religion was all in all and dogma a large part of religion. Zwingli approached the problem of salvation from a less personal, certainly from a less agonized, and from a more legal, liberal, empiric standpoint. He felt for liberty and for the value of common action in the state. He interpreted the Bible by reason; Luther placed his reason under the tuition of the Bible in its apparent meaning.

Anabaptists, 1522

Next came the turn of the Anabaptists—those Bolsheviki of the sixteenth century. Their first leaders appeared at Zurich and were for a while bosom friends of Zwingli. But a parting of the ways was inevitable, for the humanist could have little sympathy with an uncultured and ignorant group—such they were, in spite of the fact that a few leaders were university graduates—and the statesman could not admit in his categories a purpose that was sectarian as against the state church, and democratic as against the existing aristocracy.

1523

His first work against them shows how he was torn between his desire to make the Bible his only guide and the necessity of compromising with the prevailing polity. As he was unable to condemn his opponents on any consistent grounds he was obliged to prefer against them two charges that were false, though probably believed true by himself. As they were ascetics in some particulars he branded them as monastic; for their social program he called them seditious.

The suppression of the Peasants' Revolt had the effect in Switzerland, as elsewhere, of causing the poor and oppressed to lose heart, and of alienating them from the cause of the official Protestant churches. A disputation with the Anabaptist leaders was held at Zurich; they were declared refuted, and the council passed an order for all unbaptized children to be christened within a week. The leaders were arrested and tried; Zwingli bearing testimony that they advocated communism, which he considered wrong as the Bible's injunction not to steal implied the right of private property. The Anabaptists denied that they were communists, but the leaders were bound over to keep the peace, some were fined and others banished. As persecuting measures almost always increase in severity, it was not long before the death penalty was denounced against the sectaries, and actually applied. In a polemic against the new sect entitled *In Catabaptistarum Strophas Elenchus*, Zwingli's only argument is a criticism of some inconsistencies in the Anabaptists' biblicism; his final appeal is to force. His strife with them was harder than his battle with Rome. It seems that the reformer fears no one so much as him who carries the reformer's own principles to lengths that the originator disapproves. Zwingli saw in the fearless fanatics men prepared to act in political and social matters as he had done in ecclesiastical affairs; he dreaded anarchy or, at least, subversion of the polity he preferred, and, like all the other men of his age, he branded heresy as rebellion and punished it as crime.

November 6–8, 1525

July, 1527

By this time Zurich had become a theocracy of the same tyrannical type as that later made famous by

Theocracy

Geneva. Zwingli took the position of an Old Testament prophet, subordinating state to church. At first he had agreed with the Anabaptists in separating (theoretically) church and state. But he soon came to believe that, though true Christians might need no government, it was necessary to control the wicked, and for this purpose he favored an aristocratic polity. All matters of morals were strictly regulated, severe laws being passed against taverns and gambling. The inhabitants were forced to attend church. After the suppression of the Catholics and the radicals, there developed two parties just as later in Geneva, the Evangelical and the Indifferent, the policy of the latter being one of more freedom, or laxity, in discipline, and in general a preference of political to religious ends.

Basle November, 1522

The Reformation had now established itself in other cities of German Switzerland. Oecolampadius coming to Basle as the bearer of Evangelical ideas, won such success that soon the bishop was deprived of authority, two disputations with the Catholics were held, and the monasteries abolished. Oecolampadius, after taking counsel with Zwingli on the best means of suppressing Catholic worship, branded the mass as an act worse than theft, harlotry, adultery, treason, and murder, called a meeting of the town council, and requested them to decree the abolition of Catholic worship. Though they replied that every man should be free to exercise what religion he liked, on Good Friday, 1528, the Protestants removed the images from Oecolampadius's church, and grumbled because their enemies were yet tolerated. Liberty of conscience was only assured by the fairly equal division of the membership of the town council. On December 23, 1528, two hundred citizens assembled and presented a petition, drawn up by Oecolampadius, for the suppression of

1524
1525
1527

October 27, 1527

the mass. On January 6, 1529, under pressure from the ambassadors of Berne and Zurich, the town council of Basle decreed that all pastors should preach only the Word of God, and asked them to assemble for instruction on this point. The compromise suited no one and on February 8 the long prepared revolution broke out. Under pretence that the Catholics had disobeyed the last decree, a Protestant mob surrounded the town hall, planted cannon, and forced the council to expel the twelve Catholic members, meanwhile destroying church pictures and statues. "It was indeed a spectacle so sad to the superstitious," Oecolampadius wrote to Capito, "that they had to weep blood. . . . We raged against the idols, and the mass died of sorrow."

A somewhat similar development took place in Berne, St. Gall, Schaffhausen, and Glarus. The favorite instrument for arousing popular interest and support was the disputation. Such an one was held at Baden in May and June, 1526. Zwingli declined to take part in this and the Catholics claimed the victory. This, however, did them rather harm than good, for the public felt that the cards had been stacked. A similar debate at Berne in 1528 turned that city completely to the Reformation. A synod of the Swiss Evangelical churches was formed in 1527. This made for uniformity. The publication of the Bible in a translation by Leo Jud and others, with prefaces by Zwingli, proved a help to the Evangelical cause. This translation was the only one to compete at all successfully with Luther's. 1530

The growing strength of the Protestant cantons encouraged them to carry the reform by force in all places in which a majority was in favor of it. Zwingli's far-reaching plans included an alliance with Hesse and with Francis I to whom he dedicated his two most important theological works, *True and False Religion* and *An Exposition of the Christian Faith.* The Catholic cantons replied by making a league with Austria. War seemed imminent and Zwingli was so heartily in favor of it that he threatened resignation if Zurich did not declare war. This was accordingly done on June 8. Thirty thousand Protestant soldiers marched against the Catholic cantons, which, without the expected aid from Austria, were able to put only nine thousand men into the field. Seeing themselves hopelessly outnumbered, the Catholics prudently negotiated a peace without risking a battle. The terms of this first Peace of Cappel forced the Catholics to renounce the alliance with Austria, and to allow the majority of citizens in each canton to decide the religion they would follow. Toleration for Protestants was provided for in Catholic cantons, though toleration of the old religion was denied in the Evangelical cantons.

April, 1529

First Peace of Cappel

This peace marked the height of Zwingli's power. He continued to negotiate on equal terms with Luther, and he sent missionaries into Geneva to win it to his cause and to the Confederacy. The Catholic cantons, stung to the quick, again sought aid from Austria and raised another and better army. Zwingli heard of this and advocated a swift blow to prevent it—the "offensive defence." Berne refused to join Zurich in this aggression, but agreed to bring pressure to bear on the Catholics by proclaiming a blockade of their frontiers. An army was prepared by the Forest Cantons, but Berne, whose entirely selfish policy was more disastrous to the Evangelical cause than was the hostility of the league, still refused to engage in war. Zurich was therefore obliged to meet it alone. An army of only two thousand Zurichers marched out, accompanied by Zwingli as field chaplain. Eight thousand Catholic troops attacked, utterly defeated them, and

Defeat of Zwingli

May, 1531

killed many on the field of battle. Zwingli, who, though a non-combatant, was armed, was wounded and left on the field. Later he was recognized by enemies, killed, and his body burned as that of a heretic.

October 11, 1531

The defeat was a disaster to Protestant Switzerland not so much on account of the terms of peace, which were moderate, as because of the loss of prestige and above all of the great leader. His spirit, however, continued to inspire his followers, and lived in the Reformed Church. Indeed it has been said, though with exaggeration, that Calvin only gave his name to the church founded by Zwingli, just as Americus gave his name to the continent discovered by Columbus. In many respects Zwingli was the most liberal of the Reformers. In his last work he expressed the belief that in heaven would be saved not only Christians and the worthies of the Old Testament but also "Hercules, Theseus, Socrates, Aristides, Antigonus, Numa, Camillus, the Catos and Scipios. . . . In a word no good man has ever existed, nor shall there exist a holy mind, a faithful soul, from the very foundation of the world to its consummation, whom you will not see there with God." Nevertheless, Zwingli was a persecutor and was bound by many of the dogmatic prepossessions of his time. But his religion had in it less of miracle and more of reason than that of any other founder of a church in the sixteenth century. He was a statesman, and more willing to trust the people than were his contemporaries, but yet he was ready to sacrifice his country to his creed.

For a short time after the death of so many of its leading citizens in the battle of Cappel, Zurich was reduced to impotence and despair. Nor was she much comforted or assisted by her neighbors. Oecolampadius died but a few weeks after his friend; while Luther and Erasmus sang paeans of triumph over the prostration of their rivals. Even Calvin considered it a judgment of God. Gradually by her own strength Zurich won her way back to peace and a certain influence. Zwingli's follower, Henry Bullinger, the son of a priest, was a remarkable man. He not only built up his own city but his active correspondence with Protestants of all countries did a great deal to spread the cause of the Evangelical religion. In conjunction with Myconius, he drew up the first Swiss confession, accepted by Zurich, Berne, Basle, Schaffhausen, St. Gall, Mülhausen and Biel; and later he made the agreement with Calvin known as the Consensus Tigurinus. In this the Zwinglian and Calvinistic doctrines of the eucharist were harmonized as far as possible. But while the former decreased the latter increased, and Geneva took the place of Zurich as the metropolis of the Reformed faith.

Bullinger, 1504–75

1536

1549

§ 2. Calvin

On January 15, 1527, Thomas von Hofen wrote Zwingli from Geneva that he would do all he could to exalt the gospel in that city but that he knew it would be vain, for there were seven hundred priests working against him. This letter gives an insight into the methods by which new territory was evangelized, the quarters whence came the new influences, and the forces with which they had to contend.

Among the early missionaries of "the gospel" in French-speaking lands, one of the most energetic was William Farel. He had studied at Paris under Lefèvre d'Étaples, and was converted to Lutheranism as early as 1521. He went first to Basle, where he learned to know Erasmus. Far from showing respect to the older and more famous man, he scornfully told him to his face that Froben's wife knew more theology than

Farel, 1489–1565

did he. Erasmus's resentment showed itself in the nickname Phallicus that he fastened on his antagonist. From Basle Farel went to Montbéliard and Aigle, preaching fearlessly but so fiercely that his friend Oecolampadius warned him to remember rather to teach than to curse. After attending the disputation at Berne he evangelized western Switzerland. His methods may be learned from his work at Valangin on August 15, 1530. He attended a mass, but in the midst of it went up to the priest, tore the host forcibly from his hands, and said to the people: "This is not the God whom you worship: he is above in heaven, even in the majesty of the Father." In 1532 he went to Geneva. Notwithstanding the fact that here, as often elsewhere, he narrowly escaped lynching, he made a great impression. His red hair and hot temper evidently had their uses.

1528

Calvin, 1509–64

The Reformer of French Switzerland was not destined to be Farel, however, but John Calvin. Born at Noyon, Picardy, his mother died early and his father, who did not care for children, sent him to the house of an aristocratic friend to be reared. In this environment he acquired the distinguished manners and the hauteur for which he was noted. When John was six years old his father, Gerard, had him appointed to a benefice just as nowadays he might have got him a scholarship. At the age of twelve Gerard's influence procured for his son another of these ecclesiastical livings and two years later this was exchanged for a more lucrative one to enable the boy to go to Paris. Here for some years, at the College of Montaigu, Calvin studied scholastic philosophy and theology under Noel Beda, a medieval logic-chopper and schoolman by temperament. At the university Calvin won from his fellows the sobriquet of "the accusative case," on account of his censorious and fault-finding disposition. At his father's wish John changed from theology to law. For a time he studied at the universities of Orleans and Bourges. At Orleans he came under the influence of two Protestants, Olivetan and the German Melchior Volmar. On the death of his father, in 1531, he began to devote himself to the humanities. His first work, a commentary on Seneca's *De Clementia,* witnesses his wide reading, his excellent Latin style, and his ethical interests.

It was apparently through the humanists Erasmus and Lefèvre that he was led to the study of the Bible and of Luther's writings. Probably in the fall of 1533 he experienced a "conversion" such as stands at the head of many a religious career. A sudden beam of light, he says, came to him at this time from God, putting him to the proof and showing him in how deep an abyss of error and of filth he had been living. He thereupon abandoned his former life with tears.

Institutes of the Christian Religion, 1536

In the spring of 1534 Calvin gave up the sinecure benefices he had held, and towards the end of the year left France because of the growing persecution, for he had already rendered himself suspect. After various wanderings he reached Basle, where he published the first edition of his *Institutes of the Christian Religion.* It was dedicated, like two of Zwingli's works, to Francis I, with a strong plea for the new faith. It was, nevertheless, condemned and burnt publicly in France in 1542. Originally written in Latin it was translated by the author into French in 1541, and reissued from time to time in continually larger editions, the final one, of 1559, being five times as bulky as the first impression. The thought, too, though not fundamentally changed, was rearranged and developed. Only in the redaction of 1541 was predestination made perfectly clear. The first edition, like Luther's catechism, took up in order the Decalogue, the Creed, the Lord's Prayer, and the Sacraments. To this was added a section on Christian liberty, the power of the church, and civil government. In the last edition the arrangement followed entirely the order of articles in the Apostles' Creed, all the other matter being digested in its relation to faith.

A system of theology

In the *Institutes* Calvin succeeded in summing up the whole of Protestant Christian doctrine and practice. It is a work of enormous labor and thought. Its rigid logic, comprehensiveness, and clarity have secured it the same place in the Protestant Churches that the *Summa* of Aquinas has in the Roman theology. It is like the *Summa* in other ways, primarily in that it is an attempt to derive an absolute, unchangeable standard of dogma from premises considered infallible. Those who have found great freshness in Calvin, a new life and a new realism, can do so only in comparison with the older schoolmen. Calvin simply went over their ground, introducing into their philosophy all the connotations that three centuries of progress had made necessary. This is not denying that his work was well written and that it filled a need urgently felt at the time. Calvin cultivated style, both French and Latin, with great care, for he saw its immense utility for propaganda. He studied especially brevity, and thought that he carried it to an extreme, though the French edition of the *Institutes* fills more than eight hundred large octavo pages. However, all things are relative, and compared to many other theologians Calvin is really concise and readable.

There is not one original thought in any of Calvin's works. I do not mean "original" in any narrow sense, for to the searcher for sources it seems that there is literally nothing new under the sun. But there is nothing in Calvin for which ample authority cannot be found in his predecessors. Recognizing the Bible as his only standard, he interpreted it according to the new Protestant doctors. First and foremost he was dependent on Luther, and to an extent that cannot be exaggerated. Especially from the *Catechisms, The Bondage of the Will,* and *The Babylonian Captivity of the Church,* Calvin drew all his principal doctrines even to details. He also borrowed something from Bucer, Erasmus and Schwenckfeld, as well as from three writers who were in a certain sense his models. Melanchthon's *Commonplaces of Theology,* Zwingli's *True and False Religion,* and Farel's *Brief Instruction in Christian Faith* had all done tentatively what he now did finally.

Theocentric character

The center of Calvin's philosophy was God as the Almighty Will. His will was the source of all things, of all deeds, of all standards of right and wrong and of all happiness. The sole purpose of the universe, and the sole intent of its Creator, was the glorification of the Deity. Man's chief end was "to glorify God and enjoy him forever." God accomplished this self-exaltation in all things, but chiefly through men, his noblest work, and he did it in various ways, by the salvation of some and the damnation of others. And his act was purely arbitrary; he foreknew and predestined the fate of every man from the beginning; he damned and saved irrespective of foreseen merit. "God's eternal decree" Calvin himself called "frightful."[1] The outward sign of election to grace he thought was moral behavior, and in this respect he demanded the uttermost from himself and from his followers. The elect, he thought, were certain of salvation. The highest virtue was faith, a matter more

[1] "Decretum Dei aeternum horribile."

of the heart than of the reason. The divinity of Christ, he said, was apprehended by Christian experience, not by speculation. Reason was fallacious; left to itself the human spirit "could do nothing but lose itself in infinite error, embroil itself in difficulties and grope in opaque darkness." But God has given us his Word, infallible and inerrant, something that "has flowed from his very mouth." "We can only seek God in his Word," he said, "nor think of him otherwise than according to his Word."

Inevitably, Calvin sought to use the Bible as a rigid moral law to be fulfilled to the letter. His ethics were an elaborate casuistry, a method of finding the proper rule to govern the particular act. He preached a new legalism; he took Scripture as the Pharisees took the Law, and Luther's sayings as they took the Prophets, and he turned them all into stiff, fixed laws. Thus he crushed the glorious autonomy of his predecessor's ethical principles. It was Kant, who denied all Luther's specific beliefs, but who developed his idea of the individual conscience, that was the true heir of his spirit, not Calvin who crushed the spirit in elaborating every jot and tittle of the letter. In precisely the same manner Calvin killed Luther's doctrine of the priesthood of all believers. To Calvin the church was a sacramental, aristocratic organization, with an authoritative ministry. The German rebelled against the idea of the church as such; the Frenchman simply asked what was the true church. So he brought back some of the sacramental miracle of baptism and the eucharist. In the latter he remained as medieval as Luther, never getting beyond the question of the mode of the presence of the body and blood of Christ in the bread and wine. His endeavor to rationalize the doctrine of Augsburg, especially with reference to the Zwinglians, had disastrous results. Only two posi-

Legalism

tions were possible, that the body and blood were present, or that they were not. By endeavoring to find some middle ground Calvin upheld a contradiction in terms: the elements were signs and yet were realities; the body was really there when the bread was eaten by a believer, but really not there when the same bread was eaten by an infidel. The presence was actual, and yet participation could only occur by faith. While rejecting some of Luther's explanations, Calvin was undoubtedly nearer his position than that of Zwingli, which he characterized as "profane."

As few instructed and thinking persons now accept the conclusions of the *Institutes*, it is natural to underestimate the power that they exercised in their own day. The book was the most effective weapon of Protestantism. This was partly because of the style, but still more because of the faultless logic. The success of an argument usually depends far less on the truth of the premises than on the validity of the reasoning. And the premises selected by Calvin not only seemed natural to a large body of educated European opinion of his time, but were such that their truth or falsity was very difficult to demonstrate convincingly. Calvin's system has been overthrown not by direct attack, but by the flank, in science as in war the most effective way. To take but one example out of many that might be given: what has modern criticism made of Calvin's doctrine of the inerrancy of Scripture? But this science was as yet all but unknown: biblical exegesis there was in plenty, but it was only to a minute extent literary and historical; it was almost exclusively philological and dogmatic.

His logic

Calvin's doctrine of the arbitrary dealing out of salvation and damnation irrespective of merit has often excited a moral rather than an intellectual revulsion. To his true followers, indeed, like Jonathan Ed-

Eternal damnation

wards, it seems "a delightful doctrine, exceeding bright, pleasant and sweet." But many men agree with Gibbon that it makes God a cruel and capricious tyrant and with William James that it is sovereignly irrational and mean. Even at that time those who said that a man's will had no more to do with his destiny than the stick in a man's hand could choose where to strike or than a saddled beast could choose its rider, aroused an intense opposition. Erasmus argued that damnation given for inevitable crimes would make God unjust, and Thomas More blamed Luther for calling God the cause of evil and for saying "God doth damn so huge a number of people to intolerable torments only for his own pleasure and for his own deeds wrought in them only by himself." An English heretic, Cole of Faversham, said that the doctrine of predestination was meeter for devils than for Christians. "The God of Calvin," exclaimed Jerome Bolsec, "is a hypocrite, a liar, perfidious, unjust, the abetter and patron of crimes, and worse than the devil himself."

But there was another side to the doctrine of election. There was a certain moral grandeur in the complete abandon to God and in the earnestness that was ready to sacrifice all to his will. And if we judge the tree by its fruits, at its best it brought forth a strong and good race. The noblest examples are not the theologians, Calvin and Knox, not only drunk with God but drugged with him, much less politicians like Henry of Navarre and William of Orange, but the rank and file of the Huguenots of France, the Puritans of England, "the choice and sifted seed wherewith God sowed the wilderness" of America. These men bore themselves with I know not what of lofty seriousness, and with a matchless disdain of all mortal peril and all earthly grandeur. Believing themselves chosen vessels and elect instruments of grace, they could neither be seduced by carnal pleasure nor awed by human might. Taught that they were kings by the election of God and priests by the imposition of his hands, they despised the puny and vicious monarchs of this earth. They remained, in fact, what they always felt themselves to be, an élite, "the chosen few."

Having finished his great work, Calvin set out on his wanderings again. For a time he was at the court of the sympathetic Renée de France, Duchess of Ferrara. When persecution broke out here, he again fled northward, and came, by chance, to Geneva. Here Farel was waging an unequal fight with the old church. Needing Calvin's help he went to him and begged his assistance, calling on God to curse him should he not stay. "Struck with terror," as Calvin himself confessed, he consented to do so.

Geneva

Beautifully situated on the blue waters of Lake Leman in full view of Mont Blanc, Geneva was at this time a town of 16,000 inhabitants, a center of trade, pleasure, and piety. The citizens had certain liberties, but were under the rule of a bishop. As this personage was usually elected from the house of the Duke of Savoy, Geneva had become little better than a dependency of that state. The first years of the sixteenth century had been turbulent. The bishop, John, had at one time been forced to abdicate his authority, but later had tried to resume it. The Archbishop of Vienne, Geneva's metropolitan, had then excommunicated the city and invited Duke Charles III of Savoy to punish it. The citizens rose under Bonivard, renounced the authority of the pope, expelled the bishop and broke up the religious houses. To guard against the vengeance of the duke, a league was made with Berne and Freiburg.

On October 2, 1532, William Farel arrived from Berne. At Geneva as elsewhere tumult followed his preaching, but it met with such success that by January, 1534, he held a disputation which decided the city to become evangelical. The council examined the shrines and found machinery for the production of bogus miracles; provisionally abolished the mass; and soon after formally renounced the papal religion.

1535

May 21, 1536

At this point Calvin arrived, and began preaching and organizing at once. He soon aroused opposition from the citizens, galled at his strictness and perhaps jealous of a foreigner. The elections to the council went against him, and the opposition came to a head shortly afterwards. The town council decided to adopt the method of celebrating the eucharist used at Berne. For some petty reason Calvin and Farel refused to obey, and when a riot broke out at the Lord's table, the council expelled them from the city.

Calvin expelled, February, 1538

Calvin went to Strassburg, where he learned to know Bucer and republished his *Institutes*. Here he married Idelette de Bure, the widow of an Anabaptist, who was never in strong health and died, probably of consumption, on March 29, 1549. Calvin's married life lacked tenderness and joy. The story that he selected his wife because he thought that by reason of her want of beauty she would not distract his thoughts from God, is not well founded, but it does illustrate his attitude towards her. The one or more children born of the union died in infancy.

August, 1540

Calvin attended the Colloquy at Ratisbon, in the result of which he was deeply disappointed. In the meantime he had not lost all interest in Geneva. When Cardinal Sadoleto wrote, in the most polished Latin, an appeal to the city to return to the Roman communion, Calvin answered it. The party opposed to him discredited itself by giving up the city's rights to Berne, and was therefore overthrown. The perplexities presenting themselves to the council were be-

1541

September 1, 1539

yond their powers to solve, and they felt obliged to recall Calvin, who returned to remain for the rest of his life.

Calvin returns, 1541

Theocracy

His position was so strong that he was able to make of Geneva a city after his own heart. The form of government he caused to prevail was a strict theocracy. The clergy of the city met in a body known as the Congregation, a "venerable company" that discussed and prepared legislation for the consideration of the Consistory. In this larger body, besides the clergy, the laity were represented by twelve elders chosen by the council, not by the people at large. The state and church were thus completely identified in a highly aristocratic polity.

"The office of the Consistory is to keep watch on the life of everyone." Thus briefly was expressed the delegation of as complete powers over the private lives of citizens as ever have been granted to a committee. The object of the Ecclesiastical Ordinances was to create a society of saints. The Bible was adopted as the norm; all its provisions being enforced except such Jewish ceremonies as were considered abrogated by the New Testament. The city was divided into quarters, and some of the elders visited every house at least once a year and passed in review the whole life, actions, speech, and opinions of the inmates. The houses of the citizens were made of glass; and the vigilant eye of the Consistory, served by a multitude of spies, was on them all the time. In a way this espionage but took the place of the Catholic confessional. A joke, a gesture was enough to bring a man under suspicion. The Elders sat as a regular court, hearing complaints and examining witnesses. It is true that they could inflict only spiritual punishments, such as public censure, penance, excommunication, or forcing the culprit to demand pardon in church on his knees. But when the Consistory thought necessary, it could invoke the aid of the civil courts and the judgment was seldom doubtful. Among the capital crimes were adultery, blasphemy, witchcraft, and heresy. Punishments for all offences were astonishingly and increasingly heavy. During the years 1542–6 there were, in this little town of 16,000 people, no less than fifty-eight executions and seventy-six banishments.

In judging the Genevan theocracy it is important to remember that everywhere, in the sixteenth century, punishments were heavier than they are now, and the regulation of private life minuter.[1] Nevertheless, though parallels to almost everything done at Geneva can be found elsewhere, it is true that Calvin intensified the medieval spirit in this respect and pushed it to the farthest limit that human nature would bear.

First of all, he compelled the citizens to fulfil their religious duties. He began the process by which later the Puritans identified the Jewish Sabbath and the Lord's Day. Luther had thought the injunction to rest on the Seventh Day a bit of Jewish ceremonial abrogated by the new dispensation and that, after attending church, the Christian might devote the day to what work or pleasure he thought proper. Calvin, however, forbade all work and commanded attendance on sermons, of which an abundance were offered to the devout. In addition to Sunday services there were, as in the Catholic church, morning prayers every work day and a second service three days a week. All ceremonies with a vestige of popery about them were forbidden. The keeping of Christmas was prohibited under pain of fine and imprisonment.

1555

"As I see that we cannot forbid men all diversions," sighed Calvin, "I confine myself to those that are really bad." This class was sufficiently large. The

[1] See below, Chapter X, section 3.

theater was denounced from the pulpit, especially when the new Italian habit of giving women's parts to actresses instead of to boys was introduced. According to Calvin's colleague Cop, "the women who mount the platform to play comedies are full of unbridled effrontery, without honor, having no purpose but to expose their bodies, clothes, and ornaments to excite the impure desires of the spectators. . . . The whole thing," he added, "is very contrary to the modesty of women who ought to be shamefaced and shy." Accordingly, attendance on plays was forbidden.

Supervision of conduct

Among other prohibited amusements was dancing, especially obnoxious as at that time dances were accompanied by kisses and embraces. Playing cards, cursing and swearing were also dealt with, as indeed they were elsewhere. Among the odd matters that came before the Consistory were: attempted suicide, possessing the *Golden Legend* (a collection of saints' lives called by Beza "abominable trash"), paying for masses, betrothing a daughter to a Catholic, fasting on Good Friday, singing obscene songs, and drunkenness. A woman was chastized for taking too much wine even though it did not intoxicate. Some husbands were mildly reprimanded, not for beating their wives which was tolerated by contemporary opinion, but for rubbing salt and vinegar into the wales. Luxury in clothing was suppressed; all matters of color and quality regulated by law, and even the way in which women did their hair. In 1546 the inns were put under the direct control of the government and strictly limited to the functions of entertaining—or rather of boarding and lodging—strangers and citizens in temporary need of them. Among the numerous rules enforced within them the following may be selected as typical:

If any one blasphemes the name of God or says, "By

the body, 'sblood, zounds'' or anything like, or who gives himself to the devil or uses similar execrable imprecations, he shall be punished. . . .

Rules for inns

If any one insults any one else the host shall be obliged to deliver him up to justice.

If there are any persons who make it their business to frequent the said inns, and there to consume their goods and substance, the host shall not receive them.

Item the host shall be obliged to report to the government any insolent or dissolute acts committed by the guests.

Item the host shall not allow any person of whatever quality he be, to drink or eat anything in his house without first having asked a blessing and afterwards said grace.

Item the host shall be obliged to keep in a public place a French Bible, in which any one who wishes may read, and he shall not prevent free and honest conversation on the Word of God, to edification, but shall favor it as much as he can.

Item the host shall not allow any dissoluteness like dancing, dice or cards, nor shall he receive any one suspected of being a debauché or ruffian.

Item he shall only allow people to play honest games without swearing or blasphemy, and without wasting more time than that allowed for a meal.

Item he shall not allow indecent songs or words, and if any one wishes to sing Psalms or spiritual songs he shall make them do it in a decent and not in a dissolute way.

Item nobody shall be allowed to sit up after nine o'clock at night except spies.

Of course, such matters as marriage were regulated strictly. When a man of seventy married a girl of twenty-five Calvin said it was the pastor's duty to reprehend them. The Reformer often selected the women he thought suitable for his acquaintances who wanted wives. He also drew up a list of baptismal names which he thought objectionable, including the names of "idols,"—*i. e.* saints venerated near Geneva —the names of kings and offices to whom God alone appoints, such as Angel or Baptist, names belonging to God such as Jesus and Emanuel, silly names such as Toussaint and Noel, double names and ill-sounding names. Calvin also pronounced on the best sort of stoves and got servants for his friends. In fact, there was never such a busy-body in a position of high authority before nor since. No wonder that the citizens frequently chafed under the yoke.

If we ask how much was actually accomplished by this minute regulation accompanied by extreme severity in the enforcement of morals, various answers are given. When the Italian reformer Bernardino Occhino visited Geneva in 1542, he testified that cursing and swearing, unchastity and sacrilege were unknown; that there were neither lawsuits nor simony nor murder nor party spirit, but that universal benevolence prevailed. Again in 1556 John Knox said that Geneva was "the most perfect school of Christ that ever was on earth since the days of the apostles. In other places," he continued, "I confess Christ to be truly preached, but manners and religion so sincerely reformed I have not yet seen in any place besides." But if we turn from these personal impressions to an examination of the acts of the Consistory, we get a very different impression. The records of Geneva show more cases of vice after the Reformation than before. The continually increasing severity of the penalties enacted against vice and frivolity seem to prove that the government was helpless to suppress them. Among those convicted of adultery were two of Calvin's own female relatives, his brother's wife and his step-daughter Judith. What success there was in making Geneva a city of saints was due to the fact that it gradually became a very select population. The worst of the incorrigibles were soon either executed or banished, and their places taken by a large influx of

Morals of Geneva

men of austere mind, drawn thither as a refuge from persecution elsewhere, or by the desire to sit at the feet of the great Reformer. Between the years 1549 and 1555 no less than 1297 strangers were admitted to citizenship. Practically all of these were immigrants coming to the little town for conscience's sake.

Persecution

Orthodoxy was enforced as rigidly as morality. The ecclesiastical constitution adopted in 1542 brought in the Puritan type of divine service. Preaching took the most important place in church, supplemented by Bible reading and catechetical instruction. Laws were passed enforcing conformity under pain of losing goods and life. Those who did not expressly renounce the mass were punished. A little girl of thirteen was condemned to be publicly beaten with rods for saying that she wanted to be a Catholic. Calvin identified his own wishes and dignity with the commands and honor of God. One day he forbade a citizen, Philibert Berthelier, to come to the Lord's table. Berthelier protested and was supported by the council. "If God lets Satan crush my ministry under such tyranny," shrieked Calvin, "it is all over with me." The slightest assertion of liberty on the part of another was stamped out as a crime. Sebastian Castellio, a sincere Christian and Protestant, but more liberal than Calvin, fell under suspicion because he called the Song of Songs obscene, and because he made a new French version of the Bible to replace the one of Olivetan officially approved. He was banished in 1544. Two years later Peter Ameaux made some very trifling personal remarks about Calvin, for which he was forced to fall on his knees in public and ask pardon.

But opposition only increased. The party opposing Calvin he called the Libertines—a word then meaning something like "free-thinker" and gradually getting the bad moral connotation it has now, just as the word "miscreant" had formerly done. One of these men, James Gruet, posted on the pulpit of St. Peter's church at Geneva a warning to Calvin, in no very civil terms, to leave the city. He was at once arrested and a house to house search made for his accomplices. This method failing to reveal anything except that Gruet had written on one of Calvin's tracts the words "all rubbish," his judges put him to the rack twice a day, morning and evening, for a whole month. The frightful torture failed to make Gruet incriminate anyone else, and he was accordingly tried for heresy. He was charged with "disparaging authors like Moses, who by the Spirit of God wrote the divine law, saying that Moses had no more power than any other man. . . . He also said that all laws, human and divine, were made at the pleasure of man." He was therefore sentenced to death for blasphemy and beheaded on July 26, 1547, "calling on God as his Lord." After his death one of his books was found and condemned. To justify this course Calvin alleged that Gruet said that Jesus Christ was a good-for-nothing, a liar, and a false seducer, and that he (Gruet) denied the existence of God and immortality. Evangelical freedom had now arrived at the point where its champions first took a man's life and then his character, merely for writing a lampoon!

January, 1547

Naturally such tyranny produced a reaction. The enraged Libertines nicknamed Calvin Cain, and saved from his hands the next personal enemy, Ami Perrin, whom he caused to be tried for treason. A still more bitter dose for the theocrat was that administered by Jerome Bolsec, who had the audacity to preach against the doctrine of predestination. Calvin and Farel refuted him on the spot and had him arrested. Berne, Basle and Zurich intervened and, when solicited for

October 16, 1551

an expression on the doctrine in dispute, spoke indecisively. The triumph of his enemies at this rebuke was hard for Calvin to bear and prepared for the commission of the most regrettable act of his career.

Servetus 1531

The Spanish physician Michael Servetus published, in Germany, a work on the *Errors concerning the Trinity.* His theory was not that of a modern rationalist, but of one whose starting point was the authority of the Bible, and his unitarianism was consequently of a decidedly theological brand, recalling similar doctrines in the early church. Leaving Germany he went to Vienne, in France, and got a good practice under an assumed name. He later published a work called, perhaps in imitation of Calvin's *Institutio, The Restitution of Christianity,* setting forth his ideas about the Trinity, whch he compared to the three-headed monster Cerberus, but admitting the divinity of Christ. He also denied the doctrine of original sin and asserted that baptism should be for adults only. He was poorly advised in sending this book to the Reformer, with whom he had some correspondence. With Calvin's knowledge and probably at his instigation, though he later issued an equivocating denial, William Trie, of Geneva, denounced Servetus to the Catholic inquisition at Vienne and forwarded the material sent by the heretic to Calvin. On June 17, 1553, the Catholic inquisitor, expressly stating that he acted on this material, condemned Servetus to be burnt by slow fire, but he escaped and went to Geneva.

1553

Here he was recognized and arrested. Calvin at once appeared as his prosecutor for heresy. The charges against him were chiefly concerned with his denial of the Trinity and of infant baptism, and with his attack on the person and teaching of Calvin. As an example of the point to which Bibliolatry could suppress candor it may be mentioned that one of the charges against him was that he had asserted Palestine to be a poor land. This was held to contradict the Scriptural statement that it was a land flowing with milk and honey. The minutes of the trial are painful reading. It was conducted on both sides with unbecoming violence. Among other expressions used by Calvin, the public prosecutor, were these: that he regarded Servetus's defence as no better than the braying of an ass, and that the prisoner was like a villainous cur wiping his muzzle. Servetus answered in the same tone, his spirit unbroken by abuse and by his confinement in a horrible dungeon, where he suffered from hunger, cold, vermin, and disease. He was found guilty of heresy and sentenced to be burnt with slow fire. Calvin said that he tried to alter the manner of execution, but there is not a shred of evidence, in the minutes of the trial or elsewhere, that he did so. Possibly, if he made the request, it was purely formal, as were similar petitions for mercy made by the Roman inquisitors. At any rate, while Calvin's alleged effort for mercy proved fruitless, he visited his victim in prison to read him a self-righteous and insulting lecture. Farel, also, reviled him on the way to the stake, at which he perished on October 26, 1553, crying, "God preserve my soul! O Jesus, Son of the eternal God, have mercy on me!" Farel called on the bystanders to witness that these words showed the dying man to be still in the power of Satan.

Death of Servetus

This act of persecution, one of the most painful in the history of Christianity, was received with an outburst of applause from almost all quarters. Melanchthon, who had not been on speaking terms with Calvin for some years, was reconciled to him by what he called "a signal act of piety." Other leading Protestants congratulated Calvin, who continued persecution systematically. Another victim of his was Matthew

Gribaldi, whom he delivered into the hands of the government of Berne, with a refutation of his errors. Had he not died of the plague in prison he would probably have suffered the same fate as Servetus.

1564

Complete theocracy, 1555

Strengthened by his victory over heresy, Calvin now had the chance to annihilate his opponents. On May 15, 1555, he accused a number of them of treason, and provided proof by ample use of the rack. With the party of Libertines completely broken, Calvin ruled from this time forth with a rod of iron. The new Geneva was so cowed and subservient that the town council dared not install a new sort of heating apparatus without asking the permission of the theocrat. But a deep rancor smouldered under the surface. "Our incomparable theologian Calvin," wrote Ambrose Blaurer to Bullinger, "labors under such hatred of some whom he obscures by his light that he is considered the worst of heretics by them." Among other things he was accused of levying tribute from his followers by a species of blackmail, threatening publicly to denounce them unless they gave money to the cause.

International Calvinism

At the same time his international power and reputation rose. Geneva became the capital of Protestantism, from which mandates issued to all the countries of Western Europe. Englishmen and Frenchmen, Dutchmen and Italians, thronged to "this most perfect school of Christ since the apostles" to learn the laws of a new type of Christianity. For Calvin's Reformation was more thorough and logical than was Luther's. The German had regarded all as permitted that was not forbidden, and allowed the old usages to stand in so far as they were not repugnant to the ordinances of the Bible. But Calvin believed that all was forbidden save what was expressly allowed, and hence abolished as superstitious accretions all the elements of the medieval cult that could find no warrant in the

Bible. Images, vestments, organs, bells, candles, ritual, were swept away in the ungarnished meeting-house to make way for a simple service of Bible-reading, prayer, hymn and sermon. The government of the church was left by Calvin in close connection with the state, but he apparently turned around the Lutheran conception, making the civil authority subordinate to the spiritual and not the church to the state.

Whereas Lutheranism appealed to Germans and Scandinavians, Calvinism became the international form of Protestantism. Even in Germany Calvin made conquests at the expense of Luther, but outside of Germany, in France, in the Netherlands, in Britain, he moulded the type of reformed thought in his own image. It is difficult to give statistics, for it is impossible to say how far each particular church, like the Anglican for example, was indebted to Calvin, how far to Luther, and how far to other leaders, and also because there was a strong reaction against pure Calvinism even in the sixteenth century. But it is safe to say that the clear, cold logic of the *Institutes,* the good French and Latin of countless other treatises and letters, and the political thought which amalgamated easily with rising tides of democracy and industrialism, made Calvin the leader of Protestantism outside of the Teutonic countries of the north. His gift for organization and the pains he took to train ministers and apostles contributed to this success.

Death of Calvin, May 27, 1564

On May 27, 1564 Calvin died, worn out with labor and ill health at the age of fifty-five. With a cold heart and a hot temper, he had a clear brain, an iron will, and a real moral earnestness derived from the conviction that he was a chosen vessel of Christ. Constantly tortured by a variety of painful diseases, he drove himself, by the demoniac strength of his will, to perform labor that would have taxed the strongest.

The way he ruled his poor, suffering body is symbolic of the way he treated the sick world. To him the maladies of his own body, or of the body politic, were evils to be overcome, at any cost of pain and sweat and blood, by a direct effort of the will. As he never yielded to fever and weakness in himself, so he dealt with the vice and frivolity he detested, crushing it out by a ruthless application of power, hunting it with spies, stretching it on the rack and breaking it on the wheel. But a gentler, more understanding method would have accomplished more, even for his own purpose.

Beza, 1519–1605

His successor at Geneva, Theodore Beza, was a man after his own heart but, as he was far weaker, the town council gradually freed itself from spiritual tyranny. Towards the end of the century the pastors had been humbled and the questions of the day were far less the dogmatic niceties they loved than ethical ones such as the right to take usury, the proper penalty for adultery, the right to make war, and the best form of government.

CHAPTER IV

FRANCE

§ 1. Renaissance and Reformation

France

Though, at the opening of the sixteenth century, the French may have attained to no greater degree of national self-consciousness than had the Germans, they had gone much farther in the construction of a national state. The significance of this evolution, one of the strongest tendencies of modern history, is that it squares the outward political condition of the people with their inward desires. When once a nation has come to feel itself such, it cannot be happy until its polity is united in a homogeneous state, though the reverse is also true,—that national feeling is sometimes the result as well as the cause of political union. With the growth of a common language and of common ideals, and with the improvement of the methods of communication, the desire of the people for unity became stronger and stronger, until it finally overcame the centrifugal forces of feudalism and of particularism. These were so strong in Germany that only a very imperfect federation could be formed by way of national government, but in France, though they were still far from moribund, external pressure and the growth of the royal power had forged the various provinces into a nation such as it exists today. The most independent of the old provinces, Brittany, was now united to the crown by the marriage of its duchess Anne to Louis XII.

Louis XII, 1498–1515

Geographically, France was nearly the same four hundred years ago as it is today, save that the eastern

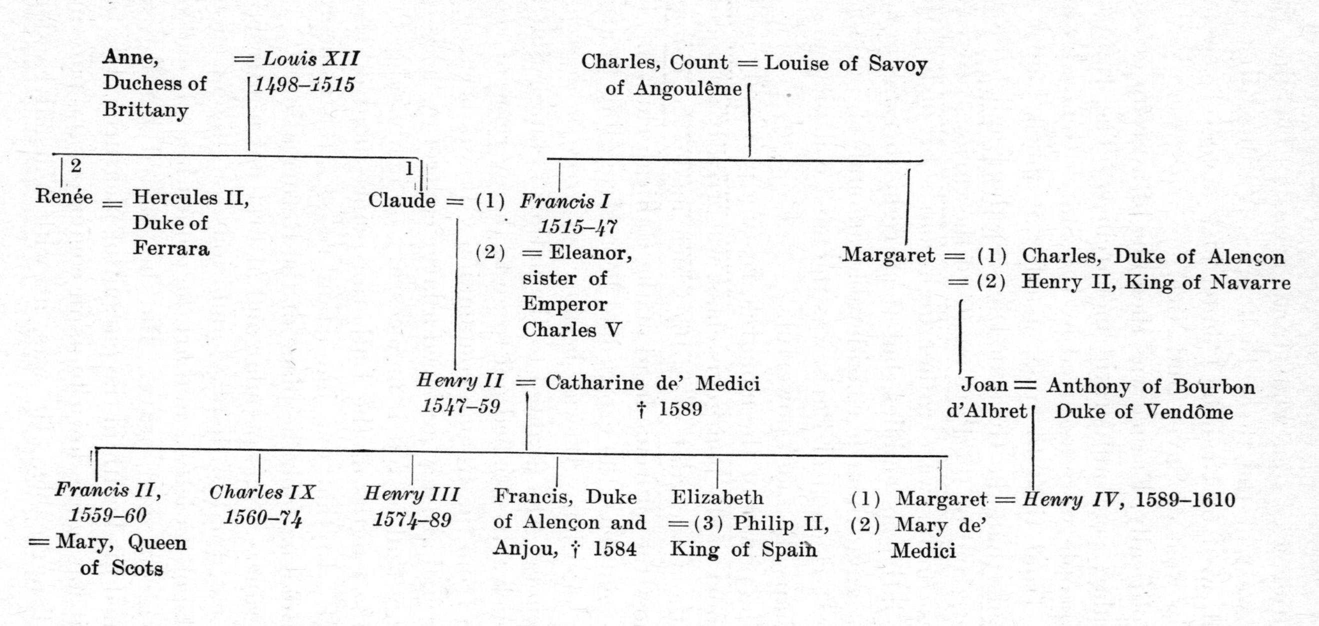

Anne, Duchess of Brittany = Louis XII 1498–1515
Charles, Count of Angoulême = Louise of Savoy
2
1
Renée = Hercules II, Duke of Ferrara
Claude = (1) Francis I 1515–47
(2) = Eleanor, sister of Emperor Charles V
Margaret = (1) Charles, Duke of Alençon
= (2) Henry II, King of Navarre
Henry II 1547–59 = Catharine de' Medici † 1589
Joan d'Albret = Anthony of Bourbon Duke of Vendôme
Francis II, 1559–60 = Mary, Queen of Scots
Charles IX 1560–74
Henry III 1574–89
Francis, Duke of Alençon and Anjou, † 1584
Elizabeth = (3) Philip II, King of Spain
(1) Margaret = Henry IV, 1589–1610
(2) Mary de' Medici

frontier was somewhat farther west. The line then ran west of the three Bishoprics, Verdun, Metz and Toul, west of Franche Comté, just east of Lyons and again west of Savoy and Nice.

Politically, France was then one of a group of semi-popular, semi-autocratic monarchies. The rights of the people were asserted by the States General which met from time to time, usually at much longer intervals than the German Diets or the English Parliaments, and by the Parlements of the various provinces. These latter were rather high courts of justice than legislative assemblies, but their right to register new laws gave them a considerable amount of authority. The Parlement of Paris was the most conspicuous and perhaps the most powerful.

Concordat, 1516

The power of the monarch, resting primarily on the support of the bourgeois class, was greatly augmented by the Concordat of 1516, which made the monarch almost the supreme head of the Gallican church. For two centuries the crown had been struggling to attain this position. It was because so large a degree of autonomy was granted to the national church that the French felt satisfied not to go to the extreme of secession from the Roman communion. It was because the king had already achieved a large control over his own clergy that he felt it unnecessary or inadvisable to go to the lengths of the Lutheran princes and of Henry VIII. In that one important respect the Concordat of Bologna took the place of the Reformation.

Francis I, 1515–47

Francis I was popular and at first not unattractive. Robust, fond of display, ambitious, intelligent enough to dabble in letters and art, he piqued himself on being chivalrous and brave. But he wasted his life and ruined his health in the pursuit of pleasure. His face, as it has come down to us in contemporary paintings, is disagreeable. He was, as with unusual candor a contemporary observer put it, a devil even to the extent of considerably looking it.

While to art and letters Francis gave a certain amount of attention, he usually from mere indolence allowed the affairs of state to be guided by others. Until the death of his mother, Louise of Savoy, he was ruled by her. Thereafter the Constable Anne de Montmorency was his chief minister. The policy followed was the inherited one which was, to a certain point, necessary in the given conditions. In domestic affairs, the king or his advisors endeavored to increase the power of the crown at the expense of the nobles. The last of the great vassals strong enough to assert a quasi-independence of the king was Charles of Bourbon. He was arrested and tried by the Parlement of Paris, which consistently supported the crown. Fleeing from France he entered the service of Charles V, and his restoration was made an article of the treaty of Madrid. His death in the sack of Rome closed the incident in favor of the king.

1531

1523–4

1526

May, 1527

The foreign policy of France was a constant struggle, now by diplomacy, now by arms, with Charles V. The principal remaining powers of Europe, England, Turkey and the pope, threw their weight now on one side now on the other of the two chief antagonists. Italy was the field of most of the battles. Francis began his reign by invading that country and defeating the Swiss at Marignano, thus conquering Milan. The campaigns in Italy and Southern France culminated in the disastrous defeat of the French at Pavia. Francis fought in person and was taken prisoner. "Of all things nothing is left me but honor and life," he wrote his mother.

September 13–14, 1515

February 24, 1525

Francis hoped that he would be freed on the payment of ransom according to the best models of chivalry. He found, however, when he was removed to

Madrid in May, that his captor intended to exact the last farthing of diplomatic concession. Discontent in France and the ennui and illness of the king finally forced him to sign a most disadvantageous treaty, renouncing the lands of Burgundy, Naples and Milan, and ceding lands to Henry VIII. The king swore to the document, pledged his knightly honor, and as additional securities married Eleanor the sister of Charles and left two of his sons as hostages.

January 14, 1526

Even when he signed it, however, he had no intention of executing the provisions of the treaty which, he secretly protested, had been wrung from him by force. The deputies of Burgundy refused to recognize the right of France to alienate them. Henry VIII at once made an alliance against the "tyranny and pride" of the emperor. Charles was so chagrined that he challenged Francis to a duel. This opera bouffe performance ended by each monarch giving the other "the lie in the throat."

Though France succeeded in making with new allies, the pope and Venice, the League of Cognac, and though Germany was at that time embarrassed by the Turkish invasion, the ensuing war turned out favorably to the emperor. The ascendancy of Charles was so marked that peace again had to be made in his favor in 1529. The treaty of Cambrai, as it was called, was the treaty of Madrid over again except that Burgundy was kept by France. She gave up, however, Lille, Douai and other territory in the north and renounced her suzerainty over Milan and Naples. Francis agreed to pay a ransom of two million crowns for his sons. Though he was put to desperate straits to raise the money, levying a 40 per cent. income tax on the clergy and a 10 per cent. income tax on the nobles, he finally paid the money and got back his children in 1530.

May, 1526

By this time France was so exhausted, both in

money and men, that a policy of peace was the only one possible for some years. Montmorency, the principal minister of the king, continued by an active diplomacy to stir up trouble for Charles. While suppressing Lutherans at home he encouraged the Schmalkaldic princes abroad, going to the length of inviting Melanchthon to France in 1535. With the English minister Cromwell he came to an agreement, nothwithstanding the Protestant tendencies of his policy. An alliance was also made with the Sultan Suleiman, secretly in 1534, and openly proclaimed in 1536. In order to prepare for the military strife destined to be renewed at the earliest practical moment, an ordinance of 1534 reorganized and strengthened the army.

Reformation

Far more important for the life of France than her incessant and inconclusive squabbling with Spain was the transformation passing over her spirit. It is sometimes said that if the French kings brought nothing else back from their campaigns in Italy they brought back the Renaissance. There is a modicum of truth in this, for there are some traces of Italian influence before the reign of Francis I. But the French spirit hardly needed this outside stimulus. It was awakening of itself. Scholars like William Budé and the Estiennes, thinkers like Dolet and Rabelais, poets like Marot, were the natural product of French soil. Everywhere, north of the Alps no less than south, there was a spontaneous efflorescence of intellectual activity.

The Reformation is often contrasted or compared with the Renaissance. In certain respects, where a common factor can be found, this may profitably be done. But it is important to note how different in kind were the two movements. One might as well compare Darwinism and Socialism in our own time. The one was a new way of looking at things, a fresh intellectual start, without definite program or organization. The other was primarily a thesis: a set of tenets the object of which was concrete action. The Reformation began in France as a school of thought, but it soon grew to a political party and a new church, and finally it evolved into a state within the state.

Christian Renaissance

Though it is not safe to date the French Reformation before the influence of Luther was felt, it is possible to see an indigenous reform that naturally prepared the way for it. Its harbinger was Lefèvre d'Étaples. This "little Luther" wished to purify the church, to set aside the "good works" thereof in favor of faith, and to make the Bible known to the people. He began to translate it in 1521, publishing the Gospels in June 1523 and the Epistles and Acts and Apocalypse in October and November. The work was not as good as that of Luther or Tyndale. It was based chiefly on the Vulgate, though not without reference to the Greek text. Lefèvre prided himself on being literal, remarking, with a side glance at Erasmus's *Paraphrases,* that it was dangerous to try to be more elegant than Scripture. He also prided himself on writing for the simple, and was immensely pleased with the favorable reception the people gave his work. To reach the hearts of the poor and humble he instituted a reform of preaching, instructing his friends to purge their homilies of the more grossly superstitious elements and of the scholastic theology. Instead of this they were to preach Christ simply with the aim of touching the heart, not of dazzling the mind.

Like-minded men gathering around Lefèvre formed a new school of thought. It was a movement of revival within the church; its leaders, wishing to keep all the old forms and beliefs, endeavored to infuse into them a new spirit. To some extent they were in conscious reaction against the intellectualism of Erasmus and the Renaissance. On the other hand they were far from wishing to follow Luther, when he appeared, in his schism.

Among the most famous of these mystical reformers were William Briçonnet, Bishop of Meaux, and his disciple, Margaret d'Angoulême, sister of Francis I. Though a highly talented woman Margaret was weak and suggestible. She adored her dissolute brother and was always, on account of her marriages, first with Charles, duke of Alençon, and then with Henry d'Albret, king of Navarre, put in the position of a suppliant for his support. She carried on an assiduous correspondence with Briçonnet as her spiritual director, being attracted first by him and then by Luther, chiefly, as it seems, through the wish to sample the novelty of their doctrines. She wrote *The Mirror of the Sinful Soul* in the best style of penitent piety. Its central idea is the love of God and of the "debonnaire" Jesus. She knew Latin and Italian, studied Greek and Hebrew, and read the Bible regularly, exhorting her friends to do the same. She coquetted with the Lutherans, some of whom she protected in France and with others of whom in Germany she corresponded. She was strongly suspected of being a Lutheran, though a secret one. Capito dedicated to her a commentary on Hosea; Calvin had strong hopes of winning her to an open profession, but was disappointed. Her house, said he, which might have become the family of Jesus Christ, harbored instead servants of the devil. Throughout life she kept the accustomed Catholic rites, and wrote with much respect to Pope Paul III. But fundamentally her religious idealism was outside of any confession.

1509
1527
1531

This mystically pious woman wrote, in later life, the *Heptameron*, a book of stories published posthumously. Modelled on the *Decameron*, it consists almost entirely of licentious stories, told without reprobation and with gusto. If the mouth speaketh from the fullness of the heart she was as much a sensualist in thought as her brother was in deed. The apparent contradictions in her are only to be explained on the theory that she was one of those impressionable natures that, chameleon-like, always take on the hue of their environment.

But though the work of Lefèvre and of Briçonnet, who himself gave his clergy an example of simple, biblical preaching, won many followers not only in Meaux but in other cities, it would never have produced a religious revolt like that in Germany. The Reformation was an importation into France; "The key of heresy," as John Bouchet said in 1531, "was made of the fine iron of Germany." At first almost all the intellectuals hailed Luther as an ally. Lefèvre sent him a greeting in 1519, and in the same year Budé spoke well of him. His books were at this time approved even by some doctors of the Sorbonne. But it took a decade of confusion and negation to clarify the situation sufficiently for the French to realize the exact import of the Lutheran movement, which completely transformed the previously existing policy of Lefèvre. The chief sufferer by the growth of Lutheranism was not at first the Catholic church but the party of Catholic reform. The schism rent the French evangelicals before it seriously affected the church. Some of them followed the new light and others were forced back into a reactionary attitude.

Luther's books

The first emissaries of Luther in France were his books. Froben exported a volume containing nearly all he had published up to October, 1518, immediately and in large quantities to Paris. In 1520 a student there wrote that no books were more quickly bought. At first only the Latin ones were intelligible to the

French, but there is reason to believe that very early translations into the vernacular were made, though none of this period have survived. It was said that the books, which kept pouring in from Frankfort and Strassburg and Basle, excited the populace against the theologians, for the people judged them by the newly published French New Testament. A bishop complained that the common people were seduced by the vivacity of the heretic's style. 1523

It did not take the Sorbonne long to define its position as one of hostility. The university, which had been lately defending the Gallican liberties and had issued an appeal from pope to future council, was one of the judges selected by the disputants of the Leipzig debate. Complete records of the speeches, taken by notaries, were accordingly forwarded to Paris by Duke George of Saxony, with a request for an opinion. After brief debate the condemnation of Luther by the university was printed. April 15 1521

Neither was the government long in taking a position. That it should be hostile was a foregone conclusion. Francis hated Lutheranism because he believed that it tended more to the overthrow of kingdoms and monarchies than to the edification of souls. He told Aleander, the papal nuncio, that he thought Luther a rascal and his doctrine pernicious. March, 1521

The king was energetically seconded by the Parlement of Paris. A royal edict provided that no book should be printed without the imprimatur of the university. The king next ordered the extirpation of the errors of Martin Luther of Saxony, and, having begun by burning books, continued, as Erasmus observed was usually the case, by burning people. The first to suffer was John Vallière. At the same time Briçonnet was summoned to Paris, sharply reprimanded for leniency to heretics and fined two hundred livres, in April, 1523 1523 consequence of which he issued two decrees against the heresy, charging it with attempting to subvert the hierarchy and to abolish sacerdotal celibacy. When Lefèvre's doctrines were condemned, he submitted; those of his disciples who failed to do so were proscribed. But the efforts of the government became more strenuous after 1524. Francis was at this time courting the assistance of the pope against the emperor, and moreover he was horrified by the outbreak of the Peasants' War in Germany. Convinced of the danger of allowing the new sect to propagate itself any further he commanded the archbishops and bishops of his realm to "proceed against those who hold, publish and follow the heresies, errors and doctrines of Martin Luther." Lefèvre and some of his friends fled to Strassburg. Arrests and executions against those who were sometimes called "heretics of Meaux," and sometimes Lutherans, followed.

1524

1525

The theologians did not leave the whole burden of the battle to the government. A swarm of anti-Lutheran tracts issued from the press. Not only the heresiarch, but Erasmus and Lefèvre were attacked. Their translations of the Bible were condemned as blasphemies against Jerome and against the Holy Ghost and as subverting the foundations of the Christian religion. Luther's sacramental dogmas and his repudiation of monastic vows were refuted.

Nevertheless the reform movement continued. At this stage it was urban, the chief centers being Paris, Meaux, and Lyons. Many merchants and artisans were found among the adherents of the new faith. While none of a higher rank openly professed it, theology became, under the lead of Margaret, a fashionable subject. Conventicles were formed to read the Bible in secret not only among the middle classes but also at court. Short tracts continued to be the best methods of propaganda, and of these many were translations. Louis de Berquin of Artois, a layman, proved the most formidable champion of the new opinions. Though he did little but translate other men's work he did that with genius. His version of Erasmus's *Manual of a Christian Knight* was exquisitely done, and his version of Luther's *Tesseradecas* did not fall short of it. Tried and condemned in 1523, he was saved by the king at the behest of Margaret. The access of rigor during the king's captivity gave place to a momentary tolerance. Berquin, who had been arrested, was liberated, and Lefèvre recalled from exile. But the respite was brief. Two years later, Berquin was again arrested, tried, condemned, and executed speedily to prevent reprieve on April 17, 1529. But the triumph of the conservatives was more apparent than real. Lutheranism continued to gain silently but surely.

Berquin 1490–1529

1526

While the Reformation was growing in strength and numbers, it was also becoming more definite and coherent. Prior to 1530 it was almost impossible to tell where Lutheranism began and where it ended. There was a large, but vague and chaotic public opinion of protest against the existing order. But after 1530 it is possible to distinguish several parties, three of which at first reckoned among the supporters of the Reformation, now more or less definitely separated themselves from it. The first of these was the party of Meaux, the leaders of which submitted to the government and went their own isolated way. Then there was a party of Erasmian reform, mainly intellectual but profoundly Christian. Its leader, William Budé, felt, as did Erasmus, that it was possible to unite the classical culture of the Renaissance with a purified Catholicism. Attached to the church, and equally repelled by some of the dogmas and by the apparent social effects of the Reformation, Budé, who had spoken well of Luther in 1519, repudiated him in 1521.

Humanists

Finally there was the party of the "Libertines" or free-thinkers, the representatives of the Renaissance pure and simple. Revolutionaries in their own way, consciously rebels against the older culture of the Middle Ages, though prepared to canvass the new religion and to toy with it, even to use it as an ally against common enemies, the interest of these men was fundamentally too different from that of the Reformers to enable them to stand long on the same platform.

Marot

There was Clement Marot, a charming but rather aimless poet, a protégé of Margaret and the ornament of a frivolous court. Though his poetic translation of the Psalms became a Protestant book, his poetry is often sensual as well as sensuous. Though for a time absenting himself from court he re-entered it in 1536 at the same time "abjuring his errors."

Rabelais

Of the same group was Francis Rabelais, whose *Pantagruel* appeared in 1532. Though he wrote Erasmus saying that he owed all that he was to him, he in fact appropriated only the irony and mocking spirit of the humanist without his deep underlying piety. He became a universal skeptic, and a mocker of all things. The "esprit gaulois," beyond all others alive to the absurdities and inconsistency of things, found in him its incarnation. He ridiculed both the "pope-maniacs" and the "pope-phobes," the indulgence-sellers and the inquisitors, the decretals "written by an angel" and the Great Schism, priests and kings and doubting philosophers and the Scripture. Paul III called him "the vagabond of the age." Calvin at first reckoned him among those who "had relished the gospel," but when he furiously retorted that he considered Calvin "a demoniacal imposter," the theologian of Geneva loosed against him a furious invective in his

Treatise on Offences. Rabelais was now called "a Lucian who by his diabolic fatuity had profaned the gospel, that holy and sacred pledge of life eternal." William Farel had in mind Rabelais's recent acceptance from the court of the livings of Meudon and St. Christophe de Jambet, when he wrote Calvin on May 25, 1551: "I fear that avarice, that root of evil, has extinguished all faith and piety in the poets of Margaret. Judas, having sold Christ and taken the biretta, instead of Christ has that hard master Satan."[1]

Catholic reform

The stimulus given by the various attacks on the church, both Protestant and infidel, showed itself promptly in the abundant spirit of reform that sprang up in the Catholic fold. The clergy and bishop braced themselves to meet the enemy; they tried in some instances to suppress scandals and amend their lives; they brushed up their theology and paid more attention to the Bible and to education.

But the "Lutheran contagion" continued to spread and grow mightily. In 1525 it was found only at Paris, Meaux, Lyons, Grenoble, Bourges, Tours and Alençon. Fifteen years later, though it was still confined largely to the cities and towns, there were centers of it in every part of France except in Brittany. The persecution at Paris only drove the heretics into hiding or banished them to carry their opinions broadcast over the land. The movement swept from the north and east. The propaganda was not the work of one class but of all save that of the great nobles. It was not yet a social or class affair, but a purely intellectual and religious one. It is impossible to esti-

[1] *Harvard Theological Review*, 1919, p. 209. Margaret had died several years before, but Rabelais was called her poet because he had claimed her protection and to her wrote a poem in 1545. *Oeuvres de Rabelais*, ed. A. Lefranc, 1912, i, pp. xxiii, cxxxix. *Cf.* also Calvin's letter to the Queen of Navarre, April 28, 1545. *Opera*, xii, pp. 65f.

mate the numbers of the new sect. In 1534 Aleander said there were thirty thousand Lutherans in Paris alone. On the contrary René du Bellay said that there were fewer in 1533 than there were ten years previous. True it is that the Protestants were as yet weak, and were united rather in protest against the established order than as a definite and cohesive party. Thus, the most popular and successful slogans of the innovators were denunciation of the priests as anti-Christs and apostates, and reprobation of images and of the mass as idolatry. Other catchwords of the reformers were, "the Bible" and "justification by faith." The movement was without a head and without organization. Until Calvin furnished these the principal inspiration came from Luther, but Zwingli and the other German and Swiss reformers were influential. More and more, Lefèvre and his school sank into the background.

Protestant progress

For a time it seemed that the need of leadership was to be supplied by William Farel. His learning, his eloquence, and his zeal, together with the perfect safety of action that he found in Switzerland, were the necessary qualifications. The need for a Bible was at first met by the version of Lefèvre, printed in 1532. But the Catholic spirit of this work, based on the Vulgate, was distasteful to the evangelicals. Farel asked Olivetan, an excellent philologist, to make a new version, which was completed by February 1535. Calvin wrote the preface for it. It was dedicated to "the poor little church of God." In doctrine it was thoroughly evangelical, replacing the old "évêques" and "prêtres" by "surveillants" and "anciens," and omitting some of the Apocrypha.

Encouraged by their own growth the Protestants became bolder in their attacks on the Catholics. The situation verged more and more towards violence;

neither side, not even the weaker, thought of tolerance for both. On the night of October 17–18 some placards, written by Anthony de Marcourt, were posted up in Paris, Orleans, Rouen, Tours and Blois and on the doors of the king's chamber at Amboise. They excoriated the sacrifice of the mass as a horrible and intolerable abuse invented by infernal theology and directly counter to the true Supper of our Lord. The government was alarmed and took strong steps. Processions were instituted to appease God for the sacrilege. Within a month two hundred persons were arrested, twenty of whom were sent to the scaffold and the rest banished after confiscation of their goods.

But the government could not afford to continue an uninterruptedly rigorous policy. The Protestants found their opportunity in the exigencies of the foreign situation. In 1535 Francis was forced by the increasing menace of the Hapsburgs to make alliance not only with the infidel but with the Schmalkaldic League. He would have had no scruples in supporting abroad the heresy he suppressed at home, but he found the German princes would accept his friendship on no terms save those of tolerance to French Protestants. Accordingly on July 16, 1535, Francis was obliged to publish an edict ordering persecution to cease and liberating those who were in prison for conscience's sake.

But the respite did not last long. New rigors were undertaken in April 1538. Marot retracted his errors, and Rabelais, while not fundamentally changing his doctrine, greatly softened, in the second edition of his *Pantagruel,* the abusive ridicule he had poured on the Sorbonne. But by this time a new era was inaugurated. The deaths of Erasmus and Lefèvre in 1536 gave the *coup de grace* to the party of the Christian

1542

Renaissance, and the publication of Calvin's *Institutes* in the same year finally gave the French Protestants a much needed leader and standard.

§ 2. The Calvinist Party. 1536–1559

Truce of Nice, 1538

The truce of Nice providing for a cessation of hostilities between France and the Hapsburgs for ten years, was greeted with much joy in France. Bonfires celebrated it in Paris, and in every way the people made known their longing for peace. Little the king cared for the wishes of his loyal subjects when his own dignity, real or imagined, was at stake. The war with Charles, that cursed Europe like an intermittent fever, broke out again in 1542. Again France was the aggressor and again she was worsted. The emperor invaded Champagne in person, arriving, in 1544, at a point within fifty miles of Paris. As there was no army able to oppose him it looked as if he would march as a conqueror to the capital of his enemy. But he sacrificed the advantage he had over France to a desire far nearer his heart, that of crushing his rebellious Protestant subjects. Already planning war with the League of Schmalkalden he wished only to secure his own safety from attack by his great rival. The treaty made at Crépy was moderate in its terms and left things largely as they were.

Treaty of Crépy, 1544

Henry II, 1547–59

On March 31, 1547, Francis I died and was succeeded by his son, Henry II, a man of large, strong frame, passionately fond of all forms of exercise, especially of hunting and jousting. He had neither his father's versatility nor his fickleness nor his artistic interests. His policy was influenced by the aim of reversing his father's wishes and of disgracing his father's favorites.

1533

While his elder brother was still alive, Henry had married Catharine de' Medici, a daughter of Lorenzo

II de' Medici of Florence. The girl of fourteen in a foreign country was uncomfortable, especially as it was felt, after her husband became Dauphin, that her rank was not equal to his. The failure to have any children during the first ten years of marriage made her position not only unpleasant but precarious, but the birth of her first son made her unassailable. In rapid succession she bore ten children, seven of whom survived childhood. Though she had little influence on affairs of state during her husband's reign, she acquired self-confidence and at last began to talk and act as queen.

Diana of Poitiers

At the age of seventeen Henry fell in love with a woman of thirty-six, Diana de Poitiers, to whom his devotion never wavered until his death, when she was sixty. Notwithstanding her absolute ascendancy over her lover she meddled little with affairs of state.

Admiral Coligny, 1519–72

The direction of French policy at this time fell largely into the hands of two powerful families. The first was that of Coligny. Of three brothers the ablest was Gaspard, Admiral of France, a firm friend of Henry's as well as a statesman and warrior. Still more powerful was the family of Guise, the children of Claude, Duke of Guise, who died in 1527. The eldest son, Francis, Duke of Guise, was a great soldier. His brother, Charles, Cardinal of Lorraine, won a high place in the councils of state, and his sister Mary, by her marriage with James V of Scotland, brought added prestige to the family. The great power wielded by this house owed much to the position of their estates, part of which were fiefs of the French king and part subject to the Empire. As suited their convenience they could act either as Frenchmen or as foreign nobles.

Francis of Guise

Expansion

Under Henry France enjoyed a period of expansion such as she had not had for many years. The perpetual failures of Francis were at last turned into substantial successes. This was due in large part to the civil war in Germany and to the weakness of England's rulers, Edward VI and Mary. It was due in part to the irrepressible energy of the French bourgeois and gentlemen, in part to the genius of Francis of Guise. The co-operation of France and Turkey, rather an identity of interests than a formal alliance, a policy equally blamed by contemporaries and praised by historians, continued. But the successes achieved were due most of all to the definite abandonment of the hope of Italian conquests and to the turning of French arms to regions more suitable for incorporation under her government.

War having been declared on Charles, the French seized the Three Bishoprics, at that time imperial fiefs, Metz, Verdun, and Toul. A large German army under Alva besieged Metz, but failed to overcome the brilliant defence of Francis of Guise. Worn by the attrition of repulsed assaults and of disease the imperial army melted away. When the siege was finally raised Guise distinguished himself as much by the humanity with which he cared for wounded and sick enemies as he had by his military prowess.

1557
1558
Peace of Cateau-Cambrésis, 1559

Six years later Guise added fresh laurels to his fame and new possessions to France by the conquest of Calais and Guines, the last English possessions in French territory. The loss of Calais, which had been held by England since the Hundred Years War, was an especially bitter blow to the islanders. These victories were partly counterbalanced by the defeats of French armies at St. Quentin on the Somme and by Egmont at Gravelines. When peace was signed at Cateau-Cambrésis, France renounced all her conquests in the south, but kept the Three Bishoprics and Calais, all of which became her permanent possessions.

Calvinism

While France was thus expanding her borders, the internal revolution matured rapidly. The last years of Francis and the reign of Henry II saw a prodigious growth of Protestantism. What had begun as a sect now became, by an evolution similar to that experienced in Germany, a powerful political party. It is the general fate of new causes to meet at first with opposition due to habit and the instinctive reaction of almost all minds against "the pain of a new idea." But if the cause is one suited to the spirit and needs of the age, it gains more and more supporters, slowly if left to itself, rapidly if given good organization and adequate means of presenting its claims. The thorough canvassing of an idea is absolutely essential to win it a following. Now, prior to 1536, the Protestants had got a considerable amount of publicity as well through their own writings as through the attacks of their enemies. But not until Calvin settled at Geneva and began to write extensively in French, was the cause presented in a form capable of appealing to the average Frenchman. Calvin gave not only the best apology for his cause, but also furnished it with a definite organization, and a coherent program. He supplied the dogma, the liturgy, and the moral ideas of the new religion, and he also created ecclesiastical, political, and social institutions in harmony with it. A born leader, he followed up his work with personal appeals. His vast correspondence with French Protestants shows not only much zeal but infinite pains and considerable tact in driving home the lessons of his printed treatises.

Though the appeal of Calvin's dogmatic system was greater to an age interested in such things and trained to regard them as highly important, than we are likely to suppose at present, this was not Calvinism's only or even its main attraction to intelligent people. Like every new and genuine reform Calvinism had the advantage of arousing the enthusiasm of a small but active band of liberals. The religious zeal as well as the moral earnestness of the age was naturally drawn to the Protestant side. As the sect was persecuted, no one joined it save from conscientious motives. Against the laziness or the corruption of the prelates, too proud or too indifferent to give a reason for their faith, the innovators opposed a tireless energy in season and out of season; against the scandals of the court and the immorality of the clergy they raised the banner of a new and stern morality; to the fires of martyrdom they replied with the fires of burning faith.

The missionaries of the Calvinists were very largely drawn from converted members of the clergy, both secular and regular, and from those who had made a profession of teaching. For the purposes of propaganda these were precisely the classes most fitted by training and habit to arouse and instruct the people. Tracts were multiplied, and they enjoyed, notwithstanding the censures of the Sorbonne, a brisk circulation. The theater was also made a means of propaganda, and an effective one.

Picardy continued to be the stronghold of the Protestants throughout this period, though they were also strong at Meaux and throughout the north-east, at Orleans, in Normandy, and in Dauphiné. Great progress was also made in the south, which later became the most Protestant of all the sections of France.

Catholic measures

The Catholics continued to rely on force. There was a counter-propaganda, emanating from the University of Paris, but it was feeble. The Jesuits, in the reign of Henry II, had one college at Paris and two in Auvergne; otherwise there was hardly any intellectual effort made to overcome the reformers. Indeed, the Catholics hardly had the munitions for such a combat.

Apart from the great independents, holding themselves aloof from all religious controversy, the more intelligent and enterprising portion of the educated class had gone over to the enemy.

But the government did its best to supply the want of argument by the exercise of authority. New and severe edicts against "the heresies and false doctrines of Luther and his adherents and accomplices" were issued. The Sorbonne prohibited the reading and sale of sixty-five books by name, including the works of Luther, Melanchthon, Calvin, Dolet, and Marot, and all translations of the Bible issued by the publishing house of Estienne.

The south of France had in earlier centuries been prolific in sects claiming a Protestantism older than that of Augsburg. Like the Bohemian Brethren they eagerly welcomed the Calvinists as allies and were rapidly enrolled in the new church. Startled by the stirring of the spirit of reform, the Parlement of Aix, acting in imitation of Simon de Monfort, ordered two towns, Merindol and Cabrières, destroyed for their heresy. The sentence was too drastic for the French government to sanction immediately; it was therefore postponed by command of the king, but it was finally executed, at least in part. A ghastly massacre took place in which eight hundred or more of the Waldenses perished. A cry of horror was raised in Germany, in Switzerland, and even in France, from which the king himself recoiled in terror.

1540

1545

Only a few days after his accession Henry issued an edict against blasphemy, and this was followed by a number of laws against heresy. A new court of justice was created to deal with heretics. From its habit of sending its victims to the stake it soon became known as the Chambre Ardente. Its powers were so extensive that the clergy protested against them as

October 8, 1547

infringements of their rights. In its first two years it pronounced five hundred sentences,—and what sentences! Even in that cruel age its punishments were frightful. Burning alive was the commonest. If the heretic recanted on the scaffold he was strangled before the fire was lit; if he refused to recant his tongue was cut out. Those who were merely suspected were cast into dungeons from which many never came out alive. Torture was habitually used to extract confession. For those who recanted before sentence milder, but still severe, punishments were meted out: imprisonment and various sorts of penance. By the edict of Châteaubriand a code of forty-six articles against heresy was drawn up, and the magistrate empowered to put suspected persons under surveillance.

June, 1551

In the face of this fiery persecution the conduct of the Calvinists was wonderfully fine. They showed great adroitness in evading the law by all means save recantation and great astuteness in using what poor legal means of defence were at their disposal. On the other hand they suffered punishment with splendid constancy and courage, very few failing in the hour of trial, and most meeting death in a state of exaltation. Large numbers found refuge in other lands. During the reign of Henry II fourteen hundred fled to Geneva, not to mention the many who settled in the Netherlands, England, and Germany.

Protestant growth

Far from lying passive, the Calvinists took the offensive not only by writing and preaching but by attacking the images of the saints. Many of these were broken or defaced. One student in the university of Paris smashed the images of the Virgin and St. Sebastian and a stained glass window representing the crucifixion, and posted up placards attacking the cult of the saints. For this he was pilloried three times and then shut into a small hole walled in on all sides save for an aperture through which food was passed him until he died.

Undaunted by persecution the innovators continued to grow mightily in numbers and strength. The church at Paris, though necessarily meeting in secret, was well organized. The people of the city assembled together in several conventicles in private houses. By 1559 there were forty fully organized churches (*églises dressées*) throughout France, and no less than 2150 conventicles or mission churches (*églises plantées*). Estimates of numbers are precarious, but good reason has been advanced to show that early in the reign of Henry the Protestants amounted to one-sixth of the population. Like all enthusiastic minorities they wielded a power out of proportion to their numbers. Increasing continually, as they did, it is probable, but for the hostility of the government, they would have been a match for the Catholics. At any rate they were eager to try their strength. A new and important fact was that they no longer consisted entirely of the middle classes. High officers of government and great nobles began to join their ranks. In 1546 the Bishop of Nîmes protected them openly, being himself suspected, probably with justice, of Calvinism. In 1548 a lieutenant-general was among those prosecuted for heresy. Anthony of Bourbon, a descendant of Louis IX, a son of the famous Charles, Constable of France, and husband of Joan d'Albret, queen of Navarre, who was a daughter of Margaret d'Angoulême, became a Protestant. About the same time the great Admiral Coligny was converted, though it was some years before he openly professed his faith. His brother, d'Andelot, also adhered to the Calvinists but was later persuaded by the king and by his wife to go back to the Catholic fold.

1555

So strong had the Protestants become that the

French government was compelled against its will to tolerate them in fact if not in principle, and to recognize them as a party in the state with a quasi-constitutional position. The synod held at Paris in May, 1559, was evidence that the first stage in the evolution of French Protestantism was complete. This assembly drew up a creed called the *Confessio Gallicana,* setting forth in forty articles the purest doctrine of Geneva. Besides affirming belief in the common articles of Christianity, this confession asserted the dogmas of predestination, justification by faith only, and the distinctive Calvinistic doctrine of the eucharist. The worship of saints was condemned and the necessity of a church defined. For this church an organization and discipline modelled on that of Geneva was provided. The country was divided into districts, the churches within which were to send to a central consistory representatives both clerical and lay, the latter to be at least equal in number to the former. Over the church of the whole nation there was to be a national synod or "Colloque" to which each consistory was to send one clergyman and one or two lay elders.

Alarmed by the growth of the Protestants, Henry II was just preparing, after the treaty of Cateau-Cambrésis, to grapple with them more earnestly than ever, when he died of a wound accidentally received in a tournament. His death, hailed by Calvin as a merciful dispensation of Providence, conveniently marks the ending of one epoch and the beginning of another. For the previous forty years France had been absorbed in the struggle with the vast empire of the Hapsburgs. For the next forty years she was completely occupied with the wars of religion. Externally, she played a weak rôle because of civil strife and of a contemptible government. Indeed, all her interests, both foreign and domestic, were from this

July 10, 1559

time forgotten in the intensity of the passions aroused by fanaticism. The date of Henry's demise also marks a change in the evolution of the French government. Hitherto, for some centuries, the trend had been away from feudalism to absolute monarchy. The ideal, "une foi, une loi, un roi" had been nearly attained. But this was now checked in two ways. The great nobles found in Calvinism an opportunity to assert their privileges against the king. The middle classes in the cities, especially in those regions where sectionalism was still strong, found the same opportunity but turned it to the advantage of republicanism. A fierce spirit of resistance not only to the prelates but to the monarch, was born. There was even a considerable amount of democratic sentiment. The poor clergy, who had become converted to Calvinism, were especially free in denouncing the inequalities of the old régime which made of the higher clergy great lords and left the humbler ministers to starve. The fact is that the message of Calvinism was essentially democratic in that the excellence of all Christians and their perfect equality before God was preached. Interest in religion and the ability to discuss it was not confined to a privileged hierarchy, but was shared by the humblest. In a ribald play written in 1564 it is said:[1]

Equality preached

> If faut que Jeanne [a servant] entre les pots
> Parle de reformation;
> La nouvelle religion
> A tant fait que les chambrières,
> Les serviteurs et les tripières
> En disputent publiquement.

But while the gay courtier and worldling sneered at the religion of market women and scullerymaids, he had little cause to scoff when he met the Protestants

[1] Remy Belleau: *La Reconnue*, act 4, scene 2.

in debate at the town hall of his city, or on the field of battle.

Finally, the year 1559 very well marks a stage in the development of French Protestantism. Until about 1536 it had been a mere unorganized opinion, rather a philosophy than a coherent body. From the date of the publication of the *Institutes* to that of the Synod of 1559 the new church had become organized, self-conscious, and definitely political in aims. But after 1559 it became more than a party; it became an *imperium in imperio*. There was no longer one government and one allegiance in France but two, and the two were at war.

The Huguenots

It was just at this time that the name of Huguenot began to be applied to the Protestants, hitherto called "Lutherans," "heretics of Meaux" and, more rarely, "Calvinists." The origin of the word, first used at Tours in 1560, is uncertain. It may possibly come from "le roi Huguet" or "Hugon," a night spectre; the allusion then would be to the ghostly manner in which the heretics crept by night to their conventicles. Huguenot is also found as a family name at Belfort as early as 1425. It may possibly come from the term "Hausgenossen" as used in Alsace of those metal-workers who were not taken into the gild but worked at home, hence a name of contempt like the modern "scab." It may also come from the name of the Swiss Confederation, "Eidgenossen," and perhaps this derivation is the most likely, though it cannot be considered beyond doubt. Whatever the origin of the name the picture of the Huguenot is familiar to us. Of all the fine types of French manhood, that of the Huguenot is one of the finest. Gallic gaiety is tempered with earnestness; intrepidity is strengthened with a new moral fibre like that of steel. Except in the case of a few great lords, who joined the party

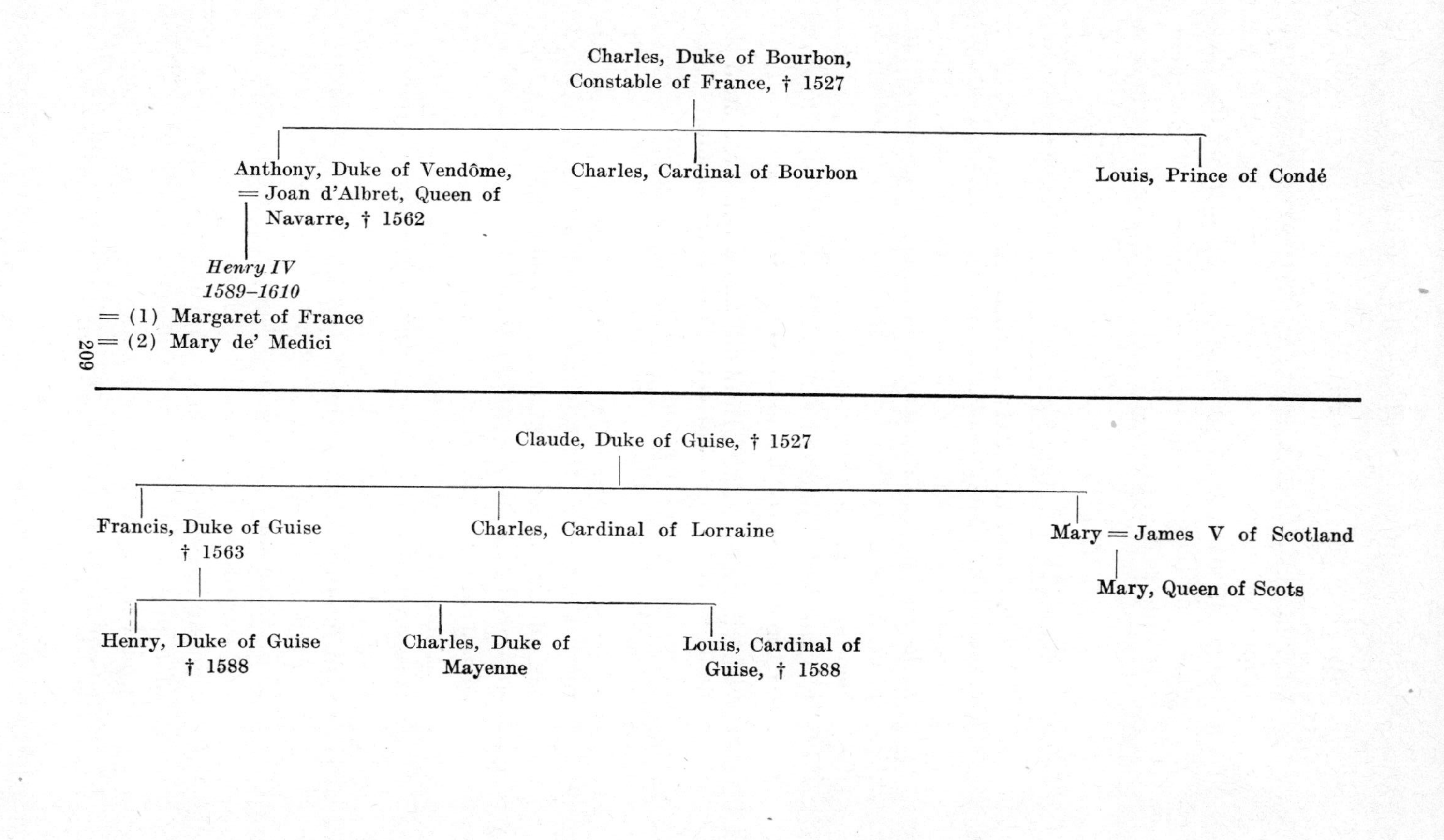
Charles, Duke of Bourbon,
Constable of France, † 1527
Anthony, Duke of Vendôme,
= Joan d'Albret, Queen of
Navarre, † 1562
Charles, Cardinal of Bourbon
Louis, Prince of Condé
Henry IV
1589–1610
= (1) Margaret of France
= (2) Mary de' Medici
Claude, Duke of Guise, † 1527
Francis, Duke of Guise
† 1563
Charles, Cardinal of Lorraine
Mary = James V of Scotland
Mary, Queen of Scots
Henry, Duke of Guise
† 1588
Charles, Duke of
Mayenne
Louis, Cardinal of
Guise, † 1588

without serious conviction, the high standard of the Huguenot morals was recognized even by their enemies. In an age of profligacy the "men of the religion," as they called themselves, walked the paths of rectitude and sobriety.

§ 3. The Wars of Religion. 1559–1598

Francis II, 1559–60

Henry II was followed by three of his sons in succession, each of them, in different degrees and ways, a weakling. The first of them was Francis II, a delicate lad of fifteen, who suffered from adenoids. Child as he was he had already been married for more than a year to Mary Stuart, a daughter of James V of Scotland and a niece of Francis of Guise and the Cardinal of Lorraine. As she was the one passion of the morose and feeble king, who, being legally of age was able to choose his own ministers, the government of the realm fell into the strong hands of "the false brood of Lorraine." Fearing and hating these men above all others the Huguenots turned to the Bourbons for protection, but the king of Navarre was too weak a character to afford them much help. Finding in the press their best weapon the Protestants produced a flood of pamphlets attacking the Cardinal of Lorraine as "the tiger of France."

A more definite plan to rid the country of the hated tyranny was that known as the Conspiracy of Amboise. Godfrey de Barry, Sieur de la Renaudie, pledged several hundred Protestants to go in a body to present a petition to the king at Blois. How much further their intentions went is not known, and perhaps was not definitely formulated by themselves. The Venetian ambassador spoke in a contemporary dispatch of a plot to kill the cardinal and also the king if he would not assent to their counsels, and said that the conspirators relied, to justify this course, on the declaration of Calvin that it was lawful to slay those who hindered the preaching of the gospel. Hearing of the conspiracy, Guise and his brother were ready. They transferred the court from Blois to Amboise, by which move they upset the plans of the petitioners and also put the king into a more defensible castle. Soldiers, assembled for the occasion, met the Huguenots as they advanced in a body towards Amboise, shot down La Renaudie and some others on the spot and arrested the remaining twelve hundred, to be kept for subsequent trial and execution. The suspicion that fastened on the prince of Condé, a brother of the king of Navarre, was given some color by his frank avowal of sympathy with the conspirators. Though the Guises pressed their advantage to the utmost in forbidding all future assemblies of heretics, the tumult of Amboise was vaguely felt, in the sultry atmosphere of pent-up passions, to be the avant-courier of a terrific storm.

The tumult of Amboise, March 1560

Charles IX, 1560–74

The early death of the sickly king left the throne to his brother Charles IX, a boy of nine. As he was a minor, the regency fell to his mother, Catharine de' Medici, who for almost thirty years was the real ruler of France. Notwithstanding what Brantôme calls "ung embonpoint très-riche," she was active of body and mind. Her large correspondence partly reveals the secrets of her power: much tact and infinite pains to keep in touch with as many people and as many details of business as possible. Her want of beauty was supplied by gracious manners and an elegant taste in art. As a connoisseur and an indefatigable collector she gratified her love of the magnificent not only by beautiful palaces and gorgeous clothes, but in having a store of pictures, statues, tapestries, furniture, porcelain, silver, books, and manuscripts.

Policy of Catharine de'Medici

A "politique" to her fingertips, Catharine had neither sympathy nor patience with the fanatics who would put their religion above peace and prosperity. Surrounded by men as fierce as lions, she showed no little of the skill and intrepidity of the tamer in keeping them, for a time, from each others' throats. Soon after Charles ascended the throne, she was almost hustled into domestic and foreign war by the offer of Philip II of Spain to help her Catholic subjects against the Huguenots without her leave. She knew if that were done that, as she scrawled in her own peculiar French, "le Roy mon fils nave jeames lantyere aubeysance,"[1] and she was determined "que personne ne peut nous brouller en lamitie en la quele je desire que set deus Royaumes demeurent pendant mauye."[2] Through her goggle eyes she saw clearly where lay the path that she must follow. "I am resolved," she wrote, "to seek by all possible means to preserve the authority of the king my son in all things, and at the same time to keep the people in peace, unity and concord, without giving them occasion to stir or to change anything." Fundamentally, this was the same policy as that of Henry IV. That she failed where he succeeded is not due entirely to the difference in ability. In 1560 neither party was prepared to yield or to tolerate the other without a trial of strength, whereas a generation later many members of both parties were sick of war.

December 13, 1560

Just as Francis was dying, the States General met at Orleans. This body was divided into three houses, or estates, that of the clergy, that of the nobles, and that of the commons. The latter was so democratically chosen that even the peasants voted. Whether they had voted in 1484 is not known, but it is certain that they did so in 1560, and that it was in the interests of the crown to let them vote is shown by the increase in

1 "The king my son will never have entire obedience."

2 "That no one may embroil us in the friendship in which I desire that these two kingdoms shall remain during my lifetime."

the number of royal officers among the deputies of the third estate. The peasants still regarded the king as their natural protector against the oppression of the nobles.

The Estates were opened by Catharine's minister, Michael de l'Hôpital. Fully sympathizing with her policy of conciliation, he addressed the Estates as follows: "Let us abandon those diabolic words, names of parties, factions and seditions:—Lutherans, Huguenots, Papists; let us not change the name of Christians." Accordingly, an edict was passed granting an amnesty to the Huguenots, nominally for the purpose of allowing them to return to the Catholic church, but practically interpreted without reference to this proviso.

February 24, 1561

But the government found it easier to pass edicts than to restrain the zealots of both parties. The Protestants continued to smash images; the Catholics to mob the Protestants. Paris became, in the words of Beza, "the city most bloody and murderous among all in the world." Under the combined effects of legal toleration and mob persecution the Huguenots grew mightily in numbers and power. Their natural leader, the King of Navarre, indeed failed them, for he changed his faith several times, his real cult, as Calvin remarked, being that of Venus. His wife, Joan d'Albret, however, became an ardent Calvinist.

At this point the government proposed a means of conciliation that had been tried by Charles V in Germany and had there failed. The leading theologians of both confessions were summoned to a colloquy at Poissy. Most of the German divines invited were prevented by politics from coming, but the noted Italian Protestant Peter Martyr Vermigli and Theodore Beza of Geneva were present. The debate turned on the usual points at issue, and was of course indecisive,

Colloquy of Poissy August, 1561

though the Huguenots did not hesitate to proclaim their own victory.

January, 1562

A fresh edict of toleration had hardly been issued when civil war was precipitated by a horrible crime. Some armed retainers of the Duke of Guise, coming upon a Huguenot congregation at Vassy in Champagne, attacked them and murdered three hundred. A wild cry of fury rose from all the Calvinists; throughout the whole land there were riots. At Toulouse, for example, fighting in the streets lasted four days and four hundred persons perished. It was one of the worst years in the history of France. A veritable reign of terror prevailed everywhere, and while the crops were destroyed famine stalked throughout the land. Bands of robbers and ravishers, under the names of Christian parties but savages at heart, put the whole people to ransom and to sack. Indeed, the Wars of Religion were like hell; the tongue can describe them better than the imagination can conceive them. The whole sweet and pleasant land of France, from the Burgundian to the Spanish frontier, was widowed and desolated, her pride humbled by her own sons and her Golden Lilies trampled in the bloody mire. Foreign levy was called in to supply strength to fratricidal arms. The Protestants, headed by Condé and Coligny, raised an army and started negotiations with England. The Catholics, however, had the best of the fighting. They captured Rouen, defended by English troops, and, under Guise, defeated the Huguenots under Coligny at Dreux.

Massacre of Vassy, March 1, 1562

December 19, 1562

Two months later, Francis of Guise was assassinated by a Protestant near Orléans. Coligny was accused of inciting the crime, which he denied, though he confessed that he was glad of it. The immediate beneficiary of the death of the duke was not the Huguenot, however, so much as Catharine de' Medici. Continu-

February 18, 1563

Edict of Amboise March 19, 1563

ing to put into practise her policy of tolerance she issued an edict granting liberty of conscience to all and liberty of worship under certain restrictions. Great nobles were allowed to hold meetings for divine service according to the reformed manner in their own houses, and one village in each bailiwick was allowed to have a Protestant chapel.

How consistently secular was Catharine's policy became apparent at this time when she refused to publish the decrees of the Council of Trent, fearing that they might infringe on the liberties of the Gallican church. In this she had the full support of most French Catholics. She continued to work for religious peace. One of her methods was characteristic of her and of the time. She selected "a flying squadron" of twenty-four beautiful maids of honor of high rank and low principles to help her seduce the refractory nobles on both sides. In many cases she was successful. Condé, in love with one—or possibly with several—of these sirens, forgot everything else, his wife, his party, his religion. His death in 1569 threw the leadership of the Huguenots into the steadier and stronger grasp of Coligny.

But such means of dealing with a profoundly dangerous crisis were of course but the most wretched palliatives. The Catholic bigots would permit no dallying with the heretics. In 1567 they were strong enough to secure the disgrace of L'Hôpital and in the following year to extort a royal edict unconditionally forbidding the exercise of the reformed cult. The Huguenots again rebelled and in 1569 suffered two severe defeats at Jarnac and at Moncontour. The Catholics were jubilant, fully believing, as Sully says, that at last the Protestants would have to submit. But nothing is more remarkable than the apparently slight effect of military success or failure on the

Huguenots defeated

strength and numbers of the two faiths. "We had beaten our enemies over and over again," cried the Catholic soldier Montluc in a rage, "we were winning by force of arms but they triumphed by means of their diabolical writings."

The Huguenots, however, did not rely entirely on the pen. Their stronghold was no longer in the north but was now in the south and west. The reason for this may be partly found in the preparation of the soil for their seed by the medieval heresies, but still more in the strong particularistic spirit of that region. The ancient provinces of Poitou and Guienne, Gascony and Languedoc, were almost as conscious of their southern and Provençal culture as they were of their French citizenship. The strength of the centralizing tendencies lay north of the Loire; in the south local privileges were more esteemed and more insisted upon. While Protestantism was persecuted by the government at Paris it was often protected by cities of the south. The most noteworthy of these was La Rochelle on the Atlantic coast near Bordeaux. Though coming late to the support of the Reformation, its conversion was thorough and lasting. To protect the new religion it successfully asserted its municipal freedom almost to the point of independence. Like the Dutch Beggars of the Sea its armed privateers preyed upon the commerce of Catholic powers, a mode of warfare from which the city derived immense booty.

La Rochelle

The Huguenots tried but failed to get foreign allies. Neither England nor Germany sent them any help. Their policy of supporting the revolt of the Low Countries against Spain turned out disastrously for themselves when the French under Coligny were defeated at Mons by the troops of Philip.

Battle of Mons, July 17, 1572

The Catholics now believed the time ripe for a decisive blow. Under the stimulus of the Jesuits they had for a short time been conducting an offensive and effective propaganda. Leagues were formed to combat the organizations of the Huguenots, armed "Brotherhoods of the Holy Spirit" as they were called. The chief obstacle in their path seemed to be a small group of powerful nobles headed by Coligny. Catharine and the Guises resolved to cut away this obstacle with the assassin's knife. Charles, who was personally on good terms with Coligny, hesitated, but he was too weak a youth to hold out long. There seems to be good reason to believe that all the queen dowager and her advisers contemplated was the murder of a few leaders and that they did not foresee one of the most extensive massacres in history.

August 22 1572

Her first attempt to have Coligny assassinated aroused the anger of the Huguenot leaders and made them more dangerous than before. A better laid and more comprehensive plan was therefore carried out on the eve of St. Bartholomew's day. Early in the evening of August 23, Henry of Guise, a son of Duke Francis, and Coligny's bitterest personal enemy, went with armed men to the house of the admiral and murdered him. From thence they proceeded to the houses of other prominent Huguenots to slay them in the same manner. News of the man-hunt spread through the city with instant rapidity, the mob rose and massacred all the Huguenots they could find as well as a number of foreigners, principally Germans and Flemings. De Thou says that two thousand were slain in Paris before noon of August 24. A general pillage followed.

Massacre of St. Bartholomew, August 24, to October 3

The king hesitated to assume responsibility for so serious a tumult. His letters of August 24 to various governors of provinces and to ambassadors spoke only of a fray between Guise and Coligny, and stated that he wished to preserve order. But with these very letters he sent messengers to all quarters with verbal orders to kill all the leading Protestants. On August 27 he again wrote of it as "a great and lamentable sedition" originating in the desire of Guise to revenge his father on Coligny. The king said that the fury of the populace was such that he was unable to bring the remedy he wished, and he again issued directions for the preservation of order. But at the same time he declared that the Guises had acted at his command to punish those who had conspired against him and against the old religion. In fact, he gave out a rapid series of contradictory accounts and orders, and in the meantime, from August 25 to October 3 terrible series of massacres took place in almost all the provinces. Two hundred Huguenots perished at Meaux, from 500 to 1000 at Orleans, a much larger number at Lyons. It is difficult to estimate the total number of victims. Sully, who narrowly escaped, says that 70,000 were slain. Hotman, another contemporary, says 50,000. Knowing how much figures are apt to be exaggerated even by judicious men, we must assume that this number is too large. On the other hand the lowest estimate given by modern Catholic investigators, 5000, is certainly too small. Probably between 10,000 and 20,000 is correct. Those who fell were the flower of the party.

Other massacres

Whatever may have been the precise degree of guilt of the French rulers, which in any case was very grave, they took no pains to conceal their exultation over an event that had at last, as they believed, ground their enemies to powder. In jubilant tone Catharine wrote to her son-in-law, Philip of Spain, that God had given her son the king of France the means "of wiping out those of his subjects who were rebellious to God and to himself." Philip sent his hearty congratulations and heard a Te Deum sung. The pope struck a medal with a picture of an avenging angel and the legend, "Ugonotorum strages," and ordered an annual Te Deum which was, in fact, celebrated for a long time. But on the other hand a cry of horror arose from Germany and England. Elizabeth received the French ambassador dressed in mourning and declared to him that "the deed had been too bloody."

Though the triumph of the Catholics was loudly shouted, it was not as complete as they hoped. The Huguenots seemed cowed for a moment, but nothing is more remarkable than the constancy of the people. Recantations were extremely few. The Reformed pastors, nourished on the Old Testament, saw in the affliction that had befallen them nothing but the means of proving the faithful. Preparations for resistance were made at once in the principal cities of the south. La Rochelle, besieged by the royal troops, evinced a heroism worthy of the cause. While the men repulsed the furious assaults of the enemy the women built up the walls that crumbled under the powerful fire of the artillery. A faction of citizens who demanded surrender was sternly suppressed and the city held out until relief came from an unhoped quarter. The king's brother, Henry Duke of Anjou, was elected to the throne of Poland on condition that he would allow liberty of conscience to Polish Protestants. In order to appear consistent the French government therefore stopped for the moment the persecution of the Huguenots. The siege of La Rochelle was abandoned and a treaty made allowing liberty of worship in that city, in Nîmes and Montauban and in the houses of some of the great nobles.

Siege of La Rochelle

In less than two years after the appalling massacre the Protestants were again strong and active. A chant of victory sounded from their dauntless ranks. More than ever before they became republican in principle.

Their pamphleteers, among them Hotman, fiercely attacked the government of Catharine, and asserted their rights.

Charles was a consumptive. The hemorrhages characteristic of his disease reminded him of the torrents of blood that he had caused to flow from his country. Broken in body and haunted by superstitious terrors the wretched man died on May 30, 1574.

Henry III, 1547–89

He was succeeded by his brother, Henry III, recently elected king of Poland, a man of good parts, interested in culture and in study, a natural orator, not destitute of intelligence. His mother's pet and spoiled child, brought up among the girls of the "flying squadron," he was in a continual state of nervous and sensual titillation that made him avid of excitement and yet unable to endure it. A thunderstorm drove him to hide in the cellar and to tears. He was at times overcome by fear of death and hell, and at times had crises of religious fervour. But his life was a perpetual debauch, ever seeking new forms of pleasure in strange ways. He would walk the streets at night accompanied by gay young rufflers in search of adventures. He had a passion for some handsome young men, commonly called "the darlings," whom he kept about him dressed as women.

His reign meant a new lease of power to his mother, who worshipped him and to whom he willingly left the arduous business of government. By this time she was bitterly hated by the Huguenots, who paid their compliments to her in a pamphlet entitled *A wonderful Discourse on the Life, Deeds and Debauchery of Catharine de' Medici,* perhaps written in part by the scholar Henry Estienne. She was accused not only of crimes of which she was really guilty, like the massacre of St. Bartholomew, but of having murdered the dauphin Francis, her husband's elder brother, and others who had died natural deaths, and of having systematically depraved her children in order to keep the reins of authority in her own hands.

Frightened by the odium in which his mother was held, Henry III thought it wise to disavow all part or lot in St. Bartholomew and to concede to the Huguenots liberty of worship everywhere save in Paris and in whatever place the court might be for the moment.

So difficult was the position of the king that by this attempt to conciliate his enemies he only alienated his friends. The bigoted Catholics, finding the crown impotent, began to take energetic measures to help themselves. In 1576 they formed a League to secure the benefit of association. Henry Duke of Guise drew up the declaration that formed the constituent act of the League. It proposed "to establish the law of God in its entirety, to reinstate and maintain divine service according to the form and manner of the holy, Catholic and apostolic church," and also "to restore to the provinces and estates of this kingdom the rights, privileges, franchises, and ancient liberties such as they were in the time of King Clovis, the first Christian king." This last clause is highly significant as showing how the Catholics had now adopted the tactics of the Huguenots in appealing from the central government to the provincial privileges. It is exactly the same issue as that of Federalism versus States' Rights in American history; the party in power emphasizes the national authority, while the smaller divisions furnish a refuge for the minority.

The League

The constituency of the League rapidly became large. The declaration of Guise was circulated throughout the country something like a monster petition, and those who wished bound themselves to support it. The power of this association of Catholics among nobles and people soon made it so formidable that Henry III reversed his former policy, recognized the League and declared himself its head.

Estates General of Blois

The elections for the States General held at Blois in 1576 proved highly favorable to the League. The chief reason for their overwhelming success was the abstention of the Protestants from voting. In continental Europe it has always been and is now common for minorities to refuse to vote, the idea being that this refusal is in itself a protest more effective than a definite minority vote would be. To an American this seems strange, for it has been proved time and again that a strong minority can do a great deal to shape legislation. But the Huguenots reasoned differently, and so seated but one Protestant in the whole assembly, a deputy to the second, or noble, estate. The privileged orders pronounced immediately for the enforcement of religious unity, but in the Third Estate there was a warm debate. John Bodin, the famous publicist, though a Catholic, pleaded hard for tolerance. As finally passed, the law demanded a return to the old religion, but added the proviso that the means taken should be "gentle and pacific and without war." So impossible was this in practice that the government was again obliged to issue a decree granting liberty of conscience and restricted liberty of worship.

1577

Under the oppression of the ruinous civil wars the people began to grow more and more restless. The king was extremely unpopular. Perhaps the people might have winked even at such outrages against decency as were perpetrated by the king had not their critical faculties been sharpened by the growing misery of their condition. The wars had bankrupted both them and the government, and the desperate expedients of the latter to raise money only increased the poverty of the masses. Every estate, every province, was urged to contribute as much as possible, and most of them replied, in humble and loyal tone, but firmly, begging for relief from the ruinous exactions. The sale of offices, of justice, of collectorships of taxes, of the administration, of the army, of the public domain, was only less onerous than the sale of monopolies and inspectorships of markets and ports. The only prosperous class seemed to be the government agents and contractors. In fact, for the first time in the history of France the people were becoming thoroughly disaffected and some of them semi-republican in feeling.

1584

The king had no sons and when his only remaining brother died a new element of discord and perplexity was introduced in that the heir to the throne, Henry of Navarre, was a Protestant. Violent attacks on him were published in the pamphlet press. The League was revived in stronger form than before. Its head, Guise, selected as candidate for the throne the uncle of Henry of Navarre, Charles, Cardinal of Bourbon, a stupid and violent man of sixty-four. The king hastened to make terms with the League and commanded all Protestants to leave the country in six months. At this point the pope intervened to strengthen his cause by issuing the "Bull of Deprivation" declaring Henry of Navarre incapable, as a heretic, of succeeding to the throne. Navarre at once denounced the bull as contrary to French law and invalid, and he was supported both by the Parlement of Paris and by some able pamphleteers. Hotman published his attack on the "vain and blind fulmination" of the pontiff.

1585

Battle of Coutras, October 20, 1587

An appeal to arms was inevitable. At the battle of Coutras, the Huguenots, led by Henry of Navarre, won their first victory. While this increased Navarre's power and his popularity with his followers, the majority of the people rallied to the League. In the "war of the three Henrys" as it was called, the king had more to fear from Henry of Guise than from the Huguenot. Cooped up at the Tuileries the monarch was under so irksome a restraint that he was finally obliged to regain freedom by flight, on May 12, 1588. The elections for the States General gave an enormous majority to the League. In an evil hour for himself the king resorted again to that much used weapon, assassination. By his order Guise was murdered. "Now I am king," he wrote with a sigh of relief. But he was mistaken. The League, more hostile than ever, swearing to avenge the death of its captain, was now frankly revolutionary.

It continued to exercise its authority under the leadership of a Committee of Sixteen. These gentlemen purged the still royalist Parlement of Paris. By the hostility of the League the king was forced to an alliance with Henry of Navarre. This is interesting as showing how completely the position of the two leading parties had become reversed. The throne, once the strongest ally of the church, was now supported chiefly by the Huguenots who had formerly been in rebellion. Indeed by this time "the wars of religion" had become to a very large extent dynastic and social.

On August 1, 1589, the king was assassinated by a Dominican fanatic. His death was preceded shortly by that of Catharine de' Medici.

Henry IV, 1589–1610

Henry IV was a man of thirty-five, of middle stature, but very hardy and brave. He was one of the most intelligent of the French kings, vigorous of brain as of body. Few could resist his delicate compliments and the promises he knew how to lavish. The glamour of his personality has survived even until now. In a song still popular he is called "the gallant king who knew how to fight, to make love and to drink." He is also remembered for his wish that every peasant might have a fowl in his pot. His supreme desire was to see France, bleeding and impoverished by civil war, again united, strong and happy. He consistently subordinated religion to political ends. To him almost alone is due the final adoption of tolerance, not indeed as a natural right, but as a political expedient.

The difficulties with which he had to contend were enormous. The Catholics, headed by the Duke of Mayenne, a brother of Guise, agreed to recognize him for six months in order that he might have the opportunity of becoming reconciled to the church. But Mayenne, who wished to be elected king by the States General, soon commenced hostilities. The skirmish at Arques between the forces of Henry and Mayenne, resulting favorably to the former, was followed by the battle of Ivry. Henry, with two thousand horse and eight thousand foot, against eight thousand horse and twelve thousand foot of the League, addressed his soldiers in a stirring oration: "God is with us. Behold his enemies and ours; behold your king. Charge! If your standards fail you, rally to my white plume; you will find it on the road to victory and honor." At first the fortune of war went against the Huguenots, but the personal courage of the king, who, with "a terrible white plume" in his helmet led his cavalry to the attack, wrested victory from the foe.

Battle of Ivry, March 14, 1590

From Ivry Henry marched to Paris, the headquarters of the League. With thirteen thousand soldiers he besieged this town of 220,000 inhabitants, garrisoned by fifty thousand troops. With their usual self-sacrificing devotion, the people of Paris held out against the horrors of famine. The clergy aroused the fanaticism of the populace, promising heaven to those who died; women protested that they would eat

Siege of Paris

their children before they would surrender. With provisions for one month, Paris held out for four. Dogs, cats, rats, and grass were eaten; the bones of animals and even of dead people were ground up and used for flour; the skins of animals were devoured. Thirteen thousand persons died of hunger and twenty thousand of the fever brought on by lack of food. But even this miracle of fanaticism could not have saved the capital eventually, but for the timely invasion of France from the north by the Duke of Parma, who joined Mayenne on the Marne. Henry raised the siege to meet the new menace, but the campaign of 1591 was fruitless for both sides.

Anarchy

France seemed to be in a state of anarchy under the operation of many and various forces. Pope Gregory XIV tried to influence the Catholics to unite against Henry, but he was met by protests from the Parlements in the name of the Gallican Liberties. The "Politiques" were ready to support any strong *de facto* government, but could not find it. The cities hated the nobles, and the republicans resented the "courteous warfare" which either side was said to wage on the other, sparing each other's nobles and slaughtering the commons.

1593

At this point the States General were convoked at Paris by the League. So many provinces refused to send deputies that there were only 128 members out of a normal 505. A serial publication by several authors, called the *Satyre Menippée,* poured ridicule on the pretentions of the national assembly. Various solutions of the deadlock were proposed. Philip II of Spain offered to support Mayenne as Lieutenant General of France if the League would make his daughter, as the heiress through her mother, Elizabeth of Valois, queen. This being refused, Philip next proposed that the young Duke of Guise should marry his daughter and become king. But this proposal also won little support. The enemies of Henry IV were conscious of his legitimate rights and jealous of foreign interference; the only thing that stood in the way of their recognizing him was his heresy.

Henry's conversion

Henry, finding that there seemed no other issue to an intolerable situation, at last resolved, though with much reluctance, to change his religion. On July 25, 1593, he abjured the Protestant faith, kneeling to the Archbishop of Bourges, and was received into the bosom of the Roman church. That his conversion was due entirely to the belief that "Paris was worth a mass" is, of course, plain. Indeed, he frankly avowed that he still scrupled at some articles, such as purgatory, the worship of the saints, and the power of the pope. And it must be remembered that his motives were not purely selfish. The alternative seemed to be indefinite civil war with all its horrors, and Henry deliberately but regretfully sacrificed his confessional convictions on the altar of his country.

The step was not immediately successful. The Huguenots were naturally enraged. The Catholics doubted the king's sincerity. At Paris the preachers of the League ridiculed the conversion from the pulpit. "My dog," sneered one of them, "were you not at mass last Sunday? Come here and let us offer you the crown." But the "politiques" rallied to the throne and the League rapidly melted away. The *Satyre Menippée,* supporting the interests of Henry, did much to turn public opinion in his favor.

A further impression was made by his coronation at Chartres in 1594. When the surrender of Paris followed, the king entered his capital to receive the homage of the Sorbonne and the Parlement of Paris. The superstitious were convinced of Henry's sincerity when he touched some scrofulous persons and they were said to be healed. Curing the "king's evil" was one of the oldest attributes of royalty, and it could not be imagined that it would descend to an impostor.

Henry showed the wisest statesmanship in consolidating his power. He bought up those who still held out against him at their own price, remarking that whatever it cost it would be cheaper than fighting them. He showed a wise clemency in dealing with his enemies, banishing only about 130 persons. Next came absolution by Pope Clement VIII, who, after driving as hard a bargain as he could, finally granted it on September 17, 1595.

But even yet all danger was not past. Enraged at seeing France escape from his clutches, Philip of Spain declared war, and he could still count on the support of Mayenne and the last remnant of the League. The daring action of Henry at Fontaine-Française on June 5, 1595, where with three hundred horse he routed twelve hundred Spaniards, so discouraged his enemies that Mayenne hastened to submit, and peace was signed with Spain in 1598. The finances of the realm, naturally in a chaotic state, were brought to order and solvency by a Huguenot noble, the Duke of Sully, Henry's ablest minister.

The legal status of the Protestants was still to be settled. It was not changed by Henry's abjuration, and the king was determined at all costs to avoid another civil war. He therefore published the Edict of Nantes, declared to be perpetual and irrevocable. By it liberty of conscience was granted to all "without being questioned, vexed or molested," and without being "forced to do anything contrary to their religion." Liberty of worship was conceded in all places in which it had been practised for the last two years; *i.e.* in two places in every bailiwick except large towns, where services were to be held outside the walls, and

Edict of Nantes, April 13, 1598

in the houses of the great nobles. Protestant worship was forbidden at Paris and for five leagues (twelve and one-half miles) outside the walls. Protestants had all other legal rights of Catholics and were eligible to all offices. To secure them in these rights a separate court of justice was instituted, a division of the Parlement of Paris to be called the Edict Chamber and to consist of ten Catholic and six Protestant judges. But a still stronger guarantee was given in their recognition as a separately organized state within the state. The king agreed to leave two hundred towns in their hands, some of which, like Montpellier, Montauban, and La Rochelle, were fortresses in which they kept garrisons and paid the governors. As they could raise 25,000 soldiers at a time when the national army in time of peace was only 10,000, their position seemed absolutely impregnable. So favorable was the Edict to the Huguenots that it was bitterly opposed by the Catholic clergy and by the Parlement of Paris. Only the personal insistence of the king finally carried it.

Reasons for failure of French Protestantism

Protestantism was stronger in the sixteenth century in France than it ever was thereafter. During the eighty-seven years while the Edict of Nantes was in force it lost much ground, and when that Edict was revoked by a doting king and persecution began afresh, the Huguenots were in no condition to resist. From a total constituency at its maximum of perhaps a fifth or a sixth of the whole population, the Protestants have now sunk to less than two per cent. (650,000 out of 39,000,000). The history of the rise and decline of the Huguenot movement is a melancholy record of persecution and of heroism. How great the number of martyrs was can never be known accurately. Apart from St. Bartholomew there were several lesser massacres, the wear and tear of a generation of war, and

1685

the unremitting pressure of the law that claimed hundreds of victims a year.

Hostility of the Government

Three principal causes can be assigned for the failure of the Reformation to do more than fight a drawn battle in France. The first and least important of these was the steady hostility of the government. This hostility was assured by the mutually advantageous alliance between the throne and the church sealed in the Concordat of Bologna of 1516. But that the opposition of the government, heavily as it weighed, was not and could not be the decisive force in defeating Protestantism is proved, in my judgment, by the fact that even when the Huguenots had a king of their own persuasion they were unable to obtain the mastery. Had their faith won the support not only of a considerable minority, but of the actual majority of the people, they could surely at this time have secured the government and made France a Protestant state.

Protestantism came too late

The second cause of the final failure of the Reformation was the tardiness with which it came to France. It did not begin to make its really popular appeal until some years after 1536, when Calvin's writings attained a gradual publicity. This was twenty years later than the Reformation came forcibly home to the Germans, and in those twenty years it had made its greatest conquests north of the Rhine. Of causes as well as of men it is true that there is a tide in their affairs which, taken at the flood, leads on to fortune, but which, once missed, ebbs to defeat. Every generation has a different interest; to every era the ideals of that immediately preceding become stale and old-fashioned. The writings of every age are a polemic against those of their fathers; every dogma has its day, and after every wave of enthusiam a reaction sets in. Thus it was that the Reformation missed, though it narrowly missed, the propitious moment for conquering France. Enough had been said of it during the reign of Francis to make the people tired of it, but not enough to make them embrace it. By the time that Calvin had become well known, the Catholics had awakened and had seized many of the weapons of their opponents, a fresh statement of belief, a new enthusiasm, a reformed ethical standard. The Council of Trent, the Jesuits, the other new orders, were only symptoms of a still more widely prevalent Catholic revival that came, in France, just in the nick of time to deprive the Protestants of many of their claims to popular favor.

Beaten by the Renaissance

But probably the heaviest weight in the scale against the Reformation was the Renaissance—far stronger in France than in Germany. The one marched from the north, while the other was wafted up from Italy. They met, not as hostile armies but rather—to use a humble, commercial illustration—as two competing merchants. The goods they offered were not the same, not even similar, but the appeal of each was of such a nature that few minds could be the whole-hearted devotees of both. The new learning and the beauties of Italian art and literature sapped away the interest of just those intelligent classes whose support was needed to make the triumph of the Reformation complete. Terrible as were the losses of the Huguenots by fire and sword, considerable as were the defections from their ranks of those who found in the reformed Catholic church a spiritual refuge, still greater was the loss of the Protestant cause in failing to secure the adherence of such minds as Dolet and Rabelais, Ronsard and Montaigne, and of the thousands influenced by them. And a study of just these men will show how the Italian influence worked and how it grew stronger in its rivalry with the religious interest.

Whereas Marot had found something to interest him in the new doctrines, Ronsard bitterly hated them. Passionately devoted, as he and the rest of the Pléiade were, to the sensuous beauties of Italian poetry, he had neither understanding of nor patience with dogmatic subtleties. In the Huguenots he saw nothing but mad fanatics and dangerous fomentors of rebellion. In his *Discourses on the Evils of the Times,* he laid all the woes of France at the door of the innovators. And powerfully his greater lyrics seduced the mind of the public from the contemplation of divinity to the enjoyment of earthly beauty.

Montaigne's aloofness

The same intensification of the contrast between the two spirits is seen in comparing Montaigne with Rabelais. It is true that Rabelais ridiculed all positive religion, but nevertheless it fascinated him. His theological learning is remarkable. But Montaigne ignored religion as far as possible. Nourished from his earliest youth on the great classical writers, he had no interest apart from "the kingdom of man." He preferred to remain in the old faith because that course caused him the least trouble. He had no sympathy with the Protestants, but he did not hate them, as did Ronsard. During the wars of religion, he maintained friendly relations with the leaders of both parties. And he could not believe that creed was the real cause of the civil strife. "Take from the Catholic army," said he, "all those actuated by pure zeal for the church or for the king and country, and you will not have enough men left to form one company." It is strange that beneath the evil passions and self-seeking of the champions of each party he could not see the fierce flame of popular heroism and fanaticism; but that he, and thousands of men like him, could not do so, and could not enter, even by imagination, into the causes which, but a half century earlier, had set the world on fire, largely explains how the religious issue had lost its savour and why Protestantism failed in France.

CHAPTER V

THE NETHERLANDS

§ 1. The Lutheran Reform

The Netherlands

The Netherlands have always been a favorite topic for the speculation of those philosophers who derive a large part of national character from geographical conditions. A land that needed reclaiming from the sea by hard labor, a country situated at those two great outlets of European commerce, the mouths of the Rhine and the Scheldt, a borderland between German and Latin culture, naturally moulded a brave, stubborn, practical and intelligent people, destined to play in history a part seemingly beyond their scope and resources.

The people of the Netherlands became, to all intents, a state before they became a nation. The Burgundian dukes of the fourteenth and fifteenth century added to their fiefs counties, dukedoms and bishoprics, around the nucleus of their first domain, until they had forged a compact and powerful realm. Philip the Good, Duke of Burgundy and lord, under various titles, of much of the Netherlands, deserved the title of *Conditor Belgii* by his successful wars on France and by his statesmanlike policy of centralization. To foster unity he created the States General—borrowing the name and function thereof from France—in which all of the seventeen provinces [1] of the Netherlands were represented on great occasions. Continually increas-

Philip the Good, 1419–67

[1] Brabant, Limburg, Luxemburg, Guelders, Flanders, Artois, Hainaut, Holland, Zeeland, Malines, Namur, Lille, Tournay, Friesland, Utrecht, Overyssel and Groningen.

ing in power with reference to the various localities, it remained subordinate to the prince, who had the sole right of initiating legislation. At first it met now in one city, then in another, but after 1530 always convened at Brussels, and always used the French language officially.

Charles the Bold, 1467–77

Charles the Bold completed and yet endangered the work of Philip, for he was worsted in mortal strife with Louis XI of France and, dying in battle, left his dominions to his daughter, Mary. Her husband, the Emperor Maximilian, and her son, Philip the Handsome, added to her realms those vast dominions that made her grandson, Charles, the greatest potentate in Europe. Born in Ghent, reared in the Netherlands, and speaking only the French of the Walloons, Charles was always regarded by his subjects as one of themselves. He almost completed the unification of the Burgundian state by the conquest of Tournay from France (1521), and the annexation of the independent provinces of Friesland (1523), Overyssel and Utrecht (1528), Groningen (1536) and Guelders (1543). Liège still remained a separate entity under its prince-bishops. But even under Charles, notwithstanding a general feeling of loyalty to the house of Hapsburg, each province was more conscious of its own individuality than were the people as a whole of common patriotism. Some of the provinces lay within the Empire, others were vassals of France, a few were independent. Dutch was regarded as a dialect of German. The most illustrious Netherlander of the time, Erasmus, in discussing his race, does not even contemplate the possibility of there being a nation composed of Dutch and Flemish men. The only alternative that presents itself to him is whether he is French or German and, having been born at Rotterdam, he decides in favor of the latter.

Maximilian, 1477–93
Philip the Handsome, 1493–1506

Classes

The Burgundian princes found their chief support in the nobility, in a numerous class of officials, and in the municipal aristocracies. The nobles, transformed from a feudal caste to a court clique, even though they retained, as satellites of the monarch, much wealth and power, had relatively lost ground to the rising pretensions of the cities and of the commercial class. The clergy, too, were losing their old independence in subservience to a government which regulated their tithes and forbade their indulgence-trade. In 1515 Charles secured from Leo X and again in 1530 from Clement VII the right of nomination to vacant benefices. He was able to make of the bishops his tools and to curtail the freedom, jurisdiction, and financial privileges of the clergy considerably because the spiritual estate had lost favor with the people and received no support from them.

As the two privileged classes surrendered their powers to the monarch, the third estate was coming into its own. Not until the war of independence, however, was it able to withstand the combination of bureaucracy and plutocracy that made common cause with the central government against the local rights of the cities and the customary privileges of the gilds. Almost everywhere the prince was able, with the tacit support of the wealthier burghers, to substitute for the officers elected by the gilds his own commissioners. But this usurpation, together with a variety of economic ills for which the commoners were inclined, quite wrongly, to blame the government, caused general discontent and in one case open rebellion. The gilds of Ghent, a proud and ancient city, suffering from the encroachments of capitalism and from the decline of the Flemish cloth industry, had long asserted among their rights that of each gild to refuse to pay one of the taxes, any one it chose, levied by the government. The attempt

Revolt of Ghent

1539

of the government to suppress this privilege caused a rising which took the characteristically modern form of a general strike. The regent of the Netherlands, Mary, yielded at first to the demands of the gilds, as she had no means of coercion convenient. Charles was in Spain at the time, but hurried northward, being granted free passage through France by the king who felt he had an interest in aiding his fellow monarch to put down rebellious subjects. Early in 1540 Charles entered Ghent at the head of a sufficient army. He soon meted out a sanguinary punishment to the "brawlers" as the strikers were called, humbled the city government, deprived it of all local privileges, suppressed all independent corporations, asserted the royal prerogative of nominating aldermen, and erected a fortress to overawe the burghers. Thus the only overt attempt to resist the authority of Charles V, apart from one or two insignificant Anabaptist riots, was crushed.

In matters of foreign policy the people of the Netherlands naturally wished to be guided in reference to their own interests and not to the larger interests of the emperor's other domains. Wielding immense wealth—during the middle decades of the sixteenth century Antwerp was both the first port and the first money-market of Europe—and cherishing the sentiment that Charles was a native of their land, they for some time sweetly flattered themselves that their interests were the center around which gravitated the desires and needs of the Empire and of Spain. Indeed, the balance of these two great states, and the regency of Margaret of Austria, a Hapsburg determined to give the Netherlands their due, for a time allowed them at least the semblance of getting their wishes. But when Charles's sister, Mary of Hungary, succeeded Margaret as regent, she was too entirely de-

Margaret of Austria Regent, 1522–31

pendent on her brother, and he too determined to consult larger than Burgundian interests, to allow the Netherlands more than the smallest weight in larger plans. The most that she could do was to unify, centralize and add to the provinces, and to get what commercial advantages treaties could secure. Thus, she redeemed Luxemburg from the Margrave of Baden to whom Maximilian had pawned it. Thus, also, she negotiated fresh commercial treaties with England and unified the coinage. But with all these achievements, distinctly advantageous to the people she governed, her efforts to increase the power of the crown and the necessity she was under of subordinating her policy to that of Germany and Spain, made her extremely unpopular.

The relationship of the Netherlands to the Empire was a delicate and important question. Though the Empire was the feudal suzerain of most of the Burgundian provinces, Charles felt far more keenly for his rights as an hereditary, local prince than for the aggrandizement of his Empire, and therefore tried, especially after he had left Austria to his brother Ferdinand, to loosen rather than to strengthen the bond. Even as early as 1512, when the Imperial Diet demanded that the "common penny" be levied in the Netherlands, Charles's council aided and abetted his Burgundian subjects in refusing to pay it. In 1530 the Netherlands, in spite of urgent complaints from the Diet, completely freed itself from imperial jurisdiction in the administration of justice. Matters became still more complicated when Utrecht, Friesland, Groningen and Guelders, formerly belonging to the Westphalian district of the Empire, were annexed by Charles as Burgundian prince. Probably he would not have been able to vindicate these acts of power, had not his victory at Mühlberg freed him from the re-

September 7, 1522

1547

straints of the imperial constitution. A convention was made at the next Diet of Augsburg, providing that henceforth the Netherlands should form a separate district, the "Burgundian circle," of the Empire, and that their prince, as such, should be represented in the Diet and in the Imperial Supreme Court. Taxes were so apportioned that in time of peace the Netherlands should contribute to the imperial treasury as much as did two electors, and in time of war as much as three. This treaty nominally added to the Empire two new counties, Flanders and Artois, and it gave the whole Netherlands the benefit of imperial protection. But, though ratified by the States General promptly, the convention remained almost a dead letter, and left the Netherlands virtually autonomous. As long as they were unmolested the Netherlands forgot their union entirely, and when, under the pressure of Spanish rule, they later remembered and tried to profit by it, they found that the Empire had no wish to revive it.

Convention of June 26, 1548

The general causes of the religious revolution were the same in the Low Countries as in other lands. The ground was prepared by the mystics of the earlier ages, by the corruption of and hatred for the clergy, and by the Renaissance. The central situation of the country made it especially open to all currents of European thought. Printing was early introduced from Germany and expanded so rapidly in these years that no less than fifty new publishing houses were erected. As Antwerp was the most cosmopolitan of cities, so Erasmus was the most nearly the citizen of the world in that era. The great humanist, who did so much to prepare for the Reformation, spent in his native land just those early years of its first appearance when he most favored Luther.

Reformation

1525–55

A group to take up with the Wittenberg professor's doctrines were the Augustinians, many of whom had been in close relations with the Saxon friaries. One of them, James Probst, had been prior of Wittenberg where he learned to know Luther well and when he became prior of the convent at Antwerp he started a rousing propaganda in favor of the reform. Another Augustinian, Henry of Zütphen, made his friary at Dordrecht the center of a Lutheran movement. Hoen at the Hague, Hinne Rode at Utrecht, Gerard Lister at Zwolle, Melchior Miritzsch at Ghent, were soon in correspondence with Luther and became missionaries of his faith. His books, which circulated among the learned in Latin, were some of them translated into Dutch as early as 1520.

1515

1518

The German commercial colony at Antwerp was another channel for the infiltration of the Lutheran gospel. The many travelers, among them Albert Dürer, brought with them tidings of the revolt and sowed its seeds in the soil of Flanders and Holland. Singularly enough, the colony of Portuguese Jews, the Marranos as they were called, became, if not converts, at least active agents in the dissemination of Lutheran works.

1520–1

Catholic answers

A vigorous counter-propaganda was at once started by the partisans of the pope. This was directed against both Erasmus and Luther and consisted largely, according to the reports of the former, in the most violent invective. Nicholas of Egmont, "a man with a white pall but a black heart" stormed in the pulpit against the new heretics. Another man interspersed a sermon on charity with objurgations against those whom he called "geese, asses, stocks, and Antichrists." One Dominican said he wished he could fasten his teeth in Luther's throat, for he would not fear to go to the Lord's supper with that blood on his

1533

mouth. It was at Antwerp, a little later, that were first coined, or at least first printed, the so celebrated epigrams that Erasmus was Luther's father, that Erasmus had laid the eggs and Luther had hatched the chickens, and that Luther, Zwingli, Oecolampadius and Erasmus were the four soldiers who had crucified Christ.

The principal literary opposition to the new doctrines came from the University of Louvain. Luther's works were condemned by Cologne, and this sentence was ratified by Louvain. A number of the leading professors wrote against him, among them the ex-professor Adrian of Utrecht, recently created Bishop of Tortosa and cardinal, and soon to be pope.

August 30, 1519

November 7

The conservatives, however, could do little but scold until the arrival of Charles V in June 1520, and of the papal nuncio Aleander in September. The latter saw Charles immediately at Antwerp and found him already determined to resist heresy. Acting under the edict procured at that time, though not published until the following March 22, Aleander busied himself by going around and burning Lutheran works in various cities and preaching against the heresy. He found far more opposition than one would think probable, and the burning of the books, as Erasmus said, removed them from the bookstores only, not from the hearts of the people. The nuncio even discovered, he said, at this early date, heretics who denied the real presence in the eucharist: evidently independent spirits like Hoen who anticipated the doctrine later taken up by Carlstadt and Zwingli.

October, 1520

The validity of the Edict of Worms was affirmed for the Burgundian provinces. The edict was read publicly at Antwerp while four hundred of Luther's books were burnt, three hundred confiscated from the shops and one hundred brought by the people.

July 13, 1521

Whereas spiritual officers were at first employed, civil magistrates now began to act against the innovators. In the beginning, attention was paid to municipal privileges, but these soon came to be disregarded, and resistance on any pretext was treated as rebellion and treason. The first persons to be arrested were the Prior of Antwerp, Probst, who recanted, but later escaped and relapsed, and two other intimate friends of Erasmus.

1522

The Inquisition

Charles wished to introduce the Spanish inquisition, but his councillors were all against it. Under a different name, however, it was exactly imitated when Francis van der Hulst was appointed chief inquisitor by the state, and was confirmed by a bull of Adrian VI. The original inquisitorial powers of the bishops remained, and a supreme tribunal of three judges was appointed in 1524.

April 23, 1522

June 1, 1523

Martyrs, July 1, 1523

The first martyrs, Henry Voes and John Esch of Brussels, said Erasmus, made many Lutherans by their death. Luther wrote a hymn on the subject and published an open letter to the Christians of the Netherlands. Censorship of the press was established in Holland in vain, for everything goes to show that Lutheranism rapidly increased. Popular interest in the subject seemed to be great. Every allusion to ecclesiastical corruption in speeches or in plays was applauded. Thirty-eight laborers were arrested at Antwerp for assembling to read and discuss the gospel. Iconoclastic outbreaks occurred in which crucifixes were desecrated. In the same year an Italian in Antwerp wrote that though few people were openly Lutheran many were secretly so, and that he had been assured by leading citizens that if the revolting peasants of Germany approached Antwerp, twenty thousand armed men would rise in the city to assist them. When a Lutheran was drowned in the Scheldt,

1524

1525

July 31

the act precipitated a riot. In 1527 the English ambassador wrote Wolsey from the Netherlands that two persons out of three "kept Luther's opinions," and that while the English New Testament was being printed in that city, repeated attempts on his part to induce the magistrates to interfere came to nothing. Protestant works also continued to pour from the presses. The Bible was soon translated into Dutch, and in the course of eight years four editions of the whole Bible and twenty-five editions of the New Testament were called for, though the complete Scriptures had never been printed in Dutch before.

October 14, 1529

Alarmed by the spread of heresy, attributed to too great mildness, the government now issued an edict that inaugurated a reign of terror. Death was decreed not only for all heretics but for all who, not being theologians, discussed articles of faith, or who caricatured God, Mary, or the saints, and for all who failed to denounce heretics known to them. While the government momentarily flattered itself that heresy had been stamped out, at most it had been driven under ground. One of the effects of the persecution was to isolate the Netherlands from the Empire culturally and to some small extent commercially.

Anabaptists

But heresy proved to be a veritable hydra. From one head sprang many daughters, the Anabaptists, harder to deal with than their mother. For while Lutheranism stood essentially for passive obedience, and flourished nowhere save as a state church, Anabaptism was frankly revolutionary and often socialistic. Melchior Hoffmann, the most striking of their early leaders, a fervent and uneducated fanatic, driven from place to place, wandered from Sweden and Denmark to Italy and Spain preaching chiliastic and communistic ideas. Only for three years was he much in the Netherlands, but it was there that he won his greatest suc-

1530–1533

cesses. Appealing, as the Anabaptists always did, to the lower classes, he converted thousands and tens of thousands of the very poor—beggars, laborers and sailors—who passionately embraced the teaching that promised the end of kings and governments and the advent of the "rule of the righteous." Mary of Hungary was not far wrong when she wrote that they planned to plunder all churches, nobles, and wealthy merchants, in short, all who had property, and from the spoil to distribute to every individual according to his need. A new and severer edict would have meant a general massacre, had it been strictly enforced, but another element entered into the situation. The city bourgeoisies that had previously resisted the government, now supported it in this one particular, persecution of the Anabaptists. When at Amsterdam the sectaries rose and very nearly mastered the city, death by fire was decreed for the men, by water for the women. From Antwerp they were banished by a general edict especially aimed at them supplemented by massacres in the northern provinces. After the crisis at Münster, though the Anabaptists continued to be a bugbear to the ruling classes, their propaganda lost its dangerously revolutionary character. Menno Simons of Friesland, after his conversion in 1536, became the leader of the movement and succeeded in gathering the smitten people into a large and harmless body. The Anabaptists furnished, however, more martyrs than did any other sect.

October 7, 1531

1534

June 24, 1535

Lutheranism also continued to spread. The edict of 1540 confesses as much while providing new and sterner penalties against those who even interceded for heretics. The fact is that the inquisition as directed against Lutherans was thoroughly unpopular and was resisted in various provinces on the technical ground of local privileges. The Protestants managed to keep unnoticed amidst a general intention to connive at them, and though they did not usually flinch from martyrdom they did not court it. The inquisitors were obliged to arrest their victims at the dead of night, raiding their houses and hauling them from bed, in order to avoid popular tumult. When Enzinas printed his Spanish Bible at Antwerp the printer told him that in that city the Scriptures had been published in almost every European language, doubtless an exaggeration but a significant one. Arrested and imprisoned at Brussels for this cause, Enzinas received while under duress visits from four hundred citizens of that city who were Protestants. To control the book trade an oath was exacted of every bookseller not to deal in heretical works and the first "Index of prohibited books," drawn up by the University of Louvain, was issued. A censorship of plays was also attempted. This was followed by an edict of 1550 requiring of every person entering the Netherlands a certificate of Catholic belief. As Brabant and Antwerp repudiated a law that would have ruined their trade, it remained, in fact, a dead letter.

1543

1546

Charles's policy of repression had been on the whole a failure, due partly to the cosmopolitan culture of the Netherlands and their commercial position making them open to the importation of ideas as of merchandise from all Europe. It was due in part to the local jealousies and privileges of the separate provinces, and in part to the strength of certain nobles and cities. The persecution, indeed, had a decidedly class character, for the emperor well knew Protestant nobles whom he did not molest, while the poor seldom failed to suffer. And yet Charles had accomplished something. Even the Protestants were loyal, strange to say, to him personally. The number of martyrs in his reign has been estimated at barely one thousand, but it must be remembered that for every one put to death there were a number punished in other ways. And the body of the people was still Catholic, even in the North. It is noteworthy that the most popular writer of this period, as well as the first to use the Dutch tongue with precision and grace, was Anna Bijns, a lay nun, violently anti-Lutheran in sentiment.

Anna Bijns, 1494–1575

§ 2. The Calvinist Revolt

When Charles V, weary of the heaviest scepter ever wielded by any European monarch from Charlemagne to Napoleon, sought rest for his soul in a monk's cell, he left his great possessions divided between his brother Ferdinand and his son Philip. To the former went Austria and the Empire, to the latter the Burgundian provinces and Spain with its vast dependencies in the New World.

Spain and the Netherlands

The result of this was to make the Netherlands practically a satellite of Spain. Hitherto, partly because their interests had largely coincided with those of the Empire, partly because by balancing Germany against Spain they could manage to get their own rights, they had found prosperity and had acquired a good deal of national power. Indeed, with their wealth, their central position, and growing strength as province after province was annexed, and their consciousness that their ruler was a native of Flanders, their pride had been rather gratified than hurt by the knowledge that he possessed far larger dominions. But when Charles, weeping copiously and demanding his subjects' pardon, descended from the throne supported by the young Prince of Orange, and when his son Philip II had replied to his father in Spanish, even those present had an uneasy feeling that the situation had changed for the worse, and that the Netherlands were being handed over from a Burgundian to a Spanish ruler. From

Abdication of Charles

October 25, 1555

this time forth the interests and sentiments of the two countries became more and more sharply divergent, and, as the smaller was sacrificed to the larger, a conflict became inevitable. The revolt that followed within ten years after Philip had permanently abandoned the Netherlands to make his home in Spain was first and foremost a nationalist revolt. Contrasted with the particularistic uprising of 1477 it evinced the enormous growth, in the intervening century, of a national self-consciousness in the Seventeen Provinces.

1559

Religious issue

But though the catastrophe was apparently inevitable from political grounds, it was greatly complicated and intensified by the religious issue. Philip was determined, as he himself said, either to bring the Netherlands back to the fold of Rome or "so to waste their land that neither the natives could live there nor should any thereafter desire the place for habitation." And yet the means he took were even for his purpose the worst possible, a continual vacillation between timid indulgence and savage cruelty. Though he insisted that his ministers should take no smallest step without his sanction, he could never make up his mind what to do, waited too long to make a decision and then, with fatal fatuity, made the wrong one.

Calvinism

At the same time the people were coming under the spell of a new and to the government more dangerous form of Protestantism. Whereas the Lutherans had stood for passive obedience and the Anabaptists for revolutionary communism, the Calvinists appealed to the independent middle classes and gave them not only the enthusiasm to endure martyrdom but also—what the others had lacked—the will and the power to resist tyranny by force. Calvin's polity, as worked out in Geneva, was a subordination of the state to the church. His reforms were thorough and consciously social and political. Calvinism in all lands aroused republican passions and excited rebellion against the powers that be. This feature was the more prominent in the Netherlands in that its first missionaries were French exiles who irrigated the receptive soil of the Low Countries with doctrines subversive of church and state alike. The intercourse with England, partly through the emigration from that land under Mary's reign, partly through the coming and going of Flemings and Walloons, also opened doors to Protestant doctrine.

1545

At first the missionaries came secretly, preaching to a few specially invited to some private house or inn. People attended these meetings disguised and after dark. First mentioned in the edict of 1550, nine years later the Calvinists drew up a *Confessio Belgica,* as a sign and an aid to union. Calvin's French writings could be read in the southern provinces in the original. Though as early as 1560 some nobles had been converted, the new religion undoubtedly made its strongest appeal, as a contemporary put it, "to those who had grown rich by trade and were therefore ready for revolution." It was among the merchants of the great cities that it took strongest root and from the middle class spread to the laborers; influenced not only by the example of their masters, but sometimes also by the policy of Protestant employers to give work only to co-religionists. In a short time it had won a very considerable success, though perhaps not the actual majority of the population. Many of the poor, hitherto Anabaptists, thronged to it in hopes of social betterment. Many adventurers with no motive but to stir the waters in which they might fish joined the new party. But on the whole, as its appeal was primarily moral and religious, its constituency was the more substantial, progressive, and intelligent part of the community.

The greatest weakness of the Protestants was their

division. Lutheran, Calvinist, and Anabaptist continued to compete for the leadership and hated each other cordially. The Calvinists themselves were divided into two parties, the "Rekkelijken" or "Compromisers" and the "Preciesen" or "Stalwarts." Moreover there were various other shades of opinion, not amounting quite to new churches. The pure Erasmians, under Cassander, advocated tolerance. More pronounced was the movement of Dirck Volckertszoon Coornheert a merchant of Amsterdam who, in addition to advising his followers to dissimulate their views rather than to court martyrdom, rejected the Calvinist dogma of predestination and tried to lay the emphasis in religion on the spirit of Jesus rather than on either dogma or ritual.

Coornheert, 1522–90

Though the undertow was slowly but surely carrying the Low Countries adrift from Spain, for the moment their new monarch, then at the age of twenty-eight, seemed to have the winds and waves of politics all in his favor. He was at peace with France; he had nothing to fear from Germany; his marriage with Mary of England made that country, always the best trader with the Netherlands, an ally. His first steps were to relieve Mary of Hungary of her regency and to give it to Emanuel Philibert, to issue a new edict against heresy and to give permission to the Jesuits to enter the Low Countries.

1556

The chief difficulties were financial. The increase in the yield of the taxes in the reign of Charles had been from 1,500,000 guilders [1] to 7,000,000 guilders. In addition to this, immense loans had exhausted the credit of the government. The royal domain was mortgaged. As the floating debt of the Provinces rose rapidly the

[1] The guilder, also called the "Dutch pound," at this time was worth 40 cents intrinsically. Money had many times the purchasing power that it has in 1920.

government was in need of a grant to keep up the army. The only way to meet the situation was to call the States General. When they met, they complained that they were taxed more heavily than Spain and demanded the removal of the Spanish troops, a force already so unpopular that William of Orange refused to take command of it. In presenting their several grievances one province only, Holland, mentioned the religious question to demand that the powers of the inquisitors be curtailed. To obtain funds Philip was obliged to promise, against his will, to withdraw the soldiers. This was only done, under pressure, on January 10, 1561.

March, 1556

1559

Philip had left the Netherlands professing his intention of returning, but hoping and resolving in his heart never to do so. His departure made easier the unavoidable breach, but the struggle had already begun. Wishing to leave a regent of royal blood Philip appointed Margaret of Parma, a natural daughter of Charles V. Born in 1522, she had been married at the age of fourteen to Alexander de' Medici, a nephew of Clement VII; becoming a widow in the following year she was in 1538 married to Ottavio Farnese, a nephew of Paul III, at that time only fourteen years old. Given as her dower the cities of Parma and Piacenza, she had become thoroughly Italian in feeling.

Anthony Perrenot Cardinal Granvelle, 1517–86

To guide her Philip left, besides the Council of State, a special "consulta" or "kitchen cabinet" of three members, the chief of whom was Granvelle. The real fatherland of this native of the Free County of Burgundy was the court. As a passionate servant of the crown and a clever and knowing diplomat, he was in constant correspondence with Philip, recommending measures over the head of Margaret. His acts made her intensely unpopular and her attempts to coax and cozen public opinion only aroused suspicion.

Egmont, 1522–68

Three members in the Council of State, Granvelle and two others, were partisans of the crown; three other members may be said to represent the people. One of them was Lamoral Count of Egmont, the most brilliant and popular of the high nobility. Though a favorite of Charles V on account of his proved ability as a soldier, his frankness and generosity, he was neither a sober nor a weighty statesman. The popular proverb, "Egmont for action and Orange for counsel," well characterized the difference between the two leading members of the Council of State. William, Prince of Orange, lacking the brilliant qualities of Egmont, far surpassed him in acumen and in strength of character. From his father, William Count of Nassau-Dillenburg, he inherited important estates in Germany near the Netherlands, and by the death of a cousin he became, at the age of eleven, Prince of Orange—a small, independent territory in southern France—and Lord of Breda and Gertruidenberg in Holland. With an income of 150,000 guilders per annum he was by far the richest man in the Netherlands, Egmont coming next with an income of 62,000. William was well educated. Though he spoke seven languages and was an eloquent orator, he was called "the Silent" because of the rare discretion that never revealed a secret nor spoke an imprudent word. In religion he was indifferent, being first a Catholic, then a Lutheran, then a Calvinist, and always a man of the world. His broad tolerance found its best, or only, support in the Erasmian tendencies of Coornheert. His second wife, Anne of Saxony, having proved unfaithful to him, he married, while she was yet alive, Charlotte of Bourbon. This act, like the bigamy of Philip of Hesse, was approved by Protestant divines. Behind them Egmont and Orange had the hearty support of the patriotic and well educated native nobility.

William the Silent, 1533–84

The rising generation of the aristocracy saw only the bad side of the reign of Charles; they had not shared in his earlier victories but had witnessed his failure to conquer either France or Protestantism.

New bishoprics

In order to deal more effectively with the religious situation Granvelle wished to bring the ecclesiastical territorial divisions into harmony with the political. Hitherto the Netherlands had been partly under the Archbishop of Cologne, partly under the Archbishop of Rheims. But as these were both foreigners Granvelle applied for and secured a bull creating fourteen new bishoprics and three archbishoprics, Cambrai, Utrecht, and Malines, of which the last held the primacy. His object was doubtless in large part to facilitate the extirpation of heresy, but it was also significant as one more instance of the nationalization of the church, a tendency so strong that neither Catholic nor Protestant countries escaped from it. In this case all the appointments were to be made by the king with consent of the pope. The people resented the autocratic features of a plan they might otherwise have approved; a cry was raised throughout the provinces that their freedom was infringed upon, and that the plan furnished a new instrument to the hated inquisition.

March 12, 1559

February, 1561

Granvelle, more than ever detested when he received the cardinal's hat, was dubbed "the red devil," "the archrascal," "the red dragon," "the Spanish swine," "the pope's dung." In July Egmont and Orange sent their resignations from the Council of State to Philip, saying that they could no longer share the responsibility for Granvelle's policy, especially as everything was done behind their backs. Philip, however, was slow to take alarm. For the moment his attention was taken up with the growth of the Huguenot party in France and his efforts centered on helping the French Catholics against them. But the Netherlands were importunate. In voicing the wishes of the people the province of Brabant, with the capital, Brussels, the metropolitan see, Malines, and the university, Louvain, took as decided a lead as the Parlement of Paris did in France. The estates of Brabant demanded that Orange be made their governor. The nobles began to remember that they were legally a part of the Empire. The marriage of Orange, on August 26, 1561, with the Lutheran Anne of Saxony, was but one sign of the *rapprochement.* Though the prince continued to profess Catholicism, he entertained many Lutherans and emphasized as far as possible his position as vassal of the Empire. Philip, indeed, believed that the whole trouble came from the wounded vanity of a few nobles.

1561 But Granvelle saw deeper. When the Estates of Brabant stopped the payment of the principal tax or "Bede,"[1] and when the people of Brussels took as a party uniform a costume derived from the carnival, a black cloak covered with red fool's heads, the cardinal, whose red hat was caricatured thereby, stated that nothing less than a republic was aimed at. This was true, though in the anticipation of the nobles, at least, the republic should have a decidedly aristocratic character. But Granvelle had no policy to propose but repression. In order to prevent condemned heretics from preaching and singing on the scaffold a gag was put into their mouths. How futile a measure! The Calvinists no longer disguised, but armed—a new and significant fact—thronged to their conventicles. Emigration continued on a large scale. By 1556 it was estimated that thirty thousand Protestants from the Low Countries were settled in or near London. Elizabeth encouraged them to come, assigning them

[1] The word, meaning "prayer," indicated, like the English "benevolence" and the French "don gratuit," that the tax had once been voluntarily granted.

Norwich as a place of refuge. She also began to tax imports from the Netherlands, a blow to which Philip replied by forbidding all English imports.

1563

Revolt

Hitherto the resistance to the government had been mostly passive and constitutional. But from 1565 may be dated the beginning of the revolt that did not cease until it had freed the northern provinces forever from Spanish tyranny. The rise of the Dutch Republic is one of the most inspiring pages in history. Superficially it has many points of resemblance with the American War of Independence. In both there was the absentee king, the national hero, the local jealousies of the several provinces, the economic grievances, the rising national feeling and even the religious issue, though this had become very small in America. But the difference was in the ferocity of the tyranny and the intensity of the struggle. The two pictures are like the same landscape as it might be painted by Millet and by Turner: the one is decent and familiar, the other lurid and ghastly. With true Anglo-Saxon moderation the American war was fought like a game or an election, with humanity and attention to rules; but in Holland and Belgium was enacted the most terrible frightfulness in the world; over the whole land, mingled with the reek of candles carried in procession and of incense burnt to celebrate a massacre, brooded the sultry miasma of human blood and tears. On the one side flashed the savage sword of Alva and the pitiless flame of the inquisitor Tapper; on the other were arrayed, behind their dykes and walls, men resolved to win that freedom which alone can give scope and nobility to life.

The Intellectuals

And in the melée those suffered most who would fain have been bystanders, the humanists. Persecuted by both sides, the intellectuals, who had once deserted the Reform now turned again to it as the lesser of the two evils. They would have been glad to make terms with any church that would have left them in liberty, but they found the whips of Calvin lighter than the scorpions of Philip. Even those who, like Van Helmont, wished to defend the church and to reconcile the Tridentine decrees with philosophy, found that their labors brought them under suspicion and that what the church demanded was not harmony of thought but abnegation of it.

The Compromise, 1565

The first act of the revolt may be said to be a secret compact, known as the Compromise, originally entered into by twenty nobles at Brussels and soon joined by three hundred other nobles elsewhere. The document signed by them denounced the Edicts as surpassing the greatest recorded barbarity of tyrants and as threatening the complete ruin of the country. To resist them the signers promised each other mutual support. In this as in subsequent developments the Calvinist minority took the lead, but was supported by strong Catholic forces. Among the latter was the Prince of Orange, not yet a Protestant. His conversion really made little difference in his program; both before and after it he wanted tolerance or reconciliation on Cassander's plan of compromise. He would have greatly liked to have seen the Peace of Augsburg, now the public law of the Empire, extended to the Low Countries, but this was made difficult even to advocate because the Peace of Augsburg provided liberty only for the Lutheran confession, whereas the majority of Protestants in the Netherlands were now Calvinists. For the same reason little help could be expected from the German princes, for the mutual animosity that was the curse of the Protestant churches prevented their making common cause against the same enemy.

As the Huguenots—for so they began to be called in Brabant as well as in France—were as yet too few to rebel, the only course open was to appeal to the government once more. A petition to make the Edicts milder was presented to Margaret in 1566. One of her advisers bade her not to be afraid of "those beggars." Originating in the scorn of enemies, like so many party names, the epithet "Beggars" (Gueux) presently became the designation, and a proud one, of the nobles who had signed the Compromise, and later of all the rebels.

Encouraged by the regent's apparent lack of power to coerce them, the Calvinist preachers became daily bolder. Once again their religion showed its remarkable powers of organization. Lacking nothing in funds, derived from a constituency of wealthy merchants, the preachers of the Reformation were soon able to forge a machinery of propaganda and party action that stood them in good stead against the greater numbers of their enemies. Especially in critical times, discipline, unity, and enthusiasm make headway against the deadly hatred of enemies and the deadlier apathy and timidity of the mass of mankind. It is true that the methods of the preachers often aroused opposition.

Iconoclasm

The zeal of the Calvinists, inflamed by oppression and encouraged by the weakness of the government, burst into an iconoclastic riot, first among the unemployed at Armentières, but spreading rapidly to Antwerp, Brussels, Ghent, and then to the northern provinces, Holland and Zeeland. The English agent at Brussels wrote: "Coming into Oure Lady Church, yt looked like hell wher were above 1000 torches brannyng and syche a noise as yf heven and erth had gone together with fallyng of images and fallyng down of costly works." Books and manuscripts as well as pictures were destroyed. The cry "Long live the Beggars" resounded from one end of the land to the

August 11, 1566

other. But withal there was no pillage and no robbery. The gold in the churches was left untouched. Margaret feared a *jacquerie* but, lacking troops, had to look on with folded hands at least for the moment. By chance there arrived just at this time an answer from Philip to the earlier petition of the Beggars. The king promised to abolish the Spanish inquisition and to soften the edicts. Freedom of conscience was tacitly granted, but the government made an exception, as soon as it dared, of those who had committed sacrilege in the recent riots. These men were outlawed.

Civil war

No longer fearing a religious war the Calvinists started it themselves. Louis of Nassau, a brother of Prince William, hired German mercenaries and invaded Flanders, where he won some slight successes. In Amsterdam the great Beggar Brederode entered into negotiations with Huguenots and English friends. The first battle between the Beggars and the government troops, near Antwerp, ended in a rout for the former.

March 13, 1567

Philip now ordered ten thousand Spanish veterans, led by Alva, to march from Italy to the Netherlands. Making their way through the Free County of Burgundy and Lorraine they entered Brussels on August 9, 1567. Ferdinand Alvarez de Toledo, Duke of Alva, had won experience and reputation as a soldier in the German wars. Though self-controlled and courtly in manner, his passionate patriotism and bigotry made him a fit instrument to execute Philip's orders to make the Netherlands Spanish and Catholic. He began with no uncertain hand, building forts at Antwerp and quartering his troops at Brussels where their foreign manners and Roman piety gave offence to the citizens. On September 9 he arrested the counts of Egmont and Horn, next to Orange the chief leaders of the patriotic party. Setting up a tribunal, called the Council of

Alva 1508–83

Troubles, to deal with cases of rebellion and heresy, he inaugurated a reign of terror. He himself spent seven hours a day in this court trying cases and signing death-warrants. Not only heretics were punished but also agitators and those who had advocated tolerance. Sincere Catholics, indeed, noted that the crime of heresy was generally the mere pretext for dealing with patriots and all those obnoxious to the government.

Executions

For the first time we have definite statistics of the numbers executed. For instance, on January 4, 1568, 48 persons were sentenced to death, on February 20, 37; on February 21, 71; on March 20, 55; and so on for day after day, week in and week out. On March 3 at the same hour throughout the whole land 1500 men were executed. The total number put to death during the six years of Alva's administration has been variously estimated at from 6,000 to 18,000. The lower number is probably nearer the truth, though not high enough. Emigration on a hitherto unknown scale within the next thirty or forty years carried 400,000 persons from the Netherlands. Thousands of others fled to the woods and became freebooters. The people as a whole were prostrated with terror. The prosperity of the land was ruined by the wholesale confiscations of goods. Alva boasted that by such means he had added to the revenues of his territories 500,000 ducats per annum.

William of Orange retired to his estates at Dillenburg not to yield to the tyrant but to find a *point d'appui* from which to fight. Wishing to avoid anything that might cause division among the people he kept the religious issue in the background and complained only of foreign tyranny. He tried to enlist the sympathies of the Emperor Maximilian II and to collect money and men. William's friend Villiers invaded the Burgundian State near Maastricht and Louis of Nassau marched with troops into Friesland. By this time Alva had increased his army by 10,000 German cavalry and both the rebel leaders were severely defeated.

April, 1568

This triumph was followed by an act of power and defiance on Alva's part sometimes compared to the execution of Louis XVI by the French Republicans. Hitherto the sufferers from his reign of blood had not in any case been men of the highest rank. The first execution of nobles took place at Brussels on June 1, that of the captured Villiers followed on June 2, and that of Egmont and Horn on June 5.

Orange himself now took the field with 25,000 troops, a motley aggregate of French, Flemish, and Walloon Huguenots and of German mercenaries. But he had no genius for war to oppose to the veterans of Alva. Continually harassed by the Spaniards he was kept in fear for his communications, dared not risk a general engagement and was humiliated by seeing his retreat, in November, turned into a rout.

July 16, 1570

Finding that severity did not pacify the provinces, Alva issued a proclamation that on the face of it was a general amnesty with pardon for all who submitted. But he excepted by name several hundred emigrants, all the Protestant clergy, all who had helped them, all iconoclasts, all who had signed petitions for religious liberty, and all who had rebelled. As these exceptions included the greater portion of those who stood in need of pardon the measure proved illusory as a means of reconciliation. Coupled with it were other measures, including the prohibition to subjects to attend foreign universities, intended to put a check on free trade in ideas.

Taxation

Alva's difficulties and the miseries of the unhappy land entrusted to his tender mercies were increased by want of money. Notwithstanding the privilege of

March 21, 1569

granting their own taxes the States General were summoned and forced to accept new imposts of one per cent. on all property real and personal, ten per cent. on the sale of all movable goods and five per cent. on the sale of real estate. These were Spanish taxes, exorbitant in any case but absolutely ruinous to a commercial people. A terrible financial panic followed. Houses at Antwerp that had rented for 300 gulden could now be had for 50 gulden. Imports fell off to such an extent that at this port they yielded but 14,000 gulden per annum instead of 80,000 as formerly. The harbor was filled with empty boats; the market drugged with goods of all sorts that no one would buy.

Beggars of the Sea

The cause of the patriots looked hopeless. Orange, discredited by defeat, had retired to Germany. At one time, to avoid the clamors of his troops for pay, he was obliged to flee by night from Strassburg. But in this dark hour help came from the sea. Louis of Nassau, not primarily a statesman like his brother but a passionate crusader for Protestantism, had been at La Rochelle and had there seen the excellent work done by privateers. In emulation of his French brethren he granted letters of marque to the sailors of Holland and Zeeland. Recruits thronged to the ships, Huguenots, men from Liège, and the laborers of the Walloon provinces thrown out of work by the commercial crisis. These men promptly won striking successes in preying on Spanish commerce. Their many and rich prizes were taken to England or to Emden and sold. Often they landed on the coasts and attacked small Catholic forces, or murdered priests. On the night of March 31–April 1, 1572, these Beggars of the Sea seized the small town of Brielle on a large island at the mouth of the Meuse not far from the Hague. This success was immediately followed by the insurrection of Rotterdam and Flushing. The war was conducted with combined heroism and frightfulness. Receiving no quarter the Beggars gave none, and to avenge themselves on the unspeakable wrongs committed by Alva they themselves at times massacred the innocent. But their success spread like wildfire. The coast towns "fell away like beads from a rosary when one is gone." Fortifications in all of them were strengthened and, where necessary, dykes were opened. Reinforcements also came from England.

Revolution

By this time the revolt had become a veritable revolution. It found its battle hymn in the Wilhelmuslied and its Washington in William of Orange. As all the towns of Holland save Amsterdam were in his hands, in June the provincial Estates met—albeit illegally, for there was no one authorized to convene them—assumed sovereign power and made William their Statholder. They voted large taxes and forced loans from rich citizens, and raised money from the sale of prizes taken at sea. All defect in prescriptive and legal power was made up by the popularity of the prince, deeply loved by all classes, not only on account of his affability to all, even the humblest, but still more because of confidence in his ability. Never did his versatility, patience and skill in management shine more brightly. Among the troops raised by the patriots he kept strict discipline, thus making by contrast more lurid the savage pillage by the Spaniards. He kept far from fanatics and swashbucklers of whom there were plenty attracted to the revolt. His master idea was to keep the Netherlands together and to free them from the foreigner. Complete independence of Spain was not at first planned, but it soon became inevitable.

For a moment there was a prospect of help from Coligny's policy of prosecuting a war with Spain, but these hopes were destroyed by the defeat of the French Huguenots near Mons and by the massacre of Saint

July 17, 1572

August 24, 1572

Bartholomew. Freed from menace in this quarter and encouraged by his brilliant victory, Alva turned north with an army now increased to 40,000 veterans. First he took Malines and delivered it to his soldiers for "the most dreadful and inhuman sack of the day" as a contemporary wrote. The army then marched to Guelders and stormed Zutphen under express orders from their general "not to leave one man alive or one building unburnt." "With the help of God," as Alva piously reported, the same punishment was meted out to Naarden. Then he marched to the still royalist Amsterdam from which base he proceeded to invest Haarlem. The siege was a long and hard one for the Spaniards, harassed by the winter weather and by epidemics. Alva wrote Philip that it was "the bloodiest war known for long years" and begged for reinforcements. At last famine overcame the brave defenders of the city and it capitulated. Finding that his cruelty had only nerved the people to the most desperate resistance, and wishing to give an example of clemency to a city that would surrender rather than await storming, Alva contented himself with putting to death to the last man 2300 French, English, and Walloon soldiers of the garrison, and five or six citizens. He also demanded a ransom of 100,000 dollars [1] in lieu of plunder. Not content with this meager largess the Spanish troops mutinied, and only the promise of further cities to sack quieted them. The fortunes of the patriots were a little raised by the defeat of the Spanish fleet in the Zuiderzee by the Beggars on October 12, 1573.

July 12, 1573

Requesens

For some time Philip had begun to suspect that Alva's methods were not the proper ones to win back the affectionate loyalty of his people. Though he hesitated long he finally removed him late in 1573 and

[1] The dollar, or Thaler, is worth 75 cents, intrinsically.

appointed in his stead Don Louis Requesens. Had Philip come himself he might have been able to do something, for the majority professed personal loyalty to him, and in that age, as Shakespeare reminds us, divinity still hedged a king. But not having the decision to act in person Philip picked out a favorite, known from his constant attendance on his master as "the king's hour-glass," in whom he saw the slavishly obedient tool that he thought he wanted. The only difference between the new governor and the old was that Requesens lacked Alva's ability; he had all the other's narrowly Spanish views, his bigotry and absolutism.

Once arrived in the provinces committed to his charge, he had no choice but to continue the war. But on January 27, 1574, Orange conquered Middelburg and from that date the Spanish flag ceased to float over any portion of the soil of Holland or Zeeland. In open battle at Mook, however, the Spanish veterans again achieved success, defeating the patriots under Louis of Nassau, who lost his life. The beginning of the year saw the investment of Leyden in great force. The heroism of the defence has become proverbial. When, in September, the dykes were cut to admit the sea, so that the vessels of the Beggars were able to sail to the relief of the city, the siege was raised. It was the first important military victory for the patriots and marks the turning-point of the revolt. Henceforth the Netherlands could not be wholly subdued.

April 14, 1574

Requesens summoned the States General and offered a pardon to all who would submit. But the people saw in this only a sign of weakness. A flood of pamphlets calling to arms replied to the advances of the government. Among the pamphleteers the ablest was Philip van Marnix, a Calvinist who turned his powers of satire against Spain and the Catholic

Marnix, 1538–98

church. William of Orange, now a Protestant, living at Delft, inspired the whole movement. Requesens, believing that if he were out of the way the revolt would collapse, like Alva offered public rewards for his assassination. That there was really no common ground was proved at a conference between the two foes, broken off without result. In the campaign of 1575 the Spanish army again achieved great things, taking Oudewater, Schoonhoven and other places. But the rebels would not give up.

March 5, 1576

The situation was changed by the death of Requesens. Before his successor could be appointed events moved rapidly. After taking Zierikzee on June 29, the Spanish army turned to Aalst, quartered the soldiers on the inhabitants, and forced the loyal city to pay the full costs of their maintenance. If even the Catholics were alienated by this, the Protestants went so far as to preach that any Spaniard might be murdered without sin. In the concerted action against Spain the Estates of Brabant now took the leading part; meeting at Brussels they intimidated the Council of State and raised an army of 3000 men. By this time Holland and Zeeland were to all intents and purposes an independent state. The Calvinists, strong among the native population, were recruited by a vast influx of immigrants from other provinces until theirs became the dominant religion. Holland and Zeeland pursued a separate military and financial policy. Alone among the provinces they were prosperous, for they had command of the rich sea-borne commerce.

The growth of republican theory kept pace with the progress of the revolt. Orange was surrounded by men holding the free principles of Duplessis-Mornay and corresponding with him. Dutchmen now openly voiced their belief that princes were made for the sake of their subjects and not subjects for the sake of princes. Even though they denied the equal rights of the common people they asserted the sovereignty of the representative assembly. The Council of State, having assumed the authority of the viceroy during the interim, was deluged with letters petitioning them to shake off the Spanish yoke entirely. But, as the Council still remained loyal to Philip, on September 4 its members were arrested, a *coup d'état* planned in the interests of Orange and doubtless with his knowledge. It was, of course, tantamount to treason. The Estates General now seized sovereign powers. Still protesting their loyalty to the monarch's person and to the Catholic religion, they demanded virtual independence and the withdrawal of the Spanish troops. To enforce their demands they collected an army and took possession of several forts. But the Spanish veterans never once thought of giving way. Gathering at Antwerp where they were besieged by the soldiers of the States General, they attacked and scattered the bands sent against them and then proceeded to sack Antwerp like a captured town. In one dreadful day 7000 of the patriots, in part soldiers, in part noncombatants, perished. The wealth of the city was looted. The army of occupation boasted as of a victory of this deed of blood, known to the Netherlanders as "the Spanish fury."

November 4, 1576

Naturally, such a blow only welded the provinces more firmly together and steeled their temper to an even harder resistance. Its immediate result was a treaty, known as the Pacification of Ghent, between the provinces represented in the States General on the one hand and Holland and Zeeland on the other, for the purposes of union and of driving out the foreigner. The religious question was left undecided, save that the northern provinces agreed to do nothing for the present against the Roman church. But, as heretofore, the Calvinists, now inscribing "Pro fide et patria" on their banners, were the more active and patriotic party.

Don John, 1547–78

On May 1, 1577, the new Governor General, Don John of Austria, entered Brussels. A natural son of Charles V, at the age of twenty-four he had made himself famous by the naval victory of Lepanto, and his name still more celebrated in popular legend on account of his innumerable amours. That he had some charm of manner must be assumed; that he had ability in certain directions cannot be denied; but his aristocratic hauteur, his contempt for a nation of merchants and his disgust at dealing with them, made him the worst possible person for the position of Governor. Philip's detailed instructions left nothing to the imagination: the gist of them was to assure the Catholic religion and obedience of his subjects "as far as possible," to speak French, and not to take his mistresses from the most influential families, nor to alienate them in any other way. After force had been tried and failed the effect of gentleness was to be essayed. Don John was to be a dove of peace and an angel of love.

But even if a far abler man had been sent to heal the troubles in the Netherlands, the breach was now past mending. In the States General, as in the nation at large, there were still two parties, one for Orange and one for Philip, but both were determined to get rid of the devilish incubus of the Spanish army. The division of the two parties was to some extent sectional, but still more that class division that seems inevitable between conservatives and liberals. The king still had for him the clergy, the majority of the nobles and higher bourgeoisie; with William were ranged the Calvinists, the middle and lower classes and most of the "intellectuals," lawyers, men of learning and those publicists known as the "monarchomachs." Many of these were still Catholics who wished to distinguish sharply between the religious and the national issue. At the very moment of Don John's arrival the Estates passed a resolution to uphold the Catholic faith.

February, 1577

Even before he had entered his capital Don John issued the "Perpetual Edict" agreeing to withdraw the Spanish troops in return for a grant of 600,000 guilders for their pay. He promised to respect the privileges of the provinces and to free political prisoners, including the son of Orange. In April the troops really withdrew. The small effect of these measures of conciliation became apparent when the Estates General voted by a majority of one only to recognize Don John as their Statholder. So little influence did he have that he felt more like a prisoner than a governor; he soon fled from his capital to the fortress of Namur whence he wrote urging his king to send back the troops at once and let him "bathe in the blood of the traitors."

May 12

William was as much pleased as John was enraged at the failure of the policy of reconciliation. While the majority of the Estates still hoped for peace William was determined on independence at all costs. In August he sent a demand to the representatives to do their duty by the people, for he did not doubt that they had the right to depose the tyrant. Never did his prospects look brighter. Help was offered by Elizabeth and the tide of republican feeling began to rise higher. In proportion as the laborers were drawn to the party of revolt did the doctrine of the monarchomachs become liberal. No longer satisfied with the democracy of corporations and castes of the Middle Ages, the people began to dream of the individualistic democracy of modern times.

The executive power, virtually abandoned by Don John, now became centered in a Committee of Eighteen, nominally on fortifications, but in reality, like the French Committee of Public Safety, supreme in all matters. This body was first appointed by the citizens of Brussels, but the States General were helpless against it. It was supported by the armed force of the patriots and by the personal prestige of Orange. His power was growing, for, with the capitulation of the Spanish garrison at Utrecht he had been appointed Statholder of that province. When he entered Brussels on September 23, he was received with the wild acclamations of the populace. Opposition to him seemed impossible. And yet, even at this high-water mark of his power, his difficulties were considerable. Each province was jealous of its rights and, as in the American Revolution, each province wished to contribute as little as possible to the common fund. Moreover, the religious question was still extremely delicate. Orange's permission to the Catholics to celebrate their rites on his estates alienated as many Protestant fanatics as it conciliated those of the old religion.

Archduke Matthew

The Netherlands were not yet strong enough to do without powerful foreign support, nor was public opinion yet ripe for the declaration of an independent republic. Feeling that a statholder of some sort was necessary, the States General petitioned Philip to remove Don John and to appoint a legitimate prince of the blood. This petition was perhaps intentionally impossible of fulfilment in a way agreeable to Philip, for he had no legitimate brother or son. But a prince of the House of Hapsburg offered himself in the person of the Archduke Matthew, a son of the Emperor Maximilian, recently deceased. Though he had neither ability of his own nor support from his brother, the Emperor Rudolph II, and though but nineteen years old, he offered his services to the Netherlands and immediately went thither. With high statecraft William

October 12, 1576

drew Matthew into his policy, for he saw that the dangers to be feared were anarchy and disunion. In some cities, notably Ghent, where another Committee of Eighteen was appointed on the Brussels model, the lowest classes assumed a dictatorship analagous to that of the Bolsheviki in Russia. At the same time the Patriots' demand that Orange should be made Governor of Brabant was distasteful to the large loyalist element in the population. William at once saw the use that might be made of Matthew as a figure-head to rally those who still reverenced the house of Hapsburg and who saw in monarchy the only guarantee of order at home and consideration abroad. Promptly arresting the Duke of Aerschot, a powerful noble who tried to use Matthew's name to create a separate faction, Orange induced the States General first to decree Don John an enemy of the country and then to offer the governorship of the Netherlands to the archduke, at the same time begging him, on account of his youth, to leave the administration in the hands of William. After Matthew's entry into Brussels the States General swore allegiance to this puppet in the hands of their greatest statesman.

December 7, 1577

January 18, 1578

Almost immediately the war broke out again. Both sides had been busy raising troops. At Gembloux Don John with 20,000 men defeated about the same number of Patriot troops. But this failed to clarify a situation that tended to become ever more complicated. Help from England and France came in tiny dribblets just sufficient to keep Philip's energies occupied in the cruel civil war. But the vacancy, so to speak, on the ducal throne of the Burgundian state, seemed to invite the candidacy of neighboring princes and a chance of seriously interesting France came when the ambition of Francis, Duke of Anjou, was stirred to become ruler of the Low Countries. William attempted also to make

January 31

use of him. In return for the promise to raise 12,000 troops, Anjou received from the States General the title of "Defender of the Freedom of the Netherlands against the tyranny of the Spaniards and their allies." The result was that the Catholic population was divided in its support between Matthew and Anjou, and that Orange retained the balance of influence.

Protestant schism

The insuperable difficulty in the way of success for the policy of this great man was still the religious one. Calvinism had been largely drawn off to Holland and Zeeland, and Catholicism remained the religion of the great majority of the population in the other provinces. At first sight the latter appeared far from being an intractable force. In contrast with the fiery zeal of the Calvinists on the one hand and of the Spaniards on the other, the faith of the Catholic Flemings and Walloons seemed lukewarm, an old custom rather than a living conviction. Most were shocked by the fanaticism of the Spaniards, who thus proved the worst enemies of their faith, and yet, within the Netherlands, they were very unwilling to see the old religion perish. When the lower classes at Ghent assumed the leadership they rather forced than converted that city to the Calvinist confession. Their acts were taken as a breach of the Pacification of Ghent and threatened the whole policy of Orange by creating fresh discord. To obviate this, William proposed to the States General a religious peace on the basis of the *status quo* with refusal to allow further proselyting. But this measure, acceptable to the Catholics, was deeply resented by the Calvinists. It was said that one who changed his religion as often as his coat must prefer human to divine things and that he who would tolerate Romanists must himself be an atheist.

July, 1578

Division of the Netherlands

It was, therefore, a primarily religious issue, and no difference of race, language or material interest, that divided the Netherlands into two halves. For a time the common hatred of all the people for the foreigner welded them into a united whole; but no sooner was the pressure of the Spanish yoke even slightly relaxed than the mutual antipathy of Calvinist and Catholic showed itself. If we look closely into the causes why the North should become predominantly Protestant while the South gradually reverted to an entirely Catholic faith, we must see that the reasons were in part racial, in part geographical and in part social. Geographically and linguistically the Northern provinces looked for their culture to Germany, and the Southern provinces to France. Moreover the easy defensibility of Holland and Zeeland, behind their moats, made them the natural refuge of a hunted sect and, this tendency once having asserted itself, the polarization of the Netherlands naturally followed, Protestants being drawn and driven to their friends in the North and Catholics similarly finding it necessary or advisable to settle in the South. Moreover in the Southern provinces the two privileged classes, clergy and nobility, were relatively stronger than in the almost entirely bourgeois and commercial North. And the influence of both was thrown into the scale of the Roman church, the first promptly and as a matter of course, the second eventually as a reaction from the strongly democratic tendency of Calvinism. In some of the Southern cities there ensued at this time a desperate struggle between the Protestant democracy and the Catholic aristocracy. The few Protestants of gentle birth in the Walloon provinces felt ill at ease in company with their Dutch co-religionists and were called by them "Malcontents" because they looked askance at the political principles of the North.

January, 1579

The separatist tendencies on both sides crystallized as some of the Southern provinces signed a league at

Arras on January 5 for the protection of the Catholic religion. On the 29th this was answered by the Union of Utrecht, signed by the representatives of Holland, Zeeland, Utrecht, Friesland, Guelders, Zutphen, and the city of Ghent, binding the said provinces to resist all foreign tyranny. Complete freedom of worship was granted, a matter of importance as the Catholic minority was, and has always remained, large. By this act a new state was born. Orange still continued to labor for union with the Southern provinces, but he failed. A bitter religious war broke out in the cities of the South. At Ghent the churches were plundered anew. At Brussels and Antwerp the Protestant proletariat won a temporary ascendancy and Catholic worship was forbidden in both cities. A general emigration from them ensued. Under the stress of the religious war which was also a class war, the last vestiges of union perished. The States General ceased to have power to raise taxes or enforce decrees, and presently it was no more regarded.

1581

Even William of Orange now abandoned his show of respect for the monarch and became wholly the champion of liberty and of the people. The States General recognized Anjou as their prince, but at the same time drew up a very republican constitution. The representatives of the people were given not only the legislative but also the executive powers, including the direction of foreign affairs. The States of the Northern Provinces formally deposed Philip, who could do nothing in reply. A proclamation had already been issued offering 25,000 dollars and a patent of nobility to anyone who would assassinate Orange, who was branded as "a traitor and rascal" and as "the enemy of the human race."

1580

Deposition of Philip, 1581

October 1, 1578

Don John, having died unlamented, was succeeded by Alexander Farnese, a son of the ex-regent Margaret of Parma. Though an Italian in temperament he united a rare diplomatic pliability with energy as a soldier. Moreover, whereas his predecessors had despised the people they were sent to govern and had hated the task of dealing with them, he set his heart on making a success. By this time the eyes of all Europe were fixed on the struggle in the Low Countries and it seemed a worthy achievement to accomplish what so many famous soldiers and statesmen had failed in. It is doubtless due to the genius of Farnese that the Spanish yoke was again fixed on the neck of the southern of the two confederacies into which the Burgundian state had spontaneously separated. Welcomed by a large number of the signers of the Treaty of Arras, he promptly raised an army of 31,000 men, mostly Germans, attacked and took Maastricht. A sickening pillage followed in which no less than 1700 women were slaughtered. Seeing his mistake, on capturing the next town, Tournai, he restrained his army and allowed even the garrison to march out with the honors of war. Not one citizen was executed, though an indemnity of 200,000 guilders was demanded. His clemency helped his cause more than his success in arms.

Farnese 1545–92

1579

Slowly but surely his campaign of conquest progressed. It was a war of sieges only, without battles. Bruges was taken after a long investment, and was mildly treated. Ghent surrendered and was also let off with an indemnity but without bloody punishment. After a hard siege Antwerp capitulated. Practically the whole of the Southern confederacy had been reduced to obedience to the king of Spain. The Protestant religion was forbidden by law but in each case when a city was conquered the Protestants were given from two to four years either to become reconciled or to emigrate.

Conquest of the South

1584

1585

But the land that was reconquered was not the land that had revolted. A ghastly ruin accompanied by a numbing blight on thought and energy settled on the once happy lands of Flanders and Brabant. The civil wars had so wasted the country that wolves prowled even at the gates of great cities. The *coup de grace* was given to the commerce of Antwerp by the barring of the Scheldt by Holland. Trade with the East and West Indies was forbidden by Spain until 1640.

Freedom of the North

But the North, after a desperate struggle and much suffering, vindicated its freedom. Anjou tried first to make himself their tyrant; his soldiers at Antwerp attacked the citizens but were beaten off after frightful street fighting. The "French fury" as it was called, taught the Dutch once again to distrust foreign governors, though the death of Anjou relieved them of fear.

January 17, 1583

June, 1584

But a sterner foe was at hand. Having reduced what is now called Belgium, Farnese attacked the Reformation and the republicans in their last strongholds in Holland, Zeeland, and Utrecht. The long war, of a high technical interest because of the peculiar military problems to be solved, was finally decided in favor of the Dutch. The result was due in part to the heroic courage of the people, in part to the highly defensible nature of their country, saved time and again by that great ally, the sea.

July 10, 1584

A cruel blow was the assassination of Orange whose last words were "God have pity on this poor people." His life had been devoted to them in no spirit of ambition or vulgar pride; his energy, his patience, his breadth had served the people well. And at his death they showed themselves worthy of him and of the cause. Around his body the Estates of Holland convened and resolved to bear themselves manfully without abatement of zeal. Right nobly did they aquit themselves.

1586 Leicester

The bad ending of a final attempt to get foreign help taught the Dutch Republic once and for all to rely only on itself. Robert Dudley, Earl of Leicester, Elizabeth's favorite, was inaugurated as Governor General. His assumption of independent power enraged his royal mistress, whereas the Dutch were alienated by the suspicion that he sacrificed their interests to those of England, and by his military failures. In less than two years he was forced to return home.

1587

Oldenbarneveldt, 1547–1619

Under the statesmanlike guidance of John van Oldenbarneveldt, since 1586 Pensionary of Holland, a Republic was set up founded on the supremacy of the Estates. Under his exact, prudent, and resolute leadership internal freedom and external power were alike developed. Though the war continued long after 1588 the defeat of the Armada in that year crippled Spain beyond hope of recovery and made the new nation practically safe.

The Dutch Republic

The North had suffered much in the war. The frequent inundation of the land destroyed crops. Amsterdam long held out against the rest of Holland in loyalty to the king, but she suffered so much by the blockade of the Beggars of the Sea and by the emigration of her merchants to nearby cities, that at last she gave in and cast her lot with her people. From that time she assumed the commercial hegemony once exercised by Antwerp. Recovering rapidly from the devastations of war, the Dutch Republic became, in the seventeenth century, the first sea-power and first money-power in the world. She gave a king to England and put a bridle in the mouth of France. She established colonies in America and in the East Indies. With her celebrated new university of Leyden, with publicists like Grotius, theologians like Jansen, painters like Van Dyke and Rembrandt, philosophers like Spinoza, she took the lead in many of the fields of thought. Her material and spiritual power, her tolerance and freedom, became the envy of the world.

CHAPTER VI

ENGLAND

§ 1. Henry VIII and the National Church. 1509–47

Henry VIII 1509–47

"The heavens laugh, the earth exults; all is full of milk and honey and nectar." With these words the accession of Henry VIII was announced to Erasmus by his pupil and the king's tutor, Lord Mountjoy. This lover of learning thought the new monarch would be not only Octavus but Octavius, fostering letters and cherishing the learned. There was a general feeling that a new era was beginning and a new day dawning after the long darkness of the Middle Age with its nightmares of Black Deaths and Peasants' Revolts and, worst of all, the civil war that had humbled England's power and racked her almost to pieces within.

It was commonly believed that the young prince was a paragon: handsome, athletic, learned, generous, wise, and merciful. That he was fond of sports, strong and in early life physically attractive, is well attested. The principal evidences of his learning are the fulsome testimony of Erasmus and his work against Luther. But it has been lately shown that Erasmus was capable of passing off, as the work of a powerful patron, compositions which he knew to be written by Latin secretaries; and the royal author of the *Defence of the Seven Sacraments,* which evinces but mediocre talent, received much unacknowledged assistance.

If judged by his foreign relations Henry's statesmanship was unsuccessful. His insincerity and perfidy often overreached themselves, and he was often deceived. Moreover, he was inconstant, pursuing no worthy end whatever. England was by her insular location and by the nearly equal division of power on the Continent between France and the emperor, in a wonderfully safe and advantageous place. But, so far was Henry from using this gift of fortune, that he seems to have acted only on caprice.

Domestic policy

In domestic policy Henry achieved his greatest successes, in fact, very remarkable ones indeed. Doubtless here also he was favored by fortune, in that his own ends happened in the main to coincide with the deeper current of his people's purpose, for he was supported by just that wealthy and enterprising bourgeois class that was to call itself the people and to make public opinion for the next three centuries. In time this class would become sufficiently conscious of its own power to make Parliament supreme and to demand a reckoning even from the crown, but at first it needed the prestige of the royal name to conquer the two privileged classes, the clergy and the nobility. The merchants and the moneyed men only too willingly became the faithful followers of a chief who lavishly tossed to them the wealth of the church and the political privileges of the barons. And Henry had just one strong quality that enabled him to take full advantage of this position; he seemed to lead rather than to drive, and he never wantonly challenged Parliament. The atrocity of his acts was only equaled by their scrupulous legality.

On Henry's morals there should be less disagreement than on his mental gifts. Holbein's faithful portraits do not belie him. The broad-shouldered, heavy-jowled man, standing so firmly on his widely parted feet, has a certain strength of will, or rather of boundless egotism. Francis and Charles showed themselves persecuting, and were capable of having a defaulting minister or a rebel put to death; but neither Charles nor Francis, nor any other king in modern times, has to answer for the lives of so many nobles and ministers, cardinals and queens, whose heads, as Thomas More put it, he kicked around like footballs.

Empson and Dudley executed, April 25, 1509

The reign began, as it ended, with political murder. The miserly Henry VII had made use of two tools, Empson and Dudley, who, by minute inquisition into technical offences and by nice adjustment of fines to the wealth of the offender, had made the law unpopular and the king rich. Four days after his succession, Henry VIII issued a proclamation asking all those who had sustained injury or loss of goods by these commissioners, to make supplication to the king. The floodgates of pent-up wrath were opened, and the two unhappy ministers swept away by an act of attainder.

War with France and Scotland

The pacific policy of the first years of the reign did not last long. The young king felt the need of martial glory, of emulating the fifth Henry, of making himself talked about and enrolling his name on the list of conquerors who, in return for plaguing mankind, have been deified by them. It is useless to look for any statesmanlike purpose in the war provoked with France and Scotland, but in the purpose for which he set out Henry was brilliantly successful: the French were so quickly routed near Guinegate that the action has been known in history as the Battle of the Spurs. While the king was still absent in France and his queen regent in England, his lieutenants inflicted a decisive defeat on the Scots and slew their king, James IV, at Flodden. England won nothing save military glory by these campaigns, for the invasion of France was at once abandoned and that of Scotland not even undertaken.

August 13, 1513

September

Wolsey, c. 1475–1530

The gratification of the national vanity redounded to the profit not only of Henry but of his minister,

Thomas Wolsey. A poor man, like the other tools of the Tudor despot, he rose rapidly in church and state partly by solid gifts of statesmanship, partly by baser arts. By May, 1515, Erasmus described him as all-powerful with the king and as bearing the main burden of public affairs on his shoulders, and fifteen years later Luther spoke of him as "the demigod of England, or rather of Europe." His position at home he owed to his ability to curry favor with the king by shouldering the odium of unpopular acts. When the Duke of Buckingham was executed for the crime of standing next in succession to the throne, Wolsey was blamed; many people thought, as it was put in a pun attributed to Charles V, that "it was a pity so noble a *buck* should have been slain by such a hound." Wolsey lost the support of the nobles by the pride that delighted to humble them, and of the commons by the avarice that accumulated a corrupt fortune. But, though the rich hated him for his law in regard to enclosures, and the poor for not having that law enforced, he recked little of aught, knowing himself secure under the royal shield.

May, 1521

To make his sovereign abroad as great as at home, he took advantage of the nice balance of power existing on the Continent. "Nothing pleases him more than to be called the arbiter of Christendom," wrote Giustiniani, and such, in fact, he very nearly was. His diplomatic gifts were displayed with immense show during the summer of 1520, when Henry met both Francis and Charles V, and promised each secretly to support him against his rival. The camp where the royalties of France and England met, near Guines, amid scenes of pageantry and chivalry so resplendent as to give it the name of The Field of Cloth of Gold, saw an alliance cemented by oath, only to be followed by a solemn engagement between Henry and Charles, repugnant in every particular to that with France. When war actually broke out between the two, England preferred to throw her weight against France, thereby almost helping Charles to the throne of universal empire and raising up for herself an enemy to menace her safety in many a crisis to come. In the end, then, Wolsey's perfidious policy failed; and his personal ambition for the papacy was also frustrated.

But while "the congress of kings," as Erasmus called it, was disporting itself at Guines and Calais, the tide of a new movement was swiftly and steadily rising, no more obeying them than had the ocean obeyed Canute. More in England than in most countries the Reformation was an imported product. Its "dawn came up like thunder" from across the North Sea.

Luther's Theses on Indulgences were sent by Erasmus to his English friends Thomas More and John Colet little more than four months after their promulgation. By February, 1519, Froben had exported to England a number of volumes of Luther's works. One of them fell into the hands of Henry VIII or his sister Mary, quondam Queen of France, as is shown by the royal arms stamped on it. Many others were sold by a bookseller at Oxford throughout 1520, in which year a government official in London wrote to his son in the country, "there be heretics here which take Luther's opinions." The universities were both infected at the same time. At Cambridge, especially, a number of young men, many of them later prominent reformers, met at the White Horse Tavern regularly to discuss the new ideas. The tavern was nicknamed "Germany" and the young enthusiasts "Germans" in consequence. But surprisingly numerous as are the evidences of the spread of Lutheranism in these early years, naturally it as yet had few prominent adherents. When Erasmus wrote Luther that he had well-wishers

March 5, 1518

March 3, 1520

1521

May, 1519

in England, and those of the greatest, he was exaggerating or misinformed. At most he may have been thinking of John Colet, whose death in September, 1519, came before he could take any part in the religious controversy.

At an early date the government took its stand against the heresy. Luther's books were examined by a committee of the University of Cambridge, condemned and burnt by them, and soon afterwards by the government. At St. Paul's in London, in the presence of many high dignitaries and a crowd of thirty thousand spectators Luther's books were burnt and his doctrine "reprobated" in addresses by John Fisher, Bishop of Rochester, and Cardinal Wolsey. A little later it was forbidden to read, import or keep such works, and measures were taken to enforce this law. Commissions searched for the said pamphlets; stationers and merchants were put under bond not to trade in them; and the German merchants of the Steelyard were examined. When it was discovered that these foreigners had stopped "the mass of the body of Christ," commonly celebrated by them in All Hallows' Church the Great, at London, they were haled before Wolsey's legatine court, forced to acknowledge its jurisdiction, and dealt with.

1520

May 12, 1521

1526

With one accord the leading Englishmen declared against Luther. Cuthbert Tunstall, a mathematician and diplomatist, and later Bishop of London, wrote Wolsey from Worms of the devotion of the Germans to their leader, and sent to him *The Babylonian Captivity* with the comment, "there is much strange opinion in it near to the opinions of Boheme; I pray God keep that book out of England." Wolsey himself, biassed perhaps by his ambition for the tiara, labored to suppress the heresy. Most important of all, Sir Thomas More was promptly and decisively alienated.

January 21, 1521

It was More, according to Henry VIII, who "by subtle, sinister slights unnaturally procured and provoked him" to write against the heretic. His *Defence of the Seven Sacraments,* in reply to the *Babylonian Captivity,* though an extremely poor work, was greeted, on its appearance, as a masterpiece. The handsome copy bound in gold, sent to Leo X, was read to the pope and declared by him the best antidote to heresy yet produced. In recognition of so valuable an arm, or of so valiant a champion, the pope granted an indulgence of ten years and ten periods of forty days to the readers of the book, and to its author the long coveted title Defender of the Faith. Luther answered the king with ridicule and the controversy was continued by Henry's henchmen More, Fisher, and others. Stung to the quick, Henry, who had already urged the emperor to crush the heretic, now wrote with the same purpose to the elector and dukes of Saxony and to other German princes.

July, 1521

Growth of Lutheranism

But while the chief priests and rulers were not slow to reject the new "gospel," the common people heard it gladly. The rapid diffusion of Lutheranism is proved by many a side light and by the very proclamations issued from time to time to "resist the damnable heresies" or to suppress tainted books. John Heywood's *The Four P's: a merry Interlude of a Palmer, a Pardoner, a Potycary and a Pedlar,* written about 1528 though not published until some years later, is full of Lutheran doctrine, and so is another book very popular at the time, Simon Fish's *Supplication of Beggars.* John Skelton's *Colyn Clout,* a scathing indictment of the clergy, mentions that

c. 1522

Some have smacke
Of Luther's sacke,
And a brennyng sparke
Of Luther's warke.

William Tyndale's Bible

But the acceptance of the Reformation, as apart from mere grumbling at the church, could not come until a Protestant literature was built up. In England as elsewhere the most powerful Protestant tract was the vernacular Bible. Owing to the disfavor in which Wyclif's doctrines were held, no English versions had been printed until the Protestant divine William Tyndale highly resolved to make the holy book more familiar to the ploughboy than to the bishop.

Educated at both Oxford and Cambridge, Tyndale imbibed the doctrines first of Erasmus, then of Luther, and finally of Zwingli. Applying for help in his project to the bishop of London and finding none, he sailed for Germany where he completed a translation of the New Testament, and started printing it at Cologne. Driven hence by the intervention of Cochlaeus and the magistrates, he went to Worms and got another printer to finish the job. Of the six thousand copies in the first edition many were smuggled to England, where Cuthbert Tunstall, Bishop of London, tried to buy them all up, "thinking," as the chronicler Hall phrased it, "that he had God by the toe when he indeed had the devil by the fist." The money went to Tyndale and was used to issue further editions, of which no less than seven appeared in the next ten years.

1524

1526

The government's attitude was that

> Having respect to the malignity of this present time, with the inclination of the people to erroneous opinions, the translation of the New Testament should rather be the occasion of continuance or increase of errors among the said people than any benefit or commodity towards the weal of their souls.

But the magistrates were unable to quench the fiery zeal of Tyndale who continued to translate parts of the Old Testament and to print them and other tracts at Antwerp and at Cologne, until his martyrdom at Vilvorde, near Brussels, on October 6, 1536. In 1913 a monument was erected on the place of his death.

Under the leadership of Tyndale on the one side and of More on the other the air became dark with a host of controversial tracts. They are half filled with theological metaphysic, half with the bitterest invective. Luther called Henry VIII "a damnable and rotten worm, a snivelling, drivelling swine of a sophist"; More retorted by complaining of the violent language of "this apostate, this open incestuous lecher, this plain limb of the devil and manifest messenger of hell." Absurd but natural tactic, with a sure effect on the people, which relishes both morals and scandal! To prove that faith justifies, the Protestants pointed to the debauchery of the friars; to prove the mass a sacrifice their enemies mocked at "Friar Martin and Cate Callate his nun lusking together in lechery." But with all the invective there was much solid argument of the kind that appealed to an age of theological politics. In England as elsewhere the significance of the Reformation was that it was the first issue of supreme importance to be argued by means of the press before the bar of a public opinion sufficiently enlightened to appreciate its importance and sufficiently strong to make a choice and to enforce its decision.

Controversial tracts

The party of the Reformation in England at first consisted of two classes, London tradesmen and certain members of what Bismarck long afterward called "the learned proletariat." In 1532 the bishops were able to say:

> In the crime of heresy, thanked be God, there hath no notable person fallen in our time. Truth it is that certain apostate friars and monks, lewd priests, bankrupt merchants, vagabonds and lewd, idle fellows of corrupt nature have embraced the abominable and erroneous

opinions lately sprung in Germany and by them have been some seduced in simplicity and ignorance.

Anti-clerical feeling

But though both anti-clerical feeling and sympathy with the new doctrines waxed apace, it is probable that no change would have taken place for many years had it not been for the king's divorce. The importance of this episode, born of the most strangely mingled motives of conscience, policy, and lust, is not that, as sometimes said, it proved the English people ready to follow their government in religious matters as sheep follow their shepherd. Its importance is simply that it loosed England from its ancient moorings of papal supremacy, and thus established one, though only one, of the cardinal principles of the Protestant revolt. The Reformation consisted not only in a religious change but in an assertion of nationalism, in a class revolt, and in certain cultural revolutions. It was only the first that the government had any idea of sanctioning, but by so doing it enabled the people later to take matters into their own hands and add the social and cultural elements. Thus the Reformation in England ran a course quite different from that in Germany. In the former the cultural revolution came first, followed fast by the rising of the lower and the triumph of the middle classes. Last of all came the successful realization of a national state. But in England nationalism came first; then under Edward the economic revolution; and lastly, under the Puritans, the transmutation of spiritual values.

Divorce of Catherine of Aragon

The occasion of the breach with Rome was the divorce of Henry from Catharine of Aragon, who had previously married his brother Arthur when they were both fifteen, and had lived with him as his wife for five months until his death. As marriage with a brother's widow was forbidden by Canon Law, a dispensation from the pope had been secured, to enable Catharine to marry Henry. The king's scruples about the legality of the act were aroused by the death of all the queen's children, save the Princess Mary, in which he saw the fulfilment of the curse denounced in Leviticus xx, 21: "If a man shall take his brother's wife . . . they shall be childless." Just at this time Henry fell in love with Anne Boleyn, and this further increased his dissatisfaction with his present estate.

Anne Boleyn

He therefore applied to the pope for annulment of marriage, but the unhappy Clement VII, now in the emperor's fist, felt unable to give it to him. He writhed and twisted, dallied with the proposals that Henry should take a second wife, or that his illegitimate son the Duke of Richmond should marry his half sister Mary; in short he was ready to grant a dispensation for anything save for the one horrible crime of divorce—as the annulment was then called. His difficulties in getting at the rights of the question were not made easier by the readiness of both parties to commit a little perjury or to forge a little bull to further their cause.

Seeing no help in sight from Rome Henry began to collect the opinions of universities and "strange doctors." The English, French, and Italian universities decided as the king wished that his marriage was null; Wittenberg and Marburg rendered contrary opinions. Many theologians, including Erasmus, Luther, and Melanchthon, expressed the opinion that bigamy would be the best way to meet the situation.

But more was needed to make the annulment legal than the verdict of universities. Repulsed by Rome Henry was forced to make an alliance, though it proved but a temporary one, with the Reforming and anticlerical parties in his realm. At Easter, 1529, Lutheran books began to circulate at court, books advocating the confiscation of ecclesiastical property and the reduction of the church to a state of primitive simplicity. To Chapuis, the imperial ambassador, Henry pointedly praised Luther, whom he had lately called "a wolf of hell and a limb of Satan," remarking that though he had mixed heresy in his books that was not sufficient reason for reproving and rejecting the many truths he had brought to light. To punish Wolsey for the failure to secure what was wanted from Rome, the pampered minister was arrested for treason, but died of chagrin before he could be executed. "Had I served my God," said he, "as diligently as I have served my king, he would not have given me over in my grey hairs."

November 4, 1530

Reformation Parliament, November 3, 1529

In the meantime there had already met that Parliament that was to pass, in the seven years of its existence, the most momentous and revolutionary laws as yet placed upon the statute-books. The elections were free, or nearly so; the franchise varied from a fairly democratic one in London to a highly oligarchical one in some boroughs. Notwithstanding the popular feeling that Catharine was an injured woman and that war with the Empire might ruin the valuable trade with Flanders, the "government," as would now be said, that is, the king, received hearty support by the majority of members. The only possible explanation for this, apart from the king's acknowledged skill as a parliamentary leader, is the strength of the anti-clerical feeling. The rebellion of the laity against the clergy, and of the patriots against the Italian yoke, needed but the example of Germany to burst all the dykes and barriers of medieval custom. The significance of the revolution was that it was a forcible reform of the church by the state. The wish of the people was to end ecclesiastical abuses without much regard to doctrine; the wish of the king was to make himself "emperor and pope" in his own dominions. While Henry studied Wyclif's program, and the people read the English Testament, the lessons they derived from these sources were at first moral and political, not doctrinal or philosophic.

Submission of the clergy, December, 1530

The first step in the reduction of the church was taken when the attorney-general filed in the court of King's Bench an information against the whole body of the clergy for violating the statutes of Provisors and Praemunire by having recognized Wolsey's legatine authority. Of course there was no justice in this; the king himself had recognized Wolsey's authority and anyone who had denied it would have been punished. But the suit was sufficient to accomplish the government's purposes, which were, first to wring money from the clergy and then to force them to declare the king "sole protector and supreme head of the church and clergy of England." Reluctantly the Convocation of Canterbury accepted this demand in the form that the king was, "their singular protector, only and supreme lord and, as far as the law of Christ allows, even Supreme Head." Henry further proposed that the oaths of the clergy to the pope be abolished and himself made supreme legislator. Convocation accepted this demand also in a document known as "the submission of the clergy."

May 15, 1532

If such was the action of the spiritual estate, it was natural that the temporal peers and the Commons in parliament should go much further. A petition of the Commons, really emanating from the government and probably from Thomas Cromwell, complained bitterly of the tyranny of the ordinaries in ecclesiastical jurisdiction, of excessive fees and vexations and frivolous charges of heresy made against unlearned laymen. Abuses of like nature were dealt with in statutes limiting the fees exacted by priests and regulating

1532

May, 1532

pluralities and non-residence. Annates were abolished with the proviso that the king might negotiate with the pope,—the intention of the government being thus to bring pressure to bear on the curia. No wonder the clergy were thoroughly frightened. Bishop Fisher, their bravest champion, protested in the House of Lords: "For God's sake, see what a realm the kingdom of Boheme was, and when the church fell down, there fell the glory of the kingdom. Now with the Commons is nothing but 'Down with the church,' and all this meseemeth is for lack of faith only."

Marriage with Anne Boleyn

It had taken Henry several years to prepare the way for his chief object, the divorce. His hand was at last forced by the knowledge that Anne was pregnant; he married her on January 25, 1533, without waiting for final sentence of annulment of marriage with Catharine. In so doing he might seem, at first glance, to have followed the advice so freely tendered him to discharge his conscience by committing bigamy; but doubtless he regarded his first marriage as illegal all the time and merely waited for the opportunity to get a court that would so pronounce it. The vacancy of the archbishopric of Canterbury enabled him to appoint to it Thomas Cranmer, the obsequious divine who had first suggested his present plan. Cranmer was a Lutheran, so far committed to the new faith that he had married; he was intelligent, learned, a wonderful master of language, and capable at last of dying for his belief. But that he showed himself pliable to his master's wishes beyond all bounds of decency is a fact made all the more glaring by the firm and honorable conduct of More and Fisher. His worst act was possibly on the occasion of his nomination to the province of Canterbury; wishing to be confirmed by the pope he concealed his real views and took an oath of obedience to the Holy See, having previously signed

Cranmer

a protest that he considered the oath a mere form and not a reality.

The first use he made of his position was to pronounce sentence that Henry and Catharine had never been legally married, though at the same time asserting that this did not affect the legitimacy of Mary because her parents had believed themselves married. Immediately afterwards it was declared that Anne was a lawful wife, and she was crowned queen, amid the smothered execrations of the populace, on June 1. On September 7, the Princess Elizabeth was born. Catharine's cause was taken up at Rome; Clement's brief forbidding the king to remarry was followed by final sentence in Catharine's favor. Her last years were rendered miserable by humiliation and acts of petty spite. When she died her late husband, with characteristic indecency, celebrated the joyous event by giving a ball at which he and Anne appeared dressed in yellow.

1533

January, 1536

The feeling of the people showed itself in this case finer and more chivalrous than that prevalent at court. The treatment of Catharine was so unpopular that Chapuis wrote that the king was much hated by his subjects. Resolved to make an example of the murmurers, the government selected Elizabeth Barton, the "Holy Maid of Kent." After her hysterical visions and a lucky prophecy had won her an audience, she fell under the influence of monks and prophesied that the king would not survive his marriage with Anne one month, and proclaimed that he was no longer king in the eyes of God. She and her accomplices were arrested, attainted without trial, and executed. She may pass as an English Catholic martyr.

March, 1534

January, 1536

April 1, 1534

Continuing its course of making the king absolute master the Parliament passed an Act in Restraint of Appeals, the first constitutional break with Rome.

Act in Restraint of Appeals, February, 1533

The theory of the government was set forth in the preamble:

> Whereas by divers sundry old authentic histories and chronicles, it is manifestly declared and expressed, that this realm of England is an Empire, and so hath been accepted in the world, governed by one supreme head and king . . . unto whom a body politic compact of all sorts and degrees of people, divided in terms, and by names of spirituality and temporalty, be bounden and ought to bear, next to God, a natural and humble obedience. . . .

therefore all jurisdiction of foreign powers was denied.

January 15, 1534

When, after a recess, Parliament met again there were forty vacancies to be filled in the Lower House, and this time care was taken that the new members should be well affected. Scarcely a third of the spiritual lords assembled, though whether their absence was commanded, or their presence not required, by the king, is uncertain. As, in earlier Parliaments, the spiritual peers had outnumbered the temporal, this was a matter of importance. Another sign of the secularization of the government was the change in the character of the chancellors. Wolsey was the last great ecclesiastical minister of the reign; More and Cromwell who followed him were laymen.

The severance with Rome was now completed by three laws. In the first place the definite abolition of the annates meant that henceforth the election of archbishops and bishops must be under licence by the king and that they must swear allegiance to him before consecration. A second act forbade the payment of Peter's pence and all other fees to Rome, and vested in the Archbishop of Canterbury the right to grant licences previously granted by the pope. A third act, for the subjection of the clergy, put convocation under the royal power and forbade all privileges inconsistent with this. The new pope, Paul III, struck back, though

1535–8

with hesitation, excommunicating the king, declaring all his children by Anne Boleyn illegitimate, and absolving his subjects from their oath of allegiance.

1534
Act of Succession

Two acts entrenched the king in his despotic pretensions. The Act of Succession, notable as the first assertion by crown and Parliament of the right to legislate in this constitutional matter, vested the inheritance of the crown in the issue of Henry and Anne, and made it high treason to question the marriage. The Act of Supremacy declared that the king's majesty "justly and rightfully is and ought to be supreme head of the church of England," pointedly omitting the qualification insisted on by Convocation,—"as far as the law of Christ allows." Exactly how far this supremacy went was at first puzzling. That it extended not only to the governance of the temporalities of the church, but to issuing injunctions on spiritual matters and defining articles of belief was soon made apparent; on the other hand the monarch never claimed in person the power to celebrate mass.

Act of Supremacy

That the abrogation of the papal authority was accepted so easily is proof of the extent to which the national feeling of the English church had already gone. An oath to recognize the supremacy of the king was tendered to both convocations, to the universities, to the clergy and to prominent laymen, and was with few exceptions readily taken. Doubtless many swallowed the oath from mere cowardice; others took it with mental reservations; and yet that the majority complied shows that the substitution of a royal for a papal despotism was acceptable to the conscience of the country at large. Many believed that they were not departing from the Catholic faith; but that others welcomed the act as a step towards the Reformation cannot be doubted. How strong was the hold of Luther on the country will presently be shown, but here only one instance of the exuberance of the will for a purely national religion need be quoted. "God hath showed himself the God of England, or rather an English God," wrote Hugh Latimer, a leading Lutheran; not only the church but the Deity had become insular!

1537

Fisher

But there were a few, and among them the greatest, who refused to become accomplices in the break with Roman Christendom. John Fisher, Bishop of Rochester, a friend of Erasmus and a man of admirable steadfastness, had long been horrified by the tyranny of Henry. He had stoutly upheld the rightfulness of Catharine's marriage, and now he refused to see in the monarch the fit ruler of the church. So strongly did he feel on these subjects that he invited Charles to invade England and depose the king. This was treason, though probably the government that sent him to the tower was ignorant of the act. When Paul III rewarded Fisher by creating him a cardinal Henry furiously declared he would send his head to Rome to get the hat. The old man of seventy-six was accordingly beheaded.

May 20, 1535

June 22,

Sir Thomas More executed, July 6

This execution was followed by that of Sir Thomas More, the greatest ornament of his country. As More has been remembered almost entirely by his noble *Utopia* and his noble death, it is hard to estimate his character soberly. That his genius was polished to the highest perfection, that in a hard age he had an altogether lovely sympathy with the poor, and in a servile age the courage of his convictions, would seem enough to excuse any faults. But a deep vein of fanaticism ran through his whole nature and tinctured all his acts, political, ecclesiastical, and private. Not only was his language violent in the extreme, but his acts were equally merciless when his passions were aroused. Appointed chancellor after the fall of Wolsey, he did not scruple to hit the man who was down, describing him, in a scathing speech in Parliament, as the scabby wether separated by the careful shepherd from the sound sheep. In his hatred of the new opinions he not only sent men to death and torture for holding them, but reviled them while doing it. "Heretics as they be," he wrote, "the clergy doth denounce them. And as they be well worthy, the temporality doth burn them. And after the fire of Smithfield, hell doth receive them, where the wretches burn for ever."

As chancellor he saw with growing disapproval the course of the tyrant. He opposed the marriage with Anne Boleyn. The day after the submission of the clergy he resigned the great seal. He could not long avoid further offence to his master, and his refusal to take the oath of supremacy was the crime for which he was condemned. His behaviour during his last days and on the scaffold was perfect. He spent his time in severe self-discipline; he uttered eloquent words of forgiveness of his enemies, messages of love to the daughter whom he tenderly loved, and brave jests.

Anabaptist martyrs, 1536

But while More's passion was one that any man might envy, his courage was shared by humbler martyrs. In the same year in which he was beheaded thirteen Dutch Anabaptists were burnt, as he would have approved, by the English government. Mute, inglorious Christs, they were led like sheep to the slaughter and as lambs dumb before their shearers. They had no eloquence, no high position, to make their words ring from side to side of Europe and echo down the centuries; but their meek endurance should not go unremembered.

Thomas Cromwell, 1485?–1540

To take More's place as chief minister Henry appointed the most obsequious tool he could find, Thomas Cromwell. To good purpose this man had studied Machiavelli's *Prince* as a practical manual of tyranny. His most important service to the crown was the

Dissolution of the monasteries

next step in the reduction of the medieval church, the dissolution of the monasteries. Like other acts tending towards the Reformation this was, on the whole, popular, and had been rehearsed on a small scale on several previous occasions in English history. The pope and the king of France taught Edward II to dissolve the preceptories, to the number of twenty-three, belonging to the Templars; in 1410 the Commons petitioned for the confiscation of all church property; in 1414 the alien priories in England fell under the animadversion of the government; their property was handed over to the crown and they escaped only by the payment of heavy fines, by incorporation into English orders, and by partial confiscation of their land. The idea prevailed that mortmain had failed of its object and that therefore the church might rightfully be relieved of her ill-gotten gains. These were grossly exaggerated, a pamphleteer believing that the wealth of the church amounted to half the property of the realm. In reality the total revenue of the spirituality amounted to only £320,000; that of the monasteries to only £140,000. There had been few endowments in the fifteenth century; only eight new ones, in fact, in the whole period 1399–1509. Colleges, schools, and hospitals now attracted the money that had previously gone to the monks.

Moreover, the monastic life had fallen on evil days. The abbeys no longer were centers of learning and of the manufacture of books. The functions of hospitality and of charity that they still exercised were not sufficient to redeem them in the eyes of the people for the "gross, carnal, and vicious living" with which they were commonly and quite rightly charged. Visitations undertaken not by hostile governments but by bishops in the fifteenth century prove that much immorality obtained within the cloister walls. By 1528 they had become so intolerable that a popular pamphleteer, Simon Fish, in his *Supplication of Beggars*, proposed that the mendicant friars be entirely suppressed.

January 21, 1535

A commission was now issued to Thomas Cromwell, empowering him to hold a general visitation of all churches, monasteries, and collegiate bodies. The evidence gathered of the shocking disorders obtaining in the cloisters of both sexes is on the whole credible and well substantiated. Nevertheless these disorders furnished rather the pretext than the real reason for the dissolutions that followed. Cromwell boasted that he would make his king the richest in Christendom, and this was the shortest and most popular way to do it.

1536

Accordingly an act was passed for the dissolution of all small religious houses with an income of less than £200 a year. The rights of the founders were safe-guarded, and pensions guaranteed to those inmates who did not find shelter in one of the larger establishments. By this act 376 houses were dissolved with an aggregate revenue of £32,000, not counting plate and jewels confiscated. Two thousand monks or nuns were affected in addition to about eight thousand retainers or servants. The immediate effect was a large amount of misery, but the result in the long run was good. Perhaps the principal political importance of this and the subsequent spoliations of the church was to make the Reformation profitable and therefore popular with an enterprising class. For the lion's share of the prey did not go to the lion, but to the jackals. From the king's favorites to whom he threw the spoils was founded a new aristocracy, a class with a strong vested interest in opposing the restoration of the papal church. To the Protestant citizens of London was now added a Protestant landed gentry.

Union with Wales, 1536

Before the "Reformation Parliament" had ceased to exist, one more act of great importance was passed. Wales was a wild country, imperfectly governed by irregular means. By the first Act of Union in British history, Wales was now incorporated with England and the anomalies, or distinctions, in its legal and administrative system, wiped out. By severe measures, in the course of which 5000 men were sent to the gallows, the western mountaineers were reduced to order during the years 1534–40; and in 1543 their union with England was completed. The measure was statesmanlike and successful; it was undoubtedly aided by the loyalty of the Welsh to their own Tudor dynasty.

April 14, 1536

When Parliament dissolved after having accomplished, during its seven years, the greatest permanent revolution in the history of England, it had snapped the bands with Rome and determined articles of religious belief; it had given the king more power in the church than the pope ever had, and had exalted his prerogative in the state to a pitch never reached before or afterwards; it had dissolved the smaller monasteries, abridged the liberties of the subject, settled the succession to the throne, created new treasons and heresies; it had handled grave social problems, like enclosures and mendicancy; and had united Wales to England.

Execution of Anne Boleyn

And now the woman for whose sake, one is tempted to say, the king had done it all—though of course his share in the revolution does not represent the real forces that accomplished it—the woman he had won with "such a world of charge and hell of pain," was to be cast into the outer darkness of the most hideous tragedy in history. Anne Boleyn was not a good woman. And yet, when she was accused of adultery with four men and of incest with her own brother,

May 19, 1536

though she was tried by a large panel of peers, condemned, and beheaded, it is impossible to be sure of her guilt.

Jane Seymour

On the day following Anne's execution or, as some say, on May 30, Henry married his third wife, Jane Seymour. On October 12, 1537, she bore him a son, Edward. Forced by her husband to take part in the christening, an exhausting ceremony too much for her strength, she sickened and died soon afterwards.

Lutheran tracts

In the meantime the Lutheran movement was growing apace in England. In the last two decades of Henry's reign seven of Luther's tracts and some of his hymns were translated into English. Five of the tracts proved popular enough to be reprinted. One of them was *The Liberty of a Christian Man,* turned into English by John Tewkesbury whom, having died for his faith, More called "a stinking martyr." The hymns and some of the other tracts were Englished by Miles Coverdale. In addition to this there was translated an account of Luther's death in 1546, the Augsburg Confession and four treatises of Melanchthon, and one each of Zwingli, Oecolampadius and Bullinger,—this last reprinted. Of course these versions are not a full measure of Lutheran influence, but a mere barometer. The party now numbered powerful preachers like Latimer and Ridley; Thomas Cranmer the Archbishop of Canterbury and Thomas Cromwell, since May, 1534, the king's principal secretary. The adherence of the last named to the Reforming party is perhaps the most significant sign of the times. As his only object was to be on the winning side, and as he had not a bit of real religious interest, it makes it all the more impressive that, believing the cat was about to jump in the direction of Lutheranism, he should have tried to put himself in the line of its trajectory by doing all he could to foster the Reformers at home and the Protestant alliance abroad.

Coverdale, 1488?–1569

One of the decisive factors in the Reformation again proved to be the English Bible, completed, after the end of Tyndale's labors by a man of less scholarship but equally happy mastery of language, Miles Coverdale. Of little original genius, he spent his life largely in the labor of translating tracts and treatises by the German Reformers into his native tongue. His first great work was the completion of the English Bible which was published by Christopher Froschauer of Zurich in 1535, the title-page stating that it had been translated "out of Douche and Latyn"—the "Douche" being, of course, Luther's German version. For the New Testament and for the Old Testament as far as the end of Chronicles, Tyndale's version was used; the rest was by Coverdale. The work was dedicated to the king, and, as Cromwell had already been considering the advisability of authorizing the English Bible, this was not an unwelcome thing. But as the government was as yet unprepared to recognize work avowedly based on German Protestant versions, they resorted to the device of re-issuing the Bible with the name of Thomas Matthew as translator, though in fact it consisted entirely of the work of Tyndale and Coverdale. A light revision of this work was re-issued as the Great Bible, and Injunctions were issued by Cromwell ordering a Bible of the largest size to be set up in every church, and the people to be encouraged to read it. They were also to be taught the Lord's prayer and creed in English, spiritual sermons were to be preached, and superstitions, such as going on pilgrimages, burning candles to saints, and kissing and licking relics, were to be discouraged.

The English Bible, 1535

1537

1538–9

October 11, 1538

At the same time Cromwell diligently sought a *rapprochement* with the German Protestants. The idea was an obvious one that, having won the enmity of Charles, England should support his dangerous intestine enemies, the Schmalkaldic princes. In that day of theological politics it was natural to try to find cement for the alliance in a common confession. Embassy after embassy made pilgrimages to Wittenberg, where the envoys had long discussions with the Reformers both about the divorce and about matters of faith. They took back with them to England, together with a personal letter from Luther to Cromwell, a second opinion unfavorable to the divorce and a confession drawn up in Seventeen Articles. In this, though in the main it was, as it was called, "a repetition and exegesis of the Augsburg Confession," considerable concessions were made to the wishes of the English. Melanchthon was the draughtsman and Luther the originator of the articles.

January, 1536

April

This symbol now became the basis of the first definition of faith drawn up by the government. Some such statement was urgently needed, for, amid the bewildering acts of the Reformation Parliament, the people hardly knew what the king expected them to believe. The king therefore presented to Convocation a Book of Articles of Faith and Ceremonies, commonly called the Ten Articles, drafted by Fox on the basis of the memorandum he had received at Wittenberg, in close substantial and frequently in verbal agreement with it. By this confession the Bible, the three creeds, and the acts of the first four councils were designated as authoritative; the three Lutheran sacraments of baptism, penance, and the altar were retained; justification by faith and good works jointly was proclaimed; the use of images was allowed and purgatory disallowed; the real presence in the sacrament was strongly affirmed. The significance of the articles, however, is not so much in their Lutheran provenance, as in their promulgation

July 11
The Book of Articles

by the crown. It was the last step in the enslavement of religion. "This king," as Luther remarked, "wants to be God. He founds articles of faith, which even the pope never did."

The Pilgrimage of Grace

It only remained to see what the people would say to the new order. Within a few months after the dissolution of the Reformation Parliament and the publication of the Ten Articles, the people in the north spread upon the page of history an extremely emphatic protest. For this is really what the Pilgrimage of Grace was—not a rebellion against king, property, or any established institution, but a great demonstration against the policy for which Cromwell became the scapegoat. In those days of slow communication opinions travelled on the beaten roads of commerce. As late as Mary's reign there is proof that Protestantism was confined to the south, east, and midlands,—roughly speaking to a circle with London as its center and a radius of one hundred miles. In these earlier years, Protestant opinion was probably even more confined; London was both royalist and anti-Roman Catholic; the ports on the south-eastern coast, including Calais, at that time an English station in France, and the university towns had strong Lutheran and still stronger anti-clerical parties.

But in the wilds of the north and west it was different. There, hardly any bourgeois class of traders existed to adopt "the religion of merchants" as Protestantism has been called. Perhaps more important was the mere slowness of the diffusion of ideas. The good old ways were good enough for men who never knew anything else. The people were discontented with the high taxes, and the nobles, who in the north retained feudal affections if not feudal power, were outraged by the ascendency in the royal councils of low-born upstarts. Moreover, it seems that the clergy were stronger in the north even before the inroads of the new doctrines. In the suppression of the lesser monasteries Yorkshire, the largest county in England, had lost the most foundations, 53 in all, and Lincolnshire the next most, 37. Irritation at the suppression itself was greatly increased among the clergy by the insolence and thoroughness of the visitation, in which not only monasteries but parish priests had been examined. In resisting the king in the name of the church the priests had before them the example of the most popular English saint, Thomas Becket. They were the real fomenters of the demonstration, and the gentlemen, not the people, its leaders.

Rioting began in Lincolnshire on October 1, 1536, and before the end of the month 40,000 men had joined the movement. A petition to the king was drawn up demanding that the church holidays be kept as before, that the church be relieved of the payment of first-fruits and tithes, that the suppressed houses be restored except those which the king "kept for his pleasure only," that taxes be reduced and some unpopular officials banished.

Henry thundered an answer in his most high and mighty style: "How presumptuous then are ye, the rude commons of one shire, and that one of the most brute and beastly of the whole realm, and of least experience to find fault with your prince in the electing of his councillors and prelates!" He at once dispatched an army with orders "to invade their countries, to burn, spoil and destroy their goods, wives and children." Repression of the rising in Lincolnshire was followed by the execution of forty-six leaders.

March, 1537

But the movement had promptly spread to Yorkshire, where men gathered as for a peaceable demonstration, and swore not to enter "this pilgrimage of grace for the commonwealth, save only for the main-

October, 1536

tenance of God's faith and church militant, preservation of the king's person, and purifying the nobility of all villein's blood and evil counsellors, to the restitution of Christ's church and the suppression of heretics' opinions." In Yorkshire it was feared that the money extorted from the abbeys was going to London; and that the new treason's acts would operate harshly. Cumberland and Westmoreland soon joined the rising, their special grievance being the economic one of the rise of rents, or rather of the heavy fines exacted by landlords on the renewal of leases. An army of 35,000 was raised by the insurgents but their leader, Robert Aske, did not wish to fight, though he was opposed by only 8,000 royal troops. He preferred a parley and demanded, in addition to a free pardon, the acceptance of the northern demands, the summons of a free Parliament, the restoration of the papal supremacy as touching the cure of souls, and the suppression of the books of Tyndale, Huss, Luther, and Melanchthon. The king invited Aske to a personal interview, and promised to accede to the demand for a Parliament if the petitioners would disperse. An act of violence on a part of a few of the northerners was held to absolve the government, and Henry, having gathered his forces, demanded, and secured, a "dreadful execution" of vengeance.

Though the Pilgrimage of Grace had some effect in warning Henry not to dabble in foreign heresies, the policy he had most at heart, that of making himself absolute in state and church, went on apace. The culmination of the growth of the royal power is commonly seen in the Statute of Proclamations apparently giving the king's proclamations the same validity as law save when they touched the lives, liberty, or property of subjects or were repugnant to existing statutes. Probably, however, the intent of Parliament was not

Statute of Proclamations, 1539

to confer new powers on the crown but to regulate the enforcement of already existing prerogatives. As a matter of fact no proclamations were issued during the last years of Henry's reign that might not have been issued before.

But the reform of the church by the government, in morals and usages, not in doctrine, proceeded unchecked. The larger monasteries had been falling into the king's hands by voluntary surrender ever since 1536; a new visitation and a new Act for the dissolution of the greater monasteries completed the process.

1539

War on relics

An iconoclastic war was now begun not, as in other countries, by the mob, but by the government. Relics like the Blood of Hailes were destroyed, and the Rood of Boxley, a crucifix mechanically contrived so that the priests made it nod and smile or shake its head and frown according to the liberality of its worshipper, was taken down and the mechanism exposed in various places. At Walsingham in Norfolk was a nodding image of the Virgin, a bottle of her milk, still liquid, and a knuckle of St. Peter. The shrine, ranking though it did with Loretto and Compostella in popular veneration, was now destroyed. With much zest the government next attacked the shrine of St. Thomas Becket at Canterbury, thus revenging the humiliation of another Henry at the hands of the church. The martyr was now declared to be a rebel who had fled from the realm.

1536

The definition of doctrine, coupled with negotiations with the Schmalkaldic princes, continued briskly. The project for an alliance came to nothing, for John Frederic of Saxony wrote that God would not allow them to have communication with Henry. Two embassies to England engaged in assiduous, but fruitless, theological discussion. Henry himself, with the aid of Cuthbert Tunstall, drew up a long statement "against the opinions of the Germans on the sacrament in both kinds, private masses, and sacerdotal marriage.'' The reactionary tendency of the English is seen in the *Institution of the Christian Man,* published with royal authority, and still more in the Act of the Six Articles. In the former the four sacraments previously discarded are again ''found.'' In the latter, transubstantiation is affirmed, the doctrine of communion in both kinds branded as heresy, the marriage of priests declared void, vows of chastity are made perpetually binding, private masses and auricular confessions are sanctioned. Denial of transubstantiation was made punishable by the stake and forfeiture of goods; those who spoke against the other articles were declared guilty of felony on the second offence. This act, officially entitled ''for abolishing diversity in opinions'' was really the first act of uniformity. It was carried by the influence of the king and the laity against the parties represented by Cromwell and Cranmer. It ended the plans for a Schmalkaldic alliance. Luther thanked God that they were rid of that blasphemer who had tried to enter their league but failed.

Definitions of Faith

1537

1539

July 10, 1539

By a desperate gamble Cromwell now tried to save what was left of his pro-German policy. Duke William of Cleves-Jülich-Berg had adopted an Erasmian compromise between Lutheranism and Romanism, in some respects resembling the course pursued by Henry. In this direction Cromwell accordingly next turned and induced his master to contract a marriage with Anne, the duke's sister. As Henry had offered to the European audience three tragedies in his three former marriages, he now, in true Greek style, presented in his fourth a farce or ''satyric drama.'' The monarch did not like his new wife in the least, and found means of ridding himself of her more speedily than was usual even with him. Having shared her bed for six months

January 6, 1540

he divorced her on the ground that the marriage had not been consummated. The ex-queen continued to live as "the king's good sister" with a pension and establishment of her own, but Cromwell vicariously expiated her failure to please. He was attainted, without trial, for treason, and speedily executed.

July 28, 1540

On the same day Henry married Catharine Howard, a beautiful girl selected by the Catholics to play the same part for them that Anne Boleyn had played for the Lutherans, and who did so more exactly than her backers intended. Like her predecessor she was beheaded for adultery on February 13, 1542. On July 12, 1543, Bluebeard concluded his matrimonial adventures by taking Catharine Parr, a lady who, like Sieyès after the Terror, must have congratulated herself on her rare ability in surviving.

Bluebeard's wives

As a Catholic reaction marked the last eight years of Henry's reign, it may perhaps be well to say a few words about the state of opinion in England at that time. The belief that the whole people took their religion with sheepish meekness from their king is too simple and too dishonorable to the national character to be believed. That they *appeared* to do this is really a proof that parties were nearly divided. Just as in modern times great issues are often decided in general elections by narrow majorities, so in the sixteenth century public opinion veered now this way, now that, in part guided by the government, in part affecting it even when the channels by which it did so are not obvious. We must not imagine that the people took no interest in the course of affairs. On the contrary the burning issues of the day were discussed in public house and marketplace with the same vivacity with which politics are now debated in the New England country store. "The Word of God was disputed, rhymed, sung and jangled in every alehouse and tav-

Catholic reaction

ern,'' says a contemporary state paper. In private, graver men argued with the high spirit reflected in More's dialogues.

Four parties may be plainly discerned. First and most numerous were the strict Anglicans, orthodox and royalist, comprising the greater part of the crown-loving, priest-hating and yet, in intellectual matters, conservative common people. Secondly, there were the pope's followers, still strong in numbers especially among the clergy and in the north. Their leaders were among the most high-minded of the nation, but were also the first to be smitten by the king's wrath which, as his satellites were always repeating in Latin proverb, meant death. Such men were More and Fisher and the London Carthusians executed in 1535 for refusing the oath of supremacy. Third, there were the Lutherans, an active and intelligent minority of city merchants and artisans, led by men of conspicuous talents and generally of high character, like Coverdale, Ridley, and Latimer. With these leaders were a few opportunists like Cranmer and a few Machiavellians like Cromwell. Lastly there was a very small contingent of extremists, Zwinglians and Anabaptists, all classed together as blasphemers and as social agitators. Their chief notes were the variety of their opinions and the unanimity of their persecution by all other parties. Some of them were men of intelligible social and religious tenets; others furnished the "lunatic fringe" of the reform movement. The proclamation banishing them from England on pain of death merely continued the previous practice of the government.

1538

The fall of the Cromwell ministry, if it may be so termed by modern analogy, was followed by a government in which Henry acted as his own prime minister.

He had made good his boast that if his shirt knew his counsel he would strip it off.[1] Two of his great ministers he had cast down for being too Catholic, one for being too Protestant. Having procured laws enabling him to burn Romanists as traitors and Lutherans as heretics, he established a régime of pure Anglicanism, the only genuine Anglican Catholicism, however much it may have been imitated in after centuries, that ever existed.

Anti-Protestant measures

Measures were at once taken towards suppressing the Protestants and their Bible. One of the first martyrs was Robert Barnes, a personal friend of Luther. Much stir was created by the burning, some years later, of a gentlewoman named Anne Askewe and of three men, at Smithfield. The revulsion naturally caused by this cruelty prepared the people for the Protestant rule of Edward. The Bible was also attacked. The translation of 1539 was examined by Convocation in 1540 and criticized for not agreeing more closely with the Latin. In 1543 all marginal notes were obliterated and the lower classes forbidden to read the Bible at all.

Henry's reign ended as it began with war on France and Scotland, but with little success. The government was put to dire straits to raise money. A forced loan of 10 per cent. on property was exacted in 1542 and repudiated by law the next year. An income tax rising from four pence to two shillings in the pound on goods and from eight pence to three shillings on revenue from land, was imposed. Crown lands were sold or mortgaged. The last and most disastrous expedient was the debasement of the coinage, the old equivalent of the modern issue of irredeemable paper. As a consequence of this prices rose enormously.

[1] The metaphor came from Erasmus, *De Lingua*, 1525, *Opera*, iv, 682, where the words are attributed to Caecilius Metellus.

§ 2. The Reformation Under Edward VI. 1547–1553

Accession of Edward VI, January 28, 1547

The real test of the popularity of Henry's double revolution, constitutional and religious, came when England was no longer guided by his strong personality, but was ruled by a child and governed by a weak and shifting regency. It is significant that, whereas the prerogative of the crown was considerably relaxed, though substantially handed on to Edward's stronger successors, the Reformation proceeded at accelerated pace.

Somerset Regent

Henry himself, not so much to insure further change as to safeguard that already made, appointed Reformers as his son's tutors and made the majority of the Council of Regency Protestant. The young king's maternal uncle, Edward Seymour, Earl of Hertford, was chosen by the council as Protector and created Duke of Somerset. Mildness was the characteristic of his rule. He ignored Henry's treason and heresy acts even before they had been repealed.

1547

Repeal of treason and heresy laws

The first general election was held with little government interference. Parliament may be assumed to have expressed the will of the nation when it repealed Henry's treason and heresy laws, the ancient act *De Haeretico comburendo,* the Act of the Six Articles, and the Statute of Proclamations.

To ascertain exactly what, at a given time, is the "public opinion" of a political group, is one of the most difficult tasks of the historian.[1] Even nowadays it is certain that the will of the majority is frequently not reflected either in the acts of the legisature or in the newspaper press. It cannot even be said that the wishes of the majority are always public opinion. In expressing the voice of the people there is generally some section more vocal, more powerful on account

[1] See A. L. Lowell: *Public Opinion and Popular Government,* 1914.

of wealth or intelligence, and more deeply in earnest than any other; and this minority, though sometimes a relatively small one, imposes its will in the name of the people and identifies its voice with the voice of God.

Protestant public opinion

Therefore, when we read the testimony of contemporaries that the majority of England was still Catholic by the middle of the sixteenth century, a further analysis of popular opinion must be made to account for the apparently spontaneous rush of the Reformation. Some of these estimates are doubtless exaggerations, as that of Paget who wrote in 1549 that eleven Englishmen out of twelve were Catholics. But conceding, as we must, that a considerable majority was still anti-Protestant, it must be remembered that this majority included most of the indifferent and listless and almost all those who held their opinions for no better reason than they had inherited them and refused the trouble of thinking about them. Nearly the solid north and west, the country districts and the unrepresented and mute proletariat of the cities, counted as Catholic but hardly counted for anything else. The commercial class of the towns and the intellectual class, which, though relatively small, then as now made public opinion as measured by all ordinary tests, was predominantly and enthusiastically Protestant.

If we analyse the expressed wishes of England, we shall find a mixture of real religious faith and of worldly, and sometimes discreditable, motives. A new party always numbers among its constituency not only those who love its principles but those who hate its opponents. With the Protestants were a host of allies varying from those who detested Rome to those who repudiated all religion. Moreover every successful party has a number of hangers-on for the sake of political spoils, and some who follow its fortunes with no purpose save to fish in troubled waters.

But whatever their constituency or relative numbers, the Protestants now carried all before them. In the free religious debate that followed the death of Henry, the press teemed with satires and pamphlets, mostly Protestant. From foreign parts flocked allies, while the native stock of literary ammunition was reinforced by German and Swiss books. In the reign of Edward there were three new translations of Luther's books, five of Melanchthon's, two of Zwingli's, two of Oecolampadius's, three of Bullinger's and four of Calvin's. Many English religious leaders were in correspondence with Bullinger, many with Calvin, and some with Melanchthon. Among the prominent European Protestants called to England during this reign were Bucer and Fagius of Germany, Peter Martyr and Bernardino Ochino of Italy, and the Pole John Laski.

1547

The purification of the churches began promptly. Images, roods and stained glass windows were destroyed, while the buildings were whitewashed on the inside, properly to express the austerity of the new cult. Evidence shows that these acts, countenanced by the government, were popular in the towns but not in the country districts.

Book of Common Prayer, 1549

Next came the preparation of an English liturgy. The first Book of Common Prayer was the work of Cranmer. Many things in it, including some of the most beautiful portions, were translations from the Roman Breviary; but the high and solemn music of its language must be credited to the genius of its translator. Just as the English Bible popularized the Reformation, so the English Prayer Book strengthened and broadened the hold of the Anglican church. Doctrinally, it was a compromise between Romanism, Lutheranism and Calvinism. Its use was enforced by

1549

the Act of Uniformity, the first and mildest of the

statutes that bore that name. Though it might be celebrated in Greek, Latin or Hebrew as well as in English, priests using any other service were punished with loss of benefices and imprisonment.

At this time there must have been an unrecorded struggle in the Council of Regency between the two religious parties, followed by the victory of the innovators. The pace of the Reformation was at once increased; between 1550 and 1553 England gave up most of what was left of distinctively medieval Catholicism. For one thing, the marriage of priests was now legalized. That public opinion was hardly prepared for this as yet is shown by the act itself in which celibacy of the clergy is declared to be the better condition, and marriage only allowed to prevent vice. The people still regarded priests' wives much as concubines and the government spoke of clergymen as "sotted with their wives and children." There is one other bit of evidence, of a most singular character, showing that this and subsequent Acts of Uniformity were not thoroughly enforced. The test of orthodoxy came to be taking the communion occasionally according to the Anglican rite. This was at first expected of everyone and then demanded by law; but the law was evaded by permitting a conscientious objector to hire a substitute to take communion for him.

End of 1549

Accelerated Reformation

In 1552 the Prayer Book was revised in a Protestant sense. Bucer had something to do with this revision, and so did John Knox. Little was now left of the mass, nothing of private confession or anointing the sick. Further steps were the reform of the Canon Law and the publication of the Forty-two Articles of Religion. These were drawn up by Cranmer on the basis of thirteen articles agreed upon by a conference of three English Bishops, four English doctors, and two German missionaries, Boyneburg and Myconius, in

May, 1538. Cranmer hoped to make his statement irenic; and in fact it contained some Roman and Calvinistic elements, but in the main it was Lutheran. Justification by faith was asserted; only two sacraments were retained. Transubstantiation was denounced as repugnant to Scripture and private masses as "dangerous impostures." The real presence was maintained in a Lutheran sense: the bread was said to be the Body of Christ, and the wine the Blood of Christ, but only after a heavenly and spiritual manner. It was said that by Christ's ordinance the sacrament is not reserved, carried about, lifted up, or worshipped.

A reform of the clergy was also undertaken, and was much needed. In 1551 Bishop Hooper found in his diocese of 311 clergymen, 171 could not repeat the Ten Commandments, ten could not say the Lord's Prayer in English, seven could not tell who was its author, and sixty-two were absentees, chiefly because of pluralities.

The notable characteristic of the Edwardian Reformation was its mildness. There were no Catholic martyrs. It is true that heretics coming under the category of blasphemers or deniers of Christianity could still be put to death by common law, and two men were actually executed for speculations about the divinity of Christ, but such cases were wholly exceptional.

Social disorders

The social disorders of the time, coming to a head, seemed to threaten England with a rising of the lower classes similar to the Peasants' War of 1525 in Germany. The events in England prove that, however much these ebullitions might be stimulated by the atmosphere of the religious change, they were not the direct result of the new gospel. In the west of England and in Oxfordshire the lower classes rebelled under the leadership of Catholic priests; in the east the rising, known as Kett's rebellion, took on an Anabaptist character. The real causes of discontent were the same in both cases. The growing wealth of the commercial classes had widened the gap between rich and poor. The inclosures continued to be a grievance, by the ejection of small tenants and the appropriation of common lands. But by far the greatest cause of hardship to the poor was the debasement of the coinage. Wheat, barley, oats and cattle rose in price to two or three times their previous cost, while wages, kept down by law, rose only 11 per cent. No wonder that the condition of the laborer had become impossible.

The demands of the eastern rising, centering at Norwich, bordered on communism. The first was for the enfranchisement of all bondsmen for the reason that Christ had made all men free. Inclosures of commons and private property in game and fish were denounced and further agrarian demands were voiced. The rebels committed no murder and little sacrilege, but vented their passions by slaughtering vast numbers of sheep. All the peasant risings were suppressed by the government, and the economic forces continued to operate against the wasteful agricultural system of the time and in favor of wool-growing and manufacture.

Execution of Somerset, January 22, 1552

After five years under Protector Somerset there was a change of government signalized, as usual under Henry VIII, by the execution of the resigning minister. Somerset suffered from the unpopularity of the new religious policy in some quarters and from that following the peasants' rebellion in others. As usual, the government was blamed for the economic evils of the time and for once, in having debased the coinage, justly. Moreover the Protector had been involved by scheming rivals in the odium more than in the guilt of fratricide, for this least bloody of all English ministers in that century, had executed his brother, Thomas, Baron Seymour, a rash and ambitious man rightly supposed to be plotting his own advancement by a royal marriage.

Among the leaders of the Reformation belonging to the class of mere adventurers, John Dudley, Earl of Warwick, was the ablest and the worst. As the Protector held quasi-royal powers, he could only be deposed by using the person of the young king. Warwick ingratiated himself with Edward and brought the child of thirteen to the council. Of course he could only speak what was taught him, but the name of royalty had so dread a prestige that none dared disobey him. At his command Warwick was created Duke of Northumberland, and his confederate, Henry Grey Marquis of Dorset, was created Duke of Suffolk. A little later these men, again using the person of the king, had Somerset tried and executed.

Northumberland and Suffolk

The conspirators did not long enjoy their triumph. While Edward lived and was a minor they were safe, but Edward was a consumptive visibly declining. They had no hope of perpetuating their power save to alter the succession, and this they tried to do. Another Earl of Warwick had been a king-maker, why not the present one? Henry VIII's will appointed to succeed him, in case of Edward's death without issue, (1) Mary, (2) Elizabeth, (3) the heirs of his younger sister Mary who had married Charles Brandon, Duke of Suffolk. Of this marriage there had been born two daughters, the elder of whom, Frances, married Henry Grey, recently created Duke of Suffolk. The issue of this marriage were three daughters, and the eldest of them, Lady Jane Grey, was picked by the two dukes as the heir to the throne, and was married to Northumberland's son, Guilford Dudley. The young king was now appealed to, on the ground of his religious feeling, to alter the succession so as to exclude not only his Catholic sister Mary but his lukewarm sister Elizabeth in favor of the strongly Protestant Lady Jane. Though his lawyers told him he could not alter the succession to the crown, he intimidated them into drawing up a "devise" purporting to do this.

§ 3. The Catholic Reaction Under Mary. 1553–58

Proclamation of Queen Jane, July 10, 1553

When Edward died on July 6, 1553, Northumberland had taken such precautions as he could to ensure the success of his project. He had gathered his own men at London and tried to secure help from France, whose king would have been only too glad to involve England in civil war. The death of the king was concealed for four days while preparations were being made, and then Queen Jane was proclaimed. Mary's challenge arrived the next day and she (Mary) at once began raising an army. Had her person been secured the plot might have succeeded, but she avoided the set snares. Charles V wished to support her for religious reasons, but feared to excite patriotic feeling by dispatching an army and therefore confined his intervention to diplomatic representations to Northumberland.

Accession of Mary

There was no doubt as to the choice of the people. Even the strongest Protestants hated civil turmoil more than they did Catholicism, and the people as a whole felt instinctively that if the crown was put up as a prize for unscrupulous politicians there would be no end of strife. All therefore flocked to Mary, and almost without a struggle she overcame the conspirators and entered her capital amid great rejoicing. Northumberland, after a despicable and fruitless recantation, was executed and so were his son and his son's wife, Queen Jane. Sympathy was felt for her on account of her youth, beauty and remarkable talents, but none for her backers.

The relief with which the settlement was regarded gave the new queen at least the good will of the nation to start with. This she gradually lost. Just as Elizabeth instinctively did the popular thing, so Mary seemed almost by fatality to choose the worst course possible. Her foreign policy, in the first place, was both un-English and unsuccessful. Almost at once Charles V proposed his son Philip as Mary's husband, and, after about a year of negotiation, the marriage took place. The tremendous unpopularity of this step was due not so much to hostility to Spain, though Spain was beginning to be regarded as the national foe rather than France, but to the fear of a foreign domination. England had never before been ruled by a queen, if we except the disastrous reign of Mathilda, and it was natural to suppose that Mary's husband should have the prerogative as well as the title of king. In vain Philip tried to disabuse the English of the idea that he was asserting any independent claims; in some way the people felt that they were being annexed to Spain, and they hated it.

Marriage of Mary and Philip, July 25, 1554

The religious aim of the marriage, to aid in the restoration of Catholicism, was also disliked. Cardinal Pole frankly avowed this purpose, declaring that

> as Christ, being heir of the world, was sent down by his Father from the royal throne, to be at once Spouse and Son of the Virgin Mary and to be made the Comforter and Saviour of mankind; so, in like manner, the greatest of all princes upon earth, the heir of his father's kingdom, departed from his own broad and happy realms that he, too, might come hither into this land of trouble, to be the spouse and son of this virgin Mary . . . to aid in the reconciliation of this people to Christ and the church.

For Mary herself the marriage was most unhappy.

She was a bride of thirty-eight, already worn and aged by grief and care; her bridegroom was only twenty-seven. She adored him, but he almost loathed her and made her miserable by neglect and unfaithfulness. Her passionate hopes for a child led her to believe and announce that she was to have one, and her disappointment was correspondingly bitter.

So unpopular was the marriage coupled with the queen's religious policy, that it led to a rebellion under Sir Thomas Wyatt. Though suppressed, it was a dangerous symptom, especially as Mary failed to profit by the warning. Her attempts to implicate her sister Elizabeth in the charge of treason failed.

Had Mary's foreign policy only been strong it might have conciliated the patriotic pride of the ever present jingo. But under her leadership England seemed to decline almost to its nadir. The command of the sea was lost and, as a consequence of this and of the military genius of the Duke of Guise, Calais, held for over two centuries, was conquered by the French. With the subsequent loss of Guines the last English outpost on the continent was reft from her.

1558

Religious policy

Notwithstanding Mary's saying that "Calais" would be found in her heart when she died, by far her deepest interest was the restoration of Catholicism. To assist her in this task she had Cardinal Reginald Pole, in whose veins flowed the royal blood of England and whom the pope appointed as legate to the kingdom. Though Mary's own impulse was to act strongly, she sensibly adopted the emperor's advice to go slowly and, as far as possible, in legal forms. Within a month of her succession she issued a proclamation stating her intention to remain Catholic and her hope that her subjects would embrace the same religion, but at the same time disclaiming the intention of forcing them and forbidding strife and the use of "those new-found devilish terms of papist or heretic or such like."

Elections to the first Parliament were free; it passed two noteworthy Acts of Repeal, the first restoring the *status quo* at the death of Henry VIII, the second restoring the *status quo* of 1529 on the eve of the Reformation Parliament. This second act abolished eighteen statutes of Henry VIII and one of Edward VI, but it refused to restore the church lands. The fate of the confiscated ecclesiastical property was one of the greatest obstacles, if not the greatest, in the path of reconciliation with Rome. The pope at first insisted upon it, and Pole was deeply grieved at being obliged to absolve sinners who kept the fruits of their sins. But the English, as the Spanish ambassador Renard wrote, "would rather get themselves massacred than let go" the abbey lands. The very Statute of Repeal, therefore, that in other respects met Mary's demands, carefully guarded the titles to the secularized lands, making all suits relating to them triable only in crown courts.

Repeal of Reforming acts

The second point on which Parliament, truly representing a large section of public opinion, was obstinate, was in the refusal to recognize the papal supremacy. The people as a whole cared not what dogma they were supposed to believe, but they for the most part cordially hated the pope. They therefore agreed to pass the acts of repeal only on condition that nothing was said about the royal supremacy. To Mary's insistence they returned a blank refusal to act and she was compelled to wait "while Parliament debated articles that might well puzzle a general council," as a contemporary wrote.

Lords and Commons were quite willing to pass acts to strengthen the crown and then to leave the responsibility for further action to it. Thus the divorce of Henry and Catharine of Aragon was repealed and the treason laws were revived. Going even beyond the limit of Henry VIII it was made treason to "pray or desire" that God would shorten the queen's days. Worse than that, Parliament revived the heresy laws. It is a strange comment on the nature of legislatures that they have so often, as in this case, protected property better than life, and made money more sacred than conscience. However, it was not Parliament but the executive that carried out to its full extent the policy of persecution and religious reaction.

Revival of treason laws

The country soon showed its opposition. A temporary disarray that might have been mistaken for disintegration had been produced in the Protestant ranks by the recantation of Northumberland. The restoration of the mass was accomplished in orderly manner in most places. The English formulas had been patient of a Catholic interpretation, and doubtless many persons regarded the change from one liturgy to the other as a matter of slight importance. Moreover the majority made a principle of conformity to the government, believing that an act of the law relieved the conscience of the individual of responsibility. But even so, there was a large minority of recusants. Of 8800 beneficed clergy in England, 2000 were ejected for refusal to comply. A very large number fled to the Continent, forming colonies at Frankfort-on-the-Main and at Geneva and scattering in other places. The opinion of the imperial ambassador Renard that English Protestants depended entirely on support from abroad was tolerably true for this reign, for their books continued to be printed abroad, and a few further translations from foreign reformers were made. It is noteworthy that these mostly treat of the question, then so much in debate, whether Protestants might innocently attend the mass.

Other expressions of the temper of the people were the riots in London. On the last day of the first Parliament a dog with a tonsured crown, a rope around its neck and a writing signifying that priests and bishops should be hung, was thrown through a window into the queen's presence chamber. At another time a cat was found tonsured, surpliced, and with a wafer in its mouth in derision of the mass. The perpetrators of these outrages could not be found.

Passive resistance

A sterner, though passive, resistance to the government was gloriously evinced when stake and rack began to do their work. Mary was totally unprepared for the strength of Protestant feeling in the country. She hoped a few executions would strike terror into the hearts of all and render further persecution unnecessary. But from the execution of the first martyr, John Rogers, it was plain that the people sympathized with the victims rather than feared their fate. Not content with warring on the living, Mary even broke the sleep of the dead.[1] The bodies of Bucer and Fagius were dug up and burned. The body of Peter Martyr's wife was also exhumed, though, as no evidence of heresy could be procured, it was thrown on a dunghill to rot.

Martyrs, October 16, 1555

The most famous victims were Latimer, Ridley and Cranmer. The first two were burnt alive together, Latimer at the stake comforting his friend by assuring him, "This day we shall light such a candle, by God's grace, in England, as I trust, shall never be put out." A special procedure was reserved for Cranmer, as primate. Every effort was made to get him to recant. He at first signed four submissions recognizing the

[1] The canon law forbade the burial of heretics in consecrated ground, but it is said that Charles V refused to dig up Luther's body when he took Wittenberg.

power of the pope as and if restored by Parliament. He then signed two real recantations, and finally drew up a seventh document, repudiating his recantations, re-affirming his faith in the Protestant doctrine of the sacraments and denouncing the pope. By holding his right hand in the fire, when he was burned at the stake, he testified his bitter repentance for its act in signing the recantations.

March 21, 1556

The total number of martyrs in Mary's reign fell very little, if at all, short of 300. The lists of them are precise and circumstantial. The geographical distribution is interesting, furnishing, as it does, the only statistical information available in the sixteenth century for the spread of Protestantism. It graphically illustrates the fact, so often noticed before, that the strongholds of the new opinions were the commercial towns of the south and east. If a straight line be drawn from the Wash to Portsmouth, passing about twenty miles west of London, it will roughly divide the Protestant from the Catholic portions of England. Out of 290 martyrdoms known, 247 took place east of this line, that is, in the city of London and the counties of Essex, Hertford, Kent, Sussex, Norfolk, Suffolk and Cambridge. Thirteen are recorded in the south center, at Winchester and Salisbury, eleven at the western ports of the Severn, Bristol and Gloucester. There were three in Wales, all on the coast at St. David's; one in the south-western peninsula at Exeter, a few in the midlands, and not one north of Lincolnshire and Cheshire.

When it is said that the English changed their religion easily, this record of heroic opposition must be remembered to the contrary. Mary's reign became more and more hateful to her people until at last it is possible that only the prospect of its speedy termination prevented a rebellion. The popular epithet of "bloody" rightly distinguishes her place in the estimate of history. It is true that her persecution sinks into insignificance compared with the holocausts of victims to the inquisition in the Netherlands. But the English people naturally judged by their own history, and in all of that such a reign of terror was unexampled. The note of Mary's reign is sterility and its achievement was to create, in reaction to the policy then pursued, a ferocious and indelible hatred of Rome.

§ 3. The Elizabethan Settlement. 1558–88.

Elizabeth, 1558–1603

However numerous and thorny were the problems pressed for solution into the hands of the maiden of twenty-five now called upon to rule England, the greatest of all questions, that of religion, almost settled itself. It is extremely hard to divest ourselves of the wisdom that comes after the event and to put ourselves in the position of the men of that time and estimate fairly the apparent feasibility of various alternatives. But it is hard to believe that the considerations that seem so overwhelming to us should not have forced themselves upon the attention of the more thoughtful men of that generation.

In the first place, while the daughter of Anne Boleyn was predestined by heredity and breeding to oppose Rome, yet she was brought up in the Anglican Catholicism of Henry VIII. At the age of eleven she had translated Margaret of Navarre's *Mirror of the Sinful Soul,* a work expressing the spirit of devotion joined with liberalism in creed and outward conformity in cult. The rapid vicissitudes of faith in England taught her tolerance, and her own acute intellect and practical sense inclined her to indifference. She did not scruple to give all parties, Catholic, Lutheran and Calvinist, the impression, when it suited her, that she was almost in agreement with each of them. The accusation that she was "an atheist and a maintainer of atheism" meant no more than that her interests were secular. She once said that she would rather hear a thousand masses than be guilty of the millions of crimes perpetrated by some of those who had suppressed the mass. She liked candles, crucifixes and ritual just as she inordinately loved personal display. And politically she learned very early to fear the republicanism of Knox.

1601

Most of people Catholic

The conservatism of Elizabeth's policy was determined also by the consideration that, though the more intelligent and progressive classes were Protestant, the mass of the people still clung to the Roman faith, and, if they had no other power, had at least the *vis inertiae.* Accurate figures cannot be obtained, but a number of indications are significant. In 1559 Convocation asserted the adherence of the clergy to the ancient faith. Maurice Clenoch estimated in 1561 that the majority of the people would welcome foreign intervention in favor of Mary Stuart and the old faith. Nicholas Sanders, a contemporary Catholic apologist, said that the common people of that period were divided into three classes: husbandmen, shepherds and mechanics. The first two classes he considered entirely Catholic; the third class, he said, were not tainted with schism as a whole, but only in some parts, those, namely of sedentary occupation such as weavers, cobblers and some lazy "aulici," *i. e.* servants and humble retainers of the great. The remote parts of the kingdom, he added, were least tainted with heresy and, as the towns were few and small, he estimated that less than one per cent. of the population was Protestant. Though these figures are a tremendous exaggeration of the proportion of Catholics, some support may be found for them in the information sent to the Curia in 1567 that 32 English nobles were Catholic, 20 well affected to the Catholics and 15 Protestants. Only slightly different is the report sent in 1571 that at that time 33 English peers were Catholic, 15 doubtful and 16 heretical. As a matter of fact, in religious questions we find that the House of Lords would have been Catholic but for the bishops, a solid phalanx of government nominees.

But most powerful class Protestants

But if the masses were Catholic, the strategically situated classes were Reformed. The first House of Commons of Elizabeth proved by its acts to be strongly Protestant. The assumption generally made that it was packed by the government has been recently exploded. Careful testing shows that there was hardly any government interference. Of the 390 members, 168 had sat in earlier Parliaments of Mary, and that was just the normal proportion of old members. It must be remembered that the parliamentary franchise approached the democratic only in the towns, the strongholds of Protestantism, and that in the small boroughs and in some of the counties the election was determined by just that middle class most progressive and at this time most Protestant.

Another test of the temper of the country is the number of clergy refusing the oath of supremacy. Out of a total number of about nine thousand only about two hundred lost their livings as recusants, and most of these were Mary's appointees.

The same impression of Protestantism is given by the literature of the time. The fifty-six volumes of Elizabethan divinity published by the Parker Society testify to the number of Reformation treaties, tracts, hymns and letters of this period. During the first thirty years of Elizabeth's reign there were fifteen new translations of Luther's works, not counting a number of reprints, two new translations from Melanchthon, thirteen from Bullinger and thirty-four from Calvin. Notwithstanding this apparently large foreign influence, the English Reformation at this time resumed the national character temporarily lost during Mary's reign. John Jewel's *Apologia Ecclesiae Anglicanae* has been called by Creighton, "the first methodical statement of the position of the church of England against the church of Rome, and the groundwork of all subsequent controversy."

1562

Finally, most of the prominent men of the time, and most of the rising young men, were Protestants. The English sea-captains, wolves of the sea as they were, found it advisable to disguise themselves in the sheep's clothing of zeal against the idolater. More creditable to the cause was the adherence of men like Sir William Cecil, later Lord Burghley, a man of cool judgment and decent conversation. Coverdale, still active, was made a bishop. John Foxe published, all in the interests of his faith, the most popular and celebrated history of the time. Roger Ascham, Elizabeth's tutor, still looked to Lutheran Germany as "a place where Christ's doctrine, the fear of God, punishment of sin, and discipline of honesty were held in special regard." Edmund Spenser's great allegory, as well as some of his minor poems, were largely inspired by Anglican and Calvinistic purposes.

Conversion of the masses

It was during Elizabeth's reign that the Roman Catholics lost the majority they claimed in 1558 and became the tiny minority they have ever since remained. The time and to some extent the process through which this came to pass can be traced with fair accuracy. In 1563 the policy of the government, till then wavering, became more decided, indicating that the current had begun to set in favor of Protestantism. The failure of the Northern rising and of the papal bull in 1569–70, indicated the weakness of the ancient faith. In 1572 a careful estimate of the

Carleton's estimate

religious state of England was made by a contemporary, who thought that of the three classes into which he divided the population, papist, Protestant and atheist (by which he probably meant, indifferent) the first was smaller than either of the other two. Ten years later (1580–85) the Jesuit mission in England claimed 120,000 converts. But in reality these adherents were not new converts, but the remnant of Romanism remaining faithful. If we assume, as a distinguished historian has done, that this number included nearly all the obstinately devoted, as the population of England and Wales was then about 4,000,000, the proportion of Catholics was only about 3 per cent. of the total, at which percentage it remained constant during the next century. But there were probably a considerable number of timid Roman Catholics not daring to make themselves known to the Jesuit mission. But even allowing liberally for these, it is safe to say that by 1585 the members of that church had sunk to a very small minority.

Those who see in the conversion of the English people the result merely of government pressure must explain two inconvenient facts. The first is that the Puritans, who were more strongly persecuted than the papists, waxed mightily notwithstanding. The second is that, during the period when the conversion of the masses took place, there were no martyrdoms and there was little persecution. The change was, in fact, but the inevitable completion and consequence of the conversion of the leaders of the people earlier. With the masses, doubtless, the full contrast between the old and the new faiths was not realized. Attending the same churches if not the same church, using a liturgy which some hoped would obtain papal sanction, and ignorant of the changes made in translation from the Latin ritual, the uneducated did not trouble themselves about abstruse questions of dogma or even about more obvious matters such as the supremacy of the pope and the marriage of the clergy. Moreover, there were strong positive forces attracting them to the Anglican communion. They soon learned to love the English prayer-book, and the Bible became so necessary that the Catholics were obliged to produce a version of their own. English insularity and patriotism drew them powerfully to the bosom of their own peculiar communion.

Elizabeth's policy

Though we can now see that the forces drawing England to the Reformation were decisive, the policy of Elizabeth was at first cautious. The old services went on until Parliament had spoken. As with Henry VIII, so with this daughter of his, scrupulous legality of form marked the most revolutionary acts. Elizabeth had been proclaimed "Queen of England, France and Ireland, Defender of the Faith &c," this "&c" being chosen to stand in place of the old title "Supreme Head of the Church," thus dodging the question of its assumption or omission. Parliament, however, very soon passed supremacy and uniformity acts to supply the needed sanction. The former repealed Philip and Mary's Heresy Act and Repealing Statute, revived ten acts of Henry VIII and one of Edward VI, but confirmed the repeal of six acts of Henry VIII. Next, Parliament proceeded to seize the episcopal lands. Its spirit was just as secular as that of Henry's Parliaments, only there was less ecclesiastical property left to grab.

The Book of Common Prayer was revised by introducing into the recension of 1552 a few passages from the first edition of 1549, previously rejected as too Catholic. Three of the Forty-two Articles of Religion of Edward were dropped, thus making the Thirty-nine Articles that have ever since been the authoritative

The Thirty-nine Articles 1563

statement of Anglican doctrine. Thus it is true to some extent that the Elizabethan settlement was a compromise. It took special heed of various parties, and tried to avoid offence to Lutherans, Zwinglians, and even to Roman Catholics. But far more than a compromise, it was a case of special development. As it is usually compared with the English Dissenting sects, the church of England is often said to be the most conservative of the reformed bodies. It is often said that it is Protestant in doctrine and Catholic in ritual and hierarchy. But compared with the Lutheran church it is found to be if anything further from Rome. In fact the Anglicans of the sixteenth and seventeenth centuries abhorred the Lutherans as "semi-papists."

The Church of England

And yet the Anglican church was like the Lutheran not only in its conservatism as compared with Calvinism, but in its political aspects. Both became the strong allies of the throne; both had not only a markedly national but a markedly governmental quality. Just as the Reformation succeeded in England by becoming national in opposition to Spain, and remaining national in opposition to French culture, so the Anglican church naturally became a perfect expression of the English character. Moderate, decorous, detesting extremes of speculation and enthusiasm, she cares less for logic than for practical convenience.

Succession

Closely interwoven with the religious settlement were the questions of the heir to the throne and of foreign policy. Elizabeth's life was the only breakwater that stood between the people and a Catholic, if not a disputed, succession. The nearest heir was Mary Stuart, Queen of Scots, a granddaughter of Margaret Tudor, Henry VIII's sister. As a Catholic and a Frenchwoman, half by race and wholly by her first marriage to Francis II, she would have been most distasteful to the ruling party in England. Elizabeth was therefore desired and finally urged by Parliament to marry. Her refusal to do this has been attributed to some hidden cause, as her love for Leicester or the knowledge that she was incapable of bearing a child. But though neither of these hypotheses can be disproved, neither is necessary to account for her policy. It is true that it would have strengthened her position to have had a child to succeed her; but it would have weakened her personal sway to have had a husband. She wanted to rule as well as to reign. Her many suitors were encouraged just sufficiently to flatter her vanity and to attain her diplomatic ends. First, her brother-in-law Philip sought her hand, and was promptly rejected as a Spanish Catholic. Then, there was Robert Dudley, Earl of Leicester, apparently her favorite in spite of his worthless character, but his rank was not high enough. Then, there were princes of Sweden and Denmark, an Archduke of Austria and two sons of Catharine de' Medici's. The suit of one of the latter began when Elizabeth was thirty-nine years old and he was nineteen and continued for ten years with apparent zest on both sides. Parliament put all the pressure it could upon the queen to make her flirtations end in matrimony, but it only made Elizabeth angry. Twice she forbade discussion of the matter, and, though she afterwards consented to hear the petition, she was careful not to call another Parliament for five years.

1566

Financial measures

Vexatious financial difficulties had been left to Elizabeth. Largely owing to the debasement of the currency royal expenditure had risen from £56,000 per annum at the end of Henry's reign to £345,000 in the last year of Mary's reign. The government's credit was in a bad way, and the commerce of the kingdom deranged. By the wise expedient of calling in the de-

1560

based coins issued since 1543, the hardest problems were solved.

Underhand war

Towards France and Spain Elizabeth's policy was one well described by herself as "underhand war." English volunteers, with government connivance, but nominally on their own responsibility, fought in the ranks of Huguenots and Netherlanders. Torrents of money poured from English churches to support their fellow-Protestants in France and Holland. English sailors seized Spanish galleons; if successful the queen secretly shared the spoil; but if they were caught they might be hanged as pirates by Philip or Alva. This condition, unthinkable now, was allowed by the inchoate state of international law; the very idea of neutrality was foreign to the time. States were always trying to harm and overreach each other in secret ways. In Elizabethan England the anti-papal and anti-Spanish ardor of the mariners made possible this buccaneering without government support, had not the rich prizes themselves been enough to attract the adventurous. Doubtless far more energy went into privateering than into legitimate commerce.

Peace was officially made with France, recognizing the surrender of Calais at first for a limited period of years. Though peace was still nominally kept with Spain for a long time, the shift of policy from one of hostility to France to one of enmity to Spain was soon manifest. As long, however, as the government relied chiefly on the commercial interests of the capital and other large towns, and as long as Spain controlled the Netherlands, open war was nearly impossible, for it would have been extremely unpopular with the merchants of both London and the Low Countries. In times of crisis, however, an embargo was laid on all trade with Philip's dominions.

1569

Elizabeth's position was made extremely delicate by

the fact that the heiress to her throne was the Scotch Queen Mary Stuart, who, since 1568, had been a refugee in England and had been kept in a sort of honorable captivity. On account of her religion she became the center of the hopes and of the actual machinations of all English malcontents. In these plots she participated as far as she dared.

The Catholic Powers

Elizabeth's crown would have been jeoparded had the Catholic powers, or any one of them, acted promptly. That they did not do so is proof, partly of their mutual jealousies, party of the excellence of Cecil's statesmanship. Convinced though he was that civil peace could only be secured by religious unity, for five years he played a hesitating game in order to hold off the Catholics until his power should be strong enough to crush them. By a system of espionage, by permitting only nobles and sailors to leave the kingdom without special licence, by welcoming Dutch Protestant refugees, he clandestinely fostered the strength of his party. His scheme was so far successful that the pope hesitated more than eleven years before issuing the bull of deprivation. For this Elizabeth had also to thank the Catholic Hapsburgs; in the first place Philip who then hoped to marry her, and in the second place the Emperor Ferdinand who said that if Elizabeth were excommunicated the German Catholics would suffer for it and that there were many German Protestant princes who deserved the ban as much as she did.

Matters were clarified by the calling of the Council of Trent. Asked to send an embassy to this council Elizabeth refused for three reasons: (1) because she had not been consulted about calling the council; (2) because she did not consider it free, pious and Christian; (3) because the pope sought to stir up sedition in her realms. The council replied to this snub by excommunicating her, but it is a significant sign of the times that neither they nor the pope as yet dared to use spiritual weapons to depose her, as the pope endeavored to do a few years later.

Anti-Catholic laws, 1563

Whether as a reply to this measure or not, Parliament passed more stringent laws against Catholics. Cecil's policy, inherited from Thomas Cromwell, to centralize and unify the state, met with threefold opposition; first from the papists who disliked nationalizing the church, second from the holders of medieval franchises who objected to their absorption in a centripetal system, and third from the old nobles who resented their replacement in the royal council by upstarts. All these forces produced a serious crisis in the years 1569–70. The north, as the stronghold of both feudalism and Catholicism, led the reaction. The Duke of Norfolk, England's premier peer, plotted with the northern earls to advance Mary's cause, and thought of marrying her himself. Pope Pious V warmly praised their scheme which culminated in a rebellion. The nobles and commons alike were filled with the spirit of crusaders, bearing banners with the cross and the five wounds of Christ. At the same time they voiced the grievance of the old-fashioned farmer against the new-fangled merchant. Their banners inscribed "God speed the plough" bear witness to the agrarian element common to so many revolts. Their demands were the restoration of Catholicism, intervention in Scotland to put Mary back on her throne, and her recognition as heiress of England, and the expulsion of foreign refugees. Had they been able to secure Mary's person or had the Scotch joined them, it is probable that they would have seceded from the south of England.

Rebellion, 1561

But the new Pilgrimage of Grace was destined to no more success than the old one. Moray, Regent of Scotland, forcibly prevented assistance going to the rebels from North Britain. Elizabeth prepared an overwhelming army, but it was not needed. The rebels, seeing the hopelessness of their cause, dispersed and were pursued by an exemplary punishment, no less than eight hundred being executed. Three years later Norfolk trod the traitor's path to the scaffold. His death sealed the ruin of the old nobility whose privileges were incompatible with the new régime. In the same year a parliamentary agitation in favor of the execution of Mary witnessed how dead were medieval titles to respect.

Papal Bull, February 25, 1570

Too late to have much effect, Pius V issued the bull *Regnans in excelsis,* declaring that whereas the Roman pontiff has power over all nations and kingdoms to destroy and ruin or to plant and build up, and whereas Elizabeth, the slave of vice, has usurped the place of supreme head of the church, has sent her realm to perdition and has celebrated the impious mysteries of Calvin, therefore she is cut off from the body of Christ and deprived of her pretended right to rule England, while all her subjects are absolved from their oaths of allegiance. The bull also reasserted Elizabeth's illegitimacy, and echoed the complaint of the northern earls that she had expelled the old nobility from her council. The promulgation of the bull, without the requisite warning and allowance of a year for repentance, was contrary to the canon law.

The fulmination was sent to Alva to the Netherlands and a devotee was found to carry it to England. Forthwith Elizabeth issued a masterly proclamation vouchsafing that,

> her majesty would have all her loving subjects to understand that, as long as they shall openly continue in the observation of her laws, and shall not wilfully and manifestly break them by open actions, her majesty's means is not to have any of them molested by any inquisition or

examination of their consciences in causes of religion, but to accept and entreat them as her good and obedient subjects.

Anti-papal laws

But to obviate the contamination of her people by political views expressed in the bull, and to guard against the danger of a further rising in the interests of Mary Stuart, the Parliament of 1571 passed several necessary laws. One of these forbade bringing the bull into England; another made it treasonable to declare that Elizabeth was not or ought not to be queen or that she was a heretic, usurper or schismatic.

The first seventeen years of Elizabeth's reign had been blessedly free from persecution. The increasing strain between England and the papacy was marked by a number of executions of Romanists. A recent Catholic estimate is that the total number of this faith who suffered under Elizabeth was 189, of whom 128 were priests, 58 laymen and three women; and to this should be added 32 Franciscans who died in prison of starvation. The contrast of 221 victims in Elizabeth's forty-five years as against 290 in Mary's five years, is less important than the different purpose of the government. Under Mary the executions were for heresy; under Elizabeth chiefly for treason. It is true that the whole age acted upon Sir Philip Sidney's maxim that it was the highest wisdom of statesmanship never to separate religion from politics. Church and state were practically one and the same body, and opinions repugnant to established religion naturally resulted in acts inimical to the civil order. But the broad distinction is plain. Cecil put men to death not because he detested their dogma but because he feared their politics.

Jesuit mission

Nothing proves more clearly the purposes of the English government than its long duel with the Jesuit mission. It is unfair to say that the primary purpose of the Curia was to get all the privileges of loyalty for English Catholics while secretly inciting them to rise and murder their sovereign. But the very fact that the Jesuits were instructed not to meddle in politics and yet were unable to keep clear of the law, proves how inextricably politics and religion were intertwined. Immediately drawing the suspicion of Burghley, they were put to the "bloody question" and illegally tortured, even while the government felt called upon to explain that they were not forced to the rack to answer "any question of their supposed conscience" but only as to their political opinions. But one of these opinions was whether the pope had the right to depose the queen.

Character of Jesuits

The history of these years is one more example of how much more accursed it is to persecute than to be persecuted. The Jesuits sent to England were men of the noblest character, daring and enduring all with fortitude, showing charity and loving-kindness even to their enemies. But the character of their enemies correspondingly deteriorated. That sense of fair play that is the finest English quality disappeared under the stress of fanaticism. Not only Jesuits, but Catholic women and children were attacked; one boy of thirteen was racked and executed as a traitor. The persecution by public opinion supplied what the activity of the government overlooked. In fact it was the government that was the moderating factor. The act passed in 1585 banishing the Jesuits was intended to obviate sterner measures. In dealing with the mass of the population Burghley made persecution pay its way by resorting to fines as the principal punishment. During the last twenty years of the reign no less than £6,000 per annum was thus collected.

The helpless rage of the popes against "the Jezebel of the north" waxed until one of them, Gregory XIII,

Conspiracies

sanctioned an attempt at her assassination. In 1580 there appeared at the court of Madrid one Humphrey Ely, later a secular priest. He informed the papal nunciature that some English nobles, mentioned by name, had determined to murder Elizabeth but wished the pope's own assurance that, in case they lost their lives in the attempt, they should not have fallen into sin by the deed. After giving his own opinion that the bull of Pius V gave all men the right to take arms against the queen in any fashion, the nuncio wrote to Rome. From the papal secretary, speaking in the pope's name, he received the following reply:

> As that guilty woman of England rules two so noble realms of Christendom, is the cause of so much harm to the Catholic faith, and is guilty of the loss of so many million souls, there is no doubt that any one who puts her out of the world with the proper intention of serving God thereby, not only commits no sin but even wins merit, especially seeing that the sentence of the late Pius V is standing against her. If, therefore, these English nobles have really decided to do so fair a work, your honor may assure them that they commit no sin. Also we may trust in God that they will escape all danger. As to your own irregularity [caused to the nuncio as a priest by conspiracy to murder] the pope sends you his holy blessing.[1]

A conspiracy equally unsuccessful but more famous, because discovered at the time, was that of Anthony Babington. Burghley's excellent secret service apprised the government not only of the principals but also of aid and support given to them by Philip II and Mary Queen of Scots. Parliament petitioned for the execution of Mary. Though there was no doubt of her guilt, Elizabeth hesitated to give the dangerous example of sending a crowned head to the block.

[1] A. O. Meyer: *England und die katholische Kirche unter Elizabeth*, p. 231.

With habitual indirection she did her best to get Mary's jailer, Sir Amyas Paulet, to put her to death without a warrant. Failing in this, she finally signed the warrant, but when her council acted upon it in secret haste lest she should change her mind, she flew into a rage and, to prove her innocence, heavily fined and imprisoned one of the privy council whom she selected as scapegoat.

Mary beheaded, February 8, 1587

The war with Spain is sometimes regarded as the inevitable consequence of the religious opposition of the chief Catholic and the chief Protestant power. But probably the war would never have gone beyond the stage of privateering and plots to assassinate in which it remained inchoate for so long, had it not been for the Netherlands. The corner-stone of English policy has been to keep friendly, or weak, the power controlling the mouths of the Rhine and the Scheldt. The war of liberation in the Netherlands had a twofold effect; in the first place it damaged England's best customer, and secondly, Spanish "frightfulness" shocked the English conscience. For a long time the policy of the queen herself was as cynically selfish as it could possibly be. She not only watched complacently the butcheries of Alva, but she plotted and counterplotted, now offering aid to the Prince of Orange, now betraying his cause in a way that may have been sport to her but was death to the men she played with. Her aim, as far as she had a consistent one, was to allow Spain and the Netherlands to exhaust each other.

War with Spain

Not only far nobler but, as it proved in the end, far wiser, was the action of the Puritan party that poured money and recruits into the cause of their oppressed fellow-Calvinists. But an equally great service to them, or at any rate a greater amount of damage to Spain, was done by the hardy buccaneers, Hawkins and Drake, who preyed upon the Spanish treasure galleons and pillaged the Spanish settlements in the New World. These men and their fellows not only cut the sinews of Spain's power but likewise built the fleet.

England's sea power

The eventual naval victory of England was preceded by a long course of successful diplomacy. As the aggressor England forced the haughtiest power in Europe to endure a protracted series of outrages. Not only were rebels supported, not only were Spanish fleets taken forcibly into English harbors and there stripped of moneys belonging to their government, but refugees were protected and Spanish citizens put to death by the English queen. Philip and Alva could not effectively resent and hardly dared to protest against the treatment, because they felt themselves powerless. As so often, the island kingdom was protected by the ocean and by the proved superiority of her seamen. After a score of petty fights all the way from the Bay of Biscay to the Pacific Ocean, Spanish sailors had no desire for a trial of strength in force.

But in every respect save in sea power Spain felt herself immeasurably superior to her foe. Her wealth, her dominions, recently augmented by the annexation of Portugal, were enormous; her army had been tried in a hundred battles. England's force was doubtless underestimated. An Italian expert stated that an army of 10,000 to 12,000 foot and 2,000 horse would be sufficient to conquer her. Even to the last it was thought that an invader would be welcomed by a large part of the population, for English refugees never wearied of picturing the hatred of the people for their queen.

But the decision was long postponed for two reasons. First, Spain was fully employed in subduing the Netherlands. Secondly, the Catholic powers hoped for the accession of Mary. But after the assassination of Orange in 1584, and after the execution of the Queen of Scots, these reasons for delay no longer existed. Drake carried the naval war to the coasts of Spain and to her colonies. The consequent bankruptcy of the Bank of Seville and the wounded national pride brought home to Spaniards the humiliation of their position. All that Philip could do was to pray for help and to forbid the importation of English wares. In reply Drake fell upon the harbor of Cadiz and destroyed twenty-four or more warships and vast military stores.

1585

April, 1587

So at last the decision was taken to crush the one power that seemed to maintain the Reformation, to uphold the Huguenots and the Dutch patriots and to harry with impunity the champions of Catholicism. Pope Sixtus V, not wishing to hazard anything, promised a subsidy of 1,000,000 crowns of gold, the first half payable on the landing of the Spanish army, the second half two months later. Save this, Philip had no promise of help from any Catholic power.

The huge scale of his preparations was only equaled by their vast lack of intelligence, insuring defeat from the first. The type of ship adopted was the old galley, intended to ram and grapple the enemy but totally unfitted for manoeuvring in the Atlantic gales. The 130 ships carried 2500 guns, but the artillery, though numerous, was small, intended rather to be used against the enemy crews than against the ships themselves. The necessary geographical information for the invasion of Britain in the year 1588 was procured from Caesar's *De Bello Gallico.* The admiral in chief, the Duke of Medina Sidonia, had never even commanded a ship before and most of the high officers were equally innocent of professional knowledge, for sailors were despised as inferior to soldiers. Three-fourths of the crews were soldiers, all but useless in naval warfare of the new type. Blind zeal did little to supply the lack of foresight, though Philip spent hours on his knees before the host in intercession for the success of his venture. The very names of the ships, though quite in accordance with Spanish practice, seem symbolic of the holy character of the crusade: *Santa Maria de Gracia, Neustra Señora del Rosario, San Juan Baptista, La Concepcion.*

On the English side there was also plenty of fanatical fury, but it was accompanied by practical sense. The grandfathers of Cromwell's *Ironsides* had already learned, if they had not yet formulated, the maxim, "Fear God and keep your powder dry." Some of the ships in the English navy had religious names, but many were called by more secular appellations: *The Bull, The Tiger, The Dreadnought, The Revenge.* To meet the foe a very formidable and self-confident force of about forty-five ships of the best sort had gathered from the well-tried ranks of the buccaneers. It is true that patronage did some damage to the English service, but it was little compared to that of Spain. Lord Howard of Effingham was made admiral on account of his title, but the vice-admiral was Sir Francis Drake, to whom the chief credit of the action must fall.

July, 1588

The battle in the Channel was fought for nine days. There was no general strategy or tactics; the English simply sought to isolate and sink a ship wherever they could. Their heavier cannon were used against the enemy, and fire-ships were sent among his vessels. When six Spanish ships had foundered in the Channel, the fleet turned northward to the coasts of Holland. During their flight an uncertain number were destroyed by the English, and a few more fell a prey to the Sea Beggars of Holland. The rest, much battered, turned north to sail around Scotland. In the storms nineteen ships were wrecked on the coasts of Scotland and Ireland; of thirty-five ships the Spaniards themselves could give no account. For two months Philip was in suspense as to the fate of his great Armada, of which at last only a riddled and battered remnant returned to home harbors.

The importance of the victory over the Armada, like that of most dramatic events, has been overestimated. To contemporaries, at least to the victors and their friends it appeared as the direct judgment of God: "Flavit Deus et dissipati sunt." The gorgeous rhetoric of Ranke and Froude has painted it as one of the turning points in world history. But in reality it rather marked than made an epoch. Had Philip's ships won, it is still inconceivable that he could have imposed his dominion on England any more than he could on the Netherlands. England was ripening and Spain was rotting for half a century before the collision made this fact plain to all. The Armada did not end the war nor did it give the death blow to Spanish power, much less to Catholicism. On the Continent of Europe things went on almost unchanged.

But in England the effect was considerable. The victory stimulated national pride; it strengthened the Protestants, and the left wing of that party. Though the Catholics had shown themselves loyal during the crisis they were subjected, immediately thereafter, to the severest persecution they had yet felt. This was due partly to nervous excitement of the whole population, partly to the advance towards power of the Puritans, always the war party.

Puritans

Even in the first years of the great queen there had been a number of Calvinists who looked askance at the Anglican settlement as too much of a compromise with Catholicism and Lutheranism. The Thirty-nine Articles passed Convocation by a single vote as against a more Calvinistic confession. Low-churchmen (as they would now be called) attacked the "Aaronic" vest-

1563

ments of the Anglican priests, and prelacy was detested as but one degree removed from papacy.

The Puritans were not dissenters but were a party in the Anglican communion thoroughly believing in a national church, but wishing to make the breach with Rome as wide as possible. They found fault with all that had been retained in the Prayer Book for which there was no direct warrant in Scripture, and many of them began to use, in secret conventicles, the Genevan instead of the English liturgy. Their leader, Thomas Cartwright, a professor of divinity at Cambridge until deprived of his chair by the government, had brought back from the Netherlands ideals of a presbyterian form of ecclesiastical polity. In his view many "Popish Abuses" remained in the church of England, among them the keeping of saints' days, kneeling at communion, "the childish and superstitious toys" connected with the baptismal service, the words then used in the marriage service by the man, "with my body I thee worship" by which the husband "made an idol of his wife," the use of such titles as archbishop, archdeacon, lord bishop.

Cartwright, 1535–1603

It was because of their excessively scrupulous conscience in these matters, that the name "Puritan" was given to the Calvinist by his enemy, at first a mocking designation analogous to "Catharus" in the Middle Ages. But the tide set strongly in the Puritan direction. Time and again the Commons tried to initiate legislation to relieve the consciences of the stricter party, but their efforts were blocked by the crown. From this time forth the church of England made an alliance with the throne that has never been broken. As Jewel had been compelled, at the beginning of Elizabeth's reign, to defend the Anglican church against Rome, so Richard Hooker, in his famous *Ec-*

1562

clesiastical Polity was now forced to defend it from the extreme Protestants. In the very year in which this finely tempered work was written, a Jesuit reported that the Puritans were the strongest body in the kingdom and particularly that they had the most officers and soldiers on their side. The coming Commonwealth was already casting its shadow on the age of Shakespeare.

1594

As a moral and religious influence Puritanism was of the utmost importance in moulding the English—and American—character and it was, take it all in all, a noble thing. If it has been justly blamed for a certain narrowness in its hostility, or indifference, to art and refinement, it more than compensated for this by the moral earnestness that it impressed on the people. To bring the genius of the Bible into English life and literature, to impress each man with the idea of living for duty, to reduce politics and the whole life of the state to ethical standards, are undoubted services of Puritanism. Politically, it favored the growth of self-reliance, self-control and a sense of personal worth that made democracy possible and necessary.

Browne, 1550?–1633?

To the left of the Puritans were the Independents or Brownists as they were called from their leader Robert Browne, the advocate of *Reformation without Tarrying for Any.* He had been a refugee in the Netherlands, where he may have come under Anabaptist influence. His disciples differed from the followers of Cartwright in separating themselves from the state church, in which they found many "filthy traditions and inventions of men." Beginning to organize in separate congregations about 1567, they were said by Sir Walter Raleigh to have as many as 20,000 adherents in 1593. Though heartily disliked by re-actionaries and by the *beati possidentes* in both church and state, they were, nevertheless, the party of the future.

§ 5. Ireland

If the union of England and Wales has been a marriage—after a courtship of the primitive type; if the union with Scotland has been a successful partnership—following a long period of cut-throat competition; the position of Ireland has been that of a captive and a slave. To her unwilling mind the English domination has always been a foreign one, and this fact makes more difference with her than whether her master has been cruel, as formerly, or kind, as of late.

English rule

The saddest period in all Erin's sad life was that of the sixteenth and seventeenth centuries, when to the old antagonism of race was added a new hatred of creed and a new commercial competition. The policy of Henry was "to reduce that realm to the knowledge of God and obedience of Us." The policy of Elizabeth was to pray that God might "call them to the knowledge of his truth and to a civil polity," and to assist the Almighty by the most fiendish means to accomplish these ends. The government of the island was a crime, and yet for this crime some considerations must be urged in extenuation. England then regarded the Irish much as the Americans have seemed to regard the Indians, as savages to be killed and driven off to make room for a higher civilization. Had England been able to apply the method of extermination she would doubtless have done so and there would then be no Irish question today. But in 1540 it was recognized that "to enterprise the whole extirpation and total destruction of all the Irishmen in the land would be a marvellous sumptious charge and great difficulty."

Being unable to accomplish this or to put Ireland at

the bottom of the sea, where Elizabeth's minister Walsingham often wished that it were, the English had the alternatives of half governing or wholly abandoning their neighbors. The latter course was felt to be too dangerous, but had it been adopted, Ireland might have evolved an adequate government and prosperity of her own. It is true that she was more backward than England, but yet she had a considerable trade and culture. Certain points, like Dublin and Waterford, had much commerce with the Continent. And yet, as to the nation as a whole, the report of 1515 probably speaks true in saying: "There is no common folk in all this world so little set by, so greatly despised, so feeble, so poor, so greatly trodden under foot, as the king's poor common folk of Ireland." There was no map of the whole of Ireland; the roads were few and poor and the vaguest notions prevailed as to the shape, size and population of the country. The most civilized part was the English Pale around Dublin; the native Irish lived "west of the Barrow and west of the law," and were governed by more than sixty native chiefs. Intermarriage of colonists and natives was forbidden by law. The only way the Tudor government knew of asserting its suzerainty over these septs, correctly described as "the king's Irish enemies," was to raid them at intervals, slaying, robbing and raping as they went. It was after one of these raids in 1580 that the poet Spencer wrote:

Irish misery

> The people were brought to such wretchedness that any strong heart would have rued the same. Out of every corner of the woods and glens they came, creeping forth upon their hands, for their legs would not bear them. They looked like anatomies of death; they spoke like ghosts crying out of their graves. They did eat the dead carrions, happy where they could find them; yea and one

> another soon after, inasmuch as the very carcasses they spared not to scrape out of their graves; and if they found a plot of watercresses or shamrocks, there they thronged as to a feast for a time.

The Irish chiefs were not to be tamed by either kindness or force. Henry and Elizabeth scattered titles of "earl" and "lord" among the O's and Macs of her western island, only to find that the coronet made not the slightest difference in either their affections or their manners. They still lived as marauding chiefs, surrounded by wild kerns and gallowglasses fighting each other and preying on their own poor subjects. "Let a thousand of my people die," remarked one of them, Neil Garv, "I pass not a pin. . . . I will punish, exact, cut and hang where and whenever I list." Had they been able to make common cause they might perhaps have shaken the English grasp from their necks, for it was commonly corrupt and feeble. Sir Henry Sidney was the strongest and best governor sent to the island during the century, but he was able to do little. Though the others could be bribed and though one of them, the Earl of Essex, conspired with the chiefs to rebel, and though at the very end of Elizabeth's reign a capable Spanish army landed in Ireland to help the natives, nothing ever enabled them to turn out the hated "Sassenach."

English colonization

England had already tried to solve the Irish problem by colonization. Leinster had long been a center of English settlement, and in 1573 the first English colony was sent to Ulster. But as it consisted chiefly of bankrupts, fugitives from justice and others "of so corrupt a disposition as England rather refuseth," it did not help matters much but rather "irrecuperably damnified the state." The Irish Parliament continued to represent only the English of the Pale and of a few towns outside of it. Though the inhabitants of the

Pale remained nominally Catholic, the Parliament was so servile that in 1541 it destroyed the monasteries and repudiated the pope, shortly after which the king took the title of Head of the Irish Church. Not one penny of the confiscated wealth went to endow an Irish university until 1591, when Trinity College was founded in the interests of Protestantism. Though almost every other country of Europe had its own printing presses before 1500, Ireland had none until 1551, and then the press was used so exclusively for propaganda that it made the very name of reading hateful to the natives. There were, however, no religious massacres and no martyrs of either cause. The persecuting laws were left until the following century.

Religion

Commercial exploitation

The rise of the traders to political power was more ominous than the inception of a new religion. The country was drained of treasure by the exaction of enormous ransoms for captured chiefs. The Irish cloth-trade and sea-borne commerce were suppressed. The country was flooded with inferior coin, thus putting its merchants at a vast disadvantage. Finally, there was little left that the Irish were able to import save liquors, and those "much corrupted."

With every plea in mitigation of judgment that can be offered, it must be recognized that England's government of Ireland proved a failure. If she did not make the Irish savage she did her best to keep them so, and then punished them for it. By exploiting Erin's resources she impoverished herself. By trying to impose Protestantism she made Ireland the very stronghold of papacy. By striving to destroy the septs she created the nation.

CHAPTER VII

SCOTLAND

One of the most important effects of modern means of easy communication between all parts of the world has been to obliterate or minimize distinctions in national character and in degrees of civilization. The manner of life of England and Australia differ less now than the manner of life of England and Scotland differed in the sixteenth century. The great stream of culture then flowed much more strongly in the central than in the outlying parts of Western Europe. The Latin nations, Italy and France, lay nearest the heart of civilization. But slightly less advanced in culture and in the amenities of life, and superior in some respects, were the Netherlands, Switzerland, England and the southern and central parts of Germany. In partial shadow round about lay a belt of lands: Spain, Portugal, Northern Germany, Prussia, Poland, Hungary, Scandinavia, Scotland, and Ireland.

Scotland

Scotland, indeed, had her own universities, but her best scholars were often found at Paris, or in German or Italian academies. Scotch humanists on the continent, the Scotch guard of the French king, and Scotch monasteries, such as those at Erfurt and Würzburg, raised the reputation of the country abroad rather than advanced its native culture. Printing was not introduced until 1507. Brantôme in the sixteenth century, like Aeneas Silvius in the fifteenth, remarked the uncouthness of the northern kingdom.

Most backward of all was Scotland's political development. No king arose strong enough to be at once the tyrant and the saviour of his country; under the weak rule of a series of minors, regents and wanton women a feudal baronage with a lush growth of intestine war and crime, flourished mightily to curse the poor people. When Sir David Lyndsay asked, Why are the Scots so poor? he gave the correct answer:

1528

> Wanting of justice, policy and peace,
> Are cause of their unhappiness, alas!

Something may also be attributed to the poverty of the soil and the lack of important commerce or industries.

Relations with England

The policy of any small nation situated in dangerous proximity to a larger one is almost necessarily determined by this fact. In order to assert her independence Scotland was forced to make common cause with England's enemies. Guerrilla warfare was endemic on the borders, breaking out, in each generation, into some fiercer crisis. England, on the other hand, was driven to seek her own safety in the annexation of her small enemy, or, failing that, by keeping her as impotent as possible. True to the maxims of the immoral political science that has commonly passed for statesmanship, the Tudors consistently sought by every form of deliberate perfidy to foster factions in North Britain, to purchase traitors, to hire stabbers, to subsidize rebels, to breed mischief, and to waste the country, at opportune intervals, with armies and fleets. Simply to protect the independence that England denied and attacked, Scotch rulers became fast allies of France, to be counted on, in every war between the great powers, to stir up trouble in England's rear.

On neither side was the policy one of sheer hatred. North and south the purpose increased throughout the century to unite the two countries and thus put an end to the perennial and noxious war. If the early Tudors were mistaken in thinking they could assert a suzerainty by force of arms, they also must be credited with laying the foundations of the future dynastic union. Margaret Tudor, Henry VIII's sister, was married to James IV of Scotland. Somerset hoped to effect the union more directly by the marriage of Edward VI and Mary Queen of Scots. That a party of enlightened statesmen in England should constantly keep the union in mind, is less remarkable under the circumstances than that there should have been built up a considerable body of Scotchmen aiming at the same goal. Notwithstanding the vitality of patriotism and the tenacity with which small nations usually refuse to merge their own identity in a larger whole, very strong motives called forth the existence of an English party. One favorable condition was the feudal disorganization of society. Faction was so common and so bitter that it was able to call in the national enemy without utterly discrediting itself. A second element was jealousy of France. For a time, with the French marriages of James V with Mary of Lorraine, a sister of the Duke of Guise, and of Mary Queen of Scots with Francis II, there seemed more danger that the little kingdom should become an appanage of France than a satellite of her southern neighbor. The licentiousness of French officers and French soldiers on Scotch soil made their nation least loved when it was most seen. But the great influence overcoming national sentiment was religion. The Reformation that brought not peace but a sword to so much of Europe in this case united instead of divided the nations.

Influence of religion

It is sometimes said that national character reveals itself in the national religion. This is true to some extent, but it is still more important to say that a nation's history reveals itself in its forms of faith. From religious statistics of the present day one could deduce with considerable accuracy much of the history of any people.

The contrast between the churches of England and Scotland is the more remarkable when it is considered that the North of England was the stronghold of Catholicism, and that the Lowland Scot, next door to the counties of the Northern Earls who rose against Elizabeth, flew to the opposite extreme and embraced Protestantism in its most pronounced form. To say that Calvinism, uncompromising and bare of adornment, appealed particularly to the dour, dry, rationalistic Scot, is at best but a half truth and at worst a begging of the question. The reasons why England became Anglican and Scotland Presbyterian are found immediately not in the diversity of national character but in the circumstances of their respective polities and history. England cast loose from Rome at a time when the conservative influence of Luther was predominant; Scotland was swept into the current of revolution under the fiercer star of Calvin. The English Reformation was started by the crown and supported by the new noblesse of commerce. The Scotch revolution was markedly baronial in tone. It began with the humanists, continued and flourished in the junior branches of great families, among the burgesses of the towns and among the more vigorous of the clergy, both regular and secular. The crown was consistently against the new movement, but the Scottish monarch was too weak to impose his will, or even to have a will of his own. Neither James V nor his daughter could afford to break with Rome and with France. James V, especially, was thrown into the arms of his clergy by the hostility of his nobles. Moreover, after the death of many nobles at the battle of Flodden, the clergy became, for a time, the strongest estate in the kingdom. **1513**

Reformation

Like the other estates the clergy were still in the Middle Ages when the Reformation came on them like a thief in the night. In no country was the corruption greater. The bishops and priests took concubines and ate and drank and were drunken and buffeted their fellow men. They exacted their fees to the last farthing, an especially odious one being the claim of the priest to the best cow on the death of a parishioner. As a consequence the parsons and monks were hated by the laity.

Humanism shed a few bright beams on the hyperborean regions of Dundee and Glasgow. Some Erasmians, like Hector Boece, prepared others for the Reformation without joining it themselves; some, like George Buchanan, threw genius and learning into the scales of the new faith. The unlearned, too, were touched with reforming zeal. Lollardy sowed a few seeds of heresy. About 1520 Wyclif's version of the New Testament was turned into Scots by one John Nesbit, but it remained in manuscript.

In the days before newspapers tidings were carried from place to place by wandering merchants and itinerant scholars. Far more than today propaganda was dependent on personal intercourse. One of the first preachers of Lutheranism in Scotland was a Frenchman named La Tour, who was martyred on his return to his own country. The noble Patrick Hamilton made a pilgrimage to the newly founded University of Marburg, and possibly to Wittenberg. Filled, as his Catholic countryman, Bishop John Leslie put it, "with venom very poisonable and deadly . . . soaked out of Luther and other archheretics," he returned to find the martyr's crown in his native land. "The reek of Patrick Hamilton" infected all upon whom it blew. Other young men visited Germany. Some, like Alexander Alesius and John MacAlpine, found positions in

February 29, 1528

foreign universities. Others visited Wittenberg for a short time to carry thence the new gospel. A Scotch David[1] appears at Wittenberg in January 1528. Another Scot, "honorably born and well seen in scholastic theology, exiled from his land on account of the Word," made Luther's acquaintance in May, 1529. Another of the Reformer's visitors was James Wedderburn whose brother, John, translated some of the German's hymns, and published them as "Ane compendious Booke of Godly and spiritual Songs." 1540–2

While men like these were bringing tidings of the new faith back to their countrymen, others were busy importing and distributing Lutheran books. The Parliament prohibited all works of "the heretic Luther and his disciples," but it could not enforce this law. The English agent at Antwerp reported to Wolsey that New Testaments and other English works were bought by Scottish merchants and sent to Edinburgh and St. Andrews. The popularity and influence of Tyndale's and Coverdale's Bible is proved by the rapid anglicizing, from this date onward, of the Scots dialect. The circulation of the Scriptures in English is further proved by the repetition of the injunctions against using them. But the first Bible printed in Scotland was that of Alexander Arbuthnot in 1579, based on the Geneva Bible in 1561.

July 17, 1525

February 20, 1527

Another indication of the growth of Lutheranism is the request of King James V to Consistory for permission to tax his clergy one-third of their revenues in order to raise an army against the swarm of his Lutheran subjects. As these Protestants met in private houses, Parliament passed a law, "That none hold nor let be holden in their houses nor other ways, congregations or conventicles to commune or dispute of

March 14, 1531

1540

[1] Could he have been David Borthwick or David Lyndsay? See Luther's letters and *Dictionary of National Biography*.

the Holy Scripture, without they be theologians approved by famous universities."

Pamphlets

As the new party grew the battle was joined. At least twelve martyrs perished in the years 1539–40. The field was taken on either side by an army of pamphlets, ballads and broadsides, of which the best known, perhaps, is David Lyndsay's *Ane Satire of the thrie Estatis.* In this the clergy are mercilessly attacked for greed and wantonness. The New Testament is highly praised by some of the characters introduced into the poem, but a pardoner complains that his credit has been entirely destroyed by it and wishes the devil may take him who made that book. He further wishes that "Martin Luther, that false loon, Black Bullinger and Melanchthon" had been smothered in their chrisom-cloths and that St. Paul had never been born.

1540

Mary Stuart, born Dec. 8, 1542

When James V died, he left the crown to his infant daughter of six days old, that Mary whose beauty, crimes and tragic end fixed the attention of her contemporaries and of posterity alike. For the first three years of her reign the most powerful man in the kingdom was David Beaton, Cardinal Archbishop of St. Andrews. His policy, of course, was to maintain the Catholic religion, and this implied the defence of Scotch independence against England. Henry VIII, with characteristic lack of scruple, plotted to kidnap the infant queen and either to kidnap or to assassinate the cardinal. Failing in both, he sent an army north with orders to put man, woman and child to the sword wherever resistance was made. Edinburgh castle remained untaken, but Holyrood was burned and the country devastated as far as Sterling.

Cardinal Beaton

Defeated by England, Beaton was destined to perish in conflict with his other enemy, Protestantism. During this time of transition from Lutheranism to Calvinism, the demands of the Scotch reformers would have been more moderate than they later became. They would doubtless have been content with a free Bible, free preaching and the sequestration of the goods of the religious orders. Under George Wishart, who translated the First Helvetic Confession, the Kirk began to assume its Calvinistic garb and to take the aspect of a party with a definite political program. The place of newspapers, both as purveyors of information and as organs of public opinion, was taken by the sermons of the ministers, most of them political and all of them controversial. Of this party Beaton was the scourge. He himself believed that in 1545 heresy was almost extinct, and doubtless his belief was confirmed when he was able to put Wishart to death. In revenge for this a few fanatics murdered him.

1536 or 1537

March 1, 1546

May 29

John Knox

In the consummation of the religious revolution during the next quarter of a century, one factor was the personality of John Knox. A born partisan, a man of one idea who could see no evil on his own side and no good on the other, as a good fighter and a good hater he has had few equals. His supreme devotion to the cause he embraced made him credulous of evil in his foes, and capable of using deceit and of applauding political murder. Of his first preaching against Romanism it was said, "Other have sned [snipped] the branches, but this man strikes at the root," and well nigh the latest judgment passed upon him, that of Lord Acton, is that he differed from all other Protestant founders in his desire that the Catholics should be exterminated, either by the state or by the self-help of all Christian men. His not to speak the words of love and mercy from the gospel, but to curse and thunder against "those dumb dogs, the poisoned and pestilent papists" in the style of the Old Testament prophet or psalmist. But while the harshness of his character has repelled many, his fundamental consistency and his courage have won admiration. As a great preacher, "or he had done with his sermon he was so active and vigorous that he was like to ding the pulpit in blads and fly out of it." His style was direct, vigorous, plain, full of pungent wit and biting sarcasm.

Even the year of his birth is in dispute. The traditional date is 1505; but it has been shown with much reason that the more likely date is 1513 or 1514. That he had a university education and that he was ordained priest is all that is known of him until about 1540. During the last months of Wishart's life Knox was his constant attendant. His own preaching continued the work of the martyr until June, 1547, when St. Andrews was captured by the French fleet and Knox was made a galley slave for nineteen months. Under the lash and, what grieved him even more, constantly plied with suggestions that he should "commit idolatry" in praying to the image of Mary, his heart grew bitter against the French and their religion.

January, 1549

Released, either through the influence of the English government, or by an exchange of prisoners, Knox spent the next five years in England. After filling positions as preacher at Berwick and Newcastle, he was appointed royal chaplain and was offered the bishopric of Rochester, which he declined because he foresaw the troubles under Mary. As the pioneer of Puritanism in England he used his influence to make the Book of Common Prayer more Protestant. Not long after Mary's accession Knox fled to the Continent, spending a few years at Frankfort and Geneva. He was much impressed by "that notable servant of

1551

God, John Calvin" whose system he adopted with political modifications of his own.

In the meantime things were not going well in Scotland. The country had suffered another severe defeat at the hands of the English in the battle of Pinkie. The government was largely in the hands of the Queen Dowager, Mary of Lorraine, who naturally favored France, and who married her daughter, the Queen of Scots, to the Dauphin Francis, both of them being fifteen years old. By treaty she conveyed Scotland to the king of France, acting on the good old theory that her people were a chattel. Though the pact, with its treason to the people, was secret, its purport was guessed by all. Whereas the accession of Francis II momentarily bound Scotland closer to France, his death in the following year again cut her loose, and allowed her to go her own way.

September 10, 1547

April 24, 1558

All the while the Reformed party had been slowly growing in strength. Somerset took care to send plenty of English Bibles across the Cheviot Hill, rightly seeing in them the best emissaries of the English interest. The Scotch were drawn towards England by the mildness of her government as much as they were alienated from France by the ferocity of hers. In Scotland the English party, when it had the chance, made no Catholic martyrs, but the French party continued to put heretics to death. The execution of the aged Walter Milne, the last of the victims of the Catholic persecution, excited especial resentment.

1558

Knox now returned to his own country for a short visit. He there preached passionately against the mass and addressed a letter to the Regent Mary of Lorraine, begging her to favor the gospel. This she treated as a joke, and, after Knox had departed, she sentenced him to death and burnt him in effigy. From Geneva he continued to be the chief adviser of the

Knox, August, 1555

December 3, 1557

Protestant party, whose leaders drew up a "Common Band," usually known as the First Scottish Covenant. The signers, including a large number of nobles and gentlemen headed by the earls of Argyle, Glencairn and Morton, promised to apply their whole power, substance and lives to maintain, set forward and establish "the most blessed Word of God and his congregation." Under the protection of this bond, reformed churches were set up openly. The Lords of the Congregation, as they were called, demanded that penal statutes against heretics be abrogated and "that it be lawful to us to use ourselves in matters of religion and conscience as we must answer to God." This scheme of toleration was too advanced for the time.

1557

1558

May 2, 1559

As the assistance of Knox was felt to be desirable, the Lords of the Congregation urgently requested his return. Before doing so he published his "Appellation" to the nobles, estates and commonalty against the sentence of death recently passed on him. When he did arrive in Edinburgh, his preaching was like a match set to kindling wood. Wherever he went burst forth the flame of iconoclasm. Images were broken and monasteries stormed not, as he himself wrote, by gentlemen or by "earnest professors of Christ," but by "the rascal multitude." In reckoning the forces of revolution, the joy of the mob in looting must not be forgotten. From Perth Knox wrote: "The places of idolatry were made equal with the ground; all monuments of idolatry that could be apprehended, consumed with fire; and priests commanded, under pain of death, to desist from their blasphemous mass." Similar outbursts occurred at St. Andrews, and when Knox returned to Edinburgh, civil war seemed imminent. Pamphlets of the time, like *The Beggars' Warning,* distinctly made the threat of social revolution.

May 11

1559

But as a matter of fact the change came as the most bloodless in Europe. The Reformers, popular with the middle and with part of the upper classes, needed only to win English support to make themselves perfectly secure. The difficulty in this course lay in Queen Elizabeth's natural dislike of Knox on account of his *First Blast of the Trumpet against the Monstrous Regiment of Women.* In this war-whoop, aimed against the Marys of England and Scotland, Knox had argued that "to promote a woman to bear rule, superiority, dominion or empire above any realm is repugnant to nature, contrary to God, and, finally, it is the subversion of good order and of all equity and justice." The author felt not a little embarrassment when a Protestant woman ascended the throne of England and he needed her help. But to save his soul he "that never feared nor flattered any flesh" could not admit that he was in the wrong, nor take back aught that he had said. He seems to have acted on Barry Lyndon's maxim that "a gentleman fights but never apologizes." When he wrote Elizabeth, all he would say was that he was not her enemy and had never offended her or her realm maliciously or of purpose. He seasoned this attempt at reconciliation by adding a stinging rebuke to the proud young queen for having "declined from God and bowed to idolatry," during her sister's reign, for fear of her life.

July 20, 1559

But the advantages of union outweighed such minor considerations as bad manners, and early in 1560 a league was formed between England and the Lords of the Congregation. Shortly after the death of Mary of Lorraine the Treaty of Edinburgh was signed between the queen of England and the lords of Scotland. This provided: (1) that all English and French troops be sent out of Scotland except 120 French; (2) that all warlike preparations cease; (3) that the

June 11, 1560

Treaty of Edinburgh, July 6

Berwickshire citadel of the sea, Eyemouth, be dismantled; (4) that Mary and Francis should disuse the English title and arms; (5) that Philip of Spain should arbitrate certain points, if necessary; (6) that Elizabeth had not acted wrongfully in making a league with the Lords of the Congregation. Mary and Francis refused to ratify this treaty.

A supplementary agreement was proposed between Mary Stuart and her rebellious Protestant subjects. She promised to summon Parliament at once, to make neither war nor peace without the consent of the estates, and to govern according to the advice of a council of twelve chosen jointly by herself and the estates. She promised to give no high offices to strangers or to clergymen; and she extended to all a general amnesty.

Revolution

The summons of Parliament immediately after these negotiations proved as disastrous to the old régime as the assembly of the French Estates General in 1789. Though bloodless, the Scotch revolution was as thorough, in its own small way, as that of Robespierre. Religion was changed and a new distribution of political power secured, transferring the ascendency of the crown and of the old privileged orders to a class of "new men," low-born ministers of the kirk, small "lairds" and burgesses. The very constitution of the new Parliament was revolutionary. In the old legislative assemblies between ten and twenty greater barons were summoned; in the Parliament of 1560 no less than 106 small barons assembled, and it was to them, together with the burgesses of the cities, that the adoption of the new religion was due. A Confession of Faith, on extreme Calvinistic lines, had been drawn up by Knox and his fellows; this was presented to Parliament and adopted with only eight dissenting voices, those of five laymen and three bishops. The minority was overawed, not only by the majority in

Scottish Confession

Parliament but by the public opinion of the capital and of the whole Lowlands.

Laws of the estates

Just a week after the adoption of the Confession, the estates passed three laws: (1) Abolishing the pope's authority and all jurisdiction by Catholic prelates; (2) repealing all previous statutes in favor of the Roman church; (3) forbidding the celebration of mass. The law calls it "wicked idolatry" and provides that "no manner of person nor persons say mass, nor yet hear mass, nor be present thereat under pain of confiscation of all their goods movable and immovable and punishing their bodies at the discretion of the magistrate." The penalty for the third offence was made death, and all officers were commanded to "take diligent suit and inquisition" to prevent the celebration of the Catholic rite. In reality, persecution was extremely mild, simply because there was hardly any resistance. Scarcely three Catholic martyrs can be named, and there was no Pilgrimage of Grace. This is all the more remarkable in that probably three-fourths of the people were still Catholic. The Reformation, like most other revolutions, was the work not of the majority, but of that part of the people that had the energy and intelligence to see most clearly and act most strongly. For the first time in Scotch history a great issue was submitted to a public opinion sufficiently developed to realize its importance. The great choice was made not by counting heads but by weighing character.

The burgher class having seized the reins of government proceeded to use them in the interests of their kirk. The prime duty of the state was asserted to be the maintenance of the true religion. Ministers were paid by the government. Almost any act of government might be made the subject of interference by the church, for Knox's profession, "with the policy, mind us to meddle no further than it hath religion mixed in it,'' was obviously an elastic and self-imposed limitation.

Theocracy

The character of the kirk was that of a democratic, puritanical theocracy. The real rulers of it, and through it of the state, were the ministers and elders elected by the people. The democracy of the kirk consisted in the rise of most of these men from the lower ranks of the people; its theocracy in the claim of these men, once established in Moses' seat, to interpret the commands of God. ''I see,'' said Queen Mary, after a conversation with Knox, ''that my subjects shall obey you rather than me.'' ''Madam,'' replied Knox, ''my study is that both princes and people shall obey God''—but, of course, the voice of the pulpit was the voice of God. As a contemporary put it: ''Knox is king; what he wills obeyit is.'' Finally the kirk was a tyranny, as a democracy may well be. In life, in manners, in thought, the citizen was obliged, under severe social penalty, to conform exactly to a very narrow standard.

Queen Mary in Scotland, August 19, 1561

When Queen Mary, a widow eighteen years old, landed in Scotland, she must have been aware of the thorny path she was to tread. It is impossible not to pity her, the spoiled darling of the gayest court of Europe, exposed to the bleak skies and bleaker winds of doctrines at Edinburgh. Endowed with high spirit, courage, no little cleverness and much charm, she might have mastered the situation had her character or discretion equaled her intellect and beauty. But, thwarted, nagged and bullied by men whose religion she hated, whose power she feared and whose low birth she despised, she became more and more reckless in the pursuit of pleasure until she was tangled in a network of vice and crime, and delivered helpless into the hands of her enemies.

Her true policy, and the one which she began to follow, was marked out for her by circumstances. Scotland was to her but the stepping-stone to the throne of England. As Elizabeth's next heir she might become queen either through the death of the reigning sovereign, or as the head of a Catholic rebellion. At first she prudently decided to wait for the natural course of events, selecting as her secretary of state Maitland, "the Scottish Cecil," a staid politician bent on keeping friends with England. But at last growing impatient, she compromised herself in the Catholic plots and risings of the disaffected southerners.

So, while aspiring to three crowns, Mary showed herself incapable of keeping even the one she had. Not religion but her own crimes and follies caused her downfall, but it was over religion that the first clash with her subjects came. She would have liked to restore Catholicism, though this was not her first object, for she would have been content to be left in the private enjoyment of her own worship. Even on this the stalwarts of the kirk looked askance. Knox preached as Mary landed that one mass was more terrible to him than ten thousand armed invaders. Mary sent for him, hoping to win the hard man by a display of feminine and queenly graciousness. In all he had five interviews with her, picturesquely described by himself. On his side there were long, stern sermons on the duties of princes and the wickedness of idolatry, all richly illustrated with examples drawn from the sacred page. On her side there was "howling together with womanly weeping," "more howling and tears above that the matter did require," "so many tears that her chamber-boy could scarce get napkins enough to dry her eyes." With absurdly unconscious offensiveness and egotism Knox began acquaintance with his sovereign by remarking that he was as well

August, 1561–December, 1563

content to live under her as Paul under Nero. Previously he had maintained that the government was set up to control religion; now he informed Mary that "right religion took neither original nor authority from worldly princes but from the Eternal God alone." "'Think ye,' quoth she, 'that subjects, having power, may resist their princes?' 'If princes exceed their bounds, madam, they may be resisted and even deposed,'" replied Knox. Mary's marriage was the most urgent immediate question of policy. When Knox took the liberty of discussing it with her she burst out: "What have you to do with my marriage? Or what are you within this commonwealth?" "A subject born within the same," superbly retorted the East Lothian peasant, "and though neither earl, lord nor baron, God has made me a profitable member."

Marriage with Darnley, July, 1565

Determined, quite excusably, to please herself rather than her advisers in the choice of a husband, Mary selected her cousin Henry Stuart Lord Darnley; a "long lad" not yet twenty. The marriage was celebrated in July, 1565; the necessary papal dispensation therefor was actually drawn up on September 25 but was thoughtfully provided with a false date as of four months earlier. Almost from the first the marriage was wretchedly unhappy. The petulant boy insisted on being treated as king, whereas Mary allowed him only "his due." Darnley was jealous, probably with good cause, of his wife's Italian secretary, David Riccio, and murdered him in Mary's presence; "an action worthy of all praise," pontificated Knox.

March 9, 1566

With this crime begins in earnest that sickening tale of court intrigue and blackest villainy that has commonly passed as the then history of Scotland. To revenge her beloved secretary Mary plotted with a new paramour, the Earl of Bothwell, an able soldier, a nominal Protestant and an evil liver. On the night of February 9–10, 1567, the house of Kirk o' Field near Edinburgh where Darnley was staying and where his wife had but just left him, was blown up by gunpowder and later his dead body was found near by. Public opinion at once laid the crime at the right doors, and it did not need Mary's hasty marriage with Bothwell to confirm the suspicion of her complicity.

Marriage with Bothwell, May 15, 1567

The path of those opposed to the queen was made easier by the fact that she now had an heir, James, of Scotland the sixth and afterwards of England the first. The temper of the people of Edinburgh was indicated by the posting up of numerous placards accusing Bothwell and Mary. One of these was a banner on which was painted a little boy kneeling and crowned, and thereon the legend: "Avenge the death of my father!" Deeds followed words; Parliament compelled the queen under threat of death to abdicate in favor of her son and to appoint her half-brother, the Earl of Moray, regent. At the coronation of the infant king Knox preached. A still more drastic step was taken when Parliament declared Mary guilty of murder and formally deposed her from the throne. That Mary really was guilty in the fullest degree there can be no reasonable doubt. An element of mystery has been added to the situation by a dispute over the genuineness of a series of letters and poems purporting to have been written by Mary to Bothwell and known collectively as the Casket Letters. They were discovered in a suspiciously opportune way by her enemies. The originals not being extant, some historians have regarded them in whole or in part as forgeries, but Robertson, Ranke, Froude, Andrew Lang and Pollard accept them as genuine. This is my opinion, but it seems to me that the fascination of

James VI, June 19, 1566

July 16

July 29

December 15

mystery has lent the documents undue importance. Had they never been found Mary's guilt would have been established by circumstantial evidence.

Mary was confined for a short time in the castle of Lochleven, but contrived to escape. As she approached Glasgow she risked a battle, but her troops were defeated and she fled to England. Throwing herself on Elizabeth's mercy she found prison and finally, after nineteen years, the scaffold. An inquiry was held concerning her case, but no verdict was rendered because it did not suit Elizabeth to degrade her sister sovereign more than was necessary. Not for the murder of her husband, but for complicity in a plot against Elizabeth, was Mary finally condemned to die. In spite of the fact that she did everything possible to disgrace herself more deeply than ever, such as pensioning the assassin of her brother Moray, her sufferings made her the martyr of sentimentalists, and pieces of embroidery or other possessions of the beautiful queen have been handed down as the precious relics of a saint.[1]

May, 1568

All the murderous intrigues just narrated contributed thoroughly to disgrace the Catholic and royalist party. The revolution had left society dissolved, full of bloodthirsty and false men. But though the Protestants had their share of such villains, they also had the one consistent and public-spirited element in the kingdom, namely Knox and his immediate followers. Moray was a man rather above the average respectability and he confirmed the triumph of Protestantism in the Lowlands in the few short years preceding his assassination in January, 1570. But by this time the revolution had been so firmly accomplished that nothing could shake it. The deposition of a queen, though

1 Such a piece of embroidery has been kept in my mother's family from that day to this.

a defiance of all the Catholic powers and of all the royalist sentiment of Europe, had succeeded. The young king was brought up a Protestant, and his mind was so thoroughly turned against his mother that he acquiesced without a murmur in her execution. At last peace and security smiled upon North Britain. The coming event of the union with England cast its beneficent shadow over the reign of Elizabeth's successor.

Preparation for union with England

The Reformation ran the same course as in England earlier; one is almost tempted to hypostatize it and say that it took the bit between its teeth and ran away with its riders. Actually, the man cast for the rôle of Henry VIII was James VI; the slobbering pedant without drawing the sword did what his abler ancestors could not do after a life-time of battle. He made himself all but absolute, and this, demonstrably, as head of the kirk.

Absolution

In 1584 Parliament passed a series of statutes known as the Black Acts, putting the bodies and souls of the Scotch under the yoke of the king, who was now pope as well. In 1587 the whole property of the pre-Reformation church, with some trifling exceptions, was confiscated and put at the king's disposition. As in England, so here, the lands of abbeys and of prelates was thrown to new men of the pushing, commercial type. Thus was founded a landed aristocracy with interests distinct from the old barons and strong in supporting both king and Reformation.

It is true that this condition was but temporary. Just as in England later the Parliament and the Puritans called the crown to account, so in Scotland the kirk continued to administer drastic advice to the monarch and finally to put direct legal pressure upon him. The Black Acts were abrogated by Parliament in 1592 and from that time forth ensued a struggle between the

Reaction in the kirk, 1592

king and the presbyteries which, in the opinion of the former, agreed as well together as God and the devil. Still more after his accession to the English throne James came to prefer the episcopal form of church government as more subservient, and to act on the maxim, "no bishop, no king."

CHAPTER VIII

THE COUNTER-REFORMATION

§ 1. Italy

It is sometimes so easy to see, after the event, why things should have taken just the course they did take, that it may seem remarkable that political foresight is so rare. It is probable, however, that the study of history not only illumines many things, and places them in their true perspective, but also tends to simplify too much, overemphasizing, to our minds, the elements that finally triumphed and casting those that succumbed into the shadow.

Italy

However this may be, Italy of the sixteenth century appears to offer an unusually clear case of a logical sequence of effects due to previously ascertainable causes. That Italy should toy with the Reformation without accepting it, that she should finally suppress it and along with it much of her own spiritual life, seems to be entirely due to her geographical, political and cultural condition at the time when she felt the impact of the new ideas.

In all these respects, indeed, there was something that might at first blush have seemed favorable to the Lutheran revolt. Few lands were more open to German and Swiss influences than was their transalpine neighbor. Commercially, Italy and Germany were united by a thousand bonds, and a constant influx of northern travellers, students, artists, officials and soldiers, might be supposed to carry with them the contagion of the new ideas. Again, the lack of political unity might be supposed, as in Germany, so in Italy, to facilitate sectional reformation. Finally, the Renaissance, with its unparalleled freedom of thought and its strong anti-clerical bias, would at least insure a fair hearing for innovations in doctrine and ecclesiastical ideals.

And yet, as even contemporaries saw, there were some things which weighed far more heavily in the scale of Catholicism than did those just mentioned in the scale of Protestantism. In the first place the autonomy of the political divisions was more apparent than real. Too weak and too disunited to offer resistance to any strong foreign power, contended for by the three greatest, Italy became gradually more and more a Spanish dependency. After Pavia and the treaty of Cateau-Cambrésis French influence was reduced to a threat rather than a reality. Naples had long been an appendage of the Spanish crown; Milan was now wrested from the French, and one after another most of the smaller states passed into Spain's "sphere of influence." The strongest of all the states, the papal dominions, became in reality, if not nominally, a dependency of the emperor after the sack of Rome. Tuscany, Savoy and Venetia maintained a semblance of independence, but Savoy was at that time hardly Italian. Venice had passed the zenith of her power, and Florence, even under her brilliant Duke Cosimo de' Medici was amenable to the pressure of the Spanish soldier and the Spanish priest.

1525
1529

1527

Cosimo de' Medici, 1537–74

Enormous odds were thrown against the Reformers because Italy was the seat of the papacy. In spite of all hatred of Roman morals and in spite of all distrust of Roman doctrine, this was a source of pride and of advantage of the whole country. As long as tribute flowed from all Western Europe, as long as kings and emperors kissed the pontiff's toe, Rome was still in a sense the capital of Christendom. An example of how the papacy was both served and despised has been left us by the Florentine statesman and historian Guicciardini: "So much evil cannot be said of the Roman curia," he wrote, "that more does not deserve to be said of it, for it is an infamy, an example of all the shame and wickedness of the world." He might have been supposed to be ready to support any enemy of such an institution, but what does he say?

Guicciardini, 1483–1540

> No man dislikes more than do I the ambition, avarice and effeminacy of the priests, not only because these vices are hateful in themselves but because they are especially unbecoming to men who have vowed a life dependent upon God. . . . Nevertheless, my employment with several popes has forced me to desire their greatness for my own advantage. But for this consideration I should have loved Luther like myself, not to free myself from the silly laws of Christianity as commonly understood, but to put this gang of criminals under restraint, so that they might live either without vices or without power.

From this precious text we learn much of the inner history of contemporary Italy. As far as the Italian mind was liberated in religion it was atheistic, as far as it was reforming it went no further than rejection of the hierarchy. The enemies to be dreaded by Rome were, as the poet Luigi Alamanni wrote, not Luther and Germany, but her own sloth, drunkenness, avarice, ambition, sensuality and gluttony.

Alamanni, 1495–1556

The great spiritual factor that defeated Protestantism in Italy was not Catholicism but the Renaissance. Deeply imbued with the tincture of classical learning, naturally speculative and tolerant, the Italian mind had already advanced, in its best representatives, far beyond the intellectual stage of the Reformers. The hostility of the Renaissance to the Reformation was a deep and subtle antithesis of the interests of this world

Renaissance vs. Reformation

and of the next. It is notable that whereas some philosophical minds, like that of the brilliant Olympia Morata, who had once been completely skeptical, later came under the influence of Luther, there was not one artist of the first rank, not one of the greatest poets, that seems to have been in the least attracted by him. A few minor poets, like Folengo, showed traces of his influence, but Ariosto and Tasso were bitterly hostile. The former cared only for his fantastic world of chivalry and faery, and when he did mention, in a satire dedicated to Bembo, that Friar Martin had become a heretic as Nicoletto had become an infidel, the reason in both cases is that they had overstrained their intellects in the study of metaphysical theology, "because when the mind soars up to see God it is no wonder that it falls down sometimes blind and confused." Heresy he elsewhere pictures as a devastating monster.

Folengo, 1491–1544

Ariosto, 1531

But there was a third reason why the Reformation could not succeed in Italy, and that was that it could not catch the ear of the common people. If for the churchman it was a heresy, and for the free-thinker a superstition, for the "general public" of ordinarily educated persons it was an aristocratic fad. Those who did embrace its doctrines and read its books, and they were not a few of the second-rate humanists, cherished it as their fathers had cherished the neo-Platonism of Pico della Mirandola, as an esoteric philosophy. So little inclined were they to bring their faith to the people that they preferred to translate the Bible into better Greek or classical Latin rather than into the vulgar Tuscan. And just at the moment when it seemed as if a popular movement of some sort might result from the efforts of the Reformers, or in spite of them, came the Roman Inquisition and nipped the budding plant.

Christian Renaissance

But between the levels of the greatest intellectual leaders and that of the illiterate masses, there was a surprising number of groups of men and women more or less tinctured with the doctrines of the north. And yet, even here, one must add that their religion was seldom pure Lutheranism or Calvinism; it was Christianized humanism. There was the brilliant woman Vittoria Colonna, who read with rapture the doctrine of justification by faith, but who remained a conforming Catholic all her life. There was Ochino, the general of the Capuchins, whose defection caused a panic at Rome but who remained, nevertheless, an independent rather than an orthodox Protestant. Of like quality were Peter Martyr Vermigli, an exile for his faith, and Jerome Bolsec, a native of France but an inhabitant of Ferrara, whence he took to Geneva an eccentric doctrine that caused much trouble to Calvin. Finally, it was perfectly in accordance with the Italian genius that the most radical of Protestant dissenters, the unitarians Lelio and Fausto Sozzini, should have been born in Siena.

Among the little nests of Lutherans or Christian mystics the most important were at Venice, Ferrara and Naples. As early as 1519 Luther's books found their way to Venice, and in 1525 one of the leading canon lawyers in the city wrote an elaborate refutation of them, together with a letter to the Reformer himself, informing him that his act of burning the papal decretals was worse than that of Judas in betraying, or of Pilate in crucifying, Christ. The first sufferer for the new religion was Jerome Galateo. Nevertheless, the new church waxed strong, and many were executed for their opinions. A correspondence of the brethren with Bucer and Luther has been preserved. In one letter they deeply deplore the schisms on the doctrine of the eucharist as hurtful to their cause. The

1530

1540

famous artist Lorenzo Lotto was employed to paint pictures of Luther and his wife, probably copies of Cranach. The appearance of the Socinians about 1550, and the mutual animosity of the several sects, including the Anabaptist, was destructive. Probably more fatal was the disaster of the Schmalkaldic war and the complete triumph of the emperor. The Inquisition finished the work of crushing out what remained of the new doctrines.

Naples

That Naples became a focus of Protestantism was due mainly to John de Valdes, a deeply religious Spaniard. From his circle went out a treatise on justification entitled *The Benefit of Christ's Death,* by Benedict of Mantua, of which no less than 40,000 copies were sold, for it was the one reforming work to enjoy popularity rivalling that of Luther and Erasmus. Influenced by Valdes, also, Bartholomew Forzio translated Luther's *Address to the German Nobility* into Italian.

Ferrara

At the court of Ferrara the duchess, Renée de France, gathered a little circle of Protestants. Calvin himself spent some time here, and his influence, together with the high protection of his patroness, made the place a fulcrum against Rome. Isabella d'Este, originally of Ferrara and later Marchioness of Mantua, one of the brilliant women of the Renaissance, for a while toyed with the fashionable theology. Cardinal Bembo saw at her castle at Mantua paintings of Erasmus and Luther. One of the courtly poets of Northern Italy, Francis Berni, bears witness to the good repute of the Protestants. In his *Rifacimento* of Boiardo's *Orlando Inamorato,* he wrote: "Some rascal hypocrites snarl between their teeth, 'Freethinker! Lutheran!' but Lutheran means, you know, good Christian."

1537

Roman prelates affected by Luther

The most significant sign of the times, and the most ominous for the papacy, was that among those affected by the leaven of Lutheranism were many of the leading luminaries in the bosom of the church. That the Florentine chronicler Bartholomew Cerratani expressed his hope that Luther's distinguished morals, piety and learning should reform the curia was bad enough; that the papal nuncio Vergerio, after being sent on a mission to Wittenberg, should go over to the enemy, was worse; that cardinals like Contarini and Pole should preach justification by faith and concede much that the Protestants asked, was worst of all. "No one now passes at Rome," wrote Peter Anthony Bandini about 1540, "as a cultivated man or a good courtier who does not harbor some heretical opinions." Paul Sarpi, the eminent historian of Trent, reports that Luther's arguments were held to be unanswerable at Rome, but that he was resisted in order that authority might be upheld. For this statement he appeals to a diary of Francis Chieregato, an eminent ecclesiastic who died on December 6, 1539. As the diary has not been found, Lord Acton rejects the assertion, believing that Sarpi's word cannot be taken unsupported. But a curious confirmation of Sarpi's assertion, and one that renders it acceptable, is found in Luther's table talk. Speaking on February 22, 1538, he says that he has heard from Rome that it was there believed to be impossible to refute him until St. Paul had been deposed. He regarded this as a signal testimony to the truth of his doctrines; to us it is valuable only as an evidence of Roman opinion. It is not too much to say that at about that time the most distinguished Italian prelates were steering for Wittenberg and threatened to take Rome with them. How they failed is the history of the Counter-reformation.

Sarpi's assertion

§ 2. The Papacy. 1522–1590

Nothing can better indicate the consternation caused at Rome by the appearance of the Lutheran revolt than the fact that for the first time in 144 years and for the last time in history the cardinals elected as supreme pontiff a man who was not an Italian, Adrian of Utrecht. After teaching theology at Louvain he had been appointed tutor to Prince Charles and, on the accession of his pupil to the Spanish throne was created Bishop of Tortosa, and shortly thereafter cardinal and Inquisitor General of Spain. While in this country he distinguished himself equally by the justness of his administration and by his bitter hatred of Luther, against whom he wrote several letters both to his imperial master and to his old colleagues at Louvain.

Adrian VI, January, 1522–September, 1523

December, 1521

The death of Leo X was followed by an unusually long conclave, on account of the even balance of parties. At last, despairing of agreement, and feeling also that extraordinary measures were needed to meet the exigencies of the situation, the cardinals, in January, offered the tiara to Adrian, who, alone among modern popes, kept his baptismal name while in office. The failure of Adrian VI to accomplish much was due largely to the shortness of his pontificate of only twenty months, and still more to the invincible corruption he found at Rome. His really high sense of duty awakened no response save fear and hatred among the courtiers of the Medicis. When he tried to restore the ruined finances of the church he was accused of niggardliness; when he made war on abuses he was called a barbarian; when he frankly confessed, in his appeal to the German Diets, that perchance the whole evil infecting the church came from the rottenness of the Curia, he was assailed as putting arms into the arsenal of the enemy. His greatest crime in the eyes of his court was that he was a foreigner, an austere, phlegmatic man, who could understand neither their tongue nor their ways.

Exhausted by the fruitless struggle, Adrian sank into his grave, a good pope unwept and unhonored as few bad popes have ever been. On his tomb the cardinals wrote: "Here lies Adrian VI whose supreme misfortune in life was that he was called upon to rule." A like judgment was expressed more wittily by the people, who erected a monument to Adrian's physician and labeled it, "Liberatori Patriae."

Clement VII, 1523–34

The swing of the pendulum so often noticed in politics was particularly marked in the elections to the papacy of the sixteenth century. In almost every instance the new pope was an opponent, and in some sort a contrast, to his predecessor. In no case was this more true than in the election of 1523. Deciding that if Adrian's methods were necessary to save the church the medicine was worse than the disease, the cardinals lost no time in raising another Medici to the throne. Like all of his race, Clement VII was a patron of art and literature, and tolerant of abuses. Personally moral and temperate, he cared little save for an easy life and the advancement of the Three Balls. He began that policy, which nearly proved fatal to the church, of treating the Protestants with alternate indulgence and severity. But for himself the more immediate trouble came not from the enemy of the church but from its protector. Though Adrian was an old officer of Charles V, it was really in the reign of Clement that the process began by which first Italy, then the papacy, then the whole church was put under the Spanish yoke.

Spanish influence, 1525–6

After Pavia and the treaty of Madrid had eliminated French influence, Charles naturally felt his power and naturally intended to have it respected even by the pope. Irritated by Clement's perpetual deceit and intrigue with France, Charles addressed to him, in 1526, a document which Ranke calls the most formidable ever used by any Catholic prince to a pope during the century, containing passages "of which no follower of Luther need be ashamed."

Sack of Rome, May and September, 1527

Rather to threaten the pope than to make war on him, Charles gathered a formidable army of German and Spanish soldiers in the north under the command of his general Frundsberg. All the soldiers were restless and mutinous for want of pay, and in addition to this a powerful motive worked among the German landsknechts. Many of them were Lutheran and looked to the conquest of Rome as the triumph of their cause. As they loudly demanded to be lead against Antichrist, Frundsberg found that his authority was powerless to stop them. When he died of rage and mortification the French traitor Charles, Constable of Bourbon, was appointed by the emperor in his place, and, finding there was nothing else to do, led the army against Rome and promised the soldiers as much booty as they could take. Twice, in May and September, the city was put to the horrors of a sack, with all the atrocities of murder, theft and rapine almost inseparable from war. In addition to plundering, the Lutherans took particular pleasure in desecrating the objects of veneration to the Catholics. Many an image and shrine was destroyed, while Luther was acclaimed pope by his boisterous champions. But far away on the Elbe he heard of the sack and expressed his sorrow for it.

March 16, 1527

The importance of the sack of Rome, like that of other dramatic events, is apt to be exaggerated. It has been called the end of the Renaissance and the beginning of the Catholic reaction. It was neither the one nor the other, but only one incident in the long, stubborn process of the Hispanization of Italy and the church. For centuries no emperor had had so much power in Italy as had Charles. With Naples and Milan were now linked Siena and Genoa under his rule; the states of the church were virtually at his disposal, and even Florence, under its hereditary duke, Alexander de' Medici, was for a while under the control of the pope and through him, of Charles.

Nor did the fall of the holy city put the fear of God into the hearts of the prelates for more than a moment. The Medici, Clement, who never sold his soul but only pawned it from time to time, without entirely abandoning the idea of reform, indefinitely postponed it. Procrastinating, timid, false, he was not the man to deal with serious abuses. He toyed with the idea of a council but when, on the mere rumor that a council was to be called the prices of all salable offices dropped in a panic, he hesitated. Moreover he feared the council would be used by the emperor to subordinate him even in spiritual matters. Perhaps he meant well, but abuses were too lucrative to be lightly affronted. As to Lutheranism, Clement was completely misinformed and almost completely indifferent. While he and the emperor were at odds it grew mightily. Here as elsewhere he was irresolute; his pontificate, as a contemporary wrote, was "one of scruples, considerations and discords, of buts and ifs and thens and moreovers, and plenty of words without effect."

Paul III, 1534–49

The pontificate of Paul III marks the turning point in the Catholic reaction. Under him the council of Trent was at last opened; the new orders, especially the Jesuits, were formed, and such instrumentalities as the Inquisition and Index of prohibited books put on a new footing. Paul III, a Farnese from the States of the Church, owed his election partly to his strength of character, partly to the weakness of his health, for the cardinals liked frequent vacancies in the Holy See. Cautious and choleric, prolix and stubborn, he had a real desire for reform and an earnest wish to avoid quarrels with either of the great powers that menaced him, the emperor and France. The reforming spirit of the pope showed itself in the appointment of several men of the highest character to the cardinalate, among them Gaspar Contarini and Fisher, Bishop of Rochester. In other cases, however, the exigencies of politics induced the nomination of bad men, such as Del Monte and David Beaton. At the same time a commission was named to recommend practical reforms. The draft for a bull they presented for this purpose was rejected by the Consistory, but some of their recommendations, such as the prohibition of the Roman clergy to visit taverns, theaters and gambling dens, were adopted.

May, 1535
Consilium delectorum cardinalium et aliorum praelatorum

A second commission of nine ecclesiastics of high character, including John Peter Caraffa, Contarini, Pole and Giberti, was created to make a comprehensive report on reform. The important memorial they drew up fully exposed the prevalent abuses. The root of all they found in the exaggeration of the papal power of collation and the laxity with which it was used. Not only were morally unworthy men often made bishops and prelates, but dispensations for renunciation of benefices, for absenteeism and for other hurtful practices were freely sold. The commission demanded drastic reform of these abuses as well as of the monastic orders, and called for the abolition of the venal exercise of spiritual authority by legates and nuncios. But the reform memorial, excellent and searching as it was, led to nothing. At most it was of some use as a basis of reforms made by the Council of Trent later. But for the moment it only rendered the position of the church more difficult. The reform of the Dataria, for example, the office which sold graces, privileges, indults, dispensations and benefices, was considered impossible because half of the papal revenue, or 110,000 ducats annually, came from it. Nor could the fees of the Penitentiary be abolished for fear of bankruptcy, though in 1540 they were partially reduced. The most obvious results of the *Consilium* was to put another weapon into the hands of the Lutherans. Published by an unauthorized person, it was at once seized upon by the Reformers as proof of the hopeless depravity of the Curia. So dangerous did it prove to simple-minded Catholics that it was presently put on the Index!

1538

Paul's diplomacy tried to play off the Empire against France and to divert the attention of both to a crusade against the Turk. Hoping to advance the cause of the church by means of the war declared by Charles V on the Schmalkaldic League, the pope, in return for a subsidy, exacted a declaration in the treaty, that the reason of the war was religious and the occasion for it the refusal of the Protestants to recognize the Council of Trent's authority. But when Charles was victor he used his advantage only to strengthen his own prerogative, not effectively to suppress heresy. Paul now dreaded the emperor more than he did the Protestants and his position was not made easier by the threat of Charles to come to terms with the Lutherans did Paul succeed in rousing France against him. In fact, with all his squirming, Paul III only sank deeper into the Spanish vassalage, while the championship of the church passed from his control into that of new agencies that he had created.

Julius III, 1550–5

It was perhaps an effort to free the Holy See from the Spanish yoke that led the cardinals to raise to the purple, as Julius III, Cardinal John Mary Ciocchi del Monte who as one of the presidents of the oecumenical council had distinguished himself by his opposition to the emperor. Nevertheless his pontificate marked a relaxation of the church's effort, for policy or strength to pursue reform he had none.

Marcellus II, April 9–May 1, 1555

Marcellus II, who was pope for twenty-two days, would hardly be remembered save for the noble Mass of Pope Marcellus dedicated to him by Palestrina.

Paul IV, 1555–9

With the elevation of Cardinal Caraffa to the tiara Peter's keys were once more restored to strong hands and a reforming heart. The founder of the Theatines was a hot-blooded Neapolitan still, in spite of his seventy-nine years, hale and hearty. Among the reforms he accomplished were some regulations relating to the residence of bishops and some rules for the bridling of Jews, usurers, prostitutes, players and mountebanks. But he was unable to reform himself. He advanced his young kinsmen shamelessly to political office. His jealousy of the Jesuits, in whom he saw a rival to his own order, not only caused him to neglect to use them but made him put them in a very critical position. Nor did he dare to summon again the council that had been prorogued, for fear that some stronger power should use it against himself. He chafed under the Spanish yoke, coming nearer to a conflict with Charles V and his son Philip II than any pope had ventured to do. He even thought of threatening Philip with the Inquisition, but was restrained by prudence. In his purpose of freeing Italy from foreign domination he accomplished nothing whatever.

Pius IV, 1560–5

Pius IV was a contrast to the predecessor whom he hated. John Angelo Medici, of Milan, not connected with the Florentine family, was a cheerful, well-wishing, beneficent man, genial and fond of life, a son of the Renaissance, a patron of art and letters. The choice of a name often expresses the ideals and tendencies of a pope; that of Pius was chosen perhaps in imitation of Pius II, Aeneas Sylvius Piccolomini, the most famous humanist to sit on the fisherman's throne. And yet the spirit of the times no longer allowed the gross licentiousness of the earlier age, and the cause of reform progressed not a little under the diplomatic guidance of the Milanese. In the first place, doubtless from personal motives, he made a fearful example of the kinsmen of his predecessor, four of whom he executed chiefly for the reason that they had been advanced by papal influence. This salutary example practically put an end to nepotism; at least the unfortunate nephews of Paul IV were the last to aspire to independent principalities solely on the strength of kinship to a pope.

Reforms

The demand for the continuation and completion of the general council, which had become loud, was acceded to by Pius who thought, like the American boss, that at times it was necessary to "pander to the public conscience." The happy issue of the council, from his point of view, in its complete submissiveness to the papal prerogative, led Pius to emphasize the spiritual rather than the political claims of the hierarchy. In this the church made a great gain, for, as the history of the time shows plainly, in the game of politics the papacy could no longer hold its own against the national states surrounding it. Pius leaned heavily on Philip, for by this time Spain had become the acknowledged champion of the church, but he was able to do so without loss of prestige because of the gradual separation of the temporal from the spiritual power.

Among his measures the most noteworthy was one regulating the powers of the college of cardinals, while their exclusive right to elect the pontiff was maintained against the pretensions of the council. The best Catholic spirit of the time was represented in

Cardinal Charles Borromeo, Archbishop of Milan, an excellent prelate who sought to win back members of Christ to the fold by his good example, while he did not disdain to use the harsher methods of persecution when necessary. Among the amiable weaknesses of Pius was the belief, inherited from a bygone age, that the Protestants might still be reunited to the church by a few concessions, such as those of the marriage of the clergy and the use of the cup by the laity.

Pius V, 1566–72

With Pius V a sterner spirit entered into the councils of the church. The election of the Dominican and Chief Inquisitor Michael Ghislieri was a triumph for the policy of Borromeo. His pitiless hatred of the heretics hounded Catharine de' Medici against the Huguenots, and Philip II against the Dutch. Contrary to the dictates of prudence and the wishes of the greatest Catholic princes, he issued the bull deposing Elizabeth. But he was severe to himself, an ascetic nicknamed for his monkish narrowness "Friar Wooden-shoe" by the Roman populace. He ruthlessly reformed the Italian clergy, meting out terrible punishments to all sinners. Under his leadership Catholicism took the offensive in earnest and accomplished much. His zeal won him the name of saint, for he was the last of the Roman pontiffs to be canonized.

But the reign of sainthood coupled with absolutism is apt to grow irksome, and it was with relief that the Romans hailed the election of Hugo Buoncompagno as

Gregory XIII, 1572–85

Gregory XIII. He did little but follow out, somewhat weakly, the paths indicated by his predecessors. So heavily did he lean on Spain that he was called the chaplain of Philip, but, as the obligations were mutual, and the Catholic king came also to depend more and more upon the spiritual arms wielded by the papacy, it might just as well have been said that Philip was the executioner employed by Gregory. The mediocrity of his rule did not prevent notable achievement by the Jesuits in the cause of the church. His reform of the calendar will be described more fully elsewhere.

Gregory XIII offers an opportunity to measure the moral standard of the papacy after half a century of reform. His policy was guided largely by his ruling passion, love of a natural son, born before he had taken priest's orders, whom he made Gonfaloniere of the church and would have advanced to still further preferment had not his advisers objected. Gregory was the pope who thanked God "for the grace vouchsafed unto Christendom" in the massacre of St. Bartholomew. He was also the pope who praised and encouraged the plan for the assassination of Elizabeth.[1]

Sixtus V, 1585–90

In the person of Sixtus V the spirit of Pius V returned to power. Felix Peretti was a Franciscan and an Inquisitor, an earnest man and a hard one. Like his predecessors pursuing the goal of absolutism, he had an advantage over them in the blessing disguised as the disaster of the Spanish Armada. From this time forward the papacy was forced to champion its cause with the spiritual weapons at its command, and the gain to it as a moral and religious power was enormous. In some ways it assumed the primacy of Catholic Europe, previously usurped by Spain, and attained an influence that it had not had since the Great Schism of the fourteenth century.

The reforms of Sixtus are important rather for their comprehensive than for their drastic quality. The whole machinery of the Curia was made over, the routine of business being delegated to a number of standing committees known as Congregations, such as the Congregation of Ceremonies to watch over matters of precedence at the papal court, and the Congregation

[1] *Ante*, p. 338.

of the Consistory to prepare the work of the Consistory. The number of cardinals was fixed at seventy. New editions of the breviary and of the Index were carefully prepared. At the same time the moral reforms of Trent were laxly carried out, for while decrees enforcing them were promulgated by Sixtus with one hand, with the other he sold dispensations and privileges.

§ 3. The Council of Trent

While the popes were enjoying their *jus incorrigibilitatis*—as Luther wittily expressed it—the church was going to rack and ruin. Had the safety of Peter's boat been left to its captains, it would apparently have foundered in the waves of schism and heresy. No such dangerous enemy has ever attacked the church as that then issuing from her own bosom. Neither the medieval heretics nor the modern philosophers have won from her in so short a time such masses of adherents. Where Voltaire slew his thousands Luther slew his ten thousands, for Voltaire appealed only to the intellect, Luther appealed to the conscience.

Decline of Protestantism

The extraordinary thing about the Protestant conquests was their sudden end. Within less than fifty years the Scandinavian North, most of Germany including Austria, parts of Hungary, Poland, most of Switzerland, and Great Britain had declared for the "gospel." France was divided and apparently going the same road; even in Italy there were serious symptoms of disaffection. That within a single generation the tide should be not only stopped but rolled back is one of the most dramatic changes of fortune in history The only country which Protestantism gained after 1560 was the Dutch Republic. Large parts of Germany and Poland were won back to the church, and Catholicism made safe in all the Latin countries.

Spanish revival

The spirit that accomplished this work was the spirit of Spain. More extraordinary than the rapid growth of her empire was the conquest of Europe by her ideals. The character of the Counter-reformation was determined by her genius. It was not, as it started to be in Italy, a more or less inwardly Christianized Renaissance. It was a distinct and powerful religious revival, and one that showed itself, as many others have done, by a mighty reaction. Medievalism was restored, largely by medieval methods, the general council, the emphasis on tradition and dogma, coercion of mind and body, and the ministrations of a monastic order, new only in its discipline and effectiveness, a reduplication of the old mendicant orders in spirit and ideal.

Preparation for calling a council

The Oecumenical Council was so double-edged a weapon that it is not remarkable that the popes hesitated to grasp it in their war with the heretic. They had uncomfortable memories of Constance and Basle, of the election and deposition of popes and of decrees limiting their prerogatives. And, moreover, the council was the first authority invoked by the heretic himself. Adrian might have been willing to risk such a synod, but before he had time to call one, his place was taken by the vacillating and pusillanimous Clement. Perpetually toying with the idea he yet allowed the pressure of his courtiers and the difficulties of the political situation—for France was opposed to the council as an imperial scheme—indefinitely to postpone the summons.

The more serious-minded Paul III found another lion in his path. He for the first time really labored to summon the general synod, but he found that the Protestants had now changed their position and would no longer consent to recognize its authority under any conditions to which he could possibly assent. Though his nuncio Vergerio received in Germany and even in Wittenberg a cordial welcome, it was soon discovered that the ideas of the proper constitution of the council entertained by the two parties were irreconciliable. Fundamentally each wanted a council in which its own predominance should be assured. The Schmalkaldic princes, on the advice of their theologians, asked for a free German synod in which they should have a majority vote, and in this they were supported by Francis I and Henry VIII. Naturally no pope could consent to any such measures; under these discouraging circumstances, the opening of the council was continually postponed, and in place of it the emperor held a series of religious colloquies that only served to make the differences of the two parties more prominent.

Summons of Council, November 19, 1544

After several years of negotiation the path was made smooth and the bull *Laetare Hierusalem* summoned a general synod to meet at Trent on March 15, 1545, and assigned it three tasks: (1) The pacification of religious disputes by doctrinal decisions; (2) the reform of ecclesiastical abuses; (3) the discussion of a crusade against the infidel. Delay still interfered with the opening of the assembly, which did not take place until December 15, 1545.

First period 1545–7

The council was held at three separate periods with long intervals. The first period was 1545–7, the second 1551–2, the third 1562–3. The city of Trent was chosen in order to yield to the demand for a German town while at the same time selecting that one nearest to Italy, for the pope was determined to keep the action of the synod under control. Two measures were adopted to insure this end, the initiative and presidency of the papal legates and packing the membership. The faculties to be granted the legates were already decided upon in 1544; these lieutenants were to be, according to Father Paul Sarpi, angels of peace to preside, make all necessary regulations, and publish them "according to custom." The phrase that the council should decide on measures, "legatis proponentibus" was simply the constitutional expression of the principal familiar in many governments, that the legislative should act only on the initiative of the executive, thus giving an immense advantage to the latter. The second means of subordinating the council was the decision to vote by heads and not by nations and to allow no proxies. This gave a constant majority to the Italian prelates sent by the pope. So successful were these measures that the French ambassador bitterly jested of the Holy Ghost coming to Trent in the mailbags from Rome.

Membership

At the first session there were only thirty-four members entitled to vote: four cardinals, four archbishops, twenty-one bishops and five generals of orders. There were also present other personages, including an ambassador from King Ferdinand, four Spanish secular priests and a number of friars. The first question debated was the precedence of dogma or reform. Regarding the council chiefly as an instrument for condemning the heretics, the pope was in favor of taking up dogma first. The emperor, on the other hand, wishing rather to conciliate the Protestants and if possible to lure them back to the old church, was in favor of starting with reform. The struggle, which was carried on not so much on the floor of the synod as behind the members' backs in the intrigues of courts, was decided by a compromise to the effect that both dogma and reform should be taken up simultaneously. But all enactments dealing with ecclesiastical irregularities were to bear the proviso "under reservation of the papal authority."

Dogmatic decrees

The dogmatic decrees at Trent were almost wholly oriented by the polemic against Protestantism. Practically nothing was defined save what had already been taken up in the Augsburg Confession or in the writings of Calvin, of Zwingli and of the Anabaptists. Inevitably, a spirit so purely defensive could not be animated by a primarily philosophical interest. The guiding star was not a system but a policy, and this policy was nothing more nor less than that of re-establishing tradition. The practice of the church was the standard applied; many an unhistorical assertion was made to justify it and many a practice of comparatively recent growth was sanctioned by the postulate that "it had descended from apostolic use." "By show of antiquity they introduce novelty," was Bacon's correct judgment.

Bible and tradition

Quite naturally the first of the important dogmatic decrees was on the basis of authority. The Protestants had acknowledged the Bible only; over against them the Tridentine fathers declared for the Bible *and* the tradition of the church. The canon of Scripture was different from that recognized by the Protestants in that it included the Apocrypha.

Justification

After passing various reform decrees on preaching, catechetical instruction, privileges of mendicants and indulgences, the council took up the thorny question of justification. Discussion was postponed for some months out of consideration for the emperor, who feared it might irritate the Protestants, and only gave his consent to it in the hope that some ambiguous form acceptable to that party, might be found. How deeply the solifidian doctrine had penetrated into the very bosom of the church was revealed by the storminess of the debate. The passions of the right reverend fathers were so excited by the consideration of a fundamental article of their faith that in the course of disputation they accused one another of conduct unbecoming to Christians, taunted one another with plebeian origin and tore hair from one another's beards. The decree as finally passed established the position that faith and works together justify, and condemned the semi-Lutheran doctrines of "duplicate justice" and imputed righteousness hitherto held by such eminent theologians as Contarini and Cajetan.

Having accomplished this important work the council appeared to the pope ready for dissolution. The protests of the emperor kept it together for a few months longer, but an outbreak of the spotted fever and the fear of a raid during the Schmalkaldic war, served as sufficient excuses to translate the council to Bologna. Though nothing was accomplished in this city the assembly was not formally prorogued until September 13, 1549.

March, 1547

Second period, 1551–2

Under pressure from the emperor Pope Julius III convoked the synod for a second time at Trent on May 1, 1551. The personnel was different. The Jesuits Lainez and Salmeron were present working in the interests of the papacy. No French clergy took part as Henry II was hostile. The Protestants were required to send a delegation, which was received on January 24, 1552. They presented a confession, but declined to recognize the authority of a body in which they were not represented. Several dogmatic decrees were passed on the sacraments, reasserting transubstantiation and all the doctrines and usages of the church. A few reform decrees were also passed, but before a great deal could be accomplished the revolt of Maurice of Saxony put both emperor and council in a precarious position and the latter was consequently prorogued for a second time on April 28, 1552.

Third period, 1562–3

When, after ten long years, the council again convened at the command of Pius IV, in January, 1562, it is extraordinary to see how little the problems confronting it had changed. Not only was the struggle for power between pope and council and between pope and emperor still going on, but hopes were still entertained in some quarters of reconciling the schismatics. Pius invited all princes, whether Catholic or heretical, to send delegates, but was rebuffed by some of them. The argument was then taken up by the Emperor Ferdinand who sent in an imposing demand for reforms, including the authorization of the marriage of priests, communion in both kinds, the use of the vulgar tongue in divine service, and drastic rules for the improvement of the convents and of the papal courts.

Jesuits present

The contention over this bone among the fathers, now far more numerous than in the earlier days, waxed so hot that for ten whole months no session could be held. Mobs of the partisans of the various factions fought in the streets and bitter taunts of "French diseases" and "Spanish eruptions" were exchanged between them. For a time the situation seemed inextricable and one cardinal prophesied the impending downfall of the papacy. But in the nick of time to prevent such a catastrophe the pope was able to send into the field the newly recruited praetorian guards of the Society of Jesuits. Under the command of Cardinal Morone these indefatigable zealots turned the flank of the opposing forces partly by intrigue at the imperial court, partly by skilful manipulation of debate. The emperor's mind was changed; reforms demanded by him were dropped.

The questions actually taken up and settled were dogmatic ones, chiefly concerning the sacrifice of the mass and the perpetuation of the Catholic customs of communion in one kind, the celebration of masses in honor of saints, the celebration of masses in which the priest only communicates, the mixing of water with the wine, the prohibition of the use of the vulgar tongue, and the sanction of masses for the dead. Other decrees amended the marriage laws, and enjoined the preparation of an Index of prohibited books, of a catechism and of standard editions of missal and breviary.

Subjection to papacy

How completely the council in its last estate was subdued to the will of the pope is shown by its request that the decrees should all be confirmed by him. This was done by Pius IV in the bull *Benedictus Deus.* Pius also caused to be prepared a symbol known as the Tridentine Profession of Faith which was made binding on all priests. Save that it was slightly enlarged in 1877 by the pronouncement on Papal Infallibility, it stands to the present day.

January 26, 1564

Reception of decrees

The complete triumph of the papal claims was offset by the cool reception which the decrees received in Catholic Europe. Only the Italian states, Poland, Portugal and Savoy unreservedly recognized the authority of all of them. Philip II, bigot as he was, preferred to make his own rules for his clergy and recognized the laws of Trent with the proviso "saving the royal rights." France sanctioned only the dogmatic, not the practical decrees. The emperor never officially recognized the work of the council at all. Nor were the governments the only recalcitrants. According to Sarpi the body of German Catholics paid no attention to the prescribed reforms and the council was openly mocked in France as claiming an authority superior to that of the apostles.

To Father Paul Sarpi, indeed, the most intelligent observer of the next generation, the council seemed to have been a failure if not a fraud. Its history he calls an Iliad of woes. The professed objects of the council, healing the schism and asserting the episcopal power he thinks frustrated, for the schism was made irreconciliable and the church reduced to servitude.

But the judgment of posterity has reversed that of

Constructive work

the great historian, at least as far as the value of the work done at Trent to the cause of Catholicism is concerned. If the church shut out the Protestants and recognized her limited domain, she at least took appropriate measures to establish her rule over what was left. Her power was now collected; her dogma was unified and made consistent as opposed to the mutually diverse Protestant creeds. In several points, indeed, where the opinion of the members was divided, the words of the decrees were ambiguous, but as against the Protestants they were distinct and so comprehensive as rather to supersede than to supplement earlier standards.

Nor should the moral impulse of the council be underestimated, ridiculed though it was by its opponents as if expressed in the maxim, "si non caste, tamen caute." Sweeping decrees for urgent reforms were passed, and above all a machinery set up to carry on the good work. In providing for a catechism, for authoritative editions of the Vulgate, breviary and other standard works, in regulating moot points, in striking at lax discipline, the council did a lasting service to Catholicism and perhaps to the world. Not the least of the practical reforms was the provision for the opening of seminaries to train the diocesan clergy. The first measure looking to this was passed in 1546; Cardinal Pole at once began to act upon it, and a decree of the third session ordered that each diocese should have such a school for the education of priests. The Roman seminary, opened two years later, was a model for subsequent foundations.

1563

1565

§ 4. The Company of Jesus

If the Counter-reformation was in part a pure reaction to medievalism it was in part also a religious revival. If this was stimulated by the Protestant example, it was also the outcome of the rising tide of Catholic pietism in the fifteenth century. Still more was it the answer to a demand on the part of the church for an instrument with which to combat the dangers of heresy and to conquer spiritually the new worlds of heathenism.

Great crises in the church have frequently produced new revivals of monasticism. From Benedict to Bernard, from Bernard to Francis and Dominic, from the friars to the Jesuits, there is an evolution in the adaptation of the monastic life to the needs of Latin Christianity. Several new orders, all with more or less in common, started in the first half of the sixteenth century. Under Leo X there assembled at Rome a number of men united by the wish to renew their spiritual lives by religious exercises. From this Oratory of Divine Love, as it was called, under the inspiration of Gaetano di Tiene and John Peter Caraffa, arose the order of Theatines, a body of devoted priests, dressing not in a special garb but in ordinary priest's robes, who soon attained a prominent position in the Catholic reformation. Their especial task was to educate the clergy.

New monastic orders

1524

The order of the Capuchins was an offshoot of the Franciscans. It restored the relaxed discipline of the early friars and its members went about teaching the poor. Notwithstanding the blow to it when its third vicar Bernardino Ochino became a Calvinist, it flourished and turned its energies especially against the heretics.

c. 1526

Of the other orders founded at this time, the Barnabites (1530), the Somascians (1532), the Brothers of Mercy (1540), the Ursulines (1537), only the common characteristics can be pointed out. It is notable that they were all animated by a social ideal; not only the salvation of the individual soul but also the amelioration of humanity was now their purpose. Some of the orders devoted themselves to the education of children, some to home missions or foreign missions, some to nursing the sick, some to the rescue of fallen women. The evolution of monasticism had already pointed the way to these tasks; its apogee was reached with the organization of the Company of Jesus.

Typical Jesuit

The Jesuit has become one of those typical figures, like the Puritan and the buccaneer. Though less exploited in fiction than he was in the days of Dumas, Eugène Sue and Zola, the mention of his name calls to the imagination the picture of a tall, spare man, handsome, courteous, obliging, but subtle, deceitful, dangerous, capable of nursing the blackest thoughts and of sanctioning the worst actions for the advancement of his cause. The *Lettres Provinciales* of Pascal first stamped on public opinion the idea that the Jesuit was necessarily immoral and venomous; the implacable hatred of Michelet and Symonds has brought them as criminals before the bar of history. On the other hand they have had their apologists and friends even outside their own order. Let us neither praise nor blame, but seek to understand them.

Loyola c. 1493–1556

In that memorable hour when Luther said his everlasting nay at Worms one of his auditors was—or might have been for she was undoubtedly present in the city—Germaine de Foix, the wife of the Margrave John of Brandenburg. The beautiful and frivolous young woman had been by a former marriage the second wife of Ferdinand the Catholic and at his court she had been known and worshipped by a young page of good family, Iñigo de Loyola. Like the romantic Spaniard that he was he had taken, as he told later, for his lady "no duchess nor countess but one far higher" and to her he paid court in the genuine spirit of old chivalry. Not that this prevented him from addressing less disinterested attentions to other ladies, for, if something of a Don Quixote he was also something of a Don Juan. Indeed, at the carnival of 1515, his "enormous misdemeanors" had caused him to be tried before a court of justice and little did his plea of benefit of clergy avail him, for the judge failed to find a tonsure on his head "even as large as a seal on a papal bull," and he was probably punished severely.

Loyola was a Basque, and a soldier to his fingertips. When the French army invaded Spain he was given command of the fortress of Pampeluna. Defending it bravely against desperate odds he was wounded in the leg with a cannon ball and forced to yield. The leg was badly set and the bone knit crooked. With indomitable courage he had it broken and reset, stretched on racks and the protruding bone sawed off, but all the torture, in the age before anaesthetics, was in vain. The young man of about twenty-eight—the exact year of his birth is unknown—found himself a cripple for life.

May 21, 1521

To while away the long hours of convalescence he asked for the romances of chivalry but was unable to get them and read in their place legends of the saints and a life of Christ by Ludolph of Saxony. His imagination took fire at the new possibilities of heroism and of fame. "What if you should be a saint like Dominic or Francis?" he asked himself, "ay, what if you should even surpass them in sanctity?" His choice was fixed. He took Madonna for his lady and determined to become a soldier of Christ.

As soon as he was able to move he made a pilgrimage to Seville and Manresa and there dedicated his arms in a church in imitation of the knights he had read about in *Amadis of Gaul*. Then, with a general confession and much fasting and mortification of the flesh, began a period of doubt and spiritual anguish that has sometimes been compared with that of Luther. Both were men of strong will and intellect, both suffered from the sense of sin. But Luther's development was somewhat quieter and more normal—if, indeed, in the psychology of conversion so carefully studied by James, the quieter is the more normal. At any rate where Luther had one vision on an exceptional occasion, Loyola had hundreds and had them daily. Ignatius saw the Trinity as a clavichord with three strings, the miracle of transubstantiation as light in bread, Satan as a glistening serpent covered with bright, mysterious eyes, Jesus as "a big round form shining as gold," and the Trinity again as "a ball of fire."

But with all the visions he kept his will fixed on his purpose. At first this took the form of a vow to preach to the infidels and he made a pilgrimage to Jerusalem, only to be turned back by the highest Christian authority in that region, the politically-minded Franciscan vicar.

1523

1524

On returning to Spain he went to Barcelona and started to learn Latin with boys, for his education as a gentleman had included nothing but reading and writing his own tongue. Thence he went to the university of Alcalá where he won disciples but was imprisoned for six weeks by the Inquisition and forbidden to hold meetings with them. Practically the same experience was repeated at Salamanca where he was detained by the Holy Office for twenty-two days and again prohibited from holding religious meetings. Thus he was chased out of Spain by the church he sought to serve. Turning his steps to Paris he entered the College of Montaigu, and, if he here was free from the Inquisition he was publicly whipped by the college authorities as a dangerous fanatic. Nevertheless, here he gathered his first permanent disciples, Peter Le Fèvre of Savoy, Francis Xavier of Pampeluna and two Castilians,

James Laynez and Alfonso Salmeron. The little man, hardly over five feet two inches high, deformed and scarred, at the age of thirty-five, won men to him by his smile, as of a conqueror in pain, by his enthusiasm, his mission and his book.

The Spiritual Exercises

If one reckons the greatness of a piece of literature not by the beauty of the style or the profundity of the thought but by the influence it has exercised over men, the *Spiritual Exercises* of Ignatius will rank high. Its chief sources were the meditation and observation of its author. If he took some things from Garcia de Cisneros, some from *The Imitation of Christ,* some from the rules of Montaigu, where he studied, far more he took from the course of discipline to which he had subjected himself at Manresa. The psychological soundness of Loyola's method is found in his discovery that the best way to win a man to an ideal is to kindle his imagination. His own thought was imaginative to the verge of abnormality and the means which he took to awaken and artificially to stimulate this faculty in his followers were drastic in the extreme.

The purpose of the *Exercises* is stated in the axiom that "Man was created to praise, reverence and serve God our Lord and thereby to save his soul." To fit a man for this work the spiritual exercises were divided into four periods called weeks, though each period might be shortened or lengthened at the discretion of the director. The first week was devoted to the consideration of sin; the second to that of Christ's life as far as Palm Sunday; the third to his passion; and the fourth to his resurrection and ascension. Knowing the tremendous power of the stimulant to be administered Ignatius inserted wise counsels of moderation in the application of it. But, subject only to the condition that the novice was not to be plied beyond what he could bear, he was directed in the first week of solitary meditation to try to see the length, breadth and depth of hell, to hear the lamentations and blasphemies of the damned, to smell the smoke and brimstone, to taste the bitterness of tears and of the worm of conscience and to feel the burnings of the unquenchable fire. In like manner in the other weeks he was to try to picture to himself in as vivid a manner as possible all the events brought before his mind, whether terrible or glorious. The end of all this discipline was to be the complete subjection of the man to the church. The Jesuit was directed ever "to praise all the precepts of the church, holding the mind ready to find reasons for her defence and nowise in her offence." There must be an unconditional surrender to her not only of the will but of the intelligence. "To make sure of being right in all things," says Loyola, "we ought always to hold by the principle that the white I see I should believe to be black if the hierarchical church were so to rule it."

Inspired by this ideal the small body of students, agreeing to be called henceforth the Company of Jesus —a military term, the *socii* being the companions or followers of a chief in arms—took vows to live in poverty and chastity and to make a pilgrimage to Jerusalem. With this object they set out to Venice and then turned towards Rome for papal approbation of their enterprise. Their first reception was chilling, but they gradually won a few new recruits and Ignatius drafted the constitution for a new order which was handed to the pope by Contarini and approved in the bull *Regimini militantis ecclesiae,* which quotes from the formula of the Jesuits:

August 15, 1540

September 27, 1540

> Whoever wishes to fight for God under the standard of the cross and to serve the Lord alone and his vicar on earth the Roman pontiff shall, after a solemn vow of perpetual chastity, consider that he is part of a society instituted chiefly for these ends, for the profit of souls in

> life and Christian doctrine, for the propagation of the faith through public preaching, the ministry of God's word, spiritual exercises and works of charity, and especially for the education of children and ignorant persons in Christianity, for the hearing of confession and for the giving of spiritual consolation.

Moreover it is stated that the members of the new order should be bound by a vow of special obedience to the pope and should hold themselves ready at his behest to propagate the faith among Turks, infidels, heretics or schismatics, or to minister to believers.

April, 1541

Ignatius was chosen first general of the order. The pope then cancelled the previous limitation of the number of Jesuits to 60 and later issued a large charter of privileges for them. They were exempted from taxes and episcopal jurisdiction; no member was to be allowed to accept any dignity without the general's consent, nor could any member be assigned to the spiritual direction of women. Among many other grants was one to the effect that the faithful might confess to them and receive communion without permission of their parish priests. A confirmation of all privileges and a grant of others was made in a bull of July 21, 1550.

1544

1549

Organization of Society of Jesus, 1550

The express end of the order being the world-domination of the church, its constitution provided a marvellously apt organization for this purpose. Everything was to be subordinate to efficiency. Detachment from the world went only so far as necessary for the completer conquest of the world. Asceticism, fasting, self-discipline were to be moderate so as not to interfere with health. No special dress was prescribed, for it might be a hindrance rather than a help. The purpose being to win over the classes rather than the masses, the Jesuits were particular to select as members only robust men of agreeable appearance, calm minds and eloquence. That an aspirant to the order should also be rich and of good family was not requisite but was considered desirable. Men of bad reputation, intractible, choleric, or men who had ever been tainted with heresy, were excluded. No women were recruited.

After selection, the neophyte was put on a probation of two years. He was then assigned to the class of scholars for further discipline. He was later placed either as a temporal coadjutor, a sort of lay brother charged with inferior duties, or as a spiritual coadjutor, who took the three irrevocable vows. Finally, there was a class, to which admission was gained after long experience, the Professed of Four Vows, the fourth being one of special obedience to the pope. A small number of secret Jesuits who might be considered as another class, were charged with dangerous missions and with spying.

General

Over the order was placed a General who was practically, though not theoretically, absolute. On paper he was limited by the possibility of being deposed and by the election, independently of his influence, of an "admonitor" and some assistants. In practice the only limitations of his power were the physical ones inherent in the difficulties of administering provinces thousands of miles away. From every province, however, he received confidential reports from a multitude of spies.

The spirit of the order was that of absolute, unquestioning, blind obedience. The member must obey his superior "like a corpse which can be turned this way or that, or a rod that follows every impulse, or a ball of wax that might be moulded in any form." The ideal was an old one; the famous *perinde ac cadaver* itself dates back to Francis of Assisi, but nowhere had the ideal been so completely realized as by the companions of Ignatius. In fact, in this as in other respects, the

Jesuits were but a natural culmination of the evolution of monasticism. More and more had the orders tended to become highly disciplined, unified bodies, apt to be used for the service of the church and of the pope.

Growth

The growth of the society was extraordinarily rapid. By 1544 they had nine establishments, two each in Italy, Spain and Portugal and one each in France, Germany and the Netherlands. When Loyola died Jesuits could be found in Japan and Brazil, in Abyssinia and on the Congo; in Europe they were in almost every country and included doctors at the largest universities and papal nuncios to Poland and Ireland. There were in all twelve provinces, about 65 residences and 1500 members.

July 31, 1556

Their work was as broad as their field, but it was dedicated especially to three several tasks: education, war against the heretic, and foreign missions. Neither of the first two was particularly contemplated by the founders of the order in their earliest period. At that time they were rather like the friars, popular preachers, catechists, confessors and charitable workers. But the exigencies of the time called them to supply other needs. The education of the young was the natural result of their desire to dominate the intellectual class. Their seminaries, at first adapted only to their own uses, soon became famous.

Combating heresy

In the task of combating heresy they were also the most successful of the papal cohorts. Though not the primary purpose of the order, it soon came to be regarded as their special field. The bull canonizing Loyola speaks of him as an instrument raised up by divine providence especially to combat that "foulest of monsters" Martin Luther. Beginning in Italy the Jesuits revived the nearly extinct popular piety. Going among the poor as missionaries they found many who knew no prayers, many who had not confessed for

1623

thirty or forty years, and a host of priests as blind as their flocks.

In most other Catholic countries they had to fight for the right to exist. In France the Parlement of Paris was against them, and even after the king had granted them permission to settle in the country in 1553, the Parlement accused them of jeoparding the faith, destroying the peace of the church, supplanting the old orders and tearing down more than they built up. Nevertheless they won their way to a place of great power, until, sitting at the counsels of the monarch, they were able to crush their Catholic opponents, the Jansenists, as completely as their Protestant enemies were crushed by the revocation of the Edict of Nantes.

In the Netherlands the Jesuits were welcomed as allies of the Spanish power. The people were impressed by their zeal, piety, and disinterestedness, and in the Southern provinces they were able to bear away a victory after a fierce fight with Calvinism.

In England, where they showed the most devotion, they met with the least success. The blood of their martyrs did not sow the ground with Catholic seed, and they were expelled by statute under Elizabeth.

Jesuit victories

The most striking victories of the Jesuits were won in Central Europe. When the first of their company, Peter Faber, entered Germany in 1540, he found nearly the whole country Lutheran. The Wittelsbachs of Bavaria were almost the only reigning family that never compromised with the Reformers and in them the Jesuits found their starting point and their most constant ally. Called to the universities of Ingolstadt and Vienna their success was great and from these foci they radiated in all directions, to Poland, to Hungary, to the Rhine. One of their most eminent missionaries was Peter Canisius, whose catechism, published in 1555 in three forms, short, long and middle, and in two languages, German and Latin, became the chief spiritual text-book of the Catholics. The idea and selection of material was borrowed from Luther and he was imitated also in the omission of all overt polemic material. This last feature was, of course, one of the strongest.

Missions to heathens

But the conquests of the Company of Jesus were as notable in lands beyond Europe as they were in the heart of civilization. They were not, indeed, pioneers in the field of foreign missions. The Catholic church showed itself from an early period solicitous for the salvation of the natives of America and of the Far East. The bull of Alexander VI stated that his motive in dividing the newly discovered lands between Spain and Portugal was chiefly to assist in the propagation of the faith. That the Protestants at first developed no activity in the conversion of the heathen was partly because their energies were fully employed in securing their own position, and still more, perhaps, because, in the sixteenth century, Spain and Portugal had a practical monopoly of the transoceanic trade and thus the only opportunities of coming into contact with the natives.

Very early Dominican and Franciscan friars went to America. Though some of them exemplified Christian virtues that might well have impressed the natives, the greater number relied on the puissant support of the Toledo sword. Though the natives, as heathen born in invincible ignorance, were exempt from the jurisdiction of the inquisitor, they were driven by terror if not by fire, into embracing the religion of their conquerors. If some steadfast chiefs told the missionaries that they would rather go to hell after death than live for ever with the cruel Christians, the tribes as a whole, seeing their dreaded idols overthrown and their temples uprooted, embraced the religion of the stronger God, as they quailed before his votaries. Little could they understand of the mysteries of the faith, and in some places long continued to worship Christ and Mary with the ritual and attributes of older deities. But nominally a million of them were converted by 1532, and when the Jesuits arrived a still more successful effort was made to win over the red man. The important mission in Brazil, served by brave and devoted brothers of Ignatius, achieved remarkable results, whereas in Paraguay the Jesuits founded a state completely under their own tutelage.

In the Far East the path of the missionary was broken by the trader. At Goa the first ambassadors of Christ were friars, and here they erected a cathedral, a convent, and schools for training native priests. But the greatest of the missionaries to this region was Francis Xavier, the companion of Loyola. Not forgetting the vow which he, together with all the first members of the society, had taken, he sailed from Lisbon, clothed with extraordinary powers. The pope made him his vicar for all the lands bathed by the Indian Ocean, and the king of Portugal gave him official sanction and support. Arriving at Goa he put himself in touch with the earlier missionaries and began an earnest fight against the immorality of the port, both Christian and native. His motto "Amplius" led him soon to virgin fields, among the natives of the coast and of Ceylon. In 1545 he went to Cochin-China, thence to the Moluccas and to Japan, preaching in every place and baptizing by the thousand and ten thousand.

Xavier, 1506–52

April, 1541

May, 1542

Though Xavier was a man of brilliant endowments and though he was passionately devoted to the cause, to neither of his good qualities did he owe the successes, whether solid or specious, with which he has been credited. In the first place, judged by the standards of modern missions, the superficiality of his work was almost inconceivable. He never mastered one of the languages of the countries which he visited. He learned by rote a few sentences, generally the creed and some phrases on the horrors of hell, and repeated them to the crowds attracted to him by the sound of a bell. He addressed himself to masses rather than to individuals and he regarded the culmination of his work as being merely the administration of baptism and not the conversion of heart or understanding. Thus, he spent hours in baptizing, with all possible speed, sick and dying children, believing that he was thus rescuing their souls from limbo. Probably many of his adult converts never understood the meaning of the application of water and oil, salt and spittle, that make up the ritual of Catholic baptism.

Use of force

In the second place, what permanent success he achieved was due largely to the invocation of the aid of the civil power. One of the most illuminating of Xavier's letters is that written to King John of Portugal on January 20, 1548, in which he not only makes the reasonable request that native Christians be protected from persecution by their countrymen, but adds that every governor should take such measures to convert them as would insure success to his preaching, for without such support, he says, the cause of the gospel in the Indies would be desperate, few would come to baptism and those who did come would not profit much in religion. Therefore he urges that every governor, under whose rule many natives were not converted, should be mulcted of all his goods and imprisoned on his return to Portugal. What the measures applied by the Portugese officers must have been, under such pressure, can easily be inferred from a slight knowledge of their savage rule.

It has been said that every organism carries in it-

Decay of Jesuits

self the seeds of its own decay. The premature corruption of the order was noticed by its more earnest members quite early in its career. The future general Francis Borgia wrote: "The time will come when the Company will be completely absorbed in human sciences without any application to virtue; ambition, pride and arrogance will rule." The General Aquaviva said explicitly, "Love of the things of this world and the spirit of the courtier are dangerous diseases in our Company. Almost in spite of us the evil creeps in little by little under the fair pretext of gaining princes, prelates, and the great ones of the world."

1560

1587

A principal cause of the ultimate odium in which the Jesuits were held as well as of their temporary successes, was their desire for speedy results. Every one has noticed the immense versatility of the Jesuits and their superficiality. They produced excellent scholars of a certain rank, men who could decipher Latin inscriptions, observe the planets, publish libraries of historical sources, of casuistry and apologetic, or write catechisms or epigrams. They turned with equal facility to preaching to naked savages and to the production of art for the most cultivated peoples in the world. And yet they have rarely, if ever, produced a great scholar, a great scientist, a great thinker, or even a great ascetic. They were not founded for such purposes; they were founded to fight for the church and they did that with extraordinary success.

Efficiency

Failure

But their very efficiency became, as pursued for its own sake it must always become, soulless. In terms suggested by the Great War, the Jesuits were the incarnation of religious militarism. To set up an ideal of aggrandizement, to fill a body of men with a fanatical enthusiasm for that ideal and then to provide an organization and discipline marvellously adapted to conquest, that is what the Prussian schoolmaster who proverbially won Sadowa, and the Jesuits who beat back the Reformation, have known how to do better than anyone else. Their methods took account of everything except the conscience of mankind.

Moreover, there can be no doubt that in their eager pursuit of tangible results they lowered the ethical standards of the church. Wishing to open her doors as widely as possible to all men, and finding that they could not make all men saints, they brought down the requirements for admission to the average human level. One cannot take the denunciations of Jesuitical "casuistry" and "probabilism" at their face value, but one can find in Jesuit works on ethics, and in some of their early works, very dangerous compromises with the world. One reads in their books how the bankrupt, without sinning mortally, may defraud his creditors of his mortaged goods; how the servant may be excused for pilfering from his master; how a rich man may pardonably deceive the tax-collector; how the adulteress may rightfully deny her sin to her husband, even on oath.[1] Doubtless these are extreme instances, but that they should have been possible at all is a melancholy warning to all who would, even for pious ends, substitute inferior imitations for genuine morality.

Jesuitical compromises

§ 5. The Inquisition and Index

Not only by propaganda appealing to the mind and heart did the Catholic church roll back the tides of Reformation and Renaissance, but by coercion also. In this the church was not alone; the Protestants also persecuted and they also censored the press with the object of preventing their adherents from reading the arguments of their opponents. But the Catholic

[1] Substantiation of these statements in excerpts from Jesuit works of moral theology, printed in C. Mirbt: *Quellen zur Geschichte des Papsttums*[3], 1911, pp. 447ff.

church was not only more consistent in the application of her intolerant theories but she almost always assumed the direction of the coercive measures directly instead of applying them through the agency of the state. Divided as they were, dependent on the support of the civil government and hampered, at least to some slight extent, by their more liberal tendencies, the Protestants never had instrumentalities half as efficient or one-tenth as terrible as the Inquisition and the Index.

The Inquisition was a child of the Middle Ages. For centuries before Luther the Holy Office had cauterized the heretical growths on the body of Mother Church. The old form was utilized but was given a new lease of life by the work it was called upon to perform against the Protestants. Outside of the Netherlands the two forms of the Inquisition which played the largest part in the battles of the sixteenth century were the Spanish and the Roman.

Spanish Inquisition

The Inquisition was licensed in Spain by a bull of Sixtus IV of 1478, and actually established by Ferdinand and Isabella in Castile in 1480, and soon afterwards in their other dominions. It has sometimes been said that the Spanish Inquisition was really a political rather than an ecclesiastical instrument, but the latest historian of the subject, whose deep study makes his verdict final, has disposed of this theory. Though occasionally called upon to interfere in political matters, this was exceptional. Far more often it asserted an authority and an independence that embarrassed not a little the royal government. On the other hand it soon grew so great and powerful that it was able to ignore the commands of the popes. On account of its irresponsible power it was unpopular and was only tolerated because it was so efficient in crushing out the heresy that the people hated.

The annals of its procedure and achievements are one long record of diabolical cruelty, of protracted confinement in dungeons, of endless delay and browbeating to break the spirit, of ingenious tortures and of racked and crushed limbs and of burning flesh. In mitigation of judgment, it must be remembered that the methods of the civil courts were also cruel at that time, and the punishments severe.

Procedure

As the guilt of the suspected person was always presumed, every effort was made to secure confession, for in matters of belief there is no other equally satisfactory proof. Without being told the nature of his crime or who was the informant against him, the person on trial was simply urged to confess. An advocate was given him only to take advantage of his professional relations with his client by betraying him. The enormous, almost incredible procrastination by which the accused would be kept in prison awaiting trial sometimes for five or ten or even twenty years, usually sufficed to break his spirit or to unbalance his mind. Torture was first threatened and then applied. All rules intended to limit its amount proved illusory, and it was applied practically to any extent deemed necessary, and to all classes; nobles and clergy were no less obnoxious to it than were commons. Nor was there any privileged age, except that of the tenderest childhood. Men and women of ninety and boys and girls of twelve or fourteen were racked, as were young mothers and women with child. Insanity, however, if recognized as genuine, was considered a bar to torture.

Acquittal was almost, though not quite, unknown. Sometimes sentence was suspended and the accused discharged without formal exoneration. Very rarely acquittal by compurgation, that is by oath of the accused supported by the oaths of a number of persons that they believed he was telling the truth, was allowed.

Practically the only plea open to the suspect was that the informers against him were actuated by malice. As he was not told who his accusers were this was difficult for him to use.

Penalties

The penalties were various, including scourging, the galleys and perpetual imprisonment. Capital punishment by fire was pronounced not only on those who were impenitent but on those who, after having been once discharged, had relapsed. In Spain, heretics who recanted before execution were first strangled; the obstinately impenitent were burned alive. Persons convicted of heresy who could not be reached were burnt in effigy.

Acting on the maxim *ecclesia non sitit sanguinem* the Inquisitors did not put their victims to death by their own officers but handed them over to the civil authorities for execution. With revolting hypocrisy they even adjured the hangmen to be merciful, well knowing that the latter had no option but to carry out the sentence of the church. Magistrates who endeavored to exercise any discretion in favor of the condemned were promptly threatened with excommunication.

If anything could be wanting to complete the horror it was supplied by the festive spirit of the executions.

Auto da Fe

The *Auto da Fe,* or act of faith, was a favorite spectacle of the Spaniards; no holiday was quite complete without its holocaust of human victims. The staging was elaborate, and the ceremony as impressive as possible. Secular and spiritual authorities were ordered to be present and vast crowds were edified by the horrible example of the untimely end of the unbeliever. Sundays and feast days were chosen for these spectacles and on gala occasions, such as royal weddings and christenings, a special effort was made to celebrate one of these holy butcheries.

The number of victims has been variously estimated.

An actual count up to the year 1540, that is, before Protestantism became a serious factor, shows that 20,226 were burned in person and 10,913 in effigy, and these figures are incomplete. It must be remembered that for every one who paid the extreme penalty there were a large number of others punished in other ways, or imprisoned and tortured while on trial. When Adrian of Utrecht, afterwards the pope, was Inquisitor General 1516–22, 1,620 persons were burned alive, 560 in effigy and 21,845 were sentenced to penance or other lighter punishments. Roughly, for one person sentenced to death ten suffered milder penalties.

Crimes punished

Heresy was not the only crime punished by the Inquisition; it also took charge of blasphemy, bigamy and some forms of vice. In its early years it was chiefly directed against the Jews who, having been forced to the baptismal font, had relapsed. Later the Moriscos or christened Moors supplied the largest number of victims. As with the Jews, race hatred was so deep an ingredient of the treatment meted out to them that the nominal cause was sometimes forgotten, and baptism often failed to save "the new Christian" who preserved any, even the most innocent, of the national customs. Many a man and woman was tortured for not eating pork or for bathing in the Moorish fashion.

As Protestantism never obtained any hold in Spain, the Inquisition had comparatively little trouble on that account. During the sixteenth century a total number of 1995 persons were punished as Protestants of whom 1640 were foreigners and only 355 were Spaniards. Even these figures exaggerate the hold that the Reformation had in Spain, for any error remotely resembling the tenets of Wittenberg immediately classed its maintainer as Lutheran. The first case known was found in Majorca in 1523, but it was not until 1559 that any considerable number suffered for this faith. In that year 24 Lutherans were burnt at Rodrigo and Seville, 32 in 1562, and 19 Calvinists in 1569.

The dread of the Spanish Inquisition was such that only in those dependencies early and completely subdued could it be introduced. Established in Sicily in 1487 its temporal jurisdiction was suspended during the years 1535–46, when it was revived by the fear of Protestantism. Even during its dark quarter, however, it was able to punish heretics. In an *auto* celebrated at Palermo, of the twenty-two culprits three were Lutherans and nineteen Jews. The capitulation of Naples in 1503 expressly excluded the Spanish Inquisition, nor could it be established in Milan. The Portuguese Inquisition was set up in 1536.

May 30, 1541

New World

The New World was capable of offering less resistance. Nevertheless, for many years the inquisitorial powers were vested in the bishops sent over to Mexico and Peru, and when the Inquisition was established in both countries in 1570 it probably meant no increase of severity. The natives were exempt from its jurisdiction and it found little combustible material save in captured Protestant Europeans. A Fleming was burned at Lima in 1548, and at the first *auto* held at Mexico in 1574 thirty-six Lutherans were punished, all English captives, two by burning and the rest by scourging or the galleys.

Roman Inquisition

The same need of repelling Protestantism that had helped to give a new lease of life to the Spanish Inquisition called into being her sister the Roman Inquisition. By the bull *Licet ab initio,* Paul IV reconstituted the Holy Office at Rome, directing and empowering it to smite all who persisted in condemned opinions lest others should be seduced by their example, not only in the papal states but in all the nations of Christendom. It was authorized to pronounce

July 21, 1542

sentence on culprits and to invoke the aid of the secular arm to punish them with prison, confiscation of goods and death. Its authority was directed particularly against persons of high estate, even against heretical princes whose subjects were loosed from their obligation of obedience and whose neighbors were invited to take away their heritage.

Procedure

The procedure of the Holy Office at Rome was characterized by the Augustinian Cardinal Seripando as at first lenient, but later, he continues, "when the superhuman rigor of Caraffa [one of the first Inquisitors General] held sway, the Inquisition acquired such a reputation that from no other judgment-seat on earth were more horrible and fearful sentences to be expected." Besides the attention it paid to Protestants it instituted very severe processes against Judaizing Christians and took cognizance also of seduction, of pimping, of sodomy, and of infringment of the ecclesiastical rules for fasting.

Italy

The Roman Inquisition was introduced into Milan by Michael Ghislieri, afterwards pope, and flourished mightily under the protecting care of Borromeo, cardinal archbishop of the city. It was established by Charles V, notwithstanding opposition, in Naples. (1547) Venice also fought against its introduction but nevertheless finally permitted it. (1544) During the sixteenth century in that city there were no less than 803 processes for Lutheranism, 5 for Calvinism, 35 against Anabaptists, 43 for Judaism and 199 for sorcery. In countries outside of Italy the Roman Inquisition did not take root. Bishop Magrath endeavored in 1567 to give Ireland the benefit of the institution, but naturally the English Government allowed no such thing.

Censorship of the press

A method of suppressing given opinions and propagating others probably far more effective than the mauling of men's bodies is the guidance of their minds through direction of their reading and instruction. Naturally, before the invention of printing, and in an illiterate society, the censorship of books would have slight importance. Plato was perhaps the first to propose that the reading of immoral and impious books be forbidden, but I am not aware that his suggestion was acted upon either in the states of Greece or in pagan Rome. Examples of the rejection of certain books by the early church are not wanting. Paul induced the Ephesian sorcerers to burn their books; certain fathers of the church advised against the reading of heathen authors; Pope Gelasius made a decree on the books received and those not received by the church, and Manichaean books were publicly burnt.

c. 496

Fourth century

Printing

The invention of printing brought to the attention of the church the danger of allowing her children to choose their own reading matter. The first to animadvert upon it was Berthold, Archbishop of Mayence, the city of Gutenberg. On the 22d of March, 1485, he promulgated a decree to the effect that, whereas the divine art of printing had been abused for the sake of lucre and whereas by this means even Christ's books, missals and other works on religion, were thumbed by the vulgar, and whereas the German idiom was too poor to express such mysteries, and common persons too ignorant to understand them, therefore every work translated into German must be approved by the doctors of the university of Mayence before being published.

June 1, 1501

The example of the prelate was soon followed by popes and councils. Alexander VI forbade as a detestable evil the printing of books injurious to the Catholic faith, and made all archbishops official censors for their dioceses. This was enforced by a decree of the Fifth Lateran Council setting forth that although printing has brought much advantage to the church it has also disseminated errors and pernicious dogmas contrary to the Christian religion. The decree forbids the printing of any book in any city or diocese of Christendom without license from the local bishop or other ecclesiastical authority.

May 4, 1515

This sweeping edict was supplemented by others directed against certain books or authors, but for a whole generation the church left the censorship chiefly to the discretion of the several national governments. This was the policy followed also by the Protestants, both at this time and later. Neither Luther, nor any other reformer for a long time attempted to draw up regular indices of prohibited books. Examples of something approaching this may be found in the later history of Protestantism, but they are so unimportant as to be negligible.

Protestant Censorship

The national governments, however, laid great stress on licensing. The first law in Spain was followed by an ever increasing strictness under the inquisitor who drew up several indices of prohibited books, completely independent of the official Roman lists. The German Diets and the French kings were careful to give their subjects the benefit of their selection of reading matter. In England, too, lists of prohibited books were drawn up under all the Tudors. Mary restricted the right to print to licensed members of the Stationers' Company; Elizabeth put the matter in the hands of Star Chamber. A special license was required by the Injunctions, and a later law was aimed at "seditious, schismatic or libellous books and other fantastic writings."

National censorship, 1502

1559

1588

The idea of a complete catalogue of heretical and dangerous writings under ecclesiastical censure took its rise in the Netherlands. After the works of various authors had been severally prohibited in distinct

Catalogues of dangerous books

proclamations, the University of Louvain, at the emperor's command, drew up a fairly extensive list in 1546 and again, somewhat enlarged, in 1550. It mentions a number of Bibles in Greek, Latin and the vernaculars, the works of Luther, Carlstadt, Osiander, Ochino, Bullinger, Calvin, Oecolampadius, Jonas, Calvin, Melanchthon, Zwingli, Huss and John Pupper of Goch, a Dutch author of the fifteenth century revived by the Protestants. It is remarkable that the works of Erasmus are not included in this list. Furthermore it is stated that certain approved works, even when edited or translated by heretics, might be allowed to students. Among the various scientific works condemned are an *Anatomy* printed at Marburg by Eucharius Harzhorn, H. C. Agrippa's *De vanitate scientiarum,* and Sebastian Münster's *Cosmographia universalis,* a geography printed in 1544. The Koran is prohibited, and also a work called "Het paradijs van Venus," this latter presumably as indecent. Finally, all books printed since 1525 without name of author, printer, time, and place, are prohibited.

Roman Index

Partly in imitation of this work of Louvain, partly in consequence of the foundation of the Inquisition, the Roman Index of Prohibited Books was promulgated. Though the bull founding the Roman Inquisition said nothing about books, their censure was included in practice. Under the influence of the Holy Office at Lucca a list of forbidden works was drawn up by the Senate at Lucca, including chiefly the tracts of Italian heretics and satires on the church. The fourth session of the Council of Trent prohibited the printing of all anonymous books whatever and of all others on religion until licensed. A further indication of increasing severity may be found in a bull issued by Julius III who complained that authors licensed to read heretical

1545

April 8, 1546

1550

books for the purpose of refuting them were more likely to be seduced by them, and who therefore revoked all licenses given up to that time.

September, 1557

When the Roman Inquisition issued a long list of volumes to be burnt publicly, including works of Erasmus, Machiavelli and Poggio, this might be considered the first Roman Index of Prohibited Books; but the first document to bear that name was issued by Paul IV. It divided writings into three classes: (1) Authors who had erred *ex professo* and whose whole works were forbidden; (2) Authors who had erred occasionally and some of whose books only were mentioned; (3) Anonymous books. In addition to these classes 61 printers were named, all works published by whom were banned. The Index strove to be as complete as possible. Its chief though not its only source was the catalogue of Louvain. Many editions and versions of the Bible were listed and the printing of any translation without permission of the Inquisition was prohibited. Particular attention was paid to Erasmus, who was not only put in the first class by name but was signalized as having "all his commentaries, notes, annotations, dialogues, epistles, refutations, translations, books and writings" forbidden.

1559

Tridentine censorship, February 26, 1562

The Council of Trent again took up the matter, passing a decree to the effect that inasmuch as heresy had not been cured by the censorship this should be made much stricter, and appointing a commission in order, as, regardless of the parable,[1] it was phrased, to separate the tares from the wheat. The persons appointed for this delicate work comprised four archbishops, nine bishops, two generals of orders and some "minor theologians." After much sweat they brought forth a report on most of the doubtful authors though

[1] Matthew xiii, 28–30.

the most difficult of all, Erasmus, they relinquished to the theological faculties of Louvain and Paris for expurgation.

1564 The results of their labors were published by Paul IV under the name of the Tridentine Index. It was more sweeping, and at the same time more discriminating than the former Index. Erasmus was changed to the second class, only a portion of his works being now condemned. Among the non-ecclesiastical authors banned were Machiavelli, Guicciardini and Boccaccio. It is noteworthy that the *Decameron* was expurgated not chiefly for its indecency but for its satire of ecclesiastics. Thus, a tale of the seduction of an abbess is rendered acceptable by changing the abbess into a countess; the story of how a priest led a woman astray by impersonating the angel Gabriel is merely changed by making the priest a layman masquerading as a fairy king.

The principles upon which the prohibition of books rested were set forth in ten rules. The most interesting are the following: (1) Books printed before 1515 condemned by popes or council; (2) Versions of the Bible; (3) books of heretics; (4) obscene books; (5) works on witchcraft and necromancy.

In order to keep the Index up to date continual revision was necessary. To insure this Pius V appointed a special Congregation of the Index, which has lasted until the present day. From his time to ours more than forty Indices have been issued. Those of the sixteenth century were concerned mainly with Protestant books, those of later centuries chiefly deal, for the purposes of internal discipline, with books written by Catholics. One of the functions of the Congregation was to expurgate books, taking out the offensive passages. A separate *Index expurgatorius,* pointing out the passages to be deleted or corrected was published, and this name has sometimes incorrectly been applied to the Index of prohibited books.

Effect of the censorship

The effect of the censorship of the press has been variously estimated. The Index was early dubbed *sica destricta in omnes scriptores* and Sarpi called it "the finest secret ever discovered for applying religion to the purpose of making men idiotic." Milton thundered against the censorship in England as "the greatest discouragement and affront that can be offered to learning and learned men." The evil of the system of Rome was, in his opinion, double, for, as he wrote in his immortal *Areopagitica,* "The Council of Trent and the Spanish Inquisition engendering together brought forth and perfected those catalogues and expurging indexes that rake through the entrails of many an old good author with a violation worse than any that could be offered to his tomb." When we remember that the greatest works of literature, such as the *Divine Comedy,* were tampered with, and that, in the Spanish Expurgatorial Index of 1640 the list of passages to be deleted or to be altered in Erasmus's works takes 59 double-columned, closely printed folio pages, we can easily see the point of Milton's indignant protest. But, to his mind, it was still worse to subject a book to the examination of unfit men before it could secure its *imprimatur.* Not without reason has liberty of the press been made one of the cornerstones of the temple of freedom.

Various writers have labored to demonstrate the blighting effect that the censorship was supposed to have on literature. But it is surprising how few examples they can bring. Lea, who ought to know the Spanish field exhaustively, can only point to a few professors of theology who were persecuted and silenced for expressing unconventional views on biblical criticism. He conjectures that others must have remained mute through fear. But, as the golden age of Spanish literature came after the law made the printing of unlicensed books punishable by death, it is hard to see wherein literature can have suffered. The Roman Inquisition did not prevent the appearance of Galileo's work, though it made him recant afterwards. The strict English law that playwrights should not "meddle with matters of divinity or state" made Shakespeare careful not to express his religious and political views, but it is hard to see in what way it hampered his genius.

1558

And yet the influence of the various press laws was incalculably great and was just what it was intended to be. It affected science less than one would think, and literature hardly at all, but it moulded the opinions of the masses like putty in their rulers' hands. That the rank and file of Spaniards and Italians remained Catholic, and the vast majority of Britons Protestant, was due more to the bondage of the press than to any other one cause. Originality was discouraged, the people to some degree unfitted for the free debate that is at the bottom of self-government, the hope of tolerance blighted, and the path opened that led to religious wars.

CHAPTER IX

THE IBERIAN PENINSULA AND THE EXPANSION OF EUROPE

§ 1. Spain

Reformation, Renaissance and Exploration

If, through the prism of history, we analyse the white light of sixteenth-century civilization into its component parts, three colors particularly emerge: the azure "light of the Gospel" as the Reformers fondly called it in Germany, the golden beam of the Renaissance in Italy, and the blood-red flame of exploration and conquest irradiating the Iberian peninsula. Which of the three contributed most to modern culture it is hard to decide. Each of the movements started separately, gradually spreading until it came into contact, and thus into competition and final blending with the other movements. It was the middle lands, France, England and the Netherlands that, feeling the impulses from all sides, evolved the sanest and strongest synthesis. While Germany almost committed suicide with the sword of the spirit, while Italy sank into a voluptuous torpor of decadent art, while Spain reeled under the load of unearned Western wealth, France, England and Holland, taking a little from each of their neighbors, and not too much from any, became strong, well-balanced, brilliant states. But if eventually Germany, Italy and Spain all suffered from over-specialization, for the moment the stimulus of new ideas and new possibilities gave to each a sort of leadership in its own sphere. While Germany and Italy were busy winning the realms of the spirit and of the mind, Spain very nearly conquered the empire of the land and of the sea.

Ferdinand, 1479–1516 and Isabella, 1474–1504

The foundation of her national greatness, like that of the greatness of so many other powers, was laid in the union of the various states into which she was at one time divided. The marriage of Ferdinand of Aragon and Isabella of Castile was followed by a series of measures that put Spain into the leading position in Europe, expelled the alien racial and religious elements of her population, and secured to her a vast colonial empire. The conquest of Granada from the Moors, the acquisition of Cerdagne and Roussillon from the French, and the annexation of Naples, doubled the dominions of the Lions and Castles, and started the proud land on the road to empire. It is true that eventually Spain exhausted herself by trying to do more than even her young powers could accomplish, but for a while she retained the hegemony of Christendom. The same year that saw the discovery of America and the occupation of the Alhambra, was also marked by the expulsion or forced conversion of the Jews, of whom 165,000 left the kingdom, 50,000 were baptized, and 20,000 perished in race riots. The statesmanship of Ferdinand showed itself in a more favorable light in the measures taken to reduce the nobles, feudal anarchs as they were, to fear of the law. To take their place in the government of the country he developed a new bureaucracy, which also, to some extent, usurped the powers of the Cortes of Aragon and of the Cortes of Castile. In the meantime a notable reform of the church, in morals and in learning if not in doctrine, was carried through by the great Cardinal Ximénez.

1492

Francis Ximénez de Cisneros, 1436–1517

Charles V, 1516–56

When Charles, the grandson of the Catholic Kings, succeeded Ferdinand he was already, through his father, the Archduke Philip, the lord of Burgundy and of the Netherlands, and the heir of Austria. His election as emperor made him, at the age of nineteen, the greatest prince of Christendom. To his gigantic task he brought all the redeeming qualities of dullness, for his mediocrity and moderation served his peoples and his dynasty better than brilliant gifts and boundless ambition would have done. "Never," he is reported to have said in 1556, "did I aspire to universal monarchy, although it seemed well within my power to attain it." Though the long war with France turned ever, until the very last, in his favor, he never pressed his advantage to the point of crushing his enemy to earth. But in Germany and Italy, no less than in Spain and the Netherlands, he finally attained something more than hegemony and something less than absolute power.

Revolt of the Communes

Though Spain benefited by his world power and became the capital state of his far flung empire, "Charles of Ghent," as he was called, did not at first find Spaniards docile subjects. Within a very few years of his accession a great revolt, or rather two great synchronous revolts, one in Castile and one in Aragon, flared up. The grievances in Castile were partly economic, the *servicio* (a tax) and the removal of money from the realm, and partly national as against a strange king and his foreign officers. Not only the regent, Adrian of Utrecht, but many important officials were northerners, and when Charles left Spain to be crowned emperor, the national pride could no longer bear the humiliation of playing a subordinate part. The revolt of the Castilian Communes began with the gentry and spread from them to the lower classes. Even the grandees joined forces with the rebels, though more from fear than from sympathy. The various revolting communes formed a central council, the Santa Junta, and put forth a program re-asserting the rights of the Cortes to redress grievances. Meeting for a time with no resistance, the rebellion disintegrated

1520

through the operation of its own centrifugal forces, disunion and lack of leadership. So at length when the government, supplied with a small force of German mercenaries, struck on the field of Villalar, the rebels suffered a severe defeat. A few cities held out longer, Toledo last of all; but one by one they yielded, partly to force, partly to the wise policy of concession and redress followed by the government.

April, 1521

In our own time Barcelona and the east coast of Spain has been the hotbed of revolutionary democracy and radical socialism. Even so, the rising in Aragon known as the Hermandad (Brotherhood) contemporary with that in Castile, not only began earlier and lasted longer, but was of a far more radical stamp. Here were no nobles airing their slights at the hands of a foreign king, but here the trade-gilds rose in the name of equality against monarch and nobles alike. Two special causes fanned the fury of the populace to a white heat. The first was the decline of the Mediterranean trade due to the rise of the Atlantic commerce; the other was the racial element. Valencia was largely inhabited by Moors, the most industrious, sober and thrifty, and consequently the most profitable of Spanish laborers. The race hatred so deeply rooted in human nature added to the ferocity of the class conflict. Both sides were ruined by the war which, beginning in 1519, dragged along for several years until the proletariat was completely crushed.

The Hermandad

The Cortes

The armed triumph of the government hardly damaged popular liberties as embodied in the constitution of the Cortes of Castile. When Charles became king this body was not, like other parliaments, ordinarily a representative assembly of the three estates, but consisted merely of deputies of eighteen Castilian cities. Only on special occasions, such as a coronation, were nobles and clergy summoned to participate. Its great power was that of granting taxes, though somehow it never succeeded, as did the English House of Commons, in making the redress of grievances conditional upon a subsidy. But yet the power amounted to something and it was one that neither Charles nor Philip commonly ventured to violate. Under both of them meetings of the Cortes were frequent.

Though never directly attacked, the powers of the Cortes declined through the growth of vast interests outside their competence. The direction of foreign policy, so absorbing under Charles, and the charge of the enormous and growing commercial interests, was confided not to the representatives of the people, but to the Royal Council of Castile, an appointative body of nine lawyers, three nobles, and one bishop. Though not absolutely, yet relatively, the functions of the Cortes diminished until they amounted to no more than those of a provincial council.

What reconciled the people to the concentration of new powers in the hands of an irresponsible council was the apparently dazzling success of Spanish policy throughout the greater part of the sixteenth century. No banner was served like that of the Lions and Castles; no troops in the world could stand against her famous regiments; no generals were equal to Cortez and Alva; no statesmen abler than Parma, no admirals, until the Armada, more daring than Magellan[1] and Don John, no champions of the church against heretic and infidel like Loyola and Xavier.

The Spanish Empire

That such an empire as the world had not seen since Rome should within a single life-time rise to its zenith and, within a much shorter time, decline to the verge of ruin, is one of the melodramas of history. Perhaps, in reality, Spain was never quite so great as she looked, nor was her fall quite so complete as it seemed. But

[1] A Portuguese in Spanish service.

the phenomena, such as they are, sufficiently call for explanation.

First of all one is struck by the fortuitous, one might almost say, unnatural, character of the Hapsburg empire. While the union of Castile and Aragon, bringing together neighboring peoples and filling a political need, was the source of real strength, the subsequent accretions of Italian and Burgundian territories rather detracted from than added to the effective power of the Spanish state. Philip would have been far stronger had his father separated from his crown not only Austria and the Holy Roman Empire of Germany, but the Netherlands as well. The revolt of the Dutch Republic was in itself almost enough to ruin Spain. Nor can it be said that the Italian states, won by the sword of Ferdinand or of Charles, were valuable accessions to Spanish power.

Colonies

Quite different in its nature was the colonial empire, but in this it resembled the other windfalls to the house of Hapsburg in that it was an almost accidental, unsought-for acquisition. The Genoese sailor who went to the various courts of Europe begging for a few ships in which to break the watery path to Asia, had in his beggar's wallet all the kingdoms of a new world and the glory of them. For a few years Spain drank until she was drunken of conquest and the gold of America. That the draught acted momentarily as a stimulant, clearing her brain and nerving her arm to deeds of valor, but that she suffered in the end from the riotous debauch, cannot be doubted. She soon learned that all that glittered was not wealth, and that industries surfeited with metal and starved of raw materials must perish. The unearned coin proved to be fairy gold in her coffers, turning to brown leaves and dust when she wanted to use it. It became a drug in her markets; it could not lawfully be exported, and no amount of it would purchase much honest labor from an indolent population fed on fantasies of wealth. The modern King Midas, on whose dominions the sun never set, was cursed with a singular and to him inexplicable need of everything that money was supposed to buy. His armies mutinied, his ships rotted, and never could his increasing income catch up with the far more rapidly increasing expenses of his budget.

The poverty of the people was in large part the fault of the government which pursued a fiscal policy ideally calculated to strike at the very sources of wealth. While, under the oppression of an ignorant paternalism, unhappy Spain suffered from inanition, she was tended by a physician who tried to cure her malady by phlebotomy. There have been worse men than Philip II, but there have been hardly any who have caused more blood to flow from the veins of their own people. His life is proof that a well-meaning bigot can do more harm than the most abandoned debauchee. "I would rather lose all my kingdoms," he averred, "than allow freedom of religion." And again, to a man condemned by the Inquisition for heresy, "If my own son were as perverse as you, I myself would carry the faggot to burn him." Consistently, laboriously, undeterred by any suffering or any horror, he pursued his aim. He was not afraid of hard work, scribbling reams of minute directions daily to his officers. His stubborn calm was imperturbable; he took his pleasures—women, *autos-da-fe* and victories—sadly, and he suffered such chagrins as the death of four wives, having a monstrosity for a son, and the loss of the Armada and of the Netherlands, without turning a hair.

Philip II, 1556–98

Spain's foreign policy came to be more and more polarized by the rise of English sea-power. Even under Charles, when France had been the chief enemy,

Spain *vs.* England

the Hapsburgs saw the desirability of winning England as a strategic point for their universal empire. This policy was pursued by alternating alliance with hostility. For six years of his boyhood Charles had been betrothed to Mary Tudor, Henry VIII's sister, to whom he sent a ring inscribed, "Mary hath chosen the better part which shall not be taken away from her." His own precious person, however, was taken from her to be bestowed on Isabella of Portugal, by whom he begot Philip. When this son succeeded him, notwithstanding the little unpleasantness of Henry VIII's divorce, he advised him to turn again to an English marriage, and Philip soon became the husband of Queen Mary. After her death without issue, he vainly wooed her sister, until he was gradually forced by her Protestant buccaneers into an undesired war.

Notwithstanding all that he could do to lose fortune's favors, she continued for many years to smile on her darling Hapsburg. After a naval disaster inflicted by the Turks on the Spaniard off the coast of Tripoli, the defeated power recovered and revenged herself in the great naval victory of Lepanto, in October 1571. The lustre added to the Lions and Castles by this important success was far outshone by the acquisition of Portugal and all her colonies, in 1581. Though not the nearest heir, Philip was the strongest, and by bribery and menaces won the homage of the Portuguese nobles after the death of the aged king Henry on January 31, 1580. For sixty years Spain held the lesser country and, what was more important to her, the colonies in the East Indies and in Africa. So vast an empire had not yet been heard of, or imagined possible, in the history of the world. No wonder that its shimmer dazzled the eyes not only of contemporaries, but of posterity. According to Macaulay,

Philip's power was equal to that of Napoleon, and its ruin is the most instructive lesson in history of how not to govern.

How hollow was this semblance of might was demonstrated by the first stalwart peoples that dared to test it, first by the Dutch and then by England. The story of the Armada has already been told. Its preparation marked the height of Philip's effort and the height of his incompetence. Its annihilation was a cruel blow to his pride. But in Spain, barring a temporary financial panic, things went much the same after 1588 as before it. The full bloom of Spanish culture, gorgeous with Velasquez and fragrant with Cervantes and Calderon, followed hard upon the defeat of the Armada.

War with the Moors

The fact is that Spain suffered much more from internal disorders than from foreign levy. The chief occasion of her troubles was the presence among her people of a large body of Moors, hated both for their race and for their religion. With the capitulation of Granada, the enjoyment of Mohammedanism was guaranteed to the Moors, but this tolerance only lasted for six years, when a decree went out that all must be baptized or must emigrate from Andalusia. In Aragon, however, always independent of Castile, they continued to enjoy religious freedom. Charles at his coronation took a solemn oath to respect the faith of Islam in these lands, but soon afterwards, frightened by the rise of heresy in Germany, he applied to Clement to absolve him from his oath. This sanction of bad faith, at first creditably withheld, was finally granted and was promptly followed by a general order for expulsion or conversion. Throughout the whole of Spain the poor Moriscos now began to be systematically pillaged and persecuted by whoever chose to do it. All manner of taxes, tithes, servitudes and fines

1524

were demanded of them. The last straw that broke the endurance of a people tried by every manner of tyranny and extortion, was an edict ordering all Moors to learn Castilian within three years, after which the use of Arabic was to be forbidden, prohibiting all Moorish customs and costumes, and strictly enjoining attendance at church.

As the Moors had been previously disarmed and as they had no military discipline, rebellion seemed a counsel of despair, but it ensued. The populace rose in helpless fury, and for three years defied the might of the Spanish empire. But the result could not be doubtful. A naked peasantry could not withstand the disciplined battalions that had proved their valor on every field from Mexico to the Levant and from Saxony to Algiers. It was not a war but a massacre and pillage. The whole of Andalusia, the most flourishing province in Spain, beautiful with its snowy mountains, fertile with its tilled valleys, and sweet with the peaceful toil of human habitation, was swept by a universal storm of carnage and of flame. The young men either perished in fighting against fearful odds, or were slaughtered after yielding as prisoners. Those who sought to fly to Africa found the avenues of escape blocked by the pitiless Toledo blades. The aged were hunted down like wild beasts; the women and young children were sold into slavery, to toil under the lash or to share the hated bed of the conqueror. The massacre cost Spain 60,000 lives and three million ducats, not to speak of the harm that it did to her spirit.

§ 2. Exploration

Division of the New World between Spain and Portugal

When Columbus returned with glowing accounts of the "India" he had found, the value of his work was at once appreciated. Forthwith began that struggle for colonial power which has absorbed so much of the energies of the European nations. In view of the Portuguese discoveries in Africa, it was felt necessary to mark out the "spheres of influence" of the two powers at once, and, with an instinctive appeal to the one authority claiming to be international, the Spanish government immediately applied to Pope Alexander VI for confirmation in the new-found territories. Acting on the suggestion of Columbus that the line of Spanish influence be drawn one hundred leagues west of any of the Cape Verde Islands or of the Azores, the pope, with magnificent self-assurance, issued a bull, *Inter caetera divinae,* of his own mere liberality and in virtue of the authority of Peter, conferring on Castile forever "all dominions, camps, posts, and villages, with all the rights and jurisdictions pertaining to them," west of the parallel, and leaving to Portugal all that fell to the east of it. Portugal promptly protested that the line was too far east, and by the treaty of Tordesillas, it was moved to 370 leagues west of the Cape Verde Islands, thus falling between the 48th and 49th parallel of longitude. The intention was doubtless to confer on Spain all land immediately west of the Atlantic, but, as a matter of fact, South America thrusts so far to the eastward, that a portion of her territory, later claimed as Brazil, fell to the lot of Portugal.

May 4, 1493

1494

Spanish adventurers

Spain lost no time in exploiting her new dominions. During the next century hundreds of ships carried tens of thousands of adventurers to seek their fortune in the west. For it was not as colonists that most of them went, but in a spirit compounded of that of the crusader, the knight-errant, and the pirate. If there is anything in the paradox that artists have created natural beauty, it is a truer one to say that the Spanish romances created the Spanish colonial empire. The men who sailed on the great adventure had feasted on tales of paladins and hippogrifs, of enchanted palaces and fountains of youth, and miraculously fair women to be rescued and then claimed by knights. They read in books of travel purporting to tell the sober truth of satyrs and of purple unicorns and of men who spread their feet over their heads for umbrellas and of others whose heads grew between their shoulders. No wonder that when they went to a strange country they found the River of Life in the Orinoco, colonies of Amazons in the jungle, and El Dorado, the land of gold, in the riches of Mexico and Peru! It is a testimony to the imaginative mood of Europe, as well as to the power of the pen, that the whole continent came to be called, not after its discoverer, but after the man who wrote the best romances—mostly fictions—about his travels in it.

Exploitation of natives

In the Greater Antilles, where Spain made her first colonies, her rule showed at its worst. The soft native race, the Caribs, almost completely disappeared within half a century. The best modern authority estimates that whereas the native population of Española (Haiti) was between 200,000 and 300,000 in 1493, by 1548 hardly 5000 Indians were left. In part the extinction of the natives was due to new diseases and to the vices of civilization, but far more to the heartless exploitation of them by the conquerors. Bartholomew de las Casas, the first priest to come to this unfortunate island, tells stories of Spanish cruelty that would be incredible were they not so well supported. With his own eyes he saw 3000 inoffensive Indians slaughtered at a single time; of another batch of 300 he observed that within a few months more than half perished at hard labor. Again, he saw 6000 Indian children condemned to work in the mines, of whom few or none long survived. In vain a bull of Paul III declared the Indians capable of becoming

Christians and forbade their enslavement. In vain the Spanish government tried to mitigate at least some of the hardships of the natives' lot, ordering that they should be well fed and paid. The temptation to exploit them was too strong; and when they perished the Spaniards supplied their place by importing negroes from Africa, a people of tougher fibre.

1537

Spanish exploration, followed by sparse settlement, soon opened up the greater part of the Americas south of the latitude of the present city of San Francisco. Of many expeditions into the trackless wilderness, only a few were financially repaying; the majority were a drain on the resources of the mother country. In every place where the Spaniard set foot the native quailed and, after at most one desperate struggle, went down, never again to loose the conqueror's grip from his throat or to move the conqueror's knee from his chest. Even the bravest were as helpless as children before warriors armed with thunder and riding upon unknown monsters.

But in no place, save in the islands, did the native races wholly disappear as they did in the English settlements. The Spaniards came not like the Puritans, as artisans and tillers of the soil intent on founding new homes, but as military conquerors, requiring a race of helots to toil for them. For a period anarchy reigned; the captains not only plundered the Indians but fought one another fiercely for more room—more room in the endless wilderness! Eventually, however, conditions became more stable; Spain imposed her effective control, her language, religion and institutions on a vast region, doing for South America what Rome had once done for her.

The lover of adventure will find rich reward in tracing the discovery of the Mississippi by De Soto, of Florida by Ponce de Leon, and of the whole course of the Amazon by Orellana who sailed down it from Peru, or in reading of Balboa, "when with eagle eyes he stared at the Pacific." A resolute man could hardly set out exploring without stumbling upon some mighty river, some vast continent, or some unmeasured ocean. But among all these fairly-tales there are some that are so marvellous that they would be thought too extravagant by the most daring writers of romance. That one captain with four hundred men, and another with two hundred, should each march against an extensive and populous empire, cut down their armies at odds of a hundred to one, put their kings to the sword and their temples to the torch, and after it all reap a harvest of gold and precious stones such as for quantity had never been heard of before—all this meets us not in the tales of Ariosto or of Dumas, but in the pages of authentic history.

Conquest of Mexico

In the tableland of Mexico dwelt the Aztecs, the most civilized and warlike of North American aborigines. Their polity was that of a Spartan military despotism, their religion the most grewsome known to man. Before their temples were piled pyramids of human skulls; the deities were placated by human sacrifice, and at times, according to the deicidal and theophagous rites common to many primitive superstitions, themselves sacrificed in effigy or in the person of a beautiful captive and their flesh eaten in sacramental cannibalism. Though the civilization of the Aztecs, derived from the earlier and perhaps more advanced Mayans, was scarcely so high as that of the ancient Egyptians, they had cultivated the arts sufficiently to work the mines of gold and silver and to hammer the precious metals into elaborate and massive ornaments.

When rumors of their wealth reached Cuba it seemed at last as if the dream of El Dorado had come true. Hernando Cortez, a cultured, resolute, brave and politic leader, gathered a force of four hundred white men, with a small outfit of artillery and cavalry, and, on Good Friday, 1519, landed at the place now called Vera Cruz and marched on the capital. The race of warriors who delighted in nothing but slaughter, was stupefied, partly by an old prophecy of the coming of a god to subdue the land, partly by the strange and terrible arms of the invaders. Moreover their neighbors and subjects were ready to rise against them and become allies of the Spaniards. In a few months of crowded battle and massacre they lay broken and helpless at the feet of the audacious conqueror, who promptly sent to Spain a glowing account of his new empire and a tribute of gold and silver. Albert Dürer in August, 1520, saw at Brussels the "things brought the king from the new golden land," and describes them in his diary as including "a whole golden sun, a fathom in breadth, and a whole silver moon of the same size, and two rooms full of the same sort of armour, and also all kinds of weapons, accoutrements and bows, wonderful shields . . . altogether valued at a hundred thousand gulden. And all my life," he adds, "I have never seen anything that so rejoiced my heart as did these things."

Conquest of Peru

If an artist, familiar with kings and courts and the greatest marts of Europe could write thus, what wonder that the imagination of the world took fire? The golden sun and the silver moon were, to all men who saw them, like Helen's breasts, the sun and moon of heart's desire, to lure them over the western waves. Twelve years after Cortez, came Pizarro who, with a still smaller force conquered an even wealthier and more civilized empire. The Incas, unlike the Mexicans, were a mild race, living in a sort of theocratic socialism, in which the emperor, as god, exercised absolute power over his subjects and in return cared for at least their common wants. The Spaniards outdid themselves in acts of treachery and blood. In vain the emperor, Atahualpa, after voluntarily placing himself in the hands of Pizarro, filled the room used as his prison nine feet high with gold as ransom; when he could give no more he was tried on the preposterous charges of treason to Charles V and of heresy, and suffered death at the stake. Pizarro coolly pocketed the till then undreamed of sum of 4,500,000 ducats,[1] worth in our standards more than one hundred million dollars.

Circumnavigation of the globe, 1519–22

But the crowning act of the age of discovery was the circumnavigation of the globe. The leader of the great enterprise that put the seal of man's dominion on the earth, was Ferdinand Magellan, a Portuguese in Spanish service. With a fleet of five vessels, only one of which put a ring around the world, and with a crew of about 275 men of whom only 18 returned successful, he sailed from Europe. Coasting down the east of South America, exploring the inlets and rivers, he entered the straits that bear his name and covered their 360 miles in thirty-eight days. After following the coast up some distance north, he struck across the Pacific, the breadth of which he much underestimated. For ninety-eight days he was driven by the east trade-wind without once sighting land save two desert islands, while his crew endured extremities of hunger, thirst and scurvy. At last he came to the islands he called, after the thievish propensities of their inhabitants, the Ladrones, making his first landing at Guam. Spending but three days here to refit and provision, he sailed again on March 9, and a week later discovered the islands known, since 1542, as the Philippines.

September 20, 1519

October 21, 1520

1521

[1] Allowing $2.40 to a ducat this would be $10,800,000 intrinsically at a time when money had ten times the purchasing power that it has today.

In an expedition against a savage chief the great leader met his death on April 27, 1521. As other sailors and as he, too, had previously been as far to the east as he now found himself, he had practically completed the circumnavigation of the globe. The most splendid triumph of the age of discovery coincided almost to a day with the time that Luther was achieving the most glorious deed of the Reformation at Worms.

September, 1522

Magellan's ship, the *Vittoria,* proceeded under Sebastian del Cano, and finally, with thirty-one men, of whom only eighteen had started out in her, came back to Portugal. The men who had burst asunder one of the bonds of the older world, were, nevertheless, deeply troubled by a strange, medieval scruple. Having mysteriously lost a day by following the sun in his westward course, they did penance for having celebrated the fasts and feasts of the church on the wrong dates.

Portugese Exploration

While Spain was extending her dominions westward, little Portugal was building up an even greater empire in both hemispheres. In the fifteenth century, this hardy people, confined to their coast and without possibility of expanding inwards, had seen that their future lay upon the water. To the possessor of sea power the ocean makes of every land bordering on it a frontier, vulnerable to them and impervious to the enemy. The first ventures of the Portuguese were naturally in the lands near by, the North African coast and the islands known as the Madeiras and the Azores. Feeling their way southward along the African coast they reached the Cape of Good Hope but did not at once go much further. This path to India was not broken until eleven years later, when Vasco da Gama, after a voyage of great daring—he was ninety-three days at sea on a course of 4500 miles from the Cape Verde Islands to South Africa—reached Calicut on May 20, 1498. This city, now sunken in the sea, was

1486 or 1488

1497–8

then the most flourishing port on the Malabar Coast, exploited entirely by Mohammedan traders. Spices had long been the staple of Venetian trade with the Orient, and when he returned with rich cargo of them the immediate effect upon Europe was greater than that of the voyage of Columbus. Trade seeks to follow the line of least resistance, and the establishment of a water way between Europe and the East was like connecting two electrically charged bodies in a Leyden jar by a copper wire. The current was no longer forced through a poor medium, but ran easily through the better conductor. With more rapidity than one would think possible in that age, the commercial consequences of the discovery were appreciated. The trade of the Levant died away, and the center of gravity was transferred from the Mediterranean to the Atlantic. While Venice decayed Lisbon rose with mushroom speed to the position of the great emporium of European ocean-borne trade, until she in her turn was supplanted by Antwerp.

1500 Da Gama was soon imitated by others. Cabral made commercial settlements at Calicut and the neighboring town of Cochin, and came home with unheard-of riches 1503 in spice, pearls and gems. Da Gama returned and bombarded Calicut, and Francis d'Almeida was made 1505 Governor of India and tried to consolidate the Portuguese power there on the correct principle that who was lord of the sea was lord of the peninsula. The rough methods of the Portuguese and their competition with the Arab traders made war inevitable between the two rivals. To the other causes of enmity that of religion was added, for, like the Spaniards, the Portuguese tried to combine the characters of merchants and missionaries, of pirates and crusaders. When the first of Da Gama's sailors to land at Calicut was asked what he sought, his laconic answer, "Christians and spices," had in it as much of truth as of epigrammatic neatness.

Portugese cruelty to Indians

Had the Portuguese but treated the Hindoos humanely they would have found in them allies against the Mohammedan traders, but all of them, not excepting their greatest statesman, Alphonso d'Albuquerque, pursued a policy of frightfulness. When Da Gama met an Arab ship, after sacking it, he blew it up with gunpowder and left it to sink in flames while the women on board held up their babies with piteous cries to touch the heart of this knight of Christ and of mammon. Without the least compunction Albuquerque tells in his commentaries how he burned the Indian villages, put part of their inhabitants to death and ordered the noses and ears of the survivors cut off.

Trade

Nevertheless, the Portuguese got what they wanted, the wealthy trade of the East. Albuquerque, failing to storm Calicut, seized Goa farther north and made it the chief emporium. But they soon felt the need of stations farther east, for, as long as the Arabs held Malacca, where spices were cheaper, the intruders did not have the monopoly they desired. Accordingly Albuquerque seized this city on the Malay Straits, which, (1511) though now it has sunk into insignificance, was then the Singapore or Hong-Kong of the Far East. Sumatra, Java and the northern coast of Australia were explored, the Moluccas were bought from Spain for 350,000 ducats, and even Japan and China were reached by the daring traders. In the meantime posts were established along the whole western and eastern coasts of Africa and in Madagascar. But wherever they went the Portuguese sought commercial advantage not permanent settlement. Aptly compared by a Chinese observer to fishes who died if taken from the sea, they founded an empire of vast length out of incredible thinness.

Brazil

The one exception to this rule, and an important one, was Brazil. The least showy of the colonies and the one that brought in the least quick profit eventually became a second and a greater Portugal, outstripping the mother country in population and dividing South America almost equally with the Spanish. In many ways the settlement of this colony resembled that of North America by the English more than it did the violent and superficial conquests of Spain. Settlers came to it less as adventurers than as home-seekers and some of them fled from religious persecution. The great source of wealth, the sugar-cane, was introduced from Madeira in 1548 and in the following year the mother country sent a royal governor and some troops.

Decadence of Portugal

But even more than Spain Portugal overtaxed her strength in her grasp for sudden riches. The cup that her mariners took from the gorgeous Eastern enchantress had a subtle, transforming drug mingled with its spices, whereby they were metamorphosed, if not into animals, at least into orientals, or Africans. While Lisbon grew by leaps and bounds the countryside was denuded, and the landowners, to fill the places of the peasants who had become sailors, imported quantities of negro slaves. Thus not only the Portuguese abroad, but those at home, undeterred by racial antipathy, adulterated their blood with that of the dark peoples. Add to this that the trade, immensely lucrative as it seemed, was an enormous drain on the population of the little state; and the causes of Portugal's decline, almost as sudden as its rise, are in large part explained. So rapid was it, indeed, that it was noticed not only by foreign travellers but by the natives. Camoens, though he dedicated his life to composing an epic in honor of Vasco da Gama, lamented his country's decay in these terms:

> O pride of empire! O vain covetise
> Of that vain glory that we men call fame . . .
> What punishment and what just penalties
> Thou dost inflict on those thou dost inflame . . .
> Thou dost depopulate our ancient state
> Till dissipation brings debility.

Nor were artificial causes wanting to make the colonies expensive and the home treasury insolvent. The governors as royal favorites regarded their appointments as easy roads to quick wealth, and they plundered not only the inhabitants but their royal master. The inefficient and extravagant management of trade, which was a government monopoly, furnished a lamentable example of the effects of public ownership. And when possible the church interfered to add the burden of bigotry to that of corruption. An amusing example of this occurred when a supposed tooth of Buddha was brought to Goa, to redeem which the Rajah of Pegu offered a sum equal to half a million dollars. While the government was inclined to sell, the archbishop forbade the acceptance of such tainted money and ordered the relic destroyed.

1521–80

Within Portugal itself other factors aided the decline. From the accession of John III to the amalgamation with Spain sixty years later, the Cortes was rarely summoned. The expulsion of many Jews in 1497, the massacre and subsequent exile of the New Christians or Marranos, most of whom went to Holland, commenced an era of destructive bigotry completed by the Inquisition. Strict censorship of the press and the education of the people by the Jesuits each added their bit to the forces of spiritual decadence.

1506–7

The Inquisition established, 1536

For the fury of religious zeal ill supplied the exhausted powers of a state fainting with loss of blood and from the intoxication of corruption. Gradually her grasp relaxed on North Africa until only three small posts in Morocco were left her, those of Ceuta, Arzila and Tangier. A last frantic effort to recover them and to punish the infidel, undertaken by the young King Sebastian, ended in disaster and in his death in 1578. After a short reign of two years by his uncle Henry, who as a cardinal had no legitimate heirs, Portugal feebly yielded to her strongest suitor, Philip II, and for sixty years remained a captive of Spain.

1580–1640

Other nations explore

Other nations eagerly crowded in to seize the trident that was falling from the hands of the Iberian peoples. There were James Cartier of France, and Sebastian Cabot and Sir Martin Frobisher and Sir Francis Drake of England, and others. They explored the coast of North America and sought a Northwest Passage to Asia. Drake, after a voyage of two years and a half, duplicated the feat of Magellan, though he took quite a different course, following the American western coast up to the Golden Gate. He, too, returned "very richly fraught with gold, silver, silk and precious stones," the best incentive to further endeavor. But no colonies of permanence and consequence were as yet planted by the northern nations. Until the seventeenth century their voyages were either actuated by commercial motives or were purely adventurous. The age did not lack daring explorers by land as well as by sea. Lewis di Varthema rivalled his countryman Marco Polo by an extensive journey in the first decade of the century. Like Burckhardt and Burton in the nineteenth century he visited Mecca and Medina as a Mohammedan pilgrim, and also journeyed to Cairo, Beirut, Aleppo and Damascus and then to the distant lands of India and the Malay peninsula.

1577–80

Russia

It may seem strange to speak of Russia in connection with the age of discovery, and yet it was precisely in the light of a new and strange land that our English ancestors regarded it. Cabot's voyage to the

White Sea in the middle of the century was every whit as new an adventure as was the voyage to India. Richard Chancellor and others followed him and established a regular trade with Muscovy, and through it and the Caspian with Asia. The rest of Europe, west of Poland and the Turks, hardly heard of Russia or felt its impact more than they now do of the Tartars of the Steppes.

1553

But it was just at this time that Russia was taking the first strides on the road to become a great power. How broadly operative were some of the influences at work in Europe lies patent in the singular parallel that her development offers to that of her more civilized contemporaries. Just as despotism, consolidation, and conquest were the order of the day elsewhere, so they were in the eastern plains of Europe. Basil III struck down the rights of cities, nobles and princes to bring the whole country under his own autocracy. Ivan the Terrible, called Czar of all the Russias, added to this policy one of extensive territorial aggrandizement. Having humbled the Tartars he acquired much land to the south and east, and then turned his attention to the west, where, however, Poland barred his way to the Baltic. Just as in its subsequent history, so then, one of the great needs of Russia was for a good port. Another of her needs was for better technical processes. Anticipating Peter the Great, Ivan endeavored to get German workmen to initiate good methods, but he failed to accomplish much, partly because Charles V forbade his subjects to go to add strength to a rival state.

Basil III, 1505–33

Ivan IV, 1533–84

Europe vs. Asia

While Europe found most of the other continents as soft as butter to her trenchant blade, she met her match in Asia. The theory of Herodotus that the course of history is marked by alternate movements east and west has been strikingly confirmed by subsequent events. In a secular grapple the two continents have heaved back and forth, neither being able to conquer the other completely. If the empires of Macedon and Rome carried the line of victory far to the orient, they were avenged by the successive inroads of the Huns, the Saracens, the Mongols and the Turks. If for the last four centuries the line has again been pushed steadily back, until Europe dominates Asia, it is far from certain that this condition will be permanent.

In spiritual matters Europe owes a balance of indebtedness to Asia, and by far the greater part of it to the Semites. The Phoenician alphabet and Arabian numerals are capital borrowed and yielding how enormous a usufruct! Above all, Asiatic religions—albeit the greatest of them was the child of Hellas as well as of Judaea—have conquered the whole world save a few savage tribes. Ever since the cry of "There is no God but Allah and Mahomet is his prophet" had aroused the Arabian nomads from their age-long slumber, it was as a religious warfare that the contest of the continents revealed itself. After the scimitar had swept the Greek Empire out of Asia Minor and had cut Spain from Christendom, the crusades and the rise of the Spanish kingdoms had gradually beaten it back. But while the Saracen was being slowly but surely driven from the western peninsula, the banner of the Crescent in the east was seized by a race with a genius for war inversely proportional to its other gifts. The Turks, who have never added to the arts of peace anything more important than the fabrication of luxurious carpets and the invention of a sensuous bath, were able to found cannon and to drill battalions that drove the armies of nobler races before them. From the sack of Constantinople in 1453 to the siege of Vienna in 1529 and even to some extent long after that, the ma-

The Turks

jestic and terrible advance of the janizaries threatened the whole fabric of Europe.

Selim I, 1512–20

Under Sultan Selim I the Turkish arms were turned to the east and south. Persia, Kurdistan, Syria and Egypt were crushed, while the title of Caliph, and with it the spiritual leadership of the Mahommetan world, was wrested from the last of the Abassid dynasty.

Suleiman, 1520–6

But it was under his successor, Suleiman the Magnificent, that the banner of the prophet, "fanned by conquest's crimson wing," was borne to the heart of Europe. Belgrade and Rhodes were captured, Hungary completely overrun, and Vienna besieged. The naval exploits of Khair-ed-din, called Barbarossa, carried the terror of the Turkish arms into the whole Mediterranean, subdued Algiers and defeated the Christian fleets under Andrew Doria.

On the death of Suleiman the Crescent Moon had attained the zenith of its glory. The vast empire was not badly administered; some authorities hold that justice was better served under the Sultan than under any contemporary Christian king. A hierarchy of officials, administrative, ecclesiastical, secretarial and military, held office directly under the Sultan, being wisely granted by him sufficient liberty to allow initiative, and yet kept under control direct enough to prevent the secession of distant provinces.

The international position of the infidel power was an anomalous one. Almost every pope tried to revive the crusading spirit against the arch-enemy of Christ, and the greatest epic poet of the sixteenth century chose for his subject the Delivery of Jerusalem in a holy war. On the other hand the Most Christian King found no difficulty in making alliances with the Sublime Porte, and the same course was advocated, though not adopted, by some of the Protestant states of Germany. Finally, that champion of the church, Philip

1580 II, for the first time in the history of his country, made a peace with the infidel Sultan recognizing his right to exist in the society of nations.

The sixteenth century, which in so much else marked a transition from medieval to modern times, in this also saw the turning-point of events, inasmuch as the tide drawn by the Half Moon to its flood about 1529, from that time onwards has steadily, if very slowly, ebbed.

CHAPTER X

SOCIAL CONDITIONS

§ 1. Population

Political history is that of the state; economic and intellectual history that of a different group. In modern times this group includes all civilized nations. Even in political history there are many striking parallels, but in social development and in culture the recent evolution of civilized peoples has been nearly identical. This fundamental unity of the nations has grown stronger with the centuries on account of improving methods of transport and communication. Formally it might seem that in the Middle Ages the white nations were more closely bound together than they are now. They had one church, a nearly identical jurisprudence, one great literature and one language for the educated classes; they even inherited from Rome the ideal of a single world-state. But if the growth of national pride, the division of the church and the rise of modern languages and literatures have been centrifugal forces, they have been outweighed by the advent of new influences tending to bind all peoples together. The place of a single church is taken by a common point of view, the scientific; the place of Latin as a medium of learning has been taken by English, French, and German, each one more widely known to those to whom it is not native now than ever was Latin in the earlier centuries. The fruits of discovery are common to all nations, who now live under similar conditions, reading the same books and (under different names) the same newspapers, doing the same busi-

Unity of civilized world

ness and enjoying the same luxuries in the same manner. Even in matters of government we are visibly approaching the perhaps distant but apparently certain goal of a single world-state.

Changes in population

In estimating the economic and cultural conditions of the sixteenth century it is therefore desirable to treat Western Europe as a whole. One of the marked differences between all countries then and now is in population. No simple law has been discovered as to the causes of the fluctuations in the numbers of the people within a given territory. This varies with the wealth of the territory, but not in direct ratio to it; for it can be shown that the wealth of Europe in the last four hundred years has increased vastly more than its population. Nor can it be discovered to vary directly in proportion to the combined amount and distribution of wealth, for in sixteenth-century England while the number of the people was increasing wealth was being concentrated in fewer hands almost as fast as it was being created. It is obvious that sanitation and transportation have a good deal to do with the population of certain areas. The largest cities of our own times could not have existed in the Middle Ages, for they could not have been provisioned, nor have been kept endurably healthy without elaborate aqueducts and drains.

Other more obscure factors enter in to complicate the problems of population. Some nations, like Spain in the sixteenth and Ireland in the nineteenth century, have lost immensely through emigration. The cause of this was doubtless not that the nation in question was growing absolutely poorer, but that the increase of wealth or in accessibility to richer lands made it relatively poorer. It is obvious again that great visitations like pestilence or war diminish population directly, though the effect of such factors is usually temporary. How much voluntary sterility operates is problematical. Aegidius Albertinus, writing in 1602, attributed the growth in population of Protestant countries since the Reformation to the abolition of sacerdotal celibacy, and this has also been mentioned as a cause by a recent writer. Probably the last named forces have a very slight influence; the primary one being, as Malthus stated, the increase of means of subsistence.

As censuses were almost unknown to sixteenth-century Europe outside of a few Italian cities, the student is forced to rely for his data on various other calculations, in some cases tolerably reliable, in others deplorably deficient. The best of these are the enumerations of hearths made for purposes of taxation in several countries. Other counts were sometimes made for fiscal or military, and occasionally for religious, purposes. Estimates by contemporary observers supplement our knowledge, which may be taken as at least approximately correct.

England and Wales

The religious census of 1603 gave the number of communicants in England and Wales as 2,275,000, to which must be added 8475 recusants. Adding 50 per cent. for non-communicants, we arrive at the figure of 3,425,000, which is doubtless too low. Another calculation based on a record of births and deaths yields the figure 4,812,000 for the year 1600. The average, 4,100,000, is probably nearly correct, of which about a tenth in Wales. England had grown considerably during the century, this increase being especially remarkable in the large towns. Whereas, in 1534, 150,000 quarters of wheat were consumed in London annually, the figure for 1605 is 500,000. The population in the same time had probably increased from 60,000 to 225,000. No figures worth anything can be given for Ireland, and for Scotland it is only safe to say that in 1500 the population was about 500,000 and in 1600 about 700,000.

The Netherlands

Enumerations of hearths and of communicants give good bases for reckoning the population of the Netherlands. Holland, the largest of the Northern provinces, had about 200,000 people in 1514; Brabant the greatest of the Southern, in 1526 had 500,000. The population of the largest town, Antwerp, in 1526 was 88,000, in 1550 about 110,000. At the same time it is remarkable that in 1521 Ghent impressed Dürer as the greatest city he had seen in the Low Countries. For the whole territory of the Netherlands, including Holland and Belgium, and a little more on the borders, the population was in 1560 about 3,000,000. This is the same figure as that given for 1567 by Lewis Guicciardini. Later in the century the country suffered by war and emigration.

Germany

The lack of a unified government, and the great diversity of conditions, makes the population of Germany more difficult to estimate. Brandenburg, having in 1535 an area of 10,000 square miles, and a population between 300,000 and 400,000, has been aptly compared for size and numbers to the present state of Vermont. Bavaria had in 1554 a population of 434,000; in 1596 of 468,000. Würzburg had in 1538 only 12,000; Hamburg in 1521 12,000 and in 1594 19,000. Danzig had in 1550 about 21,000. The largest city in central Germany, if not in the whole country—as a chronicler stated in 1572—was Erfurt, with a population of 32,000 in 1505. It was the center of the rising Saxon industries, mining and dying, and of commerce. Lübeck, Cologne, Nuremberg and Augsburg equalled or perhaps surpassed it in size, and certainly in wealth. The total population of German Switzerland was over 200,000. The whole German-speaking population of Central Europe amounted to perhaps twenty millions in 1600, though it had been reckoned by the imperial government in 1500 as twelve millions.

France

The number of Frenchmen did not greatly increase in France in the 16th century. Though the borders of the state were extended, she suffered terribly by religious wars, and somewhat by emigration. Not only did many Huguenots flee from her to Switzerland, the Netherlands and England, but economic reasons led to large movements from the south and perhaps from the north. To fill up the gap caused by emigration from Spain a considerable number of French peasants moved to that land; and it is also possible that the same class of people sought new homes in Burgundy and Savoy to escape the pressure of taxes and dues. Various estimates concur in giving France a population of 15,000,000 to 16,000,000. The Paris of Henry II was by far the largest city in the world, numbering perhaps 300,000; but when Henry IV besieged it it had been reduced by war to 220,000. After that it waxed mightily again.

Italy

Italy, leader in many ways, was the first to take accurate statistics of population, births and deaths. These begin by the middle of the fifteenth century, but are rare until the middle of the sixteenth, when they become frequent. Notwithstanding war and pestilence the numbers of inhabitants seemed to grow steadily, the apparent result in the statistics being perhaps in part due to the increasing rigor of the census. Herewith follow specimens of the extant figures: The city of Brescia had 65,000 in 1505, and 43,000 in 1548. During the same period, however, the people in her whole territory of 2200 square miles had increased from 303,000 to 342,000. The city of Verona had 27,000 in 1473 and 52,000 in 1548; her land of 1200 square miles had in the first named year 99,000, in the last 159,000. The kingdom of Sicily grew from 600,000 in 1501 to 800,-

000 in 1548, and 1,180,000 in 1615. The kingdom of Naples, without the capital, had about 1,270,000 people in 1501; 2,110,000 in 1545; the total including the capital amounted in 1600 to 3,000,000. The republic of Venice increased from 1,650,000 in 1550 to 1,850,000 in 1620. Florence with her territory had 586,000 in 1551 and 649,000 in 1622. In the year 1600 Milan with Lombardy had 1,350,000 inhabitants; Savoy in Italy 800,000; continental Genoa 500,000; Parma, Piacenza and Modena together 500,000; Sardinia 300,000; Corsica 150,000; Malta 41,000; Lucca 110,000. The population of Rome fluctuated violently. In 1521 it is supposed to have been about 55,000, but was reduced by the sack to 32,000. After this it rapidly recovered, reaching 45,000 under Paul IV (1558), and 100,000 under Sixtus V (1590). The total population of the States of the Church when the first census was taken in 1656 was 1,880,000.

Spain

The final impression one gets after reading the extremely divergent estimates of the population of Spain is that it increased during the first half of the century and decreased during the latter half. The highest figure for the increase of population during the reign of Charles V is the untrustworthy one of Häbler, who believes the number of inhabitants to have doubled. This belief is founded on the conviction that the wealth of the kingdom doubled in that time. But though population tends to increase with wealth, it certainly does not increase in the same proportion as wealth, so that, considering this fact and also that the increase in wealth as shown by the doubling of income from royal domains was in part merely apparent, due to the falling value of money, we may dismiss Häbler's figure as too high. And yet there is good evidence for the belief that there was a considerable increment. The cities especially gained with the new stimulus to commerce and industry. In 1525 Toledo employed 10,000 workers in silk, who had increased fivefold by 1550. Unfortunately for accuracy these figures are merely contemporary guesses, but they certainly indicate a large growth in the population of Toledo, and similar figures are given for Seville, Burgos and other manufacturing and trading centers. From such estimates, however, combined with the censuses of hearths, peculiarly unsatisfactory in Spain as they excluded the privileged classes and were, as their violent fluctuations show, carelessly made, we may arrive at the conclusion that in 1557 the population of Spain was barely 9,000,000.

Decline

More difficult, if possible, is it to measure the amount of the decline in the latter half of the century. It was widely noticed and commented on by contemporaries, who attributed it in part to the increase in sheep-farming (as in England) and in part to emigration to America. There were doubtless other more important and more obscure causes, namely the increasing rivalry in both commerce and industry of the north of Europe and the consequent decay of Spain's means of livelihood. The emigration amounted on the average to perhaps 4000 per annum throughout the century. The total Spanish population of America was reckoned by Velasco in 1574 at 30,500 households, or 152,500 souls. This would, however, imply a much larger emigration, probably double the last number, to account for the many Spaniards lost by the perils of the sea or in the depths of the wilderness. It is known, for example, that whereas the Spanish population of Venezuela was reckoned at 200 households at least 2000 Spaniards had gone to settle there. An emigration of 300,000 before 1574, or say 400,000 for the whole century, would have left a considerable gap at home. Add to this the industrial decline by which

Altamira reckons that the cities of the center and north, which suffered most, lost from one-half to one-third of their total population, and it is evident that a very considerable shrinkage took place. The census of 1594 reported a population of 8,200,000.

Portugal

The same tendency to depopulation was noticed to a much greater degree by contemporary observers of Portugal. Unfortunately, no even approximately accurate figures can be given. Two million is almost certainly too large for 1600.

General table

The following statistical table will enable the reader to form some estimate of the movements of population. Admitting that the margin of error is fairly large in some of the earlier estimates, it is believed that they are sufficiently near the truth to be of real service.

Country	*1500*	*1600*
England and Wales	3,000,000	4,100,000
Scotland	500,000	700,000
The Netherlands (Holland and Belgium) (1550)		3,000,000
Germany (including Austria, German Switzerland, Franche Comté and Savoy north of the Alps, but excluding Hungary, the Netherlands, East and West Prussia)	12,000,000	20,000,000
France (1550)		16,000,000
Italy	10,000,000	13,000,000
Spain (1557 and 1594)	9,000,000 [1]	8,200,000
Poland with East and West Prussia		3,000,000
Denmark		600,000
Sweden, Norway and Finland		1,400,000

§ 2. Wealth and Prices

Gigantic increase in wealth since 16th century

If the number of Europe's inhabitants has increased fourfold since Luther's time, the amount of her wealth has increased in a vastly greater ratio. The difference

[1] For a higher estimate—ten to twelve millions in 1500—see note in bibliography.

between the twentieth and the sixteenth centuries is greater than anyone would at first blush believe possible. Moreover it is a difference that is, during times of peace, continually increasing. During the century from the close of the Napoleonic to the opening of the Great War, the wealth of the white races probably doubled every twenty-five years. The new factors that made this possible were the exploited resources of America, and the steam-engine. Prior to 1815 the increase of the world's wealth was much slower, but if it doubled once a century,—as would seem not improbable—we should have to allow that the world of 1914 was one hundred and twenty-eight times as rich as it was in 1514.

Change from poverty to affluence emphasized

Of course such a statement cannot pretend to anything like exactitude; the mathematical figure is a mere figure of speech; it is intended only to emphasize the fact that one of the most momentous changes during the last four centuries has been that from poverty to affluence. That the statement, surprising as it may seem, is no exaggeration, may be borne out by a few comparisons.

War a test of a nation's financial strength

One of the tests of a nation's financial strength is that of war. Francis I in time of war mustered at most an army of 100,000, and he reached this figure, or perhaps slightly exceeded it, only once during his reign, in the years 1536–7. This is only half the number of soldiers, proportionately to the population, that France maintained in time of peace at the opening of the twentieth century. And for more than four years, at a time when war was infinitely more expensive than it was when Pavia was fought, France kept in the field about an even five millions of men, more than an eighth of her population instead of about one one-hundred-and-fiftieth. Similar figures could be given for Germany and England. It is true that the power of modern states is multiplied by their greater facilities for borrowing, but with all allowances the contrast suggests an enormous difference of wealth.

Labor power of the world

Take, as a standard of comparison, the labor power of the world. In 1918 the United States alone produced 685,000,000 tons of coal. Each ton burned gives almost as much power as is expended by two laborers working for a whole year. Thus the United States from its coal only had command of the equivalent of the labor of 1,370,000,000 men, or more than thrice the adult male labor power of the whole world; more than fifty times the whole labor power of sixteenth-century Europe. This does not take account of the fact that labor is far more productive now than then, even without steam. The comparison is instructive because the population of the United States in 1910 was about equal to that of the whole of Europe in 1600.

The same impression would be given by a comparison of the production of any other standard product. More gold was produced in the year 1915 than the whole stock of gold in the world in 1550, perhaps in 1600. More wheat is produced annually in Minnesota than the granaries of the cities of the world would hold four centuries ago.

Poverty of the Middle Ages

In fact, there was hardly wealth at all in the Middle Ages, only degrees of poverty, and the sixteenth century first began to see the accumulation of fortunes worthy of the name. In 1909 there were 1100 persons in France with an income of more than $40,000 per annum; among them were 150 with an income of more than $200,000. In England in 1916 seventy-nine persons paid income taxes on estates of more than $125,000,000. On the other hand the richest man in France, Jacques Coeur, whose fortune was proverbial like that of Rockefeller today, had in 1503 a capital of only

$5,400,000. The total wealth of the house of Fugger about 1550 has been estimated at $32,000,000, though the capital of their bank was never anything like that. The contrast was greatest among the very richest class, but it was sufficiently striking in the middle classes. Such a condition as comfort hardly existed.

The same impression will be given to the student of public finance. As more will be said in another paragraph on the revenues of the principal states, only one example need be given here for the sake of contrast. The total revenue of Francis I was $256,000 per annum, that of Henry II even less, $228,000. The revenue of France in 1905 was $750,000,000. Henry VIII often had more difficulty in raising a loan of £50,000 than the English government had recently in borrowing six billions.

Value of money

It is impossible to say which is the harder task, to compare the total wealth of the world at two given periods, or to compare the value of money at different times. Even the mechanical difficulties in the comparison of prices are enormous. When we read that wheat at Wittenberg sold at one gulden the scheffel, it is necessary to determine in the first place how much a gulden and how much a scheffel represented in terms of dollars and bushels. When we discover that there were half a dozen different guldens, and half a dozen separate measures known as scheffels, varying from province to province and from time to time, and varying widely, it is evident that great caution is necessary in ascertaining exactly which gulden and exactly which scheffel is meant.

When coin and measure have been reduced to known quantities, there remains the problem of fixing the quality. Cloth is quoted in the sixteenth century as of standard sizes and grades, but neither of these important factors is accurately known to any modern economist. One would think that in quoting prices of animals an invariable standard would be secured. Quite the contrary. So much has the breed of cattle improved that a fat ox now weighs two or three times what a good ox weighed four centuries ago. Horses are larger, stronger and faster; hens lay many more eggs, cows give much more milk now than formerly. Shoes, clothes, lumber, candles, are not of the same quality in different centuries, and of course there is an ever increasing list of new articles in which no comparison can be made.

Fluctuation in coinage

Nevertheless, some allowance can be made for all factors involved, as far as they are mechanical; some comparisons can be given that bear a sufficiently close relation to exactitude to form the basis from which certain valid deductions can be drawn. Now first as to the intrinsic value, in amounts of gold and silver in the several coins. The vast fluctuation in the value of the English shilling, due to the successive debasements and final restitution of the coinage, is thus expressed:

Year	*Troy grains*	*Year*	*Troy grains*
1461	133	1551	20
1527	118	1552	88
1543	100	1560	89
1545	60	1601	86
1546	40	1919	87.27

A similar depreciation, more gradual but never rectified, is seen in the value of French money. The standard of reckoning was the livre tournois, which varied intrinsically in value of the silver put into it as follows:

Years	*Intrinsic value of silver*
1500	93 cents
1512–40	78 cents
1541–60	66 cents
1561–72	62 cents

Years	*Intrinsic value of silver*
1573–79	57 cents
1580–1600	51 cents

The standard Spanish gold coin after 1497 was the ducat, which had 3.485 grammes of gold (value in our money $2.40). This was divided into 375 maravedis, which therefore had a value of about two-thirds of a cent each. A Castilian marc of gold had 230 grammes or a value of about $16. After 1537 a handsome silver coin, known as the peso fuerte or "piece of eight" because each contained eight reals, was minted in America. Its value was about $1.06 of our money, it being the predecessor of our dollar.

Value of Spanish coins

The great difficulty with the coinage of Germany and Italy is not so much in its fluctuation as in the number of mints. The name gulden was given to almost any coin, originally, as its etymology signifies, a gold piece, but later also to a silver piece. Among gold guldens there was the Rhenish gulden intrinsically worth $1.34; the Philip's gulden in the Netherlands of 96¢ and the Carolus gulden coined after 1520 and worth $1.14. But the coin commonly used in reckoning was the silver gulden, worth intrinsically 56¢. This was divided into 20 groschen. Other coins quite ordinarily met with in the literature of the times are pounds (7.5¢), pfennigs (various values), stivers, crowns, nobles, angels ($2), and Hungarians ducats ($1.75). Since 1518 the chief silver coin was the thaler, at first considered the equal of a silver gulden. The law of 1559, however, made them two different coins, restoring the thaler to what had probably been its former value of 72¢, and leaving the imperial gulden in law, what it had commonly become in fact, a lesser amount of silver.

Gulden a general term

The coinage of Italy was dominated by the gold gulden or florin of Florence and the ducat of Venice, each worth not far from $2.25 of our money. Both these coins, partly on account of their beauty, partly because of the simple honesty with which they were kept at the nominal standard, attained just fame throughout the Middle Ages and thereafter, and became widely used in other lands.

Wheat

The standard of value determined, it is now possible to compare the prices of some staple articles. First in importance comes wheat, which fluctuated enormously within short periods at the same place and in terms of the same amounts of silver. From Luther's letters we learn that wheat sold at Wittenberg for one gulden a scheffel in 1539 and for three groschen a scheffel in 1542, the latter price being considered "so cheap as never before," the former reached in a time almost of famine and calling for intervention on the part of the government. However we interpret these figures (and I believe them to mean that wheat sold at from twelve cents to eighty cents a bushel) they certainly indicate a tremendous instability in prices, due to the poor communications and backward methods of agriculture, making years of plenty alternate with years of hunger. In the case of Wittenberg, the lower level was nearer the normal, for in 1527 wheat was there sold at twenty cents a bushel. In other parts of Germany it was dearer; at Strassburg from 1526–50 it averaged 30 cents a bushel; from 1551–75 it went up to an average of 58 cents, and from 1576–1600 the average again rose to 80 cents a bushel.

Prices also rose in England throughout the century even in terms of silver. Of course part of the rise in the middle years was due to the debasement of the coinage. Reduced to bushels and dollars, the following table shows the tendency of prices:

1530	17 cents a bushel
1537	30 cents

1544	45 cents
1546	69 cents
1547	12 cents
1548	24 cents
1549	48 cents
1550	54 cents
1572	66 cents
1595	$1.14

Wheat in France averaged 23 cents a bushel prior to 1540, after which it rose markedly in price, touching $1.50 in 1600, under exceptional conditions. In order to compare with prices nowadays we must remember that $1 a bushel was a remarkably good price before the late war, during which it was fixed at $2.20 by the American government. Barley in England rose from 6 cents a bushel in 1530 to 10 cents in 1547 and 33 cents in 1549. It was in 1913 70 cents a bushel. Oats rose from 5 cents a bushel in England in 1530 to 18 cents in 1549; in 1913 38 cents.

Animals

Animals sold much lower in the sixteenth century than they do now, though it must be remembered that they are worth more after several centuries of careful breeding. Horses then sold at $2.50 in England and at $4 to $11 in France; the average price in 1913 was $244 for working animals. Cows were worth $2 in England in 1530; from $4 to $6.40 in France; oxen apparently came considerably higher, averaging in England $10 a head in 1547 and in France from $9 to $16 a yoke. At present they are sold by weight, averaging in 1913 9¢ per lb., or $90 for one weighing a thousand pounds. Beef then cost about 2/3 of a cent a pound instead of 40¢ as in 1914. A sheep was sold in 1585 at $1.60, a large swine at $5, and pigs at 26¢ apiece. Pork cost 2¢ a pound; hens sold in England at 12¢ a piece and geese and ducks for the same; at Wittenberg geese fetched only 6¢ in 1527. Eggs might have been bought at 2¢ a dozen.

Groceries

Wholesale prices of groceries, taken mostly from an English table drawn up about 1580, were as follows: Oil was $140 the ton, or 55 cents a gallon; train-oil was just half that price; Newfoundland fish cost then $2.50 the quintal dry, as against $7.81 in 1913. Gascon wines (claret) varied according to quality, from 16 cents to 24 cents a quart. Salt fetched $7.50 a ton, which is very close to the price that it was in 1913 ($1.02 per bbl. of 280 lbs.). Soap was $13 the hundredweight. Pepper and sugar cost nearly the same, about $70 the hundredweight, or far higher than they were in 1919, when each cost $11 the hundredweight. Spices also cost more in the sixteenth century than they do now, and rose throughout the century. By 1580 the wholesale price per hundredweight was $224 for cloves, the same for nutmegs, $150 for cinnamon, $300 for mace. Ginger was $90 the hundredweight, and candles 6.6¢ the lb. as against 7.25¢ now.

Drygoods

Drygoods varied immensely in cost. Raw wool sold in England in 1510 for 4 cents per lb., as against 26 cents just four hundred years later. Fine cloth sold at $65 "the piece," the length and breadth of which it is unfortunately impossible to determine accurately. Different grades came in different sizes, averaging a yard in width, but from 18 yards to 47 yards in length, the finer coming in longer rolls. Sorting cloths were $45 the piece. Linen cost 20 cents a yard in 1580; Mary, Queen of Scots, five years later paid $6.50 the yard for purple velvet and 28 cents the yard for buckram to line the same. The coarse clothes of the poor were cheaper, a workman's suit in France costing $1.80 in 1600, a child's whole wardrobe $3.40, and a soldier's uniform $4.20. The prices of the poorest women's dresses ranged from $3 to $6 each. In 1520 Albert Dürer paid in the Netherlands 17 cents for one pair of shoes, 33 cents for another and 20 cents for a pair of woman's gloves. A pair of spectacles cost him 22 cents, a pair of gloves for himself 38 cents.

Metals were dearer in the sixteenth century than they are now. Iron cost $60 a ton in 1580 against $22 a ton in 1913. Lead fetched $42 the ton and tin $15 the cwt. The ratio of gold to silver was about 1 to 11. The only fuel much used was wood, which was fairly cheap but of course not nearly as efficient as our coal.

Metals

Interest, as the price of money, varied then as it does now in inverse ratio to the security offered by the debtor, and on the whole within much the same range that it does now. The best security was believed to be that of the German Free Cities, governed as they were by the commercial class that appreciated the virtue of prompt and honest payment. Accordingly, we find that they had no trouble in borrowing at 5 per cent., their bonds taking the form of perpetual annuities, like the English consols. So eagerly were these investments sought that they were apportioned on petition as special favors to the creditors. The cities of Paris and London also enjoyed high credit. The national governments had to pay far higher, owing to their poverty and dishonesty. Francis I borrowed at 10 per cent.; Charles V paid higher in the market of Antwerp, the extreme instance being that of 50 per cent. per annum. In 1550 he regularly paid 20 per cent., a ruinous rate that foreshadowed his bankruptcy and was partly caused by its forecast. Until the recent war we were accustomed to think of the great nations borrowing at 2–4 per cent., but during the war the rate immensely rose. Anglo-French bonds, backed by the joint and several credit of the two nations, sold on the New York Stock Exchange in 1918 at a price that would yield the investor more than 12 per cent., and City of Paris bonds at a rate of more than 16 per cent.

Interest

Commercial paper, or loans advanced by banks to merchants on good security, of course varied. The lowest was reached at Genoa where from time to time merchants secured accommodation at 3 per cent. The average in Germany was 6 per cent. and this was made the legal rate by Brandenburg in 1565. But usurers, able to take advantage of the necessities of poor debtors, habitually exacted more, as they do now, and loans on small mortgages or on pawned articles often ran at 30 per cent. On the whole, the rate of interest fell slightly during the century.

Real estate

The price of real estate is more difficult to compare than almost anything, owing to the individual circumstances of each purchase. Land in France sold at rates ranging from $8 to $240 the acre. Luther bought a little farm in the country for $340, and a piece of property in Wittenberg for $500. After his death, in 1564, the house he lived in, a large and handsome building formerly the Augustinian Cloister, fetched $2072. The house can be seen today[1] and would certainly, one would think, now bring fifteen times as much.

Books

Books were comparatively cheap. The Greek Testament sold for 48 cents, a Latin Testament for half that amount, a Latin folio Bible published in 1532 for $4, Luther's first New Testament at 84 cents. One might get a copy of the Pandects for $1.60, of Vergil for 10 cents, a Greek grammar for 8 cents, Demosthenes and Aeschines in one volume at 20 cents, one of Luther's more important tracts for 30 cents and the condemnation of him by the universities in a small pamphlet at 6 cents. One of the things that has gone down most in price since that day is postage. Dürer while in the Netherlands paid a messenger 17 cents to deliver a

[1] See the photograph in my *Life and Letters of Luther*, p. 364.

letter (or several letters?), presumably sent to his home in Nuremberg.

Wages

In accordance with the general rule that wages follow the trend of prices sluggishly, whether upwards or downwards, there is less change to be observed in them throughout the sixteenth century than there is in the prices of commodities. Subject to government regulation, the remuneration of all kinds of labor remained nearly stationary while the cost of living was rising. Startling is the difference in the rewards of the various classes, that of the manual laborers being cruelly low, that of professional men somewhat less in proportion to the cost of living than it is today, and that of government officers being very high. No one except court officials got a salary over $5000 a year, and some of them got much more. In 1553 a French chamberlain was paid $51,000 per annum.

A French navvy received 8 cents a day in 1550, a carpenter as much as 26 cents. A male domestic was given $7 to $12 a year in addition to his keep and a woman $5 to $6. As the number of working days in Catholic countries was only about 250 a year, workmen made from $65 to as low as $20. If anything, labor was worse paid in Germany than it was in France. Agricultural labor in England was paid in two scales, one for summer and one for winter. It varied from 3 cents to 7 cents a day, the smaller sum being paid only to men who were also boarded. In summer freemasons and master carpenters got from 8 cents to 11 cents for a terribly long day, in winter 6 cents to 9 cents for a shorter day. The following scale was fixed by law in England in 1563: A hired farmer was to have $10 a year and $2 for livery; a common farm hand was allowed $8.25 and $1.25 extra for livery; a "mean servant" $6 and $1.25 respectively, a man child

$4 and $1; a chief woman cook $5 and $1.60, a mean or simple woman $3 and $1; a woman child $2.50 and $1. All were of course boarded and lodged.

The pay of French soldiers under Francis I was for privates $28 a year in time of war; this fell to $14 a year in time of peace; for captains $33 a month in time of peace and $66 in time of war. Captains in the English navy received $36 a month; common seamen $1.25 a month for wages and the same allowance for food.

Pay of clergymen

The church fared little better than the army. In Scotland, a poor country but one in which the clergy were respected, by the law of 1562, a parson if a single man was given $26 a year, if a married man a maximum of $78 a year; probably a parsonage was added. Doubtless many Protestant ministers eked out their subsistence by fees, as the Catholic priests certainly did. Dürer gave 44 cents to a friar who confessed his wife. Every baptism, marriage and burial was taxed a certain amount. In France one could hire a priest to say a mass at from 60 cents to $7 in 1500, and at from 30 to 40 cents in 1600. At this price it has remained since, a striking instance of religious conservatism working to the detriment of the priest, for the same money represents much less in real wages now than it did then.

Physicians

Fees for physicians ranged from 33 to 44 cents a visit in Germany about 1520. Treatment and medicine were far higher. At Antwerp Dürer paid $2.20 for a small quantity of medicine for his wife. Fees were sometimes given for a whole course of attendance. In England we hear of such "cures" paid for at from $3.30 to $5. Very little, if any, advice was given free to the poor. The physicians for the French king received a salary of $200 a year and other favors. William Butts, physician to Henry VIII, had $500 per annum, in addition to a knighthood; and his salary was increased to over $600 for attending the Duke of Richmond.

Teachers

Teachers in the lower schools were regarded as lackeys and paid accordingly. Nicholas Udal, head master of Eton, received $50 per annum and various small allowances. University professors were treated more liberally. Luther and Melanchthon at Wittenberg got a maximum of $224 per annum, which was about the same as the stipend of leading professors in other German universities and at Oxford and Cambridge. The teacher also got a small honorarium from each student. When Paul III restored the Sapienza at Rome he paid a minimum of $17 per annum to some friars who taught theology and who were cared for by their order, but he gave high salaries to the professors of rhetoric and medicine. Ordinarily these received $476 a year, but one professor of the classics reached the highwater-mark with nearly $800.

Royalties

The rewards of literary men were more consistently small in the sixteenth century than they are now, owing to the absence of effective copyright. An author usually received a small sum from the printer to whom he first offered his manuscript, but his subsequent royalties, if any, depended solely on the goodwill of the publisher. A Wittenberg printer offered Luther $224 per annum for his manuscripts, but the Reformer declined it, wishing to make his books as cheap as possible. In 1512 Erasmus got $8.40 from Badius the Parisian printer for a new edition of his *Adages*. In fact, the rewards of letters, such as they were, were indirect, in the form of pensions, gifts and benefices from the great. Erasmus got so many of these favors that he lived more than comfortably. Luther died almost a rich man, so many *honoraria* did he collect from noble admirers. Rabelais was given a benefice, though he only lived two years afterwards to enjoy its fruits. Henry VIII gave $500 to Thomas Murner for writing against Luther. But the lot of the average writer was hard. Fulsome flattery was the most lucrative production of the muse.

Artists

Artists fared better. Dürer sold one picture for $375 and another for $200, not counting the "tip" which his wife asked and received on each occasion from the patron. Probably his woodcuts brought him more from the printers than any single painting, and when he died he left the then respectable sum of $32,000. He had been offered a pension of $300 per annum and a house at Antwerp by that city if he would settle there, but he preferred to return to Nuremberg, where he was pensioned $600 a year by the emperor. Leonardo da Vinci and Michelangelo both received $129 a month for work done for a prince, and the latter was given a pension of $5200 a year by Paul III. Raphael in 1520 left an estate of $140,000.

Value of money

If a comparison of the value of money is made, the final impression that one gets is that an ounce of gold was in 1563, let us say, expected to do about ten times as much work as the same weight of precious metal performed in 1913.[1] If a few articles were then actually dearer, they were comparatively unimportant and were balanced by other articles even more than ten times as cheap. But a dollar will buy so many articles now which did not exist in former ages that a plausible case can be made out for the paradox that money is now worth more than it ever was before. If an ounce of gold would in Luther's time exchange for a much larger quantity of simple necessaries than it will purchase now, on the other hand a man with an income of $5000 a year is far better off than a man with the

[1] No valid comparison can be made for the years after 1913, for in most nations paper currencies have ousted gold.

same income, or indeed with any income, was then.

Trend of prices

Notwithstanding the great difficulties of making out any fair index number representing the cost of living and applicable to long periods, owing to the fact that articles vary from time to time, as when candles are replaced by gas and gas by electricity, yet the general trend of prices can be pretty plainly ascertained. Generally speaking, prices—measured in weight of gold and not in coin—sank slowly from 1390 till 1520 under the influence of better technical methods of production and possibly of the draining of gold and silver to the Orient. From 1520 till 1560 prices rose quite slowly on account of the increased production of gold and silver and its more rapid circulation by means of better banking. From 1560 to 1600 prices rose with enormous rapidity, partly because of the destruction of wealth and increase in the cost of production following in the wake of the French and Dutch wars of religion, and still more, perhaps, on account of the torrent of American silver suddenly poured into the lap of Europe. Taking the century as a whole, we find that wheat rose the most, as much as 150 per cent. in England, 200 per cent. in France and 300 per cent. in Germany. Other articles rose less, and in some cases remained stationary, or sank in price. Money wages rose slowly, far less than the cost of living.

Increase in volume of precious metals

Apart from special circumstances affecting the production of particular classes of goods, the main cause of the general trend of prices upwards was probably the increase in the volume of the precious metals. Just how great this was, it is impossible to determine, and yet a calculation can be made, yielding figures near enough the actual to be of service. From the middle of the fifteenth century there had been a considerable increase in the production of silver from German, Bohemian and Hungarian mines. Although this increase was much more than is usually allowed for—equalling, in the opinion of one scholar, the produce of American mines until nearly the middle of the sixteenth century—it was only enough to meet the expanding demands of commerce. Before America entered the market, there was also a considerable import of gold from Asia and Africa. The tide of Mexican treasure began to flood Spain about 1520, but did not reach the other countries in large quantities until about 1560, When we consider the general impression concerning the increase of the currency immediately following the pillage of the Aztecs and Incas, the following statistics of the English mint are instructive, if they are not enigmatical. During the first fourteen years of Henry VIII (1509–23) the average amount of gold minted in England was 24,666 troy pounds per annum, and of silver 31,225 troy pounds. But in the years 1537–40, before the great debasement of the currency had taken place, the amount of gold coined fell to 3,297 Troy pounds per annum, and that of silver rose only to 52,974 troy pounds. As each pound of gold was at that time worth as much as eleven pounds of silver, this means that the actual amount of new money put into circulation each year in the latter period was less than a third of that minted in the earlier years. The figures also indicate the growing cheapness of silver, stimulating its import, while the import of gold was greatly restricted, according to Gresham's law that cheap money drives out dear.

Estimates of gold and silver products

The spoil of Mexico and Peru has frequently been over-estimated, by none more extravagantly than by the Conquistadores and their contemporaries. But the estimates of modern scholars vary enormously. Lexis believes that the total amount of gold produced by Europe and America from 1501 to 1550 (the greater part, of course, by America) amounted to $134,000,000.

F. de Laiglesio, on the other hand, thinks that not more than $4,320,000 was mined in America before 1555. The most careful estimate, that made by Professor Haring, arrives at the following results, the amounts being given in pesos each worth very nearly the same as our dollar. Mexican production:

Haring's estimate

	1521–44	*1545–60*
Gold	5,348,900	343,670
Silver	4,130,170	22,467,111

For Peru the proportions of gold and silver cannot be separated, but the totals taken together from 1531–1560 amounted to probably 84,350,000 pesos. Other small sums came from other parts of the New World, and the final total for production of gold *and* silver in America until 1560 is given at 139,720,000 pesos. This is a reduction to 70 per cent. of the estimate of Lexis. Assuming that the same correction must be made on all of the estimates given by Lexis we have the following figures for the world's production of precious metals in kilogrammes and in dollars: [1]

	Gold *Average per annum*		*Silver* *Average per annum*	
	in kilos	*in dollars*	*kilos*	*in pesos or dollars of 25 grammes*
1493–1520	4270	3,269,000	31,570	1,262,800
1521–44	4893	3,425,000	52,010	2,080,400
1545–60	4718	3,302,600	184,730	7,389,200
1561–80	4718	3,302,600	185,430	7,417,200
1581–1600	4641	3,268,700	230,480	9,219,200

[1] These figures are based on those of Sommerlad in the *Handwörterbuch der Staatswissenschaften*, s.v. "Preis," taken from Wiebe, who based on Lexis. Figures quite similar to those of Sommerlad are given by C. F. Bastable in the *Encyclopaedia Britannica*, s.v. "Money." I have incorporated Haring's corrections.

Combining these figures we see that the production of gold was pretty steady throughout the century, making a total output of about $330,000,000. The production of silver, however, greatly increased after 1544. From the beginning of the century to that year it amounted to $75,285,600; from 1545 to 1600 inclusive it increased to $450,955,200, making a total output for the century of $526,240,800. Of course these figures only roughly approximate the truth; nevertheless they give a correct idea of the general processes at work. Even for the first half of the century the production of the precious metals was far in excess of anything that had preceded, and this output, large as it was, was nearly tripled in the last half of the century. These figures, however, are extremely modest compared with those of recent times, when more gold is mined in a year than was then mined in a century. The total amount mined in 1915 was $470,000,000; in 1917 $428,000,000; for the period 1850 to 1916 inclusive the total amount mined was $13,678,000,000.

§ 3. Institutions

The monarchies

For a variety of reasons the sixteenth century was as monarchical in mind as the twentieth century is democratic. Immemorial prescription then had a vigor since lost, and monarchy descended from classical and biblical antiquity when kings were hedged with a genuine divinity. The study of Roman law, with its absolutist maxims, aided in the formation of royalist sentiment. The court as the center of fashion attracted a brilliant society, while the small man satisfied his cravings for gentility by devouring the court gossip that even then clogged the presses. It is probable that one reason why the throne became so popular was that it was, next to the church, the best advertised article in the world. But underlying these sentimental reasons for loyalty there was a basis of solid utility, predisposing men to support the scepter as the one power strong enough to overawe the nobles. One tyrant was better than many; one lion could do less harm than a pack of wolves and hyaenas. In the greater states men felt perfectly helpless without a king to rule the anarchical chaos into which society would have dissolved without him. When the Spanish Communes rebelled against Charles V they triumphed in the field, but their attempt simply collapsed in face of their utter inability to solve the problem of government without a royal governor. They were as helpless as bees without a queen. Indeed, so strong was their instinct to get a royal head that they tried to preserve themselves by kidnapping Charles's mother, poor, mad Joanna, to fill the political vacuum that they had made. So in the civil wars in France; notwithstanding the more promising materials for the formation of a republic in that country, all parties were, in fact, headed by claimants to the throne.

Councils of State

Next to the king came the Council of State, composed of princes of the blood, cardinals, nobles and some officers and secretaries of state, not always of noble blood but frequently, especially in the cases of the most powerful of them, scions of the middle class. What proportion of the executive power was wielded by the Council depended on the personal character of the monarch. Henry VIII was always master; Elizabeth was more guided than guiding; the Councils of the Valois and Hapsburgs profited by the preoccupation or the stupidity of their masters to usurp the royal power for themselves. In public opinion the Council occupied a great place, similar to that of an English Cabinet today. The first Anglican prayerbook contains petitions for the Council, though it did not occur to the people to pray for Parliament until the next century.

The countries were governed no longer by the nobles as such but by officials appointed by the crown. It is an indication of the growing nationalization of policy that the sixteenth century saw the first establishment of permanent diplomatic agents. The first ambassadors, selected largely from a panel of bishops, magistrates, judges and scholars, were expected to function not only as envoys but also as spies. Under them was a host of secret agents expected to do underhand work and to take the responsibility for it themselves so that, if found out, they could be repudiated.

Parliaments

Very powerful was the national popular assembly: the Parliament, the Diet, the States General, or the Cortes. Its functions, prescriptive and undefined, were commonly understood to include the granting of taxes. The assent of the body was also required, to a varying degree, for the sanction of other laws. But the real power of the people's representatives lay in the fact that they were the chief organ for the expression of that public opinion which in all countries and at all times it is unsafe for governments to disregard. Sitting in two or more chambers to represent the several estates or sometimes—as in the German Diet—subdivisions of these estates, the representatives were composed of members of the privileged orders, the clergy and nobility, and of the elected representatives of the city aristocracies. The majority of the population, the poor, were unrepresented. That this class had as great a stake in the commonwealth as any other, and that they had a class consciousness capable of demanding reforms and of taking energetic measures to secure them, is shown by a number of rebellions of the proletariat, and yet it is not unfair to them, or disdainful, to say that on most matters they were too uninstructed, too powerless and too mute to contribute much to that body of sentiment called public opinion, one condition of which seems to be that to exist it must find expression.

Influence of the Estates General

The Estates General, by whatever name they were called, supplemented in France by provincial bodies called Parlements partaking of the nature of high courts of justice, and in Germany by the local Diets (Landtag) of the larger states, exercised a very real and in some cases a decisive influence on public policy. The monarch of half the world dared not openly defy the Cortes of Aragon or of Castile; the imperious Tudors diligently labored to get parliamentary sanction for their tyrannical acts, and, on the few occasions when they could not do so, hastened to abandon as gracefully as possible their previous intentions. In Germany the power of the Diet was not limited by the emperor, but by the local governments, though even so it was considerable. When a Diet, under skilful manipulation or by unscrupulous trickery, was induced by the executive to pass an unpopular measure, like the Edict of Worms, the law became a dead letter. In some other instances, notably in its long campaign against monopolies, even when it expressed the popular voice the Diet failed because the emperor was supported by the wealthy capitalists. Only recently it has been revealed how the Fuggers of Augsburg and their allies endeavored to manipulate or to frustrate its work in the matter of government regulation of industry and commerce.

Public finance

The finances of most countries were managed corruptly and unwisely. The taxes were numerous and complicated and bore most heavily on the poor. From ordinary taxes in most countries the privileged orders were exempt, though they were forced to contribute special sums levied by themselves. The general property tax (taille) in France yielded 2,400,000 livres tournois in 1517 and 4,600,000 in 1543. The taxes were farmed; that is, the right of collecting them was sold at auction, with the natural result that they were put into the hands of extortioners who made vast fortunes by oppressing the people. Revenues of the royal domain, excises on salt and other articles, import and export duties, and the sale of offices and monopolies, supplemented the direct taxes. The system of taxation varied in each country. Thus in Spain the 10 per cent. tax on the price of an article every time it was sold and the royalty on precious metals—20 per cent. after 1504—proved important sources of revenue. Rome drove a lucrative trade in spiritual wares. Everywhere, fines for transgressions of the law figured more largely as a source of revenue than they do nowadays.

Wasteful expenditures

Expenditures were both more wasteful and more niggardly than they are today. Though the service of the public debt was trifling compared with modern standards, and though the administration of justice was not expensive because of the fee system, the army and navy cost a good deal, partly because they were composed largely of well paid mercenaries. The personal extravagances of the court were among the heaviest burdens borne by the people. The kings built palaces; they wallowed in cloth of gold; they collected objects of art; they squandered fortunes on mistresses and minions; they made constant progresses with a retinue of thousands of servants and horses. The two greatest states, France and Spain, both went into bankruptcy in 1557.

Public order

The great task of government, that of keeping public order, protecting life and property and punishing the criminal, was approached by our forbears with more gusto than success. The laws were terrible, but they were unequally executed. In England among capital crimes were the following: murder, arson, escape from prison, hunting by night with painted faces or visors, embezzling property worth more than 40 shillings, carrying horses or mares into Scotland, conjuring, practising witchcraft, removing landmarks, desertion from the army, counterfeiting or mutilating coins, cattle-lifting, house-breaking, picking of pockets. All these were punished by hanging, but crimes of special heinousness, such as poisoning, were visited with burning or boiling to death. The numerous laws against treason and heresy have already been described. Lesser punishments included flogging, pillory, branding, the stocks, clipping ears, piercing tongues, and imprisonment in dungeons made purposely as horrible as possible, dark, noisome dens without furniture or conveniences, often too small for a man to stand upright or to lie at full length.

Number of executions

With such laws it is not surprising that 72,000 men were hanged under Henry VIII, an average of nearly 2,000 a year. The number at present, when the population of England and Wales has swollen to tenfold of what it was then, is negligible. Only nine men were hanged in the United Kingdom in the years 1901–3; about 5,000 are now on the average annually convicted of felony. If anything, the punishments were harsher on the Continent than in Britain. The only refuge of the criminal was the greed of his judges. At Rome it was easy and regular to pay a price for every crime, and at other places bribery was more or less prevalent.

Cruel trial methods

The methods of trying criminals were as cruel as their punishments. On the Continent the presumption was held to be against the accused, and the rack and its ghastly retinue of instruments of pain were freely used to procure confession. Calvin's hard saying that when men felt the pain they spoke the truth merely expressed the current delusion, for legislators and judges, their hearts hardened in part by the example of the church, concurred in his opinion. The exceptional protest of Montaigne deserves to be quoted for its humanity: "All that exceeds simple death is absolute cruelty, nor can our laws expect that he whom the fear of decapitation or hanging will not restrain should be awed by imagining the horrors of a slow fire, burning pincers or breaking on the wheel."

The spirit of the English law was against the use of torture, which, however, made progress, especially in state trials, under the Tudors. A man who refused to plead in an English court was subjected to the *peine forte et dure,* which consisted in piling weights on his chest until he either spoke or was crushed to death. To enforce the laws there was a constabulary in the country, supplemented by the regular army, and a police force in the cities. That of Paris consisted of 240 archers, among them twenty-four mounted men. The inefficiency of some of the English officers is amusingly caricatured in the persons of Dogberry and Verges who, when they saw a thief, concluded that he was no honest man and the less they had to meddle or make with him the more for their honesty.

Blue laws

If, in all that has just been said, it is evident that the legislation of that period and of our own had the same conception of the function of government and only differed in method and efficiency, there was one very large class of laws spread upon the statute-books of medieval Europe that has almost vanished now. A paternal statesmanship sought to regulate the private lives of a citizen in every respect: the fashion of his clothes, the number of courses at his meals, how many guests he might have at wedding, dinner or dance, how long he should be permitted to haunt the tavern, and how much he should drink, how he should spend Sunday, how he should become engaged, how dance, how part his hair and with how thick a stick he should be indulged in the luxury of beating his wife.

The "blue laws," as such regulations on their moral side came to be called, were no Protestant innovation. The Lutherans hardly made any change whatever in this respect, but Calvin did give a new and biting intensity to the medieval spirit. His followers, the Puritans, in the next century, almost succeeded in reducing the staple of a Christian man's legitimate recreation to "seasonable meditation and prayer." But the idea originated long before the evolution of "the non-conformist conscience."

The fundamental cause of all this legislation was sheer conservatism. Primitive men and savages have so strong a feeling of the sanction of custom that they have, as Bagehot expresses it, fairly screwed themselves down by their unreasoning demands for conformity. A good deal of this spirit has survived throughout history and far more of it, naturally, was found four centuries ago than at present, when reason has proved a solvent for so many social institutions. There are a good many laws of the period under survey—such as that of Nuremberg against citizens parting their hair—for which no discoverable basis can be found save the idea that new-fangled fashions should not be allowed.

Spirit of conservatism

Economic reasons also played their part in the regulation of the habits of the people. Thus a law of Edward VI, after a preamble setting forth that divers kinds of food are indifferent before God, nevertheless commands all men to eat fish as heretofore on fast days, not as a religious duty but to encourage fishermen, give them a livelihood and thus train men for the navy.

A third very strong motive in the mind of the sixteenth-century statesmen, was that of differentiating the classes of citizens. The blue laws, if they may be so called in this case, were secretions of the blue blood. To make the vulgar know their places it was essential to make them dress according to their rank. The intention of An Act for the Reformation of excess in Apparel, passed by the English Parliament in 1532, was stated to be,

Apparel according to rank

> the necessary repressing and avoiding and expelling of the excess daily more used in the sumptuous and costly apparel and array accustomably worn in this Realm, whereof hath ensued and daily do chance such sundry high and notorious detriments of the common weal, the subversion of good and politic order in knowledge and distinction of people according to their estates, pre-eminences, dignities and degrees to the utter impoverishment and undoing of many inexpert and light persons inclined to pride, mother of all vices.

The tenor of the act prescribes the garb appropriate to the royal family, to nobles of different degree, to citizens according to their income, to servants and husbandmen, to the clergy, doctors of divinity, soldiers, lawyers and players. Such laws were common in all countries. A Scotch act provides "that it be lauchful to na wemen to weir [clothes] abone [above] their estait except howries." This law was not only "apprevit" by King James VI, but endorsed with his own royal hand, "This acte is verray gude."

Excessive fare at feasts was provided against for similar reasons and with almost equal frequency. By an English proclamation the number of dishes served was to be regulated according to the rank of the highest person present. Thus, if a cardinal was guest or host, there might be nine courses, if a lord of Parliament six, for a citizen with an income of five hundred pounds a year, three. Elsewhere the number of guests at all

1517

ordinary functions as well as the number and price of gifts at weddings, christenings and like occasions, was prescribed.

Games of chance were frequently forbidden. Francis I ordered a lieutenant with twenty archers to visit taverns and gaming houses and arrest all players of cards, dice and other unlawful games. This did not prevent the establishment of a public lottery, a practice justified by alleging the examples of Italian cities in raising revenue by this means. Henry III forbade all games of chance "to minors and other debauched persons," and this was followed six years later by a crushing impost on cards and dice, interesting as one of the first attempts to suppress the instruments of vice through the taxing power. Merry England also had many laws forbidding "tennis, bowles, dicing and cards," the object being to encourage the practice of archery.

1526

1539

1577

Tippling was the subject of occasional animadversion by the various governments, though there seemed to be little sentiment against it until the opening of the following century. The regulation of the number of taverns and of the amount of wine that might be kept in a gentleman's cellar, as prescribed in an English law, mentions not the moral but the economic aspect of drinking. The purchase of French wines was said to drain England of money.

1553

Though the theater also did not suffer much until the time of Cromwell, plays were forbidden in the precincts of the city of London. The Book of Discipline in Scotland forbade attendance at theaters. Calvin thoroughly disapproved of them, and even Luther considered them "fools' work" and at times dangerous.

1574

Commendable efforts to suppress the practice of duelling were led by the Catholic church. Clement

1524 VII forbade it in a bull, confirmed by a decree of the 1563 Council of Trent. An extraordinarily worded French proclamation of 1566 forbade "all gentlemen and others to give each other the lie and, if they do give each other the lie, to fight a duel about it." Other governments took the matter up very sluggishly. Scotland forbade "the great liberty that sundry persons take in provoking each other to singular combats upon sudden and frivol occasions," without license from his majesty.

1551 Two matters on which the Puritans felt very keenly, blasphemy and Sabbath-breaking, were but scantily looked after in the century of the Reformation. Scotland forbade "grievous and abominable oaths, swearing, execrations and blasphemation," and somewhat similar laws can be found in other countries. Scotland was also a pioneer in forbidding on the Sabbath all work, "gaming, playing, passing to taverns and alehouses and wilful remaining away from the parish kirk in time of sermon."

Mail

Government has other functions than the enforcement of the civil and criminal law. Almost contemporary with the opening of the century was the establishment of post offices for the forwarding of letters. After Maximilian had made a start in the Netherlands other countries were not slow to follow his example. Though under special government supervision at first these letter-carriers were private men.

Sanitation

In the Middle Ages there had been efforts to safeguard public sanitation. The sixteenth century did not greatly improve on them. Thus, Geneva passed a law that garbage and other refuse should not be allowed to lie in the streets for more than three days in summer or eight days in winter. In extreme cases quarantine was adopted as a precaution against epidemics.

War

It is the most heart-breaking or the most absurd fact in human history, according as the elements involved are focused in a humane or in a cynical light, that the chief energies of government as well as the most zealous forces of peoples, have been dedicated since civilization began to the practice of wholesale homicide. As we look back from the experience of the Great War to the conflicts of other times, they seem to our jaded imaginations almost as childish as they were vicious. In the sixteenth century, far more than in the nineteenth, the nations boiled and bubbled with spleen and jealousy, hurled Thrasonical threats and hyperbolic boasts in each other's teeth, breathing out mutual extermination with no compunctious visitings of nature to stay their hungry swords—but when they came to blows they had not the power of boys. The great nations were always fighting but never fought to a finish. In the whole century no national capital west of Hungary, save Rome and Edinburgh, was captured by an enemy. The real harm was not done on the battlefield, where the carnage was incredibly small, but in the raids and looting of town and country by the professional assassins who filled the ranks of the hireling troops. Then, indeed, cities were burned, wealth was plundered and destroyed, men were subjected to nameless tortures and women to indescribable outrages, and children were tossed on pikes. Nor did war seem then to shock the public conscience, as it has at last succeeded in doing. The people saw nothing but dazzling glory in the slaughter of foemen on the stricken field, in the fanfare of the trumpets and the thunder of the captains and the shouting. Soldiers, said Luther, founding his opinion on the canon law, might be in a state of grace, for war was as necessary as eating, drinking or any other business. Statesmen like Machiavelli and Bacon were keen for the largest armies possible, as the mainstay of a nation's power. Only Erasmus was a clear-sighted pacifist, always declaiming against war and once asserting that he agreed with Cicero in thinking the most unjust peace preferable to the justest war. Elsewhere he admitted that wars of self-defence were necessary.

Arms

Fire-arms had not fully established their ascendancy in the period of Frundsberg, or even of Alva. As late as 1596 an English soldier lamented that his countrymen neglected the bow for the gun. Halberdiers with pikes were the core of the army. Artillery sometimes inflicted very little damage, as at Flodden, sometimes considerable, as at Marignano, where, with the French cavalry, it struck down the till then almost invincible Swiss infantry. In battle arquebusiers and musketeers were interspersed with cross-bowmen. Cannon of a large type gave way to smaller field-guns; even the idea of the machine-gun emerged in the fifteenth century. The name of them, "organs," was taken from their appearance with numerous barrels from which as many as fifty bullets could be discharged at a time. Cannon were transported to the field on carts. Rifles were invented by a German in 1520, but not much used. Pistols were first manufactured at Pistoia—whence the name—about 1540. Bombs were first used in 1588.

The arts of fortification and of siege were improved together, many ingenious devices being called into being by the technically difficult war of the Spaniards against the Dutch. Tactics were not so perfect as they afterwards became and of strategy there was no consistent theory. Machiavelli, who wrote on the subject, based his ideas on the practice of Rome and therefore despised fire-arms and preferred infantry to cavalry. Discipline was severe, and needed to be, notwithstanding which there were sporadic and often very annoying mutinies. Punishments were terrible, as in civil life. Blasphemy, cards, dicing, duelling and women were forbidden in most regular armies, but in time of war the soldiers were allowed an incredible license in pillaging and in foraging. Rings and other decorations were given as rewards of valor. Uniforms began first to be introduced in England by Henry VIII.

Personnel of the armies

The personnel of the armies was extremely bad. Not counting the small number of criminals who were allowed to expiate their misdeeds by military service, the rank and file consisted of mercenaries who only too rapidly became criminals under the tutelage of Mars. There were a few conscripts, but no universal training such as Machiavelli recommended. The officers were nobles or gentlemen who served for the prestige and glory of the profession of arms, as well as for the good pay.

Size of armies compared

But the most striking difference between armies then and now is not in their armament nor in their quality but in the size. Great battles were fought and whole campaigns decided with twenty or thirty thousand troops. The French standing army was fixed by the ordinance of 1534 at seven legions of six thousand men each, besides which were the mercenaries, the whole amounting to a maximum, under Francis I, of about 100,000 men. The English official figures about 1588 gave the army 90,000 foot soldiers and 9000 horse, but these figures were grossly exaggerated. In fact only 22,000 men were serviceable at the crisis of England's war with Spain. Other armies were proportionately small. The janizaries, whose intervention often decided battles, numbered in 1520 only 12,000. They were perhaps the best troops in Europe, as the Turkish artillery was the most powerful known. What all these figures show, in short, is that the phenomenon of nations with every man physically fit in the army, engaging in a death grapple until one goes down in complete exhaustion, is a modern development.

Sea power

The influence of sea power upon history has become proverbial, if, indeed, it has not been overestimated since Admiral Mahan first wrote. It may be pointed out that this influence is far from a constant factor. Sea power had a considerable importance in the wars of Greece and of Rome, but in the Middle Ages it became negligible. Only with the opening of the seven seas to navigation was the command of the waves found to secure the avenues to wealth and colonial expansion. In Portugal, Spain, and England, "the blue water school" of mariners speedily created navies whose strife was apparently more decisive for the future of history than were the battles of armies on land.

When the trade routes of the Atlantic superseded those of the Mediterranean in importance, naturally methods of navigation changed, and this involved a revolution in naval warfare greater than that caused by steam or by the submarine. From the time that Helen's beauty launched a thousand ships until the battle of Lepanto, the oar had been the chief instrument of locomotion, though supplemented, even from Homeric times, by the sail. Naval battles were like those on land; the enemy keels approached and the soldiers on each strove to board and master the other's crew. The only distinctly naval tactic was that of "ramming," as it was called in a once vivid metaphor.

But the wild winds and boisterous waves of the Atlantic broke the oar in the galley-slave's hand and the muscles in his back. Once again man harnessed the hostile forces of nature; the free breezes were broken to the yoke and new types of sailing ships were driven at racing speed across the broad back of the sea. Swift, yare vessels were built, at first smaller than the old galleons but infinitely more manageable. And the new boats, armed with thunder as they were clad with wings, no longer sought to sink or capture enemies at close quarters, but hurled destruction from afar. Heavy guns took the place of small weapons and of armed prow.

It was England's genius for the sea that enabled her to master the new conditions first and most completely and that placed the trident in her hands so firmly that no enemy has ever been able to wrest it from her. Henry VIII paid great attention to the navy. He had fifty-three vessels with an aggregate of 11,268 tons, an average of 200 tons each, carrying 1750 soldiers, 1250 sailors and 2085 guns. Under Elizabeth the number of vessels had sunk to 42, but the tonnage had risen to 17,055, and the crews numbered 5534 seamen, 804 gunners and 2008 soldiers. The largest ships of the Tudor navy were of 1000 tons; the flagship of the Spanish Armada was 1150 tons, carrying 46 guns and 422 men. How tiny are these figures! A single cruiser of today has a larger tonnage than the whole of Elizabeth's fleet; a large submarine is greater than the monsters of Philip.

§ 4. Private Life and Manners

Of all the forces making for equality among men probably the education of the masses by means of cheap books and papers has been the strongest. But this force has been slow to ripen; at the close of the Middle Ages the common man was still helpless. The old privileged orders were indeed weakened and despoiled of part of their prerogatives, but it was chiefly by the rise of a new aristocracy, that of wealth.

Nobility

The decay of feudalism and of ecclesiastical privilege took the form of a changed and not of an abolished position for peer and priest. They were not cashiered, but they were retained on cheaper terms. The feudal baron had been a petty king; his descendant had the option of becoming either a highwayman or a courtier. As the former alternative became less and less rewarding, the greater part of the old nobles abandoned their pretensions to independence and found a congenial sphere as satellities of a monarch, "le roi soleil," as a typical king was aptly called, whose beams they reflected and around whom they circled.

As titles of nobility began now to be quite commonly given to men of wealth and also to politicians, the old blood was renewed at the expense of the ancient pride. Not, indeed, that the latter showed any signs of diminishing. The arrogance of the noble was past all toleration. Men of rank treated the common citizens like dirt beneath their feet, and even regarded artists and other geniuses as menials. Alphonso, duke of Ferrara, wrote to Raphael in terms that no king would now use to a photographer, calling him a liar and chiding him for disrespect to his superior. The same duke required Ariosto to prostitute his genius by writing an apology for a fratricide committed by his grace. The duke of Mayenne poniarded one of his most devoted followers for having aspired to the hand of the duke's widowed daughter-in-law. So difficult was it to conceive of a "gentleman" without gentle blood that Castiglione, the arbiter of manners, lays down as the first prerequisite to a perfect courtier that he shall be of high birth. And of course those who had not this advantage pretended to it. An Italian in London noticed in 1557 that all gentlemen without other title insisted on being called "mister."

Professions

One sign of the break-up of the old medieval castes was the new classification of men by calling, or profession. It is true that two of the professions, the higher offices in army and church, became apanages of the nobility, and the other liberal vocations were almost as completely monopolized by the children of the moneyed middle class; nevertheless it is significant that there were new roads by which men might rise. No class has profited more by the evolution of ideas than has the intelligentsia. From a subordinate, semi-menial position, lawyers, physicians, educators and journalists, not to mention artists and writers, have become the leading, almost the ruling, body of our western democracies.

Clergy

Half way between a medieval estate and a modern calling stood the clergy. In Catholic countries they remained very numerous; there were 136 episcopal or archiepiscopal sees in France; there were 40,000 parish priests, with an equal number of secular clergy in subordinate positions, 24,000 canons, 34,000 friars, 2500 Jesuits (in 1600), 12,000 monks and 80,000 nuns. Though there were doubtless many worthy men among them, it cannot honestly be said that the average were fitted either morally or intellectually for their positions. Grossly ignorant of the meaning of the Latin in which they recited their masses and of the main articles of their faith, many priests made up for these defects by proficiency in a variety of superstitious charms. The public was accustomed to see nuns dancing at bridals and priests haunting taverns and worse resorts. Some attempts, serious and partially successful, at reform, have been already described. Profane and amatory plays were forbidden in nunneries, bull-fights were banished from the Vatican and the dangers of the confessional were diminished by the invention of the closed box in which the priest should sit and hear his penitent through a small aperture instead of having her kneeling at his knees. So depraved was public opinion on the subject of the confession that a prolonged controversy took place in Spain as to whether minor acts of impurity perpetrated by the priest while confessing women were permissible or not.

Conditions of the Protestant clergy

Neither was the average Protestant clergyman a shining and a burning light. So little was the calling regarded that it was hard to fill it. At one time a third of the parishes of England were said to lack incumbents. The stipends were wretched; the social position obscure. The wives of the new clergy had an especially hard lot, being regarded by the people as little better than concubines, and by Parliament called "necessary evils." The English government had to issue injunctions in 1559 stating that because of the offence that has come from the type of women commonly selected as helpmates by parsons, no manner of priest or deacon should presume to marry without consent of the bishop, of the girl's parents, "or of her master or mistress where she serveth." Many clergymen, nevertheless, afterwards married domestics.

Very little was done to secure a properly trained ministry. Less than half of the 2000 clergymen ordained at Wittenberg from 1537–60 were university men; the majority were drapers, tailors and cobblers, "common idiots and laymen" as they were called—though the word "idiot" did not have quite the same disparaging sense that it has now. Nor were the reverend gentlemen of unusually high character. As nothing was demanded of them but purity of doctrine, purity of life sank into the background. It is really amazing to see how an acquaintance of Luther's succeeded in getting one church after he had been dismissed from another on well-founded charges of seduction, and how he was thereafter convicted of rape. This was perhaps an extreme case, but that the majority of clergymen were morally unworthy is the melancholy conviction borne in by contemporary records.

Character of sermons

Sermons were long, doctrinal and political. Cranmer advised Latimer not to preach more than an hour and a half lest the king grow weary. How the popular preacher—in this case a Catholic—appealed to his audience, is worth quoting from a sermon delivered at Landau in 1550.

> The Lutherans [began the reverend gentleman] are opposed to the worship of Mary and the saints. Now, my friends, be good enough to listen to me. The soul of a man who had died got to the door of heaven and Peter shut it in his face. Luckily, the Mother of God was taking a stroll outside with her sweet Son. The deceased addresses her and reminds her of the Paters and Aves he has recited in her glory and the candles he has burnt before her images. Thereupon Mary says to Jesus: "It's the honest truth, my Son." The Lord, however, objected and addressed the suppliant: "Hast thou never heard that I am the way and the door to life everlasting?" he asks. "If thou art the door, I am the window," retorted Mary, taking the "soul" by the hair and flinging it through the open casement. And now I ask you whether it is not the same whether you enter Paradise by the door or by the window?

There was a naïve familiarity with sacred things in our ancestors that cannot be imitated. Who would now name a ship "Jesus," as Hawkins's buccaneering slaver was named? What serious clergyman would now compare three of his friends to the Father, the Son and the Holy Ghost, as did Luther? The Reformer also wrote a satire on the calling of a council, in the form of a letter from the Holy Ghost signed by Gabriel as notary and witnessed by Michael the Provost of Paradise and Raphael, God's Court Physician. At another time he made a lampoon on the collection of relics made by his enemy the Archbishop of Mayence, stating that they contained such things as "a fair piece of Moses' left horn, a whole pound of the wind that blew for Elijah in the cave on Mount Horeb and two feathers and an egg of the Holy Ghost" as a dove. All this, of course, not in ribald profanity, but in works intended for edification. . . .

The city

Though beautiful, the city of our ancestors was far from admirable in other ways. Filth was hidden under its comely garments, so that it resembled a Cossack prince—all ermine and vermin. Its narrow streets, huddled between strong walls, were over-run with pigs and chickens and filled with refuse. They were often ill-paved, flooded with mud and slush in winter. Moreover they were dark and dangerous at night, infested with princes and young nobles on a spree and with other criminals.

The house

Like the exterior, the interior of the house of a substantial citizen was more pretty than clean or sweet smelling. The high wainscoting and the furniture, in various styles, but frequently resembling what is now known as "mission," was lovely, as were the ornaments—tapestries, clocks, pictures and flowers. But the place of carpets was supplied by rushes renewed from time to time without disturbing the underlying mass of rubbish beneath. Windows were fewer than they are now, and fires still fewer. Sometimes there was an open hearth, sometimes a huge tile stove. Most houses had only one or two rooms heated, sometimes, as in the case of the Augustinian friary at Wittenberg, only the bathroom, but usually also the living room.

Dress

The dress of the people was far more various and picturesque than nowadays. Both sexes dressed in gaudy colors and delighted in strange fashions, so that, as Roger Ascham said, "he thought himself most brave that was most monstrous in misorder." For women the fashion of decolleté was just coming in, as so many fashions do, from the demi-monde. To Catharine de' Medici is attributed the invention of the corset, an atrocity to be excused only by her own urgent need of one.

Food

The day began at five in summer and at seven in winter. A heavy breakfast was followed by a heavier dinner at ten, and supper at five, and there were between times two or three other tiffins or "drinkings." The staple food was meat and cereal; very few of our vegetables were known, though some were just beginning to be cultivated. The most valuable article of food introduced from the new world was the potato. Another importation that did not become thoroughly acclimatized in Europe was the turkey. Even now they are rare, but there are several interesting allusions to them in the literature of that time, one of the year 1533 in Luther's table talk. Poultry of other sorts was common, as were eggs, game and fish. The cooking relied for its highest effects on sugar and spices. The ordinary fruits—apples, cherries and oranges—furnished a wholesome and pleasing variety to the table. Knives and spoons were used in eating, but forks were unknown, at least in northern Europe.

1585–6

Drink

All the victuals were washed down with copious potations. A water-drinker, like Sir Thomas More, was the rarest of exceptions. The poor drank chiefly beer and ale; the mildest sort, known as "small beer," was recommended to the man suffering from too strong drink of the night before. Wine was more prized, and there were a number of varieties. There being no champagne, Burgundy was held in high esteem, as were some of the strong, sweet, Spanish and Portuguese wines. The most harmless drinks were claret and Rhine wine. There were some "mixed drinks," such as sack or hippocras, in which beer or wine was sophisticated with eggs, spices and sugar. The quantities habitually drunk were large. Roger Ascham records that Charles V drank the best he ever saw, never less than a quart at a draft. The breakfast table of an English nobleman was set out with a quart of wine and a quart of beer, liquor then taking the place of tea, coffee, chocolate and all the "soft" beverages that now furnish stimulation and sociability.

Tobacco, 1573

"In these times," wrote Harrison, "the taking-in of the smoke of an Indian herb called 'Tobaco' by an instrument formed like a little ladle . . . is greatly taken up and used in England against rewmes [colds] and some other diseases." Like other drugs, tobacco soon came to be used as a narcotic for its own sake, and was presently celebrated as "divine tobacco" and "our holy herb nicotian" by the poets. What, indeed, are smoking, drinking, and other wooings of pure sensation at the sacrifice of power and reason, but a sort of pragmatized poetry? Some ages, and those the most poetical, like that of Pericles and that of Rabelais, have deified intoxication and sensuality; others, markedly our own, have preferred the accumulation of wealth and knowledge to sensual indulgence. It is a psychological contrast of importance.

Could we be suddenly transported on Mr. Wells's time machine four hundred years back we should be less struck by what our ancestors had than by what they lacked. Quills took the place of fountain pens, pencils, typewriters and dictaphones. Not only was postage dearer but there were no telephones or telegrams to supplement it. The world's news of yesterday, which we imbibe with our morning cup, then sifted down slowly through various media of communication, mostly oral. It was two months after the battle before Philip of Spain knew the fate of his own Armada. The houses had no steam heat, no elevators; the busy housewife was aided by no vacuum cleaner, sewing machine and gas ranges; the business man could not ride to his office, nor the farmer to his market, in automobiles. There were neither railways nor steamships to make travel rapid and luxurious.

Travel

Nevertheless, journeys for purposes of piety, pleasure and business were common. Pilgrimages to Jerusalem, Rome, Compostella, Loretto, Walsingham and many other shrines were frequent in Catholic countries. Students were perpetually wandering from one university to another; merchants were on the road, and gentlemen felt the attractions of sight-seeing. The cheap and common mode of locomotion was on foot. Boats on the rivers and horses on land furnished the alternatives. The roads were so poor that the horses were sometimes "almost shipwrecked." The trip from Worms to Rome commonly took twelve days, but could be made in seven. Xavier's voyage from Lisbon to Goa took thirteen months. Inns were good in France and England; less pleasant elsewhere. Erasmus particularly abominated the German inns, where a large living and dining room would be heated to a high temperature by a stove around which travelers would dry their steaming garments. The smells caused by these operations, together with the fleas and mice with which the poorer inns were infested, made the stay anything but luxurious. Any complaint was met by the retort, "If you don't like it, go somewhere else," a usually impracticable alternative. When the traveller was escorted to his bedroom, he found it very cold in winter, though the featherbeds kept him warm enough. He would see his chamber filled with other beds occupied by his travelling companions of both sexes, and he himself was often forced to share his bed with a stranger. The custom of the time was to take one bath a week. For this there were public bath-houses, frequented by both sexes. A common form of entertainment was the "bath-party."

Baths

Sports

With the same insatiable gusto that they displayed in other matters the contemporaries of Luther and Shakespeare went in for amusements. Never has the theater been more popular. Many sports, like bear-baiting and bull-baiting, were cruel. Hunting was also much relished, though humane men like Luther and More protested against the "silly and woeful beastes' slaughter and murder." Tennis was so popular that there were 250 courts in Paris alone. The game was different from the modern in that the courts were 121 feet long, instead of 78 feet, and the wooden balls and "bats"—as racquets are still called in England—were much harder. Cards and dice were passionately played, a game called "triumph" or "trump" being the ancestor of our whist. Chess was played nearly as now.

Young people loved dances and some older people shook their heads over them, then as now. Melanchthon danced, at the age of forty-four, and Luther approved of such parties, properly chaperoned, as a means of bringing young people together. On the other hand dances were regulated in many states and prohibited in others, like Zurich and Geneva. Some of the dances were quite stately, like the minuet, others were boisterous romps, in which the girls were kissed, embraced and whirled around giddily by their partners. The Scotch ambassador's comment that Queen Elizabeth "danced very high" gives an impression of agility that would hardly now be considered in the best taste.

The veneer of courtesy was thin. True, humanists,

Manners

publicists and authors composed for each other eulogies that would have been hyperboles if addressed to the morning stars singing at the dawn of creation, but once a quarrel had been started among the touchy race of writers and a spouting geyser of inconceivable scurrility burst forth. No imagery was too nasty, no epithet too strong, no charge too base to bring against an opponent. The heroic examples of Greek and Roman invective paled before the inexhaustible resources of learned billingsgate stored in the minds of the humanists and theologians. To accuse an enemy of atheism and heresy was a matter of course; to add charges of unnatural vice or, if he were dead, stories of suicide and of the devils hovering greedily over his deathbed, was extremely common. Even crowned heads exchanged similar amenities.

Withal, there was growing up a strong appreciation of the merits of courtesy. Was not Bayard, the captain in the army of Francis I a "knight without fear and without reproach"? Did not Sir Philip Sidney do one of the perfect deeds of gentleness when, dying on the battle field and tortured with thirst, he passed his cup of water to a common soldier with the simple words, "Thy need is greater than mine"? One of the most justly famous and most popular books of the sixteenth century was Baldessare Castiglione's *Book of the Courtier,* called by Dr. Johnson the best treatise on good breeding ever written. Published in Italian in 1528, it was translated into Spanish in 1534, into French in 1537, into English and Latin in 1561, and finally into German in 1566. There have been of it more than 140 editions. It sets forth an ideal of a Prince Charming, a man of noble birth, expert in games and in war, brave, modest, unaffected, witty, an elegant speaker, a good dancer, familiar with literature and accomplished in music, as well as a man of honor and courtesy. It is significant that this ideal appealed to the time, though it must be confessed it was rarely reached. Ariosto, to whom the first book was dedicated by the author, depicts, as his ideals, knights in whom the sense of honor has completely replaced all Christian virtues. They were always fighting each other about their loves, much like the bulls, lions, rams and dogs to whom the poet continually compares them. Even the women were hardly safe in their company.

Sometimes a brief anecdote will stamp a character as no long description will do. The following are typical of the manners of our forbears:

One winter morning a stately matron was ascending the steps of the church of St. Gudule at Brussels. They were covered with ice; she slipped and took a precipitate and involuntary seat. In the anguish of the moment, a single word, of mere obscenity, escaped her lips. When the laughing bystanders, among whom was Erasmus, helped her to her feet, she beat a hasty retreat, crimson with shame. Nowadays ladies do not have such a vocabulary at their tongue's end.

The Spanish ambassador Enriquez de Toledo was at Rome calling on Imperia de Cugnatis, a lady who, though of the demi-monde, lived like a princess, cultivated letters and art, and had many poets as well as many nobles among her friends. Her floors were carpeted with velvet rugs, her walls hung with golden cloth, and her tables loaded with costly bric-à-brac. The Spanish courtier suddenly turned and spat copiously in the face of his lackey and then explained to the slightly startled company that he chose this objective rather than soil the splendor he saw around him. The disgusting act passed for a delicate and successful flattery.

1538 Among the students at Wittenberg was a certain Simon Lemchen, or Lemnius, a lewd fellow of the baser sort who published two volumes of scurrilous epigrams bringing unfounded and nasty charges against Luther, Melanchthon and the other Reformers and their wives. When he fled the city before he could be arrested, Luther revenged himself partly by a Catilinarian sermon, partly by composing, for circulation among his friends, some verses about Lemnius in which the scurrility and obscenity of the offending youth were well overtrumped. One would be surprised at similar measures taken by a professor of divinity today.

Morals

In measuring the morals of a given epoch statistics are not applicable; or, at any rate, it is probably true that the general impression one gets of the moral tone of any period is more trustworthy than would be got from carefully compiled figures. And that one does get such an impression, and a very strong one, is undeniable. Everyone has in his mind a more or less distinct idea of the ethical standards of ancient Athens, of Rome, of the Middle Ages, the Renaissance, the Puritan Commonwealth, the Restoration, the Victorian Age.

The sixteenth century was a time when morals were perhaps not much worse than they are now, but when vice and crime were more flaunted and talked about. Puritanism and prudery have nowadays done their best to conceal the corruption and indecency beneath the surface. But our ancestors had no such delicacy. The naïve frankness of the age, both when it gloried in the flesh and when it reproved sin, gives a full-blooded complexion to that time that is lacking now. The large average consumption of alcohol—a certain irritant to moral maladies—and the unequal administration of justice, with laws at once savage and corruptly dispensed, must have had bad consequences.

The Reformation had no permanent discernible effect on moral standards. Accompanied as it often was with a temporary zeal for righteousness, it was too often followed by a breaking up of conventional standards and an emphasis on dogma at the expense of character, that operated badly. Latimer thought that the English Reformation had been followed by a wave of wickedness. Luther said that when the devil of the papacy had been driven out, seven other devils entered to take its place, and that at Wittenberg a man was considered quite a saint who could say that he had not broken the first commandment, but only the other nine. Much of this complaint must be set down to disappointment at not reaching perfection, and over against it may be set many testimonies to the moral benefits assured by the reform.

Violence

It was an age of violence. Murder was common everywhere. On the slightest provocation a man of spirit was expected to whip out a rapier or dagger and plunge it into his insulter. The murder of unfaithful wives was an especial point of honor. Benvenuto Cellini boasts of several assassinations and numerous assaults, and he himself got off without a scratch from the law, Pope Paul III graciously protesting that "men unique in their profession, like Benvenuto, were not subject to the laws." The number of unique men must have been large in the Holy City, for in 1497 a citizen testified that he had seen more than a hundred bodies of persons foully done to death thrown into the Tiber, and no one bothered about it.

Brigandage

Brigandage stalked unabashed through the whole of Europe. By 1585 the number of bandits in the papal states alone had risen to 27,000. Sixtus V took energetic means to repress them. One of his stratagems is too characteristic to omit mentioning. He had a train of mules loaded with poisoned food and then drove them along a road he knew to be infested by highwaymen, who, as he had calculated, actually took them and ate of the food, of which many died.

Other countries were perhaps less scourged by robbers, but none was free. Erasmus's praise of Henry VIII, in 1519, for having cleared his realm of freebooters, was premature. In the wilder parts, especially on the Scotch border, they were still rife. In 1529 the Armstrongs of Lidderdale, just over the border, could boast that they had burned 52 churches, besides making heavy depredations on private property. When James V took stern measures to suppress them, and instituted a College of Justice for that purpose, the good law was unpopular.

1532

Bands of old soldiers and new recruits wandered through France, Spain and the Netherlands. The worst robbers in Germany were the free knights. From their picturesque castles they emerged to pillage peaceful villages and trains of merchandise going from one walled city to another. In doing so they inflicted wanton mutilations on the unfortunate merchants whom they regarded as their natural prey. Even the greatest of them, like Francis von Sickingen, were not ashamed to "let their horses bite off travellers' purses" now and then. But it was not only the nobles who became gentlemen of the road. A well-to-do merchant of Berlin, named John Kohlhase, was robbed of a couple of horses by a Saxon squire, and, failing to get redress in the corrupt courts, threw down the gauntlet to the whole of Electoral Saxony in a proclamation that he would rob, burn and take reprisals until he was given compensation for his loss. For six years he maintained himself as a highwayman, but was finally taken and executed in Brandenburg.

1534–40

Fraud

Fraud of all descriptions was not less rampant than force. When Machiavelli reduced to a reasoned theory the practice of all hypocrisy and guile, the courts of Europe were only too ready to listen to his advice. In fact, they carried their mutual attempts at deception to a point that was not only harmful to themselves, but ridiculous, making it a principle to violate oaths and to debase the currency of good faith in every possible way. There was also much untruth in private life. Unfortunately, lying in the interests of piety was justified by Luther, while the Jesuits made a soul-rotting art of equivocation.

Unchastity

The standard of sexual purity was disturbed by a reaction against the asceticism of the Middle Ages. Luther proclaimed that chastity was impossible, while the humanists gloried in the flesh. Public opinion was not scandalized by prostitution; learned men occasionally debated whether fornication was a sin, and the Italians now began to call a harlot a "courteous woman" (courtesan) as they called an assassin a "brave man" (bravo). Augustine had said that harlots were remedies against worse things, and the church had not only winked at brothels, but frequently licensed them herself. Bastardy was no bar to hereditary right in Italy.

c. 1500

The Reformers tried to make a clean sweep of the "social evil." Under Luther's direction brothels were closed in the reformed cities. When this was done at Strassburg the women drew up a petition, stating that they had pursued their profession not from liking but only to earn bread, and asked for honest work. Serious attempts were made to give it to them, or to get them husbands. At Zurich and some other cities the brothels were left open, but were put under the supervision of an officer who was to see that no married men frequented them. The reformers had a strange ally in the growing fear of venereal diseases. Other countries followed Germany in their war on the prostitute. In London the public houses of ill fame were closed in 1546, in Paris in 1560. An edict of July 23, 1566 commanded all prostitutes to leave Rome, but when 25,000 persons, including the women and their dependents, left the city, the loss of public revenue induced the pope to allow them to return on August 17 of the same year.

Polygamy

One of the striking aberrations of the sixteenth century, as it seems to us, was the persistent advocacy of polygamy as, if not desirable in itself, at least preferable to divorce. Divorce or annulment of marriage was not hard to obtain by people of influence, whether Catholic or Protestant, but it was a more difficult matter than it is in America now. In Scotland there was indeed a sort of trial marriage, known as "handfasting," by which the parties might live together for a year and a day and then continue as married or separate. But, beginning with Luther, many of the Reformers thought polygamy less wrong than divorce, on the biblical ground that whereas the former had been practised in the Old Testament times and was not clearly forbidden by the New Testament, divorce was prohibited save for adultery. Luther advanced this thesis as early as 1520, when it was purely theoretical, but he did not shrink from applying it on occasion. It is extraordinary what a large body of reputable opinion was prepared to tolerate polygamy, at least in exceptional cases. Popes, theologians, humanists like Erasmus, and philosophers like Bruno, all thought a plurality of wives a natural condition.

Marriage

But all the while the instincts of the masses were sounder in this respect than the precepts of their guides. While polygamy remained a freakish and exceptional practice, the passions of the age were absorbed to a high degree by monogamous marriage. Matrimony having been just restored to its proper dignity as the best estate for man, its praises were sounded highly. The church, indeed, remained true to her preference for celibacy, but the Inquisition found much business in suppressing the then common opinion that marriage was better than virginity. To the Reformers marriage was not only the necessary condition of happiness to mankind, but the typically holy estate in which God's service could best be done. From all sides paeans arose celebrating matrimony as the true remedy for sin and also as the happiest estate. The delights of wedded love are celebrated equally in Luther's table talk and letters and in the poems of the Italian humanist Pontano. "I have always been of the opinion," writes Ariosto, "that without a wife at his side no man can attain perfect goodness or live without sin." "In marriage there is one mind in two bodies," says Henry Cornelius Agrippa, "one harmony, the same sorrows, the same joys, an identical will, common riches, poverty and honors, the same bed and the same table. . . . Only a husband and wife can love each other infinitely and serve each other as long as both do live, for no love is either so vehement or so holy as theirs."

Remarriage common

The passion for marriage in itself is witnessed by the practice of widows and widowers of remarrying as soon and as often as possible. Luther's friend, Justus Jonas, married thrice, each time with a remark to the effect that it was better to marry than to burn. The English Bishop Richard Cox excused his second marriage, at an advanced age, by an absurd letter lamenting that he had not the gift of chastity. Willibrandis Rosenblatt married in succession Louis Keller, Oecolampadius, Capito and Bucer, the ecclesiastical eminence of her last three husbands giving her, one would think, an almost official position. Sir Thomas More married a second wife just one month after his first wife's death.

Treatment of wives

Sad to relate, the wives so necessary to men's happiness were frequently ill treated after they were won. In the sixteenth century women were still treated as minors; if married they could make no will; their husbands could beat them with impunity, for cruelty was no cause for divorce. Sir Thomas More's home-life is lauded by Erasmus as a very paragon, because "he got more compliance from his wife by jokes and blandishments than most husbands by imperious harshness." One of these jokes, a customary one, was that his wife was neither pretty nor young; one of the "blandishments," I suppose, was an epigram by Sir Thomas to the effect that though a wife was a heavy burden she might be useful if she would die and leave her husband money. In Utopia, he assures us, husbands chastise their wives.

Position of woman

In the position of women various currents crossed each other. The old horror of the temptress, inherited from the early church, the lofty scorn exhibited by the Greek philosophers, mingled with strands of chivalry and a still newer appreciation of the real dignity of woman and of her equal powers. Ariosto treated women like spoiled children; the humanists delighted to rake up the old jibes at them in musty authors; the divines were hardest of all in their judgment. "Nature doth paint them forth," says John Knox of women, "to be weak, frail, impatient, feeble and foolish, and experience hath declared them to be unconstant, variable, cruel and void of the spirit of council and regimen." "If women bear children until they become sick and eventually die," preaches Luther, "that does no harm. Let them bear children till they die of it; that is what they are for." In 1595 the question was debated at Wittenberg as to whether women were human beings. The general tone was one of disparagement. An anthology might be made of the proverbs recommending (à la Nietzsche) the whip as the best treatment for the sex.

But withal there was a certain chivalry that revolted against all this brutality. Castiglione champions courtesy and kindness to women on the highest and most beautiful ground, the spiritual value of woman's love. Ariosto sings:

> No doubt they are accurst and past all grace
> That dare to strike a damsel in the face,
> Or of her head to minish but a hair.

Certain works like T. Elyot's *Defence of Good Women* and like Cornelius Agrippa's *Nobility and Excellence of the Female Sex,* witness a genuine appreciation of woman's worth. Some critics have seen in the last named work a paradox, like the *Praise of Folly,* such as was dear to the humanists. To me it seems absolutely sincere, even when it goes so far as to proclaim that woman is as superior to man as man is to beast and to celebrate her as the last and supreme work of the creation.

Children

The family was far larger, on the average, in the sixteenth century than it is now. One can hardly think of any man in this generation with as many as a dozen children; it is possible to mention several of that time with over twenty. Anthony Koberger, the famous Nuremberg printer had twenty-five children, eight by his first and seventeen by his second wife. Albert Dürer was the third of eighteen children of the same couple, of whom apparently only three reached maturity. John Colet, born in 1467, was the eldest of twenty-two brothers and sisters of whom by 1499 he was the only survivor. Of course these families were exceptional, but not glaringly so. A brood of six to twelve was a very common occurrence.

Children were brought up harshly in many families,

strictly in almost all. They were not expected to sit in the presence of their parents, unless asked, or to speak unless spoken to. They must needs bow and crave a blessing twice a day. Lady Jane Grey complained that if she did not do everything as perfectly as God made the world, she was bitterly taunted and presently so nipped and pinched by her noble parents that she thought herself in hell. The rod was much resorted to. And yet there was a good deal of natural affection. Few fathers have even been better to their babies than was Luther, and he humanely advised others to rely as much on reward as on punishment—on the apple as on the switch—and above all not to chastise the little ones so harshly as to make them fear or hate their parents.

The *patria potestas* was supposed to extend, as it did in Rome, during the adult as during the callow years. Especially did public opinion insist on children marrying according to the wishes of their parents. Among the nobility child-marriage was common, a mere form, of course, not at once followed by cohabitation. A betrothal was a very solemn thing, amounting to a definite contract. Perfect liberty was allowed the engaged couple, by law in Sweden and by custom in many other countries. All the more necessary, in the opinion of the time, to prevent youths and maidens betrothing themselves without their parents' consent.

Health

Probably the standard of health is now higher than it was then, and the average longevity greater. It is true that few epidemics have ever been more fatal than the recent influenza; and on the other hand one can point to plenty of examples of sixteenth-century men who reached a crude and green old age. Statistics were then few and unreliable. In 1905 the death-rate in London was 15.6 per thousand; in the years 1861–1880 it averaged 23 per thousand. It has been calculated that this is just what the death-rate was in London in a healthy year under Elizabeth, but it must be remembered that a year without some sort of epidemic was almost exceptional.

Epidemics

Bubonic plague was pandemic at that time, and horribly fatal. Many of the figures given—as that 200,000 people perished in Moscow in 1570, 50,000 at Lyons in 1572, and 50,000 at Venice during the years 1575–7, must be gross exaggerations, but they give a vivid idea of the popular idea of the prevalent mortality. Another scourge was the sweating sickness, first noticed as epidemic in 1485 and returning in 1507, 1517, 1528 and 1551. Tuberculosis was probably as wide-spread in the sixteenth as it is in the twentieth century, but it figured less prominently on account of worse diseases and because it was seldom recognized until the last stages. Smallpox was common, unchecked as it was by vaccination, and with it were confounded a variety of zymotic diseases, such as measles, which only began to be recognized as different in the course of the sixteenth century. One disease almost characteristic of former ages, so much more prevalent was it in them, due to the more unwholesome food and drink, was the stone.

Venereal diseases became so prominent in the sixteenth century that it has often been thought that the syphilis was imported from America. This, however, has been denied by authorities who believe that it came down from classical antiquity, but that it was not differentiated from other scourges. The Latin name variola, like the English pox, was applied indiscriminately to syphilis, small-pox, chicken-pox, etc. Gonorrhea was also common. The spread of these diseases was assisted by many causes besides the prevalent moral looseness; by lack of cleanliness in public baths, for example.

Useless to go through the whole roster of the plagues. Suffice it to say that whatever now torments poor mortals, from tooth-ache to cold in the head, and from rheumatism to lunacy, was known to our ancestors in aggravated forms. Deleterious was the use of alcohol, the evils of which were so little understood that it was actually prescribed for many disorders of which it is a certain irritant. Add to this the lack of sanitary measures, not only of disinfection but of common cleanliness, and the etiology of the phenomena is satisfactorily accounted for.

Medicine

If even now medicine as a science and an art seems backward compared with surgery, it has nevertheless made considerable advances since it began to be empirical. In the Middle Ages it was almost purely dogmatic; men did not ask their eyes and minds what was the nature of the human body and the effect of this or that drug on it, they asked Aristotle, or Hippocrates, or Galen or Avicenna. The chief rivalries, and they were bitter, were between the Greek and the Arabian schools. Galenism finally triumphed just before the beginnings of experiment and research were made. The greatest name in the first half of the century was that of Theophrastus Paracelsus, as arrant a quack as ever lived, but one who did something to break up the strangle-hold of tradition. He worked out his system *a priori* from a fantastic postulate of the parallelism between man and the universe, the microcosm and the macrocosm. He held that the Bible gave valuable prescriptions, as in the treatment of wounds by oil and wine.

c. 1550

Paracelsus, 1493–1541

Surgery

Paré, 1510–90

Under the leadership of Ambroise Paré surgery improved rather more than medicine. Without anaesthetics, indeed, operations were difficult, but a good deal was accomplished. Paré first made amputation on a large scale possible by inventing a ligature for large arteries that effectively controlled hemorrhage. This barber's apprentice, who despised the schools and wrote in the vernacular, made other important improvements in the surgeon's technique. It is noteworthy that each discovery was treated as a trade secret to be exploited for the benefit of a few practitioners and not given freely to the good of mankind.

In obstetrics Paré also made discoveries that need not be detailed here. Until his time it was almost universal for women to be attended in childbirth only by midwives of their own sex. Indeed, so strong was the prejudice on this point that women were known to die of abdominal tumors rather than allow male physicians to examine them. The admission of men to the profession of midwife marked a considerable improvement in method.

Lunacy

The treatment of lunacy was inept. The poor patients were whipped or otherwise tormented for alluding to the subject of their monomania. Our ancestors found fun in watching the antics of crazed minds, and made up parties to go to Bedlams and tease the insane. Indeed, some of the scenes in Shakespeare's plays, in which madness is depicted, and which seem tragic to us, probably had a comic value for the groundlings before whom the plays were first produced.

Hospitals

As early as 1510 Luther saw one of the hospitals at Florence. He tells how beautiful they were, how clean and well served by honorable matrons tending the poor freely all day without making known their names and at night returning home. Such institutions were the glory of Italy, for they were sadly to seek in other lands. When they were finally established elsewhere, they were too often left to the care of ignorant and evil menials. The stories one may read of the Hôtel-Dieu, at Paris, are fairly hair-raising.

CHAPTER XI

THE CAPITALISTIC REVOLUTION

§ 1. The Rise of the Power of Money

Reformation and economic revolution

Parallel with the Reformation was taking place an economic revolution even deeper and more enduring in its consequences. Both Reformation and Revolution were manifestations of the individualistic spirit of the age; the substitution, in the latter case, of private enterprise and competition for common effort as a method of producing wealth and of distributing it. Both were prepared for long before they actually upset the existing order; both have taken several centuries to unfold their full consequences, and in each the truly decisive steps were taken in the sixteenth century.

It is doubtless incorrect to see either in the Reformation or in the economic revolution a direct and simple cause of the other. They interacted and to a certain extent joined forces; but to a greater degree each sought to use the other, and each has at times been credited, or blamed, with the results of the other's operations. Contemporaries noticed the effects, mostly the bad effects, of the rise of capitalism, and often mistakenly attributed them to the Reformation; and the new kings of commerce were only too ready to hide behind the mask of Protestantism while despoiling the church. Like other historical forces, while easily separable in thought, the two movements were usually inextricably interwoven in action.

Rise of capitalism

Capitalism supplanted gild-production because of its fitness as a social instrument for the production and storing of wealth. In competition with capital the medieval communism succumbed in one line of business after another—in banking, in trade, in mining, in industry and finally in agriculture—because it was unable to produce the results that capital produced. By the vast reward that the newer system gave to individual enterprise, to technical improvement and to investment, capitalism proved the aptest tool for the creation and preservation of wealth ever devised. It is true that the manifold multiplication of riches in the last four centuries is due primarily to inventions for the exploitation of natural resources, but the capitalistic method is ideally fitted for the utilization of these new discoveries and for laying up of their increment for ultimate social use. And this is an inestimable service to any society. Only a fairly rich people can afford the luxuries of beauty, knowledge, and power, that enhance the value of life and allow it to climb to ever greater heights. To balance this service, it must be taken into account that capitalism has lamentably failed justly to distribute rewards. Its tendency is to intercept the greater part of the wealth it creates for the benefit of a single class, and thereby to rob the rest of the communitiy of their due dividend.

Primary cause of the capitalistic revolution

So delicate is the adjustment of society that an apparently trivial new factor will often upset the whole equilibrium and produce the most incalculable results. Thus, the primary cause of the capitalistic revolution appears to have been a purely mechanical one, the increase in the production of the precious metals. Wealth could not be stored at all in the Middle Ages save in the form of specie; nor without it could large commerce be developed, nor large industry financed, nor was investment possible. Moreover the rise of prices consequent on the increase of the precious metals gave a powerful stimulus to manufacture and a fillip to the merchant and to the entrepreneur such as they have rarely received before or since. It was, in short, the development of the power of money that gave rise to the money power.

In the earlier Middle Ages there prevailed a "natural economy," or system in which payments were made chiefly in the form of services and by barter; this gave place very gradually to our modern "money economy" in which gold and silver are both the normal standards of value and the sole instruments of exchange. Already in the twelfth century money was being used in the towns of Western Europe; not until the late fourteenth or fifteenth did it become a dominant factor in rural life. This change was not the great revolution itself, but was the indispensable prerequisite of it, and in large part its direct cause.

Money-making kings

Gold and silver could now be hoarded in the form of money, and so the first step was taken in the formation of large fortunes, known to the ancient world, but almost absent in the Middle Ages. The first great fortunes were made by kings, by nobles with large landed estates, and by officers in government service. Henry VII left a large fortune to his son. Some of the popes and some of the princes of Germany and Italy hoarded money even when they were paying interest on a debt, —a testimony to the increasing estimate of the value of hard cash. The chief nobles were scarcely behind the kings in accumulating treasure. Their vast revenues from land were much more like government imposts than like rents. Thus Montmorency in France gave his daughter a dowry amounting to $420,000. The duke of Gandia in Spain owned estates peopled by 60,000 Moriscos and yielding a princely revenue. Vast ransoms were exacted in war, and fines, confiscation and pillage filled the coffers of the lords. After the atrocious war against the Moriscos, the duke of

Lerma sold their houses on his estates for 500,000 ducats.

Officials

In the monarchies of Europe the only avenue to wealth at first open to private men was the government service. Offices, benefices, naval and military commands, were bought with the expectation, often justified, of making money out of them. The farmed revenues yielded immense profit to the collectors. No small fortunes were reaped by Empson and Dudley, the tools of Henry VII, but they were far surpassed by the hoards of Wolsey and of Cromwell. Such was the great fortune made in France by Semblançay, the son of a plain merchant of Tours, who turned the offices of treasurer and superintendent of finances to such good account that he bought himself large estates and baronies. Fortunes on a proportionately smaller scale were made by the servants of the German princes, as by John Schenitz, a minion of the Archbishop Elector Albert of Mayence. So insecure was the tenure of riches accumulated in royal or princely service that most of the men who did so, including all those mentioned in this paragraph, ended on the scaffold, save, indeed, Wolsey, who would have done so had he not died while awaiting trial.

It is to be noted that, though land was the principal form of wealth in the Middle Ages, no great fortunes were made from it at the beginning of the capitalistic era, save by the titled holders of enormous domains. The small landlords suffered at the expense of the burghers in Germany, and not until these burghers turned to the country and bought up landed estates did agriculture become thoroughly profitable.

Banking

The intimate connection of government and capitalism is demonstrated by the fact that, next to officials, government concessionaires and bankers were the first to make great fortunes. At this time banking was closely dependent on public loans and was therefore the first great business to be established on the capitalistic basis. The first "trust" was the money trust. Though banking had been well started in the Middle Ages, it was still in an imperfect state of development. Jews and goldsmiths made a considerable number of commercial loans but these loans were always regarded by the borrower as temporary expedients; the habitual conduct of business on borrowed capital was unknown. But, just as the new output of the German mines was increasing the supply of precious metals, the greater costliness of war, due to the substitution of mercenaries and fire-arms for feudal levies equipped with bows and pikes, made the governments of Europe need money more than ever before. They made great loans at home and abroad, and it was the interest on these that expanded the banking business until it became an international power. Well before the sixteenth century men had made a fine art of receiving deposits, loaning capital and performing other financial operations, but it was not until the late fifteenth century that the bankers reaped the full reward of their skill and of the new opportunities. The three balls in the arms of the Medici testify to the heights to which a profession, once humble, might raise its experts. In Italy the science of accounting, or of double-entry bookkeeping, originated; it was slowly adopted in other lands. The first English work on the subject is that by John Gouge in 1543, entitled: "A Profitable Treatyce called the Instrument or Boke to learn to know the good order of the keeping of the famouse reconnynge, called in Latin, Dare et Habere, and, in Englyshe, Debitor and Creditor." It was in Italy that modern technique of clearing bills was developed; the simple system by which balances are settled not by full payment of each debt in money, but by comparing

Science of accounting

the paper certificates of indebtedness. This immense saving, as developed by the Genoese, was soon extended from their own city to the whole of Northern Italy, so that the bankers would meet several times a year in the first international clearing-house. From Genoa the same system was then applied to distant cities, with great profit, even more in security than in saving of capital. If bills payable at Antwerp were bought at Genoa, they were paid at Antwerp by selling bills on Lisbon, perhaps, and these in turn by selling exchange on Genoa. These processes seem simple and are now universal, but how vastly they facilitated the development of banking and business when first discovered can hardly be over-estimated.

From the improvement of exchange the Genoese soon proceeded to arbitrage, a transaction more profitable and more socially useful at that time when poor communications made the differences in prices between bills of exchange, bullion, coins, stocks and bonds in distant markets more considerable than they are now. The Genoese bankers also invented the first substitutes for money in the form of circulating notes. In all this, and in other ways, they made enormous profits that soon induced others to copy them.

Great firms

Though the Italians invented modern banking they were eventually surpassed by the Germans, if not in technique at least in the size of the firms established. The largest Florentine bank in 1529 was that of Thomas Guadegni with a capital of 520,000 florins ($1,170,000). The capital of the house of Fugger at Augsburg, distinct from the personal fortunes of its members, was in 1546, 4,700,000 gold gulden ($11,500,000). The average annual profits of the Fuggers during the years 1511–27 were 54.5 per cent.; from 1534–6, 2.2 per cent.; from 1540–46, 19 per cent.; from 1547–53, 5.6 per cent. Another Augsburg firm, the Welsers, averaged 9 per cent. for the fifteen years 1502–17. Dividends were not declared annually, but a general casting up of accounts was made every few years and a new balance struck, each partner withdrawing as much as he wished, or leaving it to be credited to his account as new capital.

Risks of banking

Though the Fuggers and other firms soon went into large business of all sorts, they remained primarily bankers. As such they enjoyed boundless credit with the public from whom they received deposits at regular interest. The proportion of these deposits to the capital continually rose. This general tendency, together with the habit of changing the amount of capital every few years, is evident from the following table of the liabilities of the Fuggers in gold gulden at several different periods:

Year	*Capital*	*Deposits*
1527	2,000,000	290,000
1536	1,500,000	900,000
1546	4,700,000	1,300,000
1563	2,000,000	3,100,000
1577	1,300,000	4,000,000

A smaller Augsburg firm, the Haugs, had in 1560, a capital of 140,000 florins and deposits of 648,000. As all these deposits were subject to be withdrawn at sight, and as the firms usually kept a very small reserve of specie, it would seem that banking was subject to great risks. The unsoundness of the method was counterbalanced by the fact that most of the deposits were made by members of the banker's family, or by friends, who harbored a strong sentiment against embarrassing the bank by withdrawing at inconvenient seasons. Doubtless the almost uniformly profitable career of most firms for many years concealed many dangers.

The crash came finally as the result of the bankruptcy

Bankruptcy of France and Spain, 1557

of the Spanish and French governments. Spain's repudiation of her debt was partial, taking the form of consolidation and conversion; France, however, simply stopped all payments of interest and amortization. Many banks throughout Europe failed, and drew down with them their creditors. The years 1557–64 saw the first of these characteristically modern phenomena, international financial crises. There were hard times everywhere. Other states followed the example of the French and Spanish governments, England constituting the fortunate exception. Recovery followed at length, however, and speculation boomed; but a second

1575

Spanish state bankruptcy brought on another crisis, and there was a third, following the defeat of the Armada. The failure of many of the great private companies was followed by the institution of state banks. The first to be erected was the Banco di

1587

Rialto in Venice.

The banks were the agencies for the spread of the capitalistic system to other fields. The great firms either bought up, or obtained as concessions from some government, the natural resources requisite for the production of wealth. One of the very first things

Mining

seized by them were the mines. Indeed, the profitable exploitation of the German mines especially dates from their acquisition by the Fuggers and other bankers late in the fifteenth century. Partly by the development of new methods of refining ore, but chiefly by driving large numbers of laborers to their maximum effort, the new mine-owners increased the production of metal almost at a bound, and thereby poured untold wealth into their own coffers. The total value of metals produced in Germany in 1525 amounted to $4,800,000 per annum, and employed over 100,000 men. Until 1545 the German production of silver was greater than the American, and copper was almost as valuable a product. Notwithstanding its increased production, its value doubled between 1527 and 1557. The shares in these great companies were, like the "Fugger letters," or certificates of interest-bearing deposits in banks, assignable and were actively traded in on various bourses. Each share was a certificate of partnership which then carried with it unlimited liability for the debts of the company. One of the favorite speculative issues was found in the shares of the Mansfeld Copper Co., established in 1524 with a capital of 70,000 gulden, which was increased to 120,000 gulden in 1528.

Commerce

Whereas, in banking and in mining, capital had almost created the opportunities for its employment, in commerce it partly supplanted the older system and partly entered into new paths. In the Middle Ages domestic, and to some extent international, commerce was carried on by fairs adapted to bring producer and consumer together and hence reduce the functions of middleman to the narrowest limits. Such was the annual fair at Stourbridge; such the famous bookmart at Frankfort-on-the-Main, and such were the fairs in Lyons, Antwerp, and many other cities. Only in the larger towns was a market perpetually open. Foreign commerce was also carried on by companies formed on the analogy of the medieval gilds.

New conditions called for fresh means of meeting them. The great change in sea-borne trade effected by the discovery of the new routes to India and America, was not so much in the quantity of goods carried as in the paths by which they traveled. The commerce of the two inland seas, the Mediterranean and the Baltic, relatively declined, while that of the Atlantic seaboard grew by leaps and bounds. New and large companies came into existence, formed on the joint-stock principle. Over them the various governments exercised a large control, giving them a semi-political character.

Portugal

As Portugal was the first to tap the wealth of the gorgeous East, into her lap fell the stream of gold from that quarter. The secret of her windfall was the small bulk and enormous value of her cargoes. From Malabar she fetched pepper and ginger, from Ceylon cinnamon and pearls, from Bengal opium, the only known conqueror of pain, and with it frankincense and indigo. Borneo supplied camphor, Amboyna nutmegs and mace, and two small islands, Temote and Tidor, offered cloves. These products sold for forty times as much in London or in Antwerp as they cost in the Orient. No wonder that wealth came in a gale of perfume to Lisbon. The cost of the ship and of the voyage, averaging two years from departure to return, was $20,000, and any ship might bring back a cargo worth $750,000. But the risks were great. Of the 104 ships that sailed from 1497–1506 only 72 returned. In the following century of about 800 Portuguese vessels engaged in the India trade nearly one-eighth were lost. Even the risk of loss in sailing from Lisbon to the ports of northern Europe was appreciable. The king of Portugal insured ships on a voyage from Lisbon to Antwerp for a premium of six per cent.

Spain

Spain found the path towards the setting sun as golden as Portugal had found the reflection of his rising beams. At her height she had a thousand merchant galleons. The chief imports were the precious metals, but they were not the only ones. Cochineal, selling at $370 a hundredweight in London, surpassed in value any spice from Celebes. Dye-wood, ebony, some drugs, nuts and a few other articles richly repaid importation. There was also a very considerable export trade. Cadiz and Seville sent to the Indies annually 2,240,000 gallons of wine, with quantities of oil, clothes and other necessities. Many ships, not only Spanish but Portuguese and English, were weighted with human flesh from Africa as heavily as Christian with his black load of sin, and in the case of Portugal, at least, the load almost sent its bearer to the City of Destruction.

But Spanish keels made other wakes than westward. To Flanders oil and wool were sent to be exchanged for manufactured wares, tapestries and books. Italy asked hides and dyes in return for her brocades, pearls and linen. The undoubtedly great extent of Spanish commerce even in places where it had no monopoly, is all the more remarkable in that it was at the first burdened by what in the end choked it, government regulation. Cadiz had the best harbor, but Seville was favored by the king; even ships allowed to unload at Cadiz could do so only on condition that their cargoes be transported directly to Seville. A particularly crushing tax was the alcabala, or 10 per cent. impost on all sales. Other import duties, royalties on metals, excise on food, monopolies, and petty regulations finally handicapped Spain's merchants so effectually that they fell behind those of other countries in the race for supremacy.

France

As the mariners of the Iberian peninsula drooped under the shackles of unwise laws, hardy sailors sprang into their places. Neither of the other Latin nations, however, was able to do so. The once proud supremacy of Venice and of Genoa was gone; the former sank as Lisbon rose and the latter, who held her own at least as a money market until 1540, was about that time surpassed, though she was never wholly superseded, by Antwerp. Italy exported wheat, flax, woad and other products, but chiefly by land routes or in foreign keels. Nor was France able to take any great part in maritime trade. Content with the freight brought her by other nations, she sent out few expeditions, and those few, like that of James Cartier, had no present result either in commerce or in colonies. Her greatest mart was Lyons, the fairs there being carefully fostered by the kings and being naturally favored by the growth of manufacture, while the maritime harbors either declined or at least gained nothing. For a few years La Rochelle battened on religious piracy, but that was all.

Germany

In no country is the struggle for existence between the medieval and the modern commercial methods plainer than in Germany. The trade of the Hanse towns failed to grow, partly for the reason that their merchants had not command of the fluid wealth that raised to pre-eminence the southern cities. There were, indeed, other causes for the decline of the Hanseatic Baltic trade. The discovery of new routes, especially the opening of Archangel on the White Sea, short-circuited the current that had previously flowed through the Kattegat and the Skager Rak. Moreover, the development of both wheat-growing and of commerce in the Netherlands and in England proved disastrous to the Hanse. The shores of the Baltic had at one time been the granary of Europe, but they suffered somewhat by the greater yield of the more intensive agriculture introduced at that time elsewhere. Even then their export continued to be considerable, though diverted from the northern to the southern ports of Europe. In 1563, for example, 6630 loads of grain were exported from Königsberg, and in 1573 7730 loads.

The Hanse towns lost their English trade in competition with the new companies there formed. A bitter diplomatic struggle was carried on by Henry VIII. The privileges to the Germans of the Steelyard confirmed and extended by him were abridged by his son, partly restored by Mary and again taken away by Elizabeth. The emperor, in agreement with the cities' senates, started retaliatory measures against English merchants, endeavoring to assure the Hanse towns that they should at least "continue the ancient concord of their dear native country and the good Dutches that now presently inhabit it.'" He therefore ordered English merchants banished, against which Elizabeth protested.

While the North of Germany was suffering from its failure to adapt itself to new conditions, a power was rising in the South capable of levying tribute not only from the whole Empire but from the habitable earth. Among the merchant princes who, in Augsburg, in Nuremberg, in Strassburg, placed on their own brows the golden crown of riches, the Fuggers were both typical and supreme. James Fugger "the Rich," springing from a family already opulent, was one of those geniuses of finance that turn everything touched into gold. He carried on a large banking business, he loaned money to emperors and princes, he bought up mines and fitted out fleets, he re-organized great industries, he speculated in politics and religion. For the princes of the empire he farmed taxes; for the pope he sold indulgences at a 33 1/3 per cent. commission, and collected annates and other dues. In Hungary, in Spain, in Italy, in the New World, his agents were delving for money and skilfully diverting it into his coffers. He was also a pillar of the church and a philanthropist, founding a library at Augsburg and building model tenements for poor workers. He became the incarnation of a new Great Power, that of international finance. A contemporary chronicler says: "emperors, kings, princes and governors have sent ambassage unto him; the pope hath greeted him as his beloved son and hath embraced him; cardinals have risen before him. . . . He hath become the glory

James Fugger, 1459–1525

of the whole German land." His sons, Raymond, Anthony and Jerome, were raised by Charles V to the rank and privileges of counts, bannerets and barons.

Throughout the century corporations became less and less family partnerships and more and more impersonal or "soulless." They were semi-public, semi-private affairs, resting on special charters and actively promoted, not only in Germany but in England and other countries, by the emperor, king, or territorial prince. On the other hand the capital was largely subscribed by private business men and the direction of the companies' affairs was left in their hands. Liability was unlimited.

Monopolies

In their methods many of the sixteenth century corporations were surprisingly "modern." Monopolies, corners, trusts and agreements to keep up prices flourished, notwithstanding constant legislation against them, as that against secret schedules of prices passed by the Diet of Nuremberg. Particularly noteworthy were the number of agreements to create a monopoly price in metals. Thus a ring of German mine-owners was formed artificially to raise the price of silver, a measure defended publicly on the ground that it enriched Germany at the expense of the foreigner. Another example was the formation of a tinning company under the patronage of Duke George of Saxony. It proposed agreements with its Bohemian rivals to fix the price of tin, but these usually failed even after a monopoly of Bohemian tin had been granted by Ferdinand to Conrad Mayr of Augsburg.

1522–3

1524

1518

1549

Corners

The immense difficulty of cornering any of the larger articles of commerce was not so well appreciated in the earlier time as it is now. Nothing is more instructive than the history of the mercury "trusts" of those years. When the competing companies owning mines at Idria in Carniola amalgamated for the purpose of

1523

enhancing the price of quicksilver, the attempt broke down by reason of the Spanish mines. Accordingly, one Ambrose Höchstetter of Augsburg conceived the ambitious project of cornering the whole supply of the world. As has happened so often since, the higher price brought forth a much larger quantity of the article than had been reckoned with, the so-called "invisible supply"; the corner broke down and Höchstetter failed with enormous liabilities of 800,000 gulden, and died in prison. The crash shook the financial world, but was nevertheless followed by still better planned and better financed efforts of the Fuggers to put the whole quicksilver product of the world into an international trust. These final attempts were more or less successful. Another ambitious scheme, which failed, was that of Conrad Rott of Augsburg to get a monopoly of pepper. He agreed to buy six hundred tons of pepper from the king of Portugal one year and one thousand tons the next, at the rate of 680 ducats the ton, but even this failed to give him the desired monopoly.

1528

1570 ff.

Regulation of monopolies

Just as in our own memory the trusts have aroused popular hatred and have brought down on their heads many attempts, usually unsuccessful, of governments to deal with them, so at the beginning of the capitalistic era, intense unpopularity was the lot of the new commercial methods and their exponents. Monopolies were fiercely denounced in the contemporary German tracts and every Diet made some effort to deal with them. First of all the merchants had to meet not only the envy and prejudices of the old order, but the positive teachings of the church. The prohibition of usury, and the doctrine that every article had a just or natural price, barred the road of the early entrepreneur. Aquinas believed that no one should be allowed to make more money than he needed and that profits on commerce should be scaled down to such a point that they would give only a reasonable return. This idea was shared by Catholic and Protestant alike in the first years of the Reformation; it can be found in Geiler of Kaiserberg and in Luther. In the Reformer's influential tract, *To the German Nobility*, usury and "Fuggerei" are denounced as the greatest misfortunes of Germany. Ulrich von Hutten said that of the four classes of robbers, free-booting knights, lawyers, priests and merchants, the merchants were the worst.

1520

The imperial Diets reflected popular opinion faithfully enough to try their best to bridle the great companies. The Diet of Trèves-Cologne asked that monopolies and artificial enhancement of the prices of spice, copper and woolen cloth be prohibited. To effect this acts were passed intended to insure competition. This law against monopolies, however, was not vigorously enforced until the Imperial Treasurer cited before his tribunal many merchants of Augsburg accused of violating it. The panic-stricken offenders feverishly hastened to make interest with the princes and city magistrates. But their main support was the emperor, who intervened energetically in their favor. From this time the bankers and great merchants labored hard at each Diet to place the control of monopolies in the hands of the monarch. In return for his constant support he was made a large sharer in the profits of the great houses.

1512

1523

In the struggle with the Diets, at last the capitalists were thoroughly successful. The Imperial Council of Regency passed an epoch-making ordinance, kept secret for fear of the people, expressly allowing merchants to sell at the highest prices they could get and recognizing certain monopolies said to be in the national interest as against other countries, and justified for the wages they provided for labor. About this

1525

time, for some reason, the agitation gradually died down. It is probable that the religious controversy took the public's mind off economic questions and the Peasant's War, like all unsuccessful but dangerous risings of the poor, was followed by a strong reaction in favor of the conservative rich. Moreover, it is evident that the currents of the time were too strong to be resisted by the feeble methods proposed by the reformers. When we remember that the chief practical measure recommended by Luther was the total prohibition of trading in spices and other foreign wares that took money out of the country, it is easy to see that the regulation of a complex industry was beyond the scope of his ability. And little, if any, enlightenment came from other quarters.

The Netherlands

While the towns of southern Germany were becoming the world's banking and industrial centers, the cities of the Netherlands became its chief staple ports. For generations Antwerp had had two fairs a year, but in 1484 it started a perpetual market, open to all merchants, even to foreigners, the whole year round, and in addition to this it increased its fairs to four. Later a new Merchants' Exchange or Bourse was built in which almost all the transactions now seen on our stock or produce exchanges took place. There was wild speculation, partly on borrowed money, especially in pepper, the price of which furnished a sort of barometer of bourse feeling. Bets on prices and on events were made, and from this practice various forms of insurance took their rise.

1531

Antwerp

The discovery of the new world brought an era of prosperity to Antwerp that doubtless put her at the head of all commercial cities until the Spanish sword cut her down. In 1560 there were commonly 2500 ships anchored in her harbor, as against 500 at Amsterdam, her chief rival and eventual heir. Of these not uncommonly as many as 500 sailed in one day, and, it is said, 12,000 carriages came in daily, 2000 with passengers and 10,000 with wares. Even if these statements are considerable exaggerations, a reliable account of the exports in the single year 1560 shows the real greatness of the town. The total imports in that year amounted to 31,870,000 gulden ($17,848,000), divided as follows: Italian silks, satins and ornaments 6,000,000 gulden; German dimities 1,200,000; German wines 3,000,000; Northern wheat 3,360,000; French wine 2,000,000; French dyes 600,000; French salt 360,000; Spanish wool 1,250,000; Spanish wine 1,600,000; Portuguese spices 2,000,000; English wool 500,000; English cloth 10,000,000. The last named article indicates the decay of Flemish weaving due to English competition. For a time there had been war to the knife with English merchants, following the great commercial treaty popularly called the *Malus Intercursus*. According to the theory then held that one nation's loss was another's gain, this treaty was considered a masterpiece of policy in England and the foundation of her commercial greatness. It and its predecessor, the *Magnus Intercursus,* marked the new policy, characteristic of modern times, that made commercial advantages a chief object of diplomacy and of legislation. Protective tariffs were enacted, the export of gold and silver prohibited, and sumptuary laws passed to encourage domestic industries. The policy as to export varied throughout the century and according to the article. The value of ships was highly appreciated. Sir Walter Raleigh opined that command of the sea meant command of the world's riches and ultimately of the world itself. Sir Humphrey Gilbert drew up a report advocating the acquisition of colonies as means of providing markets for home products. So little were the rights of the natives consid-

1506 Commercial policy

1496

ered that Sir Humphrey stated that the savages would be amply rewarded for all that could be taken from them by the inestimable gift of Christianity.

Buccaneering

As little regard was shown for the property of Catholics as for that of heathens. Merry England drew her dividends from slave-trading and from buccaneering as well as from honest exchange of goods. There is something fascinating about the career of a man like Sir John Hawkins whose character was as infamous as his daring was serviceable. He early learned that "negroes were very good merchandise in Hispaniola and that they might easily be had upon the coast of Guinea," and so, financed by the British aristocracy and blessed by Protestant patriots, he chartered the *Jesus of Lübeck* and went burning, stealing and body-snatching in West African villages, crowded his hold full of blacks and sold those of them who survived at $800 a head in the Indies. Quite fittingly he received as a crest "a demi-Moor, proper, in chains." He then went preying on the Spanish galleons, and at one time swindled Philip out of $200,000 by pretending to be a traitor and a renegade; thus he rose from slaver to pirate and from pirate to admiral.

English commerce

So pious, patriotic and profitable a business as buccaneering absorbed a greater portion of England's energies than did ordinary maritime commerce. A list of all ships engaged in foreign trade in 1572 shows that they amounted to an aggregate of only 51,000 tons burden, less than that of a single steamer of the largest size today. The largest ship that could reach London was of 240 tons, but some twice as large anchored at other harbors. Throughout the century trade multiplied, that of London, which profited the most, tenfold. If the customs' dues furnish an accurate barometer for the volume of trade, while London was increasing the other ports were falling behind not only relatively but positively. In the years 1506–9 London yielded to the treasury $60,000 and other ports $75,000; in 1581–2 London paid $175,000 and other ports only $25,000.

As she grew in size and wealth London, like Antwerp, felt the need of permanent fairs. From the continental city Sir Thomas Gresham, the English financial agent in the Netherlands, brought architect and materials and erected the Royal Exchange on the north side of Cornhill in London, where the same institution stands today. Built by Gresham at his own expense, it was lined by a hundred small shops rented by him. As the new was rung in, the old passed away. The ancient restrictions on the fluidity of capital were almost broken down by the end of Elizabeth's reign. The statutes of bankruptcy, giving new and strong securities to creditors, marked the advent to power of the commercial class. Capitalism took form in the chartering of large companies. The first of these, "the mistery and company of the Merchant Adventurers for the discovery of regions, dominions, islands and places unknown," commonly called the Russia Company, was a joint-stock corporation with 240 members, each with a share valued at $125. It traded principally with Russia, but, before the century was out, was followed by the Levant Company, the East India Company, and others, for the exploitation of other regions.

1568

1542 and 1571

1553

To northern Spain England sent coarse cloth, cottons, sheepskins, wheat, butter and cheese, and brought back wine, oranges, lemons and timber. To France went wax, tallow, butter, cheese, wheat, rye, "Manchester cloth," beans and biscuit in exchange for pitch, rosin, feathers, prunes and "great ynnions that be xii or xiiii ynches aboute," iron and wine. To the Russian Baltic ports, Riga, Reval and Narva went coarse cloth, "corrupt" (*i.e.,* adulterated) wine, cony-skins, salt and brandy, and from the same came flax, hemp, pitch, tar, tallow, wax and furs. Salmon from Ireland and other fish from Scotland and Denmark were paid for by "corrupt" wines. To the Italian ports of Leghorn, Barcelona, Civita Vecchia and Venice, and to the Balearic Isles went lead, fine cloth, hides, Newfoundland fish and lime, and from them came oil, silk and fine porcelain. To Barbary went fine cloth, ordnance and artillery, armor and timber for oars, though, as a memorandum of 1580 says, "if the Spaniards catch you trading with them, you shall die for it." Probably what they objected to most was the sale of arms to the infidel. From Barbary came sugar, saltpetre, dates, molasses and carpets. Andalusia demanded fine cloth and cambric in return for wines called "seckes," sweet oil, raisins, salt, cochineal, indigo, sumac, silk and soap. Portugal took butter, cheese, fine cloth "light green or sad blue," lead, tin and hides in exchange for salt, oil, soap, cinnamon, cloves, nutmegs, pepper and all other Indian wares.

While the English drove practically no trade with the East Indies, to the West Indies they sent directly oil, looking-glasses, knives, shears, scissors, linen, and wine which, to be salable, must be "singular good." From thence came gold, pearls "very orient and big withall," sugar and molasses. To Syria went colored cloth of the finest quality, and for it currants and sweet oil were taken. The establishment of an English factor in Turkey with the express purpose of furthering trade with that country is an interesting landmark in commercial history.

1582

Even as late as the reign of Elizabeth England imported almost all "artificiality," as high-grade manufactures of a certain sort were called. A famous Elizabethan play turns on the scarcity of needles, the whole household being turned upside down to look for

Gammer Gurton's Needle c. 1559

the one lost by Gammer Gurton. These articles, as well as knives, nails, pins, buttons, dolls, tennis-balls, tape, thread, glass, and laces, were imported from the Netherlands and Germany. From the same quarter came "small wares for grocers,"—by which may be meant cabbages, turnips and lettuce,—and also hops, copper and brass ware.

Manufacture

Having swept all before it in the domains of banking, mining and trade, capitalism, flushed with victory, sought for new worlds to conquer and found them in manufacture. Here also a great struggle was necessary. Hitherto the opposition to the new companies had been mainly on the part of the consumer; now the hostility of the laborer was aroused. The grapple of the two classes, in which the wage-earner went down, partly before the arquebus of the mercenary, partly under the lash and branding-iron of pitiless laws, will be described in the next section. Here it is not the strife of the classes, but of the two economic systems, that is considered. Capitalism won economically before it imposed its yoke on the vanquished by the harsh means of soldier and police. It won, in the final analysis, not because of the inherent power of concentrated wealth, though it used and abused this recklessly, but because, in the struggle for existence, it proved itself the form of life better fitted to survive in the conditions of modern society. It called forth technical improvements, it stimulated individual effort, it put an immense premium on thrift and investment, it cheapened production by the application of initially expensive but ultimately repaying, apparatus, it effected enormous economies in wholesale production and distribution. Before the new methods of business the old gilds stood as helpless, as unready, as bowmen in the face of cannon.

Each medieval "craft" or "mistery"[1] was in the hands of a gild, all the members of which were theoretically equal. Each passed through the ranks of apprentice and other lower grades until he normally became a master-workman and as such entitled to a full and equal share in the management. The gild managed its property almost like that of an endowment in the hands of trustees; it supervised the whole life of each member, took care of him when sick, buried him when dead and pensioned his widow. In these respects it was like some mutual benefit societies of our day. Almost inevitably in that age, it was under the protection of a patron saint and discharged various religious duties. It acted as a corporate whole in the government of the city and marched and acted as one on festive occasions.

Gilds

As typical of the organization of industry at the turning-point may be given the list of gilds at Antwerp drawn up by Albert Dürer: There were goldsmiths, painters, stone-cutters, embroiderers, sculptors, joiners, carpenters, sailors, fishermen, butchers, cloth-weavers, bakers, cobblers, "and all sorts of artisans and many laborers and merchants of provisions." The list is fully as significant for what it omits as for what it includes. Be it noted that there was no gild of printers, for that art had grown up since the crafts had begun to decline, and, though in some places found as a gild, was usually a combination of a learned profession and a capitalistic venture. Again, in this great banking and trading port, there is no mention of gilds of wholesale merchants (for the "merchants of provisions" were certainly not this) nor of bankers. These were two fully capitalized businesses. Finally, observe that there were many skilled and unskilled laborers

1520

[1] From the Latin *ministerium*, French *métier*, not connected with "mystery."

not included in a special gild. Here we have the beginning of the proletariat. A century earlier there would have been no special class of laborers, a century later no gilds worth mentioning.

The gilds were handicapped by their own petty regulations. Notwithstanding the fact that their high standards of craftsmanship produced an excellent grade of goods, they were over-regulated and hidebound, averse to new methods. There was as great a contrast between their meticulous traditions and the freer paths of the new capitalism as there was between scholasticism and science. They could neither raise nor administer the funds needed for foreign commerce and for export industries. Presently new technical methods were adopted by the capitalists, a finer way of smelting ores, and a new way of making brass, invented by Peter von Hoffberg, that saved 50 per cent. of the fuel previously used. In the textile industries came first the spinning-wheel, then the stocking-frame. So in other manufactures, new machinery required novel organization. Significant was the growth of new towns. The old cities were often so gild-ridden that they decayed, while places like Manchester sprang up suddenly at the call of employment. The constant effort of the gild had been to suppress competition and to organize a completely stationary society. In a dynamic world that which refuses to change, perishes. So the gilds, while charging all their woes to the government, really choked themselves to death in their own bands.

Capitalistic production

There is perhaps some analogy between the progress of capitalism in the sixteenth century and the process by which the trusts have come to dominate production in our own memory. The larger industries, and especially those connected with export trade, were seized and reorganized first; for a long time, indeed throughout the century, the gilds kept their hold on small, local industries. For a long time both systems went on side by side; the encroachment was steady, but gradual. The exact method of the change was twofold. In the first place the constitution of the gild became more oligarchical. The older members tended to restrict the administration more and more; they increased the number of apprentices by lengthening the years of apprenticeship and reduced the poorer members to the rank of journeymen who were expected to work, not as before for a limited term of years, but for life, as wage-earners. When the journeymen rebelled, they were put down. The English Clothworkers' Court Book, for example, enacted the rule in 1538 that journeymen who would not work on conditions imposed by the masters should be imprisoned for the first offence and whipped and branded for the second. Nevertheless, to some extent, the master's calling was kept open to the more enterprising and intelligent laborers. It is this opportunity to rise that has always broken up the solidarity of the working class more than anything else.

Great commercial companies

But a second transforming influence worked faster from without than did the internal decay of the gild. This was the extension of the commercial system to manufacture. The gilds soon found themselves at the mercy of the great new companies that wanted wares in large quantities for export. Thus the commercial company came either to absorb or to dominate the industries that supplied it. An example of this is supplied by the Paris mercers, who, from being mainly dealers in foreign goods, gradually became employers of the crafts. Similarly the London haberdashers absorbed the crafts of the hatters and cappers. The middle man, who commanded the market, soon found the strategic value of his position for controlling the supply of articles. Commercial capital rapidly became industrial. One by one the great gilds fell under the control of commercial companies. One of the last instances was the formation of the Stationers' Company by which the printers were reduced to the rank of an industry subordinate to that of booksellers.

Legislation on gilds

Finally came the legislative attack on the gilds, that broke what little power they had left. There is now a tendency to minimise the result of legislation in this field, but the impression that one gets by perusing the statutes not only of England but of Continental countries is that, while perhaps the governments would not have admitted any hostility to the gilds as such, they were strongly opposed to many features of them, and were determined to change them in accordance with the interests of the now dominant class. The policy of the moneyed men was not to destroy the crafts, but to exploit them; indeed they often found their old franchises extremely useful in arrogating to themselves the powers that had once belonged to the gild as a whole. The town governments were elected by the wealthy burghers; Parliaments soon came to side with them, and the monarch had already been bribed into an ally.

To give specific examples of the new trend is easy. When the great tapestry manufacture of Brussels was reorganized on a basis very favorable to the capitalists, the law sanctioning this step spoke contemptuously of the mutual benefit and religious functions of the gild as "petty details." Brandenburg now regulated the terms on which entrance to a gild should be allowed instead of leaving the matter as of old to the members themselves. The Polish nobility, jealous of the cities' monopoly of trade, demanded the total abolition of the gilds. A series of measures in England weakened the power of the gilds; under Edward VI their endowments for religious purposes were at-

1544

1515

1540

1503 ff.

1547

tacked, and this hurt them far more than would appear on the surface. The important Act Touching Weavers both witnessed the unhappy condition of the misteries and, without seeming to do so, still further put them in the power of their masters. The workmen, it seems, had complained "that the rich and wealthy clothiers oppress them" by building up factories, or workshops in which many looms were installed, instead of keeping to the old commission or sweat-shop system, by which piece work was given out and done by each man at home. The gild-workmen preferred this method, because their great rival was the newly developed proletariat, masses of men who could only be accommodated in large buildings. The act, under the guise of redressing the grievance, in reality confirmed the powers of the capitalists, for, while forbidding the use of factories outside of cities, it allowed them within towns and in the four northern counties, thus fortifying the monopolists in those places where they were strong, and hitting their rivals elsewhere. Further legislation, like the Elizabethan Statute of Apprentices, strengthened the hands of the masters at the expense of the journeymen. Such examples are only typical; similar laws were enacted throughout Europe. By act after act the employers were favored at the expense of the laborers.

1555

1563

Agriculture

There remained agriculture, at that time by far the largest and most important of all the means by which man wrings his sustenance from nature. Even now the greater part of the population in most civilized countries—and still more in semi-civilized—is rural, but four hundred years ago the proportion was much larger. England was a predominantly agricultural country until the eighteenth century,—England, the most commercial and industrial of nations! Though the last field to be attacked by capital, agriculture was as thoroughly renovated in the sixteenth century by this irrigating force as the other manners of livelihood had been transformed before it.

Medieval agriculture was carried on by peasants holding small amounts of land which would correspond to the small shops and slender capital of the handicraftsman. Each local unit, whether free village or a manor, was made up of different kinds of land,—arable, commons for pasturing sheep and cattle, forests for gathering fire-wood and for herding swine and meadows for growing hay. The arable land was divided into three so-called "fields," or sections, each field partitioned into smaller portions called in England "shots," and these in turn were subdivided into acre strips. Each peasant possessed a certain number of these tiny lots, generally about thirty, ten in each field. Normally, one field would be left fallow each year in turn, one field would be sown with winter wheat or rye (the bread crop), and one field with barley for beer and oats for feeding the horses and cattle. Into this system it was impossible to introduce individualism. Each man had to plow and sow when the village decided it should be done. And the commons and woodlands were free for all, with certain regulations.[1]

Medieval farming methods

The art of farming was not quite primitive, but it had changed less since the dawn of history than it has changed since 1600. Instead of great steam-plows and all sorts of machinery for harrowing and harvesting, small plows were pulled by oxen, and hoes and rakes were plied by hand. Lime, marl and manure were used for fertilizing, but scantily. The cattle were

[1] For the substance of this paragraph, as well as for numerous suggestions on the rest of the chapter, I am indebted to Professor N. S. B. Gras, of Minneapolis.

small and thin, and after a hard winter were sometimes so weak that they had to be dragged out to pasture. Sheep were more profitable, and in the summer season good returns were secured from chickens, geese, swine and bees. Diseases of cattle were rife and deadly. The principles of breeding were hardly understood. Fitzherbert, who wrote on husbandry in the early sixteenth century, along with some sensible advice makes remarks, on the influence of the moon on horse-breeding, worthy of Hesiod. Indeed, the matter was left almost to itself until a statute of Henry VIII provided that no stallions above two years old and under fifteen hands high be allowed to run loose on the commons, and no mares of less than thirteen hands, lest the breed of horses deteriorate. It was to meet the same situation that the habit of castrating horses arose and became common about 1580.

Capitalistic change

The capitalistic attack on communistic agriculture took two principal forms. In some countries, like Germany, it was the consequence of the change from natural economy to money economy. The new commercial men bought up the estates of the nobles and subjected them to a more intense cultivation, at the same time using all the resources of law and government to make them as lucrative as possible.

Inclosures

But in two countries, England and Spain, and to some small extent in others, a profitable opportunity for investment was found in sheep-farming on a large scale. In England this manifested itself in "inclosures," by which was primarily meant the fencing in for private use of the commons, but secondarily came to be applied to the conversion of arable land into pasture [1] and the substitution of large holdings for small. The cause of the movement was the demand for wool in cloth-weaving, largely for export trade.

[1] Although some of the inclosed land was tilled; see below.

Complaint against inclosures

Contemporaries noticed with much alarm the operations of this economic change. A cry went up that sheep were eating men, that England was being turned into one great pasture to satisfy the greed of the rich, while the land needed for grain was abandoned and tenants forcibly ejected. The outcry became loudest about the years 1516–8, when a commission was appointed to investigate the "evil" of inclosures. It was found that in the past thirty years the amount of land in the eight counties most affected was 22,500 acres. This was not all for grazing; in Yorkshire it was largely for sport, in the Midlands for plowing, in the south for pasture.

The acreage would seem extremely small to account for the complaint it excited. Doubtless it was only the chief and most typical of the hardships caused to a certain class by the introduction of new methods. One is reminded of the bitter hostility to the introduction of machinery in the nineteenth century, when the vast gain in wealth to the community as a whole, being indirect, seemed cruelly purchased at the cost of the sufferings of those laborers who could not adapt themselves to the novel methods. Evolution is always hard on a certain class and the sufferers quite naturally vociferate their woes without regard to the real causes of the change or to the larger interests of society.

Certain it is that inclosures went on uninterrupted throughout the century, in spite of legislative attempts to stop them. Indeed, they could hardly help continuing, when they were so immensely profitable. Land that was inclosed for pasture brought five pounds for every three pounds it had paid under the plow. Sheep multiplied accordingly. The law of 1534 spoke of some men owning as many as 24,000 sheep, and unwittingly gave, in the form of a complaint, the cause thereof, namely that the price of wool had recently doubled. The law limited the number of sheep allowed to one man to 2000. The people arose and slaughtered sheep wholesale in one of those unwise and blind, but not unnatural, outbursts of sabotage by which the proletariat now and then seeks to destroy the wealth that accentuates their poverty. Then as always, the only causes for unwelcome alterations of their manner of life seen by them was the greed and heartlessness of a ring of men, or of the government. The deeper economic forces escaped detection, or at least, attention.

During the period 1450–1610 it is probable that about 2¾ per cent. of the total area of England had been inclosed. The counties most affected were the Midlands, in some of which the amount of land affected was 8 per cent. to 9 per cent. of the total area. But though the aggregate seems small, it was a much larger proportion, in the then thinly settled state of the realm, of the total arable land,—of this it was probably one-fifth. Under Elizabeth perhaps one-third of the improved land was used for grazing and two-thirds was under the plow.

Spain: the Mesta

In Spain the same tendency to grow wool for commercial purposes manifested itself in a slightly different form. There, not by the inclosure of commons, but by the establishment of a monopoly by the Castilian "sheep-trust," the Mesta, did a large corporation come to prevail over the scattered and peasant agricultural interests. The Mesta, which existed from 1273 to 1836, reached the pinnacle of its power in the first two-thirds of the sixteenth century. When it took over from the government the appointment of the officer supposed to supervise it in the public interest, the Alcalde Entregador, it may be said to have won a decisive victory for capitalism. At that time it owned

1568

as many as seven million sheep, and exported wool to the weight of 55,000 tons and to the value of $560,000, per annum.

Wheat growing

Having mastered the sources of wealth offered by wool-growing, the capitalists next turned to arable land and by their transformation of it took the last step in the commercializing of life. Even now, in England, land is not regarded as quite the same kind of investment as a factory or railroad; there is still the vestige of a tradition that the tenant has customary privileges against the right of the owner of the land to exploit it for all it is worth. But this is indeed a faint ghost of the medieval idea that the custom was sacred and the profit of the landlord entirely secondary. The longest step away from the medieval to the modern system was taken in the sixteenth century, and its outward and visible sign was the substitution of the leasehold for the ancient copyhold. The latter partook of the nature of a vested right or interest; the former was but a contract for a limited, often for a short, term, at the end of which the tenant could be ejected, the rent raised, or, as was most usual, an enormous fine (*i.e.*, fee) exacted for renewal of the lease.

The revolution was facilitated by, if it did not in part consist of, the acquisition of the land by the new commercial class, resulting in increased productivity. New and better methods of tillage were introduced. The scattered thirty acres of the peasant were consolidated into three ten-acre fields, henceforth to be used as the owner thought best. One year a field would be under a cereal crop; the next year converted into pasture. This improved method, known as "convertible husbandry" practiced in England and to a lesser extent on the Continent, was a big step in the direction of scientific agriculture. Regular rotation of crops was hardly a common practice before the eighteenth century, but there was something like it in places where hemp and flax would be alternated with cereals. Capitalists in the Netherlands built dykes, drained marshes and dug expensive canals. Elsewhere also swamps were drained and irrigation begun. But perhaps no single improvement in technique accounted for the greater yield of the land so much as the careful and watchful self-interest of the private owner, as against the previous semi-communistic carelessness. Several popular proverbs then gained currency in the sense that there is no fertilizer of the glebe like that put on by the master himself. Harrison's statement, in Elizabeth's reign, that an inclosed acre yielded as much as an acre and a half of common, is borne out by the English statistics of the grain trade. From 1500 to 1534, while the process of inclosure was at its height, the export of corn more than doubled; it then diminished until it almost ceased in 1563, after which it rapidly increased until 1600. During the whole century the population was growing, and it is therefore reasonable to suppose that the yield of the soil was considerably greater in 1600 than it was in 1500.

Export of grain after 1559

It must, however, be admitted that the increase in exports was in part caused by and in part symptomatic of a change in the policy of the government. When commerce became king he looked out for his own interests first, and identified these interests with the dividends of small groups of his chief ministers. Trade was regulated, by tariff and bounty, no longer in the interests of the consumer but in those of the manufacturer and merchant. The corn-laws of nineteenth-century England have their counterpart in the Elizabethan policy of encouraging the export of grain that was needed at home. As soon as the land and the Parliament both fell into the hands of the new capitalistic landlords, they used the one to enhance the profits of the other. Nor was England alone in this. France favored the towns, that is the industrial centers, by forcing the rural population to sell at very low rates, and by encouraging export of grain. Perhaps this same policy was most glaring of all in Sixtine Rome, where the Papal States were taxed, as the provinces of the Empire had been before, to keep bread cheap in the city.

§ 2. The Rise of the Money Power

Money crowned king

In modern times, Money has been king. Perhaps at a certain period in the ancient world wealth had as much power as it has now, but in the Middle Ages it was not so. Money was then ignored by the tenant or serf who paid his dues in feudal service or in kind; it was despised by the noble as the vulgar possession of Jews or of men without gentle breeding, and it was hated by the church as filthy lucre, the root of all evil and, together with sex, as one of the chief instruments of Satan. The "religious" man would vow poverty as well as celibacy.

But money now became too powerful to be neglected or despised, and too desirable to be hated. In the age of transition the medieval and modern conceptions of riches are found side by side. When Holbein came to London the Hanse merchants there employed him to design a pageant for the coronation of Anne Boleyn. In their hall he painted two allegorical pictures, The Triumph of Poverty and The Triumph of Wealth. The choice of subjects was representative of the time of transition.

Revolution

The economic innovation sketched in the last few pages was followed by a social readjustment sufficiently violent and sufficiently rapid to merit the name of revolution. The wave struck different countries at different times, but when it did come in each, it came with a rush, chiefly in the twenties in Germany and Spain, in the thirties and forties in England, a little later, with the civil wars, in France. It submerged all classes but the bourgeoisie; or, rather, it subjugated them all and forced them to follow, as in a Roman triumph, the conquering car of Wealth.

Bourgeoisie uses monarchy

The one other power in the state that was visibly aggrandized at the expense of other classes, besides the plutocracy, was that of the prince. This is sometimes spoken of as the result of a new political theory, an iniquitous, albeit unconscious, conspiracy of Luther and Machiavelli, to exalt the divine right of kings. But in truth their theories were but an expression of the accomplished, or easily foreseen, fact; and this fact was due in largest measure to the need of the commercial class for stable and for strong government. Riches, which at the dawn of the twentieth century seemed, momentarily, to have assumed a cosmopolitan character, were then bound up closely with the power of the state. To keep order, to bridle the lawless, to secure concessions and markets, a mercantile society needed a strong executive, and this they could find only in the person of the prince. Luther says that kings are only God's gaolers and hangmen, high-born and splendid because the meanest of God's servants must be thus accoutred. It would be a little truer to say that they were the gaolers and hangmen hired by the bourgeoisie to over-awe the masses and that their quaint trappings and titles were kept as an ornament to the gay world of snobbery.

And other agencies

Together with the monarchy, the new masters of men developed other instruments, parliamentary government in some countries, a bureaucracy in others, and a mercenary army in nearly all. At that time was either invented or much quoted the saying that gold was one of the nerves of war. The expensive firearms that blew up the feudal castle were equally deadly when turned against the rioting peasants.

To break the nobility

Just as the burgher was ready to shoulder his way into the front rank, he was greatly aided by the frantic civil strife that broke out in both the older privileged orders. Never was better use made of the maxim, "divide and conquer," than when the Reformation divided the church, and the civil wars, dynastic in England, feudal in Germany and nominally religious in France, broke the sword of the noble. When the earls and knights had finished cutting each others' throats there were hardly enough of them left to make a strong stand. Occasionally they tried to do so, as in the revolt of Sickingen in Germany, of the Northern Earls in England, and in the early stages of the rising of the Communeros in Spain. In every case they were defeated, and the work of the sword was completed by the axe and the dagger. Whether they trod the blood-soaked path to the Tower, or whether they succumbed to the hired assassins of Catharine, the old nobles were disposed of and the power of their caste was broken. But their places were soon taken by new men. Some bought baronies and titles outright, others ripened more gradually to these honors in the warmth of the royal smile and on the sunny slopes of manors wrested from the monks. But the end finally attained was that the coronet became a mere bauble in the hands of the rich, the final badge of social deference to success in money-making.

Plunder the church

Still more violent was the spoliation of the church. The confiscations carried out in the name of religion redounded to the benefit of the newly rich. It is true that all the property taken did not fall into their hands; some was kept by the prince, more was used to found or endow hospices, schools and asylums for the poor.

But the most and the best of the land was soon thrown to the eager grasp of traders and merchants. In England probably one-sixth of all the cultivated soil in the kingdom was thus transferred, in the course of a few years, into the hands of new men. Thus were created many of the "county families" of England, and thus the new interest soon came to dominate Parliament. Under Henry VII the House of Lords, at one important session, mustered thirty spiritual and only eighteen temporal peers. In the reign of his son the temporal peers came to outnumber the spiritual, from whom the abbots had been subtracted. The Commons became, what they remained until the nineteenth century, a plutocracy representing either landed or commercial wealth.

Somewhat similar secularizations of ecclesiastical property took place throughout Germany, the cities generally leading. The process was slow, but certain, in Electoral Saxony, Hesse and the other Protestant territories, and about the same time in Sweden and in Denmark. But something the same methods were recommended even in Roman Catholic lands and in Russia of the Eastern Church, so contagious were the examples of the Reformers. Venice forbade gifts or legacies to church or cloisters. France, where confiscation was proposed, partially attained the same ends by subjecting the clergy to the power of the crown.

1536
1557
1516

Bourgeoisie Bribes the intelligentsia

Among the groups into which society naturally falls is that of the intellectual class, the body of professional men, scientists, writers and teachers. This group, just as it came into a new prominence in the sixteenth century, at the same time became in part an annex and a servant to the money power. The high expense of education as compared with the Middle Ages, the enormous fees then charged for graduating in professional schools, the custom of buying livings in the church and practices in law and medicine, the need of patronage in letters and art, made it nearly impossible for the sons of the poor to enter into the palace of learning. Moreover the patronage of the wealthy, their assertion of a monopoly of good form and social prestige, seduced the professional class that now ate from the merchant's hand, aped his manners, and served his interests. For four hundred years law, divinity, journalism, art, and education, have cut their coats, at least to some extent, in the fashion of the court of wealth.

And subjugates the proletariat

Last of all, there remained the only power that proved itself nearly a match for money, that of labor. Far outnumbering the capitalists, in every other way the workers were their inferiors,—in education, in organization, in leadership and in material resources. One thing that made their struggle so hard was that those men of exceptional ability who might have been their leaders almost always made fortunes of their own and then turned their strength against their former comrades. Labor also suffered terribly from quacks and ranters with counsels of folly or of madness.

The social wars of the sixteenth century partook of the characteristics of both medieval and modern times. The Peasants' Revolt in Germany was both communistic and religious; the risings of Communeros and the Hermandad in Spain were partly communistic; the several rebellions in England were partly religious. But a new element marked them all, the demand on the part of the workers for better wages and living conditions. The proletariat of town and mining district joined the German peasants in 1524; the revolt was in many respects like a gigantic general strike.

Emancipation of the serfs

Great as are the ultimate advantages of freedom, the emancipation of the serfs cannot be reckoned as an immediate economic gain to them. They were freed not because of the growth of any moral sentiment, much less as the consequence of any social cataclysm, but because free labor was found more profitable than unfree. It is notable that serfs were emancipated first in those countries like Scotland where there had been no peasants' revolt; the inference is that they were held in bondage in other countries longer than it was profitable to do so for political reasons. The last serf was reclaimed in Scotland in 1365, but the serfs had not been entirely freed in England even in the reign of Elizabeth. In France the process went on rapidly in the 15th century, often against the wishes of the serfs themselves. One hundred thousand peasants emigrated from Northern France to Burgundy at that time to exchange their free for a servile state. However, they did not enjoy their bondage for long. Serfs in the Burgundian state, especially in the Netherlands, lost their last chains in the sixteenth century, most rapidly between the years 1515 and 1531. In Germany serfdom remained far beyond the end of the sixteenth century, doubtless in part because of the fears excited by the civil war of 1525.

Regulation of labor

In place of the old serfdom under one master came a new and detailed regulation of labor by the government. This regulation was entirely from the point of view, and consequently all but entirely in the interests, of the propertied classes. The form was the old form of medieval paternalism, but the spirit was the new spirit of capitalistic gain. The endeavor of the government to be fair to the laborer as well as to the employer is very faint, but it is just perceptible in some laws.

Most of the taxes and burdens of the state were loaded on the backs of the poor. Hours of labor were fixed at from 12 to 15 according to the season.

Regulation of wages was not sporadic, but was a regular part of the work of certain magistrates, in England of the justices of the peace. Parliament enforced with incredible severity the duty of the poor and able-bodied man to work. Sturdy idlers were arrested and drafted into the new proletariat needed by capital. When whipping, branding, and short terms of imprisonment, did not suffice to compel men to work, a law was passed to brand able-bodied vagrants on the chest with a "V," and to assign them to some honest neighbor "to have and to hold as a slave for the space of two years then next following." The master should "only give him bread and water and small drink and such refuse of meat as he should think meet to cause the said slave to work." If the slave still idled, or if he ran away and was caught again he was to be marked on the face with an "S" and to be adjudged a slave for life. If finally refractory he was to be sentenced as a felon. This terrible measure, intended partly to reduce lawless vagrancy, partly to supply cheap labor to employers, failed of its purpose and was repealed in two years. Its re-enactment was vainly urged by Cecil upon Parliament in 1559. As a substitute for it in this year the law was passed forbidding masters to receive any workman without a testimonial from his last employer; laborers were not allowed to stop work or change employers without good cause, and conversely employers were forbidden to dismiss servants "unduly."

1547

The proletariat

In Germany the features of the modern struggle between owners and workers are plainest. In mining, especially, there developed a real proletariat, a class of laborers seeking employment wherever it was best paid and combining and striking for higher wages. To combat them were formed pools of employers to keep down wages and to blacklist agitators. Typical of these was the agreement made by Duke George of Saxony and other large mine-owners not to raise wages, not to allow miners to go from place to place seeking work, and not to hire any troublesome agitator once dismissed by any operator.

1520

It is extraordinary how rapidly many features of the modern proletariat developed. Take, for example, the housing problem. As this became acute some employers built model tenements for their workers. Others started stores at which they could buy food and clothing, and even paid them in part in goods instead of in money. Labor tended to become fluid, moving from one town to another and from one industry to another according to demand. Such a thing had been not unknown in the previous centuries; it was strongly opposed by law in the sixteenth. The new risks run by workers were brought out when, for the first time in history, a great mining accident took place in 1515, a flood by which eighty-eight miners were drowned. Women began to be employed in factories and were cruelly exploited. Most sickening of all, children were forced, as they still are in some places, to wear out their little lives in grinding toil. The lace-making industry in Belgium, for example, fell entirely into the hands of children. Far from protesting against this outrage, the law actually sanctioned it by the provision that no girl over twelve be allowed to make lace, lest the supply of maidservants be diminished.

Strikes

Strikes there were and rebellions of all sorts, every one of them beaten back by the forces of the government and of the capitalists combined. The kings of commerce were then, more than now, a timorous and violent race, for then they were conscious of being usurpers. When they saw a Münzer or a Kett—the mad Hamlets of the people—mop and mow and stage their deeds before the world, they became frantic with terror and could do nought but take subtle counsel to kill these heirs, or pretenders, to their realms. The great rebellions are all that history now pays much attention to, but in reality the warfare on the poor was ceaseless, a chronic disease of the body politic. Louis XI spared nothing, disfranchisement, expulsion, wholesale execution, to beat down the lean and hungry conspirators against the public order, whose raucous cries of misery he detested. With somewhat gentler, because stronger, hand, his successors followed in his footsteps. But when needed the troops were there to support the rich. The great strike of printers at Lyons is one example of several in France. In the German mines there were occasional strikes, sternly suppressed by the princes acting in agreement.

Degradation of the poor

There can be no doubt that the economic developments of the sixteenth century worked tremendous hardship to the poor. It was noted everywhere that whereas wine and meat were common articles in 1500, they had become luxuries by 1600. Some scholars have even argued from this a diminution of the wealth of Europe during the century. This, however, was not the case. The aggregate of capital, if we may judge from many other indications, notably increased throughout the century. But it became more and more concentrated in a few hands.

The chief natural cause of the depression of the working class was the rise in prices. Wages have always shown themselves more sluggish in movement than commodities. While money wages, therefore, remained nearly stationary, real wages shrank throughout the century. In 1600 a French laborer was obliged to spend 55 per cent. of his wages merely on food. A whole day's labor would only buy him two and one half pounds of salt. Rents were low, because the houses were incredibly bad. At that time a year's rent for a laborer's tenement cost from ten to twenty days labor; it now costs about thirty days' labor. The new commerce robbed the peasant of some of his markets by substituting foreign articles like indigo and cochineal for domestic farm products. The commercialization of agriculture worked manifold hardship to the peasant. Many were turned off their farms to make way for herds of sheep, and others were hired on new and harder terms to pay in money for the land they had once held on customary and not too oppressive terms of service and dues.

Under all the splendors of the Renaissance, with its fields of cloth of gold and its battles like knightly jousts, with its constant stream of adulation from artists and authors, with the ostentation of the new wealth and the greedily tasted pleasures of living and enjoying, an attentive ear can hear the low, uninterrupted murmurs of the wretched, destined to burst forth, on the day of despair or of vengeance, into ferocious clamors. Nor was there then much pity for the poor. The charity and worship for "apostolic poverty" of the Middle Ages had ceased, nor had that social kindness, so characteristic of our own time that it is affected even by those who do not feel it, arisen. The rich and noble, absorbed in debauchery or art, regarded the peasant as a different race—"the ox without horns" they called him—to be cudgeled while he was tame and hunted like a wolf when he ran wild. Artists and men of letters ignored the very existence of the unlettered, with the superb Horatian, "I hate the vulgar crowd and I keep them off," or, if they were aroused for a moment by the noise of civil war merely remarked, with Erasmus, that any tyranny was better than that of the mob. Churchmen like Matthew Lang and Warham and the popes oppressed the poor whom Jesus loved. "Rustica gens optima flens" smartly observed a canon of Zurich, while Luther blurted out,

No pity for the poor

"accursed, thievish, murderous peasants" and "the gentle" Melanchthon almost sighed, "the ass *will* have blows and the people *will* be ruled by force."

There were, indeed, a few honorable exceptions to the prevalent callousness. "I praise thee, thou noble peasant," wrote an obscure German, "before all creatures and lords upon earth; the emperor must be thy equal." The little read epigrams of Euricius Cordus, a German humanist who was, by exception, also humane, denounce the blood-sucking of the peasants by their lords. Greatest of all, Sir Thomas More felt, not so much pity for the lot of the poor, as indignation at their wrongs. *The Utopia* will always remain one of the world's noblest books because it was almost the first to feel and to face the social problem.

Pauperism

This became urgent with the large increase of pauperism and vagrancy throughout the sixteenth century, the most distressing of the effects of the economic revolution. When life became too hard for the evicted tenant of a sheep-raising landlord, or for the *déclassé* journeyman of the town gild, he had little choice save to take to the road. Gangs of sturdy vagrants, led by and partly composed of old soldiers, wandered through Europe. But a little earlier than the sixteenth century that race of mendicants the Gipsies, made their début. The word "rogue" was coined in England about 1550 to name the new class. *The Book of Vagabonds,* written by Matthew Hütlin of Pfortzheim, describes twenty-eight varieties of beggars, exposes their tricks, and gives a vocabulary of their jargon. Some of these beggars are said to be dangerous, threatening the wayfarer or householder who will not pay them; others feign various diseases, or make artificial wounds and disfigurations to excite pity, or take a religious garb, or drag chains to show that they had escaped from galleys, or have other plausible tales of woe and

1510

of adventure. All contemporaries testify to the alarming numbers of these men and women; how many they really were it is hard to say. It has been estimated that in 1500 20 per cent. of the population of Hamburg and 15 per cent. of the population of Augsburg were paupers. Under Elizabeth probably from a quarter to a third of the population of London were paupers, and the country districts were just as bad. Certain parts of Wales were believed to have a third of their population in vagabondage.

In the face of this appalling situation the medieval method of charity completely broke down. In fact, with its many begging friars, with its injunction of alms-giving as a good work most pleasing to God, and with its respect for voluntary poverty, the church rather aggravated than palliated the evil of mendicancy. The state had to step in to relieve the church.

State poor-relief, 1506

This was early done in the Netherlands. A severe edict was issued and repeatedly re-enacted against tramps ordering them to be whipped, have their heads shaved, and to be further punished with stocks. An enterprising group of humanists and lawyers demanded that the government should take over the duty of poor-relief from the church. Accordingly at Lille a "common chest" was started, the first civil charitable bureau in the Netherlands. At Bruges a cloister was secularized and turned into a school for eight hundred poor children in uniform. A secular bureau of charity was started at Antwerp.

1512

1521

January, 1526

Under these circumstances the humanist Lewis Vives wrote his famous tract on the relief of the poor, in the form of a letter to the town council of Bruges. In this well thought out treatise he advocated the law that no one should eat who did not work, and urged that all able-bodied vagrants should be hired out to artisans—a suggestion how welcome to the capitalists eager to draft men into their workshops! Cases of people unable to work should also be taken up, and they should be cared for by application of religious endowments by the government. Vives' claim to recognition lies even more in his spirit than in his definite program. For almost the first time in history he plainly said that poverty was a disgrace as well as a danger to the state and should be, not palliated, but extirpated.

While Vives was still preparing his treatise the city of Ypres (tragic name!) had already sought his advice and acted upon it, as well as upon the example of earlier reforms in German cities, in promulgating an ordinance. The city government combined all religious and philanthropic endowments into one fund and appointed a committee to administer it, and to collect further gifts. These citizens were to visit the poor in their dwellings, to apply what relief was necessary, to meet twice a week to concert remedial measures and to have charge of enforcing the laws against begging and idleness. All children of the poor were sent to school or taught a trade.

1525

Though there were sporadic examples of municipal poor-relief in Germany prior to the Reformation, it was the religious movement that there first gave the cause its decisive impulse. In his *Address to the German Nobility* Luther had recommended that each city should take care of its own poor and suppress "the rascally trade of begging." During his absence at the Wartburg his more radical colleagues had taken steps to put these ideas into practice at Wittenberg. A common fund was started by the application of ecclesiastical endowments, from which orphans were to be housed, students at school and university to be helped, poor girls dowered and needy workmen loaned money at four per cent. A severe law against begging was passed. Augsburg and Nuremberg followed the example of Wittenberg almost at once and other German cities, to the number of forty-eight, one by one joined the procession. 1522

For fairly obvious reasons the state regulation of pauperism, though it did not originate in the Reformation, was much more rapidly and thoroughly developed in Protestant lands. In these the power of the state and the economic revolution attained their maximum development, whereas the Roman church was inclined, or obligated, to stand by the medieval position. "Alms-giving is papistry," said a Scotch tract. Thus Christian Cellarius, a professor at Louvain, published *A Plea for the Right of the Poor to Beg.* The Spanish monk, Lawrence da Villavicenzio in his *Sacred Economy of caring for the Poor,* condemned the whole plan of state regulation and subvention as heretical. The Council of Trent, also, put itself on the medieval side, and demanded the restoration to the church of the direction of charity. 1530 1564

But even in Catholic lands the new system made headway. As the University of Paris approved the ordinance of Ypres, in France, and in Catholic Germany, a plan comprising elements of the old order, but informed by the modern spirit, grew up. 1531

In England the problem of pauperism became more acute than elsewhere. The drastic measures taken to force men to work failed to supply all needs. After municipal relief of various sorts had been tried, and after the government had in vain tried to stimulate private munificence to co-operate with the church to meet the growing need, the first compulsory Poor Rates were laid. Three or four years later came an act for setting the poor to labor in workhouses. These measures failed of the success that met the continental method. Even compared to Scotland, England developed a disproportionate amount of pauperism. Some 1572 authorities have asserted that by giving the poor a legal right to aid she encouraged the demand for it. 1572 Probably, however, she simply furnished the extreme example of the commercialism that made money but did not make men.

CHAPTER XII

MAIN CURRENTS OF THOUGHT

Were we reading the biography of a wayward genius, we should find the significance of the book neither in the account of his quarrels and of his sins nor in the calculation of his financial difficulties and successes, but in the estimate of his contributions to the beauty and wisdom of the world. Something the same is true about the history of a race or of a period; the political and economic events are but the outward framework; the intellectual achievement is both the most attractive and the most repaying object of our study. In this respect the sixteenth century was one of the most brilliant; it produced works of science that outstripped all its predecessors; it poured forth masterpieces of art and literature that are all but matchless.

§ 1. Biblical and Classical Scholarship

Position of Bible in 16th century

It is naturally impossible to give a full account of all the products of sixteenth century genius. In so vast a panorama only the mountain peaks can be pointed out. One of these peaks is assuredly the Bible. Never before nor since has that book been so popular; never has its study absorbed so large a part of the energies of men. It is true that the elucidation of the text was not proportional to the amount of labor spent on it. For the most part it was approached not in a scientific but in a dogmatic spirit. Men did not read it historically and critically but to find their own dogmas in it. Nevertheless, the foundations were laid for both the textual and the higher criticism.

The Greek Text

The Greek text of the New Testament was first published by Erasmus in March, 1516. Revised, but not always improved, editions were brought out by him in 1519, 1522 and 1527. For the first edition he had before him ten manuscripts, all of them minuscules, the oldest of which, though he believed it might have come from the apostolic age, is assigned by modern criticism to the twelfth century. In the course of printing, some bad errors were introduced, and the last six verses of the Apocalypse, wanting in all the manuscripts, were supplied by an extremely faulty translation from the Latin. The results were such as might have been anticipated. Though the text has been vastly purified by modern critics, the edition of Erasmus was of great service and was thoroughly honest. He noted that the last verses of Mark were doubtful and that the passage on the adulteress (John vii, 53 to viii, 11) was lacking in the best authorities, and he omitted the text on the three heavenly witnesses (I John v, 7) as wanting in all his manuscripts.

For this omission he was violently attacked. To support his position he asked his friend Bombasius to consult the Codex Vaticanus, and dared to assert that were a single manuscript found with the verse in Greek, he would include it in subsequent editions. Though there were at the time no codices with the verse in question—which was a Latin forgery of the fourth century, possibly due to Priscillian—one was promptly manufactured. Though Erasmus suspected the truth, that the verse had been interpolated from the Latin text, he added it in his third edition "that no occasion for calumny be given." This one sample must serve to show how Erasmus's work was received. For every deviation from the Vulgate, whether in the Greek text or in the new Latin translation with which he accompanied it, he was ferociously assailed. His own anecdote of the old priest who, having the misprint "mumpsimus" for "sumpsimus" in his missal, refused to correct the error when it was pointed out, is perfectly typical of the position of his critics. New truth must ever struggle hard against old prejudice.

While Erasmus was working, a much more ambitious scheme for publishing the Scriptures was maturing under the direction of Cardinal Ximénez at Alcalá or, as the town was called in Latin, Complutum. The Complutensian Polyglot, as it was thence named, was published in six volumes, four devoted to the Old Testament, one to the New Testament, and one to a Hebrew lexicon and grammar. The New Testament volume has the earliest date, 1514, but was withheld from the public for several years after this. The manuscripts from which the Greek texts were taken are unknown, but they were better than those used by Erasmus. The later editors of the Greek text in the sixteenth century, Robert Estienne (Stephanus) and Theodore Beza, did little to castigate it, although one of the codices used by Beza, and now known by his name, is of great value.

Hebrew text

The Hebrew Massoretic text of the Old Testament was printed by Gerson Ben Mosheh at Brescia in 1494, and far more elaborately in the first four volumes of the Complutensian Polyglot. With the Hebrew text the Spanish editors offered the Septuagint Greek, the Syriac, and the Vulgate, the Hebrew, Syriac and Greek having Latin translations. The manuscripts for the Hebrew were procured from Rome. A critical revision was undertaken by Sebastian Münster and published with a new Latin version at Basle 1534–5. Later recensions do not call for special notice here. An incomplete text of the Syriac New Testament was published at Antwerp in 1569.

The numerous new Latin translations made during

Latin versions

this period testify to the general discontent with the Vulgate. Not only humanists like Valla, Lefèvre and Erasmus, but perfectly orthodox theologians like Pope Nicholas V, Cajetan and Sadoletus, saw that the common version could be much improved. In the new Latin translation by Erasmus many of the errors of the Vulgate were corrected. Thus, in Matthew iii, 2, he offers "resipiscite" or "ad mentem redite" instead of "poenitentiam agite." This, as well as his substitution of "sermo" for "verbum" in John i, 1, was fiercely assailed. Indeed, when it was seen what use was made by the Protestants of the new Greek texts and of the new Latin versions, of which there were many, a strong reaction followed in favor of the traditional text. Even by the editors of the Complutensian Polyglot the Vulgate was regarded with such favor that, being printed between the Hebrew and Greek, it was compared by them to Christ crucified between the two thieves. The Sorbonne condemned as "Lutheran" the assertion that the Bible could not be properly understood or expounded without knowledge of the original languages. In the decree of Trent the Vulgate was declared to be the authentic form of the Scriptures. The preface to the English Catholic version printed at Rheims defends the thesis, now generally held by Catholics, that the Latin text is superior in accuracy to the Greek, having been corrected by Jerome, preserved by the church and sanctioned by the Council of Trent. In order to have this text in its utmost purity an official edition was issued.

1530

April 8, 1546

1582

1592

Biblical scholarship

Modern critics, having far surpassed the results achieved by their predecessors, are inclined to underestimate their debts to these pioneers in the field. The manuals, encyclopaedias, commentaries, concordances, special lexicons, all that make an introduction to biblical criticism so easy nowadays, were lacking then, or were supplied only by the labor of a life-time. The professors at Wittenberg, after prolonged inquiry, were unable to find a map of Palestine. The first Hebrew concordance was printed, with many errors, at Venice in 1523; the first Greek concordance not until 1546, at Basle. To find a parallel passage or illustrative material or ancient comment on a given text, the critic then had to search through dusty tomes and manuscripts, instead of finding them accumulated for him in ready reference books. That all this has been done is the work of ten generations of scholars, among whom the pioneers of the Renaissance should not lack their due meed of honor. The early critics were hampered by a vicious inherited method. The schoolmen, with purely dogmatic interest, had developed a hopeless and fantastic exegesis, by which every text of Scripture was given a fourfold sense, the historical, allegorical, tropological (or figurative) and anagogical (or didactic).

Erasmus

Erasmus, under the tuition of Valla, felt his way to a more fruitful method. It is true that his main object was a moral one, the overthrow of superstition and the establishment of the gentle "philosophy of Christ." He used the allegorical method only, or chiefly, to explain away as fables stories that would seem silly or obscene as history. In the New Testament he sought the man Jesus and not the deified Christ. He preferred the New Testament, with its "simple, plain and gentle truth, without savor of superstition or cruelty" to the Old Testament. He discriminated nicely even among the books of the New Testament, considering the chief ones the gospels, Acts, the Pauline epistles (except Hebrews), I Peter and I John. He hinted that many did not consider the Apocalypse canonical; he found Ephesians Pauline in thought but not in style; he believed Hebrews to have been written by Clement of Rome; and he called James lacking in apostolic dignity.

Luther

By far the best biblical criticism of the century was the mature work of Martin Luther. It is a remarkable fact that a man whose doctrine of the binding authority of Scripture was so high, and who refused his disciples permission to interpret the text with the least shade of independence, should himself have shown a freedom in the treatment of the inspired writers unequaled in any Christian for the next three centuries. It is sometimes said that Luther's judgments were mere matters of taste; that he took what he liked and rejected what he disliked, and this is true to a certain extent. "What treats well of Christ, that is Scripture, even if Judas and Pilate had written it," he averred, and again, "If our adversaries urge the Bible against Christ, we must urge Christ against the Bible." His wish to exclude the epistle of James from the canon, on the ground that its doctrine of justification contradicted that of Paul, was thus determined, and excited wide protest not only from learned Catholics like Sir Thomas More, but also from many Protestants, beginning with Bullinger.

But Luther's trenchant judgments of the books of the Bible were usually far more than would be implied by a merely dogmatic interest. Together with the best scholarship of the age he had a strong intuitive feeling for style that guided him aright in many cases. In denying the Mosaic authorship of a part of the Pentateuch, in asserting that Job and Jonah were fables, in finding that the books of Kings were more credible than Chronicles and that the books of Isaiah, Jeremiah, Hosea, Proverbs and Ecclesiastes had received their final form from later editors, he but advanced theses now universally accepted. His doubts about Esther, Hebrews, and the Apocalypse have been amply confirmed. Some modern scholars agree with his most daring opinion, that the epistle of James was written by "some Jew who had heard of the Christians but not joined them." After Luther the voluminous works of the commentators are a dreary desert of arid dogmatism and fantastic pedantry. Carlstadt was perhaps the second best of the higher critics of the time; Zwingli was conservative; Calvin's exegesis slumbers in fifty volumes in deserved neglect.

German version

Among the great vernacular Protestant versions of the Bible that of Luther stands first in every sense of the word. Long he had meditated on it before his enforced retirement at the Wartburg gave him the leisure to begin it. The work of revision, in which Luther had much help from Melanchthon and other Wittenberg professors, was a life-long labor. Only recently have the minutes of the meetings of these scholars come to light, and they testify to the endless trouble taken by the Reformer to make his work clear and accurate. He wrote no dialect, but a common, standard German which he believed to have been introduced by the Saxon chancery. But he also modelled his style not only on the few good German authors then extant, but on the speech of the market-place. From the mouths of the people he took the sweet, common words that he gave back to them again, "so that they may note that we are speaking German to them." Spirit and fire he put into the German Bible; dramatic turns of phrase, lofty eloquence, poetry.

All too much Luther read his own ideas into the Bible. To make Moses "so German that no one would know that he was a Jew" insured a noble style, but involved an occasional violent wrench to the thought. Thus the Psalms are made to speak of Christ quite plainly, and of German May-festivals; and the passover is metamorphosed into Easter. Is there not even an allusion to the golden rose given by the pope in the translation of Micah iv, 8?—"Und du Thurm Eder, eine Feste der Tochter Zion, es wird deine goldene Rose kommen." Luther declared his intention of "simply throwing away" any text repugnant to the rest of Scripture, as he conceived it. As a matter of fact the greatest change that he actually made was the introduction of the word "alone" after "faith" in the passage (Romans iii, 28) "A man is justified by faith without works of the law." Luther never used the word "church" (Kirche), in the Bible, but replaced it by "congregation" (Gemeinde). Following Erasmus he turned μετανοεῖτε (Matthew iii, 2, 8) into "bessert euch" ("improve yourselves") instead of "tut Busse" ("do penance") as in the older German versions. Also, following the Erasmian text, he omitted the "comma Johanneum" (I John v, 7); this was first insinuated into the German Bible in 1575.

English Bible

None of the other vernacular versions, not even the French translation of Lefèvre and Olivetan can compare with the German save one, the English. How William Tyndale began and how Coverdale completed the work in 1535, has been told on another page. Many revisions followed: the Great Bible of 1539, the Geneva Bible of 1560 and the Bishops' Bible of 1568. Then came the Catholic, or Douai version of 1582, the only one completely differing from the others, with its foundation on the Vulgate and its numerous barbarisms: "parasceue" for "preparation," "feast of Azymes" for "feast of unleavened bread," "imposing of hands," "what to me and thee, woman" (John ii, 4), "penance," "chalice," "host," "against the spirituals of wickedness in the celestials" (Ephesians vi, 12), "supersubstantial bread" in the Lord's prayer, "he exinanited himself" (Philippians ii, 7).

We are accustomed to speak of the Authorized Version of 1610 as if it were a new product of the literary genius of Shakespeare's age. In fact, it was a mere revision, and a rather light one, of previous work. Its rare perfection of form is due to the labors of many men manipulating and polishing the same material. Like the Homeric poems, like the Greek gospels themselves probably, the greatest English classic is the product of the genius of a race and not of one man. Even from the very beginning it was such to some extent. Tyndale could hardly have known Wyclif's version, which was never printed and was rare in manuscript, but his use of certain words, such as "mote," "beam," and "strait gate," also found in the earlier version, prove that he was already working in a literary tradition, one generation handing down to another certain Scriptural phrases first heard in the mouths of the Lollards.

Both Tyndale and Coverdale borrowed largely from the German interpreters, as was acknowledged on the title-page and in the prologue to the Bible of 1535. Thus Tyndale copied not only most of the marginal notes of Luther's Bible, but also such Teutonisms as, "this is once bone of my bone," "they offered unto field-devils" (Luther, "Felt-teuffeln"), "Blessed is the room-maker, Gad" (Luther, "Raum-macher"). The English translators also followed the German in using "elder" frequently for "priest," "congregation" for "church," and "love" for "charity." By counting every instance of this and similar renderings, Sir Thomas More claimed to have found one thousand errors in the New Testament alone.

Popularity of Bible

The astounding popularity of the Bible, chiefly but not only in Protestant countries, is witnessed by a myriad voices. Probably in all Christian countries in every age it has been the most read book, but in the sixteenth century it added to an unequaled reputation for infallibility the zest of a new discovery. Edward VI demanding the Bible at his coronation, Elizabeth passionately kissing it at hers, were but types of the time. That joyous princess of the Renaissance, Isabella d'Este, ordered a new translation of the Psalms for her own perusal. Margaret of Navarre, in the Introduction to her frivolous *Heptameron,* expresses the pious hope that all present have read the Scripture. Hundreds of editions of the German and English translations were called for. The people, wrote an Englishman in 1539, "have now in every church and place, almost every man, the Bible and New Testament in their mother tongue, instead of the old fabulous and fantastical books of the Table Round . . . and such other whose impure filth and vain fabulosity the light of God hath abolished there utterly." In Protestant lands it became almost a matter of good form to own the Bible, and reading it has been called, not ineptly, "the *opus operatum* of the Evangelicals." Even the Catholics bore witness to the demand, which they tried to check. While they admonished the laity that it was unnecessary and dangerous to taste of this tree of knowledge, while they even curtailed the reading of the Scripture by the clergy, they were forced to supply vernacular versions of their own.

Bibliolatry

Along with unbounded popularity the Bible then enjoyed a much higher reputation for infallibility than it bears today. The one point on which all Protestant churches were agreed was the supremacy and sufficiency of Scripture. The Word, said Calvin, flowed from the very mouth of God himself; it was the sole foundation of faith and the one fountain of all wisdom. "What Christ says must be true whether I or any other man can understand it," preached Luther. "Scripture is fully to be believed," wrote an English theologian, "as a thing necessary to salvation, though the thing contained in Scripture pertain not merely to the faith, as that Aaron had a beard." The Swiss and the Anabaptists added their voices to this chorus of bibliolatry.

Abeunt studia in mores

Since studies pass into character, it is natural to find a marked effect from this turning loose of a new source of spiritual authority. That thousands were made privately better, wiser and happier from the reading of the gospels and the Hebrew poetry, that standards of morality were raised and ethical tastes purified thereby, is certain. But the same cause had several effects that were either morally indifferent or positively bad. The one chiefly noticed by contemporaries was the pullulation of new sects. Each man, as Luther complained, interpreted the Holy Book according to his own brain and crazy reason. The old saying that the Bible was the book of heretics, came true. It was in vain for the Reformers to insist that none but the ministers (*i. e.* themselves) had the right to interpret Scripture. It was in vain for the governments to forbid, as the Scotch statute expressed it, "any to dispute or hold opinions on the Bible"; discordant clamor of would-be expounders arose, some learned, others ignorant, others fantastic, and all pigheaded and intolerant.

1550

There can be no doubt that the Bible, in proportion to the amount of inerrancy attributed to it, became a stumbling-block in the path of progress, scientific, social and even moral. It was quoted against Copernicus as it was against Darwin. Rational biblical criticism was regarded by Luther, except when he was the critic, as a cause of vehement suspicion of atheism. Some texts buttressed the horrible and cruel superstition of witchcraft. The examples of the wars of Israel and the text, "compel them to enter in," seemed to support the duty of intolerance. Social reformers, like

Vives, in their struggle to abolish poverty, were confronted with the maxim, mistaken as an eternal verity, that the poor are always with us. Finally the great moral lapse of many of the Protestants, the permission of polygamy, was supported by biblical texts.

The classics

Next to the Bible the sixteenth century revered the classics. Most of the great Latin authors had been printed prior to 1500, the most important exception being the *Annals* of Tacitus, of which the *editio princeps* was in 1515. Between the years 1478 and 1500, the following Greek works had been published, and in this order: Aesop, Homer, Isocrates, Theocritus, the Anthology, four plays of Euripides, Aristotle, Theognis, and nine plays of Aristophanes. Follow the dates of the *editiones principes* of the other principal Greek writers:

1502: Thucydides, Sophocles, Herodotus.
1503: Euripides (eighteen plays), Xenophon's *Hellenica.*
1504: Demosthenes.
1509: Plutarch's *Moralia.*
1513: Pindar, Plato.
1516: Aristophanes, New Testament, Xenophon, Pausanias, Strabo.
1517: Plutarch's *Lives.*
1518: Septuagint, Aeschylus, four plays.
1525: Galen, Xenophon's complete works.
1528: Epictetus.
1530: Polybius.
1532: Aristophanes, eleven plays.
1533: Euclid, Ptolemy.
1544: Josephus.
1552: Aeschylus, seven plays.
1558: Marcus Aurelius.
1559: Diodorus.
1565: Bion and Moschus.
1572: Plutarch's complete works.

Naturally the first editions were not usually the best.

The labor of successive generations has made the text what it is. Good work, particularly, though not exclusively, in editing the fathers of the church, was done by Erasmus. But a really new school of historical criticism was created by Joseph Justus Scaliger, the greatest of scholars. His editions of the Latin poets first laid down and applied sound rules of textual emendation, besides elucidating the authors with a wealth of learned comment.

Scholarship

J. J. Scaliger, 1540–1609

The editing of the texts was but a small portion of the labor that went to the cultivation of the classics. The foundations of our modern lexicons were laid in the great *Thesaurus linguae Latinae* of Robert Estienne (first edition 1532, 2d improved 1536, 3d in three volumes 1543) and the *Thesaurus linguae Graecae* by Henry Estienne the younger, published in five volumes in 1572. This latter is still used, the best edition being that in nine volumes 1829–63.

So much of ancient learning has become a matter of course to the modern student that he does not always realize the amount of ground covered in the last four centuries. Erasmus once wrote to Cardinal Grimani: "The Roman Capitol, to which the ancient poets vainly promised eternity, has so completely disappeared that its very location cannot be pointed out." If one of the greatest scholars then was ignorant of a site now visited by every tourist in the Eternal City, how much must there not have been to learn in other respects? Devotedly and successfully the contemporaries and successors of Erasmus labored to supply the knowledge then wanting. Latin, Greek and Hebrew grammars were written, treatises on Roman coinage, on epigraphy, on ancient religion, on chronology, on comparative philology, on Roman law, laid deep and strong the foundations of the consummate scholarship of modern times.

November 13, 1517

Idolatry of ancients

The classics were not only studied in the sixteenth century, they were loved, they were even worshipped. "Every elegant study, every science worthy of the attention of an educated man, in a word, whatever there is of polite learning," wrote the French savant Muret, "is contained nowhere save in the literature of the Greeks." Joachim du Bellay wrote a cycle of sonnets on the antiquities of Rome, in the spirit:

1573

> Rome fut tout le monde, et tout le monde est Rome.

"The Latin allureth me by its gracious dignity," wrote Montaigne, "and the writings of the Greeks not only fill and satisfy me, but transfix me with admiration. . . . What glory can compare with that of Homer?" Machiavelli tells how he dressed each evening in his best attire to be worthy to converse with the spirits of the ancients, and how, while reading them, he forgot all the woes of life and the terror of death. Almost all learned works, and a great many not learned, were written in Latin. For those who could not read the classics for themselves translations were supplied. Perhaps the best of these were the *Lives of Famous Men* by Plutarch, first rendered into French by Amyot and thence into English by Sir Thomas North.

Value of classics in 16th century

Strong, buoyant, self-confident as was the spirit of the age, it bore plainly upon it the impress of its zealous schooling in the lore of the ancients. In supplying the imperious need of cultured men for good literature the Romans and Greeks had, in the year 1500, but few rivals—save in Italy, hardly any. To an age that had much to learn they had much to teach; to men as greedy for the things of the mind as they were for luxury and wealth the classics offered a new world as rich in spoils of wisdom and beauty as were the East Indies and

Peru in spices and gold. The supreme value of the Greek and Latin books is that which they have in common with all literature; they furnished, for the mass of reading men, the best and most copious supply of food for the intellectual and spiritual life. "Books," says Erasmus, "are both cheering and wholesome. In prosperity they steady one, in affliction console, do not vary with fortune and follow one through all dangers even to the grave. . . . What wealth or what scepters would I exchange for my tranquil reading?" "From my earliest childhood," Montaigne confides, "poetry has had the power to pierce me through and transport me."

In the best sense of the word, books are popular philosophy. All cannot study the deepest problems of life or of science for themselves, but all can absorb the quintessence of thought in the pleasant and stimulating form in which it is served up in the best literature. Books accustom men to take pleasure in ideas and to cultivate a high and noble inward life. This, their supreme value for the moulding of character, was appreciated in the sixteenth century. "We must drink the spirit of the classics," observes Montaigne, "rather than learn their precepts," and again, "the use to which I put my studies is a practical one—the formation of character for the exigencies of life."

Ancient masters of literary style

This is the service by which the ancients have put the moderns in their debt. Another gift of distinct, though lesser value, was that of literary style. So close is the correspondence between expression and thought that it is no small advantage to any man or to any age to sit at the feet of those supreme masters of the art of saying things well, the Greeks. The danger here was from literal imitation. Erasmus, with habitual wit, ridiculed the Ciceronian who spent years in constructing sentences that might have been written by his master, who speaks of Jehovah as Jupiter and of Christ as Cecrops or Iphigenia, and who transmutes the world around him into a Roman empire with tribunes and augurs, consuls and allies. It is significant that the English word "pedant" was coined in the sixteenth century.

What the classics had to teach directly was not only of less value than their indirect influence, but was often positively harmful. Those who, intoxicated with the pagan spirit, sought to regulate their lives by the moral standards of the poets, fell into the same error, though into the opposite vices, as those who deified the letter of the Bible. Like the Bible the classics were, and are, to some extent obstacles to the march of science, and this not only because they take men's interest from the study of nature, but because most ancient philosophers from the time of Socrates spoke contemptuously of natural experiment and discovery as things of little or no value to the soul.

If for the finer spirits of the age a classical education furnished a noble instrument of culture, for all too many it was prized simply as a badge of superiority. Among a people that stands in awe of learning—and this is more true of Europe than of America and was more true of the sixteenth than it is of the twentieth century—a classical education offers a man exceptional facilities for delicately impressing inferiors with their crudity.

Vernaculars

The period that marked high water in the estimation of the classics, also saw the turn of the tide. In all countries the vernacular crowded the classics ever backward from the field. The conscious cultivation of the modern tongues was marked by the publication of new dictionaries and by various works such as John Bale's history of English literature, written itself, to be sure, in Latin. The finest work of the kind was

Joachim du Bellay's *Défence et Illustration de la langue française* published in 1549 as part of a concerted effort to raise French as a vehicle of poetry and prose to a level with the classics. This was done partly by borrowing from Latin. One of the characteristic words of the sixteenth century, "patrie," was thus formally introduced.

§ 2. History

For the examination of the interests and temper of a given era, hardly any better gauge can be found than the history it produced. In the period under consideration there were two great schools, or currents, of historiography, the humanistic, sprung from the Renaissance, and church history, the child of the Reformation.

Humanistic school of historiography

The devotees of the first illustrate most aptly what has just been said about the influence of the classics. Their supreme interest was style, generally Latin. To clothe a chronicle in the toga of Livy's periods, to deck it out with the rhetoric of Sallust and to stitch on a few antitheses and epigrams in the manner of Tacitus, seemed to them the height of art. Their choice of matter was as characteristic as their manner, in that their interest was exclusively political and aristocratic. Save the doings of courts and camps, the political intrigues of governments and the results of battles, together with the virtues and vices of the rulers, they saw little in history. What the people thought, felt and suffered, was beyond their purview. Nor did most of them have much interest in art, science or literature, or even in religion. When George Buchanan, a man in the thick of the Scottish Reformation, who drafted the *Book of Articles*, came to write the history of his own time, he was so obsessed with the desire to imitate the ancient Romans that he hardly mentioned the religious controversy at all. One sarcasm on the priests who thought the *New* Testatment was written by Luther, and demanded their good *Old* Testament back again, two brief allusions to Knox, and a few other passing references are all of the Reformation that comes into a bulky volume dealing with the reigns of James V and Mary Stuart. His interest in political liberty, his conception of the struggle as one between tyranny and freedom, might appear modern were it not so plainly rooted in antique soil.

Machiavelli

The prevailing vice of the humanists—to see in the story of a people nothing but a political lesson—is carried to its extreme by Machiavelli. Writing with all the charm that conquers time, this theorist altered facts to suit his thesis to the point of composing historical romances. His *Life of Castruccio* is as fictitious and as didactic as Xenophon's *Cyropaedia;* his *Commentary on Livy* is as much a treatise on politics as is *The Prince;* the *History of Florence* is but slightly hampered by the events.

Guicciardini

If Guicciardini's interest in politics is not less exclusive than that of his compatriot, he is vastly superior as a historian to the older man in that, whereas Machiavelli deduced history *a priori* from theory, Guicciardini had a real desire to follow the inductive method of deriving his theory from an accurate mastery of the facts. With superb analytical reasoning he presents his data, marshals them and draws from them the conclusions they will bear. The limitation that vitiates many of his deductions is his taking into account only low and selfish motives. Before idealists he stands helpless; he leaves the reader uncertain whether Savonarola was a prophet or an extremely astute politician.

Jovius

The advance that Paul Jovius marks over the Florentines lies in the appeal that he made to the interests of the general public. History had hitherto been written for the greater glory of a patron or at most of a city; Jovius saw that the most generous patron of genius must henceforth be the average reader. It is true that he despised the public for whom he wrote, stuffing them with silly anecdotes. Both as the first great interviewer and reporter for the history of his own times, and in paying homage to Mrs. Grundy by assuming an air of virtue not natural to him, he anticipated the modern journalist.

Polydore Vergil

So much more modern in point of view than his contemporaries was Polydore Vergil—whose *English History* appeared in 1534—that the generalizations about humanist historiography are only partially true of him. Though his description of land and people is perhaps modelled on Herodotus, it shows a genuine interest in the life of the common man, even of the poor. He noted the geography, climate and fauna of the island; his eyes saw London Bridge with its rows of shops on either side, and they admired the parks full of game, the apple orchards, the fat hens and pheasants, the ploughs drawn by mixed teams of horses and oxen; he even observed the silver salt-cellars, spoons and cups used by the poor, and their meals of meat. His description of the people as brave, hospitable and very religious is as true now as it was then. With an antiquary's interest in old manuscripts Vergil combined a philosopher's skepticism of old legends. This Italian, though his patron was Henry VIII, balanced English and French authorities and told the truth even in such delicate matters as the treatment of Joan of Arc. Political history was for him still the most important, although to one branch of it, constitutional history, he was totally blind. So were almost all Englishmen then, even Shakespeare, whose *King John* contains no allusion to Magna Charta. In his work *On the Inventors of Things* Vergil showed the depth of his insight into the importance in history of culture and ideas. While his treatment of such subjects as the origin of myths, man, marriage, religion, language, poetry, drama, music, sciences and laws is unequal to his purpose, the intention itself bears witness to a new and fruitful spirit.

French Memoirs

Neither France nor England nor Germany produced historians equal to those of Italian or of Scottish birth. France was the home of the memoir, personal, chatty, spicy and unphilosophic. Those of Blaise de Montluc are purely military, those of Brantôme are mostly scandalous. Martin du Bellay tried to impart a higher tone to his reminiscences, while with Hotman a school of pamphleteers arose to yoke history with political theory. John Bodin attempted without much success the difficult task of writing a philosophy of history. His chief contribution was the theory of geography and climate as determinant influences.

English chronicles

It is hard to see any value, save occasionally as sources, in the popular English chronicles of Edward Hall, Raphael Hollinshed and John Stow. Full of court gossip and of pageantry, strongly royalist, conservative and patriotic, they reflect the interests of the middle-class cockney as faithfully as does a certain type of newspaper and magazine today.

Biographies

The biography and autobiography were cultivated with considerable success. Jovius and Brantôme both wrote series of lives of eminent men and women. Though the essays of Erasmus in this direction are both few and brief, they are notable as among the most exquisite pen-portraits in literature. More ambitious and more notable were the *Lives of the Best Painters, Sculptors and Architects* by George Vasari, in which the whole interest was personal and practical, with no attempt to write a history or a philosophy of art. Even criticism was confined almost entirely to vari-

1550

ations of praise. In the realm of autobiography Benvenuto Cellini attained to the *non plus ultra* of self-revelation. If he discloses the springs of a rare artistic genius, with equal naïveté he lays bare a ruffianly character and a colossal egotism.

Church history

One immense field of human thought and action had been all but totally ignored by the humanist historians —that of religion. To cultivate this field a new genre, church history, sprang into being, though the felt want was not then for a rational explanation of important and neglected phenomena, but for material which each side in the religious controversy might forge into weapons to use against the other. The natural result of so practical a purpose was that history was studied through colored spectacles, and was interpreted with strong tendency. In the most honest hands, such as those of Sleidan, the scale was unconsciously weighted on one side; by more passionate or less honorable advocates it was deliberately lightened with suppression of the truth on one side and loaded with suggestion of the false on the other.

If the mutual animosity of Catholic and Protestant narrowed history, their common detestation of all other religions than Christianity, as well as of all heresies and skepticisms, probably impoverished it still more. Orthodox Christianity, with its necessary preparation, ancient Judaism, was set apart as divinely revealed over against all other faiths and beliefs, which at best were "the beastly devices of the heathen" and at worst the direct inspiration of the devils. Few were the men who, like Erasmus, could compare Christ with Socrates, Plato and Seneca; fewer still those who could say with Franck, "Heretic is a title of honor, for truth is always called heresy." The names of Marcion and Pelagius, Epicurus and Mahomet, excited a passion of hatred hardly comprehensible to us. The refutation of the Koran issued under Luther's auspices would have been ludicrous had it not been pitiful.

In large part this vicious interpretation of history was bequeathed to the Reformers by the Middle Ages. As Augustine set the City of God over against the city of destruction, so the Protestant historians regarded the human drama as a puppet show in which God and the devil pulled the strings. Institutions of which they disapproved, such as the papacy and monasticism, were thought to be adequately explained by the suggestion of their Satanic origin. A thin, wan line of witnesses passed the truth down, like buckets of water at a fire, from its source in the Apostolic age to the time of the writer.

Even with such handicaps to weigh it down, the study of church history did much good. A vast body of new sources were uncovered and ransacked. The appeal to an objective standard slowly but surely forced its lesson on the litigants before the bar of truth. Writing under the eye of vigilant critics one cannot forever suppress or distort inconvenient facts. The critical dagger, at first sharpened only to stab an enemy, became a scalpel to cut away many a foreign growth. With larger knowledge came, though slowly, fairer judgment and deeper human interest. In these respects there was vast difference between the individual writers. To condemn them all to the Malebolge deserved only by the worst is undiscriminating.

Magdeburg Centuries, 1559–74

Among the most industrious and the most biassed must certainly be numbered Matthew Flacius Illyricus and his collaborators in producing the *Magdeburg Centuries,* a vast history of the church to the year 1300, which aimed at making Protestant polemic independent of Catholic sources. Save for the accumulation of much material it deserves no praise. Its critical principles are worse than none, for its only criterion of sources is as they are pro- or anti-papal. The latter are taken and the former left. Miracles are not doubted as such, but are divided into two classes, those tending to prove an accepted doctrine which are true, and those which support some papal institution which are branded as "first-class lies." The correspondence between Christ and King Abgarus is used as not having been proved a forgery, and the absurd legend of the female Pope Joan is never doubted. The psychology of the authors is as bad as their criticism. All opposition to the pope, especially that of the German Emperors, is represented as caused by religion.

Annales of Baronius, 1583–1607

However poor was the work of the authors of the Magdeburg Centuries, they were at least honest in arraying their sources. This is more than can be said of Caesar Baronius, whose *Annales Ecclesiastici* was the official Catholic counterblast to the Protestant work. Whereas his criticism is no whit better than theirs, he adopted the cunning policy, unfortunately widely obtaining since his day, of simply ignoring or suppressing unpleasant facts, rather than of refuting the inferences drawn from them. His talent for switching the attention to a side-issue, and for tangling instead of clearing problems, made the Protestants justly regard him as "a great deceiver" though even the most learned of them, J. J. Scaliger, who attempted to refute him, found the work difficult.

Naturally the battle of the historians waxed hottest over the Reformation itself. A certain class of Protestant works, of which Crespin's *Book of Martyrs*, 1554 Beza's *Ecclesiastical History* 1589 and John Foxe's *Acts and Monuments* (first English edition, 1563), are examples, catered to the passions of the multitude by laying the stress of their presentation on the heroism and sufferings of the witnesses to the faith and the cruelty of the persecutors. For many men the detailed description of isolated facts has a certain "thickness" of reality—if I may borrow William James's phrase—that is found by more complex minds only in the deduction of general causes. Passionate, partisan and sometimes ribald, Foxe won the reward that waits on demagogues. When it came to him as an afterthought to turn his book of martyrs into a general history, he plagiarized the *Magdeburg Centuries.* The reliability of his original narrative has been impugned with some success, though it has not been fully or impartially investigated. Much of it being drawn from personal recollection or from unpublished records, its sole value consists for us in its accuracy. I have compared a small section of the work with the manuscript source used by Foxe and have made the rather surprising discovery that though there are wide variations, none of them can be referred to partisan bias or to any other conceivable motive. In this instance, which is too small to generalize, it is possible that Foxe either had supplementary information, or that he wrote from a careless memory. In any case his work must be used with caution.

Foxe

Knox

Much superior to the work of Foxe was John Knox's *History of the Reformation of Religion within the Realm of Scotland* (written 1559–71). In style it is rapid, with a rare gift for seizing the essential and a no less rare humor and command of sarcasm. Its intention to be "a faithful rehearsal of such personages as God has made instruments of his glory," though thus equivocally stated, is carried out in an honorable sense. It is true that the writer never harbored a doubt that John Knox himself was the chiefest instrument of God's glory, nor that "the Roman Kirk is the synagogue of Satan and the head thereof, called the pope, that man of sin of whom the apostle speaketh." If, in such an avowed apology, one does not get impartiality, neither is one misled by expecting it. Knox's honor consists only in this that, as a party pamphleteer, he did not falsify or suppress essential facts as he understood them himself.

Bullinger

In glaring contrast to Knox's obtrusive bias, is the fair appearance of impartiality presented in Henry Bullinger's *History of the Reformation* 1519–32. Here, too, we meet with excellent composition, but with a studied moderation of phrase. It is probable that the author's professions of fairness are sincere, though at times the temptation to omit recording unedifying facts, such as the sacramentarian schism, is too strong for him.

Sleidan

1555

Before passing judgment on anything it is necessary to know it at its best. Probably John Sleidan's *Religious and political History of the reign of Charles V* was the best work on the German Reformation written before the eighteenth century. Bossuet was more eloquent and acute, Seckendorf more learned, Gilbert Burnet had better perspective, but none of these writers was better informed than Sleidan, or as objective. For the first and only time he really combined the two genres then obtaining, the humanistic and the ecclesiastical. He is not blind to some of the cultural achievements of the Reformation. One of the things for which he praises Luther most is for ornamenting and enriching the German language. Sleidan's faults are those of his age. He dared not break the old stiff division of the subject by years. He put in a number of insignificant facts, such as the flood of the Tiber and the explosion of ammunition dumps, nor was he above a superstitious belief in the effects of eclipses and in monsters. He cited documents broadly and on the whole fairly, but not with painstaking accuracy. He offered nothing on the causes leading up to the Reformation, nor on the course of the development of

Protestantism, nor on the characters of its leaders nor on the life and thought of the people. But he wrote fluently, acceptably to his public, and temperately.

On the whole, save for Baronius, the Catholics had less to offer of notable histories than had the Protestants. A *succès de scandale* was won by Nicholas Sanders' *Origin and Progress of the English Schism.* Among the nasty bits of gossip with which "Dr. Slanders," as he was called, delighted to regale his audience, some are absurd, such as that Anne Boleyn was Henry VIII's daughter. As the books from which he says he took these anecdotes are not extant, it is impossible to gauge how far he merely copied from others and how far he gave rein to his imagination.

Sanders 1585

Loyola

The one brilliant bit of Catholic church history that was written in the sixteenth century is the autobiography of Ignatius Loyola, dictated by him to Lewis Gonzalez and taken down partly in Spanish and partly in Italian. The great merit of this narrative is its insight into the author's own character gained by long years of careful self-observation. Its whole emphasis is psychological, on the inner struggle and not on the outward manifestations of saintliness, such as visions. It was taken over in large part verbatim in Ribadeneira's biography of Loyola. Compared to it, all other attempts at ecclesiastical biography in the sixteenth century, notably the lives of Luther by the Catholic Cochlaeus and by the Protestant Mathesius, lag far in the dusty rear.

1553–6

§ 3. Political Theory

Premises

The great era of the state naturally shone in political thought. Though there was some scientific investigation of social and economic laws, thought was chiefly conditioned by the new problems to be faced. From the long medieval dream of a universal empire and a universal church, men awoke to find themselves in the presence of new entities, created, to be sure, by their own spirits, but all unwittingly. One of these was the national state, whose essence was power and the law of whose life was expansion to the point of meeting equal or superior force. No other factor in history, not even religion, has produced so many wars as has the clash of national egotisms sanctified by the name of patriotism. Within the state the shift of sovereignty from the privileged orders to the bourgeoisie necessitated the formulation of a new theory. It was the triumph, with the rich, of the monarchy and of the parliaments, that pointed the road of some publicists to a doctrine of the divine right of kings, and others to a distinctly republican conclusions. There were even a few egalitarians who claimed for all classes a democratic régime. And, thirdly, the Reformation gave a new turn to the old problem of the relationship of church and state. It was on premises gathered from these three phenomena that the publicists of that age built a dazzling structure of political thought.

Machiavelli, 1469–1527

It was chiefly the first of these problems that absorbed the attention of Nicholas Machiavelli, the most brilliant, the most studied and the most abused of political theorists. As between monarchy and a republic he preferred, on the whole, the former, as likely to be the stronger, but he clearly saw that where economic equality prevailed political equality was natural and inevitable. The masses, he thought, desired only security of person and property, and would adhere to either form of government that offered them the best chance of these. For republic and monarchy alike Machiavelli was ready to offer maxims of statecraft, those for the former embodied in his *Discourses on Livy*, those for the latter in his *Prince*. In erecting a new science of statecraft, by which a people might arrive at supreme dominion, Machiavelli's great merit is that he looked afresh at the facts and discarded the old, worn formulas of the schoolmen; his great defect is that he set before his mind as a premise an abstract "political man" as far divorced from living, breathing, complex reality as the "economic man" of Ricardo. Men, he thought, are always the same, governed by calculable motives of self-interest. In general, he thought, men are ungrateful, fickle, false, cowardly and covetous, to be ruled partly by an appeal to their greed, but chiefly by fear.

Politics divorced from morality

Realist as he professed to be, Machiavelli divorced politics from morality. Whereas for Aristotle [1] and Aquinas alike the science of politics is a branch of ethics, for Machiavelli it is an abstract science as totally dissociated from morality as is mathematics or surgery. The prince, according to Machiavelli, should appear to be merciful, faithful, humane, religious and upright, but should be able to act otherwise without the least scruple when it is to his advantage to do so. His heroes are Ferdinand of Aragon, "a prince who always preaches good faith but never practises it," and Caesar Borgia, "who did everything that can be done by a prudent and virtuous man; so that no better precepts can be offered to a new prince than those suggested by the example of his actions." What the Florentine publicist especially admired in Caesar's statecraft were some examples of consummate perfidy and violence which he had the opportunity of observing at first hand. Machiavelli made a sharp distinction between private and public virtue. The former he professed to regard as binding on the individual, as it was necessary to the public good. It is noteworthy that this advocate of all hypocrisy and guile

[1] In Greek the words "politics" and "ethics" both have a wider meaning than they have in English.

and violence on the part of the government was in his own life gentle, affectionate and true to trust. Religion Machiavelli regarded as a valuable instrument of tyranny, but he did not hold the view, attributed by Gibbon to Roman publicists, that all religions, though to the philosopher equally false, were to the statesman equally useful. Christianity he detested, not so much as an exploded superstition, as because he saw in it theoretically the negation of those patriotic, military virtues of ancient Rome, and because practically the papacy had prevented the union of Italy. Naturally Machiavelli cherished the army as the prime interest of the state. In advocating a national militia with universal training of citizens he anticipated the conscript armies of the nineteenth century.

Public *vs.* private life

This writer, speaking the latent though unavowed ideals of an evil generation of public men, was rewarded by being openly vilified and secretly studied. He became the manual of statesmen and the bugbear of moralists. While Catharine de' Medici, Thomas Cromwell and Francis Bacon chewed, swallowed and digested his pages, the dramatist had only to put in a sneer or an abusive sarcasm at the expense of the Florentine—and there were very many such allusions to him on the Elizabethan stage—to be sure of a round of applause from the audience. While Machiavelli found few open defenders, efforts to refute him were numerous. When Reginald Pole said that his works were written by the evil one a chorus of Jesuits sang amen and the church put his writings on the Index. The Huguenots were not less vociferous in opposition. Among them Innocent Gentillet attacked not only his morals but his talent, saying that his maxims were drawn from an observation of small states only, and that his judgment of the policy suitable to large nations was of the poorest.

It is fair to try *The Prince* by the author's own standards. He did not purpose, in Bacon's phrase, to describe what men ought to be but what they actually are; he put aside ethical ideas not as false but as irrelevant. But this rejection was fatal even to his own purpose, "for what he put aside . . . were nothing less than the living forces by which societies subsist and governments are strong."[1] Calvin succeeded where the Florentine failed, as Lord Morley points out, because he put the moral ideal first.

Erasmus

The most striking contrast to Machiavelli was not forthcoming from the camp of the Reformers, but from that of the northern humanists, Erasmus and More. The *Institution of a Christian Prince,* by the Dutch scholar, is at the antipodes of the Italian thesis. Virtue is inculcated as the chief requisite of a prince, who can be considered good only in proportion as he fosters the wealth and the education of his people. He should levy no taxes, if possible, but should live parsimoniously off his own estate. He should never make war, save when absolutely necessary, even against the Infidel, and should negotiate only such treaties as have for their principal object the prevention of armed conflict.

Still more noteworthy than his moral postulates, is Erasmus's preference for the republican form of government. In the *Christian Prince,* dedicated as it was to the emperor, he spoke as if kings might and perhaps ought to be elected, but in his *Adages* he interpreted the spirit of the ancients in a way most disparaging to monarchy. Considering how carefully this work was studied by promising youths at the impressionable age, it is not too much to regard it as one of the main sources of the marked republican current of thought throughout the century. Under the heading, "Fools

[1] Lord Morley.

and kings are born such,'' he wrote: ''In all history, ancient and recent, you will scarcely find in the course of several centuries one or two princes, who, by their signal folly, did not bring ruin on humanity.'' In another place, after a similar remark, he continues:

> I know not whether much of this is not to be imputed to ourselves. We trust the rudder of a vessel, where a few sailors and some goods alone are in jeopardy, to none but skilful pilots; but the state, wherein is comprised the safety of so many thousands, we leave to the guidance of any chance hands. A charioteer must learn, reflect upon and practice his art; a prince needs only to be born. Yet government is the most difficult, as it is the most honorable, of sciences. Shall we choose the master of a ship and not choose him who is to have the care of so many cities and so many souls? . . . Do we not see that noble cities are erected by the people and destroyed by princes? that a state grows rich by the industry of its citizens and is plundered by the rapacity of its princes? that good laws are enacted by elected magistrates and violated by kings? that the people love peace and the princes foment war?

There is far too much to the same purpose to quote, which in all makes a polemic against monarchy not exceeded by the fiercest republicans of the next two generations. It is true that Erasmus wrote all this in 1515, and half took it back after the Peasants' War. ''Princes must be endured,'' he then thought, ''lest tyranny give place to anarchy, a still greater evil.''

Reformation

As one of the principal causes of the Reformation was the strengthening of national self-consciousness, so conversely one of the most marked results of the movement was the exaltation of the state. The Reformation began to realize, though at first haltingly, the separation of church and state, and it endowed the latter with much wealth, with many privileges and with high prerogatives and duties up to that time belonging to the former. It is true that all the innovators would have recoiled from bald Erastianism, which is not found in the theses of Thomas Erastus, but in the free-thinker Thomas Hobbes. Whereas the Reformers merely said that the state should be charged with the duty of enforcing orthodoxy and punishing sinners, Hobbes drew the logical inference that the state was the final authority for determining religious truth. That Hobbes's conclusion was only the *reductio ad absurdum* of the Reformation doctrine was hidden from the Reformers themselves by their very strong belief in an absolute and ascertainable religious truth.

Erastus, 1524–83
Hobbes, 1588–1679

The tendency of both Luther and Calvin to exalt the state took two divergent forms according to their understanding of what the state was. Lutheranism became the ally of absolute monarchy, whereas Calvinism had in it a republican element. It is no accident that Germany developed a form of government in which a paternal but bureaucratic care of the people supplied the place of popular liberty, whereas America, on the whole the most Calvinistic of the great states, carried to its logical conclusion the idea of the rule of the majority. The English Reformation was at first Lutheran in this respect, but after 1580 it began to take the strong Calvinistic tendency that led to the Commonwealth.

Luther

While Luther cared enormously for social reform, and did valiant service in its cause, he harbored a distrust of the people that grates harshly on modern ears. Especially after the excesses of the Peasants' War and the extravagance of Münzer, he came to believe that "Herr Omnes" was capable of little good and much evil. "The princes of this world are gods," he once said, "the common people are Satan, through whom God sometimes does what at other times he does directly through Satan, *i.e.,* makes rebellion as a punishment for the people's sins." And again: "I would rather suffer a prince doing wrong than a people doing right." Passive obedience to the divinely ordained "powers that be" was therefore the sole duty of the subject. "It is in no wise proper for anyone who would be a Christian to set himself up against his government, whether it act justly or unjustly," he wrote in 1530.

That Luther turned to the prince as the representative of the divine majesty in the state is due not only to Scriptural authority but to the fact that there was no material for any other form of government to be found in Germany. He was no sycophant, nor had he any illusions as to the character of hereditary monarchs. In his *Treatise on Civil Authority,* dedicated to his own sovereign, Duke John of Saxony, he wrote: "Since the foundation of the world a wise prince has been a rare bird and a just one much rarer. They are generally the biggest fools and worst knaves on earth, wherefore one must always expect the worst of them and not much good, especially in divine matters." They distinctly have not the right, he adds, to decide spiritual things, but only to enforce the decisions of the Christian community.

1523

Feeling the necessity for some bridle in the mouth of the emperor and finding no warrant for the people to curb him, Luther groped for the notion of some legal limitation on the monarch's power. The word "constitution" so familiar to us, was lacking then, but that the idea was present is certain. The German Empire had a constitution, largely unwritten but partly statutory. The limitations on the imperial power were then recognized by an Italian observer, Quirini. When they were brought to Luther's attention he admitted the right of the German states to resist by force im-

1507

perial acts of injustice contrary to positive laws. Moreover, he always maintained that no subject should obey an order directly contravening the law of God. In these limitations on the government's power, slight as they were, were contained the germs of the later Calvinistic constitutionalism.

Reformed Church

While many of the Reformers—Melanchthon, Bucer, Tyndale—were completely in accord with Luther's earlier doctrine of passive obedience, the Swiss, French and Scotch developed a consistent body of constitutional theory destined to guide the peoples into ordered liberty. Doubtless an influence of prime importance in the Reformed as distinct from the Lutheran church, was the form of ecclesiastical government. Congregationalism and Presbyterianism are practical object-lessons in democracy. Many writers have justly pointed out in the case of America the influence of the vestry in the evolution of the town meeting. In other countries the same cause operated in the same way, giving the British and French Protestants ample practice in representative government. Zwingli asserted that the subject should refuse to act contrary to his faith. From the Middle Ages he took the doctrine of the identity of spiritual and civil authority, but he also postulated the sovereignty of the people, as was natural in a free-born Switzer. In fact, his sympathies were republican through and through.

Zwingli

Calvin

The clear political thinking of Calvin and his followers was in large part the result of the exigencies of their situation. Confronted with established power they were forced to defend themselves with pen as well as with sword. In France, especially, the ember of their thought was blown into fierce blaze by the winds of persecution. Not only the Huguenots took fire, but all their neighbors, until the kingdom of

France seemed on the point of anticipating the great Revolution by two centuries.

With the tocsins ringing in his ears, jangling discordantly with the servile doctrines of Paul and Luther, Calvin set to work to forge a theory that should combine liberty with order. Carrying a step further than had his masters the separation of civil and ecclesiastical authority, he yet regarded civil government as the most sacred and honorable of all merely human institutions. The form he preferred was an aristocracy, but where monarchy prevailed, Calvin was not prepared to recommend its overthrow, save in extreme cases. Grasping at Luther's idea of constitutional, or contractual, limitations on the royal power, he asserted that the king should be resisted, when he violated his rights, not by private men but by elected magistrates to whom the guardianship of the people's rights should be particularly entrusted. The high respect in which Calvin was held, and the clearness and comprehensiveness of his thought made him ultimately the most influential of the Protestant publicists. By his doctrine the Dutch, English, and American nations were educated to popular sovereignty.

French republicans

The seeds of liberty sown by Calvin might well have remained long hidden in the ground, had not the soil of France been irrigated with blood and scorched by the tyranny of the last Valois. Theories of popular rights, which sprang up with the luxuriance of the jungle after the day of St. Bartholomew, were already sprouting some years before it. The Estates General that met at Paris in March, 1561, demanded that the regency be put in the hands of Henry of Navarre and that the members of the house of Lorraine and the Chancellor L'Hôpital be removed from all offices as not having been appointed by the Estates. In August of the same year, thirty-nine representatives of the three Estates of thirteen provinces met, contemporaneously with the religious Colloquy of Poissy, at Pontoise, and there voiced with great boldness the claims of constitutional government. They demanded the right of the Estates to govern during the minority of the king; they claimed that the Estates should be summoned at least biennially; they forbade taxation, alienation of the royal domain or declaration of war without their consent. The further resolution that the persecution of the Huguenots should cease, betrayed the quarter from which the popular party drew its strength.

But if the voices of the brave deputies hardly carried beyond the senate-chamber, a host of pamphlets, following hard upon the great massacre, trumpeted the sounds of freedom to the four winds. Theodore Beza published anonymously his *Rights of Magistrates,* developing Calvin's theory that the representatives of the people should be empowered to put a bridle on the king. The pact between the people and king is said to be abrogated if the king violates it.

Beza

At the same time another French Protestant, Francis Hotman, published his *Franco-Gallia,* to show that France had an ancient and inviolable constitution. This unwritten law regulates the succession to the throne; by it the deputies hold their privileges in the Estates General; by it the laws, binding even on the king, are made. The right of the people can be shown, in Hotman's opinion, to extend even to deposing the monarch and electing his successor.

Hotman, 1573

A higher and more general view was taken in the *Rights against Tyrants* published under the pseudonym of Stephen Junius Brutus the Celt, and written by Philip du Plessis-Mornay. This brief but comprehensive survey, addressed to both Catholics and Prot-

Vindiciae contra Tyrannos, 1577

estants, and aimed at Machiavelli as the chief supporter of tyranny, advanced four theses: 1. Subjects are bound to obey God rather than the king. This is regarded as self-evident. 2. If the king devastates the church and violates God's law, he may be resisted at least passively as far as private men are concerned, but actively by magistrates and cities. The author, who quotes from the Bible and ancient history, evidently has contemporary France in mind. 3. The people may resist a tyrant who is oppressing or ruining the state. Originally, in the author's view, the people either elected the king, or confirmed him, and if they have not exercised this right for a long time it is a legal maxim that no prescription can run against the public claims. Laws derive their sanction from the people, and should be made by them; taxes may only be levied by their representatives, and the king who exacts imposts of his own will is in no wise different from an enemy. The kings are not even the owners of public property, but only its administrators, are bound by the contract with the governed, and may be rightly punished for violating it. 4. The fourth thesis advanced by Mornay is that foreign aid may justly be called in against a tyrant.

La Boétie, 1530–63

Not relying exclusively on their own talents the Huguenots were able to press into the ranks of their army of pamphleteers some notable Catholics. In 1574 they published as a fragment, and in 1577 entire, *The Discourse on Voluntary Servitude,* commonly called the *Contr'un,* by Stephen de la Boétie. This gentleman, dying at the age of thirty-three, had left all his manuscripts to his bosom friend Montaigne. The latter says that La Boétie composed the work as a prize declamation at the age of sixteen or eighteen. But along with many passages in the pamphlet, which might have been suggested by Erasmus, are several

1546–8

allusions that seem to point to the character of Henry III—in 1574 king of Poland and in 1577 king of France—and to events just prior to the time of publication. According to an attractive hypothesis, not fully proved, these passages were added by Montaigne himself before he gave the work to one of his several Huguenot friends or kinsmen. La Boétie, at any rate, appealed to the passions aroused by St. Bartholomew in bidding the people no longer to submit to one man, "the most wretched and effeminate of the nation," who has only two hands, two eyes, and who will fall if unsupported. And yet, he goes on rhetorically, "you sow the fruits of the earth that he may waste them; you furnish your houses for him to pillage them; you rear your daughters to glut his lust and your sons to perish in his wars; . . . you exhaust your bodies in labor that he may wallow in vile pleasures."

As Montaigne and La Boétie were Catholics, it is pertinent here to remark that tyranny produced much the same effect on its victims, whatever their religion. The Sorbonne, consulted by the League, unanimously decided that the people of France were freed from their oath of allegiance to Henry III and could with a good conscience take arms against him. One of the doctors, Boucher, wrote to prove that the church and the people had the right to depose an assassin, a perjurer, an impious or heretical prince, or one guilty of sacrilege or witchcraft. A tyrant, he concluded, was a wild beast, whom it was lawful for the state as a whole or even for private individuals, to kill.

The Sorbonne

So firmly established did the doctrine of the contract between prince and people become that towards the end of the century one finds it taken for granted. The *Mémoires* of the Huguenot soldier, poet and historian Agrippa d'Aubigné are full of republican sentiments, as, for example, "There is a binding obligation between the king and his subjects," and "The power of the prince proceeds from the people."

But it must not be imagined that such doctrines passed without challenge. The most important writer on political science after Machiavelli, John Bodin, was on the whole a conservative. In his writings acute and sometimes profound remarks jostle quaint and abject superstitions. He hounded the government and the mob on witches with the vile zeal of the authors of the *Witches' Hammer;* and he examined all existing religions with the coolness of a philosopher. He urged on the attention of the world that history was determined in general by natural causes, such as climate, but that revolutions were caused partly by the inscrutable will of God and partly by the more ascertainable influence of planets.

Bodin, 1530–96

His most famous work, *The Republic,* is a criticism of Machiavelli and an attempt to bring politics back into the domain of morality. He defines a state as a company of men united for the purpose of living well and happily; he thinks it arose from natural right and social contract. For the first time Bodin differentiates the state from the government, defining sovereignty (*majestas*) as the attribute of the former. He classifies governments in the usual three categories, and refuses to believe in mixed governments. Though England puzzles him, he regards her as an absolute monarchy. This is the form that he decidedly prefers, for he calls the people a many-headed monster and says that the majority of men are incompetent and bad. Preaching passive obedience to the king, he finds no check on him, either by tyrannicide or by constitutional magistrates, save only in the judgment of God.

1576

It is singular that after Bodin had removed all effective checks on the tyrant in this world, he should lay it down as a principle that no king should levy taxes without his subjects' consent. Another contradiction is that whereas he frees the subject from the duty of obedience in case the monarch commands aught against God's law, he treats religion almost as a matter of policy, advising that, whatever it be, the statesman should not disturb it. Apart from the streak of superstition in his mind, his inconsistencies are due to the attempt to reconcile opposites—Machiavelli and Calvin. For with all his denunciation of the former's atheism and immorality, he, with his chauvinism, his defence of absolutism, his practical opportunism, is not so far removed from the Florentine as he would have us believe.

Dutch republicans

The revolution that failed in France succeeded in the Netherlands, and some contribution to political theory can be found in the constitution drawn up by the States General in 1580, when they recognized Anjou as their prince, and in the document deposing Philip in 1581. Both assume fully the sovereignty of the people and the omnicompetence of their elected representatives. As Oldenbarnevelt commented, "The cities and nobles together represent the whole state and the whole people." The deposition of Philip is justified by an appeal to the law of nature, and to the example of other tortured states, and by a recital of Philip's breaches of the laws and customs of the land.

Knox

Scotland, in the course of her revolution, produced almost as brilliant an array of pamphleteers as had France. John Knox maintained that, "If men, in the fear of God, oppose themselves to the fury and blind rage of princes, in doing so they do not resist God, but the devil, who abuses the sword and authority of God," and again, he asked, "What harm should the commonwealth receive if the corrupt affections of ignorant rulers were moderated and bridled by the wisdom and discretion of godly subjects?" But the duty, he thought, to curb princes in free kingdoms and realms, does not belong to every private man, but "appertains to the nobility, sworn and born counsellors of the same." Carrying such doctrines to the logical result, Knox hinted to Mary that Daniel might have resisted Nebuchadnezzar and Paul might have resisted Nero with the sword, had God given them the power.

Another Scotch Protestant, John Craig, in support of the prosecution of Mary, said that it had been determined and concluded at the University of Bologna that "all rulers, be they supreme or inferior, may be and ought to be reformed or deposed by them by whom they were chosen, confirmed and admitted to their office, as often as they break that promise made by oath to their subjects." Knox and Craig both argued for the execution of Mary on the ground that "it was a public speech among all peoples and among all estates, that the queen had no more liberty to commit murder nor adultery than any other private person." Knollys also told Mary that a monarch ought to be deposed for madness or murder.

1554

Buchanan

To the zeal for religion animating Knox, George Buchanan joined a more rational spirit of liberty and a stronger consciousness of positive right. His great work *On the Constitution of Scotland* derived all power from the people, asserted the responsibility of kings to their subjects and pleaded for the popular election of the chief magistrate. In extreme cases execution of the monarch was defended, though by what precise machinery he was to be arraigned was left uncertain; probably constitutional resistance was thought of, as far as practicable, and tyrannicide was considered as a last resort. "If you ask anyone," says our author, "what he thinks of the punishment of

Caligula, Nero or Domitian, I think no one will be so devoted to the royal name as not to confess that they rightly paid the penalty of their crimes.''

English monarchists

In England the two tendencies, the one to favor the divine right of kings, the other for constitutional restraint, existed side by side. The latter opinion was attributed by courtly divines to the influence of Calvin. Matthew Hutton blamed the Reformer because ''he thought not so well of a kingdom as of a popular state.'' ''God save us,'' wrote Archbishop Parker, ''from such a visitation as Knox has attempted in Scotland, the people to be orderers of things.'' This distinguished prelate preached that disobedience to the queen was a greater crime than sacrilege or adultery, for obedience is the root of all virtues and the cause of all felicity, and ''rebellion is not a single fault, like theft or murder, but the cesspool and swamp of all possible sins against God and man.'' Bonner was charged by the government of Mary to preach that all rebels incurred damnation. Much later Richard Hooker warned his countrymen that Puritanism endangered the prerogatives of crown and nobility.

and republicans

But there were not wanting champions of the people. Reginald Pole asserted the responsibility of the sovereign, though in moderate language. Bishop John Ponet wrote *A Treatise on Politic Power* to show that men had the right to depose a bad king and to assassinate a tyrant. The haughty Elizabeth herself often had to listen to drastic advice. When she visited Cambridge she was entertained by a debate on tyrannicide, in which one bold clerk asserted that God might incite a regicide; and by a discussion of the respective advantages of elective and hereditary monarchy, one speaker offering to maintain the former with his life and, if need be, with his death. When Elizabeth, after hearing a refractory Parliament, complained to the

Spanish ambassador that "she could not tell what those devils were after" his excellency replied, "They want liberty, madam, and if princes do not look to themselves" they will soon find that they are drifting to revolution and anarchy. Significant, indeed, was the silent work of Parliament in building up the constitutional doctrine of its own omnicompetence and of its own supremacy.

Tyrannicide

One striking aberration in the political theory of that time was the prominence in it of the appeal to tyrannicide. Schooled by the ancients who sang the praises of Harmodius and Aristogiton, by the biblical example of Ehud and Eglon, and by various medieval publicists, and taught the value of murder by the princes and popes who set prices on each other's heads, an extraordinary number of sixteenth century divines approved of the dagger as the best remedy for tyranny. Melanchthon wished that God would raise up an able man to slay Henry VIII; John Ponet and Cajetan and the French theologian Boucher admitted the possible virtue of assassination. But the most elaborate statement of the same doctrine was put by the Spanish Jesuit Mariana, in a book *On the King and his Education* published in 1599, with an official *imprimatur,* a dedication to the reigning monarch and an assertion that it was approved by learned and grave men of the Society of Jesus. It taught that the prince holds sway solely by the consent of the people and by ancient law, and that, though his vices are to be borne up to a certain point, yet when he ruins the state he is a public enemy, to slay whom is not only permissible but glorious for any man brave enough to despise his own safety for the public good.

If one may gather the official theory of the Catholic church from the contradictory statements of her doctors, she advocated despotism tempered by assassination. No Lutheran ever preached the duty of passive obedience more strongly than did the Catechism of the Council of Trent.

Radicals

A word must be said about the more radical thought of the time. All the writers just analysed saw things from the standpoint of the governing and propertied classes. But the voice of the poor came to be heard now and then, not only from their own mouths but from that of the few authors who had enough imagination to sympathize with them. The idea that men might sometime live without any government at all is found in such widely different writers as Richard Hooker and Francis Rabelais. But socialism was then, as ever, more commonly advocated than anarchy. The Anabaptists, particularly, believed in a community of goods, and even tried to practice it when they got the chance. Though they failed in this, the contributions to democracy latent in their egalitarian spirit must not be forgotten. They brought down on themselves the severest animadversions from defenders of the existing order, by whatever confession they were bound. Vives wrote a special tract to refute the arguments of the Anabaptists on communism. Luther said that the example of the early Christians did not authorize communism for, though the first disciples pooled their own goods, they did not try to seize the property of Pilate and Herod. Even the French Calvinists, in their books dedicated to liberty, referred to the Anabaptists as seditious rebels worthy of the severest repression.

1535

Utopia, 1516

A nobler work than any produced by the Anabaptists, and one that may have influenced them not a little, was the *Utopia* of Sir Thomas More. He drew partly on Plato, on Tacitus's *Germania,* on Augustine and on Pico della Mirandola, and for the outward framework of his book on the *Four Voyages of Americus Vespuc-*

cius. But he relied mostly on his own observation of what was rotten in the English state where he was a judge and a ruler of men. He imagined an ideal country, Utopia, a place of perfect equality economically as well as politically. It was by government an elective monarchy with inferior magistrates and representative assembly also elected. The people changed houses every ten years by lot; they considered luxury and wealth a reproach. "In other places they speak still of the common wealth but every man procureth his private wealth. Here where nothing is private the common affairs be earnestly looked upon." "What justice is this, that a rich goldsmith or usurer should have a pleasant and wealthy living either by idleness or by unnecessary occupation, when in the meantime poor laborers, carters, ironsmiths, carpenters and plowmen by so great and continual toil . . . do yet get so hard and so poor a living and live so wretched a life that the condition of the laboring beasts may seem much better and wealthier?" "When I consider and weigh in my mind all these commonwealths which nowadays anywhere do flourish, so God help me, I can perceive nothing but a certain conspiracy of rich men procuring their own commodities under the name and title of the commonwealth." More was convinced that a short day's labor shared by everyone would produce quite sufficient wealth to keep all in comfort. He protests explicitly against those who pretend that there are two sorts of justice, one for governments and one for private men. He repudiates the doctrine that bad faith is necessary to the prosperity of a state; the Utopians form no alliances and carry out faithfully the few and necessary treaties that they ratify. Moreover they dishonor war above all things.

The commonwealth

In the realm of pure economic and social theory

something, though not much, was done. Machiavelli believed that the growth of population in the north and its migration southwards was a constant law, an idea derived from Paulus Diaconus and handed on to Milton. He even derived "Germany" from "germinare." A more acute remark, anticipating Malthus, was made by the Spanish Jesuit John Botero who, in his *Reason of State,* pointed out that population was absolutely dependent on means of subsistence. He concluded *a priori* that the population of the world had remained stationary for three thousand years.

Botero, 1589

Mercantile economics

Statesmen then labored under the vicious error, drawn from the analogy of a private man and a state, that national wealth consisted in the precious metals. The stringent and universal laws against the export of specie and intended to encourage its import, proved a considerable burden on trade, though as a matter of fact they only retarded and did not stop the flow of coin. The striking rise in prices during the century attracted some attention. Various causes were assigned for it, among others the growth of population and the increase of luxury. Hardly anyone saw that the increase in the precious metals was the fundamental cause, but several writers, among them Bodin, John Hales and Copernicus, saw that a debased currency was responsible for the acute dearness of certain local markets.

Usury

The lawfulness of the taking of usury greatly exercised the minds of men of that day. The church on traditional grounds had forbidden it, and her doctors stood fast by her precept, though an occasional individual, like John Eck, could be found to argue for it. Luther was in principle against allowing a man "to sit behind his stove and let his money work for him," but he weakened enough to allow moderate interest in given circumstances. Zwingli would allow interest to be taken only as a form of profit-sharing. Calvin said: "If we forbid usury wholly we bind consciences by a bond straiter than that of God himself. But if we allow it the least in the world, under cover of our permission someone will immediately make a general and unbridled licence." The laws against the taking of interest were gradually relaxed throughout the century, but even at its close Bacon could only regard usury as a concession made on account of the hardness of men's hearts.

§ 4. Science

Inductive method

The glory of sixteenth-century science is that for the first time, on a large scale, since the ancient Greeks, did men try to look at nature through their own eyes instead of through those of Aristotle and the *Physiologus*. Bacon and Vives have each been credited with the discovery of the inductive method, but, like so many philosophers, they merely generalized a practice already common at their time. Save for one discovery of the first magnitude, and two or three others of some little importance, the work of the sixteenth century was that of observing, describing and classifying facts. This was no small service in itself, though it does not strike the imagination as do the great new theories.

Mathematics

In mathematics the preparatory work for the statement and solution of new problems consisted in the perfection of symbolism. As reasoning in general is dependent on words, as music is dependent on the mechanical invention of instruments, so mathematics cannot progress far save with a simple and adequate symbolism. The introduction of the Arabic as against the Roman numerals, and particularly the introduction of the zero in reckoning, for the first time, in the later Middle Ages, allowed men to perform conveniently the four fundamental processes. The use of the signs +

and — for plus and minus (formerly written p. and m.), and of the sign = for equality and of $\sqrt{}$ for root, were additional conveniences. To this might be added the popularization of decimals by Simon Stevin in 1586, which he called "the art of calculating by whole numbers without fractions." How clumsy are all things at their birth is illustrated by his method of writing decimals by putting them as powers of one-tenth, with circles around the exponents; *e.g.*, the number that we should write 237.578, he wrote $237^{0}\,5^{1}\,7^{2}\,8^{3}$. He first declared for decimal systems of coinage, weights and measures.

Algebra 1494

Algebraic notation also improved vastly in the period. In a treatise of Lucas Paciolus we find cumbrous signs instead of letters, thus no. (numero) for the known quantity, co. (cosa) for the unknown quantity, ce. (censo) for the square, and cu. (cubo) for the cube of the unknown quantity. As he still used p. and m. for plus and minus, he wrote 3co.p.4ce.m.5cu.p.2ce.ce.m.6no. for the number we should write $3x + 4x^2 - 5x^3 + 2x^4 - 6a$. The use of letters in the modern style is due to the mathematicians of the sixteenth century. The solution of cubic and of biquadratic equations, at first only in certain particular forms, but later in all forms, was mastered by Tartaglia and Cardan. The latter even discussed negative roots, whether rational or irrational.

Geometry

Geometry at that time, as for long afterwards, was dependent wholly on Euclid, of whose work a Latin translation was first published at Venice. Copernicus with his pupil George Joachim, called Rheticus, and Francis Vieta, made some progress in trigonometry. Copernicus gave the first simple demonstration of the fundamental formula of spherical trigonometry; Rheticus made tables of sines, tangents and secants

1505

of arcs. Vieta discovered the formula for deriving the sine of a multiple angle.

Cardan, 1501–76

As one turns the pages of the numerous works of Jerome Cardan one is astonished to find the number of subjects on which he wrote, including, in mathematics, choice and chance, arithmetic, algebra, the calendar, negative quantities, and the theory of numbers. In the last named branch it was another Italian, Maurolycus, who recognized the general character of mathematics as "symbolic logic." He is indeed credited with understanding the most general principle on which depends all mathematical deduction.[1] Some of the most remarkable anticipations of modern science were made by Cardan. He believed that inorganic matter was animated, and that all nature was a progressive evolution. Thus his statement that all animals were originally worms implies the indefinite variability of species, just as his remark that inferior metals were unsuccessful attempts of nature to produce gold, might seem to foreshadow the idea of the transmutation of metals under the influence of radioactivity. It must be remembered that such guesses had no claim to be scientific demonstrations.

Gesner, Zoölogy

The encyclopaedic character of knowledge was then, perhaps, one of its most striking characteristics. Bacon was not the first man of his century to take all knowledge for his province. In learning and breadth of view few men have ever exceeded Conrad Gesner, called by Cuvier "the German Pliny." His *History of Animals* (published in many volumes 1551–87) was the basis of zoölogy until the time of Darwin. He

[1] *I.e.* the principle thus formulated in the *Encyclopaedia Britannica*, *s.v.* "Mathematics": "If s is any class and zero a member of it, also if when x is a cardinal number and a member of s, also x + 1 is a member of s, then the whole class of cardinal numbers is contained in s."

drew largely on previous writers, Aristotle and Albertus Magnus, but he also took pains to see for himself as much as possible. The excellent illustrations for his book, partly drawn from previous works but mostly new, added greatly to its value. His classification, though superior to any that had preceded it, was in some respects astonishing, as when he put the hippopotamus among aquatic animals with fish, and the bat among birds. Occasionally he describes a purely mythical animal like "the monkey-fox." It is difficult to see what criterion of truth would have been adequate for the scholar at that time. A monkey-fox is no more improbable than a rhinoceros, and Gesner found it necessary to assure his readers that the rhinoceros really existed in nature and was not a creation of fancy.

Leonardo

As the master of modern anatomy and of several other branches of science, stands Leonardo da Vinci. It is difficult to appraise his work accurately because it is not yet fully known, and still more because of its extraordinary form. He left thousands of pages of notes on everything and hardly one complete treatise on anything. He began a hundred studies and finished none of them. He had a queer twist to his mind that made him, with all his power, seek byways. The monstrous, the uncouth, fascinated him; he saw a Medusa in a spider and the universe in a drop of water. He wrote his notes in mirror-writing, from right to left; he illustrated them with a thousand fragments of exquisite drawing, all unfinished and tantalizing alike to the artist and to the scientist. His mind roamed to flying machines and submarines, but he never made one; the reason given by him in the latter case being his fear that it would be put to piratical use. He had something in him of Faust; in some respects he reminds us of William James, who also started as a painter and ended as an omniverous student of outré things and as a psychologist.

Anatomy

If, therefore, the anatomical drawings made by Leonardo from about twenty bodies that he dissected, are marvellous specimens of art, he left it to others to make a really systematic study of the human body. His contemporary, Berengar of Carpi, professor at Bologna, first did this with marked success, classifying the various tissues as fat, membrane, flesh, nerve, fibre and so forth. So far from true is it that it was difficult to get corpses to work upon that he had at least a hundred. Indeed, according to Fallopius, another famous scientist, the Duke of Tuscany would occasionally send live criminals to be vivisected, thus making their punishment redound to the benefit of science. The Inquisitors made the path of science hard by burning books on anatomy as materialistic and indecent.

Servetus

Two or three investigators anticipated Harvey's discovery of the circulation of the blood. Unfortunately, as the matter is of interest, Servetus's treatment of the subject, found in his work on *The Trinity,* is too long to quote, but it is plain that, along with various fallacious ideas, he had really discovered the truth that the blood all passes through heart and lungs whence it is returned to the other organs.

Physics

While hardly anything was done in chemistry, a large number of phenomena in the field of physics were observed now for the first time. Leonardo da Vinci measured the rapidity of falling bodies, by dropping them from towers and having the time of their passage at various stages noted. He thus found, correctly, that their velocity increased. It is also said that he observed that bodies always fell a little to the eastward of the plumb line, and thence concluded that the earth revolved on its axis. He made careful experiments with billiard balls, discovering that the momentum of the impact always was preserved entire in the motion of the balls struck. He measured forces by the weight and speed of the bodies and arrived at an approximation of the ideas of mechanical "work" and energy of position. He thought of energy as a spiritual force transferred from one body to another by touch. This remarkable man further invented a hygrometer, explained sound as a wave-motion in the air, and said that the appearance known to us as "the old moon in the new moon's lap" was due to the reflection of earth-light.

Nicholas Tartaglia first showed that the course of a projectile was a parabola, and that the maximum range of a gun would be at an angle of 45°.

Some good work was done in optics. John Baptist della Porta described, though he did not invent, the camera obscura. Burning glasses were explained. Leonard Digges even anticipated the telescope by the use of double lenses.

Further progress in mechanics was made by Cardan who explained the lever and pulley, and by Simon Stevin who first demonstrated the resolution of forces. He also noticed the difference between stable and unstable equilibrium, and showed that the downward pressure of a liquid is independent of the shape of the vessel it is in and is dependent only on the height. He and other scholars asserted the causation of the tides by the moon.

Magnetism

Magnetism was much studied. When compasses were first invented it was thought that they always pointed to the North Star under the influence of some stellar compulsion. But even in the fifteenth century it was noticed independently by Columbus and by German experimenters that the needle did not point true north. As the amount of its declination varies at different places on the earth and at different times, this was one of the most puzzling facts to explain. One man believed that the change depended on climate, another that it was an individual property of each needle. About 1581 Robert Norman discovered the inclination, or dip of the compass. These and other observations were summed up by William Gilbert in his work on *The Magnet, Magnetic Bodies and the Earth as a great Magnet.* A great deal of his space was taken in that valuable destructive criticism that refutes prevalent errors. His greatest discovery was that the earth itself is a large magnet. He thought of magnetism as "a soul, or like a soul, which is in many things superior to the human soul as long as this is bound by our bodily organs." It was therefore an appetite that compelled the magnet to point north and south. Similar explanations of physical and chemical properties are found in the earliest and in some of the most recent philosophers.

Gilbert

1600

As might be expected, the science of geography, nourished by the discoveries of new lands, grew mightily. Even the size of the earth could only be guessed at until it had been encircled. Columbus believed that its circumference at the equator was 8000 miles. The stories of its size that circulated after Magellan were exaggerated by the people. Thus Sir David Lyndsay in his poem *The Dreme* quotes "the author of the sphere" as saying that the earth was 101,750 miles in circumference, each mile being 5000 feet. The author referred to was the thirteenth century Johannes de Sacro Bosco (John Holywood). Two editions of his work, *De Sphaera,* that I have seen, one of Venice, 1499, and one of Paris, 1527, give the circumference of the earth as 20,428 miles, but an edition published at Wittenberg in 1550 gives it as 5,400, probably an

Geography

1528

attempt to reduce the author's English miles to German ones. Robert Recorde calculated the earth's circumference at 21,300 miles.[1]

1551

Rough maps of the new lands were drawn by the companions of the discoverers. Martin Waldseemüller published a large map of the world in twelve sheets and a small globe about 4½ inches in diameter, in which the new world is for the first time called America. The next great advance was made by the Flemish cartographer Gerard Mercator whose globes and maps—some of them on the projection since called by his name—are extraordinarily accurate for Europe and the coast of Africa, and fairly correct for Asia, though he represented that continent as too narrow. He included, however, in their approximately correct positions, India, the Malay peninsula, Sumatra, Java and Japan. America is very poorly drawn, for though the east coast of North America is fairly correct, the continent is too broad and the rest of the coasts vague. He made two startling anticipations of later discoveries, the first that he separated Asia and America by only a narrow strait at the north, and the second that he assumed the existence of a continent around the south pole. This, however, he made far too large, thinking that the Tierra del Fuego was part of it and drawing it so as to come near the south coast of Africa and of Java. His maps of Europe were based on recent and excellent surveys.

1507

Mercator, 1512–94

Astronomy

Astronomy, the oldest of the sciences, had made much progress in the tabulation of material. The apparent orbits of the sun, moon, planets, and stars had been correctly observed, so that eclipses might be predicted, conjunction of planets calculated, and that

[1] Eratosthenes (276–196 B.C.) had correctly calculated the earth's circumference at 25,000, which Poseidonius (c. 135–50 B.C.) reduced to 18,000, in which he was followed by Ptolemy (2d century A.D.).

gradual movement of the sun through the signs of the zodiac known as the precession of the equinoxes, taken account of. To explain these movements the ancients started on the theory that each heavenly body moved in a perfect circle around the earth; the fixed stars were assigned to one of a group of revolving spheres, the sun, moon and five planets each to one, making eight in all. But it was soon observed that the movements of the planets were too complicated to fall into this system; the number of moving spheres was raised to 27 before Aristotle and to 56 by him. To these concentric spheres later astronomers added eccentric spheres, moving within others, called epicycles, and to them epicycles of the second order; in fact astronomers were compelled:

> To build, unbuild, contrive,
> To save appearances, to gird the sphere
> With centric and eccentric scribbled o'er
> Cycle and epicycle, orb in orb.

The complexity of this system, which moved the mirth of Voltaire and, according to Milton, of the Almighty, was such as to make it doubted by some thinkers even in antiquity. Several men thought the earth revolved on its axis, but the hypothesis was rejected by Aristotle and Ptolemy. Heracleides, in the fourth century B. C., said that Mercury and Venus circled around the sun, and in the third century Aristarchus of Samos actually anticipated, though it was a mere guess, the heliocentric theory.

Just before Copernicus various authors seemed to hint at the truth, but in so mystical or brief a way that little can be made of their statements. Thus, Nicholas of Cusa argued that "as the earth cannot be the center of the universe it cannot lack all motion." Leonardo believed that the earth revolved on its axis, and stated that it was a star and would look, to a man on

Nicholas of Cusa, 1400–64

the moon, as the moon does to us. In one place he wrote, "the sun does not move,"—only that enigmatical sentence and nothing more.

Copernicus, 1473–1543

Nicholas Copernicus was a native of Thorn in Poland, himself of mixed Polish and Teutonic blood. At the age of eighteen he went to the university of Cracow, where he spent three years. In 1496 he was enabled by an ecclesiastical appointment to go to Italy, where he spent most of the next ten years in study. He worked at the universities of Bologna, Padua and Ferrara, and lectured—though not as a member of the university—at Rome. His studies were comprehensive, including civil law, canon law, medicine, mathematics, and the classics. At Padua, on May 31, 1503, he was made doctor of canon law. He also studied astronomy in Italy, talked with the most famous professors of that science and made observations of the heavens.

Copernicus's uncle was bishop of Ermeland, a spiritual domain and fief of the Teutonic Order, under the supreme suzerainty, at least after 1525, of the king of Poland. Here Copernicus spent the rest of his life; the years 1506–1512 in the bishop's palace at Heilsberg, after 1512, except for two not long stays at Allenstein, as a canon at Frauenburg.

This little town, near but not quite on the Baltic coast, is ornamented by a beautiful cathedral. On the wall surrounding the close is a small tower which the astronomer made his observatory. Here, in the long frosty nights of winter and in the few short hours of summer darkness, he often lay on his back examining the stars. He had no telescope, and his other instruments were such crude things as he put together himself. The most important was what he calls the *Instrumentum parallacticum,* a wooden isosceles triangle with legs eight feet long divided into 1000 divisions by ink marks, and a hypotenuse divided into 1414 divisions. With this he determined the height of the sun, moon and stars, and their deviation from the vernal point. To this he added a square (quadrum) which told the height of the sun by the shadow thrown by a peg in the middle of the square. A third instrument, also to measure the height of a celestial body, was called the Jacob's staff. His difficulties were increased by the lack of any astronomical tables save those poor ones made by Greeks and Arabs. The faults of these were so great that the fundamental star, *i.e.*, the one he took by which to measure the rest, Spica, was given a longitude nearly 40′ out of the true one.

Copernican hypothesis

Nevertheless with these poor helps Copernicus arrived, and that very early, at his momentous conclusion. His observations, depending as they did on the weather, were not numerous. His time was spent largely in reading the classic astronomers and in working out the mathematical proofs of his hypothesis. He found hints in quotations from ancient astronomers in Cicero and Plutarch that the earth moved, but he, for the first time, placed the planets in their true position around the sun, and the moon as a satellite of the earth. He retained the old conception of the *primum mobile* or sphere of fixed stars though he placed it at an infinitely greater distance than did the ancients, to account for the absence of any observed alteration (parallax) in the position of the stars during the year. He also retained the old conception of circular orbits for the planets, though at one time he considered the possibility of their being elliptical, as they are. Unfortunately for his immediate followers the section on this subject found in his own manuscript was cut out of his printed book.

The precise moment at which Copernicus formulated his theory in his own mind cannot be told with certainty, but it was certainly before 1516. He kept back his books for a long time, but his light was not placed under a bushel nevertheless. The first rays of it shown forth in a tract by Celio Calcagnini of which only the title, "That the earth moves and the heaven is still," has survived. Some years later Copernicus wrote a short summary of his book, for private circulation only, entitled "A Short commentary on his hypotheses concerning the celestial movements." A fuller account of them was given by his friend and disciple, George Joachim, called Rheticus, who left Wittenberg, where he was teaching, to sit at the master's feet, and who published what was called *The First Account*.

1520

Narratio prima, 1540

Finally, Copernicus was persuaded to give his own work to the public. Foreseeing the opposition it was likely to call forth, he tried to forestall criticism by a dedication to the Pope Paul III. Friends at Nuremberg undertook to find a printer, and one of them, the Lutheran pastor Andrew Osiander, with the best intentions, did the great wrong of inserting an anonymous preface stating that the author did not advance his hypotheses as necessarily true, but merely as a means of facilitating astronomical calculations. At last the greatest work of the century, *On the Revolutions of the Heavenly Spheres,* came from the press; a copy was brought to the author on his death bed.

De revolutionibus orbium caelestium, 1543

The first of the six books examines the previous authorities, the second proposes the new theory, the third discusses the precession of the equinoxes, the fourth proves that the moon circles the earth, the fifth and most important proves that the planets, including the earth, move around the sun, and gives correctly the time of the orbits of all the planets then known, from Mercury with eighty-eight days to Saturn with thirty years. The sixth book is on the determination of latitude and longitude from the fixed stars. Copernicus's proofs and reasons are absolutely convincing and valid as far as they go. It remained for Galileo and Newton to give further explanations and some modifications in detail of the new theory.

Reception of the Copernican theory

When one remembers the enormous hubbub raised by Darwin's *Origin of Species,* the reception of Copernicus's no less revolutionary work seems singularly mild. The idea was too far in advance of the age, too great, too paradoxical, to be appreciated at once. Save for a few astronomers like Rheticus and Reinhold, hardly anyone accepted it at first. It would have been miraculous had they done so.

Among the first to take alarm were the Wittenberg theologians, to whose attention the new theory was forcibly brought by their colleague Rheticus. Luther alludes to the subject twice or thrice in his table talk, most clearly on June 4, 1539, when

> mention was made of a certain new astronomer, who tried to prove that the earth moved and not the sky, sun and moon, just as, when one was carried along in a boat or wagon, it seemed to himself that he was still and that the trees and landscape moved. "So it goes now," said Luther, "whoever wishes to be clever must not let anything please him that others do, but must do something of his own. Thus he does who wishes to subvert the whole of astronomy; but I believe the Holy Scriptures, which say that Joshua commanded the sun, and not the earth, to stand still.

In his *Elements of Physics,* written probably in 1545, but not published until 1549, Melanchthon said:

> The eyes bear witness that the sky revolves every twenty-four hours. But some men now, either for love of novelty, or to display their ingenuity, assert that the earth moves. . . . But it is hurtful and dishonorable to

> assert such absurdities. . . . The Psalmist says that the sun moves and the earth stands fast. . . . And the earth, as the center of the universe, must needs be the immovable point on which the circle turns.

Apparently, however, Melanchthon either came to adopt the new theory, or to regard it as possible, for he left this passage entirely out of the second edition of the same work. Moreover his relations with Rheticus continued warm, and Rheinhold continued to teach the Copernican system at Wittenberg.

1550

The reception of the new work was also surprisingly mild, at first, in Catholic circles. As early as 1533 Albert Widmanstetter had told Clement VII of the Copernican hypothesis and the pope did not, at least, condemn it. Moreover it was a cardinal, Schönberg, who consulted Paul III on the matter and then urged Copernicus to publish his book, though in his letter the language is so cautiously guarded against possible heresy that not a word is said about the earth moving around the sun but only about the moon and the bodies near it so doing. A Spanish theologian, Didacus a Stunica (Zuñiga) wrote a commentary on Job, which was licensed by the censors, accepting the Copernican astronomy.

1536

1579

But gradually, as the implications of the doctrine became apparent, the church in self-defence took a strong stand against it. The Congregation of the Index issued a decree saying, "Lest opinions of this sort creep in to the destruction of Catholic truth, the book of Nicholas Copernicus and others [defending his hypothesis] are suspended until they be corrected." A little later Galileo was forced, under the threat of torture, to recant this heresy. Only when the system had become universally accepted, did the church, in 1822, first expressly permit the faithful to hold it.

March 5, 1616

The philosophers were as shy of the new light as

the theologians. Bodin in France and Bacon in England both rejected it; the former was conservative at heart and the latter was never able to see good in other men's work, whether that of Aristotle or of Gilbert or of the great Pole. Possibly he was also misled by Osiander's preface and by Tycho Brahe. Giordano Bruno, however, welcomed the new idea with enthusiasm, saying that Copernicus taught more in two chapters than did Aristotle and the Peripatetics in all their works.

Astronomers alone were capable of weighing the evidence scientifically and they, at first, were also divided. Erasmus Reinhold, of Wittenberg, accepted it and made his calculations on the assumption of its truth, as did an Englishman, John Field. Tycho Brahe, on the other hand, tried to find a compromise between the Copernican and Ptolemaic systems. He argued that the earth could not revolve on its axis as the centrifugal force would hurl it to pieces, and that it could not revolve around the sun as in that case a change in the position of the fixed stars would be observed. Both objections were well taken, of course, considered in themselves alone, but both could be answered by a deeper knowledge. Brahe therefore considered the earth as the center of the orbits of the moon, sun, and stars, and the sun as the center of the orbits of the planets.

1556

Tycho Brahe, 1546–1601

The attention to astronomy had two practical corollaries, the improvement of navigation and the reform of the calendar. Several better forms of astrolabe, of "sun-compass" (or dial turnable by a magnet) and an "astronomical ring" for getting the latitude and longitude by observation of sun and star, were introduced.

The reform of the Julian calendar was needed on account of the imperfect reckoning of the length of the

Reform of calendar

year as exactly 365¼ days; thus every four centuries there would be three days too much. It was proposed to remedy this for the present by leaving out ten days, and for the future by omitting leap-year every century not divisible by 400. The bull of Gregory XIII, who resumed the duties of the ancient Pontifex Maximus in regulating time, enjoined Catholic lands to rectify their calendar by allowing the fifteenth of October, 1582, to follow immediately after the fourth. This was done by most of Italy, by Spain, Portugal, Poland, most of Germany, and the Netherlands. Other lands adopted the new calendar later, England not until 1752 and Russia not until 1917.

February 24, 1582

§ 5. Philosophy

Science, religion and philosophy

The interrelations of science, religion, and philosophy, though complex in their operation, are easily understood in their broad outlines. Science is the examination of the data of experience and their explanation in logical, physical, or mathematical terms. Religion, on the other hand, is an attitude towards unseen powers, involving the belief in the existence of spirits. Philosophy, or the search for the ultimate reality, is necessarily an afterthought. It comes only after man is sophisticated enough to see some difference between the phenomenon and the idea. It draws its premises from both science and religion: some systems, like that of Plato, being primarily religious fancy, some, like that of Aristotle, scientific realism.

The Reformers

The philosophical position taken by the Catholic church was that of Aquinas, Aristotelian realism. The official commentary on the *Summa* was written at this time by Cardinal Cajetan. Compared to the steady orientation of the Catholic, the Protestant philosophers wavered, catching often at the latest style in thought, be it monism or pragmatism. Luther was the spiritual child of Occam, and the ancestor of Kant. His individualism stood half-way between the former's nominalism and the latter's transcendentalism and subjectivism. But the Reformers were far less interested in purely metaphysical than they were in dogmatic questions. The main use they made of their philosophy was to bring in a more individual and less mechanical scheme of salvation. Their great change in point of view from Catholicism was the rejection of the sacramental, hierarchical system in favor of justification by faith. This was, in truth, a stupendous change, putting the responsibility for salvation directly on God, and dispensing with the mediation of priest and rite.

Attitude towards reason

But it was the only important change, of a speculative nature, made by the Reformers. The violent polemics of that and later times have concealed the fact that in most of his ideas the Protestant is but a variety of the Catholic. Both religions accepted as axiomatic the existence of a personal, ethical God, the immortality of the soul, future rewards and punishments, the mystery of the Trinity, the revelation, incarnation and miracles of Christ, the authority of the Bible and the real presence in the sacrament. Both equally detested reason.

> He who is gifted with the heavenly knowledge of faith [says the Catechism of the Council of Trent] is free from an inquisitive curiosity; for when God commands us to believe, he does not propose to have us search into his divine judgments, nor to inquire their reasons and causes, but demands an immutable faith. . . . Faith, therefore, excludes not only all doubt, but even the desire of subjecting its truth to demonstration.
>
> We know that reason is the devil's harlot [says Luther] and can do nothing but slander and harm all that God says and does. [And again] If, outside of Christ, you wish by your own thoughts to know your relation to

> God, you will break your neck. Thunder strikes him who examines. It is Satan's wisdom to tell what God is, and by doing so he will draw you into the abyss. Therefore keep to revelation and don't try to understand.

There are many mysteries in the Bible, Luther acknowledged, that seem absurd to reason, but it is our duty to swallow them whole. Calvin abhorred the free spirit of the humanists as the supreme heresy of free thought. He said that philosophy was only the shadow and revelation the substance. "Nor is it reasonable," said he, "that the divine will should be made the subject of controversy with us." Zwingli, anticipating Descartes's "finitum infiniti capax non est," stated that our small minds could not grasp God's plan. Oecolampadius, dying, said that he wanted no more light than he then had—an instructive contrast to Goethe's last words: "Mehr Licht!" Even Bacon, either from prudence or conviction, said that theological mysteries seeming absurd to reason must be believed.

Radical sects

Nor were the radical sects a whit more rational. Those who represented the protest against Protestantism and the dissidence of dissent appealed to the Bible as an authority and abhorred reason as much as did the orthodox churches. The Antitrinitarians were no more deists or free thinkers than were the Lutherans. Campanus and Adam Pastor and Servetus and the Sozinis had no aversion to the supernatural and made no claim to reduce Christianity to a humanitarian deism, as some modern Unitarians would do. Their doubts were simply based on a different exegesis of the biblical texts. Fausto Sozini thought Christ was "a subaltern God to whom at a certain time the Supreme God gave over the government of the world." Servetus defined the Trinity to be "not an illusion of three invisible things, but the manifestation of God in the Word and a communication of the substance of God in the Spirit." This is no new rationalism coming in but a reversion to an obsolete heresy, that of Paul of Samosata. It does not surprise us to find Servetus lecturing on astrology.

Spiritual Reformers

Somewhat to the left of the Antitrinitarian sects were a few men, who had hardly any followers, who may be called, for want of a better term, Spiritual Reformers. They sought, quite in the nineteenth century spirit, to make Christianity nothing but an ethical culture. James Acontius, born in Trent but naturalized in England, published his *Stratagems of Satan* in 1565 to reduce the fundamental doctrines of Christianity to the very fewest possible. Sebastian Franck of Ingolstadt found the only authority for each man in his inward, spiritual message. He sought to found no community or church, but to get only readers. These men passed almost unnoticed in their day.

1565

Franck, 1499–1542

Italian skeptics

There was much skepticism throughout the century. Complete Pyrrhonism under a thin veil of lip-conformity, was preached by Peter Pomponazzi, professor of philosophy at Padua, Ferrara and Bologna. His *De immortalitate animi* caused a storm by its plain conclusion that the soul perished with the body. He tried to make the distinction in his favor that a thing might be true in religion and false in philosophy. Thus he denied his belief in demons and spirits as a philosopher, while affirming that he believed in them as a Christian. He was in fact a materialist. He placed Christianity, Mohammedanism and Judaism on the same level, broadly hinting that all were impostures.

Pomponazzi, 1462–1525

1516

Public opinion became so interested in the subject of immortality at this time that when another philosopher, Simon Porzio, tried to lecture on meteorology at Pisa, his audience interrupted him with cries, "Quid de anima?" He, also, maintained that the soul of man was like that of the beasts. But he had few followers who dared to express such an opinion. After the Inquisition had shown its teeth, the life of the Italian nation was like that of its great poet, Tasso, whose youth was spent at the feet of the Jesuits and whose manhood was haunted by fears of having unwittingly done something that might be punished by the stake. It was to counteract the pagan opinion, stated to be rapidly growing, that the Vatican Council forbade all clerics to lecture on the classics for five years. But in vain! A report of Paul III's cardinals charged professors of philosophy with teaching impiety. Indeed, the whole literature of contemporary Italy, from Machiavelli, who treated Christianity as a false and noxious superstition, to Pulci who professed belief in nothing but pleasure, is saturated with free thought. "Vanity makes most humanists skeptics," wrote Ariosto, "why is it that learning and infidelity go hand in hand?"

German skeptics

In Germany, too, there was some free thought, the most celebrated case being that of the "godless painters of Nuremberg," Hans Sebald Beham, Bartholomew Beham, and George Penz. The first named expressed some doubts about various Protestant doctrines. Bartholomew went further, asserting that baptism was a human device, that the Scriptures could not be believed and that the preaching he had heard was but idle talk, producing no fruit in the life of the preacher himself; he recognized no superior authority but that of God. George Penz went further still, for while he admitted the existence of God he asserted that his nature was unknowable, and that he could believe neither in Christ nor in the Scriptures nor in the sacraments. The men were banished from the city.

French skeptics

In France, as in Italy, the opening of the century saw signs of increasing skepticism in the frequent trials of heretics who denied all Christian doctrines and "all principles save natural ones." But a spirit far more dangerous to religion than any mere denial incarnated itself in Rabelais. He did not philosophize, but he poured forth a torrent of the raw material from which philosophies are made. He did not argue or attack; he rose like a flood or a tide until men found themselves either swimming in the sea of mirth and mockery, or else swept off their feet by it. He studied law, theology and medicine; he travelled in Germany and Italy and he read the classics, the schoolmen, the humanists and the heretics. And he found everywhere that nature and life were good and nothing evil in the world save its deniers. To live according to nature he built, in his story, the abbey of Thélème, a sort of hedonist's or anarchist's Utopia where men and women dwell together under the rule, "Do what thou wilt," and which has over its gates the punning invitation: "Cy entrez, vous, qui le saint evangile en sens agile annoncez, quoy qu'on gronde." For Rabelais there was nothing sacred, or even serious in "revealed religion," and God was "that intellectual sphere the center of which is everywhere and the circumference nowhere."

Rabelais was not the only Frenchman to burlesque the religious quarrels of the day. Bonaventure des Périers, in a work called *Cymbalum Mundi,* introduced Luther under the anagram of Rethulus, a Catholic as Tryocan (*i.e.,* Croyant) and a skeptic as Du Clénier (*i.e.,* Incrédule), debating their opinions in a way that redounded much to the advantage of the last named.

Des Périers, † 1544

Then there was Stephen Dolet the humanist publisher of Lyons, burned to death as an atheist, because, in translating the Axiochos, a dialogue then attributed to Plato, he had written "After death you will be nothing at all" instead of "After death you will be no

Dolet, 1509–46

more," as the original is literally to be construed. The charge was frivolous, but the impression was doubtless correct that he was a rather indifferent skeptic, disdainful of religion. He, too, considered the Reformers only to reject them as too much like their enemies. No Christian church could hold the worshipper of Cicero and of letters, of glory and of humanity. And yet this sad and restless man, who found the taste of life as bitter as Rabelais had found it sweet, died for his faith. He was the martyr of the Renaissance.

Bodin

A more systematic examination of religion was made by Jean Bodin in his *Colloquy on Secret and Sublime Matters,* commonly called the *Heptaplomeres.* Though not published until long after the author's death, it had a brisk circulation in manuscript and won a reputation for impiety far beyond its deserts. It is simply a conversation between a Jew, a Mohammedan, a Lutheran, a Zwinglian, a Catholic, an Epicurean and a Theist. The striking thing about it is the fairness with which all sides are presented; there is no summing up in favor of one faith rather than another. Nevertheless, the conclusion would force itself upon the reader that among so many religions there was little choice; that there was something true and something false in all; and that the only necessary articles were those on which all agreed. Bodin was half way between a theist and a deist; he believed that the Decalogue was a natural law imprinted in all men's hearts and that Judaism was the nearest to being a natural religion. He admitted, however, that the chain of casuality was broken by miracle and he believed in witchcraft. It cannot be thought that he was wholly without personal faith, like Machiavelli, and yet his strong argument against changing religion even if the new be better than the old, is entirely worldly. With France before his eyes, it is not strange that he drew the general conclusion that any change of religion is dangerous and sure to be followed by war, pestilence, famine and demoniacal possession.

Montaigne

After the fiery stimulants, compounded of brimstone and Stygian hatred, offered by Calvin and the Catholics, and after the plethoric gorge of good cheer at Gargantua's table, the mild sedative of Montaigne's conversation comes like a draft of nepenthe or the fruit of the lotus. In him we find no blast and blaze of propaganda, no fulmination of bull and ban; nor any tide of earth-encircling Rabelaisian mirth. His words fall as softly and as thick as snowflakes, and they leave his world a white page, with all vestiges of previous writings erased. He neither asseverates nor denies; he merely, as he puts it himself, "juggles," treating of idle subjects which he believes nothing at all, for he has noticed that as soon one denies the possibility of anything, someone else will say that he has seen it. In short, truth is a near neighbor to falsehood, and the wise man can only repeat, "Que sais-je?" Let us live delicately and quietly, finding the world worth enjoying, but not worth troubling about.

Wide as are the differences between the Greek thinker and the French, there is something Socratic in the way in which Montaigne takes up every subject only to suggest doubts of previously held opinion about it. If he remained outwardly a Catholic, it was because he saw exactly as much to doubt in other religions. Almost all opinions, he urges, are taken on authority, for when men begin to reason they draw diametrically opposite conclusions from the same observed facts. He was in the civil wars esteemed an enemy by all parties, though it was only because he had both Huguenot and Catholic friends. "I have seen in Germany," he wrote, "that Luther hath left as many divisions and altercations concerning the doubt of his opinions, yea, and more, than he himself moveth about the Holy Scriptures." The Reformers, in fact, had done nothing but reform superficial faults and had either left the essential ones untouched, or increased them. How foolish they were to imagine that the people could understand the Bible if they could only read it in their own language!

Multiplicity of sects

Montaigne was the first to feel the full significance of the multiplicity of sects. "Is there any opinion so fantastical, or conceit so extravagant . . . or opinion so strange," he asked, "that custom hath not established and planted by laws in some region?" Usage sanctions every monstrosity, including incest and parricide in some places, and in others "that unsociable opinion of the mortality of the soul." Indeed, Montaigne comes back to the point, a man's belief does not depend on his reason, but on where he was born and how brought up. "To an atheist all writings make for atheism." "We receive our religion but according to our fashion. . . . Another country, other testimonies, equal promises, like menaces, might sembably imprint a clean contrary religion in us."

Piously hoping that he has set down nothing repugnant to the prescriptions of the Catholic, Apostolic and Roman church, where he was born and out of which he purposes not to die, Montaigne proceeds to demonstrate that God is unknowable. A man cannot grasp more than his hand will hold nor straddle more than his legs' length. Not only all religions, but all scientists give the lie to each other. Copernicus, having recently overthrown the old astronomy, may be later overthrown himself. In like manner the new medical science of Paracelsus contradicts the old and may in turn pass away. The same facts appear differently to different men, and "nothing comes to us but falsified and altered by our senses.'' Probability is as hard to get as truth, for a man's mind is changed by illness, or even by time, and by his wishes. Even skepticism is uncertain, for "when the Pyrrhonians say, 'I doubt,' you have them fast by the throat to make them avow that at least you are assured and know that they doubt." In short, "nothing is certain but uncertainty," and "nothing seemeth true that may not seem false." Montaigne wrote of pleasure as the chief end of man, and of death as annihilation. The glory of philosophy is to teach men to despise death. One should do so by remembering that it is as great folly to weep because one would not be alive a hundred years hence as it would be to weep because one had not been living a hundred years ago.

Charron, 1541–1603

A disciple who dotted the i's and crossed the t's of Montaigne was Peter Charron. He, too, played off the contradictions of the sects against each other. All claim inspiration and who can tell which inspiration is right? Can the same Spirit tell the Catholic that the books of Maccabees are canonical and tell Luther that they are not? The senses are fallible and the soul, located by Charron in a ventricle of the brain, is subject to strange disturbances. Many things almost universally believed, like immortality, cannot be proved. Man is like the lower animals. "We believe, judge, act, live and die on faith," but this faith is poorly supported, for all religions and all authorities are but of human origin.

English skeptics

English thought followed rather than led that of Europe throughout the century. At first tolerant and liberal, it became violently religious towards the middle of the period and then underwent a strong reaction in the direction of indifference and atheism. For the first years, before the Reformation, the *Utopia* may serve as an example. More, under the influence of the Italian Platonists, pictured his ideal people as adherents of a deistic, humanitarian religion, with few priests and holy, tolerant of everything save intolerance. They worshipped one God, believed in immortality and yet thought that "the chief felicity of man" lay in the pursuit of rational pleasure. Whether More depicted this cult simply to fulfil the dramatic probabilities and to show what was natural religion among men before revelation came to them, or whether his own opinions altered in later life, it is certain that he became robustly Catholic. He spent much time in religious controversy and resorted to austerities. In one place he tells of a lewd gallant who asked a friar why he gave himself the pain of walking barefoot. Answered that this pain was less than hell, the gallant replied, "If there be no hell, what a fool are you," and received the retort, "If there be hell, what a fool are you." Sir Thomas evidently believed there was a hell, or preferred to take no chances. In one place he argues at length that many and great miracles daily take place at shrines.

The feverish crisis of the Reformation was followed in the reign of Elizabeth by an epidemic of skepticism. Widely as it was spread there can be found little philosophical thought in it. It was simply the pendulum pulled far to the right swinging back again to the extreme left. The suspicions expressed that the queen herself was an atheist were unfounded, but it is impossible to dismiss as easily the numerous testimonies of infidelity among her subjects. Roger Ascham wrote in his *Schoolmaster* that the "incarnate devils" of Englishmen returned from Italy said "there is no God" and then, "they first lustily condemn God, then scornfully mock his Word . . . counting as fables the holy mysteries of religion. They make Christ and his Gospel only serve civil policies. . . . They boldly laugh

1563

to scorn both Protestant and Papist. They confess no Scripture. . . . They mock the pope; they rail on Luther. . . . They are Epicures in living and ἄθεοι in doctrine."

In like manner Cecil wrote: "The service of God and the sincere profession of Christianity are much decayed, and in place of it, partly papistry, partly paganism and irreligion have crept in. . . . Baptists, deriders of religion, Epicureans and atheists are everywhere." Ten years later John Lyly wrote that "there never were such sects among the heathens, such schisms among the Turks, such misbelief among infidels as is now among scholars." The same author wrote a dialogue, *Euphues and Atheos,* to convince skeptics, while from the pulpit the Puritan Henry Smith shot "God's Arrow against atheists." According to Thomas Nash (*Pierce Penniless's Supplication to the Devil*) atheists are now triumphing and rejoicing, scorning the Bible, proving that there were men before Adam and even maintaining "that there are no divells." Marlowe and some of his associates were suspected of atheism. In 1595 John Baldwin, examined before Star Chamber, "questioned whether there were a God; if there were, how he should be known; if by his Word, who wrote the same, if the prophets and the apostles, they were but men and *humanum est errare.*" The next year Robert Fisher maintained before the same court that "Christ was no saviour and that the gospel was a fable."

1569

1592

That one of the prime causes of all this skepticism was to be found in the religious revolution was the opinion of Francis Bacon. Although Bacon's philosophic thought is excluded from consideration by the chronological limits of this book, it may be permissible to quote his words on this subject. In one place he says that where there are two religions contending for

Bacon

mastery their mutual animosity will add warmth to conviction and rather strengthen the adherents of each in their own opinions, but where there are more than two they will breed doubt. In another place he says:

> Heresies and schisms are of all others the greatest scandals, yea more than corruption of manners. . . . So that nothing doth so keep men out of the church and drive men out of the church as breach of unity. . . . The doctor of the gentiles saith, "If an heathen come in and hear you speak with several tongues, will he not say that you are mad?" And certainly it is little better when atheists and profane persons hear of so many discordant and contrary opinions in religion.

But while Bacon saw that when doctors disagree the common man will lose all faith in them, it was not to religion but to science that he looked for the reformation of philosophy. Theology, in Bacon's judgment, was a chief enemy to philosophy, for it seduced men from scientific pursuit of truth to the service of dogma. "You may find all access to any species of philosophy," said Bacon, "however pure, intercepted by the ignorance of divines."

The thought here expressed but sums up the actual trend of the sixteenth century in the direction of separating philosophy and religion. In modern times the philosopher has found his inspiration far more in science than in religion, and the turning-point came about the time of, and largely as a consequence of, the new observation of nature, and particularly the new astronomy.

Revolt against Aristotle

The prologue to the drama of the new thought was the revolt against Aristotle. "The master of them who know" had become, after the definite acceptance of his works as standard texts in the universities of the thirteenth century, an inspired and infallible authority for all science. With him were associated the schoolmen who debated the question of realism versus nominalism. But as the mind of man grew and advanced, what had been once the brace became a galling bond. All parties united to make common cause against the Stagyrite. The Italian Platonists attacked him in the name of their, and his, master. Luther opined that no one had ever understood Aristotle's meaning, that the ethics of that "damned heathen" directly contradicted Christian virtue, that any potter would know more of natural science than he, and that it would be well if he who had started the debate on realism and nominalism had never been born. Catholics like Usingen protested at the excessive reverence given to Aristotle at the expense of Christ. Finally, the French scientist Peter Ramus advanced the thesis at the University of Paris that everything taught by Aristotle was false. No authority, he argued, is superior to reason, for it is reason which creates and determines authority.

Ramus, c. 1515–72

Effect of science on philosophy

In place of Aristotle men turned to nature. "Whosoever in discussion adduces authority uses not intellect but memory," said Leonardo. Vives urged that experiment was the only road to truth. The discoveries of natural laws led to a new conception of external reality, independent of man's wishes and egocentric theories. It also gave rise to the conception of uniformity of law. Copernicus sought and found a mathematical unity in the heavens. It was, above all else, his astronomy that fought the battle of, and won the victory for, the new principles of research. Its glory was not so much its positive addition to knowledge, great as that was, but its mode of thought. By pure reason a new system was established and triumphed over the testimony of the senses and of all previous authority, even that which purported to be revelation. Man was reduced to a creature of law; God was defined as an expression of law.

How much was man's imagination touched, how was his whole thought and purpose changed by the Copernican discovery! No longer lord of a little, bounded world, man crept as a parasite on a grain of dust spinning eternally through endless space. And with the humiliation came a great exaltation. For this tiny creature could now seal the stars and bind the Pleiades and sound each deep abyss that held a sun. What new sublimity of thought, what greatness of soul was not his! To Copernicus belongs properly the praise lavished by Lucretius on Epicurus, of having burst the flaming bounds of the world and of having made man equal to heaven. The history of the past, the religion of the present, the science of the future—all ideas were transmuted, all values reversed by this new and wonderful hypothesis.

But all this, of course, was but dimly sensed by the contemporaries of Copernicus. What they really felt was the new compulsion of natural law and the necessity of causation. Leonardo was led thus far by his study of mathematics, which he regarded as the key to natural science. He even went so far as to define time as a sort of non-geometrical space.

Theory of knowledge

Two things were necessary to a philosophy in harmony with the scientific view; the first was a new theory of knowledge, the second was a new conception of the ultimate reality in the universe. Paracelsus contributed to the first in the direction of modern empiricism, by defending understanding as that which comprehended exactly the thing that the hand touched and the eyes saw. Several immature attempts were made at scientific skepticism. That of Cornelius Agrippa—*De incertitudine et vanitate scientiarum et artium atque excellentia Verbi Dei declamatio*—can hardly be taken seriously, as it was regarded by the author himself rather as a clever paradox. Francis Sanchez, on the other hand, formulated a tenable theory of the impossibility of knowing anything. A riper theory of perception, following Paracelsus and anticipating Leibnitz, was that of Edward Digby, based on the notion of the active correspondence between mind and matter.

The ultimate reality

To the thinker of the sixteenth century the solution of the question of the ultimate reality seemed to demand some form of identification of the world-soul with matter. Paracelsus and Gilbert both felt in the direction of hylozoism, or the theory of the animation of all things. If logically carried out, as it was not by them, this would have meant that everything was God. The other alternative, that God was everything, was developed by a remarkable man, who felt for the new science the enthusiasm of a religious convert, Giordano Bruno.

Bruno, 1548–1600

Born at Nola near Naples, he entered in his fifteenth year the Dominican friary. This step he soon regretted, and, after being disciplined for disobedience, fled, first to Rome and then to Geneva. Thence he wandered to France, to England, and to Wittenberg and Prague, lecturing at several universities, including Oxford. In 1593 he was lured back to Italy, was imprisoned by the Inquisition, and after long years was finally burnt at the stake in Rome.

1569

February 17, 1600

In religion Bruno was an eclectic, if not a skeptic. At Wittenberg he spoke of Luther as "a second Hercules who bound the three-headed and triply-crowned hound of hell and forced him to vomit forth his poison." But in Italy he wrote that he despised the Reformers as more ignorant than himself. His *Expulsion of the Triumphant Beast,* in the disguise of an attack on the heathen mythology, is in reality an assault on revealed religion. His treatise *On the Heroic Passions* aims to show that moral virtues are not founded on religion but on reason.

The new astronomy

The enthusiasm that Bruno lacked for religion he felt in almost boundless measure for the new astronomy, "by which," as he himself wrote, "we are moved to discover the infinite cause of an infinite effect, and are led to contemplate the deity not as though outside, apart, and distant from us, but in ourselves. For, as deity is situated wholly everywhere, so it is as near us as we can be to ourselves." From Nicholos of Cusa Bruno had learned that God may be found in the smallest as in the greatest things in the world; the smallest being as endless in power as the greatest is infinite in energy, and all being united in the "Monad," or "the One." Now, Bruno's philosophy is nothing but the cosmological implication and the metaphysical justification of the Copernician theory in the conceptual terms of Nicholas of Cusa.

Liberated from the tyranny of dogma and of the senses, dazzled by the whirling maze of worlds without end scattered like blazing sparks throughout space, drunk with the thought of infinity, he poured forth a paean of breathing thoughts and burning words to celebrate his new faith, the religion of science. The universe for him was composed of atoms, tiny "minima" that admit no further division. Each one of these is a "monad," or unity, comprised in some higher unity until finally "the monad of monads" was found in God. But this was no tribal Jehovah, no personal, anthropomorphic deity, but a First Principle, nearly identical with Natural Law.

CHAPTER XIII

THE TEMPER OF THE TIMES

§ 1. Tolerance and Intolerance

Because religion has in the past protested its own intolerance the most loudly, it is commonly regarded as the field of persecution *par excellence*. This is so far from being the case that it is just in the field of religion that the greatest liberty has been, after a hard struggle, won. It is as if the son who refused to work in the vineyard had been forcibly hauled thither, whereas the other son, admitting his willingness to go, had been left out. Nowadays in most civilized countries a man would suffer more inconvenience by going bare-foot and long-haired than by proclaiming novel religious views; he would be in vastly more danger by opposing the prevalent patriotic or economic doctrines, or by violating some possibly irrational convention, than he would by declaring his agnosticism or atheism. The reason of this state of things is that in the field of religion a tremendous battle between opposing faiths was once fought, with exhaustion as the result, and that the rationalists then succeeded in imposing on the two parties, convinced that neither could exterminate the other, respect for each other's rights.

Intolerance: Catholics

This battle was fought in the sixteenth and seventeenth centuries. Almost all religions and almost all statesmen were then equally intolerant when they had the power to be so. The Catholic church, with that superb consistency that no new light can alter, has always asserted that the opinion that everyone should have freedom of conscience was "madness flowing from the most foul fountain of indifference."[1] Augustine believed that the church should "compel men to enter in" to the kingdom, by force. Aquinas argued that faith is a virtue, infidelity of those who have heard the truth a sin, and that "heretics deserve not only to be excommunicated but to be put to death." One of Luther's propositions condemned by the bull *Exsurge Domine* was that it is against the will of the Holy Ghost to put heretics to death. When Erasmus wrote: "Who ever heard orthodox bishops incite kings to slaughter heretics who were nothing else than heretics?" the proposition was condemned, by the Sorbonne, as repugnant to the laws of nature, of God and of man. The power of the pope to depose and punish heretical princes was asserted in the bull of February 15, 1559.

Freedom of conscience

The theory of the Catholic church was put into instant practice; the duty of persecution was carried out by the Holy Office, of which Lord Acton, though himself a Catholic, has said:[2]

> The Inquisition is peculiarly the weapon and peculiarly the work of the popes. It stands out from all those things in which they co-operated, followed or assented, as the distinctive feature of papal Rome. . . . It is the principal thing with which the papacy is identified and by which it must be judged. The principle of the Inquisition is murderous, and a man's opinion of the papacy is regulated and determined by his opinion about religious assassination.

But Acton's judgment, just, as it is severe, is not the judgment of the church. A prelate of the papal

[1] Gregory XVI, Encyclical, *Mirari vos*, 1832.

[2] *Letters to Mary Gladstone*, ed. H. Paul, 1904, p. 298f.

household published in 1895, the following words in the *Annales ecclesiastici*:[1]

> Some sons of darkness nowadays with dilated nostrils and wild eyes inveigh against the intolerance of the Middle Ages. But let not us, blinded by that liberalism that bewitches under the guise of wisdom, seek for silly little reasons to defend the Inquisition! Let no one speak of the condition of the times and intemperate zeal, as if the church needed excuses. O blessed flames of those pyres by which a very few crafty and insignificant persons were taken away that hundreds of hundreds of phalanxes of souls should be saved from the jaws of error and eternal damnation! O noble and venerable memory of Torquemada!

Protestants

So much for the Catholics. If any one still harbors the traditional prejudice that the early Protestants were more liberal, he must be undeceived. Save for a few splendid sayings of Luther, confined to the early years when he was powerless, there is hardly anything to be found among the leading reformers in favor of freedom of conscience. As soon as they had the power to persecute they did.

Luther

In his first period Luther expressed the theory of toleration as well as anyone can. He wrote: "The pope is no judge of matters pertaining to God's Word and the faith, but a Christian must examine and judge them himself, as he must live and die by them." Again he said: "Heresy can never be prevented by force. . . . Heresy is a spiritual thing; it cannot be cut with iron nor burnt with fire nor drowned in water." And yet again, "Faith is free. What could a heresy trial do? No more than make people agree by mouth or in writing; it could not compel the heart. For true is the proverb: 'Thoughts are free of taxes.' "

[1] C. Mirbt: *Quellen zur Geschichte des Papsttums*, [3], 1911, p. 390.

Even when the Anabaptists began to preach doctrines that he thoroughly disliked, Luther at first advised the government to leave them unmolested to teach and believe what they liked, "be it gospel or lies."

But alas for the inconsistency of human nature! When Luther's party ripened into success, he saw things quite differently. The first impulse came from the civil magistrate, whom the theologians at first endured, then justified and finally urged on. All persons save priests were forbidden by the Elector John of Saxony to preach or baptize, a measure aimed at the Anabaptists. In the same year, under this law, twelve men and one woman were put to death, and such executions were repeated several times in the following years, *e. g.* in 1530, 1532 and 1538. In the year 1529 came the terrible imperial law, passed by an alliance of Catholics and Lutherans at the Diet of Spires, condemning all Anabaptists to death, and interpreted to cover cases of simple heresy in which no breath of sedition mingled. A regular inquisition was set up in Saxony, with Melanchthon on the bench, and under it many persons were punished, some with death, some with life imprisonment, and some with exile.

February 26, 1527

While Luther took no active part in these proceedings, and on several occasions gave the opinion that exile was the only proper punishment, he also, at other times, justified persecution on the ground that he was suppressing not heresy but blasphemy. As he interpreted blasphemy, in a work published about 1530, it included the papal mass, the denial of the divinity of Christ or of any other "manifest article of the faith, clearly grounded in Scripture and believed throughout Christendom." The government should also, in his opinion, put to death those who preached sedition, anarchy or the abolition of private property.

Melanchthon

Melanchthon was far more active in the pursuit of

heretics than was his older friend. He reckoned the denial of infant baptism, or of original sin, and the opinion that the eucharistic bread did not contain the real body and blood of Christ, as blasphemy properly punishable by death. He blamed Brenz for his tolerance, asking why we should pity heretics more than does God, who sends them to eternal torment? Brenz was convinced by this argument and became a persecutor himself.

Bucer and Capito

The Strassburgers, who tried to take a position intermediate between Lutherans and Zwinglians, were as intolerant as any one else. They put to death a man for saying that Christ was a mere man and a false prophet, and then defended this act in a long manifesto asking whether all religious customs of antiquity, such as the violation of women, be tolerated, and, if not, why they should draw the line at those who aimed not at the physical dishonor, but at the eternal damnation, of their wives and daughters?

Zwingli

January 5, 1527

The Swiss also punished for heresy. Felix Manz was put to death by drowning, the method of punishment chosen as a practical satire on his doctrine of baptism of adults by immersion. At the same time George Blaurock was cruelly beaten and banished under threat of death. Zurich, Berne and St. Gall published a joint edict condemning Anabaptists to death, and under this law two Anabaptists were sentenced in 1528 and two more in 1532.

September 9, 1527

Calvin

In judicially murdering Servetus the Genevans were absolutely consistent with Calvin's theory. In the preface to the *Institutes* he admitted the right of the government to put heretics to death and only argued that Protestants were not heretics. Grounding himself on the law of Moses, he said that the death decreed by God to idolatry in the Old Testament was a universal law binding on Christians. He thought that

Christians should hate the enemies of God as much as did David, and when Renée of Ferrara suggested that that law might have been abrogated by the new dispensation, Calvin retorted that any such gloss on a plain text would overturn the whole Bible. Calvin went further, and when Castellio argued that heretics should not be punished with death, Calvin said that those who defended heretics in this manner were equally culpable and should be equally punished.

Given the premises of the theologians, their arguments were unanswerable. Of late the opinion has prevailed that his faith cannot be wrong whose life is in the right. But then it was believed that the creed was the all-important thing; that God would send to hell those who entertained wrong notions of his scheme of salvation. "We utterly abhor," says the Scots' Confession of 1560, "the blasphemy of those that affirm that men who live according to equity and justice shall be saved, what religion so ever they have professed."

Tolerance

Against this flood of bigotry a few Christians ventured to protest in the name of their master. In general, the persecuted sects, Anabaptists and Unitarians, were firmly for tolerance, by which their own position would have been improved. Erasmus was thoroughly tolerant in spirit and, though he never wrote a treatise specially devoted to the subject, uttered many *obiter dicta* in favor of mercy and wrote many letters to the great ones of the earth interceding for the oppressed. His broad sympathies, his classical tastes, his horror of the tumult, and his Christ-like spirit, would not have permitted him to resort to the coarse arms of rack and stake even against infidels and Turks.

Erasmus

The noblest plea for tolerance from the Christian standpoint was that written by Sebastian Castellio as a protest against the execution of Servetus. He collects all the authorities ancient and modern, the latter including Luther and Erasmus and even some words, inconsistent with the rest of his life, written by Calvin himself. "The more one knows of the truth the less one is inclined to condemnation of others," he wisely observes, and yet, "there is no sect which does not condemn all others and wish to reign alone. Thence come banishments, exiles, chains, imprisonments, burnings, scaffolds and the miserable rage of torture and torment that is plied every day because of some opinions not pleasing to the government, or even because of things unknown." But Christians burn not only infidels but even each other, for the heretic calls on the name of Christ as he perishes in agony.

Castellio

> Who would not think that Christ were Moloch, or some such god, if he wished that men be immolated to him and burnt alive? . . . Imagine that Christ, the judge of all, were present and himself pronounced sentence and lit the fire,—who would not take Christ for Satan? For what else would Satan do than burn those who call on the name of Christ? O Christ, creator of the world, dost thou see such things? And hast thou become so totally different from what thou wast, so cruel and contrary to thyself? When thou wast on earth, there was no one gentler or more compassionate or more patient of injuries.

Calvin called upon his henchmen Beza to answer this "blasphemy" of one that must surely be "the chosen vessel of Satan." Beza replied to Castellio that God had given the sword to the magistrate not to be borne in vain and that it was better to have even a cruel tyrant than to allow everyone to do as he pleased. Those who forbid the punishment of heresy are, in Beza's opinion, despisers of God's Word and might as well say that even parricides should not be chastized.

Two authors quoted in favor of tolerance more than

More

they deserve to be are Sir Thomas More and Montaigne. In Utopia, indeed, there was no persecution, save of the fanatic who wished to persecute others. But even in Utopia censure of the government by a private individual was punishable by death. And, twelve years after the publication of the *Utopia,* More came to argue "that the burning of heretics is lawful and well done," and he did it himself accordingly. The reason he gave, in his *Dialogue,* was that heretics also persecute, and that it would put the Catholics at an unfair disadvantage to allow heresy to wax unhindered until it grew great enough to crush them. There is something in this argument. It is like that today used against disarmament, that any nation which started it would put itself at the mercy of its rivals.

Montaigne

The spirit of Montaigne was thoroughly tolerant, because he was always able to see both sides of everything; one might even say that he was negatively suggestible, and always saw the "other" side of an opinion better than he saw his own side of it. He never came out strongly for toleration, but he made two extremely sage remarks about it. The first was that it was setting a high value on our own conjectures to put men to death for their sake. The second was thus phrased, in the old English translation: "It might be urged that to give factions the bridle to uphold their opinion, is by that facility and ease, the ready way to mollify and release them; and to blunt the edge, which is sharpened by rareness, novelty and difficulty."

Had the course of history been decided by weight of argument, persecution would have been fastened on the world forever, for the consensus of opinion was overwhelmingly against liberty of conscience. But just as individuals are rarely converted on any vital question by argument, so the course of races and of civilizations is decided by factors lying deeper than the logic of publicists can reach. Modern toleration developed from two very different sources; by one of which the whole point of view of the race has changed, and by the other of which a truce between warring factions, at first imposed as bitter necessity, has developed, because of its proved value, into a permanent peace.

Renaissance

The first cause of modern tolerance is the growing rationalism of which the seeds were sown by the Renaissance. The generation before Luther saw an almost unparalleled liberty in the expression of learned opinion. Valla could attack pope, Bible and Christian ethics; Pomponazzi could doubt the immortality of the soul; More could frame a Utopia of deists, and Machiavelli could treat religion as an instrument in the hands of knaves to dupe fools. As far as it went this liberty was admirable; but it was really narrow and "academic" in the worst sense of the word. The scholars who vindicated for themselves the right to say and think what they pleased in the learned tongue and in university halls, never dreamed that the people had the same rights. Even Erasmus was always urging Luther not to communicate imprudent truths to the vulgar, and when he kept on doing so Erasmus was so vexed that he "cared not whether Luther was roasted or boiled" for it. Erasmus's good friend Ammonius jocosely complained that heretics were so plentiful in England in 1511 before the Reformation had been heard of, that the demand for faggots to burn them was enhancing the price of fire-wood. Indeed, in this enlightened era of the Renaissance, what porridge was handed to the common people? What was free, except dentistry, to the Jews, expelled from Spain and Portugal and persecuted everywhere else? What tolerance was extended to the Hussites? What mercy was shown to the Lollards or to Savonarola?

Reformation

Paradoxical as it may seem to say it, after what has been said of the intolerance of the Reformers, the second cause that extended modern freedom of conscience from the privileged few to the masses, was the Reformation. Overclouding, as it did for a few years, all the glorious culture of the Renaissance with a dark mist of fanaticism, it nevertheless proved, contrary to its own purpose, one of the two parents of liberty. What neither the common ground of the Christians in doctrine, nor their vaunted love of God, nor their enlightenment by the Spirit, could produce, was finally wrung from their mutual and bitter hatreds. Of all the fair flowers that have sprung from a dark and noisome soil, that of religious liberty sprouting from religious war has been the fairest.

The steps were gradual. First, after the long deadlock of Lutheran and Catholic, came to be worked out the principle of the toleration of the two churches, embodied in the Peace of Augsburg. The Compact of Warsaw granted absolute religious liberty to the nobles. The people of the Netherlands, sickened with slaughter in the name of the faith, took a longer step in the direction of toleration in the Union of Utrecht. The government of Elizabeth, acting from prudential motives only, created and maintained an extra-legal tolerance of Catholics, again and again refusing to molest those who were peaceable and quiet. The papists even hoped to obtain legal recognition when Francis Bacon proposed to tolerate all Christians except those who refused to fight a foreign enemy. France found herself in a like position, and solved it by allowing the two religions to live side by side in the Edict of Nantes. The furious hatred of the Christians for each other blazed forth in the Thirty Years War, but after that lesson persecution on a large scale was at an end. Indeed, before its end, wide religious lib-

1555

1573

1579

1592

1598

erty had been granted in some of the American colonies, notably in Rhode Island and Maryland.

§ 2. Witchcraft

Some analogy to the wave of persecution and confessional war that swept over Europe at this time can be found in the witchcraft craze. Both were examples of those manias to which mankind is periodically subject. They run over the face of the earth like epidemics or as a great fire consumes a city. Beginning in a few isolated cases, so obscure as to be hard to trace, the mania gathers strength until it burns with its maximum fierceness and then, having exhausted itself, as it were, dies away, often quite suddenly. Such manias were the Children's Crusade and the zeal of the flagellants in the Middle Ages. Such have been the mad speculations as that of the South Sea Bubble and the panics that repeatedly visit our markets. To the same category belong the religious and superstitious delusions of the sixteenth century.

The history of these mental epidemics is easier to trace than their causes. Certainly, reason does nothing to control them. In almost every case there are a few sane men to point out, with perfect rationality, the nature of the folly to their contemporaries, but in all cases their words fall on deaf ears. They are mocked, imprisoned, sometimes put to death for their pains, whereas any fanatical fool that adds fuel to the flame of current passion is listened to, rewarded and followed.

Ancient magic

The original stuff from which the mania was wrought is a savage survival. Hebrew and Roman law dealt with witchcraft. The Middle Ages saw the survival of magic, still called in Italy, "the old religion," and new superstitions added to it. Something of the ancient enchantment still lies upon the fairylands of Europe. In the Apennines one sometimes comes upon a grove of olives or cypresses as gnarled and twisted as the tortured souls that Dante imagined them to be. Who can wander through the heaths and mountains of the Scotch Highlands, with their uncanny harmonies of silver mist and grey cloud and glint of water and bare rock and heather, and not see in the distance the Weird Sisters crooning over their horrible cauldron? In Germany the forests are magic-mad. Walking under the huge oaks of the Thuringian Forest or the Taunus, or in the pine woods of Hesse, one can see the flutter of airy garments in the chequered sunlight falling upon fern and moss; one can glimpse goblins and kobolds hiding behind the roots and rocks; one can hear the King of the Willows [1] and the Bride of the Wind moaning and calling in the rustling of the leaves. On a summer's day the calm of pools is so complete that it seems as if, according to Luther's words, the throwing of a stone into the water would raise a tempest. But on moonlit, windy, Walpurgis Night, witches audibly ride by, hooted at by the owls, and vast spectres dance in the cloud-banks beyond the Brocken.

The witch

The witch has become a typical figure: she was usually a simple, old woman living in a lonely cottage with a black cat, gathering herbs by the light of the moon. But she was not always an ancient beldam; some witches were known as the purest and fairest maidens of the village; some were ladies in high station; some were men. A ground for suspicion was sometimes furnished by the fact that certain charletans playing upon the credulity of the ignorant, professed to be able by sorcery to find money, "to provoke persons to love," or to consume the body and goods of a client's enemy. Black magic was occasionally resorted to to get rid

[1] Erlkönig.

of personal or political enemies. More often a wise woman would be sought for her skill in herbs and her very success in making cures would sometimes be her undoing.

The devil

If the witch was a domestic article in Europe, the devil was an imported luxury from Asia. Like Aeneas and many another foreign conquerer, when he came to rule the land he married its princess—in this case Hulda the pristine goddess of love and beauty—and adopted many of the native customs. It is difficult for us to imagine what a personage the devil was in the age of the Reformation. Like all geniuses he had a large capacity for work and paid great attention to detail. Frequently he took the form of a cat or a black dog with horns to frighten children by "skipping to and fro and sitting upon the top of a nettle"; again he would obligingly hold a review of evil spirits for the satisfaction of Benvenuto Cellini's curiosity. He was at the bottom of all the earthquakes, pestilences, famines and wars of the century, and also, if we may trust their mutual recriminations, he was the special patron of the pope on the one hand and of Calvin on the other. Luther often talked with him, though in doing so the sweat poured from his brow and his heart almost stopped beating. Luther admitted that the devil always got the best of an argument and could only be banished by some unprintably nasty epithets hurled at his head. Satan and his satellites often took the form of men or women and under the name of incubi and succubi had sexual intercourse with mortals. One of the most abominable features of the witch craze was that during its height hundreds of children of four or five years old confessed to being the devil's paramours.

So great was the power of Satan that, in the common belief, many persons bartered their souls to him in return for supernatural gifts in this life. To compensate them for the loss of their salvation, these persons, the witches, were enabled to do acts of petty spite to their neighbors, turning milk sour, blighting crops, causing sickness to man and animals, making children cry themselves to death before baptism, rendering marriages barren, procuring abortion, and giving charms to blind a husband to his wife's adultery, or philters to compel love.

Witches' Sabbath

On certain nights the witches and devils met for the celebration of blasphemous and obscene rites in an assembly known as the Witches' Sabbath. To enable themselves to ride to the meeting-place on broomsticks, the witches procured a communion wafer, applied a toad to it, burned it, mingled its ashes with the blood of an infant, the powdered bones of a hanged man and certain herbs. The meeting then indulged in a parody of the mass, for, so the grave doctors taught, as Christ had his sacraments the devil had his "unsacraments" or "execrements." His Satanic Majesty took the form of a goat, dog, cat or ape and received the homage of his subjects in a loathsome ceremony. After a banquet promiscuous intercourse of devils and witches followed.

All this superstition smouldered along in the embers of folk tales for centuries until it was blown into a devastating blaze by the breath of theologians who started to try to blow it out. The first puff was given by Innocence VIII in his bull *Summis desiderantes.* The Holy Father having learned with sorrow that many persons in Germany had had intercourse with demons and had by incantations hindered the birth of children and blasted the fruits of the earth, gave authority to Henry Institoris and James Sprenger to correct, incarcerate, punish and fine such persons, calling in, if need be, the aid of the secular arm. These gen-

December 5, 1484

tlemen acquitted themselves with unsurpassed zeal. Not content with trying and punishing people brought before them, they put forth *The Witches' Hammer*, called by Lea the most portentous monument of superstition ever produced. In the next two centuries it was printed twenty-nine times. The University of Cologne at once decided that to doubt the reality of witchcraft was a crime. The Spanish Inquisition, on the other hand, having all it could do with Jews and heretics, treated witchcraft as a diabolical delusion.

Malleus Maleficarum, 1487

Though most men, including those whom we consider the choice and master-spirits of the age, Erasmus and More, firmly believed in the objective reality of witchcraft, they were not obsessed by the subject, as were their immediate posterity. Two causes may be found for the intensification of the fanaticism. The first was the use of torture by the Inquisition. The crime was of such a nature that it could hardly be proved save by confession, and this, in general, could be extracted only by the infliction of pain. It is instructive to note that in England where the spirit of the law was averse to torture, no progress in witch-hunting took place until a substitute for the rack had been found, first in pricking the body of the witch with pins to find the anaesthetic spot supposed to mark her, and secondly in depriving her of sleep.

Inquisition

Torture

A second patent cause of the mania was the zeal and the bibliolatry of Protestantism. The religious debate heated the spiritual atmosphere and turned men's thoughts to the world of spirits. Such texts, continually harped upon, as that on the witch of Endor, the injunction, "Thou shalt not suffer a witch to live," and the demoniacs of the New Testament, weighed heavily upon the shepherds of the people and upon their flocks. Of the reality of witchcraft Luther harbored not a doubt. The first use he made of the ban was to

Bibliolatry

excommunicate reputed witches. Seeing an idiotic child, whom he regarded as a changeling, he recommended the authorities to drown it, as a body without a soul. Repeatedly, both in private talk and in public sermons, he recommended that witches should be put to death without mercy and without regard to legal niceties. As a matter of fact, four witches were burned at Wittenberg on June 29, 1540.

The other Protestants hastened to follow the bad example of their master. In Geneva, under Calvin, thirty-four women were burned or quartered for the crime in the year 1545. A sermon of Bishop Jewel in 1562 was perhaps the occasion of a new English law against witchcraft. Richard Baxter wrote on the *Certainty of a World of Spirits.* At a much later time the bad record of the Mathers is well known, as also John Wesley's remark that giving up witchcraft meant giving up the Bible.

The madness

After the mania reached its height in the closing years of the century, anything, however trivial, would arouse suspicion. A cow would go dry, or a colt break its leg, or there would be a drought, or a storm, or a murrain on the cattle or a mildew on the crops. Or else a physician, baffled by some disease that did not yield to his treatment of bleeding and to his doses of garlic and horses' dung, would suggest that witchcraft was the reason for his failure. In fact, if any contrariety met the path of the ordinary man or woman, he or she immediately thought of the black art, and considered the most likely person for denunciation. This would naturally be the nearest old woman, especially if she had a tang to her tongue and had muttered "Bad luck to you!" on some previous occasion. She would then be hauled before the court, promised liberty if she confessed, stripped and examined for some mark of Satan or to be sure that she was not hiding a charm about her person. Torture in some form was then applied, and a ghastly list it was, pricking with needles under nails, crushing of bones until the marrow spurted out, wrenching of the head with knotted cords, toasting the feet before a fire, suspending the victim by the hands tied behind the back and letting her drop until the shoulders were disjointed. The horrible work would be kept up until the poor woman either died under the torture, or confessed, when she was sentenced without mercy, usually to be burned, sometimes to lesser punishments.

When the madness was at its height, hardly anyone, once accused, escaped. John Bodin, a man otherwise enlightened and learned, earned himself the not unjust name of "Satan's attorney-general" by urging that strict proof could not be demanded by the very nature of these cases and that no suspected person should ever be released unless the malice of her accusers was plainer than day. Moreover, each trial bred others, for each witch denounced accomplices until almost the whole population of certain districts was suspected. So frequently did they accuse their judges or their sovereign of having assisted at the witches' sabbath, that this came to be discounted as a regular trick of the devil.

Persecution raged in some places, chiefly in Germany, like a visitation of pestilence or war. Those who tried to stop it fell victims to their own courage, and, unless they recanted, languished for years in prison, or were executed as possessed by devils themselves. At Trèves the persecution was encouraged by the cupidity of the magistrates who profited by confiscation of the property of those sentenced. At Bonn schoolboys of nine or ten, fair young maidens, many priests and scores of good women were done to death.

Numbers executed

No figures have been compiled for the total number

of victims of this insanity. In England, under Elizabeth, before the craze had more than well started on its career, 125 persons are known to have been tried for witchcraft and 47 are known to have been executed for the crime. In Venice the Inquisition punished 199 persons for sorcery during the sixteenth century. In the year 1510, 140 witches were burned at Brescia, in 1514, 300 at Como. In a single year the bishop of Geneva burned 500 witches, the bishop of Bamberg 600, the bishop of Würzburg 900. About 800 were condemned to death in a single batch by the Senate of Savoy. In the year 1586 the archbishop of Trèves burned 118 women and two men for this imaginary crime. Even these figures give but an imperfect notion of the extent of the midsummer madness. The number of victims must be reckoned by the tens of thousands.

Throughout the century there were not wanting some signs of a healthy skepticism. When, during an epidemic of St. Vitus's dance at Strassburg, the citizens proposed a pilgrimage to stop it, the episcopal vicar replied that as it was a natural disease natural remedies should be used. Just as witches were becoming common in England, Gosson wrote in his *School of Abuse*: "Do not imitate those foolish patients, who, having sought all means of recovery and are never the nearer, run into witchcraft." Leonardo da Vinci called belief in necromancy the most foolish of all human delusions.

1518

1578

As it was dangerous to oppose the popular mood at its height, the more honor must go to the few who wrote *ex professo* against it. The first of these, of any note, was the Protestant physician John Weyer. In his book *De praestigiis daemonum* he sought very cautiously to show that the poor "old, feeble-minded, stay-

Weyer

1563

at-home women" sentenced for witchcraft were simply the victims of their own and other people's delusions. Satan has no commerce with them save to injure their minds and corrupt their imaginations. Quite different, he thought, were those infamous magicians who really used spells, charms, potions and the like, though even here Weyer did not admit that their effects were due to supernatural agency. This mild and cautious attempt to defend the innocent was placed on the Index and elicited the opinion from John Bodin that the author was a true servant of Satan.

Scott

A far more thorough and brilliant attack on the superstition was Reginald Scott's *Discovery of Witchcraft, wherein the lewd dealings of Witches and Witchmongers is notably detected . . . whereunto is added a Treatise upon the Nature and Substance of Spirits and Devils.* Scott had read 212 Latin authors and 23 English, on his subject, and he was under considerable obligation to some of them, notably Weyer. But he endeavored to make first-hand observations, attended witch trials and traced gossip to its source. He showed, none better, the utter flimsiness and absurdity of the charges on which poor old women were done to death. He explained the performance of the witch of Endor as ventriloquism. Trying to prove that magic was rejected by reason and religion alike, he pointed out that all the phenomena might most easily be explained by wilful imposture or by illusion due to mental disturbance. As his purpose was the humanitarian one of staying the cruel persecution, with calculated partisanship he tried to lay the blame for it on the Catholic church. As the very existence of magic could not be disproved completely by empirical reasons he attacked it on *a priori* grounds, alleging that spirits and bodies are in two categories, unable to act directly upon each

1584

other. Brilliant and convincing as the work was, it produced no corresponding effect. It was burned publicly by order of James I.

Montaigne

Montaigne, who was never roused to anger by anything, had the supreme art of rebutting others' opinions without seeming to do so. It was doubtless Bodin's abominable *Demonology* that called forth his celebrated essay on witchcraft, in which that subject is treated in the most modern spirit. The old presumption in favor of the miraculous has fallen completely from him; his cool, quizzical regard was too much for Satan, who, with all his knowledge of the world, is easily embarrassed, to endure. The delusion of witchcraft might be compared to a noxious bacillus. Scott tried to kill it by heat; he held it up to a fire of indignation, and fairly boiled it in his scorching flame of reason. Montaigne tried the opposite treatment: refrigeration. He attacked nothing; he only asked, with an icy smile, why anything should be believed. Certainly, as long as the mental passions could be kept at his own low temperature, there was no danger that the milk of human kindness should turn sour, no matter what vicious culture of germs it originally held. He begins by saying that he had seen various miracles in his own day, but, one reads between the lines, he doesn't believe any of them. One error, he says, begets another, and everything is exaggerated in the hope of making converts to the talker's opinion. One miracle bruited all over France turned out to be a prank of young people counterfeiting ghosts. When one hears a marvel, he should always say, "perhaps." Better be apprentices at sixty then doctors at ten. Now witches, he continues, are the subject of the wildest and most foolish accusations. Bodin had proposed that they should be killed on mere suspicion, but Montaigne observes, "To kill human beings there is required a bright-shining and clear light." And what do the stories amount to?

> How much more natural and more likely do I find it that two men should lie than that one in twelve hours should pass from east to west? How much more natural that our understanding may by the volubility of our loose-capring mind be transported from his place, than that one of us should by a strange spirit in flesh and bone be carried upon a broom through the tunnel of a chimney? . . . I deem it a matter pardonable not to believe a wonder, at least so far forth as one may explain away or break down the truth of the report in some way not miraculous. . . . Some years past I traveled through the country of a sovereign prince, who, in favor of me and to abate my incredulity, did me the grace in his own presence and in a particular place to make me see ten or twelve prisoners of that kind, and amongst others an old beldam witch, a true and perfect sorceress, both by her ugliness and deformity, and such a one as long before was most famous in that profession. I saw both proofs, witnesses, voluntary confessions, and some insensible marks about this miserable old woman; I enquired and talked with her a long time, with the greatest heed and attention I could, and I am not easily carried away by preconceived opinion. In the end and in my conscience I should rather have appointed them hellebore than hemlock. It was rather a disease than a crime.

Montaigne goes on to argue that even when we cannot get an explanation—and any explanation is more probable than magic—it is safe to disbelieve: "Fear sometimes representeth strange apparitions to the vulgar sort, as ghosts . . . larves, hobgoblins, Robbin-good-fellows and such other bugbears and chimaeras." For Montaigne the evil spell upon the mind of the race had been broken; alas! that it took so long for other men to throw it off!

§ 3. Education

From the most terrible superstition let us turn to the noblest, most inspiring and most important work of

Education

humanity. With each generation the process of handing on to posterity the full heritage of the race has become longer and more complex.

Schools

It was, therefore, upon a very definite and highly developed course of instruction that the contemporary of Erasmus entered. There were a few great endowed schools, like Eton and Winchester and Deventer, in which the small boy might begin to learn his "grammar"—Latin, of course. Some of the buildings at Winchester and Eton are the same now as they were then, the quite beautiful chapel and dormitories of red brick at Eton, for example. Each of these two English schools had, at this time, less than 150 pupils, and but two masters, but the great Dutch school, Deventer, under the renowned tuition of Hegius, boasted 2200 scholars, divided into eight forms. Many an old woodcut shows us the pupils gathered around the master as thick as flies, sitting cross-legged on the floor, some intent on their books and others playing pranks, while there seldom fails to be one undergoing the chastisement so highly recommended by Solomon. These great schools did not suffice for all would-be scholars. In many villages there was some poor priest or master who would teach the boys what he knew and prepare them thus for higher things. In some places there were tiny school-houses, much like those now seen in rural America. Such an one, renovated, may be still visited at Mansfeld, and its quaint inscription read over the door, to the effect that a good school is like the wooden horse of Troy. When the boys left home they lived more as they do now at college, being given a good deal of freedom out of hours. The poorer scholars used their free times to beg, for as many were supported in this way then as now are given scholarships and other charitable aids in our universities.

Flogging

Though there were a good many exceptions, most of

the teachers were brutes. The profession was despised as a menial one and indeed, even so, many a gentleman took more care in the selection of grooms and game-keepers than he did in choosing the men with whom to entrust his children. Of many of the tutors the manners and morals were alike outrageous. They used filthy language to the boys, whipped them cruelly and habitually drank too much. They made the examinations, says one unfortunate pupil of such a master, like a trial for murder. The monitor employed to spy on the boys was known by the significant name of "the wolf." Public opinion then approved of harsh methods. Nicholas Udall, the talented head-master of Eton, was warmly commended for being "the best flogging teacher in England"—until he was removed for his immorality.

Latin

The principal study—after the rudiments of reading and writing the mother tongue were learned—was Latin. As, at the opening of the century, there were usually not enough books to go around, the pedagogue would dictate declensions and conjugations, with appropriate exercises, to his pupils. The books used were such as *Donatus on the Parts of Speech,* a poem called the *Facetus* by John of Garland, intended to give moral, theological and grammatical information all in one, and selecting as the proper vehicle rhymed couplets. Other manuals were the *Floretus,* a sort of abstruse catechism, the *Cornutus,* a treatise on synonyms, and a dictionary in which the words were arranged not alphabetically but according to their supposed etymology—thus *hirundo* (swallow) from *aer* (air). One had to know the meaning of the word before one searched for it! The grammars were written in a barbarous Latin of inconceivably difficult style. Can any man now readily understand the following definition of "pronoun," taken from a book intended for beginners, published in 1499? "Pronomen . . . significat substantiam seu entitatem sub modo conceptus intrinseco permanentis seu habitus et quietis sub determinatae apprehensionis formalitate."

That with all these handicaps boys learned Latin at all, and some boys learned it extremely well, must be attributed to the amount of time spent on the subject. For years it was practically all that was studied—for the medieval trivium of grammar, rhetoric and logic reduced itself to this—and they not only read a great deal but wrote and spoke Latin. Finally, it became as easy and fluent to them as their own tongue. Many instances that sound like infant prodigies are known to us; boys who spoke Latin at seven and wrote eloquent orations in it at fourteen, were not uncommon. It is true that the average boy spoke then rather a translation of his own language into Latin than the best idiom of Rome. The following ludicrous specimens of conversation, throwing light on the manners as well as on the linguistic attainments of the students, were overheard in the University of Paris: "Capis me pro uno alio"; "Quando ego veni de ludendo, ego bibi unum magnum vitrum totum plenum de vino, sine deponendo nasum de vitro"; "In prandendo non facit nisi lichare suos digitos."

Reformation

Though there was no radical reform in education during the century between Erasmus and Shakespeare, two strong tendencies may be discerned at work, one looking towards a milder method, the other towards the extension of elementary instruction to large classes hitherto left illiterate. The Reformation, which was rather poor in original thought, was at any rate a tremendous vulgarizer of the current culture. It was a popular movement in that it passed around to the people the ideas that had hitherto been the possession of the few. Its first effect, indeed, together with that of the tumults that accompanied it, was for the moment unfavorable to all sorts of learning. Not only wars and rebellions frightened the youth from school, but men arose, both in England and Germany, who taught that if God had vouchsafed his secrets to babes and sucklings, ignorance must be better than wisdom and that it was therefore folly to be learned.

Luther not only turned the tide, but started it flowing in that great wave that has finally given civilized lands free and compulsory education for all. In a *Letter to the Aldermen and Cities of Germany on the Erection and Maintenance of Christian Schools* he urged strongly the advantages of learning. "Good schools [he maintained] are the tree from which grow all good conduct in life, and if they decay great blindness must follow in religion and in all useful arts. . . . Therefore, all wise rulers have thought schools a great light in civil life." Even the heathen had seen that their children should be instructed in all liberal arts and sciences both to fit them for war and government and to give them personal culture. Luther several times suggested that "the civil authorities ought to compel people to send their children to school. If the government can compel men to bear spear and arquebus, to man ramparts and perform other martial duties, how much more has it the right to compel them to send their children to school?" Repeatedly he urged upon the many princes and burgomasters with whom he corresponded the duty of providing schools in every town and village. A portion of the ecclesiastical revenues confiscated by the German states was in fact applied to this end. Many other new schools were founded by princes and were known as "Fürstenschulen" or gymnasia.

Luther

1524

The same course was run in England. Colet's foundation of St. Paul's School in London, for 153 boys, has perhaps won an undue fame, for it was back-

England

1510

ward in method and not important in any special way, but it is a sign that people at that time were turning their thoughts to the education of the young. When Edward VI mounted the throne the dissolution of the chantries had a very bad effect, for their funds had commonly supported scholars. A few years previously Henry VIII had ordered "every of you that be parsons, vicars, curates and also chantry priests and stipendiaries to . . . teach and bring up in learning the best you can all such children of your parishioners as shall come to you, or at least teach them to read English." Edward VI revived this law in ordering chantry priests to "exercise themselves in teaching youth to read and write," and he also urged people to contribute to the maintenance of primary schools in each parish. He also endowed certain grammar schools with the revenues of the chantries.

In Scotland the *Book of Discipline* advocated compulsory education, children of the well-to-do at their parents' expense, poor children at that of the church.

Jesuit colleges

In Catholic countries, too, there was a passion for founding new schools. Especially to be mentioned are the Jesuit "colleges," "of which," Bacon confesses, "I must say, *Talis cum sis utinam noster esses.*" How well frequented they were is shown by the following figures. The Jesuit school at Vienna had, in 1558, 500 pupils, in Cologne, about the same time, 517, in Trèves 500, in Mayence 400, in Spires 453, in Munich 300. The method of the Jesuits became famous for its combined gentleness and art. They developed consummate skill in allowing their pupils as much of history, science and philosophy as they could imbibe without jeoparding their faith. From this point of view their instruction was an inoculation against free thought. But it must be allowed that their teaching of the classics was excellent. They followed the humanists' methods, but they adapted them to the purpose of the church.

The classics

All this flood of new scholars had little that was new to study. Neither Reformers nor humanists had any searching or thorough revision to propose; all that they asked was that the old be taught better: the humanities more humanely. Erasmus wrote much on education, and, following him Vives and Budé and Melanchthon and Sir Thomas Elyot and Roger Ascham; their programs, covering the whole period from the cradle to the highest degree, seem thorough, but what does it all amount to, in the end, but Latin and Greek? Possibly a little arithmetic and geometry and even astronomy were admitted, but all was supposed to be imbibed as a by-product of literature, history from Livy, for example, and natural science from Pliny. Indeed, it often seems as if the knowledge of things was valued chiefly for the sake of literary comprehension and allusion.

The educational reformers differed little from one another save in such details as the best authors to read. Colet preferred Christian authors, such as Lactantius, Prudentius and Baptista Mantuan. Erasmus thought it well to begin with the verses of Dionysius Cato, and to proceed through the standard authors of Greece and Rome. For the sake of making instruction easy and pleasant he wrote his *Colloquies*—in many respects his *chef d' oeuvre* if not the best Latin produced by anyone during the century. In this justly famous work, which was adopted and used by all parties immediately, he conveyed a considerable amount of liberal religious and moral instruction with enough wit to make it palatable. Luther, on Melanchthon's advice, notwithstanding his hatred for the author, urged the use of the

Colloquies in Protestant schools, and they were likewise among the books permitted by the Imperial mandate issued at Louvain.

1548

The method of learning language was for the instructor to interpret a passage to the class which they were expected to be able to translate the next day. Ascham recommended that, when the child had written a translation he should, after a suitable interval, be required to retranslate his own English into Latin. Writing, particularly of letters, was taught. The real advance over the medieval curriculum was in the teaching of Greek—to which the exceptionally ambitious school at Geneva added, after 1538, Hebrew. Save for this and the banishment of scholastic barbarism, there was no attempt to bring in the new sciences and arts. For nearly four hundred years the curriculum of Erasmus has remained the foundation of our education. Only in our own times are Latin and Greek giving way, as the staples of mental training, to modern languages and science. In those days modern languages were picked up, as Milton was later to recommend that they should be, not as part of the regular course, but "in some leisure hour," like music or dancing. Notwithstanding such exceptions as Edward VI and Elizabeth, who spoke French and Italian, there were comparatively few scholars who knew any living tongue save their own.

University life

When the youth went to the university he found little change in either his manner of life or in his studies. A number of boys matriculated at the age of thirteen or fourteen; on the other hand there was a sprinkling of mature students. The extreme youth of many scholars made it natural that they should be under somewhat stricter discipline than is now the case. Even in the early history of Harvard it is recorded that the president once "flogged four bachelors" for being out too late at night. At colleges like Montaigu, if one may believe Erasmus, the path of learning was indeed thorny. What between the wretched diet, the filth, the cold, the crowding, "the short-winged hawks" that the students combed from their hair or shook from their shirts, it is no wonder that many of them fell ill. Gaming, fighting, drinking and wenching were common.

Mode of government

Nominally, the university was then under the entire control of the faculty, who elected one of themselves "rector" (president) for a single year, who appointed their own members and who had complete charge of studies and discipline, save that the students occasionally asserted their ancient rights. In fact, the corporation was pretty well under the thumb of the government, which compelled elections and dismissals when it saw fit, and occasionally appointed commissions to visit and reform the faculties.

of instruction

Instruction was still carried on by the old method of lectures and debates. These latter were sometimes on important questions of the day, theological or political, but were often, also, nothing but displays of ingenuity. There was a great lack of laboratories, a need that just began to be felt at the end of the century when Bacon wrote: "Unto the deep, fruitful and operative study of many sciences, specially natural philosophy and physics, books be not only the instrumentals." Bacon's further complaint that, "among so many great foundations of colleges in Europe, I find it strange that they are all dedicated to professions, and none left free to arts and sciences at large," is an early hint of the need of the endowment of research. The degrees in liberal arts, B.A. and M.A., were then more strictly than now licences either to teach or to pursue higher professional studies in divinity, law, or medicine. Fees for graduation were heavy; in France a B.A. cost $24, an M.D. $690 and a D.D. $780.

New universities

Germany then held the primacy that she has ever since had in Europe both in the number of her universities and in the aggregate of her students. The new universities founded by the Protestants were: Marburg 1527, Königsberg 1544, Jena 1548 and again 1558, Helmstadt 1575, Altdorf 1578, Paderborn 1584. In addition to these the Catholics founded four or five new universities, though not important ones. They concentrated their efforts on the endeavor to found new "colleges" at the old institutions.

Numbers

In general the universities lost during the first years of the Reformation, but more than made up their numbers by the middle of the century. Wittenberg had 245 matriculations in 1521; in 1526 the matriculations had fallen to 175, but by 1550, notwithstanding the recent Schmalkaldic War, the total numbers had risen to 2000, and this number was well maintained throughout the century.

Erfurt, remaining Catholic in a Protestant region, declined more rapidly and permanently. In the year 1520–21 there were 311 matriculations, in the following year 120, in the next year 72, and five years later only 14. Between 1521 to 1530 the number of students fell at Rostock from 123 to 33, at Frankfort-on-the Oder from 73 to 32. Rostock, however, recovered after a reorganization in 1532. The number of students at Greifswald declined so that no lectures were given during the period 1527–39, after which it again began to pick up. Königsberg, starting with 314 students later fell off. Cologne declined in numbers, and so did Mayence until the Jesuits founded their college in 1561, which, by 1568, had 500 pupils recognized as members of the university. Vienna, also, having sunk to the number of 12 students in 1532, kept at a very low ebb until 1554, when the effects of the Jesuit revival were felt. Whereas, during the fifteen years 1508–22 there were 6485 matriculations at Leipzig, during the next fifteen years there were only 1935. By the end of the century, however, Leipzig had again become, under Protestant leadership, a large institution.

British universities

Two new universities were founded in the British Isles during the century, Edinburgh in 1582 and Trinity College, Dublin, in 1591. In England a number of colleges were added to those already existing at Oxford and Cambridge, namely Christ Church (first known, after its founder, Wolsey, as Cardinal's College, then as King's College), Brasenose, and Corpus Christi at Oxford and St. John's, Magdalen, and Trinity at Cambridge. Notwithstanding these new foundations the number of students sank. During the years 1542–8, only 191 degrees of B.A. were given at Cambridge and only 172 at Oxford. Ascham is authority for the statement that things were still worse under Mary, when "the wild boar of the wood" either "cut up by the root or trod down to the ground" the institutions of learning. The revenues of the universities reached their low-water mark about 1547, when the total income of Oxford from land was reckoned at £5 and that of Cambridge at £50, per annum. Under Elizabeth, the universities rose in numbers, while better Latin and Greek were taught. It was at this time that a college education became fashionable for young gentlemen instead of being exclusively patronized by "learned clerks." The foundation of the College of Physicians in London deserves to be mentioned.

1528

A university was founded at Zurich under the influence of Zwingli. Geneva's University opened in 1559 with Beza as rector. Connected with it was a preparatory school of seven forms, with a rigidly prescribed course in the classics. When the boy was admitted to the university proper by examination, he took what he chose; there was not even a division into classes. The courses offered to him included Greek, Hebrew, theology, dialectic, rhetoric, physics and mathematics.

French universities

The foundation of the Collège de France by Francis I represented an attempt to bring new life and vigor into learning by a free association of learned men. It was planned to emancipate science from the tutelage of theology. Erasmus was invited but, on his refusal to accept, Budé was given the leading position. Chairs of Greek, Hebrew, mathematics and Latin were founded by the king in 1530. Other institutions of learning founded in France were Rheims 1547, Douai 1562, Besançon [1] 1564, none of them now in existence. Paris continued to be the largest university in the world, with an average number of students of about 6000.

Louvain, in the Netherlands, had 3000 students in 1500 and 1521; in 1550 the number rose to 5000. It was divided into colleges on the plan still found in England. Each college had a president, three professors and twelve fellows, entertained gratis, in addition to a larger number of paying scholars. The most popular classes often reached the number of 300. The foundation of the Collegium Trilingue by Erasmus's friend Jerome Busleiden in 1517 was an attempt, as its name indicates, to give instruction in Greek and Hebrew as well as in the Latin classics. A blight fell upon the noble institution during the wars of religion. Under the supervision of Alva it founded professorships of catechetics and substituted the decrees of the Council of Trent for the *Decretum* of Gratian in the law school. Exhausted by the hemorrhages caused by the Religious War and starved by the Lenten diet of Spanish Catholicism, it gradually decayed, while its

1 Besançon was then an Imperial Free City.

place was taken in the eyes of Europe by the Protestant University of Leyden. A second Protestant foundation, Franeker, for a time flourished, but finally withered away.

1575
1585

Spanish universities were crowded with new numbers. The maximum student body was reached by Salamanca in 1584 with 6778 men, while Alcalá passed in zenith in 1547 with the respectable enrollment of 1949. The foundation of no less than nine new universities in Spain bears witness to the interest of the Iberian Peninsula in education.

Four new universities opened their doors in Italy during the year 1540–1565. The Sapienza at Rome, in addition to these, was revived temporarily by Leo X in 1513, and, after a relapse to the dormant state, again awoke to its full power under Paul III, when chairs of Greek and Hebrew were established.

Contribution to progress

The services of all these universities cannot be computed on any statistical method. Notwithstanding all their faults, their dogmatic narrowness and their academic arrogance, they contributed more to progress than any other institutions. Each academy became the center of scientific research and of intellectual life. Their influence was enormous. How much did it mean to that age to see its contending hosts marshalled under two professors, Luther and Adrian VI! And how many other leaders taught in universities:—Erasmus, Melanchthon, Reuchlin, Lefèvre, to mention only a few. Pontiffs and kings sought for support in academic pronouncements, nor could they always force the doctors to give the decision they wished. In fact, each university stood like an Acropolis in the republic of letters, at once a temple and a fortress for those who loved truth and ensued it.

§ 4. Art

Art the expression of an ideal

The significant thing about art, for the historian as for the average man, is the ideal it expresses. The artist and critic may find more to interest him in the development of technique, how this painter dealt with perspective and that one with "tactile values," how the Florentines excelled in drawing and the Venetians in color. But for us, not being professionals, the content of the art is more important than its form. For, after all, the glorious cathedrals of the Middle Ages and the marvellous paintings of the Renaissance were not mere iridescent bubbles blown by or for children with nothing better to do. They were the embodiments of ideas; as the people thought in their hearts so they projected themselves into the objects they created.

The greatest painters the world has seen, and many others who would be greatest in any other time, were contemporaries of Luther. They had a gospel to preach no less sacred to them than was his to him; it was the glad tidings of the kingdom of this world: the splendor, the loveliness, the wonder and the nobility of human life. When, with young eyes, they looked out upon the world in its spring-tide, they found it not the vale of tears that they had been told; they found it a rapture. They saw the naked body not vile but beautiful.

Leonardo, 1452–1519

Leonardo da Vinci was a painter of wonder, but not of naïve admiration of things seen. To him the miracle of the world was in the mystery of knowledge,—and he took all nature as his province. He gave his life and his soul for the mastery of science; he observed, he studied, he pondered everything. From the sun in the heavens to the insect on the ground, nothing was so large as to impose upon him, nothing too small to escape him. Weighing, measuring, experimenting, he dug deep for the inner reality of things;

he spent years drawing the internal organs of the body, and other years making plans for engineers.

When he painted, there was but one thing that fascinated him: the soul. To lay bare the mind as he had dissected the brain; to take man or woman at some self-revealing pose, to surprise the hidden secret of personality, all this was his passion, and in all this he excelled as no one had ever done, before or since. His battle picture is not some gorgeous and romantic cavalry charge, but a confused melée of horses snorting with terror, of men wild with the lust of battle or with hatred or with fear. His portraits are either caricatures or prophecies: they lay bare some trait unsuspected, or they probe some secret weakness. Is not his portrait of himself a wizard? Does not his Medusa chill us with the horror of death? Is not Beatrice d'Este already doomed to waste away, when he paints her?

The Last Supper

The Last Supper had been treated a hundred times before him, now as a eucharistic sacrament, now as a monastic meal, now as a gathering of friends. What did Leonardo make of it? A study of character. Jesus has just said, "One of you will betray me," and his divine head has sunk upon his breast with calm, immortal grief. John, the Beloved, is fairly sick with sorrow; Peter would be fiercely at the traitor's throat; Thomas darts forward, doubting, to ask, "Lord, is it I?" Every face expresses deep and different reaction. There sits Judas, his face tense, the cords of his neck standing out, his muscles taut with the supreme effort not to betray the evil purpose which, nevertheless, lowers on his visage as plainly as a thunder cloud on a sultry afternoon.

Throughout life Leonardo was fascinated with an enigmatic smile that he had seen somewhere, perhaps in Verocchio's studio, perhaps on the face of some woman he had known as a boy. His first paintings were of laughing women, and the same smile is on the lips of John the Baptist and Dionysus and Leda and the Virgin and St. Anne and Mona Lisa! What was he trying to express? Vasari found the "smile so pleasing that it was a thing more divine than human to behold"; Ruskin thought it archaic, Müntz "sad and disillusioned," Berenson supercilious, and Freud neurotic. Reymond calls it the smile of Prometheus, Faust, Oedipus and the Sphinx; Pater saw in it "the animalism of Greece, the lust of Rome, the reverie of the Middle Ages with its spiritual ambitions and imaginary loves, the return to the pagan world, the sins of the Borgias." Though some great critics, like Reinach, have asserted that Mona Lisa is only subtle as any great portrait is subtle, it is impossible to regard it merely as that. It is a psychological study. And what means the smile? In a word, sex,—not on the physical side so studied and glorified by other painters, but in its psychological aspect. For once Leonardo has stripped bare not the body but the soul of desire,—the passion, the lust, the trembling and the shame. There is something frightening about Leda caught with the swan, about the effeminate Dionysus and John the Baptist's mouth "folded for a kiss of irresistible pleasure." If the stories then told about the children of Alexander VI and about Margaret of Navarre and Anne Boleyn were true, Mona Lisa was their sister.

Mona Lisa

Everything he touched acquires the same psychological penetration. His Adoration of the Magi is not an effort to delight the eye, but is a study, almost a criticism, of Christianity. All sorts of men are brought before the miraculous Babe, and their reactions, of wonder, of amazement, of devotion, of love, of skepticism, of scoffing, and of indifference, are perfectly recorded.

The Venetians

After the cool and stormy spring of art came the warm and gentle summer. Life became so full, so beautiful, so pleasant, so alluring, that men sought for nothing save to quaff its goblet to the dregs. Venice, seated like a lovely, wanton queen, on her throne of sparkling waters, drew to her bosom all the devotees of pleasure in the whole of Europe. Her argosies still brought to her every pomp and glory of vestment with which to array her body sumptuously; her lovers lavished on her gold and jewels and palaces and rare exotic luxuries. How all this is reflected in her great painters, the Bellinis and Giorgione and Titian and Tintoretto! Life is no longer a wonder to them but a banquet; the malady of thought, the trouble of the soul is not for them. Theirs is the realm of the senses, and if man could live by sense alone, surely he must revel in what they offer. They dye their canvasses in such blaze of color and light as can be seen only in the sunset or in the azure of the Mediterranean, or in tropical flowers. How they clothe their figures in every conceivable splendor of orphrey and ermine, in jewels and shining armor and rich stuff of silk and samite, in robe of scarlet or in yellow dalmatic! Every house for them is a palace, every bit of landscape an enchanted garden, every action an ecstasy, every man a hero and every woman a paragon of voluptuous beauty.

The portrait is one of the most characteristic branches of Renaissance painting, for it appealed to the newly aroused individualism, the grandiose egotism of the so optimistic and so self-confident age. After Leonardo no one sought to make the portrait primarily a character study. Titian and Raphael and Holbein and most of their contemporaries sought rather to please and flatter than to analyse. But withal there is often a truth to nature that make many

Titian, c. 1490–1576

of the portraits of that time like the day of judgment in their revelation of character. Titian's splendid harmonies of scarlet silk and crimson satin and gold brocade and purple velvet and silvery fur enshrine many a blend of villainies and brutal stupidities. What is more cruelly realistic than the leer of the satyr clothed as Francis, King of France; than the bovine dullness of Charles V and the lizard-like dullness of his son; or than that strange combination of wolfish cunning and swinish bestiality with human thought and self-command that fascinates in Raphael's portrait of Leo X and his two cardinals? On the other hand, what a profusion of strong and noble men and women gaze at us from the canvases of that time. They are a study of infinite variety and of surpassing charm.

The secularization of art proceeded even to the length of affecting religious painting. Susanna and Magdalen and St. Barbara and St. Sebastian are no longer starved nuns and monks, bundled in shapeless clothes; they become maidens and youths of marvellous beauty. Even the Virgin and Christ were drawn from the handsomest models obtainable and were richly clothed. This tendency, long at work, found its consummation in Raphael Sanzio of Urbino.

Raphael, 1483–1520

It is one of those useful coincidences that seem almost symbolic that Raphael and Luther were born in the same year, for they were both the products of the same process—the decay of Catholicism. When, for long ages, a forest has rotted on the ground, it may form a bed of coal, ready to be dug up and turned into power, or it may make a field luxuriant in grain and fruit and flowers. From the deposits of medieval religion the miner's son of Mansfeld extracted enough energy to turn half Europe upside down; from the same fertile swamp Raphael culled the most exquisite blossoms and the most delicious berries. To change the metaphor, Luther was the thunder and Raphael the rainbow of the same storm.

Religious art

The chief work of both of them was to make religion understanded of the people; to adapt it to the needs of the time. When faith fails a man may either abandon the old religion for another, or he may stop thinking about dogma altogether and find solace in the mystical-aesthetic aspect of his cult. This second alternative was worked to its limit by Raphael. He was not concerned with the true but with the beautiful. By far the larger part of his very numerous pictures have religious subjects. The whole Bible—which Luther translated into the vernacular—was by him translated into the yet clearer language of sense. Even now most people conceive biblical characters in the forms of this greatest of illustrators. Delicacy, pathos, spirituality, idyllic loveliness—everything but realism or tragedy—are stamped on all his canvases. "Beautiful as a Raphael Madonna" is an Italian proverb, and so skilfully selected a type of beauty is there in his Virgins that they are neither too ethereal nor too sensuous. Divine tenderness, motherhood at its holiest, gazes calmly from the face of the Sistine Madonna, "whose eyes are deeper than the depths of waters stilled at even." The simple mind, unsophisticated by lore of the pre-Raphaelite school, will worship a Raphael when he will but revel in a Titian. Strangely touched by the magic of this passionate lover both of the church and of mortal women, the average man of that day, or of this, found, and will find, glad tidings for his heart in the very color of Mary's robe. "Whoever would know how Christ transfigured and made divine should be painted, must look," says Vasari, on Raphael's canvases.

The church and the papacy found an ally in Raphael,

whose pencil illustrated so many triumphs of the popes and so many mysteries of religion. In his Disputa (so-called) he made the secret of transubstantiation visible. In his great cartoon of Leo I turning back Attila he gave new power to the arm of Leo X. His Parnassus and School of Athens seemed to make philosophy easy for the people. Indeed, it is from them that he has reaped his rich reward, for while the Pharisees of art pick flaws in him, point out what they find of shallowness and of insincerity, the people love him more than any other artist has been loved. It is for them that he worked, and on every labor one might read as it were his motto, "I will not offend even one of these little ones."

Decadence of religious art

If Raphael's art was safe in his own hands there can be little doubt that it hastened the decadence of painting in the hands of his followers. His favorite pupil, Giulio Romano, caught every trick of the master and, like the devil citing Scripture, painted pictures to delight the eye so licentious that they cannot now be exhibited. Andrea del Sarto sentimentalized the Virgin, turning tenderness to bathos. Correggio, the most gifted of them all, could do nothing so well as depict sensual love. His pictures are hymns to Venus, and his women, saints and sinners alike, are houris of an erotic paradise. Has the ecstasy of amorous passion amounting almost to mystical transport ever been better suggested than in the marvellous light and shade of his Jupiter and Io? These and many other contemporary artists had on their lips but one song, a paean in praise of life, the pomps and glories of this goodly world and the delights and beauties of the body.

But to all men, save those loved by the gods, there comes some moment, perhaps in the very heyday of success and joy and love, when a sudden ruin falls upon the world. The death of one loved more than self, disease and pain, the betrayal of some trust, the failure of the so cherished cause—all these and many more are the gates by which tragedy is born. And the beauty of tragedy is above all other beauty because only in some supreme struggle can the grandeur of the human spirit assert its full majesty. In Shakespeare and Michelangelo it is not the torture that pleases us, but the triumph over circumstance.

Michelangelo, 1475–1564

No one has so deeply felt or so truly expressed this as the Florentine sculptor who, amidst a world of love and laughter, lived in wilful sadness, learning how man from his death-grapple in the darkness can emerge victor and how the soul, by her passion of pain, is perfected. He was interested in but one thing, man, because only man is tragic. He would paint no portraits—or but one or two—because no living person came up to his ideal. All his figures are strong because strength only is able to suffer as to do. Nine-tenths of them are men rather than women, because the beauty of the male is strength, whereas the strength of the woman is beauty. Only in a few of his early figures does he attain calm,—in a Madonna, in David or in the Men Bathing, all of them, including the Madonna with its figures of men in the background, intended to exhibit the perfection of athletic power.

But save in these early works almost all that Michelangelo set his hand to is fairly convulsed with passion. Leda embraces the swan at the supreme moment of conception; Eve, drawn from the side of Adam, is weeping bitterly; Adam is rousing himself to the hard struggle that is life; the slaves are writhing under their bonds as though they were of hot iron; Moses is starting from his seat for some tremendous conflict. Every figure lavished on the decoration of the Sistine Chapel reaches, when it does not surpass, the limit of human physical development. Sibyl and Prophet,

Adam and Eve, man and God are all hurled together with a riot of strength and "terribilità."

The almost supernatural terror of Michelangelo's genius found fullest scope in illustrating the idea of predestination that obsessed the Reformers and haunted many a Catholic of that time also. In the Last Judgment the artist laid the whole emphasis upon the damnation of the wicked, hurled down to external torment by the sentence, "Depart from me, ye cursed," uttered by Christ, not the meek and gentle Man of Sorrows, but the *rex tremendae majestatis,* a Hercules, before whom Mary trembles and the whole of creation shudders. A quieter, but no less tragic work of art is the sculpture on the tomb of Lorenzo de' Medici at Florence. The hero himself sits above, and both he and the four allegorical figures, two men and two women, commonly called Day and Night, Morning and Evening, are lost in pensive, eternal sorrow. So they brood for ever as if seeking in sleep and dumb forgetfulness some anodyne for the sense of their country's and their race's doom.

The Last Judgment

But it is not all pain. Titian has not made joy nor Raphael love nor Leonardo wonder so beautiful as Michelangelo has made tragedy. His sonnets breathe a worship of beauty as the symbol of divine love. He is like the great, dark angel of Victor Hugo:

> Et l'ange devint noir, et dit:—Je suis l'amour.
> Mais son front sombre était plus charmant que le jour,
> Et je voyais, dans l'ombre où brillaient ses prunelles,
> Les astres à travers les plumes de ses ailes.

The contrast between the fertility of Italian artistic genius and the comparative poverty of Northern Europe is most apparent when the northern painters copied most closely their transalpine brothers. The taste for Italian pictures was spread abroad by the many travelers, and the demand created a supply of copies and imitations. Antwerp became a regular factory of such works, whereas the Germans, Cranach, Dürer and Holbein were profoundly affected by Italy. Of them all Holbein was the only one who could really compete with the Italians on their own ground, and that only in one branch of art, portraiture. His studies of Henry VIII, and of his wives and courtiers, combine truth to nature with a high sense of beauty. His paintings of More and Erasmus express with perfect mastery the finest qualities of two rare natures.

Hans Holbein the Younger, 1497–1543

Dürer seldom succeeded in painting pictures of the most beautiful type, but a few of his portraits can be compared with nothing save Leonardo's studies. The whole of a man's life and character are set forth in his two drawings of his friend Pirckheimer, a strange blend of the philosopher and the hog. And the tragedy is that the lower nature won; in 1504 there is but a potential coarseness in the strong face; in 1522 the swine had conquered and but the wreck of the scholar is visible.

Albert Dürer, 1471–1528

As an engineer and as a student of aesthetics Dürer was also the northern Leonardo. His theory of art reveals the secret of his genius: "What beauty is, I know not; but for myself I take that which at all times has been considered beautiful by the greater number." This is making art democratic, bringing it down from the small coterie of palace and mansion to the home of the people at large. Dürer and his compeers were enabled to do this by exploiting the new German arts of etching and wood-engraving. Pictures were multiplied by hundreds and thousands and sold, not to one patron but to the many. Characteristically they reflected the life and thoughts of the common people in every homely phase. Pious subjects were numerous, because religion bulked large in the common thought, but it was the religion of the popular preacher, translating the life of Christ into contemporary German life, wholesome and a little vulgar. The people love marvels and they are very literal; what could be more marvellous and more literal than Dürer's illustrations of the Apocalypse in which the Dragon with ten horns and seven heads, and the Lamb with seven horns and seven eyes are represented exactly as they are described? Dürer neither strove for nor attained anything but realism. "I think," he wrote, "the more exact and like a man a picture is, the better the work. . . . Others are of another opinion and speak of how a man should be . . . but in such things I consider nature the master and human imaginations errors." It was life he copied, the life he saw around him at Nuremberg.

1513–14

But Dürer, to use his own famous criterion of portraiture, painted not only the features of Germany, but her soul. Three of his woodcuts depict German aspirations so fully that they are the best explanation of the Reformation, which they prophesy. The first of these, The Knight, Death and the Devil, shows the Christian soldier riding through a valley of supernatural terrors. "So ist des Menchen Leben nichts anderes dann eine Ritterschaft auf Erden," is the old German translation of Job vii, 1, following the Vulgate. Erasmus in his *Handbook of the Christian Knight* had imagined just such a scene, and so deeply had the idea of the soldier of Christ sunk into the people's mind that later generations interpreted Dürer's knight as a picture of Sickingen or Hutten or one of the bold champions of the new religion.

In the St. Jerome peacefully at work in his panelled study, translating the Bible, while the blessed sun shines in and the lion and the little bear doze contentedly, is not Luther foretold? But the German study, that magician's laboratory that has produced so much of good, has also often been the alembic of brooding and despair. More than ever before at the opening of the century men felt the vast promises and the vast oppression of thought. New science had burst the old bonds but, withal, the soul still yearned for more. The vanity of knowledge is expressed as nowhere else in Dürer's Melancholia, one of the world's greatest pictures. Surrounded by scientific instruments,—the compass, the book, the balance, the hammer, the arithmetical square, the hour-glass, the bell—sits a woman with wings too small to raise her heavy body. Far in the distance is a wonderful city, with the glory of the Northern Lights, but across the splendid vision flits the little bat-like creature, fit symbol of some disordered fancy of an overwrought mind.

The Grotesque

Closely akin to the melancholy of the Renaissance is the love of the grewsome. In Dürer it took the harmless form of a fondness for monstrosities,—rhinoceroses, bearded babies, six-legged pigs and the like. But Holbein and many other artists tickled the emotions of their contemporaries by painting long series known as the Dance of Death, in which some man or woman typical of a certain class, such as the emperor, the soldier, the peasant, the bride, is represented as being haled from life by a grinning skeleton.

Typical of the age, too, was the caricature now drawn into the service of the intense party struggles of the Reformation. To depict the pope or Luther or the Huguenots in their true form their enemies drew them with claws and hoofs and ass's heads, and devil's tails, drinking and blaspheming. Even kings were caricatured,—doubly significant fact!

Architecture

As painting and sculpture attained so high a level of maturity in the sixteenth century, one might suppose that architecture would do the same. In truth, however, architecture rather declined. Very often, if not always, each special art-form goes through a cycle of youth, perfection, and decay, that remind one strongly of the life of a man. The birth of an art is due often to some technical invention, the full possibilities of which are only gradually developed. But after the newly opened fields have been exhausted the epigoni can do little but recombine, often in fantastic ways, the old elements; public taste turns from them and demands something new.

Churches

So the supreme beauty of the medieval cathedral, as seen at Pisa or Florence or Perugia or Rheims or Cologne, was never equalled in the sixteenth century. As the Church declined, so did the churches. Take St. Peter's at Rome, colossal in conception and enormously unequal in execution. With characteristic pride and self-confidence Pope Julius II to make room for it tore down the old church, and other ancient monuments, venerable and beautiful with the hoar of twelve centuries. Even by his contemporaries the architect, Bramante, was dubbed Ruinante! He made a plan, which was started; then he died. In his place were appointed San Gallo and Raphael and Michelangelo, together or in turn, and towers were added after the close of the sixteenth century. The result is the hugest building in the world, and almost the worst proportioned. After all, there is something appropriate in the fact that, just as the pretensions of the popes expanded and their powers decreased, so their churches should become vaster and yet less impressive. St. Peter's was intended to be a marble thunderbolt; but like so many of the papal thunders of that age, it was but a *brutum fulmen* in the end!

The love for the grandiose, carried to excess in St. Peter's, is visible in other sixteenth century ecclesiastical buildings, such as the Badia at Florence. Small as this is, there is a certain largeness of line that is not Gothic, but that goes back to classical models. St. Étienne du Mont at Paris is another good example of the influence of the study of the ancients upon architecture. It is difficult to point to a great cathedral or church built in Germany during this century. In England portions of the colleges at Oxford and Cambridge date from these years, but these portions are grafted on to an older style that really determined them. The greatest glory of English university architecture, the chapel of King's College at Cambridge, was finished in the first years of the century. The noble fan-vaulting and the stained-glass windows will be remembered by all who have seen them.

Ecclesiastic architecture

After the Reformation ecclesiastical architecture followed two diverse styles; the Protestants cultivated excessive plainness, the Catholics excessive ornament. The iconoclasts had no sense for beauty, and thought, as Luther put it, that faith was likely to be neglected by those who set a high value on external form. Moreover the Protestant services necessitated a modification of the medieval cathedral style. What they wanted was a lecture hall with pews; the old columns and transepts and the roomy floor made way for a more practical form.

The Catholics, on the other hand, by a natural reaction, lavished decoration on their churches as never before. Every column was made ornate, every excuse was taken for adding some extraneous embellishment; the walls were crowded with pictures and statues and carving to delight, or at least to arrest, the eye. But it happened that the noble taste of the earlier and simpler age failed; amid all possible devices to give effect, quiet grandeur was wanting.

Castles

What the people of that secular generation really built with enthusiasm and success were their own dwellings. What are the castles of Chambord and Blois and the Louvre and Hampton Court and Heidelberg but houses of play and pleasure such as only a child could dream of? King and cardinal and noble vied in making tower and gable, gallery and court as of a fairy palace; banqueting hall and secret chamber where they and their playmates could revel to their heart's content and leave their initials carved as thickly as boys carve them on an old school desk. And how richly they filled them! A host of new arts sprang up to minister to the needs of these palace-dwellers: our museums are still filled with the glass and enamel, the vases and porcelain, the tapestry and furniture and jewelry that belonged to Francis and Catharine de' Medici and Leo X and Elizabeth. How perfect was the art of many of these articles of daily use can only be appreciated by studying at first hand the salt-cellars of Cellini, or the gold and silver and crystal goblets made by his compeers. Examine the clocks, of which the one at Strassburg is an example; the detail of workmanship is infinite; even the striking apparatus and the dials showing planetary motions are far beyond our own means, or perhaps our taste. When Peter Henlein invented the watch, using as the mainspring a coiled feather, he may not have made chronometers as exact as those turned out nowadays, but the "Nuremberg eggs"—so called from their place of origin and their shape, not a disk, but a sphere—were marvels of chasing and incrustation and jewelry.

Love of beauty

The love of the beautiful was universal. The city of that time, less commodious, sanitary, and populous than it is today, was certainly fairer to the eye. Enough of old Nuremberg and Chester and Siena and Perugia and many other towns remains to assure us that the red-tiled houses, the overhanging storeys, the high gables and quaint dormer windows, presented a far more pleasing appearance than do our lines of smoky factories and drab dwellings.

Music

The men so greedy of all delicate sights and pleasant, would fain also stuff their ears with sweet sounds. And so they did, within the limitations of a still undeveloped technique. They had organs, lutes, viols, lyres, harps, citherns, horns, and a kind of primitive piano known as the clavichord or the clavicembalo. Many of these instruments were exquisitely rich and delicate in tone, but they lacked the range and volume and variety of our music. Almost all melodies were slow, solemn, plaintive; the tune of Luther's hymn gives a good idea of the style then prevalent. When we read that the churches adopted the airs of popular songs, so that hymns were sung to ale-house jigs and catches from the street, we must remember that the said jigs and love-songs were at least as sober and staid as are many of the tunes now expressly written for our hymns. The composers of the time, especially Palestrina and Orlando Lasso, did wonders within the limits then possible to introduce richness and variety into song.

Palestrina, 1526–94

Lasso, c. 1530–1594

Art and religion

Art was already on the decline when it came into conflict with the religious revivals of the time. The causes of the decadence are not hard to understand. The generation of giants, born in the latter half of the fifteenth century, seemed to exhaust the possibilities of artistic expression in painting and sculpture, or at least to exhaust the current ideas so expressible. Guido Reni and the Caracci could do nothing but imitate and recombine.

And then came the battle of Protestant and Catholic to turn men's minds into other channels than that of beauty. Even when the Reformation was not consciously opposed to art, it shoved it aside as a distraction from the real business of life. Thus it has come about in Protestant lands that the public regards art as either a "business" or an "education." Luther himself loved music above all things and did much to popularize it,—while Erasmus shuddered at the psalm-singing he heard from Protestant congregations! Of painting the Reformer spoke with admiration, but so rarely! What could art be in the life of a man who was fighting for his soul's salvation? Calvin saw more clearly the dangers to the soul from the seductions of this world's transitory charm. Images he thought idolatrous in churches and he said outright: "It would be a ridiculous and inept imitation of the papists to fancy that we render God more worthy service in ornamenting our temples and in employing organs and toys of that sort. While the people are thus distracted by external things the worship of God is profaned." So it was that the Puritans chased all blandishments not only from church but from life, and art came to be looked upon as a bit immoral.

Counter-Reformation

But the little finger of the reforming pope was thicker than the Puritan's loins; where Calvin had chastised with whips Sixtus V chastised with scorpions. Adrian VI, the first Catholic Reformer after Luther, could not away with "those idols of the heathen," the ancient statues. Clement VII for a moment restored the old régime of art and licentiousness together, having Perino del Vaga paint his bathroom with scenes from the life of Venus in the manner of Giulio Romano. But the Council of Trent made severe regulations against nude pictures, in pursuance of which Daniel da Volterra was appointed to paint breeches on all the naked figures of Michelangelo's Last Judgment and on similar paintings. Sixtus V, who could hardly endure the Laocoon and Apollo Belvidere, was bent on destroying the monuments of heathendom. The ruin was complete when to her cruel hate the church added her yet more cruel love. Along came the Jesuits offering, like pedlars, instead of the good old article a substitute guaranteed by them to be "just as good," and a great deal cheaper. Painting was sentimentalized and "moralized" under their tuition; architecture adopted the baroque style, gaudy and insincere. The church was stuffed with gewgaws and tinsel; marble was replaced by painted plaster and saintliness by sickliness.

§ 5. Books

Numbers of books published

The sixteenth was the first really bookish century. There were then in Germany alone about 100,000 works printed, or reprinted. If each edition amounted to 1000—a fair average, for if many editions were smaller, some were much larger—that would mean that about a million volumes were offered to the German public each year throughout the century. There is no doubt that the religious controversy had a great deal to do with the expansion of the reading public, for it had the same effect on the circulation of pamphlets that a political campaign now has on the circulation of the newspaper. The following figures show how rapidly the number of books published in Germany increased during the decisive years. In 1518 there were 150, in 1519 260, in 1520 570, 1521 620, in 1522 680, 1523 935, and 1524 990.

1526

Many of these books were short, controversial tracts; some others were intended as purveyors of news pure and simple. Some of these broadsides were devoted to a single event, as the *Neue Zeitung: Die Schlacht des türkischen Kaisers,* others had several items of interest, including letters from distant parts. Occasionally a mere lampoon would appear under the title of *Neue Zeitung,* corresponding to our funny papers. But these substitutes for modern journals were both rare and irregular; the world then got along with much less information about current events than it now enjoys. Nor was there anything like our weekly and monthly magazines.

The new age was impatient of medieval literature. The schoolmen, never widely read, were widely mocked. The humanists, too, fell into deep disgrace, charged with self-conceit, profligacy and irreligion. They still wandered around, like the sophists in ancient Greece, bemoaning their hard lot and deploring the coarseness of an unappreciative time. Their real fault was that they were, or claimed to be, an aristocracy, and the people, who could read for themselves, no longer were imposed on by pretensions to esoteric learning and a Ciceronian style.

Even the medieval vernacular romances no longer suited the taste of the new generation. A certain class continued to read *Amadis of Gaul* or *La Morte d'Arthur* furtively, but the arbiters of taste declared that they would no longer do. The Puritan found them immoral; the man of the world thought them ridiculous. Ascham asserts that "the whole pleasure" of *La Morte d'Arthur,* "standeth in two special points, in open manslaughter and bold bawdry." The century was hardly out when Cervantes published his famous and deadly satire on the knight errant.

Poetry

But as the tale of chivalry decayed, the old metal was transmuted into the pure gold of the poetry of Ariosto, Tasso and Spenser. The claim to reality was abandoned and the poet quite frankly conjured up a fantastic, fairy world, full of giants and wizards and enchantments and hippogryphs, and knights of incredible pugnacity who rescue damsels of miraculous beauty. Well might the Italian, before Luther and Loyola came to take the joy out of life, lose himself in the honeyed words and the amorous adventures of the hero who went mad for love. Another generation, and

Tasso must wind his voluptuous verses around a religious epic. Edmund Spenser, the Puritan and Englishman, allegorized the whole in such fashion that while the conscience was soothed by knowing that all the knights and ladies represented moral virtues or vices, the senses were titillated by mellifluous cadences and by naked descriptions of the temptations of the Bower of Bliss. And how British that Queen Elizabeth of England should impersonate the principal virtues!

Poetry was in the hearts of the people; song was on their lips. The early spring of Italy came later to the northern latitudes, but when it did come, it brought with it Marot and Ronsard in France, Wyatt and Surrey in England. More significant than the output of the greater poets was the wide distribution of lyric talent. Not a few compilations of verses offer to the public the songs of many writers, some of them unknown by name. England, especially, was "a nest of singing birds," rapturously greeting the dawn, and the rimes were mostly of "love, whose month is always May." Each songster poured forth his heart in fresh, frank praise of his mistress's beauty, or in chiding of her cruelty, or in lamenting her unfaithfulness. There was something very simple and direct about it all; nothing deeply psychological until at the very end of the century Shakespeare's "sugared sonnets" gave his "private friends" something to think about as well as something to enjoy.

Wit

If life could not be all love it could be nearly all laughter. Wit and humor were appreciated above all things, and Satire awoke to a sense of her terrible power. Two statues at Rome, called Pasquino and Marforio, were used as billboards to which the people affixed squibbs and lampoons against the government and public men. Erasmus laughed at everything; Luther and Murner belabored each other with ridicule; a man like Peter Aretino owed his evil eminence in the art of blackmailing to his wit.

Rabelais, c. 1490–1553

But the "master of scoffing," as Bacon far too contemptuously called him, was Rabelais. His laughter is as multitudinous as the ocean billows, and as wholesome as the sunshine. He laughed not because he scorned life but because he loved it; he did not "warm both hands" before the fire of existence, he rollicked before its blaze. It cannot be said that he took a "slice of life" as his subject, for this would imply a more exquisite excision than he would care to make; rather he reached out, in the fashion of his time, and pulled with both hands from the dish before him, the very largest and fattest chunk of life that he could grasp. "You never saw a man," he said of himself, "who would more love to be king or to be rich than I would, so that I could live richly and not work and not worry, and that I might enrich all my friends and all good, wise people." Like Whitman he was so in love with everything that the mere repetition of common names delighted him. It took pages to tell what Pantagruel ate and still more pages to tell what he drank. This giant dressed with a more than royal lavishness and when he played cards, how many games do you suppose Rabelais enumerated one after the other without pausing to take breath? Two hundred and fourteen! So he treated everything; his appetite was like Gargantua's mouth. This was the very stamp of the age; it was gluttonous of all pleasures, of food and drink and gorgeous clothes and fine dwellings and merry-making without end, and adventure without stint or limit. Almost every sixteenth-century man was a Pantagruel, whose lust for living fully and hotly no satiety could cloy, no fear of consequences dampen. The ascetic gloom and terror of the Middle Ages burned away like an early fog before the summer sun. Men saw the world unfolding before them as if in a second creation, and they hurled themselves on it with but one fear, that they should be too slow or too backward to garner all its wonder and all its pleasure for themselves.

Tales of vagabonds

And the people were no longer content to leave the glory of life to their superiors. They saw no reason why all the good things should be preserved like game for the nobles to hunt, or inclosed like commons, for the pasturage of a few aristocratic mutton-heads. So in literature they were quite content to let the fastidious gentry read their fill of poetry about knights wandering in fairy-lands forlorn, while they themselves devoured books about humbler heroes. The Picaresque novel in Spain and its counterparts, Till Eulenspiegel or Reinecke Vos in the north, told the adventures of some rascal or vagabond. Living by his wits he found it a good life to cheat and to gamble, to drink and to make love.

Plays

For those who could not concentrate on a book, there was the drama. From the Middle Ages, when the play was a vehicle of religious instruction, it developed in the period of the Renaissance into a completely secular mirror of life. In Italy there was an exquisite literary drama, turning on some plot of love or tale of seduction, and there was alongside of this a popular sort of farce known as the Commedia dell' Arte, in which only the outline of the plot was sketched, and the characters, usually typical persons as the Lover, his Lady, the Bragging Captain, the Miser, would fill in the dialogue and such comic "business" as tickled the fancy of the audience.

Somewhat akin to these pieces in spirit were the

Shrovetide Farces written in Germany by the simple Nuremberger who describes himself in the verses, literally translatable:

> Hans Sachs is a shoe-
> Maker and poet, too.

The people, always moral, delighted no less in the rough fun of these artless scenes than in the apothegms and sound advice in which they abounded.

The spirit of the Sixteenth Century

The contrast of two themes much in the thought of men, typifies the spirit of the age. The one motiv is loud at the beginning of the Reformation but almost dies away before the end of the century; the other, beginning at the same time, rises slowly into a crescendo culminating far beyond the boundaries of the age. The first theme was the Prodigal Son, treated by no less than twenty-seven German dramatists, not counting several in other languages. To the Protestant, the Younger Son represented faith, the Elder Son works. To all, the exile in the far country, the riotous living with harlots and the feeding on husks with swine, meant the life of this world with its pomps and vanities, its lusts and sinful desires that become as mast to the soul. The return to the father is the return to God's love here below and to everlasting felicity above. To those who can believe it, it is the most beautiful story in the world.

Faust

And it is a perfect contrast to that other tale, equally typical of the time, the fable of Faust. Though there was a real man of this name, a charlatan and necromancer who, in his extensive wanderings visited Wittenberg, probably in 1521, and who died about 1536–7, his life was but a peg on which to hang a moral. He became the type of the man who had sold his soul to the devil in return for the power to know everything, to do everything and to enjoy everything in this world.

The first printed *Faust-book* (1587) passed for three centuries as a Protestant production, but the discovery of an older and quite different form of the legend in 1897 changed the whole literary problem. It has been asserted now that the Faust of this unknown author is a parody of Luther by a Catholic. He is a professor at Wittenberg, he drinks heartily, his marriage with Helena recalls the Catholic caricature of Luther's marriage; his compact with the devil is such as an apostate might have made. But it is truer to say that Faust is not a caricature of Luther, but his devilish counterpart, just as in early Christian literature Simon Magus is the antithesis of Peter. Faust is the man of Satan as Luther was the man of God; their adventures are somewhat similar but with the reverse purpose.

And Faust is the sixteenth century man as truly as the Prodigal or Pantagruel. To live to the full; to know all science and all mysteries, to drain to the dregs the cup crowned with the wine of the pleasure and the pride of life: this was worth more than heaven! The full meaning of the parable of salvation well lost for human experience was not brought out until Goethe took it up; but it is implied both in the German *Faust-books* and in Marlowe's play.

Greatness of the Sixteenth Century

Many twentieth-century men find it difficult to do justice to the age of the Reformation. We are now at the end of the period inaugurated by Columbus and Luther and we have reversed the judgments of their contemporaries. Religion no longer takes the place that it then did, nor does the difference between Catholic and Protestant any longer seem the most important thing in religion. Moreover, capitalism and the state, both of which started on their paths of conquest then, are now attacked.

Again, the application of any statistical method makes the former ages seem to shrink in comparison with the present. In population and wealth, in war and in science we are immeasurably larger than our ancestors. Many a merchant has a bigger income than had Henry VIII, and many a college boy knows more astronomy than did Kepler. But if we judge the greatness of an age, as we should, not by its distance from us, but by its own achievement, by what its poets dreamed and by what its strong men accomplished, the importance of the sixteenth century can be appreciated.

An age of aspiration

It was an "experiencing" age. It loved sensation with the greediness of childhood; it intoxicated itself with Rabelais and Titian, with the gold of Peru and with the spices and vestments of the Orient. It was a daring age. Men stood bravely with Luther for spiritual liberty, or they gave their lives with Magellan to compass the earth or with Bruno to span the heavens. It was an age of aspiration. It dreamed with Erasmus of the time when men should be Christlike, or with More of the place where they should be just; or with Michelangelo it pondered the meaning of sorrow, or with Montaigne it stored up daily wisdom. And of this time, bone of its bone and flesh of its flesh, was born the world's supreme poet with an eye to see the deepest and a tongue to tell the most of the human heart. Truly such a generation was not a poor, nor a backward one. Rather it was great in what it achieved, sublime in what it dreamed; abounding in ripe wisdom and in heroic deeds; full of light and of beauty and of life!

CHAPTER XIV

THE REFORMATION INTERPRETED

The historians who have treated the Reformation might be classified in a variety of ways: according to their national or confessional bias, or by their scientific methods or by their literary achievement. For our present purpose it will be convenient to classify them, according to their point of view, into four leading schools of thought which, for want of better names I may call the Religious-Political, the Rationalist, the Liberal-Romantic, and the Economic-Evolutionary. Like all categories of things human these are but rough; many, if not most, historians have been influenced by more than one type of thought. When different philosophies of history prevail at the same time, an eclecticism results. The religious and political explanations were at their height in the sixteenth and seventeenth centuries, though they survived thereafter; the rationalist critique dominates the eighteenth century and lasts in some instances to the nineteenth; the liberal-romantic school came in with the French Revolution and subsided into secondary importance about 1859, when the economists and Darwinians began to assert their claims.

§ 1. The Religious and Political Interpretations. (Sixteenth and Seventeenth Centuries)

Early Protestants

The early Protestant theory of the Reformation was a simple one based on the analogy of Scripture. God, it was thought, had chosen a peculiar people to serve him, for whose instruction and guidance, particularly in view of their habitual backsliding, he raised up a series of witnesses to the truth, prophets, apostles and martyrs. God's care for the Jews under the old dispensation was transferred to the church in the new, and this care was confined to that branch of the true church to which the particular writer and historian happened to belong.

The name "Reformation"

The word "Reformation," far older than the movement to which it applies *par éminence,* indicates exactly what its leaders intended it should be. "Reform" has been one of the perennial watchwords of mankind; in the Middle Ages it was applied to the work of a number of leaders like Rienzi, and was taken as the program of the councils of Constance and Basle. Luther adopted it at least as early as 1518, in a letter to Duke George stating that "above all things a common reformation of the spiritual and temporal estates should be undertaken," and he incorporated it in the title of his greatest German pamphlet. The other name frequently applied by Luther and his friends to their party was "the gospel." In his own eyes the Wittenberg professor was doing nothing more nor less than restoring the long buried evangel of Jesus and Paul. "Luther began," says Richard Burton, "upon a sudden to drive away the foggy mists of superstition and to restore the purity of the primitive church."

It would be easy but superfluous to multiply *ad libitum* quotations showing that the early Protestants referred everything to the general purposes of Providence and sometimes to the direct action of God, or to the impertinent but more assiduous activity of the devil. It is interesting to note that they were not wholly blind to natural causes. Luther himself saw, as early as 1523, the connection between his movement and the revival of learning, which he compared to a John the Baptist preparing the way for the preaching of the gospel. Luther also saw, what many of his followers did not, that the Reformation was no accident, depending on his own personal intervention, but was inevitable and in progress when he began to preach. "The remedy and suppression of abuses," said he in 1529, "was already in full swing before Luther's doctrine arose . . . and it was much to be feared that there would have been a disorderly, stormy, dangerous revolution, such as Münzer began, had not a steady doctrine intervened."

English Protestant historians, while fully adopting the theory of an overruling Providence, were disposed to give due weight to secondary, natural causes. Foxe, while maintaining that the overthrow of the papacy was a great miracle and an everlasting mercy, yet recognized that it was rendered possible by the invention of printing and by the "first push and assault" given by the ungodly humanists. Burnet followed Foxe's thesis in a much better book. While printing many documents he also was capable, in the interests of piety, of concealing facts damaging to the Protestants. For his panegyric he was thanked by the Parliament. The work was dedicated to Charles II with the flattering and truthful remark that "the first step that was made in the Reformation was the restoring to your royal ancestors the rights of the crown and an entire dominion over all their subjects."

The task of the contemporary German Protestant historian, Seckendorf, was much harder, for the Thirty Years War had, as he confesses, made many people doubt the benefits of the Reformation, distrust its principles, and reject its doctrines. He discharged the thankless labor of apology in a work of enormous erudition, still valuable to the special student for the documents it quotes.

Catholics

The Catholic philosophy of history was to the Protestant as a seal to the wax, or as a negative to a photograph; what was raised in one was depressed in the other, what was light in one was shade in the other. The same theory of the chosen people, of the direct divine governance and of Satanic meddling, was the foundation of both. That Luther was a bad man, an apostate, begotten by an incubus, and familiar with the devil, went to explain his heresy, and he was commonly compared to Mohammed or Arius. Bad, if often trivial motives were found for his actions, as that he broke away from Rome because he failed to get a papal dispensation to marry. The legend that his protest against indulgences was prompted by the jealousy of the Augustinians toward the Dominicans to whom the pope had committed their sale, was started by Emser in 1519, and has been repeated by Peter Martyr d'Anghierra, by Cochlaeus, by Bossuet and by most Catholic and secular historians down to our own day.

Apart from the revolting polemic of Dr. Sanders, who found the sole cause of the Reformation in sheer depravity, the Catholics produced, prior to 1700, only one noteworthy contribution to the subject, that of Bossuet, Bishop of Meaux. His *History of the Variations of the Protestant Churches,* written without that odious defamation of character that had hitherto been the staple of confessional polemic, and with much real eloquence, sets out to condemn the Reformers out of their own mouths by their mutual contradictions. Truth is one, Bossuet maintains, and that which varies is not truth, but the Protestants have almost as many varieties as there are pastors. Never before nor since has such an effective attack been made on Protestantism from the Christian standpoint. With persuasive iteration the moral is driven home: there is nothing certain in a religion without a central authority; revolt is sure to lead to indifference and atheism in opinion, and to the overthrow of all established order in civil

Bossuet

life. The chief causes of the Reformation are found in the admitted corruption of the church, and in the personal animosities of the Reformers. The immoral consequences of their theories are alleged, as in Luther's ideas about polygamy and in Zwingli's denial of original sin and his latitudinarian admission of good heathens to heaven.

Secular historians

A great deal that was not much biassed by creed was written on the Reformation during this period. It all goes to show how completely men of the most liberal tendencies were under the influence of their environment, for their comments were almost identical with those of the most convinced partisans. For the most part secular historians neglected ecclesiastical history as a separate discipline. Edward Hall, the typical Protestant chronicler, barely mentions religion. Camden apologizes for touching lightly on church history and not confining himself to politics and war, which he considers the proper subject of the annalist. Buchanan ignores the Reformation; De Thou passes over it with the fewest words, fearing to give offence to either papists or Huguenots. Jovius has only a page or two on it in all his works. In one place he finds the chief cause of the Reformation in a malignant conjunction of the stars; in another he speaks of it as a revival of one of the old heresies condemned at Constance. Polydore Vergil pays small attention to a schism, the cause of which he found in the weakness of men's minds and their propensity to novelty.

The one valuable explanation of the rise of Protestantism contributed by the secular historians of this age was the theory that it was largely a political phenomenon. That there was much truth in this is evident; the danger of the theory was in its over-statement, and in its too superficial application. How deeply the Reformation appealed to the political needs of that age has only been shown in the nineteenth century; how subtly, how unconsciously the two revolutions often worked together was beyond the comprehension of even the best minds of that time. The political explanation that they offered was simply that religion was a hypocritical pretext for the attainment of the selfish ends of monarchs or of a faction. Even in this there was some truth, but it was far from being the larger part.

1527

Vettori in his *History of Italy* mentions Luther merely to show how the emperor used him as a lever against the pope. Guicciardini accounts for the Reformation by the indignation of the Germans at paying money for indulgences. From this beginning, honest or at least excusable in itself, he says, Luther, carried away with ambition and popular applause, nourished a party. The pope might easily have allowed the revolt to die had he neglected it, but he took the wrong course and blew the tiny spark into a great flame by opposing it.

Guicciardini

A number of French writers took up the parable. Brantôme says that he leaves the religious issue to those who know more than he does about it, but he considers a change perilous, "for a new religion among a people demands afterwards a change of government." He thought Luther won over a good many of the clergy by allowing them to marry. Martin Du Bellay found the cause of the English schism in Henry's divorce and the small respect the pope had for his majesty. Davila, de Mézeray and Daniel, writing the history of the French civil wars, treated the Huguenots merely as a political party. So they were, but they were something more. Even Hugo Grotius could not sound the deeper causes of the Dutch revolt and of the religious revolution.

Sleidan

The first of all the histories of the German Reformation was also, for at least two centuries, the best. Though surpassed in some particulars by others, Sleidan united more of the qualities of a great historian than anyone else who wrote extensively on church history in the sixteenth or seventeenth centuries: fairness, accuracy, learning, skill in presentation. In words that recall Ranke's motto he declared that, though a Protestant, he would be impartial and set forth simply "rem totam, sicut est acta." "In describing religious affairs," he continues, "I was not able to omit politics, for, as I said before, they almost always interact, and in our age least of all can they be separated." Withal, he regards the Reformation as a great victory for God's word, and Luther as a notable champion of the true religion. In plain, straightforward narrative, without much philosophic reflection, he sets forth,—none better,—the diplomatic and theological side of the movement without probing its causes or inquiring into the popular support on which all the rest was based.

Sarpi

Greater art and deeper psychological penetration than Sleidan compassed is found in the writings of Paul Sarpi, "the great unmasker of the Tridentine Council," as Milton aptly called him. This friar whose book could only be published on Protestant soil, this historian admired by Macaulay as the best of modern times and denounced by Acton as fit for Newgate prison, has furnished students with one of the most curious of psychological puzzles. Omitting discussion of his learning and accuracy, which have recently been severely attacked and perhaps discredited, let us ask what was his attitude in regard to his subject? It is difficult to place him as either a Protestant, a Catholic apologist or a rationalist. The most probable explanation of his attacks on the creed in which he believed and of his favorable presentation of the acts of the heretics he must have anathematized, is that he was a Catholic reformer, one who ardently desired to purify the church, but who disliked her political entanglements. It is not unnatural to compare him with Adrian VI and Contarini who, in a freer age, had written scathing indictments of their own church; one may also find in Döllinger a parallel to him. Whatever his bias, his limitations are obviously those of his age; his explanations of the Protestant revolt, of which he gave a full history as introductory to his main subject, were exactly those that had been advanced by his predecessors: it was a divine dispensation, it was caused by the abuses of the church and by the jealousy of Augustinian and Dominican friars.

Harrington

A brilliant anticipation of the modern economic school of historical thought is found in the *Oceana* of Harrington, who suggested that the causes of the revolution in England were less religious than social. When Henry VIII put the confiscated lands of abbey and noble into the hands of scions of the people, Harrington thought that he had destroyed the ancient balance of power in the constitution, and, while leveling feudalism and the church, had raised up unto the throne an even more dangerous enemy.

§ 2. The Rationalistic Critique. (The Eighteenth Century)

While the "philosophers" of the enlightenment were not the first to judge the Reformation from a secular standpoint, they marked a great advance in historical interpretation as compared with the humanists. The latter had been able to make of the whole movement nothing but either a delusion or a fraud inspired by refined and calculated policy. The philosophers saw deeper into the matter than that; though for them, also, religion was false, originating, as Voltaire put it, when the first knave met the first fool. But they were able to see causes of religious change and to point out instructive analogies.

Montesquieu

Montesquieu showed that religions served the needs of their adherents and were thus adapted by them to the prevailing civil organization. After comparing Mohammedanism and Christianity he said that the North of Europe adopted Protestantism because it had the spirit of independence whereas the South, naturally servile, clung to the authoritative Catholic creed. The divisions among Protestants, too, corresponded, he said, to their secular polity; thus Lutheranism became despotic and Calvinism republican because of the circumstances in which each arose. The suppression of church festivals in Protestant countries he thought due to the greater need and zest for labor in the North. He accounted for the alleged fact that Protestantism produced more free-thinkers by saying that their unadorned cult naturally aroused a less warm attachment than the sensuous ritual of Romanism.

Voltaire

One of the greatest of historians was Voltaire. None other has made history so nearly universal as did he, peering into every side of life and into every corner of the earth. No authority imposed on him, no fact was admitted to be inexplicable by natural laws. It is true that he was not very learned and that he had strong prejudices against what he called "the most infamous superstition that ever brutalized man." But with it all he brought more freedom and life into the story of mankind than had any of his predecessors.

For his history of the Reformation he was dependent on Bossuet, Sarpi, and a few other general works; there is no evidence that he perused any of the sources. But his treatment of the phenomena is wonderful.

Beginning with an enthusiastic account of the greatness of the Renaissance, its discoveries, its opulence, its roll of mighty names, he proceeds to compare the Reformation with the two contemporaneous religious revolutions in Mohammedanism, the one in Africa, the other in Persia. He does not probe deeply, but no one else had even thought of looking to comparative religion for light. In tracing the course of events he is more conventional, finding rather small causes for large effects. The whole thing started, he assures us, in a quarrel of Augustinians and Dominicans over the spoils of indulgence-sales, "and this little squabble of monks in a corner of Saxony, produced more than a hundred years of discord, fury, and misfortune for thirty nations." "England separated from the pope because King Henry fell in love." The Swiss revolted because of the painful impression produced by the Jetzer scandal. The Reformation, in Voltaire's opinion, is condemned by its bloodshed and by its appeal to the passions of the mob. The dogmas of the Reformers are considered no whit more rational than those of their opponents, save that Zwingli is praised for "appearing more zealous for freedom than for Christianity. Of course he erred," wittily comments our author, "but how humane it is to err thus!" The influence of Montesquieu is found in the following early economic interpretation in the *Philosophic Dictionary:*

Comparative religion

> There are some nations whose religion is the result of neither climate nor government. What cause detached North Germany, Denmark, most of Switzerland, Holland, England, Scotland, and Ireland [sic] from the Roman communion? Poverty. Indulgences . . . were sold too dear. The prelates and monks absorbed the whole revenue of a province. People adopted a cheaper religion.

Scotch historians

Of the two Scotch historians that were the most faithful students of Voltaire, one, David Hume, imbibed perfectly his skepticism and scorn for Christianity; the other, William Robertson, everything but that. Presbyterian clergyman as was the latter, he found that the "happy reformation of religion" had produced "a revolution in the sentiments of mankind the greatest as well as the most beneficial that has happened since the publication of Christianity." Such an operation, in his opinion, "historians the least prone to superstition and credulity ascribe to divine Providence." But this Providence worked by natural causes, specially prepared, among which he enumerates: the long schism of the fourteenth century, the pontificates of Alexander VI and Julius II, the immorality and wealth of the clergy together with their immunities and oppressive taxes, the invention of printing, the revival of learning, and, last but not least, the fact that, in the writer's judgment, the doctrines of the papists were repugnant to Scripture. With breadth, power of synthesis, and real judiciousness, he traced the course of the Reformation. He blamed Luther for his violence, but praised him—and here speaks the middle-class advocate of law and order—for his firm stand against the peasants in their revolt.

Robertson

Inferior to Robertson in the use of sources as well as in the scope of his treatment, Hume was his superior in having completely escaped the spell of the supernatural. His analysis of the nature of ecclesiastical establishments, with which he begins his account of the English Reformation, is acute if bitter. He shows why it is that, in his view, priests always find it their interest to practice on the credulity and passions of the populace, and to mix error, superstition and delusion even with the deposit of truth. It was therefore incumbent on the civil power to put the church under governmental regulation. This policy, inaugurated at that time and directed against the great evil done to

Hume

mankind by the church of Rome, in suppressing liberty of thought and in opposing the will of the state, was one cause, though not the largest cause, of the Reformation. Other influences were the invention of printing and the revival of learning and the violent, popular character of Luther and his friends, who appealed not to reason but to the prejudices of the multitude. They secured the support of the masses by fooling them into the belief that they were thinking for themselves, and the support of the government by denouncing doctrines unfavorable to sovereignty. The doctrine of justification by faith, Hume thought, was in harmony with the general law by which religions tend more and more to exaltation of the Deity and to self-abasement of the worshipper. Tory as he was, he judged the effects of the Reformation as at first favorable to the execution of justice and finally dangerous by exciting a restless spirit of opposition to authority. One evil result was that it exalted "those wretched composers of metaphysical polemics, the theologians," to a point of honor that no poet or philosopher had ever attained.

Gibbon

The ablest and fairest estimate of the Reformation found in the eighteenth century is contained in the few pages Edward Gibbon devoted to that subject in his great history of *The Decline and Fall of the Roman Empire.* "A philosopher," he begins, "who calculates the degree of their merit [*i.e.* of Zwingli, Luther and Calvin] will prudently ask from what articles of faith, above or against our reason they have enfranchised the Christians," and, in answering this question he will "rather be surprised at the timidity than scandalized by the freedom of the first Reformers." They adopted the inspired Scriptures with all the miracles, the great mysteries of the Trinity and Incarnation, the theology of the four or six first councils, the Athanasian creed with its damnation of all who did not believe in the Catholic faith. Instead of consulting their reason in the article of transubstantiation, they became entangled in scruples, and so Luther maintained a corporeal and Calvin a real presence in the eucharist. They not only adopted but improved upon and popularized the "stupendous doctrines of original sin, redemption, faith, grace and predestination," to such purpose that "many a sober Christian would rather admit that a wafer is God than that God is a cruel and capricious tyrant." "And yet," Gibbon continues, "the services of Luther and his rivals are solid and important, and the philosopher must own his obligations to these fearless enthusiasts. By their hands the lofty fabric of superstition, from the abuse of indulgences to the intercession of the Virgin, has been levelled with the ground. Myriads of both sexes of the monastic profession have been restored to the liberties and labors of social life." Credulity was no longer nourished on daily miracles of images and relics; a simple worship "the most worthy of man, the least unworthy of the Deity" was substituted for an "imitation of paganism." Finally, the chain of authority was broken and each Christian taught to acknowledge no interpreter of Scripture but his own conscience. This led, rather as a consequence than as a design, to toleration, to indifference and to skepticism.

Wieland, on the other hand, frankly gave the opinion, anticipating Nietzsche, that the Reformation had done harm in retarding the progress of philosophy for centuries. The Italians, he said, might have effected a salutary and rational reform had not Luther interfered and made the people a party to a dispute which should have been left to scholars.

Goethe

Goethe at one time wrote that Lutherdom had driven quiet culture back, and at another spoke of the Reformation as "a sorry spectacle of boundless confusion, error fighting with error, selfishness with selfishness, the truth only here and there heaving in sight." Again he wrote to a friend: "The character of Luther is the only interesting thing in the Reformation, and the only thing, moreover, that made an impression on the masses. All the rest is a lot of bizarre trash we have not yet, to our cost, cleared away." In the last years of his long life he changed his opinion somewhat for, if we can trust the report of his conversations with Eckermann, he told his young disciple that people hardly realized how much they owed to Luther who had given them the courage to stand firmly on God's earth.

The treatment of the subject by German Protestants underwent a marked change under the influence of Pietism and the Enlightenment. Just as the earlier Orthodox school had over-emphasized Luther's narrowness, and had been concerned chiefly to prove that the Reformation changed nothing save abuses, so now the leader's liberalism was much over-stressed. It was in view of the earlier Protestant bigotry that Lessing apostrophized the Wittenberg professor: "Luther! thou great, misunderstood man! Thou hast freed us from the yoke of tradition, who is to free us from the more unbearable yoke of the letter? Who will finally bring us Christianity such as thou thyself would now teach, such as Christ himself would teach?"

Lessing

German Robertsons, though hardly equal to the Scotch, were found in Mosheim and Schmidt. Both wrote the history of the Protestant revolution in the endeavor to make it all natural. In Mosheim, indeed, the devil still appears, though in the background; Schmidt is as rational and as fair as any German Protestant could then be.

§ 3. THE LIBERAL-ROMANTIC APPRECIATION. (CIRCA 1794–c. 1860)

At about the end of the eighteenth century historiography underwent a profound change due primarily to three influences: 1. The French Revolution and the struggle for political democracy throughout nearly a century after 1789; 2. The Romantic Movement; 3. The rise of the scientific spirit. The judgment of the Reformation changed accordingly; the rather unfavorable verdict of the eighteenth century was completely reversed. Hardly by its extremest partisans in the Protestant camp has the importance of that movement and the character of its leaders been esteemed so highly as it was by the writers of the liberal-romantic school. Indeed, so little had confession to do with this bias that the finest things about Luther and the most extravagant praise of his work, was uttered not by Protestants, but by the Catholic Döllinger, the Jew Heine, and the free thinkers, Michelet, Carlyle, and Froude.

The French Revolution

The French Revolution taught men to see, or misled them into construing, the whole of history as a struggle for liberty against oppression. Naturally, the Reformation was one of the favorite examples of this perpetual warfare; it *was* the Revolution of the earlier age, and Luther was the great liberator, standing for the Rights of Man against a galling tyranny.

Condorcet

The first to draw the parallel between Reformation and Revolution was Condorcet in his noble essay on *The Advance of the Human Spirit,* written in prison and published posthumously. Luther, said he, punished the crimes of the clergy and freed some peoples from the yoke of the papacy; he would have freed all, save for the false politics of the kings who, feeling instinctively that religious liberty would bring political enfranchisement, banded together against the revolt. He adds that the epoch brought added strength to the government and to political science and that it purified morals by abolishing sacerdotal celibacy; but that it was (like the Revolution, one reads between the lines) soiled by great atrocities.

In the year 1802, the Institute of France announced as the subject for a prize competition, "What has been the influence of the Reformation of Luther on the political situation of the several states of Europe and on the progress of enlightenment?" The prize was won by Charles de Villers in an essay maintaining elaborately the thesis that the gradual improvement of the human species has been effected by a series of revolutions, partly silent, partly violent, and that the object of all these risings has been the attainment of either religious or of civil liberty. After arguing his position in respect to the Reformation, the author eulogizes it for having established religious freedom, promoted civil liberty, and for having endowed Europe with a variety of blessings, including almost everything he liked. Thus, in his opinion, the Reformation made Protestant countries more wealthy by keeping the papal tax-gatherers aloof; it started "that grand idea the balance of power," and it prepared the way for a general philosophical enlightenment.

Villers

Guizot

The thesis of Villers is exactly that maintained, with more learning and caution, by Guizot. According to him:

> The Reformation was a vast effort made by the human race to secure its freedom; it was a new-born desire to think and judge freely and independently of all ideas and opinions, which until then Europe had received or been bound to receive from the hands of antiquity. It was a great endeavor to emancipate the human reason and to call things by their right names. It was an insurrection of the human mind against the absolute power of the spiritual estate.

Romantic Movement

But there was more than politics to draw the sympathies of the nineteenth century to the sixteenth. A large anthology of poetical, artistic and musical tributes to Luther and the Reformation might be made to show how congenial they were to the spirit of that time. One need only mention Werner's drama on the subject of Luther's life (1805), Mendelssohn's "Reformation Symphony" (1832–3), Meyerbeer's opera "The Huguenots" (1836), and Kaulbach's painting "The Age of the Reformation" (c. 1840). In fact the Reformation was a Romantic movement, with its emotional and mystical piety, its endeavor to transcend the limits of the classic spirit, to search for the infinite, to scorn the trammels of traditional order and method.

Mme. de Staël

All this is reflected in Mme. de Staël's enthusiastic appreciation of Protestant Germany, in which she found a people characterized by reflectiveness, idealism, and energy of inner conviction. She contrasted Luther's revolution of ideas with her own countrymen's revolution of acts, practical if not materialistic. The German had brought back religion from an affair of politics to be a matter of life; had transferred it from the realm of calculated interest to that of heart and brain.

Heine

Much the same ideas, set forth with the most dazzling brilliancy of style, animate Heine's too much neglected sketch of German religion and philosophy. To a French public, unappreciative of German literature, Heine points out that the place taken in France by *belles lettres* is taken east of the Rhine by metaphysics. From Luther to Kant there is one continuous development of thought, and no less than two revolutions in spiritual values. Luther was the sword and tongue of his time; the tempest that shattered the old oaks of hoary tyranny; his hymn was the Marseillaise of the spirit; he made a revolution and not with rose-leaves, either, but with a certain "divine brutality." He gave his people language, Kant gave them thought; Luther deposed the pope; Robespierre decapitated the king; Kant disposed of God: it was all one insurrection of Man against the same tyrant under different names.

Under the triple influence of liberalism, romanticism and the scientific impulse presently to be described, most of the great historians of the middle nineteenth century wrote. If not the greatest, yet the most lovable of them all, was Jules Michelet, a free-thinker of Huguenot ancestry. His *History of France* is like the biography of some loved and worshipped genius; he agonizes in her trials, he glories in her triumphs. And to all great men, her own and others, he puts but one inexorable question, "What did you do for the people?" and according to their answer they stand or fall before him. It is just here that one notices (what entirely escaped previous generations), that the "people" here means that part of it now called, in current cant, "the bourgeoisie," that educated middle class with some small property and with the vote. For the ignorant laborer and the pauper Michelet had as little concern as he had small patience with king and noble and priest. One thing that he and his contemporaries prized in Luther was just that bourgeois virtue that made him a model husband and father, faithfully performing a daily task for an adequate reward. Luther's joys, he assures us, were "those of the heart, of the man, the innocent happiness of family and home. What family more holy, what home more pure?" But he returns ever and again to the thought that the Huguenots were the republicans of their age and that, "Luther has been the restorer of liberty. If now we exercise in all its fullness this highest prerogative of human intelligence, it is to him we are indebted for it.

Michelet

To whom do I owe the power of publishing what I am now writing, save to this liberator of modern thought?" Michelet employed his almost matchless rhetoric not only to exalt the Reformers to the highest pinnacle of greatness, but to blacken the character of their adversaries, the obscurantists, the Jesuits, Catherine de' Medici.

Froude

English liberalism found its perfect expression in the work of Froude. Built up on painstaking research, readable as a novel, cut exactly to the prejudices of the English Protestant middle class, *The History of England from the Fall of Wolsey to the Defeat of the Spanish Armada* won a resounding immediate success. Froude loved Protestantism for the enemies it made, and as a mild kind of rationalism. The Reformers, he thought, triumphed because they were armed with the truth; it was a revolt of conscience against lies, a real religion over against "a superstition which was but the counterpart of magic and witchcraft" and which, at that time, "meant the stake, the rack, the gibbet, the Inquisition dungeons and the devil enthroned." It was the different choice made then by England and Spain that accounted for the greatness of the former and the downfall of the latter, for, after the Spaniard, once "the noblest, grandest and most enlightened people in the known world," had chosen for the saints and the Inquisition, "his intellect shrivelled in his brain and the sinews shrank in his self-bandaged limbs."

Liberals

Practically the same type of opinion is found in the whole school of middle-century historians. "Our firm belief is," wrote Macaulay, "that the North owes its great civilization and prosperity chiefly to the moral effect of the Protestant Reformation, and that the decay of the Southern countries is to be mainly ascribed to the great Catholic revival." It would be pleasant, were there space, to quote similar enthusiastic appreciations from the French scholars Quinet and Thierry, the Englishman Herbert Spencer and the Americans Motley and Prescott. They all regarded the Reformation as at once an enlightenment and enfranchisement. Even the philosophers rushed into the same camp. Carlyle worshipped Luther as a hero; Emerson said that his "religious movement was the foundation of so much intellectual life in Europe; that is, Luther's conscience animating sympathetically the conscience of millions, the pulse passed into thought, and ultimated itself in Galileos, Keplers, Swedenborgs, Newtons, Shakespeares, Bacons and Miltons." Back of all this appreciation was a strong unconscious sympathy between the age of the Reformation and that of Victoria. The creations of the one, Protestantism, the national state, capitalism, individualism, reached their perfect maturity in the other. The very moderate liberals of the latter found in the former just that "safe and sane" spirit of reform which they could thoroughly approve.

German patriots

The enthusiasm generated by political democracy in France, England and America, was supplemented in Germany by patriotism. Herder first emphasized Luther's love of country as his great virtue; Arndt, in the Napoleonic wars, counted it unto him for righteousness that he hated Italian craft and dreaded French deceitfulness. Fichte, at the same time, in his fervent *Speeches to the German Nation,* called the Reformation "the consummate achievement of the German people," and its "perfect act of world-wide significance." Freytag, at a later period, tried to educate the public to search for a German state at once national and liberal. In his *Pictures from the German Past,* largely painted from sixteenth-century models, he places all the high-lights on "Deutschtum" and "Bürgertum," and all the shade on the foreigners and the Junkers. With Freytag as a German liberal may be classed D. F. Strauss, who defended the Reformers for choosing, rather than superficial culture, "the better part," "the one thing needful," which was truth.

Scientific spirit

It is now high time to say something of the third great influence that, early in the nineteenth century, transformed historiography. It was the rise of the scientific spirit, of the fruitful conception of a world lapped in universal law. For two centuries men had gradually become accustomed to the thought of an external nature governed by an unbreakable chain of cause and effect, but it was still believed that man, with his free will, was an exception and that history, therefore, consisting of the sum total of humanity's arbitrary actions, was incalculable and in large part inexplicable. But the more closely men studied the past, and the more widely and deeply did the uniformity of nature soak into their consciousness, the more "natural" did the progress of the human race seem. When it was found that every age had its own temper and point of view, that men turned with one accord in the same direction as if set by a current, long before any great man had come to create the current, the influence of personality seemed to sink into the background, and that of other influences to be preponderant.

Hegel

Quite inevitably the first natural and important philosophy of history took a semi-theological, semi-personal form. The philosopher Hegel, pondering on the fact that each age has its own unmistakable "time-spirit" and that each age is a natural, even logical, development of some antecedent, announced the Doctrine of Ideas as the governing forces in human progress. History was but the development of spirit, or the realization of its idea; and its fundamental law was the necessary "progress in the consciousness of freedom."

The Oriental knew that one is free, the Greek that some are free, the Germans that all are free. In this third, or Teutonic, stage of evolution, the Reformation was one of the longest steps. The characteristic of modern times is that the spirit is conscious of its own freedom and wills the true, the eternal and the universal. The dawn of this period, after the long and terrible night of the Middle Ages, is the Renaissance, its sunrise the Reformation. In order to prove his thesis, Hegel labors to show that the cause of the Protestant revolt in the corruption of the church was not accidental but necessary, inasmuch as, at the Catholic stage of progress, that which is adored must necessarily be sensuous, but at the lofty German level the worshipper must look for God in the spirit and heart, that is, in faith. The subjectivism of Luther is due to German sincerity manifesting the self-consciousness of the world-spirit; his doctrine of the eucharist, conservative as it seems to the rationalist, is in reality a manifestation of the same spirituality, in the assertion of an immediate relation of Christ to the soul. In short, the essence of the Reformation is said to be that man in his very nature is destined to be free, and all history since Luther's time is but a working out of the implications of his position. If only the Germanic nations have adopted Protestantism, it is because only they have reached the highest state of spiritual development.

Baur

The philosopher's truest disciple was Ferdinand Christian Baur, of whom it has been said that he rather deduced history than narrated it. With much detail he filled in the outline offered by the master, in as far as the subject of church history was concerned. He showed that the Reformation (a term to which he objected, apparently preferring Division, or Schism) was bound to come from antecedents already in full operation before Luther. At most, he admitted, the personal factor was decisive of the time and place of the inevitable revolution, but said that the most powerful personality would have been helpless but for the popularity of the ideas expressed by him. Like Hegel, he deduced the causes of the movement from the corruption of the medieval church, and like him he regarded all later history as but the tide of which the first wave broke in 1517. The true principle of the movement, religious autonomy and subjective freedom, he believed, had been achieved only for states in the sixteenth century, but thereafter logically and necessarily came to be applied to individuals.

Ranke

From the Hegelian school came forth the best equipped historian the world has ever seen. Save the highest quality of thought and emotion that is the prerogative of poetic genius, Leopold von Ranke lacked nothing of industry, of learning, of method and of talent to make him the perfect narrator of the past. It was his idea to pursue history for no purpose but its own; to tell "exactly what happened" without regard to the moral, or theological, or political lesson. Thinking the most colorless presentation the best, he seldom allowed his own opinions to appear. In treating the Reformation he was "first an historian and then a Christian." There is in his work little biography, and that little psychological; there is no dogma and no polemic. From Hegel he derived his belief in the "spirit" of the times, and nicely differentiated that of the Renaissance, the Reformation and the Counter-reformation. He was the first to generalize the use of the word "Counter-reformation"—coined in 1770 and obtaining currency later on the analogy of "counter-revolution." The causes of the Reformation Ranke found in "deeper religious and moral repugnance to the disorders of a merely assenting faith and service of 'works,' and, secondarily, in the assertion of the rights and duties residing in the state." Quite rightly, he emphasized the result of the movement in breaking down the political power of the ecclesiastical state, and establishing in its stead "a completely autonomous state sovereignty, bound by no extraneous considerations and existing for itself alone." Of all the ideas which have aided in the development of modern Europe he esteemed this the most effective. Would he have thought so after 1919?

Buckle

A new start in the search for fixed historical laws was made by Henry Thomas Buckle. His point of departure was not, like that of Hegel, the universal, but rather certain very particular sociological facts as interpreted by Comte's positivism. Because the same percentage of unaddressed letters is mailed every year, because crimes vary in a constant curve according to season, because the number of suicides and of marriages stands in a fixed ratio to the cost of bread, Buckle argued that all human acts, at least in the mass, must be calculable, and reducible to general laws. At present we are concerned only with his views on the Reformation. The religious opinions prevalent at any period, he pointed out, are but symptoms of the general culture of that age. Protestantism was to Catholicism simply as the moderate enlightenment of the sixteenth century was to the darkness of the earlier centuries. Credulity and ignorance were still common, though diminishing, in Luther's time, and this intellectual change was the cause of the religious change. Buckle makes one strange and damaging admission, namely that though, according to his theory, or, as he puts it, "according to the natural order," the "most civilized countries should be Protestant and the most uncivilized Catholic [sic]," it has not always been so. In general Buckle adopts the theory of the Reformation as an uprising of the human mind, an enlightenment, and a democratic rebellion.

Whereas Henry Hallam, who wrote on the relation of the Reformers to modern thought, is a belated eighteenth-century rationalist, doubtless Lecky is best classified as a member of the new school. His *History of the Rise and Influence of the Spirit of Rationalism* is partly Hegelian, partly inspired by Buckle. His main object is to show how little reason has to do with the adoption or rejection of any theology, and how much it is dependent on a certain spirit of the age, determined by quite other causes. He found the essence of the Reformation in its conformity to then prevalent habits of mind and morals. But he thought it had done more than any other movement to emancipate the mind from superstition and to secularize society.

Protestants

It is impossible to do more than mention by name, in the short space at my command, the principal Protestant apologists for the Reformation, in this period. Whereas Ritschl gave a somewhat new aspect to the old "truths," Merle d'Aubigné won an enormous and unmerited success by reviving the supernatural theory of the Protestant revolution, with such modern connotations and modifications as suited the still lively prejudices of the evangelical public of England and America; for it was in these countries that his book, in translation from the French, won its enormous circulation.[1]

Döllinger

An extremely able adverse judgment of the Reformation was expressed by the Catholic Döllinger, the most theological of historians, the most historically-minded of divines. He, too, thought Luther had really

[1] The preface of the English edition of 1848 claims that whereas, since 1835, only 4000 copies were sold in France, between 150,000 and 200,000 were sold in England and America.

founded a new religion, of which the center was the mystical doctrine, tending to solipsism, of justification by faith. The very fact that he said much good of Luther, and approved of many of his practical reforms, made his protest the more effective. It is noticeable that when he broke with Rome he did not become a Protestant.

§ 4. The Economic and Evolutionary Interpretations. (1859 to the Present)

The year 1859 saw the launching of two new theories of the utmost importance. These, together with the political developments of the next twelve years, completely altered the view-point of the intellectual class, as well as of the peoples. In relation to the subject under discussion this meant a reversal of historical judgment as radical as that which occurred at the time of the French Revolution. The three new influences, in the order of their immediate importance for historiography, were the following: 1. The publication of Marx's *Zur Kritik der politischen Ökonomie* in 1859, containing the germ of the economic interpretation of history later developed in *Das Kapital* (1867) and in other works. 2. The publication of Darwin's *Origin of Species,* giving rise to an evolutionary treatment of history. 3. The Bismarckian wars (1864–71), followed by German intellectual and material hegemony, and the defeat of the old liberalism. This lasted only until the Great War (1914–18), when Germany was cast down and liberalism rose in more radical guise than ever.

Marx

Karl Marx not only viewed history for the first time from the point of view of the proletariat, or working class, but he directly asserted that in the march of mankind the economic factors had always been, in the last analysis, decisive; that the material basis of life, particularly the system of production, determined, in general, the social, political and religious ideas of every epoch and of every locality. Revolutions follow as the necessary consequence of economic change. In the scramble for sustenance and wealth class war is postulated as natural and ceaseless. The old Hegelian antithesis of idea versus personality took the new form of "the masses" versus "the great man," both of whom were but puppets in the hands of overmastering determinism. As often interpreted, Marx's theory replaced the Hegelian "spirits of the time" by the classes, conceived as entities struggling for mastery.

This brilliant theory suffered at first in its application, which was often hasty, or fantastic. As the economic factor had once been completely ignored, so now it was overworked. Its major premise of an "economic man," all greed and calculation, is obviously false, or rather, only half true. Men's motives are mixed, and so are those of aggregates of men. There are other elements in progress besides the economic ones. The only effective criticism of the theory of economic determination is that well expressed by Dr. Shailer Mathews, that it is too simple. Self-interest is one factor in history, but not the only one.

Bax

Exception can be more justly taken to the way in which the theory has sometimes been applied than to its formulation. Belfort Bax, maintaining that the revolt from Rome was largely economic in its causes, gave as one of these "the hatred of the ecclesiastical hierarchy, obviously due to its increasing exactions." Luther would have produced no result had not the economic soil been ready for his seed, and with that soil prepared he achieved a world-historical result even though, in Bax's opinion, his character and intellect were below those of the average English village grocer-deacon who sold sand for sugar. Luther, in fact, did no more than give a flag to those discontented with the existing political and industrial life. Strange to say, Bax found even the most radical party, that of the communistic Anabaptists, retrograde, with its program of return to a golden age of gild and common land.

A somewhat better grounded, but still inadequate, solution of the problem was offered by Karl Kautsky. He, too, found the chief cause of the revolt in the spoliation of Germany by Rome. In addition to this was the new rivalry of commercial classes. Unlike Bax, Kautsky finds in the Anabaptists Socialists of whom he can thoroughly approve.

Kautsky

The criticism that must be made of these and similar attempts, is that the causes picked out by them are too trivial. To say that the men who, by the thousands and tens of thousands suffered martyrdom for their faith, changed that faith simply because they objected to pay a tithe, reminds one of the ancient Catholic derivation of the whole movement from Luther's desire to marry. The effect is out of proportion to the cause. But some theorists were even more fantastic than trivial. When Professor S. N. Patten traces the origins of revolutions to either over-nutrition or undernutrition, and that of the Reformation to "the growth of frugalistic concepts"; when Mr. Brooks Adams asserts that it was all due to the desire of the people for a cheaper religion, exchanging an expensive offering for justification by faith and mental anguish, which cost nothing, and an expensive church for a cheap Bible —we feel that the dish of theory has run away with the spoon of fact. The climax was capped by the German sociologist Friedrich Simmel, who explained the Reformation by the law of the operation of force along the line of least resistance. The Reformers, by sending the soul straight to God, spared it the detour via the priest, thus short-circuiting grace, as it were, and saving energy.

Lamprecht

The genius who first and most fully worked out a tenable economic interpretation of the Lutheran movement was Karl Lamprecht, who stands in much the same relation to Marx as did Ranke to Hegel, to wit, that of an independent, eclectic and better informed student. Lamprecht, as it is well known, divides history into periods according to their psychological character—perhaps an up-to-date Hegelianism—but he maintains, and on the whole successfully, that the temper of each of these epochs is determined by their economic institutions. Thus, says he, the condition of the transition from medieval to modern times was the development of a system of "money economy" from a system of "natural economy," which took place slowly throughout the 14th, 15th, 16th and 17th centuries. "The complete emergence of capitalistic tendencies, with their consequent effects on the social, and, chiefly through this, on the intellectual sphere, must of itself bring on modern times." Lamprecht shows how the rise of capitalism was followed by the growth of the cities and of the culture of the Renaissance in them, and how, also, individualism arose in large part as a natural consequence of the increased power and scope given to the ego by the possession of wealth. This individualism, he thinks, strengthened by and strengthening humanism, was made forever safe by the Reformation.

It is a momentous error, as Lamprecht rightly points out, to suppose that we are living in the same era of civilization, psychologically considered, as that of Luther. Our subjectivism is as different from his individualism as his modernity was from medievalism. The eighteenth century was a transitional period from the one to the other.

One of the chief characteristics of the Reformation, continues Lamprecht, seen first in the earlier mystics, was the change from "polydynamism," or the worship of many saints, and the mediation of manifold religious agencies, to "monodynamism" or the direct and single intercourse of the soul with God. Still more different was the world-view of the nineteenth century, built on "an extra-Christian, though not yet anti-Christian foundation."

Berger

In the very same year in which Lamprecht's volume on the German Reformation appeared, another interpretation, though less profound and less in the economic school of thought, was put forth by A. E. Berger. He found the four principal causes of the Reformation in the growth of national self-consciousness, the overthrow of an ascetic for a secular culture, individualism, and the growth of a lay religion. The Reformation itself was a triumph of conscience and of "German inwardness," and its success was due to the fact that it made of the church a purely spiritual entity.

Weber

The most brilliant essay in the economic interpretation of the origins of Protestantism, though an essay in a very narrow field, was that of Max Weber which has made "Capitalism and Calvinism" one of the watchwords of contemporary thought. The intimate connection of the Reformation and the merchant class had long been noticed, *e. g.* by Froude and by Thorold Rogers. But Weber was the first to ask, and to answer, the question what it was that made Protestantism particularly congenial to the industrial type of civilization. In the first place, Calvinism stimulated just those ethical qualities of rugged strength and self-confidence needful for worldly success. In the second place, Protestantism abolished the old ascetic ideal of labor for the sake of the next world, and substituted for it the conception of a calling, that is, of doing faithfully the work appointed to each man in this world. Indeed, the word "calling" or "Beruf," meaning God-given work, is found only in Germanic languages, and is wanting in all those of the Latin group. The ethical idea expressed by Luther and more strongly by Calvin was that of faithfully performing the daily task; in fact, such labor was inculcated as a duty to the point of pain; in other words it was "a worldly asceticism." Finally, Calvin looked upon thrift as a duty, and regarded prosperity, in the Old Testament style, as a sign of God's favor. "You may labor in that manner as tendeth most to your success and lawful gain," said the Protestant divine Richard Baxter, "for you are bound to improve all your talents." And again, "If God show you a way in which you may lawfully get more than in another way, if you refuse this and choose the less gainful way, you cross one of the ends of your calling, and you refuse to be God's steward."

It would be instructive and delightful to follow the controversy caused by Weber's thesis. Some scholars, like Knodt, denied its validity, tracing capitalism back of the spirit of Fugger rather than of Calvin; but most accepted it. Fine interpretations and criticisms of it were offered by Cunningham, Brentano, Kovalewsky and Ashley. So commonly has it been received that it has finally been summed up in a brilliant but superficial epigram used by Chesterton, good enough to have been coined by him—though it is not, I believe, from his mint—that the Reformation was "the Revolution of the rich against the poor."

Darwinism

Contemporary with the economic historiography, there was a new intellectual criticism reminding one superficially of the Voltairean, but in reality founded far more on Darwinian ideas. The older "philosophers" had blamed the Reformers for not coming up to a modern standard; the new evolutionists censured them for falling below the standard of their own age. Moreover, the critique of the new atheism was more searching than had been that of the old deism.

Until Nietzsche, the prevailing view had been that the Reformation was the child, or sister, of the Renaissance, and the parent of the Enlightenment and the French Revolution. "We are in the midst of a gigantic movement," wrote Huxley, "greater than that which preceded and produced the Reformation, and really only a continuation of that movement." "The Reformation," in the opinion of Tolstoy, "was a rude, incidental reflection of the labor of thought, striving after the liberation of man from the darkness." "The truth is," according to Symonds, "that the Reformation was the Teutonic Renaissance. It was the emancipation of the reason on a line neglected by the Italians, more important, indeed, in its political consequences, more weighty in its bearing on rationalistic developments than was the Italian Renaissance, but none the less an outcome of the same grand influence." William Dilthey, in the nineties, labored to show that the essence of the Reformation was the same in the religious fields as that of the best thought contemporary to it in other lines.

Nietzsche

But these ideas were already obsolescent since Friedrich Nietzsche had worked out, with some care, the thought that "the Reformation was a re-action of old-fashioned minds, against the Italian Renaissance." One might suppose that this furious Antichrist, as he wished to be, would have thought well of Luther because of his opinion that the Saxon first taught the Germans to be unchristian, and because "Luther's merit is greater in nothing than that he had the courage of his sensuality—then called, gently enough, 'evangelic liberty.'" But no! With frantic passion Nietzsche charged: "The Reformation, a duplication of the medieval spirit at a time when this spirit no longer had a good conscience, pullulated sects, and superstitions like the witchcraft craze." German culture was just ready to burst into full bloom, only one night more was needed, but that night brought the storm that ruined all. The Reformation was the peasants' revolt of the human spirit, a rising full of sound and fury, but signifying nothing. It was "the rage of the simple against the complex, a rough, honest misunderstanding, in which (to speak mildly) much must be forgiven." Luther unraveled and tore apart a culture he did not appreciate and an authority he did not relish. Behind the formula "every man his own priest" lurked nothing but the abysmal hatred of the low for the higher; the truly plebeian spirit at its worst.

Acceptance of Nietzsche's opinion

Quite slowly but surely Nietzsche's opinion gained ground until one may say that it was, not long ago, generally accepted. "Our sympathies are more in unison, our reason less shocked by the arguments and doctrines of Sadolet than by those of Calvin," wrote R. C. Christie. Andrew D. White's popular study of *The Warfare of Science and Theology* proved that Protestant churches had been no less hostile to intellectual progress than had the Catholic church. "The Reformation, in fact," opined J. M. Robertson, "speedily overclouded with fanaticism what new light of free thought had been glimmering before, turning into Bibliolaters those who had rationally doubted some of the Catholic mysteries and forcing back into Catholic bigotry those more refined spirits who, like Sir Thomas More, had been in advance of their age." "Before the Lutheran revolt," said Henry C. Lea, "much freedom of thought and speech was allowed in Catholic Europe, but not after." Similar opinions might be collected in large number; I mention only the works of Bezold and the brief but admirably expressed articles of Professor George L. Burr, and that of Lemonnier, who places in a strong light the battle of the Renaissance, intellectual, indifferent in religion and politics, but aristocratic in temper, and the Reformation, reactionary, religious, preoccupied with medieval questions and turning, in its hostility to the governing orders, to popular politics.

The reaction of the Reformation on religion was noticed by the critics, who thus came to agree with the conservative estimate, though they deplored what the others had rejoiced in. Long before Nietzsche, J. Burckhardt had pointed out that the greatest danger to the papacy, secularization, had been adjourned for centuries by the German Reformation. It was this that roused the papacy from the soulless debasement in which it lay; it was thus that the moral salvation of the papacy was due to its mortal enemies.

Troeltsch

The twentieth century has seen two brilliant critiques of the Reformation from the intellectual side by scholars of consummate ability, Ernst Troeltsch and George Santayana. The former begins by pointing out, with a fineness never surpassed, the essential oneness and slight differences between early Protestantism and Catholicism. The Reformers asked the same questions as did the medieval schoolmen and, though they gave these questions somewhat different answers, their minds, like those of other men, revealed themselves far more characteristically in the asking than in the reply. "Genuine early Protestantism . . . was an authoritative ecclesiastical civilization (kirchliche Zwangskultur), a claim to regulate state and society, science and education, law, commerce, and industry, according to the supernatural standpoint of revelation." The Reformers separated early and with cruel violence from the humanistic, philological, and philosophical theology of Erasmus because they were conscious of an essential opposition. Luther's sole concern was with assurance of salvation, and this could only be won at the cost of a miracle, not any longer the old, outward magic of saints and priestcraft, but the wonder of faith occurring in the inmost center of personal life. "The sensuous sacramental miracle is done away, and in its stead appears the miracle of faith, that man, in his sin and weakness, can grasp and confidently assent to such a thought." Thus it came about that the way of salvation became more important than the goal, and the tyranny of dogma became at last unbearable. Troeltsch characterizes both his own position and that of the Reformers when he enumerates among the ancient dogmas taken over naïvely by Luther, that of the existence of a personal, ethical God. Finely contrasting the ideals of Renaissance and Reformation, he shows that the former was naturalism, the latter an intensification of religion and of a convinced otherworldliness, that while the ethic of the former was based on "affirmation of life," that of the latter was based on "calling." Even as compared with Catholicism, Troeltsch thinks, supererogatory works were abolished because each Protestant Christian was bound to exert himself to the utmost at all times. The learned professor hazards the further opinion that the spirit of the Renaissance amalgamated better with Catholicism and, after a period of quiescence, burst forth in the "frightful explosion" of the Enlightenment and Revolution, both more radical in Catholic countries than in Protestant. But Troeltsch is too historically-minded to see in the Reformation only a reaction. He believes that it contributed to the formation of the modern world by the development of nationalism, individualism (qualified by the objectively conceived sanction of Bible and Christian community), moral health, and,

Renaissance vs. Reformation

indirectly, by the introduction of the ideas of tolerance, criticism, and religious progress. Moreover, it enriched the world with the story of great personalities. Protestantism was better able to absorb modern elements of political, social, scientific, artistic and economic content, not because it was professedly more open to them, but because it was weakened by the memory of one great revolt from authority. But the great change in religion as in other matters came, Troeltsch is fully convinced, in the eighteenth century.

Santayana

If Troeltsch has the head of a skeptic with the heart of a Protestant, Santayana's equally irreligious brain is biased by a sentimental sympathy for the Catholicism in which he was trained. The essence of his criticism of Luther, than whom, he once scornfully remarked, no one could be more unintelligent, is that he moved away from the ideal of the gospel. Saint Francis, like Jesus, was unworldly, disenchanted, ascetic; Protestantism is remote from this spirit, for it is convinced of the importance of success and prosperity, abominates the disreputable, thinks of contemplation as idleness, of solitude as selfishness, of poverty as a punishment, and of married and industrial life as typically godly. In short, it is a reversion to German heathendom. But Santayana denies that Luther prevented the euthanasia of Christianity, for there would have been, he affirms, a Catholic revival without him. With all its old-fashioned insistence that dogma was scientifically true and that salvation was urgent and fearfully doubtful, Protestantism broke down the authority of Christianity, for "it is suicidal to make one part of an organic system the instrument for attacking the other part." It is the beauty and torment of Protestantism that it leads to something ever beyond its ken, finally landing its adherent in a pious skepticism. Under the solvent of self-criticism

German religion and philosophy have dropped, one by one, all supernaturalism and comforting private hopes and have become absorbed in the duty of living manfully the conventional life of the world. Positive religion and frivolity both disappear, and only "consecrated worldliness" remains.

Recent opinions

Some support to the old idea that the Reformation was a progressive movement has been recently offered by eminent scholars. G. Monod says that the difference between Catholicism and Protestantism is that the former created a closed philosophy, the latter left much open. "The Reformation," according to H. A. L. Fisher, "was the great dissolvent of European conservatism. A religion which had been accepted with little question for 1200 years, which had dominated European thought, moulded European customs, shaped no small part of private law and public policy . . . was suddenly and sharply questioned in all the progressive communities of the West."

Bertrand Russell thinks that, while the Renaissance undermined the medieval theory of authority in a few choice minds, the Reformation made the first really serious breach in that theory. It is just because the fight for liberty (which he hardly differentiates from anarchism) began in the religious field, that its triumph is now most complete in that field. We are still bound politically and economically; that we are free religiously is due to Luther. It is an evil, however, in Mr. Russell's opinion, that subjectivism has been fostered in Protestant morality.

A similar opinion, in the most attenuated form, has been expressed by Salomon Reinach. "Instead of freedom of faith and thought the Reformation produced a kind of attenuated Catholicism. But the seeds of religious liberty were there, though it was only after two centuries that they blossomed and bore fruit, thanks to the breach made by Luther in the ancient edifice of Rome."

German nationalists

A judicious estimate is offered by Imbart de la Tour, to the effect that, though the logical result of some of Luther's premises would have been individual religion and autonomy of conscience, as actually worked out, "his mystical doctrine of inner inspiration has no resemblance whatever to our subjectivism." His true originality was his personality which imposed on an optimistic society a pessimistic world-view. It is true that the revolution was profound and yet it was not modern: "the classic spirit, free institutions, democratic ideals, all these great forces by which we live are not the heritage of Luther."

As the wave of nationalism and militarism swept over Europe with the Bismarckian wars, men began to judge the Reformation as everything else by its relation, real or fancied, to racial superiority or power. Even in Germany scholars were not at all clear as to exactly what this relation was. Paul de Lagarde idealized the Middle Ages as showing the perfect expression of German character and he detested "the coarse, scolding Luther, who never saw further than his two hobnailed shoes, and who by his demagogy, brought in barbarism and split Germany into fragments." Nevertheless even he saw, at times, that the Reformation meant a triumph of nationalism, and found it significant that the Basques, who were not a nation, should have produced, in Loyola and Xavier, the two greatest champions of the anti-national church.

The tide soon started flowing the other way and scholars began to see clearly that in some sort the Reformation was a triumph of "Deutschtum" against the "Romanitas" of Latin religion and culture. Treitschke, as the representative of this school, trumpeted forth that "the Reformation arose from the good

German conscience,'' and that, ''the Reformer of our church was the pioneer of the whole German nation on the road to a freer civilization.'' The dogma that might makes right was adopted at Berlin—as Acton wrote in 1886—and the mere fact that the Reformation was successful was accounted a proof of its rightness by historians like Waitz and Kurtz.

Naturally, all was not as bad as this. A rather attractive form of the thesis was presented by Karl Sell. Whereas, he thinks, Protestantism has died, or is dying, as a religion, it still exists as a mood, as bibliolatry, as a national and political cult, as a scientific and technical motive-power, and, last but not least, as the ethos and pathos of the Germanic peoples.

The Great War

In the Great War Luther was mobilized as one of the German national assets. Professor Gustav Kawerau and many others appealed to the Reformer's writings for inspiration and justification of their cause; and the German infantry sang ''Ein' feste Burg'' while marching to battle.

Even outside of Germany the war of 1870 meant, in many quarters, the defeat of the old liberalism and the rise of a new school inclined, even in America—witness Mahan—to see in armed force rather than in intellectual and moral ideas the decisive factors in history. Many scholars noticed, in this connection, the shift of power from the Catholic nations, led by France, to the Protestant peoples, Germany, England and America. Some, like Acton, though impressed by it, did not draw the conclusion ably presented by a Belgian, Emile de Laveleye, that the cause of national superiority lay in Protestantism, but it doubtless had a wide influence, partly unconscious, on the verdict of history.

Reaction against German ideals

But the recoil was far greater than the first movement. Paul Sabatier wrote (in 1913) that until 1870 Protestantism had enjoyed the esteem of thoughtful men on account of its good sense, domestic and civic virtues and its openness to science and literary criticism. This high opinion, strengthened by the prestige of German thought, was shattered, says our authority, by the results of the Franco-Prussian war, its train of horrors, and the consequences to the victors, who raved of their superiority and attributed to Luther the result of Sedan.

The Great War loosed the tongues of all enemies of Luther. "Literary and philosophic Germany," said Denys Cochin in an interview, "prepared the evolution of the state and the cult of might. . . . The haughty and aristocratic reform of Luther both prepared and seconded the aberration."

Paquier

Paquier has written a book around the thesis: "Nothing in the present war would have been alien to Luther, for like all Germans of to-day, he was violent and faithless. The theory of Nietzsche is monstrous, but it is the logical conclusion of the religious revolution accomplished by Luther and of the philosophical revolution accomplished by Kant." He finds the causal nexus between Luther and Hindenburg in two important doctrines and several corollaries. First, the doctrine of justification by faith meant the disparagement of morality and the exaltation of the end at the expense of the means. Secondly, Luther deified the state. Finally, in his narrow patriotism, Luther is thought to have inspired the reckless deeds of his posterity.

On the other hand some French Protestants, notably Weiss, have sought to show that the modern doctrines of Prussia were not due to Luther but were an apostasy from him.

Practically all the older methods of interpreting the Reformation have survived to the present; to save space they must be noticed with the utmost brevity.

Protestants

The Protestant scholars of the last sixty years have all, as far as they are worthy of serious notice, escaped from the crudely supernaturalistic point of view. Their temptation is now, in proportion as they are conservative, to read into the Reformation ideas of their own. Harnack sees in Luther, as he does in Christ and Paul and all other of his heroes, exactly his own German liberal Evangelical mind. He is inclined to admit that Luther was little help to the progress of science and enlightenment, that he did not absorb the cultural elements of his time nor recognize the right and duty of free research, but yet he thinks the Reformation more important than any other revolution since Paul simply because it restored the true, *i.e.* Pauline and Harnackian theology. Loisy's criticism of him is brilliant: "What would Luther have thought had his doctrine of salvation by faith been presented to him with the amendment 'independently of beliefs,' or with this amendment, 'faith in the merciful Father, for faith in the Son is foreign to the Gospel of Jesus'?" The same treatment of Mohammedanism, as that accorded by Harnack to Christianity would, as Loisy remarks, deduce from it the same humanitarian deism as that now fashionable at Berlin.

Harnack

I should like to speak of the work of Below and Wernle, of Böhmer and Köhler, of Fisher and Walker and McGiffert, and of many other Protestant scholars, by which I have profited. But I can only mention one other Protestant tendency, that of some liberals who find the Reformation (quite naturally) too conservative for them. Laurent wrote in this sense in 1862–70, and he was followed by one of the most thoughtful of Protestant apologists, Charles Beard. Beard saw in the Reformation the subjective form of religion over against the objectivity of Catholicism, and also, "the first great triumph of the scientific spirit"—the Ren-

Beard

aissance, in fact, applied to theology. And yet he found its work so imperfect and even hampering at the time he wrote (1883) that the chief purpose of his book was to advocate a new Reformation to bring Christianity in complete harmony with science.

Philosophers

Several philosophers have, more from tradition than creed, adopted the Protestant standpoint. Eucken thinks that "the Reformation became the animating soul of the modern world, the principle motive-force of its progress. . . . In truth, every phase of modern life not directly or indirectly connected with the Reformation has something insipid and paltry about it." Windelband believes that the Reformation arose from mysticism but conquered only by the power of the state, and that the stamp of the conflict between the inner grace and the outward support is of the *esse* of Protestanism. William James was also in warm sympathy with Luther who, he thought, "in his immense, manly way . . . stretched the soul's imagination and saved theology from puerility." James added that the Reformer also invented a morality, as new as romantic love in literature, founded on a religious experience of despair breaking through the old, pagan pride.

Catholics

While many Catholics, among them Maurenbrecher and Gasquet, labored fruitfully in the field of the Reformation by uncovering new facts, few or none of them had much new light to cast on the philosophy of the period. Janssen brought to its perfection a new method applied to a new field; the field was that of *Kulturgeschichte,* the method that of letting the sources speak for themselves, but naturally only those sources agreeable to the author's bias. In this way he represented the fifteenth century as the great blossoming of the German mind, and the Reformation as a blighting frost to both culture and morality. Pastor's work, though dense with fresh knowledge, offers no connected

Janssen

Pastor

theory. The Reformation, he thinks, was a shock without parallel, involving all sides of life, but chiefly the religious. It was due in Germany to a union of the learned classes and the common people; in England to the caprice of an autocrat. From the learned uproar of Denifle's school emerges the explanation of the revolt as the "great sewer" which carried off from the church all the refuse and garbage of the time. Grisar's far finer psychology—characteristically Jesuit—tries to cast on Luther the origin of the present destructive subjectivism. Grisar's proof that "the modern infidel theology" of Germany bases itself in an exaggerated way on the Luther of the first period, is suggestive.

Acton

Though the Reformation was one of Lord Acton's favorite topics, I cannot find on that subject any new or fruitful thought at all in proportion to his vast learning. His theory of the Reformation is therefore the old Catholic one, stripped of supernaturalism, that it was merely the product of the wickedness and vagaries of a few gifted demagogues, and the almost equally blamable obstinacy of a few popes. He thought the English Bishop Creighton too easy in his judgment of the popes, adding, "My dogma is not the special wickedness of my own spiritual superiors, but the general wickedness of men in authority—of Luther and Zwingli and Calvin and Cranmer and Knox, of Mary Stuart and Henry VIII, of Philip II and Elizabeth, of Cromwell and Louis XIV, James and Charles, William, Bossuet and Ken." Acton dated modern times from the turn of the 15th and 16th centuries, believing that the fundamental characteristic of the period is the belief in conscience as the voice of God. He says, that "Luther at Worms is the most pregnant and momentous fact in our history," but he confesses himself baffled by the problem, which is, to his mind, why Luther did not return to the church. Luther, alleges Acton, gave up all the doctrines commonly insisted on as crucial and, then or later, dropped predestination, and admitted the necessity of good works, the freedom of the will, the hierarchical constitution, the authority of tradition, the seven sacraments, the Latin Mass. In fact, says Acton, the one bar to his return to the church was his belief that the pope was Antichrist.

It is notable that none of the free minds starting from Catholicism have been attracted to the Protestant camp. Renan prophesied that St. Paul and Protestantism were coming to the end of their reign. Paul Sabatier carefully proved that the Modernists owed nothing to Luther, and their greatest scholar, Loisy, succinctly put the case in the remark, "We are done with partial heresies."

Anglicans

The Anglicans have joined the Romanists to denounce as heretics those who rebelled against the church which still calls Anglicans heretics. Neville Figgis, having snatched from Treitschke the juxtaposition "Luther and Machiavelli," has labored to build up around it a theory by which these two men shall appear as the chief supports of absolutism and "divine right of kings." Figgis thinks that with the Reformation religion was merely the "performance for passing entertainment," but that the state was the "eternal treasure." A far more judicious and unprejudiced discussion of the same thesis is offered in the works of Professor A. F. Pollard. He sees both sides of the medal for, if religion had become a subject of politics, politics had become matter of religion. He thinks the English Reformation was primarily a revolt of the laity against the clergy.

Other schools

The liberal estimate of the Reformation fashionable a hundred years ago has also been revived in an elaborate work of Mackinnon, and is assumed in obiter dicta by such eminent historians as A. W. Benn, E. P.

Cheyney, C. Borgeaud, H. L. Osgood and Woodrow Wilson. Finally, Professor J. H. Robinson has improved the old political interpretation current among the secular historians of the sixteenth and seventeenth centuries. The essence of the Lutheran movement he finds in the revolt from the Roman ecclesiastical state.

§ 5. Concluding Estimate

The reader will expect me, after having given some account of the estimates of others, to make an evaluation of my own. Of course no view can be final; mine, like that of everyone else, is the expression of an age and an environment as well as that of an individual.

Causes of the Reformation

The Reformation, like the Renaissance and the sixteenth-century Social Revolution, was but the consequence of the operation of antecedent changes in environment and habit, intellectual and economic. There was the widening and deepening of knowledge, due in one aspect to the invention of printing, in the other to the geographical and historical discoveries of the fifteenth century and the consequent adumbration of the idea of natural law. Even in the later schoolmen, like Biel and Occam, still more in the humanists, one finds a much stronger rationalism than in the representative thinkers of the Middle Ages. The general economic antecedent was the growth in wealth and the change in the system of production from gild and barter to that of money and wages. This produced three secondary results, which in turn operated as causes: the rise of the moneyed class, individualism, and nationalism.

All these tendencies, operating in three fields, the religious, the political and the intellectual, produced the Reformation and its sisters, the Renaissance and the Social Revolution of the sixteenth century. The Reformation—including in that term both the Protestant movement and the Catholic reaction—partly occupied all these fields, but did not monopolize any of them. There were some religious, or anti-religious, movements outside the Reformation, and the Lutheran impulse swept into its own domain large tracts of the intellectual and political fields, primarily occupied by Renaissance and Revolution.

Religious aspect

(1) The *gêne* felt by many secular historians in the treatment of religion is now giving way to the double conviction of the importance of the subject and of its susceptibility to scientific study. Religion in human life is not a subject apart, nor is it necessary to regard all theological revolts as obscurantist. As a rationalist [1] has remarked, it is usually priests who have freed mankind from taboos and superstitions. Indeed, in a religious age, no effective attack on the existing church is possible save one inspired by piety.

Parallels to the Reformation

Many instructive parallels to the Reformation can be found both in Christian history and in that of other religions; they all markedly show the same consequences of the same causes. The publication of Christianity, with its propaganda of monotheism against the Roman world and its accentuation of faith against the ceremonialism of the Jewish church, resembled that of Luther's "gospel." Marcion with his message of Pauline faith and his criticism of the Bible, was a second-century Reformer. The iconoclasm and nationalism of the Emperor Leo furnish striking similarities to the Protestant Revolt. The movements started by the medieval mystics and still more by the heretics Wyclif and Huss, rehearsed the religious drama of the sixteenth century. Many revivals in the Protestant church, such as Methodism, were, like the original movement, returns to personal piety and biblicism. The Old Catholic schism in its repudiation of the papal supremacy, and even Modernism, notwithstanding its

[1] S. Reinach: *Cultes, Mythes et Religions*, iv, 467.

disclaimers, are animated in part by the same motives as those inspiring the Reformers. In Judaism the Sadducees, in their bibliolatry and in their opposition to the traditions dear to the Pharisees, were Protestants; a later counterpart of the same thing is found in the reform the Karaites by Anan ben David. Mohammed has been a favorite subject for comparison with Luther by the Catholics, but in truth, in no disparaging sense, the proclamation of Islam, with its monotheism, emphasis on faith and predestination, was very like the Reformation, and so were several later reforms within Mohammedanism, including two in the sixteenth century. Many parallels could doubtless be adduced from the heathen religions, perhaps the most striking is the foundation of Sikhism by Luther's contemporary Nanak, who preached monotheism and revolted from the ancient ceremonial and hierarchy of caste.

What is the etiology of religious revolution? The principal law governing it is that any marked change either in scientific knowledge or in ethical feeling necessitates a corresponding alteration in the faith. All the great religious innovations of Luther and his followers can be explained as an attempt to readjust faith to the new culture, partly intellectual, partly social, that had gradually developed during the later Middle Ages.

Faith vs. works

The first shift, and the most important, was that from salvation by works to salvation by faith only. The Catholic dogma is that salvation is dependent on certain sacraments, grace being bestowed automatically (*ex opere operato*) on all who participate in the celebration of the rite without actively opposing its effect. Luther not only reduced the number of sacraments but he entirely changed their character. Not they, but the faith of the participant mattered, and this faith was bestowed freely by God, or not at all. In this innovation one primary cause was the individualism of the age; the sense of the worth of the soul or, if one pleases, of the ego. This did not mean subjectivism, or religious autonomy, for the Reformers held passionately to an ideal of objective truth, but it did mean that every soul had the right to make its personal account with God, without mediation of priest or sacrament. Another element in this new dogma was the simpler, and yet more profound, psychology of the new age. The shift of emphasis from the outer to the inner is traceable from the earliest age to the present, from the time when Homer delighted to tell of the good blows struck in fight to the time when fiction is but the story of an inner, spiritual struggle. The Reformation was one phase in this long process from the external to the internal. The debit and credit balance of outward work and merit was done away, and for it was substituted the nobler, or at least more spiritual and less mechanical, idea of disinterested morality and unconditioned salvation. The God of Calvin may have been a tyrant, but he was not corruptible by bribes.

We are so much accustomed to think of dogma as the *esse* of religion that it is hard for us to do justice to the importance of this change. Really, it is not dogma so much as rite and custom that is fundamental. The sacramental habit of mind was common to medieval Christianity and to most primitive religions. For the first time Luther substituted for the sacramental habit, or attitude, its antithesis, an almost purely ethical criterion of faith. The transcendental philosophy and the categorical imperative lay implicit in the famous *sola fide*.

Monism

The second great change made by Protestantism was more intellectual, that from a pluralistic to a monistic standpoint. Far from the conception of natural law, the early Protestants did little or nothing to rationalize, or explain away, the creeds of the Catholics, but they had arrived at a sufficiently monistic philosophy to find scandal in the worship of the saints, with its attendant train of daily and trivial miracles. To sweep away the vast hierarchy of angels and canonized persons that made Catholicism quasi-polytheistic, and to preach pure monotheism was in the spirit of the time and is a phenomenon for which many parallels can be found. Instructive is the analogy of the contemporary trend to absolutism; neither God nor king any longer needed intermediaries.

Political and economic aspects

(2) In two aspects the Reformation was the religious expression of the current political and economic change. In the first place it reflected and reacted upon the growing national self-consciousness, particularly of the Teutonic peoples. The revolt from Rome was in the interests of the state church, and also of Germanic culture. The break-up of the Roman church at the hands of the Northern peoples is strikingly like the break-up of the Roman Empire under pressure from their ancestors. Indeed, the limits of the Roman church practically coincided with the boundaries of the Empire. The apparent exception of England proves the rule, for in Britain the Roman civilization was swept away by the German invasions of the fifth and following centuries.

Nationalism and Teutonism

That the Reformation strengthened the state was inevitable, for there was no practical alternative to putting the final authority in spiritual matters, after the pope had been ejected, into the hands of the civil government. Congregationalism was tried and failed as tending to anarchy. But how little the Reformation was really responsible for the new despotism and the divine right of kings, is clear from a comparison with the Greek church and the Turkish Empire. In both, the same forces which produced the state churches of Western Europe operated in the same way. Selim I, a bigoted Sunnite, after putting down the Shi'ite heresy, induced the last caliph of the Abbasid dynasty to surrender the sword and mantle of the prophet; thereafter he and his successors were caliphs as well as sultans. In Russia Ivan the Terrible made himself, in 1547, head of the national church.

Capitalism

Protestantism also harmonized with the capitalistic revolution in that its ethics are, far more than those of Catholicism, oriented by a reference to this world. The old monastic ideal of celibacy, solitude, mortification of the flesh, prayer and meditation, melted under the sun of a new prosperity. In its light men began to realize the ethical value of this life, of marriage, of children, of daily labor and of success and prosperity. It was just in this work that Protestantism came to see its chance of serving God and one's neighbor best. The man at the plough, the maid with the broom, said Luther, are doing God better service than does the praying, self-tormenting monk.

Moreover, the accentuation of the virtues of thrift and industry, which made capitalism and Calvinism allies, but reflected the standards natural to the bourgeois class. It was by the might of the merchants and their money that the Reformation triumphed; conversely they benefited both by the spoils of the church and by the abolition of a privileged class. Luther stated that there was no difference between priest and layman; some men were called to preach, others to make shoes, but—and this is his own illustration—the one vocation is no more spiritual than the other. No longer necessary as a mediator and dispenser of sacramental grace, the Protestant clergyman sank inevitably to the same level as his neighbors.

Intellectual aspect

(3) In its relation to the Renaissance and to modern thought the Reformation solved, in its way, two problems, or one problem, that of authority, in two forms. Though anything but consciously rational in their purpose, the innovating leaders did assert, at least for themselves, the right of private judgment. Appealing from indulgence-seller to pope, from pope to council, from council to the Bible and (in Luther's own words) from the Bible to Christ, the Reformers finally came to their own conscience as the supreme court. Trying to deny to others the very rights they had fought to secure for themselves, yet their example operated more powerfully than their arguments, even when these were made of ropes and of thumb-screws. The delicate balance of faith was overthrown and it was put into a condition of unstable equilibrium; the avalanche, started by ever so gentle a push, swept onward until it buried the men who tried to stop it half way. Dogma slowly narrowing down from precedent to precedent had its logical, though unintended, outcome in complete religious autonomy, yes, in infidelity and skepticism.

Individualism

Vulgarization of the Renaissance

Protestantism has been represented now as the ally, now as the enemy of humanism. Consciously it was neither. Rather, it was the vulgarization of the Renaissance; it transformed, adapted, and popularized many of the ideas originated by its rival. It is easy to see now that the future lay rather outside of both churches than in either of them, if we look only for direct descent. Columbus burst the bounds of the world, Copernicus those of the universe; Luther only broke his vows. But the point is that the repudiation of religious vows was the hardest to do at that time, a feat infinitely more impressive to the masses than either of the former. It was just here that the religious movement became a great solvent of conservatism; it made the masses think, passionately if not deeply, on their own beliefs. It broke the cake of custom and made way for greater emancipations than its own. It was the logic of events that, whereas the Renaissance gave freedom of thought to the cultivated few, the Reformation finally resulted in tolerance for the masses. Logically also, even while it feared and hated philosophy in the great thinkers and scientists, it advocated education, up to a certain point, for the masses.

The Reformation a step forward

In summary, if the Reformation is judged with historical imagination, it does not appear to be primarily a reaction. That it should be such is both *a priori* improbable and unsupported by the facts. The Reformation did not give *our* answer to the many problems it was called upon to face; nevertheless it gave the solution demanded and accepted by the time, and therefore historically the valid solution. With all its limitations it was, fundamentally, a step forward and not the return to an earlier standpoint, either to that of primitive Christianity, as the Reformers themselves claimed, or to the dark ages, as has been latterly asserted.

BIBLIOGRAPHY

PRELIMINARY

1. Unpublished Sources.

The amount of important unpublished documents on the Reformation, though still large, is much smaller than that of printed sources, and the value of these manuscripts is less than that of those which have been published. It is no purpose of this bibliography to furnish a guide to archives.

Though the quantity of unpublished material that I have used has been small, it has proved unexpectedly rich. In order to avoid repetition in each following chapter, I will here summarize manuscript material used (most of it for the first time), which is either still unpublished or is in course of publication by myself. See *Luther's Correspondence*, transl. and ed. by Preserved Smith and C. M. Jacobs, 1913 ff; *English Historical Review,* July 1919; *Scottish Historical Review,* Jan. 1919; *Harvard Theological Review,* April 1919; *The N. Y. Nation*, various dates 1919.

From the Bodleian Library, I have secured a copy of an unpublished letter and other fragments of Luther, press mark, Montagu d. 20, fol. 225, and Auct. Z. ii, 2.

From the British Museum I have had diplomatic correspondence of Robert Barnes, Cotton MSS., Vitellius B XXI, foll. 120 ff.; a letter of Albinianus Tretius to Luther, Add. MS. 19, 959, fol. 4b ff; and a portion of John Foxe's *Collection of Letters and Papers,* Harleian MS 419, fol. 125.

From the Pennsylvania Historical Society, Philadelphia, collection of autographs made by Ferdinand J. Dreer, unpublished and hitherto unused letters of Erasmus, James VI of Scotland (2), Leo X, Hedio, Farel to Calvin, Forster, Melanchthon, Charles V, Albrecht of Mansfeld, Henry VIII, Francis I (3), Catherine de' Medici, Grynaeus, Viglius van Zuichem, Alphonso d'Este, Philip Marnix, Camden, Tasso, Machiavelli, Pius IV, Vassari, Borromeo, Alesandro Ottavio de' Medici (afterwards Leo XI), Clement VIII, Sarpi, Emperor Ferdinand, William of Nassau (1559), Maximilian III, Paul Eber

(2), Rudolph II, Henry III, Philip II, Emanuel Philibert, Henry IV, Scaliger, Mary Queen of Scots, Robert Dudley (Leicester), Filippo Strozzi, and others.

From Wellesley College a patent of Charles V., dated Worms, March 6, 1521, granting mining rights to the Count of Belalcazar. Unpublished.

From the American Hispanic Society of New York unpublished letter of Henry IV of France to Du Pont, on his conversion, and letter of Henry VII of England to Ferdinand of Aragon.

2. General Works

Encyclopædia Britannica.[11] 1910–1. (Many valuable articles of a thoroughly scientific character).

The New International Encyclopædia, 1915f. (Equally valuable).

Realencyklopädie für protestantische Theologie und Kirche.[3] 24 vols. Leipzig. 1896–1913. (Indispensable to the student of Church History; The Schaff-Herzog Encyclopedia of Religious Knowledge, 12 vols., 1908 ff, though in part based on this, is far less valuable for the present subject).

Wetzer und Welte: *Kirchenlexikon oder Encyklopädie der katholischen Theologie und ihrer Hülfswissenschaften.* Zweite Auflage von J. Card. Hergenröther und F. Kaulen. Freiburg im Breisgau. 1880–1901. 12 vols. (Valuable).

Die Religion in Geschichte und Gegenwart, hg. von H. Gunkel, O. Scheel, F. M. Schiele. 5 vols. 1909–13.

The Cambridge Modern History, planned by Lord Acton, edited by A. W. Ward, G. W. Prothero, Stanley Leathes. London and New York. 1902 ff. Vol. 1. *The Renaissance.* 1902. Vol. 2. *The Reformation.* 1904. Vol. 3. *The Wars of Religion.* 1905. Vol. 13. *Tables and Index.* 1911. Vol. 14. *Maps.* 1912. (A standard co-operative work, with full bibliographies).

Weltgeschichte, hg.v.J. von Pflugk-Harttung: Das Religiöse Zeitalter, 1500–1650. Berlin. 1907. (A co-operative work, written by masters of their subjects in popular style. Profusely illustrated).

E. Lavisse et A. Rambaud: *Histoire générale du IVe siècle à nos jours.* Tome IV *Renaissance et réforme, les nou-*

veaux mondes 1492–1559. 1894. Tome V. *Les guerres de religion 1559–1648.* 1895.

R. L. Poole: *Historical Atlas of Modern Europe.* 1902.

W. R. Shepherd: *Historical Atlas.* 1911.

Ramsay Muir: *Hammond's New Historical Atlas for Students.* 1914.

A list of general histories of the Reformation will be found in the bibliography to the last chapter.

An excellent introduction to the bibliography of the public documents of all countries will be found in the *Encyclopædia Britannica,* s.v. "Record."

CHAPTER I. THE OLD AND THE NEW

§ 1. *The World*

On economic changes see bibliography to chapter xi; on exploration, chapter ix; on universities, chapter xiii, 3. On printing:

J. Janssen: *A History of the German People from the Close of the Middle Ages,* transl. by M. A. Mitchell and A. M. Christie. 2d English ed. 16 volumes. 1905–10.

A. W. Pollard: *Fine Books.* 1912.

T. L. De Vinne: *The Invention of Printing.* 1878.

Veröffentlichungen der Gutenberg-Gesellschaft. 1901 ff.

H. Meisner und J. Luther: *Die Erfindung der Buchdruckerkunst.* 1900.

Article *"Typography"* in *Encyclopædia Britannica.* (The author defends the now untenable thesis that printing originated in Holland, though the numerous and valuable data given by himself point clearly to Mayence as the cradle of the art).

§§ 2 *and* 3 *The Church, Causes of the Reformation.*

SOURCES.

C. Mirbt: *Quellen zur Geschichte des Papsttums und der römischen Katholizismus.*[3] 1911. (Convenient and scholarly; indispensable to any one who has not a large library at command).

The Missal, compiled from the Missale Romanum. 1913.

The Priest's New Ritual, compiled by P. Griffith. 1902. (The rites of the Roman Church, except the Mass, partly in Latin, partly in English).

The Catechism of the Council of Trent, translated into English by J. Donovan. 1829.

Corpus Juris Canonici, post curas A. L. Richteri instruxit Aemilius Friedberg. 2 vols. 1879–81.

Codex Juris Canonici, Pii X jussu digestus, Benedicti XV auctoritate promulgatus. 1918.

Thomas Aquinas: *Summa Theologiæ.* Many editions; the best, with a commentary by Cardinal Cajetan (1469–1534) in *Opera Omnia, iussu impensaque Leonis XIII PP.* vols. 4–10. 1882 ff.

The Summa theologica of St. Thomas Aquinas, translated by the Fathers of the English Dominican Province. 1911 ff. (In course of publication, as yet, 6 vols).

Von der Hardt: *Magnum Oecumenicum Constantiense Concilium.* 6 vols. 1700.

D. Mansi: *Conciliorum nova et amplissima collectio.* Vols. 27–32. Venice. 1784 ff. (Identical reprint, Paris, 1902).

Most of the best literature of the 14th and 15th centuries, e.g., the works of Chaucer, Langland, Boccaccio and Petrach.

Special works of ecclesiastical writers, humanists, nationalists and heretics quoted below.

V. Hasak: *Der christliche Glaube des deutschen Volkes beim Schlusse des Mittelalters.* 1868. (A collection of works of popular edification prior to Luther).

G. Berbig: *"Die erste kursächsische Visitation im Ortland Franken." Archiv für Reformationsgeschichte,* iii. 336–402; iv. 370–408. 1905–6.

Treatises.

E. Friedberg: *Lehrbuch des katholischen und evangelischen Kirchenrechts.*[5] Leipzig. 1903.

L. Pastor: *History of the Popes from the close of the Middle Ages.* English translation,[2] vols. 1–6 edited by Antrobus, vols. 7–12 edited by R. Kerr. 1899 ff. (Exhaustive, brilliantly written, Catholic, a little one-sided).

Mandel Creighton: *A History of the Papacy 1378–1527.* 6 vols. 1892 ff. (Good, but in large part superseded by Pastor).

F. Gregorovius: *A History of Rome in the Middle Ages,* translated by A. Hamilton vols 7 and 8. 1900. (Brilliant).

Schaff's *History of the Christian Church.* Vol. 5, part 2. The Middle Ages. 1294–1517, by D. S. Schaff. 1910. (A scholarly summary, warmly Protestant).

J. Schnitzer: *Quellen und Forschungen zur Geschichte Savonarolas.* 3 vols. 1902–4.

J. Schnitzer: *Savonarola im Streite mit seinem Orden und seinem Kloster.* 1914.

H. Lucas: *Fra Girolamo Savonarola.*[2] 1906.

H. C. Lea: *An Historical Sketch of Sacerdotal Celibacy.*[3] 2 vols. 1907. (Lea's valuable works evince a marvelously wide reading in the sources, but are slightly marred by an insufficient use of modern scholarship).

H. C. Lea: *A History of Auricular Confession and Indulgences in the Latin Church.* 3 vols. 1896.

Aloys Schulte: *Die Fugger in Rom, 1495–1523.* 2 vols. Leipzig. 1904. (Describes the financial methods of the church. The second volume consists of documents).

E. Rodocanachi: *Rome au temps de Jules II et de Léon X.* 1912.

H. Böhmer: *Luthers Romfahrt.* 1914. (The latter part of this work gives a dark picture of the corruption of Rome at the beginning of the 16th century).

§ 4. *The Mystics*

SOURCES.

W. R. Inge: *Life, Light and Love.* 1904. (Selections from Eckart, Tauler, Suso, Ruysbroeck, etc.).

H. Denifle: *"M. Eckeharts lateinische Schriften und die Grundanschauung seiner Lehre." Archiv für Literatur- und Sprachgeschichte.* ii. 416–652.

Meister Eckeharts Schriften und Predigten aus dem Mittelhochdeutschen übersetzt von H. Buttner. 2 vols. 1912.

H. Seuses Deutsche Schriften übertragen von W. Lehmann. 2 vols. 1914.

J. Taulers Predigten, übertragen von W. Lehmann. 2 vols. 1914.

Thomas à Kempis: *imitatio Christi.* (So many editions and translations of this celebrated work that it is hardly necessary to specify one).

The German Theology, translated by Susannah Winkworth. 1854.

TREATISES.

Kuno Francke: *"Medieval German Mysticism." Harvard Theological Review*, Jan., 1912.

G. Siedel: *Die Mystik Taulers.* 1911.

M. Windstosser: *Étude sur la 'Théologie germanique.'* 1912.

W. Preger: *Geschichte der deutschen Mystik im Mittelalter.* 3 vols. 1874–93.

History and Life of the Rev. John Tauler, with 25 sermons, translated by Susannah Winkworth. 1858.

M. Maeterlinck: *Ruysbroeck and the Mystics,* with selections from Ruysbroeck, translated by J. T. Stoddard. 1894.

J. E. G. de Montmorency: *Thomas à Kempis, his Age and his Book.* 1906.

A. R. Burr: *Religious Confessions and Confessants.* 1914. (The best psychological study of mysticism).

§ 5. *Pre-Reformers*

SOURCES.

J. Wyclif's Select English Works, ed. by T. Arnold. 1869–71. 3 vols.

J. Wyclif's English Works hitherto unprinted, ed. F. Matthew. 1880.

F. Palacky: *Documenta Magistri J. Hus.* 1869.

The Letters of John Huss, translated by H. B. Workman and R. M. Pope. 1904.

Wyclif's Latin Works have been edited in many volumes by the Wyclif Society of London, the last volume being the *Opera minora,* 1913.

John Huss: *The Church,* translated by D. S. Schaff. 1915.

TREATISES.

H. C. Lea: *A History of the Inquisition in the Middle Ages.* 3 vols. 1888.

G. M. Trevelyan: *England in the Age of Wyclif* [2]. 1899.

F. A. Gasquet: *The Eve of the Reformation* [2]. 1905.

F. Palacky: *Geschichte von Böhmen.*[3] 1864 ff. 5 vols.

J. H. Wylie: *The Council of Constance to the Death of John Hus.* 1900.

H. B. Workman: *The Dawn of the Reformation.* The Age of Hus. 1902.

Count F. Lützow: *The Hussite Wars.* 1914.

Count F. Lützow. *The Life and Times of Master John Hus.* 1909.
D. S. Schaff: *The Life of John Hus.* 1915.

§ 6. *Nationalizing the Churches*

Most of the bibliography in this chapter is given below, in the chapters on Germany, England and France.

Freher et Struvius. *Rerum German icarum Scriptores.* (1717.) pp. 676–1704: "Gravamina Germanicae Nationis . . . ad Cæsarem Maximilianum contra Sedem Romanam."
C. G. F. Walch: *Monumenta medii aevi.* (1757.) pp. 101–110. "Gravamina nationis Germanicæ adversus curiam Romanam, tempore Nicolai V Papæ."
B. Gebhardt: *Die Gravamina der deutschen Nation gegen den römischen Hof.* 1895.
Documents illustrative of English Church History, compiled by Henry Gee and W. J. Hardy. 1896.
A. Werminghoff: *Geschichte der Kirchenverfassung Deutschlands im Mittelalter.* Band I.[2] 1913.
A. Störmann: *Die Städtischen Gravamina gegen den Klerus.* 1916.

§ 7. *The Humanists*

SOURCES.

The Utopia of Sir Thomas More. Ralph Robinson's translation, with Roper's Life of More and some of his letters. Edited by G. Sampson and A. Guthkelch. With Latin Text of the Utopia. 1910. (Bohn's Libraries).
Der Briefwechsel des Mutianus Rufus, bearbeitet von C. Krause. 1885.
J. Reuchlins Briefwechsel, hg. von L. Geiger. 1875.
E. Böcking: *Hutteni Opera.* 1859–66. 5 vols.
Epistolæ Obscurorum Virorum: The Latin Text with an English translation, Notes and an Historical Introduction by F. G. Stokes. 1909.
Des. Erasmi Roterodami Opera Omnia, curavit J. Clericus. 1703–6. 10 vols.
Des. Erasmi Roterodami Opus Epistolarum, ed. P. S. Allen. 1906 ff. (A wonderful edition of the letters, in course of publication. As yet 3 vols).
The Colloquies of Des. Erasmus, translated by N. Bailey, ed. by E. Johnson. 1900. 3 vols.

The Praise of Folly. Written by Erasmus 1509 and translated by John Wilson 1668, edited by Mrs. P. S. Allen. 1913.

The Epistles of Erasmus, translated by F. M. Nichols. 1901–18. 3 vols. (To 1519).

The Ship of Fools, translated by Alexander Barclay. 2 vols. 1874. (Sebastian Brandt's *Narrenschiff* in the old translation).

TREATISES.

P. Monnier: *Le Quattrocento.* 2 vols. 1908. (Work of a high order).

L. Geiger: *Renaissance und Humanismus in Italien und Deutschland.* 1882. (In Oncken's Series). 2d ed. 1899.

J. Burckhardt: *Die Cultur der Renaissance in Italien.* 20. Auflage von L. Geiger. Berlin. 1919. (Almost a classic).

P. Villari: *Niccolò Machiavelli and His Times,* translated by Mrs. Villari [2]. 4 vols. 1891.

W. H. Hutten: *Sir Thomas More.* 1900.

J. A. Froude: *The Life and Letters of Erasmus.* London. 1895. (Charmingly written, but marred by gross carelessness).

E. Emerton: *Erasmus.* New York. 1900.

G. V. Jourdan: *The Movement towards Catholic Reform in the early XVI Century.* 1914.

A. Humbert: *Les Origines de la Théologie moderne.* Paris. 1911. (Brilliant).

A. Renaudet: *Préréforme et Humanisme à Paris 1494–1517.* 1916.

CHAPTER II. GERMANY

GENERAL

List of References on the History of the Reformation in Germany, ed. by G. L. Kieffer, W. W. Rockwell and O. H. Pannkoke, 1917.

Dahlmann-Waitz: *Quellenkunde der deutschen Geschichte.*[8] 1912.

G. Wolf: *Quellenkunde der deutschen Reformationsgeschichte.* 2 vols. 1915–16.

A. Morel-Fatio: *Historiographie de Charles-Quint.* Pt. 1. 1913.

B. J. Kidd: *Documents illustrative of the Continental Reformation.* 1911.

T. M. Lindsay: *A History of the Reformation.* Vol. 1, In Germany. 1906.

J. Janssen: *op. cit.*

K. Lamprecht: *Deutsche Geschichte,* vols. 4 and 5. 1894.

T. Brieger: *Die Reformation.* (In Pflugk-Harttung's *Weltgeschichte: Das religiöse Zeitalter 1500–1650.* 1907; also printed separately in enlarged form).

G. Mentz: *Deutsche Geschichte 1493–1648.* 1913. (The best purely political summary).

M. de Foronda y Aguilera: *Estancias y viajes del Emperador Carlos V, desde el dia de su nacimiento hasta el de su muerte.* 1914.

§ 1. *Luther*

Bibliography in Catalogue of the British Museum.

Dr. Martin Luther's Werke. Kritische Gesamtausgabe, von Knaake und Andern. Weimar. 1883 ff. (The standard edition of the Reformer's writings, in course of publication, approaching completion. As yet have appeared more than fifty volumes of the Works, and, separately numbered: Die Deutsche Bibel, 4 vols., and Tischreden, 4 vols.).

Dr. Martin Luther's Briefwechsel, bearbeitet von E. L. Enders (vols. 12 ff. fortgesetzt von G. Kawerau). 1884 ff. (In course of publication; as yet 17 volumes).

Luther's Briefe, herausgegeben von W. L. M. de Wette. 6 vols. 1825–56.

Luther's Primary Works, translated by H. Wace and C. A. Buchheim. 1896.

The Works of Martin Luther, translated and edited by W. A. Lambert, J. J. Schindel, A. T. W. Steinhaeuser, A. L. Steimle and C. M. Jacobs. 1915 ff. (To be complete in ten volumes; as yet 2).

Luther's Correspondence and other Contemporary Letters, translated and edited by Preserved Smith. Vol. I, 1913. Vol. II, in collaboration with C. M. Jacobs, 1918.

Conversations with Luther, Selections from the Table Talk, translated and edited by Preserved Smith and H. P. Gallinger. 1915.

Melanchthonis Opera, ed. Bretschneider und Bindseil. 1834 ff. In Corpus Reformatorum vols. i-xxviii.

J. Köstlin: *Martin Luther,* fünfte Auflage besorgt von G. Kawerau. 2 vols. 1903. (The standard biography. The English translation made from the edition of 1883 in no wise represents the scholarship of the last edition).

A. Hausrath: *Luther's Leben,* neue Auflage von H. von Schubert. 1914. (Excellent).

H. Grisar: *Luther.* English translation by F. M. Lamond. 1913 ff. (Six volumes, representing the German three. A learned, somewhat amorphous work, from the Catholic standpoint, but not unfair).

H. Denifle: *Luther und Lutherthum in der ersten Entwicklung*[2]. 3 vols. 1904 ff. (G. P. Gooch calls "Denifle's eight hundred pages hurled at the memory of the Reformer among the most repulsive books in historical literature"; nevertheless the author is so wonderfully learned that much may be acquired from him).

A. C. McGiffert: *Martin Luther, the Man and his Work.* 1911.

Preserved Smith: *The Life and Letters of Martin Luther*[2]. 1914.

O. Scheel: *Martin Luther, vom Katholizismus zur Reformation.*[2] 2 vols. 1917. (Detailed study of Luther until 1517. Warmly Protestant).

W. W. Rockwell: *Die Doppelehe des Landgrafen Philipp von Hessen.* 1904. (Work of a high order).

§§ 2–5. *The Revolution*

Deutsche Reichstagsakten unter Karl V, herausgegeben von A. Kluckhohn and A. Wrede. 1893 ff. (Four volumes to 1524 have appeared).

Nuntiaturberichte aus Deutschland nebst ergänzenden Aktenstücken, herausgegeben durch das Königliche Preussische Institut in Rom. Erste Abtheilung 1533–59. 1892 ff. (As yet have appeared vols. 1–6, 8–12).

Emil Sehling: *Die Evangelischen Kirchenordungen des XVI Jahrhunderts.* 5 vols. 1902–13.

E. Armstrong: *The Emperor Charles V*[2]. 2 vols. 1910.

Christopher Hare: *A Great Emperor.* 1917. (Popular).

O. Clemen: *Flugschriften aus der Reformationszeit.* 4 vols. 1904–10.

O. Schade: *Satiren und Pasquille aus der Reformationszeit.*[2] 3 vols. 1863.

H. Barge: *Der deutsche Bauernkrieg in zeitgenossischen Quellenzeugnissen.* 2 vols. (No date, published about 1914. A small and cheap selection from the sources turned into modern German).

J. S. Schapiro: *Social Reform and the Reformation.* 1909. (Gives some of the texts and a good treatment of the popular movement).

E. Belfort Bax: *The Peasants' War in Germany.* 1889. (Based chiefly on Janssen, and unscholarly, but worth mentioning considering the paucity of English works). See also articles Carlstadt, Karlstadt, T. Münzer, Sickingen, etc. in the *Encyclopœdia of Religious Knowledge* and other works of reference.

W. Stolze: *Der deutsche Bauernkrieg.* 1908.

P. Wappler: *Die Täuferbewegung in Thüringen 1526–84.* 1913.

B. Bax: *Rise and Fall of the Anabaptists.* 1903.

P. Wappler: *Die Stellung Kursachsens und Landgraf Philipps von Hessen zur Täuferbewegung.* 1910.

F. W. Schirrmacher: *Briefe und Akten zur Geschicte des Religionsgespräches zu Marburg 1529 und des Reichstages zu Augsburg, 1530.* 1876.

H. von Schubert: *Bekenntnisbildung und Religionspolitik 1529–30.* 1910.

W. Gussmann: *Quellen und Forschungen zur Geschichte des Augsburgischen Glaubensbekenntnises.* Die Ratschläge der evangelischen Reichsstände zum Reichstag zu Augsburg. 3 vols. 1911.

Politische Korrespondenz des Herzog und Kurfürst Moritz von Sachsen, hg. v. E. Brandenburg. 2 vols. (as yet), 1900, 1904.

S. Cardauns: *Zur Geschichte der Kirchlichen Unions—und Reformbestrebungen 1538–42.* 1910.

P. Heidrich: *Karl V und die deutschen Protestanten am Vorabend des Schmalkaldischen Krieges.* 2 vols. 1911–12.

G. Mentz: *Johann Friedrich,* vol. 3, 1908.

See also the works cited above by Armstrong, Pflugk-Harttung, Janssen, Pastor, *The Cambridge Modern History,* and documents in Kidd.

§ 6. *Scandinavia, Poland, and Hungary*

Documents in Kidd, and treatment in *The Cambridge Modern History.*

Acta Pontificum Danica, Band VI 1513–36. Udgivet af A. Krarup og J. Lindbaek. 1915.

C. F. Allen: *Histoire de Danemark,* traduite par E. Beauvois. 2 vols. 1878.

P. B. Watson: *The Swedish Revolution under Gustavus Vasa.* 1889.

Specimen diplomatarii norvagici . . . ab vetustioribus inde temporibus usque ad finem seculi XVI. Ved Gr. Fougner Lundh. 1828.

J. Lund: *Histoire de Norvège . . .* traduite par G. Moch. 1899.

Norges historie, fremstillet for det norske folk af A. Bugge, E. Hertzberg, O. A. Johnsen, Yngvar Nielsen, J. E. Sars, A. Taranger. 1912.

C. Zivier: *Neuere Geschichte Polens.* Band I. 1506–72. 1915.

T. Wotschke: *Geschichte der Reformation in Polen.* 1911.

A. Berga. *Pierre Skarga 1536–1612* . Étude sur la Pologne du XVIe siècle et le Protestantisme polonais. 1916.

F. E. Whitton: *A History of Poland.* 1917. (Popular).

CHAPTER III.

SWITZERLAND

§ 1. *Zwingli*

Ulrichi Zwinglii opera ed. Schuler und Schulthess, 8 vols. 1828–42.

Ulrich Zwinglis Werke, hg. von Egli, Finsler und Köhler, 1904 ff. (Corpus Reformatorum, vols. 88 ff). As yet, vols. i, ii, iii, vii. viii.

Ulrich Zwingli's Selected Works, translated and edited by S. M. Jackson. 1901.

The Latin Works and Correspondence of Huldreich Zwingli, ed. S. M. Jackson. vol. i, 1912.

Vadianische Briefsammlung, hg. von E. Arbenz und H. Wartmann, 1890–1913. 7 vols. and 6 supplements.

Der Briefwechsel der Brüder Ambrosius und Thomas Blaurer, hg. von T. Schiess, 3 vols. 1908–12.

Johannes Kesslers Sabbata, hg. von E. Egli and R. Schoch.

1902. (Reliable source for the Swiss Reformation 1519–39).
Documents in Kidd.
S. M. Jackson: *Huldreich Zwingli.* 1900.
W. Köhler: *"Zwingli"* in Pflugk-Harttung's *Im Morgenrot der Reformation,* 1912.
E. Egli: *Schweizerische Reformationsgeschichte.* Band I, 1519–25. 1910.
F. Humbel: *Ulrich Zwingli und seine Reformation im Spiegel der gleichzeitigen Schweizerischen volkstümlichen Literatur.* 1913.
Cambridge Modern History, Lindsay, etc.
H. Barth: *Bibliographie der Schweizer Geschichte.* 3 vols. 1914 f.
Bibliography in G. Wolf, *Quellenkunde,* vol. 2.
On Jetzer see *Religion in Geschichte und Gegenwart,* s.v. "Jetzer Prozess," and R. Reuss: "Le Procès des Dominicains de Berne," *Revue de l'Histoire des Religions,* 1905, 237 ff.
P. Burckhardt: *H. Zwingli.* 1918.
W. Köhler: *Ulrich Zwingli.*[2] 1917.
Ulrich Zwingli: Zum Gedächtnis der Zürcher Reformation, 1519–1919, ed. H. Escher, 1919. (Sumptuous and valuable).
Amtliche Sammlung der älteren eidgenössischen Abschiede, Abt. 3 und 4. 1861 ff.
J. Strickler: *Aktensammlung zur Schweizer Reformationsgeschichte.* 1878.
J. Dierauer: *Geschichte der schweizerischen Eidgenossenschaft.* Band III. 1907.
Hadorn: *Kirchengeschichte der reform. Schweiz.* 1907.
G. Tobler: *Aktensammlung zur Geschichte der Berner Reformation.* 1918.
E. Egli: *Analecta Reformatoria.* 2 vols. 1899–1901.

§ 2. *Calvin*

Bibliography in Wolf: *Quellenkunde,* ii.
Correspondance des Réformateurs dans les Pays de langue française[2], pub. par A. L. Herminjard. 9 vols. 1878 ff.
Calvini Opera omnia, ed. G. Baum, E. Cunitz, E. Reuss, 59 vols. 1866 ff. (*Corpus Reformatorum* vols. 29–87).
John Calvin: *The Institutes of the Christian Religion,* trans-

lated by J. Allen. Ed. by B. B. Warfield. 2 vols. 1909.

The Letters of John Calvin, compiled by J. Bonnet, translated from the original Latin and French. 4 vols. 1858.

J. Calvin: *Institution de la religion chrestienne,* réimprimée, sous la direction d' A. Lefranc par H. Chatelain et J. Pannir. 1911.

The Life of John Calvin by Theodore Beza, translated by H. Beveridge. 1909.

A. Lang: *Johann Calvin.* 1909.

W. Walker: *J. Calvin.* 1906. (Best biography).

H. Y. Reyburn: *John Calvin.* 1914.

J. Doumergue: *Jean Calvin.* As yet 5 vols. 1899–1917.

E. Knodt: *Die Bedeutung Calvins und Calvinismus für die protestantische Welt.* 1913. (Extensive bibliography and review of recent works).

E. Troeltsch: "Calvin," *Hibbert Journal,* viii, 102 ff.

T. C. Hall: "Was Calvin a Reformer or a Reactionary?" *Hibbert Journal,* vi, 171 ff.

Étienne Giran: *Sébastien Castellion.* 1913. (Severe judgment of Calvin from the liberal Protestant standpoint).

Allan Menzies: *The Theology of Calvin.* 1915.

H. D. Foster: *Calvin's programme for a Puritan State in Geneva 1536–41.* 1908.

F. Brunetière: "L'oeuvre littéraire de Calvin." *Revue des Deux Mondes,* 4 série, clxi, pp. 898 ff. (1900).

E. Lobstein: *Kalvin und Montaigne.* 1909.

CHAPTER IV

FRANCE

Sources.

A. Molinier, H. Hauser, E. Bourgeois (et autres): *Les Sources de l'histoire de France depuis les origines jusqu'en 1815.* Deuxième Partie. Le XVIe siècle, 1494–1610, par. H. Hauser. 4 vols. 1906–1915. (Valuable, critical bibliography of sources).

Recueil générale des anciennes lois francaises, par Isambert, Decrusy, Armet. Tomes 12–15 (1514–1610). 1826 ff.

Ordonnances des rois de France. Règne de François I. 10 vols. 1902–8.

Michel de L'Hôpital: *Œuvres complètes,* ed. Dufey. 4 vols. 1824–5.

Journal d'un bourgeois de Paris sous le règne de François Ier (1515–36), ed. par L. Lalanne. 1854.

Commentaires de Blaise de Monluc, ed. P. Courtreault. 2 vols. 1911 ff.

Mémoires-journaux du duc de Guise 1547–61, ed. Michaud et Poujoulat. 1839.

Œuvres complètes de Pierre de Bourdeille, seigneur de Brantôme, ed. par L. Lalanne, 11 vols. 1864–82.

Histoire Ecclésiastique des Églises reformées au Royaume de France, ed. G. Baum et E. Cunitz, 3 vols. 1883–9. (This history first appeared anonymously in 1580 in 3 vols. The place of publication is given as Antwerp, but probably it was really Geneva. The author has been thought by many to be Theodore Beza.

Memoires of the Duke of Sully. English translation in Bohn's Library. 3 vols. No date.

Crespin: *Histoire des martyrs, persecutés et mis à mort pour la verité de l' Évangile.* Ed. of 1619.

Mémoires de Martin et de Guillaume du Bellay, ed. par V. L. Bourilly et F. Vindry. 4 vols. 1908–1920.

Correspondance des Réformateurs dans les pays de langue française, pub. par A. L. Herminjard. 9 vols. 1878 ff.

J. Fraikin: *Nonciatures de la France.* Vol. i, Clement VII, 1906.

Lettres de Catherine de Médicis, publiées par H. de la Ferrière et B. de Puchesse. 10 vols. Paris. 1880–1909.

Catalogue générale de la Bibliothèque Nationale. Actes Royaux. Vol. i, 1910.

Literature.

A. M. Whitehead: *Gaspard de Coligny.* 1904.

Louis Batiffol: *The Century of the Renaissance,* translated from the French by E. F. Buckley, with an introduction by J. E. C. Bodley. 1916.

J. W. Thompson: *The Wars of Religion in France 1559–76.* 1909.

E. Lavisse: *Histoire de France.* Tome Cinquième. I. Les guerres d' Italie. La France sous Charles VIII, Louis XII et François I, par H. Lemonnier. 1903. II. La lutte contre la maison d'Autriche. La France sous Henri II, par H. Lemonnier. 1904. Tome Sixième. I. La Réforme et la Ligue. L'Édit de Nantes (1559–98), par J. H. Mariéjol. 1904. (Standard work).

H. M. Baird: *The Rise of the Huguenots in France,* 2 vols. 1879.

H. M. Baird: *The Huguenots and Henry of Navarre.* 2 vols. 1886.

H. N. Williams: *Henri II.* 1910.

E. Marcks: *Gaspard von Coligny:* sein Leben und das Frankreich seiner Zeit. 1892. (Excellent, only Volume I, taking Coligny to 1560, has appeared).

P. Imbart de la Tour: *Les Origines de la Réforme.* I. La France Moderne. 1905. II. L'Eglise Catholique et la Crise de la Renaissance. 1909. III. I'Évangélisme (1521–38). 1914. (Excellent work, social and cultural rather than political).

E. Sichel: *Catherine de' Medici and the French Reformation.* 1905.

E. Sichel: *The Later Years of Catherine de' Medici.* 1908.

C. E. du Boulay: *Historia Universitatis Parisiensis.* Tomus VI. 1673.

J. Michelet: *Histoire de France.* Vols. 8–10. First edition 1855 ff. (A beautiful book; though naturally superseded in part, it may still be read with profit).

W. Heubi: *François I et le mouvement intellectuel en France.* 1914.

A. Autin: *L' Échec de la Réforme en France au XVI, siècle,* Contribution à l' Histoire du Sentiment Religieux. 1918.

L. Romier: *Les Origines Politiques des Guerres de Religion.* 2 vols. 1911–13.

L. Romier: "Les Protestants français à la veille des guerres civiles," *Revue Historique,* vol. 124, 1917, pp. 1ff, 225 ff.

E. Armstrong: *The French Wars of Religion.* 1892.

C. G. Kelley: *French Protestantism 1559–62.* Johns Hopkins University Studies, vol. xxxvi, no. 4. 1919.

N. Weiss: *La Chambre Ardente.* 1889.

CHAPTER V. THE NETHERLANDS

H. Pirenne: *Bibliographie de l'Histoire de Belgique.* Catalogue des sources et des ouvrages principaux relatifs à l'histoire de tous les Pays-Bas jusq'en 1598.[2] 1902.

SOURCES:

Kervyn de Lettenhove: *Relations politiques des Pays-Bas et* *d'Angleterre.* 10 vols. 1882–91. (Covers 1556–76).

Resolutien der Staaten-Generaal 1576–1609. Door N. Japikse. As yet 4 vols. (1576–84.) 1915–19.

Corpus documentorum Inquisitionis . . . Neerlandicae . . . Uitgegeven door P. Fredericq. Vols. 4–6, 1900 ff.

Bibliotheca Reformatoria Neerlandica . . . Uitgegeven door S. Cramer en F. Pijper. 1903–14. 10 vols.

Collectanea van Gerardus Geldenhauer Noviomagus . . . Uitgegeven . . . door J. Prinsen. 1901.

La Chasse aux Luthériens des Pays-Bas. Souvenirs de Francisco de Enzinas. Paris. 1910. (Memoirs of a Spanish Protestant in the Netherlands. This edition is beautifully illustrated).

Correspondance de Guillaume le Taciturne, publiée . . . par M. Gachard. 1847–57. 6 vols.

Correspondance de Philippe II sur les affaires des Pays-Bas, publiée . . . par M. Gachard. 5 vols. 1848–79.

H. Grotius: *The Annals and History of the Low Country-Wars,* Rendered into English by T. M[anley]. 1665.

Calendar of State Papers, Foreign, of Elizabeth, ed. J. Stevenson and others. London 1863–1916. (19 volumes to date; much material on the Netherlands).

LITERATURE.

H. Pirenne: *Histoire de Belgique.* Vols 3 and 4. 1907–11. (Standard work. A German translation by F. Arnheim was published of the third volume in 1907, before the French edition, and of the 4th volume, revised and slightly improved, in 1915).

P. J. Blok: *History of the People of the Netherlands.* Translated by Ruth Putnam. Part 2, 1907, Part 3, 1900. (Also a standard work).

E. Grossart: *Charles V et Philippe II.* 1910.

Felix Rachfahl: *Wilhelm von Oranien und der niederländische Aufstand.* Vols. 1 and 2. 1906–8.

Ruth Putnam: *William the Silent* (Heroes of the Nations). 1911.

P. Kalkoff: *Anfänge der Gegenreformation in den Niederlanden.* 1903. (Monograph of value).

Geschiedenis van de Hervorming en de Hervormde Kerk der Nederlanden, door J. Reitsma. Derde, bijgewerkte en vermeerderde Druk beworkt door L. A. von Langeraad . . . en bezorgd door F. Reitsma. 1916.

J. L. Motley: *The Rise of the Dutch Republic.* 1855. (A classic, naturally in part superseded by later research).

J. F. Motley: *The Life and Death of John of Oldenbarneveld.* 1873.

J. C. Squire: *William the Silent.* (1918).

CHAPTER VI. ENGLAND 1509–88

Bibliographies in *Cambridge Modern History,* and in the *Political History of England,* by Pollard and Fisher, for which see below.

SOURCES:

Letters and papers, foreign and domestic, of the reign of Henry VIII, arranged by J. S. Brewer, J. Gairdner and R. H. Brodie. 20 vols. (Monumental).

Similar series of "Calendars of State Papers" have been published for English papers preserved at Rome (1 vol. 1916), Spain, (15 vols.), Venice (22 vols), Ireland (10 vols.), Domestic of Edward VI, Mary, Elizabeth and James (12 vols.), Foreign Edward VI (1 vol.), Mary (1 vol.), Elizabeth (19 vols. to 1585), Milan (1 vol. 1912).

The English Garner: Tudor Tracts 1532–88, ed. E. Arber. 8 vols. 1877–96.

Documents illustrative of English Church History, compiled by H. Gee and W. J. Hardy. 1896.

Select Statutes and other Constitutional Documents 1558–1625, ed. G. W. Prothero.[2] 1898.

The Statutes of the Realm, printed by command of George III. 1819 ff.

Select Cases before the King's Council in Star Chamber, ed. I. S. Leadam. Vol. 2, 1509–44. Selden Society. 1911.

Original Letters, ed. by Sir H. Ellis. 1st series, 3 vols. 1824; 2d series 4 vols. 1827; 3 series 4 vols. 1846.

LITERATURE:

H. A. L. Fisher: *Political History of England 1485–1547.* New edition 1913. (Political History of England edited by W. Hunt and R. L. Poole, vol. 5. Standard work).

A. F. Pollard: *Political History of England 1547–1603.*

1910. (Political History of England ed. by Hunt and Poole, vol. 6. Standard work).

A. D. Innes: *England under the Tudors.* 1905.

H. Gee: *The Reformation Period.* 1909. (Handbooks of English Church History).

J. Gairdner: *Lollardy and the Reformation.* 4 vols. 1908 ff. (Written by an immensely learned man with a very strong high-church Anglican bias).

Preserved Smith: "Luther and Henry VIII," *English Historical Review,* xxv, 656 ff, 1910.

Preserved Smith: "German Opinion of the Divorce of Henry VIII," *English Historical Review,* xxvii, 671 ff, 1912.

Preserved Smith: "Hans Luft of Marburg," *Nation,* May 16, 1912.

Preserved Smith: "News for Bibliophiles," *Nation,* May 29, 1913. (On early English translations of Luther).

Preserved Smith: "Martin Luther and England," *Nation,* Dec. 17, 1914.

Preserved Smith: "Complete List of Works of Luther in English," *Lutheran Quarterly,* October, 1918.

E. R. Adair: "The Statute of Proclamations," *English Historical Review,* xxxii, 34 ff. 1917.

Lord Ernest Hamilton: *Elizabethan Ulster.* (1919).

Peter Guilday: *The English Catholic Refugees on the Continent 1558–1795.* Vol. 1. 1914. (Brilliant study).

A. F. Pollard: *England under Protector Somerset.* 1900.

A. F. Pollard: *Henry VIII.* 1902.

A. F. Pollard: *Thomas Cranmer.* 1906.

J. H. Pollen: *The English Catholics in the Reign of Elizabeth.* 1920.

F. A. Gasquet: *The Eve of the Reformation.* New ed. 1900.

R. B. Merriman: *The Life and Letters of Thomas Cromwell.* 2 vols. 1902. (Valuable).

A. O. Meyer: *England und die katholische Kirche unter Elizabeth.* 1911. (Thorough and brilliant). Said to be translated into English, 1916.

L. Trésal: *Les origines du schisme anglican 1509–71.* 1908.

A. J. Klein: *Intolerance in the Reign of Elizabeth.* 1917.

J. A. Froude: *History of England from the Fall of Wolsey to the Armada.* 12 vols. 1854–70. (Still the best picture of the time. Strongly royalist and Protestant, some errors in detail, brilliantly written).

Dictionary of National Biography, ed. by Leslie Stephens and Sidney Lee. 63 vols. 1887–1900.

Carlos B. Lumsden: *The Dawn of Modern England 1509–25.* 1910.

Richard Bagwell: *Ireland under the Tudors.* 3 vols. 1885.

H. Holloway: *The Reformation in Ireland.* 1919.

Mrs. J. R. Green: *The Making of Ireland and its Undoing 1200–1600.* First edition 1908; revised and corrected 1909. (Nationalist; interesting).

H. N. Birt: *The Elizabethan Religious Settlement.* 1907.

W. Walch: *England's Fight with the Papacy.* 1912.

R. G. Usher: *The Rise and Fall of High Commission.* 1913.

Die Wittenberger Artikel von 1536, hg. von G. Mentz. 1905.

R. G. Usher: *The Presbyterian Movement 1582–9.* 1905.

CHAPTER VII. SCOTLAND

Sources.

Acts of the Parliament of Scotland. 12 vols. 1844 ff.

B. J. Kidd: *Documents of the Continental Reformation,* 1911, pp. 686–715.

Calendar of State Papers relating to Scotland 1509–1603. 2 vols. ed. M. J. Thorpe. 1858.

State Papers relating to Scotland and Mary Queen of Scots 1542–81, ed. J. Bain and W. K. Boyd. 5 vols. 1898 ff.

Hamilton Papers, 1532–90, ed. J. Bain.

Much in the English calendars for which see bibliography to chap. VI.

John Knox's Works, ed. Laing, 1846–64.

R. Lindsay of Pitscottie: *Historie and cronicles of Scotland,* ed. A. J. G. Mackay. 1899–1911. 3 vols.

Satirical Poems of the Time of the Reformation, ed. J. Cranstoun. 2 vols. 1891.

John Knox: *The History of the Reformation of Religion in Scotland,* ed. by Cuthbert Lennox. 1905.

Literature:

P. Hume Brown: *History of Scotland.* 3 vols. 1899–1909.

W. L. Mathieson: *Politics and Religion; a study of Scottish history from Reformation to Revolution.* 2 vols. 1902.

D. H. Fleming: *The Reformation in Scotland.* 1910. (Strongly Protestant).

G. Christie: *The Influence of Letters on the Scottish Reformation.* 1908.
A. Lang: *John Knox and the Reformation.* 1905.
J. Crook: *John Knox the Reformer.* 1907.
A. B. Hart, "John Knox," in *American Historical Review,* xiii, 259–80. (Brilliant character study).
R. S. Rait: "John Knox," in *Quarterly Review,* vol. 205, 1906.
A. Lang: *The Mystery of Mary Stuart.* 1902.
Lady Blennerhassett: *Maria Stuart, Königin von Schottland.* 1907.
A. Lang: *A History of Scotland.* 4 vols. 1900–7.
P. Hume Brown: *John Knox.* 2 vols. 1895.
H. Cowan: *John Knox.* 1905.
A. R. Macewen: *A History of the Church in Scotland.* Vol. I (397–1546), 1913; Vol. II (1546–60), 1918. (Good).
A. Lang: "Casket Letters," *Encyclopædia Britannica,* 1910.
P. Hume Brown: *Surveys of Scottish History.* 1919. (Philosophical).

CHAPTER VIII. THE COUNTER REFORMATION

§§ 1 and 2. *The Papacy and Italy 1521–1590.*

SOURCES:

C. Mirbt: *op. cit.*
Consilium delectorum cardinalium et aliorum praelatorum de emendanda ecclesia 1537. In Mansi: *Sacrorum Conciliorum et Decretorum collectio nova,* 1751, Supplement 5, pp. 539–47. The same in German with Luther's notes in *Luther's Werke,* Weimar, vol. 50.

LITERATURE:

L. von Pastor: *A History of the Popes from the Close of the Middle Ages.* English translation ed. by R. F. Kerr. Vols. 9–12. 1910 ff. (These volumes cover the period 1522–1549. Standard work dense with new knowledge).
L. von Pastor: *Geschichte der Päpste seit dem Ausgang des Mittelalters.* Band VI. 1913; VII. 1920. (Of these volumes of the German, covering the years 1550–65, there is as yet no English translation).
P. Herre: *Papsttum und Papstwahl im Zeitalter Philipps, II.* 1907.

J. McCabe: *Crises in the History of the Papacy.* 1916. (Popular).

Mandel Creighton: *op. cit.*

L. von Ranke: *History of the popes, their church and state, in the sixteenth and seventeenth centuries,* translated from the German by Sarah Austin. Vol. 1, 1841. (Translation of Ranke's *Die römischen Päpste,* of which the first edition appeared 1834–6. A classic).

H. M. Vaughan: *The Medici Popes.* 1908. (Popular, sympathetic).

G. Droysen: *Geschichte der Gegenreformation.* 1893. (Oncken's Series).

E. Rodocanachi: "La Réformation en Italie," *Revue des Deux Mondes,* March, 1915.

Lord Acton: *Lectures on Modern History,* 1906, pp. 108 ff.

J. A. Symonds: *The Catholic Reaction.* 2 vols. 1887.

G. Monod: "La Réforme Catholique," *Revue Historique,* vol. cxxi (1916).

B. Wiffen: *Life and Writings of Juan de Valdes.* 1865.

C. Hare: *Men and Women of the Italian Reformation.* (1913).

Kirche und Reformation. Unter mitwirkung von L. v. Pastor, W. Schnyder, L. Schneller usw. hg. von J. Scheuber. 1917.

"Counter-Reformation" in the *Catholic Encyclopædia.*

G. Benrath: *Geschichte der Reformation in Venedig.* 1886.

J. Burckhardt: *op. cit.*

§ 3. *The Council of Trent*

SOURCES:

Concilium Tridentinum. Diariorum, actorum, epistularum, tractatuum nova collectio. Edidit Societas Goerresiana. 1901 ff. In course of publication; as yet have appeared vols. 1–5, 8, 10.

J. Šusta: *Die römische Kurie und das Konzil von Trient unter Pius IV.* Aktenstücke zur Geschichte des Konzils von Trient. 4 vols. 1904–1914.

Le Plat: *Monumenta ad historiam Concilii Tridentini spectantia.* 7 vols. 1781–7.

The Canons and Decrees of the Sacred and Ecumenical Council of Trent, translated by J. Waterworth. 1848. Reprint, Chicago, 1917.

G. Drei: "Per la Storia del Concilio de Trento. Lettere inedite del Segretario Camille Olivo 1562." *Archivio Storico Italiano* 1916.

P. Schaff: *The Creeds of Christendom.* Vol. 2, 1877. (Latin text and English translation of canons and decrees).

The Cathechism of the Council of Trent, translated into English by J. Donovan. 1829.

LITERATURE:

J. A. Froude: *Lectures on the Council of Trent.* 1899.

P. Sarpi: *The historie of the Councel of Trent.* 1620. (Translation from the Italian, which first appeared 1619).

A. Harnack: *Lehrbuch der Dogmengeschichte,*[4] 1910, vol. iii, pp. 692 ff. English translation, vol. vii, pp. 35–117.

Ranke's remark that there was no good history of the Council of Trent holds good today. The best, as far as it goes, is in Pastor.

§ 4. *The Jesuits*

SOURCES:

Bibliothèque de la Compagnie de Jésus. I ère partie: Bibliographie par les pères De Backer. 2ème partie par A. Carayan. Nouvelle ed. par C. Sommervogel. 10 vols. 1890–1909. Corrections et Additions par E. M. Rivière. 1911.

Monumenta historica Societatis Jesu, edita a Patribus ejusdem Societatis. Madrid, 1894–1913. 46 volumes.

Cartas de San Ignacio de Loyola, 6 vols. 1874–89.

Acta Sanctorum, July 7. 1731.

The Autobiography of St. Ignatius, English translation ed. by J. F. X. O'Connor. 1900.

Letters and Instructions of St. Ignatius Loyola, translated by D. F. O'Leary and ed. by A. Goodier. 1914.

The Spiritual Exercises of St. Ignatius Loyola. Spanish and English, by J. Rickaby, S. J. 1915.

Beati Petri Canisii, S. J., Epistulae et Acta, ed. O. Braunsberger. 6 vols. as yet. 1896–1913.

LITERATURE.

H. Boehmer: *Les Jésuites.* Ouvrage traduit de l'allemand avec une Introduction et des Notes par G. Monod. 1910. (Standard work though very concise).

E. Gothein: *Ignatius von Loyola und die Gegenreformation.* 1895.

A. McCabe: *A Candid History of the Jesuits.* 1913. (Hostile but not unveracious).

B. Duhr: *Geschichte der Jesuiten in den Ländern deutscher Zunge im 16ten Jahrhundert.* Band I. 1907.

H. Fouqueray: *Histoire de la Compagnie de Jésus en France.* 2 vols. 1910–13.

E. L. Taunton: *The Jesuits in England.* 1901.

Francis Thompson: *Saint Ignatius Loyola.* 1913. (I mention this book by "a seventeenth century poet born into the nineteenth century" on account of the author's fame).

S. Brou: *St. François Xavier.* 2 vols. Paris, 1912.

J. M. Cros: *St. François de Xavier,* 2 vols. Toulouse, 1900.

On Xavier see also Mirbt, *op cit.,* no. 350, A. D. White: Warfare of Science and Theology, 1896, ii, 5–22, and Pastor.

Life of St. Francis Xavier by Edith A. Stewart, with translations from his letters by D. Macdonald. 1917. (Popular and sympathetic).

W. G. Jayne: *Vasco da Gama and his successors* (1910), On Xavier, pp. 188 ff.

§ 5. *The Inquisition and the Index*

SOURCES:

P. Fredericq: *Corpus Documentorum Inquisitionis Neerlandicæ,* vols. 4, 5., 1900 ff.

L. von Pastor: *Allegemeine Dekrete der römischen Inquisition 1555–97.* 1913.

Mandament der Keyserlijcken Maiesteit, vuytghegeven int Iaer xlvi. Louvain. 1546. One hundred facsimile copies printed for A. M. Huntington at the De Vinne Press, New York, 1896.

Catalogi Librorum reprobatorum & prælegendorum ex iudicio Academiæ Louaniensis, Pinciae. MDLI. Mandato dominorum de consilio sanctae generalis Inquisitionis. One hundred facsimile copies printed for A. M. Huntington at the De Vinne Press, New York, 1895.

Catalogus librorum qui prohibentur mandato Illustrissimi & Rev. D. D. Ferdinand de Valdes, Hispalen. Archiepiscopi, Inquisitoris Generalis Hispaniæ, 1559. One hundred facsimile copies printed at De Vinne Press, 1895.

LITERATURE.

H. C. Lea: *A History of the Inquisition in Spain.* 4 vols. 1906–7. Characterized by wide reading and the use of many manuscripts which Lea had copied from all European archives. A really wonderful work. The manuscripts on which it is based are still in his library in Philadelphia. I have been kindly allowed by his son and daughter to look over those on Spanish Protestantism.

H. C. Lea: *The Inquisition in the Spanish Dependencies.* 1908.

P. Fredericq: "Les récents historiens catholiques de l'Inquisition en France," *Revue Historique,* cix, 1912), pp. 307 ff. (A scathing criticism of the apologists of the Inquisition who have written against Lea).

E. N. Adler: *Auto de Fé and the Jew.* 1908.

E. Schäfer: *Beiträge zur Geschichte des spanischen Protestantismus und der Inquisition.* 3 vols. 1902.

G. Bushbell: *Reformation und Inquisition in Italien um die Mitte des XVI Jahrhunderts.* 1910.

F. H. Reusch: *Der Index der verbotenen Bücher.* 2 vols. 1883. (Standard).

J. Hilgers: *Der Index der verbotenen Bücher.* 1904. (Apologetic).

H. C. Lea: *Chapters from the Religious History of Spain connected with the Inquisition.* 1890. (Chiefly on the Index).

Articles: "Inquisition," "Holy Office," &c. in the *Encylopædia of Religion and Ethics, Protestantische Realencyclopädie, Catholic Encyclopedia,* &c.

G. H. Putnam: *The Censorship of the Church of Rome.* 2 vols. 1906.

CHAPTER IX.

THE IBERIAN PENINSULA AND THE EXPANSION OF EUROPE

§ 1. *Spain*

SOURCES:

Colección de documentos ineditos para la historia de España. 112 vols. 1842 ff.

Nueva Colección de documentos ineditos &c. 6 vols. 1892–6.

Calendar of Letters, Despatches and State Papers, Spanish, &c., 15 vols. covering 1509–1603, except 1555–8. 1862 to date.

A. Morel-Fatio: *Historiographie de Charles Quint.* 1913. (Contains a new French version of the Commentaries of Charles V).

F. L. de Gomara: *Annals of the Emperor Charles V,* ed. by R. B. Merriman. 1912.

LITERATURE.

Rafael Altamira y Crevea: *Historia de España,* Tomo III,[3] 1913. (The best general history, very largely social, written in easy, popular style).

C. E. Chapman: *The History of Spain.* 1918. (Based on Altamira).

R. B. Merriman: *The Rise of the Spanish Empire.* 2 vols., to 1516. 1918. (Doubtless the future volumes of the excellent work will be even more valuable for our present purpose).

K. Häbler: *Geschichte Spaniens unter den Habsburgern,* Band 1, 1907. (Standard work for the period of Charles V).

Martin A. S. Hume: *Spain, its Greatness and Decay 1479–1788.* 1898. (Popular).

M. A. S. Hume: *Philip II of Spain.* 1897.

E. Gossart: *Charles V et Philip II.* 1910.

E. A. Armstrong: *Charles V.* Second ed. 1910. 2 vols.

W. H. Prescott: *History of the Reign of Philip II, King of Spain.* 1855–74. (Unfinished, a classic).

H. C. Lea: *The Moriscos in Spain: their Conversion and Expulsion.* 1901.

Bratli: *Philippe II, roi d'Espagne,* 1912. (An unhappy attempt to whitewash Philip; uses some new material).

M. Philippson: *Westeuropa im Zeitalter von Philip II, Elizabeth und Heinrich IV.* 1882.

§ 2. *The Expansion of Europe*

W. H. Prescott: *History of the Conquest of Mexico.* 1843. (A classic).

W. H. Prescott: *History of the Conquest of Peru.* 1847.

H. Vander Linden: "Alexander VI and the Bulls of Demarcation," *American Historical Review,* xxii, 1916, pp. 1 ff.

I. A. Wright: *Early History of Cuba, 1492–1586.* 1916.
C. de Lannoy et H. Van der Linden: *L'Expansion coloniale des Peuples Européens.* Vol. 1. Portugal et Espagne. 1907.
E. G. Bourne: *Spain in America.* 1904. (Excellent).
S. Ruge: *Geschichte des Zeitalters der Entdeckungen.* 1881. (Oncken: Allgemeine Geschichte).
P. Leroy-Beaulieu: *De la Colonisation chez les peuples modernes.* 1st ed. 1874. 6th ed. 1908. 2 vols.
J. Winsor: *Narrative and Critical History of America,* vols. 1, 2, 1889, 1886.
H. Morse Stephens: *The Story of Portugal.* 1891.
G. Young: *Portugal Old and Young.* 1917.
The Commentaries of the great Afonso Dalboquerque, ed. by W. de G. Birch. 4 vols. 1875–84.
K. G. Jayne: *Vasco da Gama and his Successors.* (1910).
K. Waliszewski: *Ivan le Terrible.* 1904.
The Principal Navigations, Voyages, Traffiques and Discoveries of the English Nation, by R. Hakluyt. 12 vols. 1903.
Purchas His Pilgrimes, by S. Purchas. 20 vols. 1905.
F. G. Davenport: *European Treaties bearing on the History of the United States and its Dependencies.* 1917.
W. C. Abbott: *The Expansion of Europe.* 2 vols. 1918.

CHAPTER X

SOCIAL CONDITIONS

As the sources for this chapter would include all the extant literature and documents of the period, it is impossible to do more than mention a few of those particularly referred to. Moreover, as most political histories now have chapters on social and economic conditions, a great deal on the subject will be found in the previous bibliographies.

General

SOURCES:

Wm. Harrison's *Description of England* (1577, revised and enlarged 1586) ed. F. J. Furnivall. 1877 ff. 7 parts.
Social Tracts, ed. A. Lang from Arber's *English Garner.* 1904.

LITERATURE.

Handwörterbuch der Staatswissenschaften,[3] ed. J. Conrad, W. A. Lexis, E. Loening. 8 vols. 1909–11. (Standard).

Wörterbuch der Volkswirtschaft,[3] hg. von L. Elster. 2 vols. 1911.

Social England, ed. by H. D. Traill and J. S. Mann. Vol. 3. Henry VIII to Elizabeth. 1902. (Standard work, originally published 1894).

S. B. Fay: *The Hohenzollern Household.* 1916.

A Catalogue of French Economic Documents from the 16th, 17th and 18th Centuries, published by the John Crerar Library, Chicago, 1918.

H. van Houtte: *Documents pour servir à l' histoire des prix de 1387 à 1794.* 1902.

Cavaignac: "La Population de l'Espagne vers 1500." *Séances et Travaux de l'Académie des Sciences morales et politiques, 79e Année,* 1919, pp. 491 ff. (puts the population at ten to twelve millions).

J. Culevier: *Les dénombrements de foyers en Brabant (XVIe et XVIIe siècles.)* 1912.

W. Cunningham: *Essay on Western Civilization in its Economic Aspect.* Vol. 2. 1900.

J. Beloch: "Die Bevölkerung Europas zur Zeit der Renaissance." *Zeitschrift für Sozialwissenschaft,* iii, 1900, pp. 765–86.

D. J. Hill: *A History of Diplomacy in the International Development of Europe.* Vol. 2. 1910.

C. H. Haring: "American Gold and Silver Production in the first half of the Sixteenth Century," *Quarterly Journal of Economics,* May, 1915.

C. H. Haring: *Trade and Navigation between Spain and the Indies in the Time of the Hapsburgs.* 1918.

L. Felix: *Der Einfluss von Staat und Recht auf die Entwicklung des Eigenthums.* 2te Hälfte, 2te Abteilung. 1903.

G. Wiebe: *Zur Geschichte der Preisrevolution der 16. und 17. Jahrhunderten,* in **Von Miaskowski**: *Staats und sozialwissenschaftliche Beiträge,* II, 2. 1895. (Important.)

G. d' Avenel: *Histoire économique de la propriété, des salaires, des denrées et de tous les prix en général 1200–1800.* 6 vols. 1894 ff. (Wonderfully interesting work).

G. d'Avenel: *Découvertes d'Histoire Sociale.* 1910. (Brief summary of his larger work).

W. Naudé: *Die Getreidehandelspolitik der Europäischen Staaten von 13ten bis zum 18ten Jahrhundert.* 1896.

N. S. B. Gras: *The Evolution of the English Corn Market.* 1915.

A. P. Usher: *The History of the Grain Trade in France.* 1400–1710. 1913.

K. Häbler: *Die wirtschaftliche Blüte Spaniens im 16. Jahrhundert und ihr Verfall.* 1888.

B. Moses: "The Economic Condition of Spain in the 16th Century." *American Historical Association Reports.* 1893.

E. P. Cheyney: *Social Changes in England in the Sixteenth Century as Reflected in Contemporary Literature.* Part I, Rural Changes. 1895.

A. Luschin von Ebengreuth: *Allgemeine Münzkunde und Geldgeschichte des Mittelalters und der neueren Zeit.* 1904.

§ 4. *Life of the People*

SOURCES:

Das Zimmersche Chronik,[2] hg. v. K. A. Barack. 4 vols. 1861–2.

Social Germany in Luther's Time, the Memoirs of Bartholomew Sastrow, translated by A. D. Vandam. 1902.

T. Tusser: *A Hundred Points of Good Husbandrie.* 1558. (Later expanded as: Five Hundred Points of Good Husbandry united to as many of Good Huswifery. 1573).

L. von Pastor: *Die Reise Kardinals Luigi d'Aragona 1517–8.* 1905. (Ergänzungen und Erläuterungen zu Janssens Geschichte des deutschen Volkes. Band IV, Teil 4).

Baldassare Castiglione: *The Book of the Courtier.* English translation by Opdycke. 1903.

The Seconde Parte of a Register: being a Calendar of Manuscripts under that title intended for publication by the Puritans. 1593. By A. Peel. 2 vols. 1915.

TREATISES:

E. B. Bax: *German Society at the Close of the Middle Ages.* 1894.

P. V. B. Jones: *Household of a Tudor Nobleman.* 1917.

W. B. Rye: *England as seen by Foreigners in the Days of Elizabeth and James I.* 1865.

C. L. Powell: *English Domestic Relations, 1487–1653: a study of Matrimony and Family Life in Theory and Practice as revealed in the Literature, Law and History of the Period.* 1917.

W. Kawerau: *Die Reformation und die Ehe.* 1892.

P. S. Allen: *The Age of Erasmus.* 1914.

K. R. Greenfield: *Sumptuary Laws of Nürnberg.* 1918.

Preserved Smith: "Some old Blue Laws," *Open Court,* April, 1915.

H. Almann: *Das Leben des deutschen Volkes bem Beginn der Neuzeit.* 1893.

E. S. Bates: *Touring in 1600.* 1911.

T. F. Ordish: *The Early London Theatres.* 1894.

J. Cartwright: *Baldassare Castiglione.* 2 vols. 1908.

J. L. Pagel: *Geschichte der Medizin. Zweite Auflage von K. Südhoff.* 1915.

A. H. Buck: *The Growth of Medicine from the Earliest Times to about 1800.* 1917.

H. Haeser: *Geschichte der Medicin.* Band II.[3] 1881.

F. H. Garrison: *An Introduction to the History of Medicine.* 1914.

J. Löhr: *Methodisch-kritische Beiträge zur Geschichte der Sittlichkeit des Klerus, besonders der Erzdiözese Köln am Ausgang des Mittelalters.* 1910.

H. A. Krose: *Der Einfluss der Konfession auf die Sittlichkeit nach den Ergebnissen der Statistik.* 1900.

Henri (J. A.) Baudrillart: *Histoire du luxe privé et public depuis l'antiquité jusqu' à nos jours.* Vol. 3, Moyen Age et Renaissance. 1879.

CHAPTER XI

THE CAPITALISTIC REVOLUTION

Many of the books referred to in the last chapter and many general histories have chapters on the subject. Their titles are not repeated here.

English Economic History. Select Documents ed. by A. E. Bland, P. A. Brown and R. H. Tawney. 1914. (With helpful bibliographies and well-selected material).

H. G. Rosedale: *Queen Elizabeth and the Levant Company.* 1904.

E. Levasseur: *Histoire des classes ouvrières et de l' industrie en France avant 1789.*[2] 2 vols. 1900–1.

G. Avenel: *Paysans et Ouvriers depuis sept cent ans.*[4] 1904.

W. Cunningham: *The Growth of English Industry and Commerce, during the Early and Middle Ages.*[5] 1910. Modern Times.[3] 1894.

W. J. Ashley: *The Economic Organisation of England.* 1914. (Brief, brilliant).

G. Unwin: *The Industrial Organization of England in the Sixteenth and Seventeenth Centuries.* 1904. (Scholarly).

A. P. Usher: *The Industrial History of England.* 1920.

J. W. Burgon: *Life and Times of Sir T. Gresham.* 2 vols. 1839.

O. Noël: *Histoire du commerce du monde.* 3 vols. 1891–1906.

H. G. Selfridge: *The Romance of Commerce.* 1918.

J. A. Williamson: *Maritime Enterprise 1485–1558.* 1913.

J. Strieder: *Die Inventar der Firma Fugger aus dem Jahre 1527.* 1905.

J. Strieder: *Zur Genesis des modernen Kapitalismus.* 1904.

J. Strieder: *Studien zur Geschichte kapitalistischer Organisationsformen: Monopole, Kartelle und Aktiengesellschaften im Mittelalter und zu Beginn der Neuzeit.* 1914. (Highly important).

Clive Day: *History of Commerce.* 1907.

W. Mück: *Der Mansfelder Kupferschieferbergbau.* 1910.

R. Ehrenberg: *Das Zeitalter der Fugger.* Band I, 1896.

C. A. Herrick: *History of Commerce and Industry.* 1917. (Text-book).

M. P. Rooseboom: *The Scottish Staple in the Netherlands, 1292–1676.* 1910.

W. Sombart: *Krieg und Kapitalismus.* 1913.

W. Sombart: *Der Moderne Kapitalismus?* 2 vols. in 3. 1916–7.

L. Brentano: *Die Anfänge des modernen Kapitalismus.* 1916.

A. Schulte: *Die Fugger in Rom.* 2 vols. 1904.

Maxime Kowalewsky: *Die ökonomische Entwicklung Europas bis zum Beginn der kapitalistischen Wirtschafts-*

form. Aus dem Russischen übersetzt von A. Stein. Vol. 6. 1913. (Important).

R. E. Prothero: *English Farming Past and Present.* 1912.

E. F. Gay: "Inclosures in England in the 16th Century," *Quarterly Journal of Economics,* vol. 17, 1903.

E. F. Gay: *Zur Geschichte der Einhegungen in England.* 1902. (Berlin dissertation).

J. S. Leadam: *The Domesday of Inclosures.* 1897.

J. E. T. Rogers: *Six Centuries of Work and Wages.* 1884.

J. E. T. Rogers: *A History of Agriculture and Prices in England.* Vols. iii and iv, 1400–1582. 1882. (A classic).

J. Klein: *The Mesta: A Study in Spanish Economic History.* 1920.

R. H. Tawney: *The Agrarian Problem in the Sixteenth Century.* 1912.

W. Stolze: *Zur Vorgeschichte des Bauernkrieges. (Staats- und sozialwissenschaftliche Forschungen, hg. von G. Schmoller.* Band 18, Heft 4). 1900.

J. Hayem: *Les Grèves dans les Temps Modernes. Mémoires et Documents pour servir à l'histoire du commerce et de l'industrie en France.* 1911.

L. Feuchtwanger: "Geschichte der sozialen Politik und des Armenwesens im Zeitalter der Reformation." *Jahrbuch für Gesetzgebung,* 1908, xxxii, and 1909, xxxiii.

J. S. Schapiro: *Social Reform and the Reformation.* 1909.

G. Uhlhorn: *Die Christliche Liebestätigkeit.* 1895.

E. M. Leonard: *The Early History of English Poor Relief.* 1900.

O. Winckelmann: "Die Armenordnungen von Nürnberg (1522), Kitzingen (1523), Regensburg (1523) und Ypern (1525)," *Archiv für Reformationsgeschichte,* x, 1913 and xi, 1914.

J. L. Vives: *Concerning the Relief of the Poor,* tr. by M. M. Sherwood. 1917.

Liber Vagatorum, reprinted, with Luther's preface, in Luther's Werke, Weimar, vol. xxvi, pp. 634 ff.

Brooks Adams: *The New Empire.* 1902. (Fanciful).

K. Lamprecht: *Zum Verständnis der wirtschaftlichen und sozialen Wandlungen in Deutschland vom 14–16. Jahrhundert.* 1893.

Shakespeare's England, by various authors. 2 vols. 1916. chap. xi, G. Unwin: "Commerce and Coinage."

H. Schönebaum: "Antwerpens Blütezeit im XVI. Jahrhundert." *Archiv für Kulturgeschichte*, xiii. 1917.

O. Winckelmann: "Ueber die ältesten Armenordnungen der Reformationszeit." *Historische Vierteljahrschrift*, xvii. 1914–5.

Stella Kramer: *The English Craft Gilds and the Government.* 1905.

Niederländische Akten und Urkunden zur Geschichte der Hanse und zur deutschen Seegeschichte . . . bearbeitet von R. Häpke. Band I (1531–57). 1913.

W. Cunningham: *Progress of Capitalism in England.* 1916.

CHAPTER XII

MAIN CURRENTS OF THOUGHT

§ 1. *Biblical and Classical Scholarship*

Novum Instrumentum omne, diligenter ab Erasmo Rot. recognitum et emendatum. Basileae. 1516. (Nearly 300 editions catalogued in the Bibliotheca Erasmiana. In Erasmi Opera Omnia, 1703, vol. VI.)

Novum testamentum graece et latine in academia Complutensi noviter impressum. 1514. Vetus testamentum multiplici lingua nunc primum impressum. In hac praeclarissima Complutensi universitate. 1517.

C. R. Gregory: *Die Textkritik des Neuen Testaments.* 3 parts. 1900–9.

Articles "Bible," in *Encyclopædia Britannica, Encyclopædia of Religion and Ethics, Protestantische Realencyklopädie,* and *Die Religion in Geschichte und Gegenwart.*

E. von Dobschütz: *The Influence of the Bible on Civilization.* 1913.

F. Falk: *Die Bibel am Ausgange des Mittelalters, ihre Kenntnis und ihre Verbreitung.* 1905.

Martin Luther's *Deutsche Bibel,* in Sämmtliche Werke, Weimar, separately numbered, vols. i, ii, iii, v.

K. Fullerton: "Luther's doctrine and criticism of Scripture," *Bibliotheca Sacra,* Jan. and April, 1906.

H. Zerener: *Studien über das beginnende Eindringen der lutherischen Bibelübersetzung in der deutschen Literatur.* 1911.

Lutherstudien zur 4. Jahrhundertfeier der Reformation, von den Mitarbeitern der Weimarer Lutherausgabe. 1917. pp. 203 ff.

K. A. Meissinger: *Luther's Exegese in der Frühzeit.* 1911.

O. Reichert: *Martin Luther's Deutsche Bibel.* 1910.

Sir H. H. Howorth: "The Biblical Canon according to the Continental Reformers," *Journal of Theological Studies,* ix, 188 ff. (1907–8).

J. P. Hentz: *History of the Lutheran Version of the Bible.* 1910.

D. Lortsch: *Histoire de la Bible en France.* 1910.

A. W. Pollard: *Records of the English Bible.* 1911.

S. C. Macauley: "The English Bible," *Quarterly Review,* Oct. 1911, pp. 505 ff.

W. Canton: *The Bible and the Anglo-Saxon People.* 1914.

H. T. Peck: *A History of Classical Philology.* 1911.

Sir J. E. Sandys: "Scholarship," chap. ix in *Shakespeare's England,* 1916.

Sir J. E. Sandys: *A History of Classical Scholarship.* Vol. ii, 1908. (Standard).

H. Hallam: *Introduction to the Literature of Europe in the 15th, 16th and 17th Centuries.* 1837–9. (Very comprehensive, in part antiquated, somewhat external but on the whole excellent).

§ 2. *History*

TREATISES:

E. Fueter: *Geschichte der Neueren Historiographie.* 1911. French translation, revised, 1916. (Work of brilliance: philosophical, reliable, readable).

M. Ritter: "Studien über die Entwicklung der Geschichtswissenschaft." *Historische Zeitschrift,* cit. (1912). 261 ff.

E. Menke-Glückert: *Die Geschichtschreibung der Reformation und Gegenreformation. Bodin und die Begründung der Geschichtsmethodologie durch Bartholomäus Keckermann.* 1912.

P. Joachimsen: *Geschichtsauffassung und Geschichtschreibung in Deutschland unter dem Einfluss des Humanismus.* Teil I. 1910.

G. L. Burr: "The Freedom of History," *American Historical Review,* xxii, 261 f. 1916.

A. Morel-Fatio: *Historiographie de Charles-Quint.* 1913.

F. C. Baur: *Die Epochen der kirchlichen Geschichtschreibung.* 1852.

L. von Ranke: *Zur Kritik neueren Geschichtschreiber.*[2] 1874.

G. Wolf: *Quellenkunde der deutschen Reformationsgeschichte.* Vol. i, 1915; vol. ii, 1916.

Article, "History" in *Encyclopedia Americana,* ed. of 1919.

ORIGINALS.

N. Machiavelli: *Istorie fiorentine.* (to 1492). First ed. 1561–64. Numerous editions, and English translation by C. E. Detmold: The Historical, Political and Diplomatic Writings of N. Machiavelli. 4 vols. 1882.

Francesco Guicciardini: *Storia fiorentina.* (1378–1509). First published 1859. *Istoria d' Italia.* (1492–1534). First edition 1561–64; numerous editions since, and English translation by G. Fenton: The historie of Guicciardini. 1599.

Benvenuto Cellini: *Life,* translated by R. H. H. Cust. 2 vols. 1910. (The original text first correctly published by O. Bacci, 1901. Many English translations).

Paulus Jovius: *Historiarum sui temporis libri. xlv. (1493–1547).* 1550–52.

Polydore Vergil: *Anglicae Historiae libri. xxvii, (to 1538).* First edition, to 1509, Basle, 1534; 2d ed. 1555. (I use the edition of 1570. The best criticism is in H. A. L. Fisher's Political History of England 1485–1547, pp. 152 ff.)

Polydore Vergil: *De rerum inventoribus libri octo.* 1536. 2d ed., enlarged, 1557.

Caesar Baronius: *Annales Ecclesiastici* (to 1198). Rome. 1588–1607.

Ecclesiastica Historia . . . secundum centurias, a M. Flacio, et aliis. Magdeburg. 1559–74.

H. Bullinger: *Reformationsgeschichte, hg. von J. J. Hottinger und H. H. Vögeli.* 3 vols. 1838–40. (Index to this in preparation by W. Wuhrmann; Bullinger's Correspondence will also soon appear).

Joan. Sleidani: *De statu religionis et reipublicae, Carolo Quinto Caesare, commentariorum libri xxvi.* 1555. (My edition, 1785, 3 vols., was owned formerly by I. Döllinger).

W. A. Dunning: *A History of Political Theories. Ancient and Medieval.* 1902. *From Luther to Montesquieu.* 1905.

J. N. Figgis: *Studies in Political Thought from Gerson to Grotius.*[2] 1916.

J. Mackinnon: *A History of Modern Liberty.* Vol. 2. The Age of the Reformation. 1907.

L. Cardauns: *Die Lehre vom Widerstandsrecht des Volkes gegen die rechtmässige Obrigkeit im Luthertum und im Calvinismus des sechzehnten Jahrhunderts.* 1903.

R. Chauviré: *Jean Bodin, Auteur de la République.* 1914.

J. Kreutzer: *Zwinglis Lehre von der Obrigkeit.* 1909.

F. Meinecke: "Luther über christlichen Geminwesen und christlichen Staat," *Historische Zeitschrift,* Band 121, pp. 1 ff, 1920.

J. Faulkner: "Luther and Economic Questions," *Papers of the Am. Ch. Hist. Soc.,* 2d ser. vol. ii, 1910.

K. D. Macmillan: *Protestantism in Germany.* 1917.

K. Sell: "Der Zusammenhang von Reformation und politischer Freiheit." *Abh. in Theolog. Arbeiten aus dem rhein. wiss. Predigerverein.* Neue Folge. 12. 1910.

L. H. Waring: *The Political Theories of Martin Luther.* 1910.

G. von Schulthess-Rechberg: *Luther, Zwingli und Calvin in ihren Ansichten über das Verhältnis von Staat und Kirche.* 1910.

K. Rieker: "Staat und Kirche nach lutherischer, reformierter, moderner Anschauung," *Hist. Vierteljahrschrift,* i, 370 ff. 1898.

E. Troeltsch: *Die Soziallehren der christlichen Kirchen und Gruppen.* 1912.

H. L. Osgood: "The Political Ideas of the Puritans." *Political Science Quarterly,* vi, 1891.

R. Treumann: *Die Monarchomachen. Eine Darstellung der revolutionären Staatslehren des xvi Jahrhundert 1573–1599.* 1885.

A. Elkan: *Die Publizistik der Bartholomäusnacht und Mornays Vindiciae contra tyrannos.* 1905.

H. D. Foster: "The Political Theories of the Calvinists," *American Historical Review,* xxi, 481 ff. (1916).

Paul van Dyke: "The Estates of Pontoise," *English Historical Review,* 1913, pp. 472 ff.

E. Armstrong: "Political Theory of the Huguenots," *English Historical Review,* iv, 13 ff, 1889.

K. Gläser: "Beiträge zur Geschichte der politischen Literatur Frankreichs in der zweiten Hälfte des 16. Jahrhundert." *Zeitschrift für Französische Sprache und Literatur.* Vols. 31, 32, 33, 39, 45; 1904–18.

W. Sohm: "Die Soziallehren Melanchthons," *Historische Zeitschrift,* cxv, pp. 64–76. 1915.

Lord Acton: *History of Freedom,* pp. 212–31. (Reprint of introduction to L. A. Burd's edition of the Prince of Machiavelli.) 1907.

John Morley: *Miscellanies,* 4th series. 1908. 1 ff. "Machiavelli."

Dr. Armaingaud: *Montaigne Pamphlétaire. L'Énigme du Contr'un.* 1910.

J. Jastrow: "Kopernikus' Münz- und Geld-theorie." *Archiv für Sozialwissenschaft und Sozialpolitik,* xxxviii, 734 ff. 1904.

K. Kautsky: *Communism in Central Europe in the Time of the Reformation.* 1897.

E. Jenks: *A Short History of English Law.* 1912.

A. Esmein: *Histoire du Droit Français.*[6] 1905. (And later editions).

R. Schröder: *Deutsche Rechtsgeschichte.*[5] 1907.

Walter Platzhoff: *Die Theorie von der Mordbefugnis der Obrigkeit im XVI. Jahrhundert.* Ebinger's Historische Studien, 1906.

O. H. Pannkoke: *"The Economic Teachings of the Reformation."* In a collection of essays entitled *Four Hundred Years,* 1917.

G. Schmoller: *Zur Geschichte der nationalökonomischen Ansichten in Deutschland während der Reformationsperiode.* 1860.

F. G. Ward: *Darstellung und Würdigung der Ansichten Luthers über Staat und Gesellschaft.* 1898.

§ 4. *Science.*

J. P. Richter: *The Literary Works of Leonardo da Vinci.* 2 vols. 1883.

Les Manuscrits de Léonard de Vinci de la bibliothèque de l'Institut. Publiés en facsimile avec transcription littérale, traduction française . . . par Ch. Ravaisson-Molien 6 vols. 1881–91.

Leonardo da Vinci's note-books; arranged and rendered into English by E. McCurdy. 1906.

Leonardo de Vinci: *Notes et Dessins sur la Génération.* 1901.

Léonard de Vinci: *Feuillets inédits conservés à Windsor.* 22 vols. 1901 ff.

Instituto di Studi Vinciani:—Per il IVo centenario della morte di Leonardo da Vinci. 1919.

A. C. Klebs: *Leonardo da Vinci and his anatomical studies.* 1916.

Hieronymi Cardani: *Opera Omnia.* 1663. 10 vols.

W. W. R. Ball: *A Short Account of the History of Mathematics.* 1901.

M. Cantor: *Vorlesungen über Geschichte der Mathematik.* Vol. 2 (1200–1668). 1900.

H. G. Zeuthen: *Geschichte der Mathematik in 16. und 17. Jahrhundert.* 1903.

Articles, "Algebra" and "Mathematics" in *Encyclopædia Britannica.*

Maximilien Marie: *Histoire des sciences mathématiques et physiques,* vols. 2 and 3. 1883–4.

F. Cajori: *History of Mathematics.*[2] 1919.

David E. Smith: *Rara arithmetica.* A catalogue of the arithmetics written before the year MDCI, with a description of those in the library of G. A. Plimpton. 1908.

F. Dannemann: *Grundriss einer Geschichte der Naturwissenschaften.*[2]. 2 vols. 1902.

W. A. Locy: *Biology and its makers.*[3] 1915.

W. A. Locy: *The Main Currents of Zoölogy.* 1918.

E. L. Greene: *Landmarks of Botanical History.* Part 1. 1909. (Smithsonian Miscellaneous Collections, vol. 54).

J. V. Carus: *Geschichte der Zoölogie bis auf Joh. Müller und Ch. Darwin.* 1872.

F. Cajori: *A History of Physics in Its Elementary Branches.* 1899.

Conradi Gesneri *Historiae Animalium,* libb. iii, 3 vols. 1551–8.

Wm. Gilbert . . . *on the Loadstone and Magnetic Bodies* . . . a translation by P. F. Mottelay. 1893.

E. Gerland: *Geschichte der Physik von den ältesten Zeiten bis zum Ausgange des achtzehnten Jahrhunderts.* 1913. (Work of high philosophical and scientific value).

J. C. Brown: *A History of Chemistry from the Earliest Times Till the Present Day.* 1913.

F. J. Moore: *A History of Chemistry.* 1918.

T. E. Thorpe: *A History of Chemistry.* 2 vols. 1909–10.

Quaestiones Novae in Libellum de Sphaera Johannis de Sacro Bosco, collectae ab Ariele Bicardo. Wittenberg, 1550. (Library of Mr. G. A. Plimpton, New York).

S. Günther: *Geschichte der Erdkunde.* 1904.

Articles, "Geography" and "Map" in *Encyclopædia Britannica.*

L. Gallois: *Les géographes allemands de la Renaissance,* 1890.

N. Copernici De Revolutionibus orbium cœlestium libri vi. (First edition 1543; I use the edition of Basle, 1566).

L. Prowe: *Nikolaus Coppernicus.* 3 vols. 1883–4. (Standard).

Wohlwill: "Melanchthon und Kopernicus," in *Mitteilungen zur Geschichte der Medizin und der Naturwissenschaften,* iii, 260, 1904.

Luther on Copernicus, **Bindseil:** Lutheri Colloquia, 3 vols. 1863–66, vol. ii, p. 149. (This is the best text; the stronger form of the same saying, in which Luther called Copernicus a fool, seems to have been retouched by Aurifaber).

A. D. White: *The Warfare of Science and Theology,* 2 vols. 1896. Vol. i, pp. 114 ff.

A. Müller: *Nikolaus Copernicus.* 1898.

Dorothy Stimson: *The Gradual Acceptance of the Copernican Theory of the Universe.* 1917. (Excellent).

W. W. Bryant: *History of Astronomy.* 1907.

Article, "Navigation," in *Encyclopædia Britannica.*

§ 5. *Philosophy*

The Works of Luther, Melanchthon, Calvin, Zwingli, &c.

The Workes of Sir Thomas More, 1557. (Passage quoted, p. 329h).

De Trinitatis Erroribus per M. Servetum. (Printed, 1531; I use the MS copy at Harvard).

M. Serveti Christianismi Restitutio. (I use the MS copy at Harvard).

E. F. K. Müller: *Die Bekenntnisschriften der reformierten Kirche.* 1903.

Canons and Decrees of the Council of Trent, translated by T. A. Buckley. 1851.

Thomas Cajetan's commentary on Aquinas, in the standard edition of the *Summa,* 1880 ff.

Catechism of the Council of Trent, translated into English by J. Donovan. 1829.

Altensteig: *Lexicon Theologicum.* 1583.

A. Harnack: *A History of Dogma,* translated from the third edition by N. Buchanan. 7 vols. 1901.

A. Harnack: *Lehrbuch der Dogmengeschichte.*[4] 1910. Vol. iii.

E. Troeltsch: *Geschichte der christlichen Religion.* 1909. (Kultur der Gegenwart).

R. M. Jones: *Spiritual Reformers of the 16th and 17th Centuries.* 1914.

O. Ritschl: *Dogmengeschichte des Protestantismus,* i, ii, Hälfte, 1912.

A. C. McGiffert: *Protestant Thought before Kant.* 1911.

J. Gottschick: *Luther's Theologie.* 1914.

Francis Bacon: *Novum Organum,* Bk. I, aphorisms xv, lxv, and lxxix; Essays i, (Truth), iii, (of Unity in Religion), xxxv, (Prophecy). Advancement of Learning, Bk. ix.

Montaigne's Essays, passim (numerous editions and excellent English translation by Florio).

W. Lyly: *Euphues and Atheos* (edited by E. Arber, 1904).

R. Ascham: *The Schoolmaster.* 1761.

Janssen-Pastor [20] ii, 461f (on the Godless Painters of Nuremberg; cf. also M. Thausing: A Dürer, translated by F. A. Eaton, 1882, ii, 248 f.)

François Rabelais: *Oeuvres* (numerous editions and translations).

J. M. Robertson: *A Short History of Freethought.*[2] 2 vols. 1906.

Colloque de Jean Bodin des Secrets cachez et des Choses Sublimes. Traduction française du Colloquium Heptaplomeres, par R. Chauviré. 1914.

F. von Bezold: "Jean Bodins Colloquium Heptaplomeres und der Atheismus des 16. Jahrhunderts," *Historische Zeitschrift,* cxiii, 260–315.

Jordani Bruni Opera, ed. Fiorentino. 3 vols. 1879–91.

Giordano Brunos Gesammelte Werke, verdeutscht und erläutert von L. Kuhlenbeck. 6 vols. 1907–10.

W. Boulting: *Giordano Bruno: His Life, Thought and Martyrdom.* (1916).

L. Kuhlenbeck: *Giordano Bruno, seine Lehre von Gott, von der Unsterblichkeit und von der Willensfreiheit.* 1913.

W. Pater: *Gaston de la Tour.* 1896.

J. R. Charbonnel: *L'Éthique de Giordano Bruno et le deuxième dialogue de Spaccio,* traduction. 1919.

J. Owen: *The Skeptics of the Italian Renaissance.*[2] 1893.

J. Owen: *The Skeptics of the French Renaissance.* 1893.

A. M. Fairbairn: "Tendencies of European Thought in the Age of the Reformation," *Cambridge Modern History,* ii, chap. 19.

Allegemeine Geschichte der Philosophie. (Kultur der Gegenwart, Teil i, Abt. V.) 1909. W. Windelband: Die neuere Philosophie.

E. Cassirer: *Das Erkenntnisproblem in der Philosophie und Wissenschaft der neuen Zeit.* Vol. i.[2] 1911. (Excellent. First edition, 1906–7).

R. Adamson: *A Short History of Logic.* 1911.

H. Höffding: *A History of Modern Philosophy.* English translation. 2 vols. 1900.

R. Eucken: *The Problem of Human Life as Viewed by the Great Thinkers.* English translation. 1909.

J. M. Baldwin: *Dictionary of Philosophy and Psychology.* 3 vols. 1901–5.

J. R. Charbonnel: *La pensée italienne au XVIe siècle.* 1919.

A. Bonilla y San Martin: *Luis Vives y la filosofía del renacimiento.* 1903.

CHAPTER XIII

THE TEMPER OF THE TIMES

§ 1. *Tolerance and Intolerance*

Lord Acton: *The History of Freedom.* 1907. "The Protestant Theory of Persecution," pp. 150–187. (Essay written in 1862).

F. Ruffini: *Religious Liberty,* translated by J. P. Heyes. 1912.

N. Paulus: *Protestantismus und Toleranz.* 1912.

G. L. Burr: "Anent the Middle Ages." *American Historical Review.* 1913, pp. 710–726.

P. Wappler: *Die Stellung Kursachsens und Philipps von Hessen zur Täuferbewegung.* 1910.

Encyclopædia of Religion and Ethics, ix, s. v. "Persecution."

S. Castellion: *Traité des Hérétiques.* A savoir, si on les doit persécuter. Ed. A. Olivet. Genève. 1913.

P. Wappler: *Inquisition und Ketzerprozess zu Zwickau.* 1908.

J. A. Faulkner: *"Luther and Toleration," Papers of American Church History Society,* Second Series, vol. iv, pp. 129 ff. 1914.

K. Völker: *Toleranz und Intoleranz im Zeitalter der Reformation.* 1912.

W. E. H. Lecky: *A History of the Rise and Influence of the Spirit of Rationalism in Europe.* 2 vols. 1865. chapter iv, "Persecution" (in vols. 1 and 2 both).

Erasmi opera, 1703, ix, 904 ff. Proposition iii.

H. Hermelinck: *Der Toleranzgedanke.* 1908.

The Workes of Sir Thomas More, 1557, pp. 274 ff. (A Dialogue of Sir Thomas More, 1528).

Montaigne: *Essays,* Book ii, no. xix.

A. J. Klein: *Intolerance in the Reign of Elizabeth.* 1917.

R. Lewin: *Luther's Stellung zu den Juden.* 1911.

R. H. Murray: *Erasmus and Luther: their attitude to Toleration.* 1920.

§ 2. *Witchcraft*

Papers of the American Historical Association, iv, pp. 237–66. Bibliography of witchcraft by G. L. Burr.

N. Paulus: *Hexenwahn und Hexenprozess, vornehmlich im 16. Jahrhundert.* 1910.

G. L. Burr: *The Witch Persecutions.* Translations and Reprints issued by the University of Pennsylvania, vol. 3, no. 4, 1897.

G. L. Burr: *The Fate of Dietrich Flade.* 1891.

J. Hansen: *Zauberwahn, Inquisition und Hexenprozess im Mittelalter, und die Entstehung der grossen Hexenverfolgung.* 1900.

F. von Bezold: "Jean Bodin als Okkultist und seine Demonomanie." *Historische Zeitschrift,* cv. 1 ff. (1910).

Gosson: *The School of Abuse* (1578), ed. E. Arber, 1906, p. 60.

De Praestigiis demonum . . . authore Joanne Wiero . . . 1564.

Johannis Wieri: *De lamiis.* 1582.

Reginald Scott: *The Discoverie of Witchcraft, wherein the Lewde dealing of Witches and Witchmongers is notably* *detected . . . whereunto is added a Treatise upon the Nature and Substance of Spirits and Devils.* 1584. Reprinted by B. Nicholson, 1886.

W. Notestein: *A History of Witchcraft in England 1558–1718.* 1911.

W. E. H. Lecky: *A History of the Rise and Influence of the Spirit of Rationalism in Europe.* 2 vols. 1865. Vol. 1, chaps. i, and ii.

Montaigne: *Essays,* vol. iii, no. xi.

H. C. Lea: *A History of the Inquisition in the Middle Ages.* Vol. iii, 392 ff.

G. L. Kittredge: "A Case of Witchcraft," *American Historical Review,* xxiii, pp. 1 ff, 1917.

C. Mirbt: *Quellen zur Geschichte des Papsttums und des römischen Katholizismus.*[3] 1911. p. 182. (Bull, Summis desiderantes).

G. Roskoff: *Geschichte des Teufels.* 1869.

A. Graf: *Il diavolo.* 1889.

H. C. Lea: *The Inquisition in Spain,* 1907, vol. iv, chaps. 8 and 9.

Statutes of the Realm, 5 Eliz. 16: An Act agaynst Inchantmentes and Witchcraftes. (1562–3).

T. de Cauzons: *La Magie et la Sorcellerie en France.* 4 vols. (1911).

E. Klinger: *Luther und der deutsche Volksaberglaube.* 1912. (*Palaestra,* vol. 56).

§ 3. *Education*

Album Academiæ Vitebergensis 1502–1602, Band I, ed. K. E. Förstemann, 1841. Band ii, 1895. Band iii Indices, 1905. (Reprint of vol. i, 1906).

J. C. H. Weissenborn: *Akten der Erfurter Universität.* 3 vols. 1884.

G. Buchanan: "Anent the Reformation of the University of St. Andros," in *Buchanan's Vernacular Writings,* ed. P. Hume Brown, 1892.

The Statutes of the Faculty of Arts and of the Faculty of Theology at the Period of the Reformation, of St. Andrews' University, ed. R. K. Hannay, 1910.

K. Hartfelder: *Melanchthoniana pædogogica.* 1895.

F. V. N. Painter: *Luther on Education,* including a historical introduction and a translation of the Reformer's two most important educational treatises. 1889.

Mandament der Keyserlijcker Maiesteit, vuytghegeven int Jaer xlvi. Louvain. 1546. (100 facsimiles printed for A. M. Huntington at the De Vinne Press, N. Y., 1896. Contains lists of books allowed in schools in the Netherlands).

C. Borgeaud: *Histoire de l' Université de Genève.* 2 vols. 1900, 1909.

J. M. Höfer: *Die Stellung des Des. Erasmus und J. L. Vives zur Pädagogik des Quintilian.* (Erlangen Dissertation). 1910.

F. Watson: *Vives and the Renascence education of Women.* 1912.

P. Monroe: *Cyclopedia of education.* 5 vols. 1912–3.

K. A. Schmid: *Geschichte der Erziehung vom Anfang bis auf unserer Zeit.* 5 vols. in 7. 1884–1902. (Standard).

A. Zimmermann: *Die Universitäten Englands im 16. Jahrhundert.* 1889.

A. Zimmermann: *England's "öffentliche Schulen" von der Reformation bis zur Gegenwart,* 1892 (Stimmen aus Maria-Lach. vol. 56).

F. P. Graves: *A History of Education during the Middle Ages and the Transition to Modern Times.* 1910.

"Die Frequenz der deutschen Universitäten in früherer Zeit," *Deutsches Wochenblatt,* 1897, pp. 391 ff.

P. Monroe: *A Text-Book of the History of Education.* 1905. (Standard text-book).

W. S. Monroe: *A Bibliography of Education.* 1897.

G. Mertz: *Das Schulwesen der deutschen Reformation.* 1902.

F. Paulsen: *Geschichte des gelehrten Unterrichts in Deutschland.*[2] 2 vols. 1896–7.

W. Sohm: *Die Schule Johann Sturms.* 1912.

J. Ficker: *Die Anfänge der akademischen Studien in Strassburg.* 1912.

Shakespeare's England, 1916. 2 vols. ch. 8 "Education" by Sir J. E. Sandys.

A. Roersch: *L' Humanisme belge à l' époque de la Renaissance.* 1910.

Sir T. Elyot: *The boke named the governour.* 1531. (New edition by H. H. S. Croft. 2 vols. 1880).

Melanchthonis opera omnia, xi, 12 ff. "Declamatio de corrigendis adolescentiæ studies." (1518).

R. Ascham: *The Schole Master.* 1571. (I use the reprint

in the English Works of R. Ascham, ed. J. Bennet, 1761).
M. Fournier: *Les Statuts et Privilèges des Universités françaises depuis leur fondation jusqu'en 1789.* 4 vols. 1890–4.
F. Bacon: *The Advancement of Learning,* Book ii.
Elizabethan Oxford: reprints of rare tracts ed. by C. Plumer. 1887.
Grace book Δ containing records of the University of Cambridge 1542–89, ed. by J. Venn. 1910.
Registres des procès-verbaux de la Faculté de théologie de Paris, pub. par A. Clerval. Tome I. 1917. (1505–23).
J. H. Lupton: *A Life of John Colet,* new ed. 1909. (First printed 1887. On St. Paul's School, pp. 169, 271 ff.)
W. H. Woodward: *Des. Erasmus concerning the Aim and Method of Education.* 1904. (Fine work).
F. P. Graves: *Peter Ramus and the Educational Reformation of the 16th Century.* 1912.
Encyclopædia Britannica, articles "Universities" and "Schools."
Altamira y Crevea: *Historia de España,*[3] iii, 532 ff. (1913).
F. Gribble: *The Romance of the Cambridge Colleges.* (1913).
J. B. Mullinger: *A History of the University of Cambridge.* 1888.
G. C. Brodrick: *A History of the University of Oxford.* 1886.
C. Headlam: *The Story of Oxford.* 1907.
W. H. Woodward: *Studies in Education during the Age of the Renaissance* 1400–1600.
A. Bonilla y San Martin: *Luis Vives y la filosofía del renacimiento.* 1903.
A. Lefranc: *Histoire du Collège de France depuis ses origines jusqu' à la fin du premier empire.* 1893.
P. Feret: *La Faculté de Théologie de Paris. Époque Moderne.* 7 vols. 1900–10.
W. Friedensburg: *Geschichte der Universität Wittenberg.* 1918.

§ 4. *Art*

Very fine reproductions of the works of the principal painters of the time are published in separate volumes of the series, Klassiker der Kunst in Gesamtausgaben, Deutsche Verlags-Anstalt, Stuttgart und Leipzig. A brief list of standard criticisms of art, many of them well illustrated, follows:

K. Woermann: *Geschichte der Kunst aller Zeiten und Völker.* Band 4.[2] 1919.

S. Reinach: *Apollo.*[4] 1907. (Also English translation. Marvelously compressed and sound criticism).

J. A. Symonds: *The Italian Renaissance.* The Fine Arts. 1888.

L. Pastor: *History of the Popes.* (Much on art at Rome, passim).

B. Berenson: *North Italian Painters of the Renaissance.* 1907.

B. Berenson: *Central Italian Painters of the Renaissance.* 1897.

B. Berenson: *The Venetian Painters of the Renaissance.*[3] 1902.

B. Berenson: *The Florentine Painters of the Renaissance.*[2] 1903.

Giorgio Vasari: *Lives of the Most Eminent Painters, Sculptors and Architects,* newly translated by G. du C. de Vere. 10 vols. 1912–14. (Other editions).

R. Lanciani: *The Golden Days of the Renaissance in Rome.* 1907.

E. Müntz: *Histoire de l' art pendant la Renaissance.* 3 vols. 1889–95.

J. Crowe and G. Cavalcaselle: *History of Italian Painting.* 1903 ff.

L. Dimier: *French Painting in the Sixteenth Century.* 1904.

L. F. Freeman: *Italian Sculptors of the Renaissance.* 1902.

H. Janitschek: *Geschichte der deutschen Malerei.* 1890.

H. A. Dickenson: *German Masters of Art.* 1914.

E. Bertaux: *Rome de l' avènement de Jules II à nos jours.*[2] 1908.

M. Reymond: *L' Education de Léonard.* 1910.

W. Pater: "Leonardo da Vinci," in the volume called *The Renaissance,* 1878. (Though much attacked this is, in my opinion, the best criticism of Leonardo).

S. Freud: *Leonardo da Vinci.* 1910.

W. von Seidlitz: *Leonardo da Vinci.* 2 vols. 1909. (Excellent).

Osvald Sirén: *Leonardo da Vinci.* 1916.

Leonardo da Vinci: *A treatise on painting,* translated from the Italian by J. F. Rigaud. London. 1897.

C. J. Holmes: *Leonardo da Vinci. Proceedings of the British Academy.* 1919.

E. Müntz: *Raphael, sa vie, son oeuvre et son temps.* 1881.

W. Pater: "Raphael," in *Miscellaneous Studies,* 1913. (First written 1892; fine criticism).

Edward McCurdy: *Raphael Santi.* 1917.

H. Grimm: *Life of Michael Angelo,* tr. by F. E. Bunnètt. 2 vols. New ed. 1906.

Crowe and Cavalcasselle: *Life and Times of Titian.* 1877.

H. Thode: *Michelangelo und das Ende der Renaissance.* 5 vols. 1902–13.

L. Dorez: "Nouvelles recherches sur Michel-Ange et son entourage," *Bibliothèque de l' École des Chartes.* Vol. 77, pp. 448 ff. (1916), vol. 78, pp. 179 ff. (1917).

Romain Roland: *Vie de Michel-Ange.*[4] 1913.

The Sonnets of Michael Angelo Buonarroti, translated into English by J. A. Symonds. (My copy, Venice, has no date).

R. W. Emerson: *Essay on Michaelangelo.*

A. Dürer's *Schriftliche Nachlass,* ed. E. Heidrich. 1908.

M. Thausing: *A. Dürer.*[2] 1876. (English translation from 1st ed. by F. A. Eaton. 1882).

Albrecht Dürers Niederländische Reise, hg. von J. Veth und S. Müller. 2 vols. 1918.

A. B. Chamberlain: *Hans Holbein the Younger.* 2 vols. 1913.

A. Michel: *Histoire de l'art depuis les premiers temps chrétiens jusqu' à nos jours.* 3 vols. 1905–8.

C. H. Moore: *The Character of Renaissance Architecture.* 1905.

R. Bloomfield: *A History of French Architecture from the Reign of Charles VIII till the death of Mazarin.* 2 vols. 1911.

§ 5. *Belles Lettres*

Note: The works of the humanists, theologians, biblical and classical scholars, historians, publicists and philosophers have been dealt with in other sections of this bibliography. Representative poets, dramatists and writers of fiction for the century (up to but not including the Age of Shakespeare in England or of Henry IV in France) are the following:

Italian: Ariosto, A. F. Grazzini, M. Bandello, T. Tasso, Berni, Guarini.

French: Margaret of Navarre, C. Marot, Rabelais, Joachim du Bellay, Ronsard, Montaigne.

English: Lyndesay, Skelton, Wyatt, Surrey, anonymous poets in Tottel's Miscellany, Sidney, E. Spenser, Donne, Lyly, Heywood, Kyd, Peele, Greene, Lodge, Nash, Marlowe.

German: Hans Sachs, Fischart, T. Murner, anonymous Till Eulenspiegel and Faustbuch, B. Waldis.

Spanish: The Picaresque novel, La vida de Lazarillo de Tormes y de sus fortunas y adversidades.

Portuguese: Camoens.

As it is not my purpose to give even a sketch of literary history, but merely to illustrate the temper of the times from the contemporary belles lettres, only a few suggestive works of criticism can be mentioned here.

H. Hallam: *Introduction to the Literature of Europe in the 15th, 16th and 17th Centuries.* 1838–9. (Old, but still useful).

J. A. Symonds: *Italian Literature.* 1888.

G. Lanson: *Histoire de la littérature française.*[9] 1906.

C. H. C. Wright: *A History of French Literature.* 1912.

C. Thomas: *A History of German Literature.* 1909.

E. Wolff: *Faust und Luther.* 1912.

The Cambridge History of English Literature, vol. iii, Renaissance and Reformation. 1908.

J. J. Jusserand: *Histoire Littéraire du Peuple Anglais.* Tome ii, De la Renaissance à la Guerre Civile. 1904. (Also English translation; a beautiful work).

Winifred Smith: *The Commedia dell' Arte.* 1912. (Notable).

A. Tilley: *The Literature of the French Renaissance.* 2 vols. 1904.

CHAPTER XIV

THE REFORMATION INTERPRETED

The purpose of the following list is not to give the titles of all general histories of the Reformation, but of those books and articles in which some noteworthy contribution has been made to the philosophical interpretation of the events. Many an excellent work of pure narrative character, and many of those dealing with some particular phase of the Reformation, are omitted. All the noteworthy historical works published prior to 1600 are listed in the bibliography to Chapter XII, section 2, and are not repeated here. The chronological order is here adopted, save that all the works of each writer are grouped together. In every case I enter the book under the year in which it first appeared, adding in parentheses the edition, if another, which I have used.

Francis Bacon (1561–1626): Essay lviii; also Essays i, iii, xxxv; Novum Organum Bk. i, aphorisms xv and lxv; Advancement of Learning, Bk. ix, and i.

Jacques-Auguste de Thou (Thuanus): *Historiae sui temporis.* 1604–20.

Hugo Grotius: *Annales et historiae de rebus belgicis.* 1657. (Written 1611 ff).

William Camden: *Annales Rerum Anglicarum et Hibernicarum regnante Elizabetha.* Pars I, 1615; Pars II, 1625.

Agrippa d' Aubigné: *Histoire Universelle.* 1616–20.

Paolo Sarpi: *Istoria del Concilio Tridentino.* 1619. (P. Sarpi: Histoire du Concile du Trente, French translation by Amelot de la Houssaie. 1699).

Arrigo Caterino Davila: *Storia delle guerre civili di Francia.* 1630.

Giulio Bentivoglio: *Guerra di Fiandria.* 1632–39.

Famiano Strada: *De bello belgico decades duo.* 1632–47.

François Eudes, [called] **de Mézeray:** *Histoire de France.* 1643–51.

David Calderwood (1575–1650): *History of the Kirk of Scotland,* ed. T. Thompson, 1842–9.

Lord Herbert of Cherbury: *Life and Reign of Henry VIII.* 1649.

Thomas Fuller: *Church History,* 1655. (Ed. Brewer, 6 vols. 1845).

J. Harrington: *Oceana,* 1656. (Harrington's Works, 1700, pp. 69, 388).

Sforza Pallavicino: *Istoria del Concilio di Trento.* 1656–7.

Annales ecclesiastici . . . auctore Reynaldo, ed. J. D. Mansi. Tomi 33–35. Lucae. 1755. (Oderic Reynaldus, who died 1671, was a continuator of Baronius, covering the period in church history 1198–1565).

Jean Claude: *Défense de la Réformation. . . .* 1673. (English translation: An historical defense of the Reformation. 1683).

Gilbert Burnet: *History of the Reformation of the Church of England.* 3 vols. 1679, 1681, 1715. (Ed. by Pocock, 6 vols. 1865ff).

Louis Maimbourg: *Histoire du Luthéranisme.* 1680.

Pierre Jurieu: *Histoire du Calvinisme et celle du Papisme mises en parallèle.* 1683. (English translation, 2 vols. 1823).

Veit Ludwig von Seckendorf: *Commentarius historicus et apologeticus de Lutheranismo.* 1688–92.

Jacques Benigne Bossuet: *Histoire des variations des églises protestantes.* 1688. (I have used the editions of 1812 and 1841).

Pierre Bayle: *Dictionnaire historique et critique,* 1697., s. v. "Luther," "Calvin," &c.

Gabriel Daniel: *Histoire de France.* 1703.

Jeremy Collier: *Ecclesiastical History,* 2 vols. 1708–14. (ed. Lathbury, 9 vols. 1852).

Rapin Thoyras: *Histoire d' Angleterre.* 1723ff.

Johann Lorenz Mosheim: *Institutiones historiae christianae recentiores.* 1741.

Montesquieu: *Esprit des Lois,* 1748, Livre xxiv, chaps. 2, 5, 25; Livre xxv, chap. 2, 6, 11.

Frederick II (called The Great) of Prussia: *De la Superstition et de la Religion.* 1749. (Oeuvres, 1846, i, 204 ff).

Voltaire: *Essai sur les moeurs et l' esprit des nations, et sur les principaux faits de l' histoire depuis Charlemagne jusqu'à Louis XIII.* 1754. (*Cf.* also a passage in his Dictionnaire philosophique).

David Hume: *History of England from the Invasion of Julius Caesar to the Revolution of 1688.* The volumes on the Tudor period came out in 1759.

William Robertson: *A History of Scotland.* 1759.

William Robertson: *History of the Reign of the Emperor Charles V.* 1769.

Edward Gibbon: *The Decline and Fall of the Roman Empire.* 1776–88. (On the Reformation, chap. liv, end).

Encyclopédie, 1778, s.v. "Luthéranisme." (Anonymous article).

Johann Gottfried von Herder: *Das Weimarische Gesangbuch,* 1778, Vorrede.

Herder: *Briefe das Studium der Theologie betreffend,* 1784. (Sämtliche Werke, Teil 14).

Herder: *Briefe zur Beförderung der Humanität,* 1793–7. (Sämtliche Werke, Teil 14).

Michael Ignaz Schmidt: *Geschichte der Deutschen.* Aeltere

Geschichte (to 1544), 1778 ff. Neuere Geschichte (1544–1660), 1785 ff.

Jakob Gottlieb Planck: *Geschichte des protestantischen Lehrbegriffs,* 6 vols. 1783–1800.

[M. J. A. N. de Caritat, Marquis] De Condorcet: *Esquisse d'un tableau historique des Progrès de l' Ésprit humain.* 1794. (I use the fourth edition, 1798, pp. 200 ff.)

F. A. de Chateaubriand: *Essai historique sur les Révolutions,* 1797. (Oeuvres, 1870).

Chateaubriand: *Analyse raisonnée de l' histoire de France.* (Oeuvres, 1865, Tome 8).

Friedrich von Hardenberg (called Novalis): *Die Christenheit oder Europa,* 1799 (Novalis' Schriften hg. von Minor, 1907, Band ii. Also English translation).

Johann Wolfgang von Goethe (1749–1832): *Sämtliche Werke,* Jubiläumsausgabe, no date, Stuttgart and Berlin, i, 242 and ii, 279, and other obiter dicta for which see the excellent index. See also Gespräche mit Eckermann, 1832, English translation in Bohn's library, p. 568.

Friedrich Schiller: *Geschichte des Abfalles der Vereinigten Niederlande von der spanischen Regierung.* 1788. (2d ed., much changed, 1801; translation in Bohn's library). Cf. also Schiller's letter to Goethe, Sept. 17, 1800, in Schiller's Briefe, hg. von F. Jonas, 1895, vi, 200.

Christoph Martin Wieland (1733–1813). His opinion, in 1801 is given in *Diary &c of Henry Crabb Robinson,* ed. T. Sadler, 3 vols., 1869, i, 109, and in "Charakteristik Luthers," in Pantheon der Deutschen, 1794.

Charles de Villers: *Essai sur l'esprit et l'influence de la Réforme de Luther.* 1803. (English translation by James Mill, 1805).

William Roscoe: *Life and Pontificate of Leo X.* 1805.

J. G. Fichte: *Reden an die deutsche Nation,* 1808. Nr. 6.

Mme. de Staël: *De l'Allemagne.* 1813.

E. M. Arndt: *Ansichten und Aussichten der deutschen Geschichte.* 1814.

Arndt: *Vom Worte und vom Kirchenliede.* 1819.

Arndt: *Christliches und Türkisches.* 1828, pp. 255 ff.

Arndt: *Vergleichende Völkergeschichte.* 1814.

Friedrich von Schlegel: *Geschichte der alten und neuen Literatur.* 1815. (Sämtliche Werke, 1822, ii, 244 ff).

Schlegel: *Philosophie der Geschichte.* 1829. (English translation in Bohn's Library).

Joseph de Maistre: *De l'église gallicane.* 1820, cap. 2. (Oeuvres, 1884, ii, 3 ff).

De Maistre: *Lettres sur l'Inquisition espagnole.* 1815 ff. (Oeuvres ii).

John Lingard: *History of England,* vols. 4, 5. 1820 ff.

G. W. F. Hegel: *Philosophie der Geschichte.* Lectures delivered first 1822–3, published as vol. ix of his Werke by E. Gans, 1837. (English translation by J. Sibree, 1857, in Bohn's Library).

Leopold von Ranke: *Geschichte der romanischen und germanischen Völker von 1494–1535.* Band i, (bis 1514). 1824. Appendix: Zur Kritik neuerer Geschichtschreiber.

Ranke: *Die römischen Päpste, ihre Kirche und ihr Staat im XVI. und XVII. Jahrhundert.* 1834–6. (Many editions and translations of this and other works of Ranke).

Ranke: *Deutsche Geschichte im Zeitalter der Reformation.* 1839–47.

Ranke: *Zwölf Bücher Preussischer Geschichte.* Band i und ii, 1874.

Ranke: *Die Osmannen und die Spanische Monarchie im 16. und 17. Jahrhundert.* 1877.

C. H. de Rouvroy, Comte de Saint-Simon: *Nouveau Christianisme,* Oeuvres, 1869, vii, 100 ff. (written 1825).

Henry Hallam: *Constitutional History of England from the accession of Henry VII to the death of George II.* 1827.

Hallam: *Introduction to the Literature of Europe in the 15th, 16th and 17th Centuries.* 1837–9.

A. Thierry: *Vingt-cinq letters sur l'histoire de France.* 1827.

François-Pierre-Guillaume Guizot: *Histoire de la civilisation en Europe.* 1828. (English transl. by Hazlitt. 1846).

Guizot: *Histoire de la civilisation en France.* 4 vols. 1830.

Philipp Marheineke: *Geschichte der deutschen Reformation.* 4 vols. 1831–4.

Heinrich Leo: *Geschichte der Niederlanden.* 2 vols. 1832–5.

Leo: *Lehrbuch der Universalgeschichte,* 6 vols. 1835–44.

Friedrich von Raumer: *Geschichte Europas seit dem Ende des 15. Jahrhundert.* 1832–50.

A. Vinet: *Moralistes des 16. and 17. siècles.* 1859 (Lectures given 1832–47).

H. Martin: *Histoire de France.* 1833–6.

Heinrich Heine: *Zur Geschichte der Religion und Philosophie in Deutschland.* 1834.

Jules Michelet: *Mémoires de Luther écrits par lui-même, traduits et mis en ordre.* 1835.

Michelet et Quinet: *Les Jésuites.* 1842.

Michelet: *Histoire de France,* vols. 8–10, 1855 ff.

J. H. Merle d'Aubigné: *Histoire de la Réformation du 16. siècle.* 5 vols. 1835–53. (English translation, 1846).

Thomas Babington Macauley: "On Ranke's History of the Popes," 1840, published in his *Essays,* 1842. There are also remarks on the effect of the Reformation in his *History of England,* 1848 ff.

John Carl Ludwig Gieseler: *Lehrbuch der Kirchengeschichte.* Band iii, Abteilung 1, 1840. (Many later editions, and an English translation).

Jaime Balmes: *El protestantismo comparado con el catolicismo en sus relaciones con la civilizacion Europea.* 4 vols. 1842–4. (English translation as, Protestantism and Catholicism compared, 2d ed. 1851).

Thomas Carlyle: *Heroes and Hero-worship.* 1842.

Philarète Chasle: "La Renaissance sensuelle: Luther, Rabelais, Skelton, Folengo," *Revue des deux Mondes,* March, 1842.

Edgar Quinet: *Le génie des religions.* 1842.

Quinet: (see Michelet).

Quinet: *Le Christianisme et la Révolution française.* 1845.

Johann Joseph Ignaz von Döllinger: *Die Reformation.* 3 vols. 1846–8.

Döllinger: *Luther, eine Skizze.* 1851.

Döllinger: *Kirche und Kirchen.* 1861, p. 386.

Döllinger: *Vorträge über die Wiedervereinigungsversuche zwischen den christlichen Kirchen und die Aussichten einer künftigen Union.* 1872.

F. C. Baur: *Lehrbuch der christlichen Dogmengeschichte.* 1847.

Baur: *Die Epochen der kirchlichen Geschichtschreibung.* 1852.

Baur: *Geschichte der christlichen Kirche,* Band iv, 1863.

E. Forcade: "La Réforme et la Révolution," *Revue des Deux Mondes,* Feb. 1849.

William Corbbett: *A History of the Protestant "Reformation" in England and Ireland, showing how that event has impoverished and degraded the main body of the People in these countries.* 1852.

Napoléon Roussel: *Les nations catholiques et les nations pro-*

testantes comparées sous le triple rapport du bien-être, des lumières et de la moralité. 1854.

William H. Prescott: *History of the Reign of Philip II, King of Spain.* 1855–72.

John Lothrop Motley: *The Rise of the Dutch Republic.* 1855.

Motley: *History of the United Netherlands from the death of William the Silent to the Synod of Dort.* 1860–7.

Motley: *Life and Death of John of Barneveldt.* 1874.

James Anthony Froude: *History of England from the Fall of Wolsey to the Death of Elizabeth.* (Later: To the Spanish Armada). 1856–70.

Froude: *Short Studies on Great Subjects.* 1867–83.

Froude: *The Divorce of Catharine of Aragon.* 1891.

Froude: *The Life and Letters of Erasmus.* 1894.

Froude: *Lectures on the Council of Trent.* 1896.

Henry Thomas Buckle: *History of Civilization in England.* 1857–61.

Paul de Lagarde: "Ueber das Verhältnis des deutschen Staates zu Theologie, Kirche und Religion." *Deutsche Schriften,* 1886, pp. 48 ff. (Written in 1859, first printed 1873).

David Friedrich Strauss: *Ulrich von Hutten.* 1858.

Gustav Freytag: *Bilder aus der deutschen Vergangenheit.* 1859–62.

Ferdinand Gregorovius: *Geschichte der Stadt Rom im Mittelalter.* 1859–71.

Lord Acton: Many essays and articles, beginning about 1860, mostly collected in his *History of Freedom and Other Essays,* 1906, and *Historical Essays and Studies,* 1907.

Acton: *Lectures on Modern History.* 1906. (I use the 1912 edition; the lectures were delivered in 1899–1901).

Acton: *Letters to Mary Gladstone,* ed. H. Paul, 1904.

Jacob Burckhart: *Die Cultur der Renaissance in Italien.* 1860. (English translation by S. G. C. Middlemore, 1878). Twentieth ed. by L. Geiger, 1919.

W. Stubbs: *Lectures on European History.* 1904. (Delivered 1860–70).

François Laurent: *Études sur l'histoire de l'humanité.* 18 vols. Vol. viii: La Réforme. (No date, circa 1862). Vol. xvii: La Religion de l'avenir. 1870. Vol. xviii: Philosophie de l'histoire. 1870. (pp. 340 ff).

John William Draper: *History of the Intellectual Development of Europe.* 1863.

Draper: *History of the Conflict of Science and Religion.* 1874.

W. E. H. Lecky: *History of the Rise and Influence of the Spirit of Rationalism in Europe.* 1865.

K. P. W. Maurenbrecher: *Karl V und die deutschen Protestanten.* 1865.

Maurenbrecher: *England im Reformationszeitalter.* 1866.

Maurenbrecher: *Studien und Skizzen zur Geschichte der Reformationszeit.* 1874.

Maurenbrecher: *Geschichte der katholischen Reformation.* 1880.

Henry Charles Lea: *Superstition and Force.* 1866.

Lea: *Historical Sketch of Sacerdotal Celibacy.* 1867.

Lea: *Chapters from the Religious History of Spain connected with the Inquisition.* 1890.

Lea: *History of Auricular Confession and Indulgences in the Latin Church.* 1896.

Lea: *History of the Inquisition in Spain.* 1906–7.

Lea: "The Eve of the Reformation," *Cambridge Modern History,* ii, 1902.

Ludwig Häusser: *Geschichte des Zeitalters der Reformation.* 1867–8.

Frederic Seebohm: *The Oxford Reformers,* 1867.

Seebohm: *The Era of the Protestant Revolution.* 1874.

H. H. Milman: *Savonarola, Erasmus and other Essays.* 1870.

Eichhoff: *Dr. Martin Luther: 100 Stimmen namhafter Männer aus 4 Jahrhunderten.* 1872.

George Park Fisher: *The Reformation.* 1873. (New ed. 1906).

John Richard Green: *Short History of the English People.* 1874.

Green: *History of the English People,* 4 vols. 1877–80.

John Addington Symonds: *The Renaissance in Italy,* 7 vols. 1875–86.

Symonds: "Renaissance," article in *Encyclopædia Britannica,* 9th, 10th, 11th ed.

Johannes Janssen: *Geschichte des deutschen Volkes seit dem Ausgange des Mittelalters,* 1876–88. (Twentieth ed. of vols. 1, 2; eighteenth ed. of vols. 3–8, by L. Pastor, 1913 ff).

Emile de Laveleye: *Le protestantisme et le catholicisme dans leurs rapports avec la liberté et la prosperité des peuples,* 1875.

Richard Watson Dixon: *History of the Church of England from the abolition of the Roman jurisdiction,* 6 vols. 1878–1902.

Friedrich Nietzsche: *Menschliches, Allzumenschliches.* 1878, p. 200.

Nietzsche: *Die fröhliche Wissenschaft.* 1882, §§ 35, 148, 149, 385. (And other obiter dicta, cf. Werke, vii, 401).

Pasquale Villari: *Niccolò Machiavelli e i suoi tempi.* 1878. (English transl., 1891).

Ludwig (von) Pastor: *Die kirchliche Unionsbestrebungen unter Karl V,* 1879.

Pastor: *Geschichte der Päpste seit dem Ausgange des Mittelalters,* 7 vols. 1886–1920. (English translation of German vols. 1–5, making 12 vols, ed. by Antrobus and Kerr).

H. M. Baird: *The Rise of the Huguenots in France.* 1879.

Baird: *The Huguenots and Henry of Navarre.* 1886.

Georg Christian Bernhard Pünjer: *Geschichte der christlichen Religionsphilosophie seit der Reformation.* 2 Bände. 1880–3. (English translation of the first volume as, *History of the Christian Philosophy of Religion from the Reformation to Kant,* by W. Hastie. 1887).

J. E. Thorold Rogers: *History of Agriculture and Prices in England,* vol. iv, 1882, pp. 72 ff.

Rogers: *The Economic Interpretation of History,* 1888, pp. 83 ff.

K. W. Nitzsch: *Geschichte des deutschen Volkes bis zum Augsburger Religionsfriede,* hg. von Matthäi, 1883–5.

Heinrich von Treitschke: "Luther und die deutsche Nation," 1883. (English translation in *Germany, France, Russia and Islam,* 1915, 227 ff. Other criticisms of the Reformation may be found in his other works, e.g., *Deutsche Geschichte im 19. Jahrhundert,* 1 Teil,[5] 1895, pp. 86, 391).

Charles Beard: *The Reformation of the Sixteenth Century in its relation to Modern Thought and Knowledge.* 1883.

A. Stern: *Die Socialisten der Reformationszeit.* 1883.

Matthew Arnold: *St. Paul and Protestantism.* 1883.

Adolf (von) Harnack: *Martin Luther in seiner Bedeutung für die Geschichte der Wissenschaft und der Bildung.* 1883 (Fifth ed. 1910).

Harnack: *M. Luther und die Grundlegung der Reformation.* 1917.

Harnack: *Lehrbuch der Dogmengeschichte,* Band iii, 1890. (Fourth ed. 1910, and English translation by Neil Buchanan, 1897).

Harnack: *Das Wesen des Christentums.* 1900. (English translation, *What is Christianity?* 1901).

Harnack: "Die Bedeutung der Reformation innerhalb der allgemeinen Religionsgeschichte," *Reden und Aufsätze,* Band ii, Teil ii, 1904.

Harnack: "Die Reformation," *Internationale Monatsschrift,* xi, 1917.

M. Monnier: *La Réforme, de Luther à Shakespeare.* (Histoire de la littérature moderne). 1885.

Leo Tolstoy: *Thoughts and Aphorisms.* 1886–93. Tolstoy's Works, English, 1905, xix, 137 f.

Philip Schaff: *History of the Christian Church.* Vol. VI, The German Reformation. 1888. Vol. VII, The Swiss Reformation. 1892.

F. von Bezold: *Die Reformation.* 1890. (In Oncken's Allgemeine Geschichte in Einzeldarstellungen).

F. von Bezold, E. Gotheim und R. Koser: *Staat und Gesellschaft der neueren Zeit.* 1908. (Die Kultur der Gegenwart, Teil ii, Abteilung V).

William Cunningham: *Growth of English Industry and Commerce during the early and Middle Ages.* 1890. (Fourth ed. 1905).

Cunningham: *Growth of English Industry and Commerce in Modern Times.* 1882. (3d ed. 1903).

Cunningham: *Western Civilization in its Economic Aspects in Ancient Times.* 1898.

Cunningham: *Western Civilization in its Economic Aspects in Modern Times.* 1900. (I also have the advantage of having taken notes of Dr. Cunningham's lectures at Columbia University, November, 1914).

Rudolph Cristoph Eucken: *Die Lebensanschauungen der grossen Denker.* 1890. (7th ed. 1907; English translation, *The Problem of Human Life,* by W. Hough and Boyce Gibson, 1909).

F. Simmel: *Soziale Differenzierung.* 1890.

Robert Flint: *History of the Philosophy of History.* 1893.

C. Borgeaud: *The Rise of Modern Democracy in Old and New England.* Translated by Mrs. B. Hill. Preface by C. H. Firth. 1894. (First published in French periodicals 1890–1).

Herbert L. Osgood: "The Political Ideas of the Puritans," *Political Science Quarterly,* vi, 1 ff., 201 ff., 1891.

Wilhelm Dilthey: "Auffassung und Analyse des Menschen im 15. und 16. Jahrhundert." *Archiv für die Geschichte der Philosophie,* iv, (1891) 604 ff., v, (1892), 337 ff.

Dilthey: "Die Glaubenslehre der Reformatoren," *Preussiche Jahrbücher,* lxxv, (1894), pp. 44 ff.

Dilthey: "Weltanschauung und Analyse des Menschen seit Renaissance und Reformation." *Gesammelte Schriften,* ii, 1914.

E. A. Freeman: *Historical Essays,* 4th series, 1892.

Karl Lamprecht: *Zum Verstãndnis der wirtschaftlichen und sozialen Wandlungen in Deutschland vom 14. bis zum 16. Jahrhundert.* 1893.

Lamprecht: *Deutsche Geschichte,* Band 5, 1894–5.

Otto Pfleiderer: *Philosophy and Development of Religion.* (Gifford Lectures at Edinburgh), 1894, vol. ii, pp. 321 ff.

Pfleiderer: "Luther as the founder of Protestant civilization." In *Evolution and Theology,* 1900, pp. 48–79. (Address given 1883).

E. Belfort Bax: *German Society at the Close of the Middle Ages.* 1894.

Bax: *The Peasants' War in Germany.* 1899.

Bax: *The Rise and Fall of the Anabaptists.* 1903. (Large portions of the three works by Bax have been reprinted in his *German Culture Past and Present.* 1915).

Brooks Adams: *The Law of Civilization and Decay.* 1895.

Brooks Adams: *The New Empire.* 1902.

Karl Kautsky: *Vorläufer des neuren Sozialismus,* Band i, "Der Kommunismus in der deutschen Reformation," 1895. (Communism in Central Europe in the Time of the Reformation, transl. by J. L. and E. G. Mulliken. 1897).

A. Berger: *Die Kulturaufgaben der Reformation.* 1895. ([2] 1908).

Berger: *M. Luther in kulturgeschichtlicher Darstellung,* 3 parts, 1895, 1907, 1919.

Berger: *Ursachen und Ziele der deutschen Reformation.* 1899.

Berger: *Sind Humanismus und Protestantismus gegensätzig?* 1899.

H. Hauser: "De l'humanisme et de la Réforme en France," *Revue Historique,* July-Aug. 1897.

Karl Sell: "Die wissenschaftliche Aufgaben einer Geschichte der christlichen Religion,'' *Preussische Jahrbücher,* xcviii. (1899), 12 ff.

Sell: *Christentum und Weltgeschichte seit der Reformation.* 1910.

Sell: *Der Zusammenhang von Reformation und politischer Freiheit.* Abhandlungen in Theologischen Arbeiten aus dem rheinischen wissenschaftlichen Predigerverein. N. F. 12. 1910.

John Mackinnon Robertson: *A Short History of Freethought.* 1899. ([3] 1915).

Robertson: *A Short History of Christianity.* 1901. ([2]1913).

S. N. Patten: *The Development of English Thought.* A Study in the Economic Interpretation of History. 1899. (Fanciful).

Ferdinand Brunetière: ''L'oeuvre littéraire de Calvin.'' *Revue des Deux Mondes,* Oct. 15, 1900.

Brunetière: ''L'oeuvre de Calvin.'' (1901). *Discours de Combat,* ii, 1908, pp. 121 ff.

Williston Walker: *The Reformation.* 1900.

Walker: *A History of the Christian Church.* 1918.

A. Loisy: *L'Évangile et l'Église.* 1901. (Answer to Harnack's Wesen des Christentums).

A. Lang: *History of Scotland,* i, 1901, p. 382.

A. F. Pollard: *Henry VIII.* 1902.

A. F. Pollard: *Thomas Cranmer.* 1904.

Pollard: *Political History of England 1547–1603.* 1910.

James Gairdner: *The English Church in the Sixteenth Century* (1509–58). 1902.

J. Gairdner: Chapters in the *Cambridge Modern History,* ii, 1902.

Gairdner: *Lollardy and the Reformation.* 4 vols. 1908 ff.

Mandell Creighton: *A History of the Papacy,* vol. 5, 1902.

E. Armstrong: *The Emperor Charles V.* 1902.

H. Lemonnier: *Histoire de France* (ed. par E. Lavisse), v, 1903–4.

James Harvey Robinson: ''The Study of the Lutheran Revolt,'' *American Historical Review,* viii, 205. 1903.

J. H. Robinson: ''The Reformation,'' *Encyclopædia Britannica,* 1911.

Auguste Sabatier: *Les religions d'autorité et la religion de l'esprit.* 1903. ([4] 1910. English translation 1904).

(H. M.) Alfred Baudrillart: *L'Église catholique, la Renais-*

sance, le Protestantisme. 1904. (English translation by Mrs. Philip Gibbs. 1908).

W. H. Frere: *The English Church in the Reigns of Elizabeth and James I,* 1904.

H. A. L. Fisher: *A Political History of England 1485–1547.* 1904.

Fisher: *The Republican Tradition in Europe,* 1911, pp. 34 ff.

J. H. Mariéjol: *Histoire de France* (ed. par E. Lavisse), Tome vi, 1904.

E. P. Cheyney: *The European Background of American History,* 1904, p. 168.

O. Hegemann: *Luther in katholischem Urteil.* 1904.

Friedrich Heinrich Suso Denifle: *Luther and Luthertum in der ersten Entwicklung,* i, 1904; ii, hg. von A. M. Weiss, 1909.

Max Weber: "Die protestantische Ethik und der 'Geist' des Kapitalismus," *Archiv für Sozialwissenschaft und Sozialpolitik,* xx and xxi, 1905.

George Santayana: *Reason in Religion,* 1905, pp. 114–124.

Santayana: *Winds of Doctrine,* 1913, pp. 39–46.

Santayana: *Egotism in German Philosophy,* 1917, pp. 1 ff., 23.

P. Imbart de la Tour: *Les Origines de la Réforme,* 3 vols. 1905–13.

P. Imbart de la Tour: "Luther et l'Allemagne," in *Revue de métaphysique et morale,* 1918, p. 611.

David J. Hill: *A History of Diplomacy in the International Development of Europe,* vol. 2, 1906, pp. 422 f, 460.

A. W. Benn: *A History of English Rationalism in the Eighteenth Century,* 1906, pp. 76 f.

J. Mackinnon: *A History of Modern Liberty,* Vol. iii, The Age of the Reformation, 1906.

T. M. Lindsay: *A History of the Reformation.* 2 vols. 1906–7.

H. Böhmer: *Luther im Lichte der neueren Forschung.* 1906. (2d. ed. 1909, 3d 1913, 5th 1918, each much changed).

Ernst Troeltsch: *Bedeutung des Protestantismus für die Entstehung der modernen Welt.* 1906. (2d ed. 1911; English translation, "Protestantism and Progress." 1912).

Troeltsch: *Protestantisches Christentum und Kirche in der Neuzeit,* 1906. (Kultur der Gegenwart, I, Teil iv, 1). 2d ed. 1909.

Troeltsch: "Protestantismus und Kultur," in *Die Religion in Geschichte und Gegenwart,* 1912.

Troeltsch: *Die Soziallehren der christlichen Kirchen und Gruppen,* 1912.

Troeltsch: "Renaissance und Reformation," *Historische Zeitschrift,* cx. 519 ff., 1913.

Troeltsch: "Die Kulturbedeutung des Kalvinimus," *Internationale Wochenschrift,* iv, 1910.

Troeltsch: "Luther und der Protestantismus," *Neue Rundschau,* Oct. 1917.

T. Brieger: "Die Reformation." In *Weltgeschichte 1500–1648,* ed. Pflugk-Harttung, 1907. (Published separately, enlarged, 1909).

F. Loofs: *Luther's Stellung zum Mittelalter und zur Neuzeit.* 1907.

Horst Stephan: *Luther in den Wandlungen seiner Kirche.* 1907.

A. Kalthoff: *Das Zeitalter der Reformation.* 1907.

Otto Pfleiderer: *Die Entwicklung des Christentums.* 1907.

Joseph Fabre: *La pensée moderne, de Luther à Leibnitz.* 1908.

F. Lepp: *Schlagwörter des Reformationszeitalters.* 1908.

Paul Sabatier: *Les Modernistes,* 1908 (Translated, *Modernism,* 1908, pp. 75 ff).

Paul Sabatier: *L'Orientation religieuse de la France actuelle,* 1911. (Translated, *France Today, its Religious Orientation,* 1913, pp. 49–51).

John Morley: *Miscellanies,* Fourth Series, 1908, pp. 120 ff.

R. Eckert: *Luther im Urteil bedeutender Männer.* 1908. (2d ed., expanded, 1917).

E. Boutroux: *Science et religion dans la philosophie contemporaine,* 1908, p. 13.

L. Zscharnack: "Reformation und Humanismus im Urteil der deutschen Aufklärung," *Protestantische Monatshefte,* 1908, xii, 81 ff, 153 ff.

F. Rachfahl: "Kalvinismus und Kapitalismus," *Internationale Wochenschrift,* iii, 1909.

E. Fueter: "Die Weltgeschichtliche Bedeutung des Calvinismus." *Wissen und Leben,* ii, 1909, pp. 269 ff.

E. Fueter: *Geschichte der neueren Historiographie.* 1911. (French translation, 1916).

E. Fueter: *Geschichte des Europäischen Staatensystems 1492–1559.* 1919.

W. Windelband: *Allgemeine Geschichte der Philosophie,* p. 395. (*Kultur der Gegenwart,* Teil I, Abt. 5, 1909).

Solamon Reinach: *Orpheus,* 1909.

Jacob Salwyn Schapiro: *Social Reform and the Reformation.* 1909.

F. Katzer: *Luther und Kant.* 1910.

Emil Knodt: *Die Bedeutung Calvins und des Calvinismus für die protestantische Welt.* 1910.

Jaeger: "Germanisierung des Christentums," *Religion in Geschichte und Gegenwart,* 1910.

A. Dide: *J. J. Rousseau, le Protestantisme et la Révolution française.* (1910).

J. Rivain: *Politique, Morale, Religion; Sur l'Esprit protestant; Protestantisme et progrès; l'Église et l'État.* 1910.

C. Burdach: "Sinn und Ursprung der Worte Renaissance und Reformation." Königliche-preussische Akademie der Wissenschaften, *Sitzungsberichte,* 1910, pp. 594–646.

W. Köhler: *Idee und Persönlichkeit in der Kirchengeschichte.* 1910.

W. Köhler: "Luther," in *Morgenrot der Reformation,* hg. von Pflugk-Harttung, 1912.

W. Köhler: *Martin Luther und die deutsche Reformation.* 1916.

W. Köhler in *Religion in Geschichte und Gegenwart,* 1909. i, 2117 ff.

Köhler: "Erasmus," 1918. *(Klassiker der Religion).*

Köhler: *Dr. M. Luther, der deutsche Reformator.* 1917.

H. T. Andrews: "The Social Principles and Effects of the Reformation." In *Christ and Civilization,* ed. J. B. Patten, Sir P. W. Bunting and A. E. Garvie, 1910.

Fernand Mouret: *Histoire générale de l'Église.* Tome 5. La Renaissance et la Réforme. 1910. ([2] 1914).

A. Humbert: *Les Origines de la Théologie moderne,* 1911.

Hartmann Grisar: *Luther.* 3 vols. 1911–13.

Preserved Smith: *Life and Letters of Martin Luther,* 1911. (Especially the preface to the second edition, 1914).

Preserved Smith: "Justification by Faith," *Harvard Theological Review,* 1913.

Preserved Smith: "Luther," *International Encyclopædia,* 1915.

Preserved Smith: "The Reformation 1517–1917." *Bibliotheca Sacra,* Jan. 1918.

Preserved Smith: "English Opinion of Luther," *Harvard Theological Review,* 1917.

Hillaire Belloc: "The Results of the Reformation." *Catholic World,* Jan. 1912.

P. Wernle: *Renaissance und Reformation.* 1912.

Alfred Plummer: *The Continental Reformation.* 1912.

Maxime Kowalewsky: *Die ökonomische Entwicklung Europas bis zum Beginn der kapitalistischen Wirtschaftsform.* Aus dem Russischen überstezt von A. Stein. Vol. vi, 1913, pp. 51 ff.

J. B. Bury: *A History of Freedom of Thought.* 1913.

G. L. Burr: "Anent the Middle Ages," *American Historical Review,* 1913.

Burr: "The Freedom of History," *American Historical Review,* Jan. 1917.

W. J. Ashley: *Economic Organization of England,* 1914, pp. 64 ff.

A. Elkan: "Entstehung und Entwicklung des Begriffs 'Gegenreformation,'" *Historische Zeitschrift,* cxii, pp. 473–93, 1914.

E. M. Hulme: *The Renaissance, the Protestant Revolution and the Catholic Reformation.* 1914. (Second ed. 1915).

G. Wolf: *Quellenkunde der deutschen Reformationsgeschichte,* 2 vols. 1915, 1916.

A. E. Harvey: "Economic Self-Interest in the German Anticlericalism of the 15th and 16th Centuries," *American Journal of Theology,* 1915.

Harvey: "Economic Aspects of the Reformation," *Lutheran Survey,* Aug. 1, 1917, pp. 459–64.

Harvey: "Martin Luther in the Estimate of Modern Historians," *American Journal of Theology,* July, 1918.

W. P. Paterson: "Religion," chap. 9 of *German Culture,* ed. by W. P. Paterson, 1915.

John Dewey: *German Philosophy and Politics.* 1915.

H. Cohen: *Deutschtum und Judentum.* 1915.

G. Kawerau: *Luther's Gedanken über den Krieg.* 1916.

G. Monod: "La Réforme Catholique," *Revue Historique,* cxxi, 1916, esp. pp. 314 f.

F. S. Marvin: *Progress and History,* 1916. (Essays by various authors).

Shailer Mathews: *The Spiritual Interpretation of History,* 1916, esp. pp. 57 ff.

Frank Puaux: "La Réformation jugée par Claude et Jurieu." *Bulletin de la Société de l'histoire du Protestantisme,* Juillet-Sept. 1917.

L. Marchaud: *La Réformation: ses causes, sa nature, ses consequences.* 1917.

N. Weiss: "Pour le Quatrième Centénaire de la Réformation," *Bulletin de la Société de l'histoire du Protestantisme,* 1917, pp. 178 ff.

K. D. Macmillan: *Protestantism in Germany.* 1917.

Georg von Below: *Die Ursachen der Reformation,* 1917.

H. M. Gwatkin: "Reformation," in *Encyclopædia of Religion and Ethics,* 1917.

Alfred Fawkes: "Papacy," *ibid.*

Max Lenz: "Luthers weltgeschichtliche Stellung," *Preussische Jahrbücher,* clxx, 1917.

Chalfant Robinson: "Some Economic Aspects of the Protestant Reformation Doctrines." *Princeton Theological Review,* October 1917.

Arthur Cushman McGiffert: "Luther and the Unfinished Reformation." Address given at Union Seminary Oct. 31, 1917, published in the *Union Seminary Bulletin,* 1918.

Revue de Métaphysique et Morale, Sept.-Dec., 1918. Special number on the Reformation with important articles by C. A. Bernouilli, Imbart de la Tour, N. Weiss, F. Buisson, F. Watson, Frederic Palmer, E. Doumergue and others.

W. K. Boyd: "Political and Social Aspects of Luther's Message," *South Atlantic Quarterly,* Jan., 1918.

H. Scholz: "Die Reformation und der deutsche Geist." *Preussische Jahrbücher,* clxx, 1, 1918.

F. Heiler: *Luther's Religionsgeschichtliche Bedeutung.* 1918.

F. J. Teggart: *The Processes of History,* 1918, pp. 162 ff.

Lucy H. Humphrey: "French Estimates of Luther," *Lutheran Quarterly,* April, 1918. (Interesting study).

J. Paquier: *Luther et l'Allemagne.* 1918.

Wilbur Cross Abbott: *The Expansion of Europe 1415–1789.* 2 vols. 1918.

H. E. Barnes: "History," *Encyclopædia Americana,* 1919.

George Foot Moore: *History of Religions: Judaism, Christianity, Mohammedanism.* 1919.

P. Hume Brown: *Surveys of Scottish History.* 1919. (Essays posthumously collected).

J. Haller: *Die Ursachen der Reformation.* 1919.

F. Arnold: *Die deutsche Reformation in ihren Beziehungen zu den Kulturverhältnissen des Mittelalters.* 1919.

D. H. Bauslin: *The Lutheran Movement of the Sixteenth Century.* 1919.

INDEX